The 100 Greatest Bands of All Time

The 100 Greatest Bands of All Time

A GUIDE TO THE LEGENDS WHO ROCKED THE WORLD

Volume 1
A–J

David V. Moskowitz
Editor

GREENWOOD™

An Imprint of ABC-CLIO, LLC
Santa Barbara, California • Denver, Colorado

Library of Congress Cataloging-in-Publication Data

The 100 greatest bands of all time : a guide to the legends who rocked the world / David V. Moskowitz, editor.
    pages cm
   Includes bibliographical references and index.
    ISBN 978-1-4408-0339-0 (alk. paper) — ISBN 978-1-4408-0340-6   1. Rock music—History and criticism.
2. Rock groups—Biography.   3. Rock musicians—Biography.   I. Moskowitz, David V. (David Vlado),
1969– editor.
    ML3534.A18   2016
    781.66092'2—dc23   2015009810

ISBN: 978-1-4408-0339-0
EISBN: 978-1-4408-0340-6

20 19 18 17 16   1 2 3 4 5

This book is also available on the World Wide Web as an eBook.
Visit www.abc-clio.com for details.

Greenwood
An Imprint of ABC-CLIO, LLC

ABC-CLIO, LLC
130 Cremona Drive, P.O. Box 1911
Santa Barbara, California 93116-1911

This book is printed on acid-free paper ∞

Manufactured in the United States of America

Contents

Introduction

The human predilection to create ranked favorites of any given thing is long-standing. This ranges widely from the top five cars and trucks of each year, the top 10 most popular gifts for holidays, or the top five favorite pizza toppings. Whether this ranking is done by sales, quality, or some combination of both, as long as there is an element of opinion involved, there will always be disagreement about the resulting rank orderings.

Music is certainly not exempt from this type of behavior. In fact music has long been one of the types of media that has been ordered in some type of ranking or list by quality/sales. *Billboard* magazine began publishing in 1936 and by 1940 it was printing "Music Popularity" charts. At this time the *Billboard* charts were divided by music style: so there was a separate chart for each genre, be it country, jazz, or rhythm and blues. The lists that *Billboard* published were based on sales, which it was safe to reason were tied to popularity at any given time. *Billboard* went on to publish a composite list that was not divided by style. This "top 40" type of list continues to be issued both in *Billboard,* on their website, and as the last (noncover) page of *Rolling Stone* magazine. While these charts are helpful to gauge the commercial viability of a song, they actually say very little beyond that.

There are now top 100 or top 10 lists of a great variety within the music industry and its associated media. *Rolling Stone* issues top 100 lists of albums, songs, guitarists, and bass players. *Guitar Player* and *Bass Player* magazines contain similar lists as do other types of music magazines. This type of "best of" list is much more like the list of bands contained in this encyclopedia—it is based on a degree of opinion. Certainly, each "best of" list is based in some type of more scientific method than simple opinion, but this varies from list to list.

Other "best of" lists are even more subjective, essentially coming down to a nonscientific approach to a single person's opinion. Lists of this sort still appear in mainstream media, such as *Billboard* magazine's "Top 30 Breakup Songs." This gets even more insular with things like theboot.com's list of "Top 10 Country Breakup Songs."

This human desire to create ranked/ordered lists of various kinds of favorite things was brought into tight focus by the book *Hi Fidelity*. This book, along with most of the lists discussed above, served as a creative touchstone for the encyclopedia that follows.

Nick Hornsby's 1995 book *High Fidelity* addresses a variety of kinds of list. In *High Fidelity*, the three main characters work in a London record shop called

Champion Vinyl. The shop owner and main male character is Rob Fleming. He has just lost his girlfriend Laura, and this event has pushed him into a depression that focuses on "top five" lists of songs associated with the misery in his life. He is accompanied in this endeavor by his coworkers Dick and Barry. These "top five" lists are as much opinion as musical knowledge demonstrations. In *High Fidelity,* Rob and his cohorts do not just rank their musical thoughts, they rank everything. The book begins with a list of Rob's top five worst/most memorable breakups. This eventually works him around to the most recent—Laura.

The song-oriented lists that the three characters create throughout the course of the novel relate to a variety of topics. An example comes about midway through the book when the three discuss their "top five songs about death." They surmise that the top five songs about death are "Leader of the Pack," "Dead Man's Curve," "Terry," "Honey, I Miss You," and "Tell Laura I Love Her." Of course, the boys have a good laugh at Rob's expense in reference to the last song on the list. These types of list are purpose driven, but not scientific and very specific to a certain person or small group of people with a shared experience or perspective.

The book *High Fidelity* was turned into a movie of the same name in 2000. A change to the basic premise was made in that the setting was moved to Chicago. Actor John Cusack played Rob Gordon (not Fleming in this version). Beyond this, the movie and the book are quite similar and the "top five" lists are all intact. So successful were the novel and the movie that *High Fidelity* went on to be produced as a Broadway musical in 2006 which then toured through 2012. Thus, in the spirit of *High Fidelity* and the variety of rank/ordered lists discussed above, here is *The 100 Greatest Bands of All Time: A Guide to the Legends Who Rocked the World.*

Scope and Organization of This Book

The premise for the collection here is a mix of those list types described above. The *100 Greatest Bands* included here were chosen based on some scientific research and a series of criteria: more than one member, record sales, influence, impact, and innovation. There was also an element of opinion in that the bands included in this work are specific to the author's taste—thus, the appearance of bands such as the Replacements, the Ramones, the Stooges, Frank Zappa and the Mothers of Invention, and Primus.

Regardless of taste, each band is treated the same way. Each band is introduced with the dates during which they existed. There follows a discussion of the band's membership with life dates, legal names, and instrument specialization(s). Then follows the discussion of the band's achievements from album releases to touring, culminating in an exposition of the band's achievements, impact, and legacy. After each entry there is a selected discography and list of references for further study. Of note, the bands that appear in this collection are not ordered according to who is considered "best" within the top 100—instead they are presented alphabetically.

Volume 1 begins with a series of 10 nonband specific essays. These "connector" essays tackle issues that affect larger collections of artists including the impact of MTV on traditional radio, the ways in which the evolution of recording technology changed the music industry over the past 50 years, the role of independent labels on the release of music without major label interference/assistance, the role of women in rock and roll, the impact of rap/hip-hop crossing over to the mainstream, and the importance of the supergroup. These essays are meant to help tie the individual band entries together as the musicians discussed within them often appear in individual band entries as well.

Acknowledgments

Heather (and Avery Jo), Lucas, Katie, and Jack—you guys are the best, and I am eternally grateful to have each of you in my life. Thanks also go to my sister Danielle for all the support over the years. Additionally, I thank Dr. Walter Clark for his sage advice as I began my advanced studies in musicology. If not for his assistance in studying music outside the canon, I would not be able to pursue the types of research and writing that interest me the most.

To all of the people who helped me during the extensive research that went into the writing of this collection my appreciation. This type of encyclopedic research is impossible without a great deal of assistance that came to me in the forms of Brandi Stueckrath and Bethany Amundson. Sincere thanks to all who assisted with the initial conception of and list creation for the *100 Greatest* list: Vogel and Busker, Erin Harmon, Dara and Mark Gillis, John Gibbs, John Wetzel, Ken Green, Kevin and Michelle, Johnathan Alvis, and Brandon Hendrickson. Also, thanks go to all of the good folks in Matt's basement where a great deal of woodshedding and discussion took place. I also deeply appreciate the assistance, patience, and wisdom of James Perone, Daniel Harmon, James Sherman, and Rebecca Matheson.

Further, this collection would not exist without the work of all of the contributors: Paul Lombardi, Jacob Cohen, David Blake, James Perone, Robert Schwartz, Nolan Stolz, Monica Berger, Donna Halper, Karen Fournier, Josh Rieck, Sarah Tyrell, Scott Harding, Anthony Bushard, Benjamin Franz, Kevin Fullerton, Jay Batzner, Thomas Harrison, Jonathan Borja, Brooks Kohler, Jennifer Wagner, Nathan Saunders, Julie Turley, William Blick, Mindy Clegg, Junior Tidal, Eric Mosterd, William Clay, William Knoblauch, Katherine Price, Stephen Nepa, Derek Catsam, Jonathan Robertson, Rod Carveth, and William Blick.

Additionally, I wish to thank Dave Hause.

Girls That Rock

Although female rock and roll artists are vastly outnumbered in the bands discussed in this work, there are many outstanding female rockers who have had enormous impact on rock and roll and several of its derivatives. From all-female acts in the Motown and soul styles to the Runaways' impact on rock and roll in the mid-1970s, there has been a great many powerful female musicians influencing American popular music. Additionally, there have been many outstanding females who fronted mixed-gender bands: Janis Joplin, Tina Turner, Madonna, Courtney Love, Pink, and many others.

The all-female has a long history in American popular music. All-female groups existed before the dawn of rock and roll in the 1950s. However, once the rock and roll age dawned, more and more all-female acts came on the scene. One early example is Goldie and the Gingerbreads, who flourished from 1962 to 1967. This band was significant as it was the first to break into the male-dominated rock and roll world and landed major label deals on Decca in 1963 and Atlantic in 1964.

Goldie and the Gingerbreads started releasing music as an all-female act in 1962 with their send up of Bill Haley and His Comets' song "Skinny Minnie" reworded as "Skinny Vinnie." Remaking a popular song has been and remains a tried-and-true way to break into the popular music scene whether through a straight ahead cover version or through altering the words of the known song. In 1964, the Gingerbreads stock began to grow as they played a party attended by the Rolling Stones and Atlantic Records boss Ahmet Ertegun, who promptly signed them.

Also in 1964, the band landed a European tour during which they opened for the Rolling Stones, the Animals, the Beatles, the Yardbirds, the Kinks, and several others. The band topped out with the release of their song "Can't You Hear My Heart Beat," which charted in the United Kingdom. For a variety of reasons, the Gingerbreads did not catch on in the United States, and this eventually led to their separation by the end of 1968. Although Goldie and the Gingerbreads did not take the American rock and roll scene by storm, they opened the door for other acts to come.

Another important early all-female band was the Pleasure Seekers, who formed in 1964 under the direction of Suzi Quatro. Coming from the gritty environs of Detroit, the Pleasure Seekers were cast more in the mold of their Detroit peers such as Alice Cooper, Ted Nugent, and Bob Seger. By the end of 1964, the Pleasure Seekers were signed to the Hideout Records label and had released the songs "Never Thought You'd Leave Me" b/w "What a Way to Die." On the strength of their early singles, the group was signed to Mercury Records in 1968 and began releasing charting singles. At the end of 1968, the Pleasure Seekers changed into the band Cradle when they made the purposeful decision to write their own material, which was grittier than their previous singles. Cradle experienced a degree of success but turned out to be a showcase for Suzi Quatro, who left for a successful solo career in 1971. Since leaving Cradle, Suzi Quatro has had a storied solo career. She appeared on the popular TV show *Happy Days* in a recurring role, has sold over 50 million albums (primarily outside the United States), and maintains a successful music career.

The mid-1970s witnessed the true birth of successful all-female bands. The Slits, the Raincoats, the Mo-dettes, the Innocents, Siouxsie and the Banshees, and X-Ray Spex were all successful, but none were more important than the Runaways. Formed in Los Angeles in 1975, the Runaways were the most successful and high profile all-female band in the 1970s. The early band lineup was the power trio of Joan Jett, Sandy West, and Micki Steele. They then added Lita Ford and Steele was fired (but would later reappear in the Bangles). The band was rounded out with the addition of Cherie Currie and Jackie Fox.

With this, the Runaways procured a record deal with Mercury in 1976 and had a historic run of success. Their mid-1970s output was so popular that the band played numerous sold-out shows and even had all-male opening acts. In 1976, they released a successful self-titled album, and the following year their second album, *Queens of Noise,* led to even greater fame and international touring. The band's fame was so immediate and extreme that they struggled to maintain focus. Fox quit and was replaced by Vicki Blue. In 1977, Currie left the group and Jett took over more lead vocal duties for the band's fourth album *Waitin' for the Night.* They again toured internationally in support of the album. The year 1978 saw the band fraying at the seams. Jett wanted the group to move in a more punk rock direction while Ford and West wanted to stick with heavy metal. As a result, the Runaways broke up by mid-1979. In the wake of the band's breakup, the members went on to successful individual careers. Joan Jett went on to great success with her band the Blackhearts and Lita Ford has had a long and storied solo career. With the Runaways, all-female bands were finally considered as commercially viable as male bands by the American popular music industry.

In the 1980s, several other all-female groups had success, including Girlschool, the Go-Gos, and Headgirl. The Bangles power trio of Susanna Hoffs, Debbi Peterson, and Vicki Peterson formed in 1980 in Los Angeles. The group played a mixture of folk and pop and experienced a great deal of success throughout the decade. Originally formed under the name the Bangs, legal issues led to the modification to the Bangles. In the latter half of the 1980s, the group had a series of successful albums such as *All Over the Place* and *Everything.* With the song "Walk Like an Egyptian," the Bangles had a worldwide number one song and were part of the rock music mainstream.

At the end of the 1980s, the Bangles broke up under label pressure and increasing interest by Huff to go solo. The individual members of the group did not have great success and reformed in 1998 to record soundtrack music for the movie *Austin Powers: The Spy Who Shagged Me.* Since then, the group has enjoyed a return to fame and success and continues to perform together to the present. As the Go-Gos and the Bangles had sustained mainstream success, they both moved all-female groups into the pop music realm. In the wake of this move, several bands surfaced with the intent to take the all-female group in new directions.

Anomalous in all of this was the all-female glam rock band Vixen. Formed in 1980, the four women in the band have enjoyed a long career during which they have disbanded and reformed numerous times. Formed in St. Paul, Minnesota, the group had success with their self-titled album that yielded four charting singles in 1988–1989. *Rev It Up* produced another pair of charting singles with "How Much Love" and "Love Is a Killer" both charting in the United States and the United Kingdom. In the male-dominated genre of glam rock, Vixen's long career continues today.

Klymaxx emerged in 1979 as the first all-female R&B group whose membership self-produced its material and played all of their own instruments. With this, the all-female group began making inroads beyond pop music. The 1990s saw the first serious all-female metal bands with groups such as 4 Non Blondes, Super Heroines, and L7. The band Hole was originally made up of three women and one man and moved the female musician into more punk and metal directions. Riot Grrrl surfaced in the early 1990s as an all-female punk group focused on feminist issues.

With this, a whole series of all-female bands emerged under the badge of empowering women both within and outside of the music industry. Other examples of this style include Bikini Kill, Bratmobile, and Sleater-Kinney.

The all-female hip-hop group also came on the scene in the late 1980s. Salt-N-Pepa were two Queens, New York, MCs who, along with DJ Spinderella, blazed a trail into another male-dominated type of music. Cheryl "Salt" James, Sandra "Pepa" Denton, and Deidra "Spinderella" Roper formed the group in 1985 and by the end of the decade had put the hip-hop community on its ear. From its beginnings, hip-hop has been loaded with lyrics that objectify women or degrade them as money grabbers who destroy men. Salt-N-Pepa flipped the script by talking candidly on songs such as "Let's Talk about Sex" and "Push It." Over the course of five albums, the group garnered serious accolades and created a hip-hop community that was more accepting of women—without Salt-N-Pepa there would not have been TLC in 1990. The group has received a series of awards and honors in addition to having chart-topping hits. With their early success and strong onstage and offstage personalities, Salt-N-Pepa blazed the trail that TLC, Missy Elliot, MC Lyte, Lisa Lisa, and many other female hip-hop artists have followed. After disbanding for a time, Salt-N-Pepa reformed in 2007 and continue to perform together.

Along the way there have been many famous female-fronted bands and stand-out female soloists. From Alanis Morissette to Taylor Swift, from Lauryn Hill to Cyndi Lauper, from Bjork to Beyonce, today's successful female musicians owe a debt to the seminal all-female bands that made significant inroads into the music industry and created the environment in which these modern artists now thrive. The modern rock hot 100 is now filled with female artists who benefited from their all-female group predecessors. Chart toppers like Meghan Trainor, Tove Lo, Iggy Azalea, Rita Ora, Ariana Grande, and Nicki Minaj are the beneficiaries of the impact made by the all-female bands of the first 50 years of rock and roll.

David V. Moskowitz

References

Gaar, Gillian. *She's a Rebel: The History of Women in Rock and Roll*. Seattle: Seal Press, 1992.

Steven-Taylor, Alison. *Rock Chicks: The Hottest Female Rockers from the 1960s to Now*. Melbourne: Rockpool Publishing, 2007.

How the Evolution of Recording Technology Changed the Way Bands Work

The American record industry was built on the evolving technologies of recording and sound transmission. The movement from the 78 rpm record through reel-to-reel tape to the cassette to the compact disc to the mp3 has all affected how music is made and sold. Recording technology has always had a direct effect on the final product listeners consume. Thus, the evolution of new recording technologies has also shaped the way the record industry works and how bands function within the industry.

The effect of recording technology on the recorded medium has always been significant. Early recording media was not durable. The 78 rpm recording was fragile and heat sensitive. The reel-to-reel tape had the same issues in addition to being susceptible to water damage. More durable media developed in the early days of the rock and roll era. In the 1950s and 1960s, one of the main ways of selling songs was on the 46 rpm record. These small records with big holes in the middle were inexpensive and a great way for an artist to release single songs to the public. The limitation of this format was that it could only hold about 3 minutes and 30 seconds of sound per side. So widely used was this format that it actually mitigated the length of the standard rock and roll song—one could not release a longer song on this format, and because the 45 rpm was the standard, musicians only wrote songs this length or shorter. This song length went on to affect the radio industry as it governed the number of songs that could be played in any given time slot. In the 1960s, bands such as the Grateful Dead were regularly writing and recording songs longer than three and a half minutes, but they were doing so with no

expectation for these songs to be released as singles or to be played on the radio.

Throughout the early 20th century, the American record industry was gaining strength. On the backs of blues artists and jazz bands, the American major labels were consolidating power and creating an empire. From the 1930s through the 1970s, the major labels controlled the American record industry and maintained a controlling market share. In 1975 there were five major labels—Polygram, Decca, CBS, EMI, and Warner Bros. The dominance of these majors was so all-encompassing that they controlled the musical product that reached the consumer and, as a result, also controlled taste.

This tide began to change in the 1980s with the advent of the compact disc (and subsequent CD burner technology) and the rise of MTV. With this, the consumer gained significantly more control over the musical product they consumed. As this change was occurring, musicians discovered that they had new outlets for their music—not just the pursuit of a major label record deal—so that they could get the label's studio backing and distribution.

The major label chokehold further eroded in the 1990s with the advent of file-sharing technology such as Napster. As the music industry witnessed the burgeoning online music outlet, the major labels experienced significantly decreasing sales and market shares. As this was happening, musicians experienced a creative renaissance. Because the majors were losing their hold on music, a great deal of new music release avenues opened and new musical styles were embraced. Also, because an artist did not need to get a major label deal to publish their music, more music was released. As an example, in the 1970s, between 7,000 and 8,000 new releases emerged each year. With the changes in technology and the industry, this number climbed to 37,000 in 1997 and exceeded 75,000 in 2006.

Since 2000, the changes in recording technology have all but removed the need for major record labels. A part of this has been driven by the consumer's insatiable appetite for durable and portable music formats. In the computer age, this demand has been met by the development of the mp3 format along with great advancements in the portable music player—gone are the Walkman or cassette players of the 1980s, and instead the mp3 player as well as Internet-enabled smartphone are the preferred methods of listening to music.

All of these changes have had an irreversible effect on the record industry. The modern musician only needs a powerful laptop, audio recording software, and a quality microphone to make an Internet-ready recording. Additionally, the days of the major label distribution deal are gone. Musicians now self-market their products on online retailers such as CDBaby, iTunes, or their own websites. Further, the modern musicians can give their music away directly to the consumer on their own website or through storage/streaming media sites like SoundCloud or YouTube.

All of this has had a direct effect on the music that reaches the consumer. There is a greater variety of musical styles available, and music is transmitted to its audience in highly durable and portable ways. Additionally, those who make music are no longer tied to the endless pursuit of a major label record deal and a brick-and-mortar distribution package. The Internet and the development of truly innovative recording technologies have finally leveled the playing field. Now a music listener can identify a style of music that they enjoy and find it with their mouse. The freedom of new music is back in the hands of the artists and the listeners, and this seems unlikely to change as attested to by the shrinking ranks of the majors—down to only three in 2012.

David V. Moskowitz

References

Knab, Christopher. "Changes in the Way Music Is Sold Over the Last 30 Years." *Music Biz Academy,* Last modified January 2009. Accessed November 2014. www.musicbizacademy.com.

Morton, David. "Depression and Consolidation 1925–1940." *Recording History: The History of Recording Technology.* Last modified 2006. Accessed November 2014. http://www.recording-history.org/.

How YouTube Changed the Music Industry

Begun in February 2005 by three former PayPal employees, YouTube has subsequently reshaped the way the music industry works. It has dramatically modified how music is created, marketed, and purchased. It allows music creators to upload their creations, which essentially gives everyone with a computer international distribution without the interference of a record label. As a result, YouTube exerts an enormous influence on the music industry. As an example of its power over the media and its market share, Google purchased YouTube for $1.65 billion just a year after it was created.

Founded in San Mateo, California, by Chad Hurley, Steven Chen, and Jawed Karim, YouTube was conceived of as an easy method for its creators to share video files. In 2005, there was no easily accessed online service allowing uploading, downloading, and viewing of video content. The first video uploaded on YouTube was called "Me at the Zoo." Made and uploaded by Karim, the 19-second video now has over 16 million views and is still up on the site. With this, the trio who created the coding to allow for online video sharing recognized the potential of the product they created. They then secured the www.youtube.com domain name and went public in May 2005. Within a year of its creation, more than 60,000 videos were being uploaded per day. This power has only grown over the past nine years. In 2014, YouTube's market share was estimated to be about 43 percent internationally, and the site traffics billions of videos per month.

Although the site was originally conceived of as an online video file–sharing medium, it has subsequently transformed into one of the largest repositories of online music videos in the world. Further, it has become the third-most visited site on the Internet. As such, YouTube has changed the landscape of music creation, distribution, and marketing. Now that anyone can create music and upload it—thus sharing it with the world—the traditional music industry model has crumbled.

The need for artists to struggle to procure a major label record deal (often to get the label's distribution) evaporated with the international acclaim of YouTube. In fact, so successful is the YouTube-based marketing of modern music that successful online bands no longer need the backing of a major label. This has led to an ever shrinking market share for the majors and a decrease in the number of major labels over the past 20 years (in 1999 there were six majors, in 2014 there are only three).

This essentially free distribution has allowed for a great blossoming of available music. Before YouTube, a lone singer/songwriter could toil away in obscurity and never be discovered. Now, in the YouTube era, Justin Bieber makes a perfect case study for the change in the music industry. Bieber was "discovered" on YouTube in 2007 by music manager Scooter Braun. Bieber's mother videoed 12-year-old Justin's performance of Ne-Yo's song "So Sick" and uploaded it to YouTube where Braun found it. Within a year of Braun's discovery, Bieber was in an international star. None of that would have happened without YouTube. Bieber was in Ontario, Canada, and Braun was in New York City. Without the online conduit, Braun would likely have never heard of Bieber, and subsequently Bieber may not have become famous. Bieber is now just one of many. Other YouTube success stories include Cody Simpson, Austin Mahone, Time-flies, Boyce Avenue, and many others.

Beyond the discovery of otherwise unknown artists, YouTube has vastly broadened the types of music reaching the mainstream. Because artists can upload any kind of music they make, there is no industry go-between evaluating the current viability of the musical product. As a result, YouTube has produced an enormous blossoming of new and different music styles. Whereas a record label may be leery of trying to market a new music style, YouTube does not discriminate. Once the song is uploaded, the only success gauge is number of views.

Further, because of the way YouTube is designed, once a listener/viewer finds an artist they like, the selection of "like" artists on the right-hand side of the page points the consumer to other artists they will likely enjoy. The traditional means of grouping artists in alphabetical/style oriented bins at record stores is gone. As a result the consumer is much more likely to stumble upon similar artists they are likely to enjoy. This changed the way people consume music, as now the consumer can sample music which is linked to artists that they already enjoy. This ability to click onto music that caters to one's existing taste is revolutionary. Further, the consumer can subscribe to YouTube channels containing music they know they prefer.

YouTube has certainly benefited from the proliferation of the Internet. With Internet-enabled televisions and smartphones that stream YouTube wherever the consumer goes, the consumer can now access YouTube anywhere they have an Internet connection. With this development, YouTube essentially replaced the traditional music television channels such as MTV, MTV 2, and VH1. Because YouTube allows for end-user modification, which maintains streaming videos in the style the consumer predetermines, there are far fewer reasons to watch traditional music television on which the consumer may be exposed to music they do not like. The traditional music television stations responded by reducing the number of videos they play and replacing them with serial reality shows.

The inherent difficulty with the YouTube takeover is that it lacked a mechanism for artists to be paid for the material they upload. An unknown artist can have international distribution, become popular, and have a large fan base through YouTube, but none of this results in a direct paycheck. YouTube solved this problem through the use of advertising. The more popular a person's video, the more likely that person is to essentially become sponsored by YouTube. Advertisements are then tagged to the front of the video and thus a revenue stream is created at the end of which is the artist.

It is indisputable that YouTube (as well as the Internet in general and other music-streaming services) has changed the way people consume music. It has altered the way people are exposed to music, how/if they purchase it, how it is created, and how it is marketed. Further, because YouTube does not define what styles or kinds of music can be posted on the site, it has allowed for an explosion of various musical styles as dynamic and diverse as YouTube's audience.

David V. Moskowitz

Reference

Latta, Margaret Macintyre, and Christine Marne Thompson. "The YouTube Effect: How YouTube Has Provided New Ways to Consume, Create, and Share Music." *International Journal of Education and the Arts*. Vol 12, number 6 (July 8, 2011): 2–29.

Important Early Record Labels

In the early days of the rock and roll era, several small record labels had an enormous impact on the style and carved out their places in history along the way. In the 1950s, the major labels had a general distrust for rock and roll and, as such, did not want rock and roll artists on their rosters. It was not until the end of the decade that the larger labels could no longer ignore the popular musical product being created on small labels such as Sun Records and Hi Records in Memphis, Chess Records in Chicago, and Monument Records in Washington, D.C. Together, these labels exposed the world to the emerging rock and roll sound and, in the process, spurred the careers of the first generation of the new style.

In 1952, a radio engineer left his job and opened his own studio called Sun Records in Memphis. Opened in a small space at 706 Union Avenue, Phillips named the label Sun because of his optimism for the future of the music business. Through the middle of the decade, Phillips cultivated the reputation for making records of underrepresented black artists in the rhythm and blues style. However, along the way some of rock and roll's early stars came calling on Phillips. In fact, in 1954 Elvis Presley left his job as an over-the-road truck driver and entered Sun Studios looking to press a couple of singles. With Elvis, Phillips began to define the Sun Records sound, a mixture of early rock and roll and country swing that became known as rockabilly.

By 1956, Phillips was a known record label boss, and the work he had been doing with Elvis had put the label on the regional map. On the strength of his Sun singles, Elvis had appeared on several radio shows, and the major labels had begun to notice. In that year, RCA came calling and essentially bought Elvis from Phillips and Sun. Regardless, the label had established its place, and future fame was to come. After Elvis, other significant artists recorded on Sun, such as Johnny Cash, Roy Orbison, Jerry Lee Lewis, Carl Perkins, Merle Haggard, Conway Twitty, Roger Miller, Howlin' Wolf, and many others. Also in 1956, the "Million Dollar Quartet" (Elvis, Cash, Perkins, and Lewis) recorded at Sun Records. At the end of the 1960s, Phillips sold Sun to Mercury Records after having released material by a long string of now-famous artists. The Sun Records Studio still exists and is an active studio in the evenings, serving as a museum/tourist destination during the day.

The Hi Records label was also formed in Memphis in the 1950s. Hi Records was founded by Ray Harris, Joe Coughi, Bill Cantrell, and Quinton Claunch in 1957 as rock and roll as a named style was really taking off. Cantrell and Claunch had worked with Phillips as producers for Sun Records and were ready to branch out. In the late 1960s, Willie Mitchell joined Hi Records as a producer and quickly discovered Al Green. For the rest of the decade and the early 1970s, Mitchell and Green made hits on Hi Records with the help of the label's session players called the Hi Rhythm Section. By the mid-1970s, music taste was changing. By 1975, the soul sound featured on Hi Records was being replaced by disco and funk. As such, the label went into decline. Along the way, Hi Records also spurred the careers of Ann Peebles, Bill Black, and Ace Cannon.

Outside of Memphis, there were several other small/independent labels that were important in the first two decades of the rock and roll era. In 1950, brothers Leonard and Phil Chess formed the Chess Records label in Chicago. Chicago had a long-standing music tradition and a vibrant music community. As such, the Chess brothers recognized there was room to create a label focused on the Chicago blues style, jazz, doo-wop, gospel, soul, and early rock and roll. By the early 1960s, the Chess Records roster of musicians was large and diverse including Aretha Franklin, Bo Diddley, Muddy Waters, Howlin' Wolf, Chuck Berry, Etta James, Solomon Burke, and Laura Lee. Additionally, in 1951, Chess released Jackie Breston's single "Rocket 88," which some consider to be the first rock and roll style record. Regardless of whether it is or is not a representation of the rock and roll style, it certainly was an indication that Chess was present at the birth of the style. In early 1969, the Chess brothers sold the label to General Recorded Tape, and with this the label's independent status ended.

Fred Foster started the Monument Record label in 1958 in Washington, D.C. The label focused on releasing country, rhythm and blues, and early rock and roll records. Foster took the name of the label from the Washington Monument, and its first release was a hit. "Gotta Travel On," by Billy Grammer, was released in October of 1958 and made it to *Billboard*'s Top 5.

The label's principal focus was on its marquee artist, former Sun Records artist, Roy Orbison. With Foster, Orbison scored a series of hits in the early 1960s including "Only the Lonely." Other important artists on the Monument Records roster were Dolly Parton, Willie Nelson, Larry Gatlin, and Kris Kristofferson. In 1990, Foster fell on hard financial times and was forced to sell Monument to CBS Records, which was later folded into Sony Music Group. The Monument imprint still exists under Sony's auspices, and more recent Monument artists are the Dixie Chicks and Little Big Town.

Labels such as Sun, Hi, Monument, and Chess largely built their business around a single main artist or a small handful of artists. As such, they found the

music industry in the 1950s and 1960s rather fickle. Although the small independent labels of the early rock and roll era have largely disappeared, there are modern equivalents that have emerged in the new millennium. Most successful modern rock and roll artists maintain a "vanity" imprint on which they release their music. The issue with this is that it is not a true independent label. These vanity imprints are simply subsidiaries of some major label.

All that having been said, there is actually an increasing number of smaller independent labels at this time. As the market share of the major labels continues to decrease, more and more niche labels emerge, such as Industrial Records, Factory Records, Warp, Ninja Tune, Side One Dummy, and Rhymesayers Entertainment. Another good example of a modern independent label is Jack White's Third Man Records in Detroit. White does not only release his own music on his label; he also furthers the careers of aspiring artists such as Karen Elson, the Black Belles, the Greenhornes, and others. Additionally, White lets his imprint serve as a home for several artists who could have major label deals but choose not to, such as Wanda Jackson and Tom Jones.

David V. Moskowitz

References

Chess Records Official Site. "Complete Introduction." Last modified 2010. Accessed November 2014. www.chess records.co.uk/.

Edwards, David, and Mike Callahan. "Monument Records." Monument Records Official Site, November 2014, www.bsnpubs.com/tennessee/monument.html.

Nager, Larry. "History of Hi Records." Hi Records Official Site, November 2014, www.hirecords.com.

Sun Records Official Site. "About Sun Records." Last modified 2012. Accessed November 2014. www.sun records.com.

Third Man Records Official Site. "About/Artists." Last modified 2015. Accessed November 2014, thirdmanrecords.com/about/artists.

Rap Crosses Over: Hip-Hop Takes Over White America

In the South Bronx of New York City, in the early 1970s, a new style of music was beginning to emerge. With Caribbean and West African roots stretching back decades, the notion of rhythmically delivered storytelling over some type of beat began taking root in America. Whether from the groits of Africa or the toasters and selectors of the Caribbean, "rapping" stories over a beat came into fashion in New York City and hip-hop was born.

Lending credence to the Caribbean connection, one of the earliest hip-hop luminaries was DJ Kool Herc. Herc, a Jamaican immigrant, had been exposed to the island-based tradition of introducing a new song to the public by toasting (or rapping) improvised lyrics over the beat of the new song. Once the crowd was warmed up with the new song's beat, the selector (or DJ) turned the record over and played the new song with its lyrics. Herc combined this style of presenting new music with his love for James Brown, and the resulting product was some of the earliest hip-hop records.

By the end of the 1970s, more rappers were entering the burgeoning hip-hop community. The Sugar Hill Gang came on the scene in 1973 and was one of the earliest groups to rap about excess—women, cars, material possessions. The band and the record label they ended up creating were named after their home territory, the Sugar Hill neighborhood of Harlem. The group scored a huge hit with the song "Rapper's Delight" in 1979. The song ended up charting inside the top 40 in the United States and, with this, rap music gained a foothold in the country.

At the same time the Sugar Hill Gang was rapping about living the good life, Grandmaster Flash and the Furious Five were establishing themselves as the conscious voice of the ghetto. Begun in 1978, the set of five rappers was led by Joseph "Grandmaster Flash" Saddler. The group set itself apart from more pop music–like topics by rapping about the struggles of the urban underclass in New York City. Their song "The Message" was released on July 1, 1982, and firmly established the group's urban conscientiousness. The song went to number 62 on the *Billboard* Hot 100 chart and is considered one of the landmark records in hip-hop history. Of note, "The Message" was released on the Sugar Hill Gang's Sugar Hill label.

With these early singles getting radio play and ascending the charts, hip-hop was quickly becoming a viable style of American popular music. The crisis that the new style experienced was that it was only selling in very limited markets: essentially only in black urban environments. Artists such as Kurtis Blow started getting increasing radio play, and rap's impact started to be felt outside of New York. The first rap record to really permeate the white American listening audience was also made by a white singer. New York band Blondie issued the song "Rapture" in the early days of 1981. On it, Blondie's singer Debbie Harry rapped the middle section of the song. As such, "Rapture" was the first song containing rapped lyrics that achieved mainstream success. Harry also name-checked hip-hop figures Grandmaster Flash and Fab Five Freddy on the song. The song charted inside the top 10 in 11 countries, going to number one in the United States.

In the 1980s, hip-hop exploded across the United States. Innovators like Afrika Bambaataa and Public

Enemy came on the scene. Technological advancements in sampling, recording, and turntable rigs all pushed the style into its next phase. The period from the mid-1980s to the mid-1990s is now known as the golden age of hip-hop. During this period, enormous advancements were made in the style. Innovation on all levels pushed hip-hop out of New York and into other major metropolitan areas around the country. Hip-hop spread to Los Angeles, Atlanta, Detroit, St. Louis, and New Orleans.

Even with this level of migration around the country through the early part of the 1980s, hip-hop was still largely the domain of black urban America. That all changed at the hands of Run-DMC, Rick Rubin, and Aerosmith. On July 5, 1986, Run-DMC released their "cover" of the Aerosmith song "Walk This Way." Unlike other covers, the Run-DMC version included the original members of Aerosmith, Steven Tyler and Joe Perry. The song came about while Rubin and Run-DMC were in the studio making the songs that would be their *Raising Hell* album.

Rubin suggested that Run-DMC remake the song and, after some convincing, Tyler and Perry were brought into the fold. The song went on to tremendous crossover success. The Run-DMC version of "Walk This Way" is generally credited as the song that broke hip-hop to mainstream white America. It was the first real hip-hop song to break the top five on the *Billboard* Hot 100 chart. Further, it was a direct demonstration of how much hip-hop and rock and roll had in common. After all, many seminal hip-hop songs are built on rock and roll samples. Additionally, the Run-DMC version of "Walk This Way" was turned into a MTV video that enjoyed heavy rotation and brought hip-hop to music television.

While Run-DMC's move into the white musical mainstream was revolutionary, they were actually poised to do so even without the Aerosmith component. However, in the following year an earth-shattering crossover took place. Whereas Run-DMC came across as a fairly easy crossover act, Public Enemy was a much different story. By 1988, Public Enemy was an up-and-coming hip-hop group with the release of their album

Yo! Bum Rush the Show in 1987; they followed up with *It Takes a Nation of Millions to Hold Us Back*. On the album was their song "Bring the Noise," which became quite popular. It even appeared on the soundtrack for the movie *Less Than Zero*.

Even with the movie presence and the band's increasing popularity, Public Enemy was not a viable crossover act. The group's main rapper, Chuck D, peppered his lyrics with Nation of Islam doctrine and sentiments that could be construed as abrasive by white America. Interestingly, the song contained several shout outs to other hip-hop luminaries such as LL Cool J and Run-DMC. Additionally, Chuck D also name-dropped the thrash metal band Anthrax. This Anthrax connection was telling as the two groups ended up collaborating on a crossover version of the song.

In 1991, Public Enemy and Anthrax collaborated on a remake of "Bring the Noise." The song ended up appearing on albums by both bands: for Public Enemy the song was on *Apocalypse 91 . . . The Enemy Strikes Black* and for Anthrax it appeared on the *Attack of the Killer B's* album. The groups also made an MTV video for the song and then launched a tour on which they came together on stage to perform their collaboration. While the Public Enemy and Anthrax union did not specifically create larger audiences for either group, the song does go down in history as the first rap metal song. Further, the song has gone on to enjoy a significant period of popularity since it was released.

With the intersection of white and black America through the introduction of hip-hop, many white artists adopted the hip-hop style. One of the earliest was the Beastie Boys, who formed in New York City in 1981. The popular form of the group was three white MCs and a DJ. The group experienced mainstream success with the 1986 release of the album *Licensed to Ill*. The group then had a successful run that included tours with Public Enemy, Madonna, and Run-DMC. With this, hip-hop had truly crossed the racial divide.

Whereas hip-hop started out as a specifically urban black style of music, it is currently colorblind. An example of this is the Detroit rapper Eminem.

Beginning in 1996, Eminem went on a successful run over the course of five core albums through which he ascended to the top of the hip-hop community. With Eminem as an example, there are now hip-hop groups of all colors from around the world. Additionally, hip-hop used to be the domain of the underprivileged, but even the early economic status raps are no longer a significant part of the style.

David V. Moskowitz

References

Ogg, Alex. *The Men Behind Def Jam: The Radical Rise of Russell Simons and Rick Ruben.* London: Omnibus Press, 2009.

Ogg, Alex, and David Upshal. *The Hip Hop Years: A History of Rap.* London: Fromm International, 2001.

Tanz, Jason. *Other People's Property: A Shadow History of Hip-Hop in White America.* New York: Bloomsbury Press, 2007.

The Best Bands You Never Heard of: Famous Studio Bands

The rock and roll band has long been a solitary unit. Typically, it is a collection of people unified by a single musical idea pitted against the rest of the world. Many classic examples exist over the past 60 years. Some bands went on to be so famous that each member became known. An easy example of this is the Beatles, ubiquitously known as John, Paul, George, and Ringo. Part of the reason the membership of the Beatles is easy to remember is that it was constant throughout the heyday of the band. Not all bands are that lucky, and in many cases only the name of the singer is known. Even more obscure is the membership of the so-called studio band. These are bands who work for a specific label or studio and are employed to back many singers and songwriters. Because this was a popular approach to hit making in the 1950s and 1960s, several studio bands are responsible for thousands of hits. However, the people who were actually in these studio bands and responsible for all of these hits remain largely unknown or underappreciated. Several extremely successful and influential yet largely unknown studio bands were the Wrecking Crew, the Funk Brothers, and Booker T. and the MGs.

The Wrecking Crew was nicknamed by their longtime drummer Hal Blaine. The group worked in Los Angeles throughout the 1960s and was responsible for providing the musical backdrop to dozens of hits for singers as diverse as Bing Crosby, John Denver, the Beach Boys, and the Monkees. Further, producer Phil Spector used the Wrecking Crew in the creation of his famous "Wall of Sound" studio sound. Due to their importance, the Wrecking Crew was eventually recognized by the Rock and Roll Hall of Fame into which they were inducted in 2007.

Throughout its existence, the membership of the Wrecking Crew was relatively fluid—though some members were long-standing. Focal members of the group were Carol Kaye on bass, Jack Nitzsche as arranger, Hal Blaine on drums, Glen Campbell on guitar, harmonica player Tommy Morgan, Mac Rebennack (aka Dr. John) and Leon Russell on keyboards, and Frank Capp on percussion. There were many others, including a horn line throughout the life of the Wrecking Crew. As an active and reliable studio band, the Wrecking Crew backed hit-making artists such as Elvis Presley, Frank Sinatra, Frankie Avalon, Jan and Dean, the Beach Boys, the 5th Dimension, the Monkees, Peggy Lee, Johnny Rivers, Del Shannon, Paul Anka, Cass Elliott (from the Mamas and the Papas), Sammy Davis Jr., John Denver, Ray Charles, the Captain and Tennille, Leonard Cohen, and many others. The lack of fame as the musicians behind the hits was one thing; another was that they were considered paid employees without royalty rights.

While the Wrecking Crew was not specifically associated with a certain label, Barry Gordy made consistent use of the Funk Brothers on his Motown Records label. The original Funk Brothers were the backing musicians on the majority of Motown Records output while the label was based in Detroit. When Gordy moved the label to Los Angeles, the original Funk Brothers were left in Detroit. The Los Angeles incarnation of the Motown house band actually went on to include some members who had also worked in the Wrecking Crew, such as Carol Kaye and

Tommy Tedesco. While in Detroit, the Funk Brothers backed every significant Motown artist, including the Miracles, the Temptations, the Supremes, Martha and the Vandellas, the Marvellettes, Margin Gaye, and the Four Spinners.

Notable members of the Funk Brothers included James Jamerson on bass, Benny Benjamin on drums, Joe Messina on guitar, Jack Ashford on percussion, and Dennis Coffey on guitar, among others. The name Funk Brothers was a bit of a catchall, but there was a core of 13 musicians who are recognized as the actual group. Together, these musicians backed hits such as "I Heard It Through the Grapevine," "Baby Love," "Please Mr. Postman," "Where Did Our Love Go," and "Mercy Mercy Me." Like the Wrecking Crew, the Funk Brothers were treated as employees of the label and payed per hour/session without claim to any royalty rights. Once Gordy moved the label to California, the original Funk Brothers were abandoned. Although the name continued to be used, these Los Angeles Funk Brothers were not the same as those in Detroit. Regardless, the hits kept coming behind late Motown signees such as the Jackson 5.

The collection of musicians associated with Jim Stewart and Estelle Axton's Stax Records soul music record label was known as Booker T. and the MGs. The racially integrated collection of musicians was a stable, hit-making collective for over a decade. Begun in 1962, the original Booker T. and the MGs included Booker T. Jones on organ, Steve Cropper on guitar, Lewie Steinberg on bass, and Al Jackson Jr. on drums. Over the life of the band, some changes to the lineup took place. That said, today's Booker T. and the MGs still contain Booker T. and Cropper.

In the 1960s, the group baked Stax Records stalwarts such as Wilson Pickett and Otis Redding. Along the way, Booker T. and the MGs separated themselves from the pack of other studio bands by recording and releasing their own original music. In 1962, the group began releasing their own records, the first of which was *Green Onions*. These largely instrumental releases were successful and created a unique environment for the studio band in that they were able to capture their own royalties. Since 1962, the group has gone on to release 15 more studio albums, several of which charted in the United States.

Alongside their own products, Booker T. and the MGs continued to back famous Southern soul singers. They recorded with Sam and Dave, Albert King, the Staples Singers, and Delaney and Bonnie. Their consistent chart presence, either as a backing band or as the main attraction, caused them to be considered "the" soul band. As such, Booker T. and the MGs are largely regarded as defining the groove of 1960s soul. Unlike the Funk Brothers and the Wrecking Crew, Booker T. and the MGs have evolved with the times. This benefitted them in subsequent decades as they were the backing band for the *Blues Brothers* movie. Additionally, they have gone on to play with notable musicians such as Bob Dylan, Stevie Wonder, Johnny Cash, Eric Clapton, and George Harrison. As an indication of their fame, the group was inducted into the Rock and Roll Hall of Fame in 1992.

The studio band was the unsung hero of the first few decades of the rock and roll era. Groups like the Wrecking Crew, the Funk Brothers, and Booker T. and the MGs helped to shape the Motown and soul sound, but did so largely without credit—and certainly without proper monetary compensation. The impact these groups had was enormous and many of the singers they backed would not have been as successful without their style-defining sounds.

David V. Moskowitz

References

Beesley, Johnson. "Wrecking Crew Discography." Wrecking Crew Official Website, last modified 2011. Accessed November 2014. www.halblaine.com/discography/.

Blaine, Hal. *Hal Blaine and the Wrecking Crew*. Michigan: Rebeats Press, 2010.

Justman, Paul. *Standing in the Shadows of Motown*. New York: Artisan Entertainment, 2002.

Murrells, Joseph. *The Book of Golden Discs*. London: Barrie and Jenkins, 1978.

The Role of Woodstock

The history of rock and roll is filled with pivotal events. Whether the event was an election, a war, a change of style, or the development of new instruments, the rock and roll style has always reacted to change both within and outside of the United States. Many of these pivotal events were seminal concerts that in some way changed the landscape of American popular music. While the Monterey Pop Festival of 1967 was a major watershed moment of rock and roll—with Jimi Hendrix lighting his guitar on fire and Keith Moon of the Who blowing up his drum rig—it could not overshadow the events that took place on Max Yasgur's farm outside the town of Bethel in upstate New York at the end of the summer of 1969.

The concert was called the Woodstock Music and Art Fair, An Aquarian Exposition in White Lake, New York: Three Days of Peace and Music, and was staged August 15, 16, and 17 of 1969. The music festival was the idea of Michael Lang, John Roberts, Joel Rosenman, and Artie Kornfield. Of them, the only one with any experience as a concert promoter was Lang. Roberts and Rosenman financed the initial development deal for the show. The upstate New York location was chosen because several popular artists were already in the area (Bob Dylan and the Band were living in Woodstock and recording what would become the *Basement Tapes* at the band's rental house "Big Pink"), and there was plenty of open space to stage a large-scale outdoor concert.

In the five months prior to the concert, a great deal of planning went on, from securing the venue to lining up all of the bands to actually constructing the stage. The first major act to sign on to the concert roster was Creedence Clearwater Revival, who had recently emerged as a major musical force in the Vietnam Era. The development group also secured the concert location on Max Yasgur's dairy farm. The local community opposed the concert as it was likely draw a bunch of undesirable "hippies." The concert promoters quelled fears by claiming that no more than 50,000 people would attend.

In fact, Woodstock was originally conceived as a money-making venture. It was billed as three days of music for $18 in advance or $24 at the gate. It has been reported that about 180,000 advanced tickets were sold. However, the gates were swarmed by an audience that peaked at approximately 400,000 people (some reports inflate this to 450,000 or 500,000). With this, the concert went from being paid admission to a free show for all of the overflow audience members. Part of the problem was that as the concert approached, workers at the venue had the option of either making the fence around the stage more secure or completing construction on the stage itself.

Regardless of the security issues, the concert began on Friday night with Richie Havens who was followed by other luminaries including world-famous sitar player Ravi Shankar, Arlo Guthrie, and Joan Baez. Along the way it began to rain, and the concert venue famously dissolved into a large mud pit. The Saturday performance began at noon and included Country Joe McDonald, Santana, Canned Heat, Mountain, the Grateful Dead, Creedance Clearwater Revival, Janis Joplin, Sly and the Family Stone, the Who, and Jefferson Airplane. Sunday's lineup included Joe Cocker; the Band; Johnny Winter; Crosby, Stills, Nash, and

Young; Paul Butterfield Blues Band, and others. As the concert wore on and for a variety of reasons, bands were getting further and further behind schedule. The result was that Jimi Hendrix and Gypsy Sun and Rainbows did not appear until Monday morning.

Yasgur was asked in 1970 to host another concert, but he declined. New York passed laws against mass gatherings in an effort to prevent any such festivals from occurring again. More recently, the towns of Bethel and Woodstock have both embraced their roles in American music history, and Yasgur's farm has been preserved the way it was during the concert. In 2009, a concert hall was erected up the hill from the original stage site, and the farm is a pilgrimage destination for revelers. In 2006, Crosby, Stills, and Nash played the new stage to commemorate the 37th anniversary of the his toric concert.

In 2009, 40th-anniversary concerts were staged to commemorate the original three-day festival. On August 15, an eight-hour concert was staged in Bethel, New York, and several of the original Woodstock acts performed, including Canned Heat, Mountain, and Jefferson Starship. Additionally, there are now Woodstock-like concerts around the world, including the largest outdoor concert music festival in Europe, Poland's Przystanek Woodstock.

The weather, logistical, and over-attendance issues aside, Woodstock had an enormous impact on American culture—and concert staging. The hippies who were the predominant group in attendance have subsequently been renamed the "Woodstock generation." Additionally, there are countless pop cultural references to the concert. One is Snoopy's friend, Woodstock the bird, in the *Peanuts* cartoon by Charles Schulz. Additionally, continued fascination with the event is attested to by ongoing books, articles, and references in song. Also, the concert was captured on film, and this film's release has gone on to gross over $50 million. Released by Warner Bros. Entertainment, it also won an Oscar.

The concert and associated romanticizing of the late 1960s has become a form of escapism. There are now countless references to an idyllic scenario that never really happened. The most obvious Woodstock legacy can be found in the modern music festival. Woodstock helped to set the mold for modern festivals like Bumbershoot, Bonnaroo, and Coachella. Now the modern rock festival is a well-organized and choreographed experience lacking any of the seat-of-the-pants aspects of the original Woodstock.

Possibly even more importantly, Woodstock brought American countercultural music of the late 1960s to the world. Prior to the concert, bands like Santana and Jefferson Airplane were popular on the West Coast but did not have an international audience. This all changed in the wake of Woodstock. Not only was the concert video-recorded, it was also preserved on audio and subsequently released as a three-album set. The release of this recording came in 1970 and topped the *Billboard* chart. Interestingly, Creedance Clearwater Revival refused to allow their material to appear on the release claiming that the fidelity was not up to their standard. Regardless, the three-album set stands as a monument to the hippies, the 1960s, and to the counterculture movement.

David V. Moskowitz

References

Fornatale, Pete. *Back to the Garden: The Story of Woodstock and How It Changed a Generation.* New York: Touchstone Books, 2010.

Lang, Michael. *The Road to Woodstock: From the Man Behind the Legendary Festival.* New York: Ecco Books, 2010.

The Midas Touch and Rick Rubin

Frederick Jay "Rick" Rubin was born March 10, 1963, in Lido Beach, New York. As a teenager, Rubin attended Long Beach High School and was in a punk band called the Pricks who managed a single show at CBGB during which they got thrown off stage for fighting. After high school, Rubin attended New York University. While at NYU, he met and befriended Russell Simmons, and together the pair founded Def Jam Records in 1984. He went on to superstardom as a producer of bands as varied as the Beastie Boys, Red Hot Chili Peppers, and Johnny Cash. Although possessing only rudimentary performing skills, Rubin's ear and ability to get artists to do their best work are legendary.

In 1984, Rubin was operating Def Jam out of his NYU dorm room. Their first single was T La Rack and Jazzy Jeff's song "It's Yours" that was distributed by Baker's Streetwise Record. Less than a year later, Def Jam had inked a distribution deal with Columbia Records and, thus, were able to place musical product anywhere in the country. The label then released "I Need a Beat" by LL Cool J. With these early releases, Rubin was at the forefront of the emerging hip-hop style. He quickly formed associations with the Beastie Boys and was instrumental in redirecting them from the punk rock style toward hip-hop. Additionally, he signed Public Enemy to Def Jam just as the band was breaking.

In 1986, hip-hop was the up-and-coming style of American popular music, and Rubin had very effectively positioned himself as the spearhead for the new style. In that year, the Beastie Boys released *Licensed to Ill* and Run-DMC released *Raising Hell,* and Rubin was the producer for both records. Rubin was associated with Run-DMC through his label cofounder, Russell Simmons (who is the elder brother of Joseph "Rev. Run" Simmons). In the same year, Rubin was instrumental in bringing together Aerosmith and Run-DMC on the hip-hop version of the song "Walk This Way." This had several outcomes: it put Run-DMC on the white music map and allowed hip-hop to begin crossing over to a white audience, it reignited Aerosmith's career, and it further increased Rubin's stock in both the hip-hop and rock and roll arenas.

As Rubin's name was becoming more and more ubiquitous in the music industry, he produced the Cult's 1987 release *Electric,* which included the hit song "Love Removal Machine." The following year, Rubin and Simmons split. The pair fought over Lyor Cohen who was then the president of Def Jam. With this, Rubin moved from New York to Los Angeles and founded Def American Records. The Def American signees were a departure from Rubin's earlier work, including Slayer, Danzig, the Jesus and Mary Chain, and the comedian Andrew Dice Clay. Rubin continued to keep his finger on the pulse of hip-hop by remaining associated with Public Enemy, Run-DMC, and LL Cool J, in addition to signing the Geto Boys.

In the late 1980s, he served as executive producer on Public Enemy's groundbreaking album *It Takes a Nation of Millions to Hold Us Back* and produced *Walking with a Panther* for LL Cool J. He also cowrote and directed the second Run-DMC movie *Tougher Than Leather* in 1986.

The early 1990s again found Rubin reimagining his record label. In 1993, Rubin changed the name of this label from Def American to simply American

Records. His first major project on the renamed label was the *American Recordings* of Johnny Cash in 1994. These recordings were earth shattering as they marked the first time Cash played anything other than country music in his professional career. At Rubin's behest, Cash recorded six cover songs, which were well received and critically acclaimed. This began a series of recordings between Cash and Rubin, which included the albums *Unchained, Solitary Man, The Man Comes Around,* and, released after Cash's 2003 death, *A Hundred Highways* and *Ain't No Grave.* Of specific note was the album *The Man Comes Around.* The album was largely recorded after Johnny's wife June died and included the Nine Inch Nails song "Hurt." The video for the song won a Grammy for Best Short Form Video at the 2004 awards. With this, Rubin began the period of his career during which he became a super producer who was able to bring the best out of any artist he worked with— regardless of style.

In 1991, Rubin scored another huge hit as the producer of Sir Mix-a-Lot's album *Mack Daddy.* This album included the hit song "Baby's Got Back" that has remained popular for years. Ever the chameleon, in the same year Rubin produced *Blood Sugar Sex Magik* for the Red Hot Chili Peppers. The year 1993 saw Rubin produce Mick Jagger's solo record *Wandering Spirit,* Danzig's *Thrall: Demonsweatlive,* and Joan Jett and the Blackhearts' *Flashback,* among others. The following year he produced hit records for Sir Mix-a-Lot, Slayer, Danzig, Tom Petty, Milk, Lords of Acid, and others. The year 1995 saw Rubin work with Nine Inch Nails on *Further Down the Spiral,* Red Hot Chili Peppers on *One Hot Minute,* and AC/DC on *Ballbreaker.* This level of productivity continued throughout the rest of the 1990s.

In the first 10 years of the new millennium, Rubin produced music for more than 75 releases from bands as varied as Rage against the Machine, System of a Down, Macy Gray, Weezer, Metallica, Poison, U2, Shakira, and Justin Timberlake, to name only a few. Rubin has continued his success since 2010. He produced Black Sabbath's *13* album along with new material from Lady Gaga, the Avett Brothers, Ed Sheeran, Damien Rice, and many others. After producing over 200 albums, Rubin shows no sign of slowing down, and his Midas touch in the production booth continues unabated.

In discussing how he gets artists to do their best work, Rubin says that it is a lot about listening. Not specifically listening to the music they are making but rather to their descriptions of the music they are trying to make. He queries them about why they are making music and then uses these motivations to get them to do their best work. It takes time, and Rubin is on record as saying that he must always appear nonjudgmental or the artists will recoil and the musical product will suffer. Making the artists comfortable is a big part of getting them to do their best work once their true motivations have been exposed.

Also, Rubin specializes in being a habit breaker. He works with artists to break the habits that they normally default to either in being creative or in playing songs once they are written. He works with artists to strip away their normal behavior in the studio so they can start fresh and return to the elements of their music from which they started. With this, Rubin maintains the Midas touch—part record producer, part therapist, part musical mystic.

David V. Moskowitz

References

Ankeny, Jason. "Rick Rubin." *All Music Guide.* www.all music.com, Rovi Corporation, 2012.

Blatt, Ruth. "How Super Producer Rick Rubin Gets People to Do Their Best Work." Forbes.com, April 2014. Forbes.com. Last modified April 2014. Accessed November 2014. www.forbes.com/sites/ruthblatt/2014/04/28/how-super-producer-rick-rubin-gets-people-to-do-their-best-work/.

The Supergroup

It is generally agreed that the rock and roll style has existed since the mid-1950s. Since its inception, the rock and roll medium has been creating superstars such as Elvis and Chuck Berry. Often stars experience a period of vogue or popularity that eventually runs its course, or the bands that these stars are in disband for some reason. When this happens, some artists have chosen to reinvent themselves by teaming with other superstars to form new bands—these are the supergroups. Not all supergroups are born out of negative circumstances; some are formed to benefit a specific charity or cause. Others are formed as side projects while the original group stays intact. Regardless of circumstance, these supergroups have become an essential part of the rock and roll landscape.

In the 1960s, it became popular for members of already successful bands to team up for a single album and garner additional accolades or success. Most people, such as *Rolling Stone* creator Jann Wenner, agree that the first such group was Cream. Eric Clapton had experienced success in the Yardbirds and John Mayalls's Bluesbreakers. Jack Bruce had cut his teeth in Manfred Mann's Earth Band and the Graham Bond Organization. Ginger Baker was also in the Graham Bond Organization. The three men came together in 1966 as Cream with Clapton on guitar, Bruce on bass, and Baker on drums. Together the group released a series of four successful albums before separating again. With this, the notion of the supergroup came into effect, and it was clear that this type of rock collective could be very profitable. Although the group was only together for three years, they were extremely successful and much loved—so much so that continued attempts to reform the group eventually led to four shows at the Royal Albert Hall in 2005. More recent reunion rumors were squashed when Bruce died on October 25, 2014.

Other significant supergroups in the 1960s included Crosby, Stills, Nash, and Young, who came out of the Byrds, the Hollies, and Buffalo Springfield. Another example was Blind Faith. Although they were only together long enough to produce one album, Blind Faith left an indelible impression on rock music in the late 1960s. The band members were Eric Clapton (after Cream), Ginger Baker (after Cream), Steve Winwood from Traffic and the Spencer Davis Group, and Ric Grech from Family.

In the 1970s, the number of supergroups soared. In the year 1970, Emerson, Lake, and Palmer formed from the Nice and King Crimson. Ginger Baker's Air Force formed from Blind Faith and the Moody Blues. Also, Derek and the Dominos formed from Cream, Delaney and Bonnie, and the Allman Brothers. This continued throughout the decade. In 1971, Journey formed as a supergroup although most casual fans did not realize that its membership was already famous. Journey's roots were actually found in Santana, the Steve Miller Band, and Frank Zappa and the Mothers of Invention. Other major 1970s supergroups were Bad Company, the Little River Band, and U.K.

The 1980s witnessed an even greater growth of the supergroup. In 1982, Asia formed from Yes and King Crimson. In 1984, a pair of truly monstrous groups emerged: the Firm and the Power Station. The Firm was built of parts of Free, Bad Company, and

Uriah Heep and included Jimmy Page from Led Zepplin. The Power Station included parts of Duran Duran and Chic and included singer Robert Palmer. With this, the supergroup became mainstream as these groups built their reputations on the burgeoning music video market.

As the 1980s progressed, the supergroup stopped being a niche band type and instead became a standard part of the music business. All styles were represented, from the 1985 forming of the country supergroup the Highwaymen to the British metal supergroup Gogmagog to the pop rock supergroup Mike + The Mechanics, the market was flooded. An aspect of these bands is that they are project conceived without a future plan. Typically, the supergroup makes one album together, and then the members go back to their respective bands. In 1988, the Traveling Wilburys broke that mold. Formed of Bob Dylan, George Harrison (the Beatles), Tom Petty, Jeff Lynne (Electric Light Orchestra), and Roy Orbison, the band formed with the intention of making a series of albums. They were successful at this and issued two acclaimed full-length albums in short order. The members of the group even took on fake names for each release, such as George Harrison calling himself "Nelson Wilbury" for the first album. On December 6, 1988, Roy Orbison died of a heart attack. This was the ultimate undoing of the group, but they did stay together long enough to release a second album on October 29, 1990. This second record was also successful and also went platinum. Interestingly, the Traveling Wilburys never toured, and after the release of the second album they disbanded.

The year 1990 saw the formation of a supergroup in reverse. Temple of the Dog was formed as a tribute to Mother Love Bone singer Andy Wood after he died from a heroin overdose. In 1990, the members of this band were not yet famous, but they all went on to long-standing acclaim in other bands. Temple of the Dog included Chris Cornell (Soundgarden), Stone Gossard (Pearl Jam), Jeff Ament (Pearl Jam), Matt Cameron (Soundgarden), Mike McCready (Pearl Jam), and Eddie Vedder (Pearl Jam). In reverse of all the other supergroups, at the time the Temple of the Dog album was released, there was no band called Pearl Jam. Soundgarden had formed in 1984, but Pearl Jam did not exist until after Temple of the Dog. Of note, the members of Pearl Jam (minus Eddie Vedder) had already worked together in a proto-grunge band called Green River.

In 1994, the Foo Fighters formed out of the ashes of Nirvana. Dave Grohl was the drummer for Nirvana and Pat Smear played guitar as their unofficial fourth member. After Kurt Cobain's death, Grohl moved from drums to guitar and lead vocals and built a band around himself from parts of Sunny Day Real Estate and other bands. The Foo Fighters have enjoyed a long run of eight successful albums making them an unusual supergroup in their longevity. Another major supergroup at the end of the 1990s included the alternative metal band A Perfect Circle that formed out of Tool, Devo, Nine Inch Nails, Smashing Pumpkins, and Marilyn Manson.

The new millennium has also had its fair share of supergroups, as they are now an ordinary part of the modern music scene. Oysterhead formed from Phish, the Police, and Primus for an album in 2001. Audioslave also formed in that year and went on a three-album run with a line up that was essentially Rage against the Machine with Chris Cornell as a singer. Another similar band was Velvet Revolver, which was essentially Guns n' Roses with Scott Weiland (Stone Temple Pilots) as the singer.

Not to be outdone, the folk singers got into the supergroup market in 2004 when the band Monsters of Folk formed with members of Bright Eyes, My Morning Jacket, and She & Him. At the same time, the pop-punk band Blink-182 went on hiatus and a series of bands were formed from its membership, including +44 and Angels and Airwaves.

In 2008, ex-members of Van Halen formed the band Chickenfoot. This supergroup is Sammy Hagar (Montrose, Van Halen), Joe Satriani (Deep Purple), Michael Anthony (Van Halen), and Chad Smith of the Red Hot Chili Peppers. Chickenfoot have released two albums and still work together. Also in 2008, the hip-hop community got into the supergroup game and the group Slaughterhouse formed with Crooked I, Joe

Budden, Joell Ortiz, and Royce da 5'9". Slaughter-house went on to release three successful albums. Additionally, there are now hybrid supergroups such as SuperHeavy. This group includes the Indian singer–songwriter A. R. Rahman, the Jamaican superstar Damian Marley, Dave Steward of Eurythmics fame, Mick Jagger of the Rolling Stones, and soul singer Joss Stone. Although an odd collective of musicians, their 2011 album was successful and critically acclaimed.

In the past five years, the proliferation of supergroups has been astounding. The modern music climate is much more fluid than it once was, and this allows for people to play together outside of the full-time band that they work in. A fine example is the Gaslight Anthem. Brian Fallon, the singer, fronts this band, and they have been making records and touring for the past eight years. As the Gaslight Anthem's popularity increases, Fallon has played in several other bands, including the Horrible Crowes and Molly and the Zombies. This allows for a host of creative outlets and relieves the pressures that can lead to a band's untimely undoing.

David V. Moskowitz

Reference

Thompson, Dave. *Cream: The World's First Supergroup.* London: Virgin Books, 2005.

Video Killed the Radio Star: The Role of MTV

On August 1, 1981, the world of American popular music changed forever with the launch of MTV: Music Television. The channel was conceived of and existed for many years as a station dedicated to playing music videos and interviews with musicians, all hosted by VJs: video jockeys. The channel has been on 24/7 ever since, which has created enormous impact around the world and revolutionized the music industry. In the same way Dick Clark's *American Bandstand* (begun in 1952) or Don Cornelius's *Soul Train* (begun in 1971) had an immediate impact on American popular culture, MTV revolutionized the way America consumed music and culture in the modern information age. As of 2014, more than 98 million American households received MTV, and as a result the channel exerts enormous influence over its target audience of adolescents and teenagers.

The first video on MTV was the aptly titled "Video Killed the Radio Star" by the Buggles. The format for the channel in its infancy was much like radio. Videos of a certain style were played in blocked time slots with commentary by VJs. The videos were supplied for free by the record labels as the money spent to create the videos was part of the promotional budget for any given band. The "live" performance video was quickly replaced with concept-driven videos made by now-famous directors such as Spike Jonze and Michel Gondry. Because MTV revolved around image-based content, the artists who were especially attractive or were talented dancers really accelerated their careers in the 1980s. Madonna, Prince, and Michael Jackson owe a deep debt to the exposure they received on MTV. The impact MTV created has deep resonance in the record industry. The long-standing model of releasing a single to radio to gauge or build a band's popularity was quickly replaced by filming a video for MTV.

MTV established its early reputation right away. The second video played on the station was Pat Benatar's "You Better Run," and MTV was soon credited with causing the second British Invasion due to its heavy rotation of bands such as the Human League, Flock of Seagulls, and Duran Duran. So effective was the channel, even early on, that these bands sold well in active MTV markets even though they were not being played on the radio.

So successful was MTV in its infancy, it immediately created ripples on cable television. In the year following MTV's rollout, HBO added a half-hour video block called *Video Jukebox,* NBC added its *Friday Night Videos* show, ABC launched the show *ABC Rocks,* and the Disney Channel added a video show called *D-TV*. This level of impact changed the way the American market consumed music. The radio domination of the period of the 1950s to the 1970s was over, and now consumers expected music videos on TV for 24 hours a day.

By 1984, MTV was already tweaking its formula. Originally patterned after 1970s album-oriented rock, the station instead turned toward a more singles heavy rotation and added its first set of on-air personalities: the MTV VJs (video jockeys). The first five were J.J. Jackson, Martha Quinn, Nina Blackwood, Mark Goodman, and Alan Hunter. These VJs each had a specific style of music that they work within, and they were recorded providing introductions for each video that would be aired on their program.

The mid-1980s found MTV pushing several rock and roll formats to the top of their playlists. New

Wave, hard rock, and heavy metal bands were favored, and bands such as Mötley Crüe, Van Halen, Bon Jovi, RATT, Def Leppard, the Police, and the Cars benefitted enormously from heavy rotation. Another interesting type of band that got heavy play on MTV in the mid-1980s was the supergroup. Supergroups such as the Firm, the Traveling Wilburys, and Power Station were favored as they created a strong draw based on diverse membership. For example, the Traveling Wilburys was Bob Dylan, George Harrison (the Beatles), Jeff Lynne (Electric Light Orchestra), Roy Orbison, and Tom Petty. With such a diverse band lineup, MTV recognized that the band captured a large and diverse audience.

By 1984, the music industry recognized that MTV was here to stay and that it was directly affecting the American music market. As such, more record companies asked their artists to make videos. With the influx of more videos, MTV had to create more categories of programming in order to focus the various styles it was now airing. Also at this time, MTV was grappling with issues of race. Because MTV had started out playing mostly hard and glam rock, there were no bands of color in the rotation. This did not escape notice, and by the end of 1983, the station aired the mixed race group the Specials' song "Rat Race." However, it was slow to change. It took a great deal of internal administrative grappling to get Michael Jackson's song "Billy Jean" on the channel. There were no black artists in standard rotation before 1983. It was Jackson who really affected a change on the channel. Once "Billy Jean" reached number one on the *Billboard* Hot 100, MTV relented and put it into heavy rotation. This was followed by "Beat It" and songs by Prince and Donna Summer.

MTV had evolved into an arbiter of music taste by 1984. As such, they launched the *MTV Music Awards*. This awards show was for the popular bands, songs, and videos for each year. The prizes were MTV moonman statues—the moonman had been the channel's logo since its inception. In 1985, MTV began airing special concert events. On July 13, the channel aired Bob Geldof's *Live Aid* concert. With this, MTV began airing certain mega-concerts such as *Live 8*.

Because the MTV video rotation had gotten pretty niched out and static by the mid-1980s, the station launched *120 Minutes* for the express purpose of playing videos by alternative groups. This was enhanced in 1987 with the inception of *Headbangers Ball* to focus on heavy metal videos and news. The following year, the show *Yo! MTV Raps* began for the purpose of showcasing all things rap and hip-hop. With this, MTV managed to stay on the cutting edge of the evolution of popular music styles in the United States. As such, the channel also had a hand in determining which bands were the fastest to emerge. This control extended in a variety of ways. In the same way the Grateful Dead did not have a number one hit (their songs were too long to be friendly to the radio framework) until 1987's "Touch of Grey," artists recognized that they had to make videos which were appropriate for airing on MTV—thus, some controversial acts did not make it onto the channel. Another popular and long-lasting special was *MTV Unplugged*. These acoustic performances by bands such as Nirvana were so popular that many were released on CD.

By the end of the 1980s, the all-music-all-the-time format began to change for MTV. In 1992, the channel launched their first nonmusic show, the reality show *The Real World*. In addition to providing even more reasons for American teenagers to tune into the channel, *The Real World* became a vehicle to affect popular culture through varying modes of dressing or speech. It also became a magnet for controversy, taking on issues like AIDS and homosexuality. Other early reality shows followed, including *The Osbournes* (starring Ozzy from Black Sabbath), *Newlyweds Nick and Jessica* (about the lives of Nick Lachey and Jessica Simpson), *My Super Sweet 16,* and *The Hills,* among others. Modern "reality shows" are *Got Your 6, Awkward, Faking It, Happyland,* and *Are You the One?* With this, MTV extended their brand outside the music world to include reality television and, in so doing, pushed the boundaries of popular culture and taste.

Another change in the channel was the move into West Coast hip-hop in the early 1990s. In recognition of the emerging market on the West Coast, MTV added artists such as Tupac, Ice Cube, Warren G, Dr. Dre, and Snoop Doggy Dogg. With this new style on the channel, the videos were also changing. The videos in the 1990s were more creative than those of the first decade. In 1991, Nirvana's video for "Smells Like Teen Spirit" ushered in the carefully created concept video—in addition to bringing the new grunge sound to MTV. This was followed by the growth of MTV's "Buzz Bin," which aired new and alternative music from grunge artists and the emerging alternative music sound. In 1991 and 1992, MTV pushed the West Coast grunge sound. In 1993, it picked up on the alternative music of Stone Temple Pilots, Rage against the Machine, Tool, Beck, and others. From 1994 to 1997, MTV promoted the move into pop punk with Green Day and the Offspring as well as the next ska wave with the Mighty, Mighty Bosstones and Sublime. As such, MTV was again on the front line of the emerging styles throughout the 1990s.

By the mid-1990s, MTV was reducing the number of videos the channel aired. It also refocused its programming away from alternative music and toward more pop offerings. This was the era of Britney Spears, Christina Aguilera, Mandy Moore, and Jessica Simpson. For the last few years of the 1990s, MTV steadily decreased the number of videos it aired and stuck with the pop and hip-hop formats. Since 2000, MTV has continued to decrease the amount of music it plays, instead focusing more and more attention on the ratings grabbing reality shows it helped to popularize. As an indication of MTV's new attitude, the channel should have celebrated its 30th anniversary in 2011. Instead of changing its program for the day to bask in this accomplishment, it stuck with regular programming and let the anniversary be celebrated on its sister station MTV 2. The rationale was that the channel does not age; instead it stays the age of its current viewers.

After 2008, MTV only aired music videos on the show *Total Request Live* and in blocks called *FNMTV*. *Total Request Live* also included interviews and other nonvideo programming, and it was discontinued in 2009. The *FNMTV* only lasted for one year and was replaced a year later with *AMTV*. With this, MTV is not so much music television as it is a variety of other things. Oddly, MTV largely stopped playing music and replaced it with pop cultural fare like *Jersey Shore*.

Launched in 1996, MTV 2 was set up to take up the slack for the lack of music on the original MTV. That said, it has also gone the route of sensationalism and soap opera–type programming with shows such as *Nitro Circus Live, Off the Bat, Wild 'N Out,* and *Guy Code*, among others. The music on MTV 2 now focuses primarily on modern rock and hip-hop.

Although MTV and MTV 2 were conceived of as a conduit for music on television, the stations seem to have largely abandoned that original mission. That said, during the heyday of the station in the 1980s and 1990s, MTV exerted an incredible influence on music and popular culture. The stations essentially became the arbiters of music taste for the adolescent and teenaged demographic for 20 years. They still exert a great deal of influence but have morphed into having greater impact on popular culture than on music. Along the way, MTV ushered in a change in how the modern music consumer digests new music or listens to their existing song catalog. During MTV's reign, the consumer model for music changed. The standard of buying a 45, LP, tape, CD, or DVD changed. Now the standard consumer streams their music favorites on portable devices or televisions. As such, MTV was a direct predecessor of YouTube. Perhaps the reason MTV moved away from the music videos on which they were founded was the recognition of that change. Their choice was to either reinvent the brand or go the way of *American Bandstand* and *Soul Train* and go off the air entirely.

David V. Moskowitz

References

Hoye, Jacob. *MTV Uncensored*. New York: Pocket Books, 2001.

Litwak, Mark. *Reel Power: The Struggle for Influence and Success in the New Hollywood*. New York: William Morrow and Co., 1986.

Nuzum, Eric. *Parental Advisory: Music Censorship in America*. New York: HarperCollins Publishers, 2001.

ABBA (1972–1982)

ABBA was arguably the first (and possibly the only) Swedish super group to emerge in the past 50 years. Through nine studio releases and one live album, ABBA left an indelible mark on popular music in Europe and the United States. A simple testament to their far-flung legacy can be found in more than 35 cover versions of their song "Dancing Queen" from bands as diverse as U2, Six Pence None the Richer, and Kylie Minogue (coverproject.com 2014). Further, their musical legacy, impact, popularity, and commercial viability have long been substantiated through over 380 million albums and singles sold worldwide.

The origins of ABBA can be traced back to 1966 when Benny Andersson (born Goran Bror Andersson, December 16, 1946; piano, synthesizer, vocals) teamed up with Bjorn Ulvaeus (born Bjorn Kristian Ulvaeus, April 25, 1945; guitar, vocals, banjo, mandolin). At the time, Andersson was in the Hep Stars and Ulvaeus was in the folk-rock unit called the Hootenanny Singers (Ankeny 2014). The pair joined forces as song writers and performers. Further, they were working together at Polar Music/Union Songs, which was an active label and publishing house run by Stig Anderson.

As the story of ABBA began, Andersson began dating Agnetha Faltskog (born April 5, 1950) who had recently scored a Swedish hit with the single "I Was So in Love." Meantime, Ulvaeus began a relationship with a Swedish pop and jazz singer named Anni-Frid Lyngstad (born November 15, 1945; vocals). In the run up to the creation of ABBA, various musical iterations came from members of the band.

In 1971, Andersson and Ulvaeus scored a hit single with the song "People Need Love." As the result of this success, they earned a spot on the 1973 Eurovision song contest. They entered as Bjorn, Benn, Agnetha, and Frida and became popular with the song "Ring Ring."

Along the way, the four realized that they needed a less cumbersome name, and at Stig's suggestion created the name ABBA. The band's name was an acronym of each of the band members' first names—bearing in mind that Frida's real name is Anni-Frid. With this, ABBA was poised to ascend the charts and take over the world with their breed of Europop/disco. ABBA then released its first album on Polar Records in 1973 entitled *Ring Ring*. The title track was the single they had submitted to the Eurovision contest. The other 11 songs on the album were stock early 1970s bubblegum pop. Although not an indication of their future style, singles such as "She's My Kind of Girl" and "Love Isn't Easy" did assist with the album's ultimate popularity. In fact, *Ring Ring* eventually climbed to number two in Sweden (*Encyclopedia of Popular Music* 2008).

ABBA again entered the Eurovision contest in 1974. The song the group submitted this time, "Waterloo," was a success. With this, ABBA became the first Swedish band to win the competition. The single spawned a second album with "Waterloo" as the title track. This second album began to bring ABBA's more mature style to light. Here the group collected several very catchy songs with undertones of Lennon and McCartney and Brian Wilson (of the Beach Boys) (*Encyclopedia of Popular Music* 2008). Singles such as "Waterloo" and "Honey Honey" began to foreshadow

ABBA performing (from left to right): Benny Andersson, Frida, Agnetha Faltskog, and Bjorn Ulvaeus. ABBA is an internationally known Swedish pop group and one of the most commercially successful artists of the 1970s. They have sold more than 380 million albums and singles worldwide and were inducted to the Rock and Roll Hall of Fame on March 15, 2010. (Corbis)

the band's pop leanings and their propensity for dance music. Further, the song "Hasta Mañana" was the first glimpse of their interest in Latin music, which would resurface in subsequent releases. *Waterloo* went to number one in Sweden and charted in seven other countries (including going number one in Norway). It also cracked the top 200 in the United States.

The year 1975 witnessed even more far-flung success for the band. With the release of the 1975 single "S.O.S.," ABBA scored their first true international smash hit. The single charted in the United States and the United Kingdom and many non-English-speaking countries. "S.O.S." was part of the band's 1975 eponymous album *ABBA*. Regardless of the success of

"S.O.S," *ABBA* contained several other stand-out singles, such as "Mamma Mia" and "I Do, I Do, I Do, I Do, I Do." *ABBA* exhibited the band's new compositional maturity and began to hint at the touch of sadness that marked many of the band's later hits. *ABBA* charted in nine countries and went to number one in Sweden, Australia, and Norway. Of note, by this point in their relatively young career ABBA already had enough hit singles to release a greatest hits record. In November 1975, ABBA issued *Greatest Hits*, which charted internationally and cracked the top 50 in the United States.

In 1976, ABBA released *Arrival*. As though professing their own arrival, the album was a smash hit. The style of most of the songs on *Arrival* was best described as disco—with a distinct dance feel and active rhythms. Described as their first "classic" album, *Arrival* contained the stand-out singles "Dancing Queen" and "Knowing Me, Knowing You." "Dancing Queen" was considered by many to be the perfect mid-1970s four-minute dance song with its Phil Spectorian grandeur, McCartneyesque melody, and the indescribable vocals (*Encyclopedia of Popular Music* 2008). Although the style of the songs on *Arrival* was still a dance and pop hybrid, ABBA had certainly transcended bubblegum. The album went to number one in seven countries including the United Kingdom and topped out at number 20 in the United States. On the heels of the album, ABBA went on a concert tour of Europe and Australia in early 1977. The tour was a huge success with multiple sold-out venues. The tour was accompanied by the band making a movie that premiered in December 1977 and coincided with the release of the next album (abbasite.com).

The four members of ABBA were reveling in the success of their band in the mid-1970s. Ulvaeus and Faltskog had married in 1971 and Andersson and Lyngstad were planning a 1978 union. To top this all off, the band released *The Album* in 1977. The album contained the stand-out singles "Take a Chance on Me" and "The Name of the Game." *The Album* charted in 10 countries, went to number one in five, and cracked the top 15 in the United States.

Continuing the momentum of the past several years, ABBA invaded the United States with a promotional tour in the spring of 1978. The year 1979 saw the release of their sixth album, *Voulez-Vous*. Considered the crest of ABBA's commercial success, the album was marked by the disco stylings of "I Have a Dream." "Angel Eyes" again alluded to the band's underlying melancholy, and "The King Has Lost His Crown" had a downright spiteful sentiment (*Encyclopedia of Popular Music* 2008). Another stand-out track and AM radio standard was "Chiquitita," which was recorded as part of a UNICEF benefit. The album again charted in 10 countries and went to number one in five. Further, it was certified gold in the United States and platinum in Canada, Germany, and the United Kingdom.

ABBA's next record was an interesting experiment for the group. *Gracias Por La Musica* was released in 1980 and was a collection of ABBA's hits sung by the group in Spanish. The album was issued in Spanish-speaking countries and, with it, ABBA broke through into a new market. Subsequently, ABBA's Spanish-speaking fan base grew exponentially. The album contained "Mamma Mia" and the stand-out single "Fernando."

In March of 1980, ABBA traveled to Japan for an 11 date tour, which was completely sold out. They made a six-night stand at Tokyo's Budokan, which marked the band's conquest of yet another non-English-speaking market. The group then released the single "The Winner Takes It All." The song broke the top 10 in the United States. On the heels of this success, the band released their next album, *Super Trouper*.

Super Trouper was the band's seventh and next to last studio album. It was released to acclaim from critics and audiences alike. "The Winner Takes It All" appeared on the album along with other hit singles including "Lay All Your Love on Me." It has been noted that the other songs on the album were more introspective as though foreshadowing the group's ultimate undoing. Songs such as "Our Last Summer" and "The Way Old Friends Do" seemed to be harbingers of bad things to come. It is difficult not to read into the contents of the songs. In fact, by this time the Ulvaeus–Faltskog marriage had ended (in 1979) and the Andersson–Lyngstad marriage would end in 1981. Amid this strife, it was difficult to keep the band together and to keep these sentiments out of the lyrics. However, *Super Trouper* went to number one in five countries and was certified gold or platinum in three.

The years 1981–1982 marked the end of ABBA as a singular performing force. In 1981, Ulvaeus married Lena Kallersjo. In mid-February, Andersson and Lyngstad's marriage ended and news surfaced that Benny was already involved with Mona Norklit. Norklit and Andersson were married by the end of the year. Regardless, song writing and studio sessions continued through 1981. The band's eighth and final studio album was released in November of 1981.

The Visitors exhibited a song-writing maturity and depth that previous albums did not contain. Although the songs on the album were still quite pop in style, they comprised more dense harmonies and interesting turns of phrase.

Interestingly, and not revealed at the time, the album's title actually referred to secret meetings held without the approval of the totalitarian governments in the Soviet-dominated states. Not surprisingly, several of the songs on the album tackle the topic of failed relationships. "When All Is Said and Done" and "Slipping Through My Fingers" seemed to be the swan songs of the band's now dissolved marriages. The album was also released in Spanish-speaking countries with a couple of song substitutions. The songs "No Hay A Quien Culpar" and "Se Me Esta Escapando" were substituted for "When All Is Said and Done" and "Slipping Through My Fingers," respectively.

The album cover itself appeared to speak to the trouble in the band. The image on the front cover of the album was of the four band members carefully not meeting each other's gazes. The tone of the songs was somber and much more minor-key filled than previous disco send-ups. The album was recorded amid the dissolving relationships of the band members and that reality was impossible to escape as the album unfolded. For all of the quality of the overall album, "only on the transcendently mournful single 'One of Us' does the band reach the ecstatic heights of previous singles" (*Encyclopedia of Popular Music* 2008).

Though *The Visitors* topped the charts in several countries, even going platinum in the United Kingdom and Germany, it was not the commercial success that the mid-1970s albums had been. Even so, singles from the album, including "One of Us," charted and garnered significant acclaim. "When All Is Said and Done" was released as a single in several countries and ended up being ABBA's last U.S. top 10 hit.

Regardless of the difficulty associated with the creation of *The Visitors*, ABBA soldiered on for a time. In mid-1982, song-writing sessions resumed and some recordings were done for a possible new album. The next record had the working title *Opus 10*. The band made it back into the studio in May and June and discussions were held regarding a small tour. The recording sessions yielded three songs: "You Owe Me One," "I Am the City," "and "Just Like That."

The general consensus was that this material was not up to the band's standards. With that, the songs were shelved and the band took a break for the summer. In August, the group reconvened to work on the new record. At this time, it was decided that the next album would not be of new material. Instead, ABBA decided to issue a double-album compilation of their previous singles called *The Singles: The First Ten Years*.

Again focused on new music, the band went back in the studio in late 1982. The result was several new songs released as singles with an A and B side. The first pair was "The Day before You Came" and "Cassandra," and the second was "Under Attack" and "You Owe Me One." As it turned out, "Under Attack" was the band's last release before disbanding. The song broke the top five in the Netherlands and Belgium, but was not a big commercial success.

In the wake of the release of the singles album, the group went to London to do promotion and make television appearances. They appeared on several television programs and staged several performances. Their last show was *The Late, Late Breakfast Show* with Noel Edmonds on December 11, 1982. With this, ABBA was no more. However, the members of the group continued to make music of a variety of sorts.

Andersson and Ulvaeus turned to writing music for musical theater, specifically the musical *Chess*. Faltskog and Lyngstad moved into solo careers with varying degrees of success. The musical *Abbacadabra* came next. This work used 14 ABBA songs and found the men of the group again working with Lyngstad. The musical premiered on December 8, 1983. Although the ABBA musical was maligned by critics, it was a popular success for a time.

The four people previously known as ABBA came together once more in 1986. In January of that year, the four recorded a song written by their one-time label boss Stig Anderson to celebrate his 55th birthday. At that time, the four had not been together for almost two years. Also in 1986, ABBA released an album called *Live* with selections from their major tours in 1977 and 1979. The album was simultaneously a greatest hits and live record with inclusion of "Dancing Queen," "Take a Chance," and "Fernando."

Although ABBA no longer performs together as a group, they have never officially broken up. There is still an active band website, an ABBA museum, and an ABBA museum website that markets all things associated with the group. As further testament to the band's staying power, in 1999, a musical based on the band's music was developed. Titled *Mamma Mia*, after the group's hit from 1975, the creation of the musical involved the input of Ulvaeus and Andersson and the completed work premiered in 2001. Over 54 million people have seen the musical and it has grossed in excess of 2 billion dollars worldwide. Although the story in the musical is not about ABBA, their music fills the soundtrack. Clearly, the fervor for the musical continues unabated with performances booked into 2015 (Internet Broadway Database [ibdb.com] 2015). The Broadway production was so successful that it was turned into a movie, which premiered on July 4, 2008.

Although the group has never officially broken up, there now seems little chance of any real reunion. Faltskog has an active solo career including four solo albums. As recently as May of 2013, she released a single titled "I Should've Followed You Home." Lyngstad also has an active solo career. She has continued to release new material for the past 20 years, including five solo albums. Interestingly, in the 1990s Lyngstad married into the Swedish royal family. On August 26, 1992, she married Prince Heinrich Russo Reuss of Plauen. The couple remained together until the prince's death in 1999.

Ulvaeus has diversified his interests since the late 1980s. He remains married to Kallersjo and splits his time between music associated with ABBA (such as the musicals) and his stake in the ownership of the music notation software Igor Engraver (www.noteheads.com). Andersson remains active in music in several capacities. He launched his own 16 member performing group called Benny Andersson's Orchestra (BAO) for which he composes new material.

BAO has released five albums, and Andersson periodically writes with Ulvaeus for the group.

Although the band's career only lasted 10 years, ABBA accumulated a large number of awards and accolades that continue to be heaped on the band. From their Eurovision Song Contest win in 1974, the group went on win the World Music Award for Best Selling Swedish Artist in 1993, and were inducted into the Vocal Group Hall of Fame in 2002. In 2005, the group issued an exhaustive box set called *The Complete Studio Recordings*, the demand for which attests to the continued interest in the group. In 2010, the group was inducted into the Rock and Roll Hall of Fame by presenters Barry and Robin Gibbs.

In light of their successes, it is not surprising that ABBA has had a great deal of influence on other bands. There are at least two dozen tribute albums that have been issued by groups as diverse as Erasure and the London Symphony Orchestra. Those complete albums notwithstanding, ABBAs individual songs have been covered by several hundred bands/singers ranging from Sid Vicious of the Sex Pistols to Anna Sofie von Otter to Culture Club. Their song "Money, Money, Money" exists in at least 20 different cover versions by everyone from the band Madness to Marillion. In addition to all of those cover albums/songs, several notable artists have gone on record as having been influenced by ABBA, including Elvis Costello, Madonna, Chrissie Hynde of the Pretenders, Pete Townsend of the Who, Katy Perry, and David Grohl of the Foo Fighters.

David V. Moskowitz

Selected Discography

Bjorn & Benny, Agnetha & Frida (aka *Ring Ring*), Polar POLS 242, 1973.

Waterloo, Polar POLS 252, 1974.

ABBA, Polar POLS 262, 1975.

Arrival, Polar POLS 272, 1976.

The Album, Polar POLS 282, 1977.

Voulez-Vous, Polar POLS 292, 1979.

Gracias Por La Musica, Epic EPC 86123, 1980.

Super Trouper, Polar POLS 322, 1980.

The Visitors, Polar POLS 342, 1981.

Live, Polar POLS 412, 1986.

References

ABBA Official Website. 2013. "Biography." Accessed June 2013. www.abbasite.com.

Ankeny, Jason, "ABBA," *All Music Guide*. Rovi Corporation, 2014.

The Covers Project Official Website. 2015. Accessed June 2014. www.coversproject.com/artist/abba/.

Discogs Official Website. 2015. "ABBA Discography." Accessed June 2014. www.discogs.com/artist/69866-ABBA, 2014.

Larkin, Colin, ed., "ABBA." *Encyclopedia of Popular Music*. Oxford Music Online, 2008.

Larkin, Colin, ed., "ABBA-*Ring Ring*." *Encyclopedia of Popular Music*. Oxford Music Online, 2008.

Larkin, Colin, ed., "ABBA-*Waterloo*." *Encyclopedia of Popular Music*. Oxford Music Online, 2008.

Rock and Roll Hall of Fame Official Website. 2014. "ABBA Biography." Accessed June 2013. www.rockhall.com/inductees/abba/.

AC/DC (1973–Present with Brian Johnson)

Easily identifiable as one of the most bombastic and long-lasting heavy metal bands that emerged in the 1970s—and the only one from Australia—AC/DC have been blazing an incomparable musical trail for decades. The band was begun by brothers Angus (born Angus McKinnon Young, March 31, 1955; lead guitar) and Malcolm Young (born Malcolm Mitchell Young, January 6, 1953; rhythm guitar, bass) in Sydney, Australia, in November of 1973. The brothers had been in a band called the Velvet Underground (not the band with Lou Reed), and when it dissolved, they formed their own band.

At the time that the Young brothers started gigging around Sydney, Angus was only 15 years old. The Youngs cut a single with Dave Evans as the singer and ex-Easybeats members Harry Vanda and George Young (Malcolm and Angus's eldest brother) called "Can I Sit Next to You" (Erlewine 2014). However,

they experienced little success and decided to change locale. From Sydney, the Youngs relocated the band to Melbourne, where a recognizable AC/DC took shape. In Melbourne, the Youngs added Phil Rudd (born Phillip Hugh Norman Witschke Rudzecuis, May 19, 1954; drums) and Mark Evans (born Mark Whitmore Evans, March 2, 1956; bass). Possibly more importantly, the Youngs gained some serious momentum when they hired their then chauffeur, Bon Scott (born Ronald Belford Scott, July 9, 1946, died February 19, 1980; vocals), as their lead singer. Scott had a reputation as a petty criminal and general roust about. This delinquency became a part of the bands image as they began writing songs with "crude double entendres and violent imagery, all spiked with a mischievous sense of fun" (Erlewine 2014). This was all peppered with the image of Angus dressed in a school boy uniform on the advice of his elder sister.

In 1974 and 1975, respectively, AC/DC released two albums *High Voltage* and *T.N.T.* Both were issued in Australia under the Albert Productions imprint. Selections from both of these early records became the band's first international release, *High Voltage*, on Atlantic Records in 1976. Issued in both the United States and the United Kingdom, *High Voltage* was accompanied by tours of both of these countries, which significantly enhanced the band's reputation. *High Voltage* was the first taste of AC/DC for the U.S. audience. Described by the *Encyclopedia of Popular Music*, "lead guitarist Angus Young, a spastic dwarf-like riff-monger who wore nothing but traditional schoolboy attire, was leading this band of hooligans with gleeful perversity and balls-out ambition. The group's intent is made perfectly clear from the disc's opening power chords: to distill rock and mutate the blues down to its barest essentials" (*Encyclopedia of Popular Music* 2008).

In the wake of *High Voltage*, AC/DC released *Dirty Deeds Done Dirt Cheap* in 1976. Although an international release, it did not make it to the United States until 1981—after *Let There Be Rock*. *Dirty Deeds Done Dirt Cheap* was the band's third album and was an exhibition of Bon Scott's malevolence. Angus's guitar playing was brutish and muscled to match Scott's seething lyrics. The lyrics on the album were laden with sexual innuendo and double entendre. Stephen Erlewine described the album as "a call to arms from a group who wanted nothing more than to celebrate the dirtiest, nastiest instincts humans could have, right down to the insurgent anti-authority vibe that runs throughout the record. Take 'Big Balls'— sure it's a dirty joke, but it's a dirty joke with class overthrow in mind" (Erlewine 2014). Standout singles on the album were the title track, "Big Balls," and "Jailbreak," which pushed the band's music onto the global stage.

AC/DC charted for the first time in the United States with the 1977 release *Let There Be Rock*. This release marked a turning point for the band. Not only did it experience its first international success, it also lost its first member since the album releases began. In late 1977, Mark Evans left the band and was replaced by Cliff Williams (born Clifford Williams, December 14, 1949; bass).

As AC/DC was building its following through touring marked by high-energy live performances, it also released the album *Powerage* in the spring of 1978. As a result of the fervor over the band's live performances, live albums such as *If You Want Blood You've Got It* (1978) began being released. The band's true international emergence came on 1979's *Highway to Hell*. With this release, AC/DC scored a top-20 hit in the United States and cracked the top 10 in the United Kingdom. Additionally, this album established the band as a commercially viable entity, as it was the group's first million seller (Erlewine 2014). With this album, Angus became the audacious school-uniform-wearing poster child. Sporting his, then, outdated Gibson SG, Young laid down seemingly endless riffs that stuck in the listener's ears. Standout singles from this album were the metal tinged "Love Hungry Man" and "Touch Too Much," along with the title track.

Tragedy struck in early 1980 when Bon Scott died on February 19. In keeping with the band's hard partying image, Scott essentially drank himself to death. Scott had been drinking with friends at the Music Machine club in London the night before. Too drunk to be easily moved indoors to sleep, Scott was left in the

AC/DC with original singer Bon Scott, as pictured here in 1976. After Bon's death, the Young brothers and their band mates entered a second chapter of popularity with singer Brian Johnson. The group's extreme dynamics and Angus Young's school boy outfit have kept them perennial favorites. (Photo by Martyn Goddard/Corbis)

car overnight. Found unresponsive the next morning, Scott was rushed to College hospital, and there it was realized that he had aspirated vomit and died of asphyxiation. The official cause of death was acute alcohol poisoning. Scott was buried in a small service in Fremantal, Western Australia, where he spent his childhood.

In the wake of Scott's death, the remaining members of the band briefly considered calling it quits. After further consideration, they decided to soldier on and set about the job of finding a new front man. They entertained a small list of possibilities, including Nobby Holder of Slade, Terry Slesser of Back Street Crawler, and a few others. Eventually, the band settled on Brian Johnson (born October 5, 1947; vocals) from the band Geordie. With Johnson in the fold, the band headed into the studio and recorded what can arguably be described as their most well-known album, *Back in Black*. Released in 1980, *Back in Black* sold over 10 million copies in the United States. Perhaps more importantly, it stood as proof that the band could not only continue without Scott—it would succeed at unprecedented levels. With *Back in Black*, AC/DC cemented its position as one of the premier heavy metal/hard rock bands of the 1980s. The album topped out at number four on the *Billboard 200* charts. However, it remained on the charts for a 131-week run and ultimately sold over 19 million copies.

Now universally accepted as the band's highest selling record, *Back in Black* was released as the band reeled in the wake of Bon's death. The stand-out songs, "Hell's Bells" and "You Shook Me All Night Long," contributed to the album's reputation as proof that the band's "staple lyrical diet of sex and the general pursuit of happiness, however, remained very much in tact" (*Encyclopedia of Popular Music* 2008).

Through the early 1980s, AC/DC was one of the most important touring rock bands in the world. This premier position was further substantiated with the release of *For Those About to Rock We Salute You*. Released in 1981, the new record shot up the charts in the United States and the United Kingdom. Standout singles from this album were "Let's Get It Up" and the title track. In the wake of this release, the single "For Those About to Rock We Salute You" became a perennial live show favorite with its accompanying cannon blasts, and the album ultimately went on to sell well—charting in the United States and the United Kingdom. Also in 1981, the band headlined the Monsters of Rock Festival in Donnington, England, with Whitesnake, Blue Oyster Cult, and Slade.

The pressure on the band to continue to succeed and continually outdo the previous benchmarks took its toll. Drugs and alcohol became a problem and internal relationships among the band members deteriorated. Bad feeling between Malcolm and Rudd reached a head with a physical confrontation after which Rudd was fired from the band. Rudd's replacement was Simon Wright (born June 19, 1963; drums) who was not quite 20 years old at the time. The band soldiered on and released *Flick of the Switch* in 1983.

The drumming on this album had already been tracked by Rudd, and Rudd's material was kept for the final cut of the album.

The *Flick of the Switch* release marked a turning point for AC/DC. In the wake of this release, the band's popularity started to decrease. The material released in the early 1980s—*Flick of the Switch* and *Fly on the Wall* (1985)—were considered underdeveloped and not up to the standard that the band had previously established. Standout singles on the album were "Sink the Pink" and "Shake Your Foundations," which resurfaced in the Stephen King film *Maximum Overdrive*. A turning point came with the single "Who Made Who," produced for the film, which became a success and marked a return to previous form for the band.

Blow Up Your Video was released in 1988 and marked the band's return to the limelight. With the return of their original producers, Harry Banda and George Young, the band scored a major success. The album was certified platinum in the United States and reached number two in the United Kingdom. The *Blow Up Your Video* world tour followed and was a commercial success. A twist to the tour came when Angus stepped away from the band during the North American leg of the tour to seek treatment for alcohol addiction. Angus's spot was covered by his nephew Stevie Young (Discogs.com 2014). Ultimately, *Blow Up Your Video* was nominated for a Grammy Award for Best Hard Rock/Metal Performance Vocal or Instrumental in 1989 though it lost to *Crest of a Knave* by Jethro Tull.

After the tour, Wright left the band to work with Ronnie James Dio's band Dio on their album *Lock Up the Wolves*. He was replaced by session ace Chris Slade (born Christopher Rees, October 30, 1946; drums). With Slade in the fold, the band went back to song writing in pursuit of its next album and continued fame. The 1990s album *The Razor's Edge* was AC/DC returning to old form. It produced the stand-out single "Thunderstruck" and returned the band to its previous international fame. The album marked the beginning of the band's relationship with producer Bruce Fairbairn who had previously had success with Bon Jovi and Aerosmith. With this, *The Razor's Edge* produced several stand-out singles including "Thunderstruck" and "Money Talks"—both charting singles. The album went multiplatinum and cracked the top 10 album chart in the United States. The subsequent tour was commercially successful and produced a successful live album, called *Live*, released in 1992.

Now that AC/DC was back on top, the band worked to maintain their reputation. A step in that direction was the creation of the single "Big Gun." The band recorded this song for the soundtrack to the 1993 movie *Last Action Hero*, and it was their first U.S. number one single. The latter half of the 1990s was a period of prosperity for the band. Several significant events contributed to this uptick. The band mended its fences with drummer Rudd, and he rejoined the group. Also, AC/DC began a relationship with producer Rick Rubin of Def Jam Records fame.

With Rubin at the helm, the band recorded *Ballbreaker* in 1995. The album produced three singles— "Hail Caesar," "Hard as a Rock," and "Cover You in Oil." The *Encyclopedia of Popular Music* described the album as "eternally in pursuit of the ultimate riff . . . [with] songs that glower in the corners, ready to pounce with sweaty, blues rock guitars and razor sharp hooks" (*Encyclopedia of Popular Music* 2008). This exhibition of all of AC/DC's trademarks was made possible through the continued synergy of the Young brothers, the return of Phil Rudd, and Brian Johnson's whiskey- and cigarette-soaked vocals. Next, the band released a 1997 box set called *Bonfire*. The material contained on the set was live and unreleased material from the period that Bon Scott led the band.

After this, the band issued a four-disc box set and additional live material. The album of the 2000s, *Stiff Upper Lip*, ushered AC/DC into the new millennium. Although it was a commercial success and charted in five countries, it was panned by critics for lacking originality. The single "Stiff Upper Lip" stayed at number one on the U.S. rock charts for four weeks and indicated that the band's fans were pleased with the material regardless of what the critics said. Two subsequent singles, "Satellite Blues" and "Safe in

New York City," also charted and strengthened the band's resolve that they were giving the people what they wanted.

As a testament to AC/DC's staying power, chart success, and popularity, the band signed a multi-album deal with Sony Music in 2002 (Erlewine 2014). This Sony deal allowed the band to mine its back catalogue and rerelease material after remastering. This made their previous recordings available in compact disc format with enhanced quality. A year later, AC/DC was inducted into the Rock and Roll Hall of Fame. Steven Tyler of Aerosmith was their presenter at the 18th annual induction dinner. According to Rockhall.com, AC/DC has always had a single-minded vision that they worked to achieve with an "unwavering devotion to no-frills hard rock with plenty of bawdy wit . . . [which] won them the loyalty of millions of fan, who range from the working stiff to The Rolling Stones' Keith Richards" (Rockhall.com 2014).

Although the Rock Hall induction was a highlight of 2003, the band also played the Molson Canadian Rocks Festival in that year. The concert was staged in front of an estimated half million fans and also featured the Rolling Stones and Rush. Of note, the concert maintains the distinction of being the largest paid music event in North American history (Erlewine 2014).

In 2008, the band released the album *Black Ice* on the Columbia Records imprint. The album was produced by Brendan O'Brien who has worked with bands as diverse as Kansas, the Black Crows, and the Red Hot Chili Peppers. An interesting twist on this album was how it was marketed. The album was only sold by Walmart and Sam's Club and on the band's website. The big box store chain created "Rock Again AC/DC Stores" to promote the album.

The album was another success for the band and produced the hit single "Rock 'n' Roll Train." The single was accompanied by a popular video and commercial success. The *Black Ice* album was Columbia Records' most successful release to date and has the distinction of debuting at number one in 29 countries simultaneously. The album went multiplatinum and was followed by an 18-month world tour. Of note, "with over 6.5 million copies of *Black Ice* shipped worldwide, combined with over 5.5 million in catalogue sales, AC/DC have surpassed the Beatles as the No. 1 selling catalogue artists in the United States for 2008" (acdc.com 2014).

As a further testament to AC/DC's staying power and popularity, in September of 2008, Sirius Satellite Radio launched an AC/DC channel that exclusively played the band's music and interviews with and about the band. With these additional revenue streams, AC/DC was heralded as Australia's top entertainment earner for 2009.

In 2010, AC/DC parlayed their album success and their previous forays into movie music by providing the soundtrack to the movie *Iron Man 2*. The 26-song album was a mixture of studio versions of many of the band's most famous singles and a series of live recordings. Another successful release, this album seemed to push AC/DC into rock and roll immortality—they had conquered all of the available music media of the day.

The future of the band remains open ended. Malcolm has gone on record saying that the band will likely launch another world tour and likely release another album. That having been said, there were no time limits placed on any of this activity. From 2012 to 2014, the band made several overtures in the direction of new music, but as yet nothing concrete has come of these discussions. On April 16, 2014, Malcolm announced that he was temporarily stepping away from the band due to ill health. The band released their first live album in 20 years with 2012s *Live at River Plate*.

Through the course of four decades of music making, AC/DC have carved out a distinct and inescapable legacy. They were inducted into the Rock and Roll Hall of Fame in 2003; also in that year Malcolm was honored with a Ted Albert Award for Outstanding Service to Australian Music. Additionally, according to the Record Industry Association of America, the band has sold in excess of 71 million albums with *Back in Black* certified at over 20 million units sold. The band has been nominated for 13 ARIA Music Awards and has won three. Further, they have been nominated for seven Grammy Awards and won one.

The legacy of AC/DC began with the influence of guitarists such as Chuck Berry, Johnny Lee Hooker, Freddie King, and Jimi Hendrix, according to Angus. These influences were pushed through the lens of AC/DC and in turn created a diverse list of bands that they influenced, including Soundgarden, Poison, Van Halen, Metallica, Foo Fighters, Tesla, Joan Jett, Quiet Riot, Def Leppard, Iron Maiden, and many others. Additional influence and continued stylistic legacy falls to a series of tribute albums, notably: *Thunderbolt: A Tribute to AC/DC* in 1998, *The Rock-A-Billy Tribute to AC/DC* in 2003, and *Graveyard Classics 2* in 2004—the latter of which is a death metal version of the *Back in Black* album in its entirety. Several dozen cover versions exist of AC/DC's songs. The style in which these songs were covered is as diverse. For example, Angry Samoans covered "Highway to Hell" in a punk version, Richard Cheese covered "You Shook Me All Night Long" in a lounge music style, Latin artist Shakira covered "Back in Black" with her own spin, and the list goes on. With this, AC/DC's future may be uncertain, but its musical legacy is as solid as the band's hard rock foundations.

David V. Moskowitz

Selected Discography

Note: AC/DC's albums were largely released on the Albert Productions imprint in Australia, but on labels such as Atlantic, Universal, Elektra, and EMI around the world.

High Voltage, Albert Productions APLP.009, 1974.

T.N.T., Albert Productions APLPA-016, 1975.

Dirty Deeds Done Dirt Cheap, Atlantic K 50323, 1976.

High Voltage, Atlantic K 50257, 1976.

Let There Be Rock, Albert Productions APLP.022, 1977.

Powerage, Albert Productions APLP.030, 1978.

Highway to Hell, Albert Productions APLP.040, 1979.

Back in Black, Albert Productions APLP.046, 1980.

For Those about to Rock We Salute You, Atlantic TP11111, 1981.

Flick of the Switch, Albert Productions APLP.061, 1983.

The Razor's Edge, Albert Productions A2–91413, 1990.

Ballbreaker, Albert Productions 4770992, 1995.

Stiff Upper Lip, Albert Productions 724352564521, 2000.

Black Ice, Columbia 88697 38377 1, 2008.

Iron Man 2, Columbia 88697 60952 2, 2010.

Live at River Plate, Columbia 88765 41175 2, 2012.

References

AC/DC Official Website. 2014. "Biography." Accessed June 2014. www.acdc.com/us/theband.

Discogs Official Website. 2015. "AC/DC Discography," Accessed June 2014. http://www.discogs.com/artist/84752-ACDC, 2014.

Erlewine, Stephen. "AC/DC." *All Music Guide*. Rovi Corporation, 2014.

Larkin, Colin, ed. "AC/DC—*Back in Black*." *Encyclopedia of Popular Music*. Oxford Music Online, 2008.

Rivadivia, Eduardo. "AC/DC—*T.N.T.*" *All Music Guide*. Rovi Corporation, 2014.

Walser, Robert. "AC/DC." *Grove Music Online*. Oxford University Press, 2014.

Rock and Roll Hall of Fame Official Website. 2014. "AC/DC Biography." Accessed June 2014. rockhall.com/inductees/ac-dc/bio/.

Aerosmith (1970–Present)

Virtually any source will name Aerosmith as the greatest U.S. hard rock band, having sold more than 150 million albums worldwide and more than 60 million in the United States, having navigated a bewilderingly resilient career, and reaching international and cross-generational fame. The keys to their continued success are a tricky balance between deep loyalty and artistic vision, and strong individualism and personal drive.

Except for a relatively short time in the band's history, it has primarily consisted of the five members Steven Tyler (born Steven Victor Tallarico, March 26, 1948; lead vocals, harmonica, piano, principal lyricist), 1970–present; Joe Perry (born Anthony Joseph Pereira, September 10, 1950; lead guitar, backing vocals, occasional lead vocals), 1970–1979 and 1984–present; Brad Whitford (born Bradford Ernest Whitford, February 23, 1952; rhythm guitar, lead guitar), 1971–1981 and 1984–present; Tom Hamilton (born Thomas William Hamilton, December 31, 1951; bass, occasional backing vocals), 1970–present; and Joey Kramer (born Joseph Michael Kramer, June 21, 1950; drums), 1970–present. Other band personal included Ray Tabano (born Raymond Tabano, December 23, 1946; rhythm guitar), 1970–1971; Jimmy Crespo (born James Crespo Jr., July 5, 1954; lead guitar, backing vocals), 1979–1984; and Rick Dufay (born Richard Marc Dufay, February 19, 1952; rhythm guitar, lead guitar), 1981–1984.

Over the 40 years of their existence, Aerosmith has been both stylistically flexible and musically grounded, in spite of devastating drug addiction and interpersonal turmoil. The roller-coaster of the band's history has taken them from meager beginnings, a staggering rise to glory in the late 1970s, a fracturing decline in the 1980s, to a magnificent comeback and beyond. The band's lasting popularity is largely due to their dynamic live act, centered on Steven Tyler and Joe Perry's charisma and the band's tight performances. From the beginning, Aerosmith established themselves as a touring band, and even when the studio albums met with mediocre critical reviews, their high-energy live performances contributed to their success and kept those records selling. Part of what made their popularity last through multiple generations was the band's ability to reinvent itself while retaining its core identity. Adapting their 1970s stadium rock and roll to a 1990s music-video-saturated culture not only opened the door for a new generation of followers, but also bridged the gap between those generations. Where many enduring bands such as the Beatles often are only heard on oldies stations, Aerosmith is still regularly heard on stations that feature modern alternative rock. Fathers and sons can listen to *Nine Lives* (1997) together and both feel like this was "their" music—a rare artistic agreement between generations X and Y.

Aerosmith is sometimes considered a heavy metal band, but their loose rhythms, Perry's blues-style guitar, and Tyler's diverse lyrical topics separate them from that genre. From power ballads to riff-oriented rock songs, Tyler's exceptional voice and Perry's

Aerosmith, pictured here in 1976, have long been fan favorites with their combination of hard rocking classics mixed with tender ballads. The band has sold more than 150 million albums worldwide over the course of a career spanning more than 40 years. (Photo by Fin Costello/Redferns)

always-impressive playing are the driving force of the band. A lot has been made from many angles about the dynamic duo of Tyler and Perry. They have long described themselves as brothers, or kindred spirits. The press dubbed them the "Toxic Twins" for the incessant drug use and quarrels, but their devotion to each other and their music has shown through the years as what makes Aerosmith successful.

In the beginning, the band—as well as anyone who heard them play—was convinced that they had something special to offer and were going to make it big. The amount of devotion they put into their music

and rehearsals was evident because they were so cohesive and tightly wound. In the early days, the members often felt jaded when they met with mediocre reviews, while watching the prosperousness of other bands like the New York Dolls, who made a big spectacle dressed in women's clothes and took so many drugs they could barely play. To Aerosmith, the music was of primary importance and extraneous material—like the pyrotechnics of bands like Kiss—only detracted from the quality of the product. This kind of artistic integrity brought them through personal conflicts, drug addictions, and public criticism.

Some stylistic influences differed between the members, but they all drew strong influence from Led Zeppelin, the first Jeff Beck Group, and the Rolling Stones, taking the British blues-based rock and making it truly American. Other influences were Cream and the Yardbirds. Still, Tyler tended to write more ballads than Perry would like; Perry stated that he felt as a hard rock band, they should play hard rock music and not ballads.

In the beginning, the band members wrote their own material and insisted on playing it even when they would have gotten paid more by taking gigs as a cover band. Their lyrics are typically rebellious, ultramacho, dripping with sexual innuendo, and generally about partying and having a good time. Such topics tended to attract a predominantly male audience, although there were always girls waiting backstage hoping for some personal time with the band members (but usually ending up with the crew).

Most songs started out as guitar riffs, and the lyrics almost always came last in the creative process. Tyler would have the band jam, and he would scat or make up nonsense syllables to a tune over the top. Only later would the content arise, as he tried to match cheeky turns of a phrase with the appropriate vowel sounds he used in rehearsal. Evident from interviews with Tyler, his imagination is active and he always has a catchy comeback or creative wordplay to describe even the most mundane situation. Raw, quirky imagery saturates the song texts, which often evolved from jokes and insults that the members threw at each other.

Tyler was notorious for procrastinating on his part or losing lyrics on the road—a situation that worsened along with his addiction to drugs. During the recording of *Rocks* (1976) when their drug use was really escalating, the band described their creative process as basically getting really stoned and lying on the floor, and the music or lyrics would just flow onto the page. Tyler said "it doesn't happen that way anymore and it hasn't since we put the drugs down. We were . . . more creative as a band. We still haven't solved some of the problems that the drugs cloaked . . . Today I listen to those albums . . . and all I can hear are the drugs" (Davis 253).

As devoted as the band was to their own material, it was difficult for them in their comeback when the lack of drugs hindered their creative process and their management insisted on bringing in professional songwriters or lyricists. The band complained that songwriter Holly Knight received credit on "Ragdoll" for changing only one word, and that using someone else's text was not true to their roots. Instead, Tyler and the others worked closely with the songwriters to craft the lyrics together. The continued collaborative effort with songwriters/producers like Desmond Child, Glenn Ballard, Bruce Fairbairn, and Jim Vallance was perhaps part of what has made them more accessible to a younger audience.

The band officially began in 1970, but of course the story begins before then. From a long line of professional classical musicians, Tyler's attentive ear and calculating perfectionism made him difficult to work with because he insisted on precision—particularly when the band was young. On stage, his sexual charisma, limber strutting, and mastery of playing to the audience drew crowds from all ages.

The band's roots can be traced to Lake Sunapee, New Hampshire. Hamilton's family lived in New London, New Hampshire, on the east side of the lake. Perry's family lived near Boston and owned a summer home in Sunapee. Tyler's parents lived in Yonkers, New York, but his grandparents, the Tallaricos, owned a summer property called Trow-Rico Lodge in the community of Sunapee.

Tyler already had a performing career before he joined with the other members of Aerosmith. His first band, the Strangeurs (later called Chain Reaction), were minor celebrities in the area, having opened for bands like the Byrds and the Beach Boys, and having signed a one-record contract with CBS. Tyler was offered a solo contract, but turned it down because of his loyalty to his band, and by the summer of 1967, Chain Reaction was over. Tyler played and sang off and on in various bands, but first heard Perry play in the summer of 1969.

Young Joe Perry was in several bands at his home in Hopedale, Massachusetts, and during the summers in Sunapee, joined one called the Jam Band with

Tom Hamilton. Perry dropped out of high school in late 1968 and worked a 40-hour-a-week factory job, practicing and saving money. During the summer of Woodstock, Perry quit his job and returned to Sunapee to play in the band with Hamilton, and Tyler came to see them play. He said that they were not very good, but possessed a raw energy and groove and decided on the spot that they were what he was looking for. However, it was not until the end of the following summer of 1970 that Perry and Hamilton planned to move to Boston to make it happen. Before joining with Perry, Tyler's last band had fizzled when he started choking the guitar player onstage for yawning during the performance. Soon afterward, Tyler started to play and sing with Perry; the two were forming a very deep musical and personal connection. Together with Ray Tabano, who had been in some of Tyler's previous bands, the new Jam Band moved to Boston and got an apartment at 1325 Commonwealth Avenue where they would stay until their big break.

Tyler no longer wanted to play drums, and everyone knew that he was the best asset to the band in front as the lead singer. Joey Kramer was in his first year at Berklee College of Music and had played in many groups in Boston and New York. He, like Tyler, was from Yonkers, New York, and knew Ray Tabano from the musical community. The band inducted Kramer after hearing him play. There was a meeting to come up with a name, and Kramer resurrected a made-up word he used to scribble all over his binders in high school: Aerosmith. So with that, the band was formed.

In the summer of 1971 it became apparent to the band and their backers that Tabano's playing was not up to par. Tabano had a wife and business and often did not have time to rehearse. There was difficult tension, especially for Tyler and Kramer who had longer connections with him, but after he left the band, Tabano became part of Aerosmith's publicity group, creating and selling T-shirts, buttons, and band paraphernalia from 1974 until 1979.

Brad Whitford graduated from Berklee College of Music and had been playing in bands for six years. Although the music scene at Berklee was very jazz oriented, Whitford idolized the rock band Humble Pie (English rock band formed by Steve Marriott) and was searching for a similar sound. At the time Aerosmith was looking for a new guitarist, Whitford was playing in Sunapee with one of Tyler's friends while Aerosmith was in the audience. They quickly recruited him after hearing him play, and he moved into their apartment on Commonwealth Avenue. His technique was solid and, although they were just looking for a rhythm guitarist, Whitford and Perry formed a cohesive unit that easily melded and allowed for both players to be on top.

The whole band lived together in desperate poverty in 1971. They took day jobs when they could, scraping together just enough money for rent and drugs; it was normal for them to steal food from the local supermarket. They practiced relentlessly, booked their own shows, and did their own promotion. With help from Perry's parents, they bought a hippie-era red school bus and were able to travel farther for gigs. They played in smaller venues for lower fares because they insisted on playing their own songs rather than covering established hits.

In December 1971, they were rehearsing during the daytime at the Fenway Theater; one night, the assistant manager asked them to cover a show when the scheduled band could not make it. After Aerosmith rocked the house, the manager brought in Frank Connelly, a major Boston promoter who signed them right away. Connelly managed them for a year, tightening up the band by booking them in clubs and bars. In the spring of 1972, Connelly introduced the band to Steve Leber and David Krebs, who owned a New York company called the CCC (Contemporary Communications Corporation). Leber and Krebs would manage Aerosmith for the next 12 years, and it was they who negotiated a deal with Columbia Records that summer, signing Aerosmith for $125,000.

The record deal resulted in their first album, *Aerosmith* (January 1973), an eight-track album with seven original songs that Tyler wrote or cowrote (this was the first time Steven identified himself as Tyler rather than Tallarico). The record was a mixture of rock and blues with a hint of funk, and was not an instant success. Columbia did not promote the album very well and the record lacked any real single. ("Dream On" did not become a big hit until its rerelease in 1976 and is considered one of the first power ballads along with Led Zeppelin's "Stairway to Heaven.") The album spread mostly by word of mouth and some promotion by radio DJs Maxanne Sartori in Boston and Mark Parenteau in Detroit. The media was critical of the album, making many seemingly unfair comparisons between Tyler and Mick Jagger.

It was clear that the key to the band's success was their live shows, and they became known through direct contact rather than publicity. They had a few tours as opening acts for the Kinks, which met with good reviews. When "Dream On" was finally released as a single, they started to get airplay and opened for bands outside of New England.

The next few years solidified the band's position in stardom. They started working with producer Jack Douglas during the making of their second album, *Get Your Wings* (March 1974). Douglas clicked with the band and would sometimes sit in on jam sessions, encouraging their creativity. During the support tour for *Get Your Wings*, Tyler's trademark of bunches of scarves around the microphone stand emerged, originally reported to shield against projectiles, but later to stash drugs. Constant touring with bands like the New York Dolls and Kiss solidified Aerosmith's following in the Midwest and on the West Coast.

With their rising momentum from ceaseless performing, their next album, *Toys in the Attic* (April 1975) was a commercial breakthrough. It was their first platinum album and, although it got mediocre reviews, sold millions of copies, rising to number 10 on the U.S. charts. The album includes hits "Sweet Emotion" and "Walk this Way," the latter of which has some of Tyler's sassiest double entendres. *Toys in the Attic* was their second most commercially successful and most-loved album selling eight million copies in the United States and reaching to number 11 on the *Billboard* Top 200. Even though Tyler recalled having a particularly difficult time coming up with lyrics for this album, it is often described as their creative peak, devoid of filler and generally more sophisticated than anything that had come before.

Aerosmith was now one of the hottest new bands in the United States, according to *Circus Magazine*, which pinned their success on "the purity of their roots. They are virtually the only natural heirs to the hard rock tradition founded by the Yardbirds and passed down into the seventies through Led Zeppelin" (Davis, 250). Hectic touring, fame, and drug use provided Tyler and the band with fresh material for songs on their next album, *Rocks* (May 1976), which reached number three on the U.S. charts and was their first album to ship platinum when it was released. Hamilton and Whitmore had more involvement in writing the songs, Whitmore taking credit for "Last Child," one of the album's three hits. Other hits included "Home Tonight" and "Back in the Saddle." However, the band's now extreme use of drugs and alcohol made completing *Rocks* difficult and nonstop performing was taking its toll.

Ticket sales soared from 1976 to 1979. The *Rocks* Tour (April 1976–February 1977) took them all across the United States, to the United Kingdom, Europe, and Japan. They were received poorly by the British who were offended when they closed a show with the Beatles' "Helter Skelter." In Germany, they were almost thrown out of the country for drug possession. Their trip to Japan, however, was encouraging as they were received by crazed young people, mobbed like the Beatles had been in the United States. However, drugs, excessive spending, and hotel mayhem continued to cause significant problems.

Aerosmith had trouble completing their next album, *Draw the Line* (November 1977). First they spent a month in a 100-acre New York country estate called the Cenacle with the intention of having a working vacation and churning out an album. However, after an absurd amount of drug use and partying, they set out in June 1977 for their *Aerosmith Express* tour with incomplete work and sporadically recorded tracks. The rest of the album was recorded in spurts as they toured the United States and made what would be their last trip to Europe for a decade. When the record was finally completed, it sold mainly on the band's reputation and was a disappointment because it was so disjointed. It was less commercially successful than their previous. They stayed on the road until the fall of 1978 and were feeling the difficulty of constant travel and rowdier concerts. In Philadelphia, an explosive firecracker thrown onstage burned Tyler's cornea and injured Perry's right hand.

The band went straight from grueling touring to working on *Night in the Ruts* (November 1979), which was where everything fell apart. In July 1979, right at the beginning of the *Night in the Ruts* tour, Perry left the band to pursue his own projects; he was feeling pressure from outstanding debt, while conflict with the band escalated over his wife, Elyssa, who by all accounts was a difficult, malicious woman. She and the other wives constantly bickered, and all the band members felt that she negatively influenced Perry's contribution to the band. Although his band, the Joe Perry Project, cut three records, it was unsuccessful partly because Leber and Krebs did everything they could to kill Perry's solo career in order to get him back to Aerosmith. With the high turnover of his band members, increasing heroin addiction, and the break-up of his marriage, Perry was sleeping on his manager's couch by 1984.

Without Perry, Aerosmith enlisted Jimmy Crespo to finish the album and to continue the tour, during which Tyler collapsing onstage had become a common occurrence. The tour ended in late 1980 when a drug-related motorcycle accident left Tyler hospitalized for six months. In September 1981, Whitford quit the band as conflict escalated and Tyler's drug use increased. Rick Dufay replaced Whitford for the recording of *Rock in a Hard Place* (August 1982), which rose to only number 32 on the charts.

In the time leading up to their reconciliation, Perry and Tyler both went through rehab. In 1984, partly at the urging of Perry's manager Tim Collins, Perry and Whitford returned to Aerosmith. After a shaky first rehearsal, the band was booked for the *Back in the Saddle* tour, which lasted through the beginning of 1985. Part of Perry's return to Aerosmith involved the adoption of Collins as the band's manager; Perry refused to work with Leber and Krebs after how they had squashed his solo career. This began an arduous legal struggle between managements, which went on for

some time. Collins got Columbia to drop Aerosmith's contracts and signed with Geffen Records. The band vowed to curb harmful habits, but that did not last long; Perry and Tyler were both in and out of rehab.

The band worked hard on their next album *Done with Mirrors* (November 1985) and the subsequent tour. The album, their first on the Geffen label, rose to number 36. Their performances on the tour were mediocre, yet the large established fan base made it a success. The band was on the verge of a breakthrough.

At this time, the music industry was swaying toward video, and Collins got a pitch from Def Jam records to make a video with Aerosmith. Perry and Tyler recorded a rap/heavy metal rendition of "Walk This Way" with Run-D.M.C. Receiving much play time on MTV, this video not only introduced Aerosmith to a younger audience, but also launched the rap-metal genre. For Aerosmith, this collaboration was the beginning of their self-reinvention, which solidified them with a new fan base as one of the most important U.S. bands of all time.

Soon after in 1986, Collins staged an intervention for Tyler who finally went to rehab and got sober. Perry and the rest were soon to follow and by the release of *Permanent Vacation* (August 1987), the band was drug-free. Although *Done with Mirrors* was intended to mark Aerosmith's comeback, *Permanent Vacation* is often considered their true comeback album, as it was the band's first truly popular album since their reunion. Three top-20 singles emerged from *Permanent Vacation*: "Dude (Looks Like a Lady)," "Angel," and "Rag Doll," all making use of professional songwriters. The band remained sober for the promotional tour in the United States, Asia, and Canada, which lasted through the fall of 1988. This album generally has a more pop-sounding feel than any of their other albums and was a definite turning point in the band's career. It was the first Aerosmith album to be heavily promoted on MTV, which helped it to become the band's most successful album in a decade.

On their next album, *Pump* (September 1989), Aerosmith used a more blues feel and returned to their hard rock roots, which featured hits like "Love in an

Elevator," "The Other Side," and "Janie's Got a Gun." The video to "Janie," directed by filmmaker David Fincher, won two MTV Video Music Awards and a Grammy for best Rock Performance. "Love in an Elevator" became the first Aerosmith song to hit number one on the Mainstream Rock Tracks chart. Furthermore, *Pump* reached to number five on the *Billboard* Top 200, was the fourth bestselling album of 1990, sold more than seven million copies in the United States. The tour took them back to Germany and the United Kingdom for the first time since 1978, to Japan, and to Australia.

With the success of *Permanent Vacation* and *Pump*, Aerosmith signed a $50 million six-album contract with Sony's Columbia Records even though they still owed Geffen two albums and a compilation album. Their next album for Geffen, *Get a Grip* (April 1993), was their first album to reach number one and was as successful as *Pump*. It straddled the line between pop and hard rock and boasted the hits "Eat the Rich," "Livin' on the Edge," "Cryin'," and "Crazy." The music video to "Crazy" features Alicia Silverstone and Tyler's daughter, Liv, and received ample airtime on MTV. *Pump* won them two more Grammies.

The *Get a Grip* tour (June 1993–December 1994) was their most extensive yet, taking them to South America for the first time, and back to Japan, this time with their families in tow. In general, the band was slowing down, taking longer between booking dates, and taking more time off to spend with their families. Perhaps it was this slower pace that allowed for the band's big growth over the next few years.

Although all the members had been sober since 1986, their manager Collins took their slower pace as an indication that they had relapsed into substance abuse and were not working. He accused Tyler of taking drugs again and had many of the band members isolated from each other. Depression had forced Kramer to stop working, and the band had been recording with another drummer. Their next album, *Nine Lives* (March 1997), was turned down by Sony, partly because of issues with the new digital recording methods, but also because it was not true to their hard rock

roots. In July 1996, all five members got together and worked with a mediator; they fired Collins and rerecorded the album with producer Kevin Shirley. *Nine Lives* was the first album since the 1970s where the group recorded together in the studio at the same time. It was at the top of the *Billboard* 200 for a week, and "Falling in Love (Is Hard on the Knees)" made it to the top 10. Parts of the international tour (May 1997–July 1999) were postponed when Tyler injured his knee while swinging the microphone stand in April 1998, and when Kramer suffered second-degree burns as his Ferrari ignited at the gas station in July of the same year. At the same time, the band worked with Hollywood songwriter Diane Warren on the single "I Don't Want to Miss a Thing" for the blockbuster movie *Armageddon* starring Liv Tyler. The song and video became immensely popular with the next generation and won the 1998 MTV Award for Best Video from a Film.

A quick tour took Aerosmith to Japan for a worldwide televised Y2K performance. Then their next album with Sony Columbia, *Just Push Play* (June 2001), went platinum in one month with its hit song "Jaded." They played at half time for the 2001 Super Bowl (along with Britney Spears and 'N Sync) right before the album was released, which gave them a lot of publicity. Aerosmith was inducted into the Rock and Roll Hall of Fame the same year. *Just Push Play* was followed by *Honkin' on Bobo* (March 2004), which was a blues-based cover album.

There were nearly 10 years between *Just Push Play* and their next original studio album, during which time the band members faced health problems and other turmoil. Tyler had polyps on his vocal cords that required surgery, and then later popped a blood vessel on his right vocal cord, which also required surgery. In 2006, Hamilton announced he had been diagnosed with throat cancer, and in 2008, Perry had knee-replacement surgery. In spite of these difficulties, the video game *Guitar Hero: Aerosmith* (Playstation, Wii, and Xbox) was wildly successful and is considered the best-selling video game of its kind. Whitford missed the beginning of the supporting *Guitar Hero* tour after sustaining a head injury. Performances in the tour were postponed when Tyler had surgery to treat a leg injury. Later in the tour, Tyler fell off stage in Sturgis, South Dakota, and was airlifted to the hospital; the resulting injuries caused the band to cancel the rest of the tour. At the end of 2009, Tyler entered rehab for addiction to pain medication prescribed during his treatment and recovery.

The year 2009 also brought difficulties as many of the band members were pursuing their own projects. Kramer published an autobiography *Hit Hard: A Story of Hitting Rock Bottom at the Top*, discussing his struggles with depression. Perry released a solo album and toured the United States with his band, the Joe Perry Project. Generally, this period of time seems to be very shaky, as rumors flew that Tyler was leaving and that the band would be auditioning singers. In later interviews, the members stated it was due to poor communication between band members as well as overblown hype in the press.

After the *Cocked, Locked, Ready to Rock* tour (2010) to nearly 20 countries, Tyler agreed to judge *American Idol* without consulting other band members. While the band was worried about Tyler being overcommitted, they moved their recording project to Los Angeles so that he could continue to work with them. They later commented that Tyler was energized by working with young singers, which heightened his creative process. Also, the wide exposure of the band's front man on sensationalized live TV brought the band notoriety with an even younger crowd. In 2011, Tyler published his autobiography, *Does the Noise in My Head Bother You?: A Rock 'N' Roll Memoir*. In 2012, he announced his departure from *American Idol*, stating his intention to devote himself to his "first love," Aerosmith.

After much anticipation, the band released their first studio album in a decade, *Music from Another Dimension!* (November 2012), with 15 new and original songs. The band reunited with producer Jack Douglas for this album, who had worked his magic with their classic 1970s stuff: *Get your Wings* and *Toys*. *Music from Another Dimension!* has more variety, not only returning to some long-dormant rock and roll, but also has some new tricks like "Love XXX," which

explains the advantages of frequent lovemaking and features background vocals by actor Johnny Depp. The album has some high points and is sure to appeal to wider audiences with songs like "Can't Stop Lovin' You," which was a duet with *American Idol* winner Carrie Underwood. The album also clearly shows that Tyler's voice has aged.

Aerosmith has remained true to their roots. They have become perhaps the most important U.S. hard rock band. They were very influential on subsequent bands, including Guns and Roses, Metallica, and Mötley Crüe. Their "Walk This Way" collaboration with Run-D.M.C. brought hip-hop to the mainstream. Tyler is still a popular icon, which is evident by his recent position on *American Idol*. With *Music from Another Dimension!* as the final album to complete their contract with Sony Columbia, the band has been questioned many times if their career is ending. While finishing the album, Kramer said, "Really, at this point in time, the only thing that's going to stop us is if someone out-and-out dies. Other than that, we've already been through what we've been through and stood the test of time. What else is there?" (Laban 2010).

Paul Lombardi

Selected Discography

Aerosmith, Columbia KC 32005, 1973.

Get Your Wings, Columbia KC 32847, 1974.

Toys in the Attic, Columbia PC 33479, 1975.

Rocks, Columbia PC 34165, 1976.

Draw the Line, Columbia JC 34856, 1977.

Night in the Ruts, Columbia FC 36050, 1979.

Rock in a Hard Place, Columbia FC 38061, 1982.

Done with Mirrors, Geffen GHS 24091, 1985.

Permanent Vacation, Geffen GHS 24162, 1987.

Pump, Geffen GHS 24254, 1989.

Get a Grip, Geffen GEFD-24455, 1993.

Nine Lives, Columbia CK 67547, 1997.

Just Push Play, Columbia CK 62088, 2001.

Honkin' on Bobo, Columbia CK 87025, 2004.

Music from Another Dimension!, Columbia 88725 44281 2, 2012.

References

Aerosmith Official Website. 2014. "Aerosmith Biography." Accessed February 2013. www.aerosmith.com/.

Bowler, Dave and Bryan Dray. *Aerosmith: What It Takes*. London: Boxtree, 1997.

Davis, Stephen. *Walk This Way: The Autobiography of Aerosmith*. New York: Avon Books, 1997.

Discogs Official Website. 2015. "Aerosmith Discography." Accessed January 2013. www.discogs.com/artist/484 24-Aerosmith.

Hardy, Phil. "Aerosmith." *The Faber Companion to 20th Century Popular Music*. London: Faber and Faber Ltd., 2001.

Herman, P. G. "Aerosmith." *Current Biography*, New York: H. W. Wilson, 2004.

Huxley, Martin. *Aerosmith: The Fall and the Rise of Rock's Greatest Band*. New York: St. Martin's Griffin, 1995.

Laban, Linda. "Aerosmith Hoping to Record 'Old-School' New Album in 2011." *Spinner*, 2010.

Phillips, William. "Aerosmith." *Pop Culture Universe: Icons, Idols, Ideas*. Santa Barbara, CA: ABC-CLIO, 2013.

Tyler, Steven. *Does the Noise in My Head Bother You?: A Rock 'N' Roll Memoir*. New York: HarperCollins Publishers, 2011.

Walser, Robert. "Aerosmith." *Grove Music Online*. New York: Oxford University Press, 2007.

The Allman Brothers Band (1969–Present)

The Allman Brothers Band was the first group to embody the musical style and identity of Southern rock. They were one of the first predominantly white rock bands to emerge from the American South and were the biggest rock act in the country in the mid-1970s. Their sound combines a love for African American blues-based traditions with the psychedelic spirit of the late 1960s, featuring extended jams, soulful vocals, dynamic slide guitar playing, and an atypical approach to form in their songwriting. Unlike the British invasion bands, who emulated and repackaged American blues for mainstream audiences, the Allman Brothers Band plays the black music of the American South with a more intimate, firsthand knowledge of its history and styles. It is part of their native musical dialect, ingrained into the musical upbringing of the two namesake brothers, Duane (born Howard Duane Allman, November 20, 1946, died October 29, 1971) and Gregg (born Gregory Lenoir Allman, December 8, 1947).

Born in Nashville, Tennessee, the Allmans grew up mainly in Daytona Beach, Florida, after their mother was widowed in 1949. Like many white Southerners, the boys knew the Grand Ole Opry and older hillbilly records. But it was a rhythm and blues concert in 1961 featuring Jackie Wilson, Otis Redding, B. B. King, and Patti LaBelle that especially captivated their interests (Freeman 1995, 8).

In the summer of 1960, Gregg bought a guitar and became obsessed with the instrument. A year later, his older brother followed in his footsteps, taking to the guitar with an equal fervor. Despite the local popular taste for surf rock, the Allmans were fascinated by the rhythm and blues station WLAC out of Nashville, broadcasting Ray Charles, Howlin' Wolf, and Bobby "Blue" Bland. Gregg and Duane crossed racial lines in their musical and social lives, sitting in with black bands in Daytona. With their long, straight blond hair, Gregg and Duane didn't fit the mainstream look, and felt an outsider kinship with their black friends.

After Gregg graduated from high school in 1965 (Duane dropped out a few years prior), the brothers toured around the Southeast as a four-piece band called the Allman Joys, playing mostly blues, R&B, and soul covers in clubs. Duane had surpassed Gregg in guitar ability, and Gregg switched to playing organ. Gregg had also vastly improved his singing, absorbing many of the vocal inflections and timbres of the most popular black soul singers, including his favorite, Bobby Bland.

After the Allman Joys broke up, Duane and Gregg formed Hour Glass and secured a contract with Liberty Records in Los Angeles, yet found the recording industry restrictive. Hour Glass released two unsuccessful albums in 1967 and 1968; Liberty tried to smooth over the band's rough sound and didn't allow them to record their onstage repertoire of rocked out Southern R&B (Freeman 1995, 23).

Fronted by brothers Duane and Gregg Allman, the Allman Brothers Band has spent over 40 years as the flag bearers of southern rock. The band helped to cast the mold for the jam band style of live performance still popular today. (Photo by Michael Ochs Archives/Getty Images)

Inspired by Taj Mahal's version of the Blind Willie McTell tune "Statesboro Blues," Duane starting practicing bottleneck slide guitar, and Gregg's vocals and songwriting improved. Hoping to recapture their Southern spirit, Hour Glass went to Fame Studios in Muscle Shoals, Alabama, to lay down a few tracks. The resultant "B.B. King Medley" (*Dreams*, 1989) was exactly the type of sound the band wanted, and the opposite of what their label wanted. Unwilling to capitulate to Liberty's creative control, Hour Glass broke up in the spring of 1968.

The Allman brothers joined a band called the 31st of February in Jacksonville, Florida, but Gregg returned to Los Angeles to record and write songs for Liberty. Duane continued to jam with various Jacksonville musicians, including a band called Second Coming, but was restless and without a band of his own. Pursuing stardom, he moved to Muscle Shoals in September 1968, to try to make it as a session guitarist.

Duane's breakthrough session at Muscle Shoals came two months later when Wilson Pickett recorded with Rick Hall at Fame Studios. Allman suggested Pickett cover the Beatles single "Hey Jude," and on the outro, Allman matches the passionate shouts of Pickett with his own guitar screams, often adding fast circular licks that turned the soul track into a bona fide rock song. It was the first significant soul hit to feature a rock electric guitar, and soon Duane became a fixture in Muscle Shoals, playing solos and fills on R&B records that usually featured horns in the lead role.

Allman's playing on Fame recordings impressed Phil Walden, the agent from Macon, Georgia, who managed Otis Redding until the singer's untimely death. Walden wanted to build a band around Allman, and his first move was to introduce Duane to a young African American drummer in Macon who went by the nickname Jaimoe (born Johnny Lee Johnson, July 8, 1944, aka Jai Johanny Johanson).

Jaimoe's first love was jazz, but he cut his chops on the R&B circuit, playing in Otis Redding's road band, followed by gigs for Percy Sledge and Joe Tex. Jaimoe's preference for jazz gave him an eccentric personal style that was atypical for mainstream black music. He knew Allman's guitar work on Pickett's "Hey Jude," and their playing instantly clicked.

Duane had played with Second Coming bassist Berry Oakley (born Raymond Berry Oakley III, April 4, 1948, died November 11, 1972) in Jacksonville, and his highly melodic and powerful bass meshed well with Allman's equally intense playing. Oakley grew up in Chicago playing guitar in blues clubs, and when he switched to bass, he played with a guitarist's sense of phrasing and drive. Most bass players merely accompanied Allman, but Oakley played *with* him, pushing and challenging the strong-headed Allman.

After jamming together in Muscle Shoals, Oakley, Duane, and Jaimoe moved to Jacksonville, where they regularly played with other members of Second

Coming, including guitarist Dickey Betts (born Forrest Richard Betts, December 12, 1943). Born in Florida, Betts absorbed white Southern country music then later became hooked on rock and electric blues, much like the Allmans. While in Jacksonville, Duane and Jaimoe stayed with Butch Trucks (born Claude Hudson Trucks Jr., May 11, 1947), Allman's former drummer from the 31st of February. Trucks grew up in Jacksonville as a classically trained musician but soon became obsessed with the new electric folk-rock sound of the Byrds and Bob Dylan.

On March 23, 1969, Betts, Oakley, Trucks, Jaimoe, and Duane Allman jammed together and experienced a musical high unlike anyone had felt before, what Trucks later called the "Legendary Jacksonville Jam" (Crowe 1973, 50). All they needed was a singer, and Duane convinced his brother to join them. On March 29, 1969, the group that would eventually be called the Allman Brothers Band made its debut performance.

The group soon moved to Phil Walden's home base of Macon in April 1969. Macon was a small, conservative town where the long hair and hippie styles of the band raised many eyebrows. The entire band initially lived together in an apartment they dubbed the "Hippie Crash Pad" just up the road from an old graveyard named Rose Hill Cemetery.

Like many bands of the era, the Allman Brothers used psychedelic drugs—in their case, mushrooms— and Betts recalls, "we were really putting that into what we were doing musically" (Freeman 1995, 49). Their psychedelic musical adventures were so enmeshed in the band's early development that every band member got a mushroom tattoo, a symbol that later became inseparable from the band.

Phil Walden launched Capricorn Records with the express purpose of recording the Allman Brothers, while Jerry Wexler of Atlantic Records agreed to distribute the album. In November 1969, the band played at the famed Fillmore East, the New York venue owned by rock impresario Bill Graham, lending them a legitimacy and exposure within the rock world. That same month the band released its first album, *The Allman Brothers Band*.

Betts and Allman's double lead guitars scream out in octaves on the lead track, "Don't Want You No More," a bold announcement of the Allman Brothers sound. The band demonstrates their penchant for rearranging a blues cover using a variety of textures and effects with both rhythmic and melodic complexity. The opener segues directly into the following track, the minor key gospel blues of "It's Not My Cross to Bear," which introduce Gregg Allman's powerful, soulful vocals.

"Dreams" is a mellow song that shows the band stepping beyond their blues roots. The moderate tempo and harmonic stasis are especially suited to expansive improvisation. Ethereal guitar notes add additional psychedelic touches, and the solos seem to float above the accompaniment rather than soar, focusing on color and mood rather than screaming toward a climax.

"Whipping Post" closes the album by returning to the aggressive blues of earlier tracks. Gregg wrote the song but Oakley added a diabolical introductory riff with 11 beats per measure, a complex compositional practice that breaks blues conventions. Gregg's vocals nearly scream on the chorus, while Betts and Duane answer his pleas with descending riffs in harmony. Both Duane and Betts take solos, and the track builds to an eruptive climax.

The band spent much of 1970 on the road. Along with Bill Graham's approval, a favorable *Rolling Stone* review of the debut album written by Lester Bangs led to more concert bookings. Bangs wrote about authenticity and race, noting "it's still inspiring when the real article comes along, a white group who've transcended their schooling to produce a volatile blues-rock sound of pure energy, inspiration, and love" (Bangs 1970, 52). Walden later echoed this sentiment, saying:

A lot of people said later on, "Well, how did Gregg Allman learn how to sing *black?*" He didn't. It was part of his *culture.* Gregg don't know how to sing any way *but* black. That's not foreign to him. (Graham and Greenfield 1992, 176)

The band continued to refine their sound, and Jaimoe exposed everyone to jazz, especially Miles Davis and John Coltrane. Like many of the San Francisco bands of the late 1960s, the Allman Brothers introduced jazz sensibilities into their fundamentally blues-rock sound, evident in both their ecstatic and lengthy improvisational styles and also in the increasingly complex songwriting of the band's originals.

Idlewild South was recorded during breaks from touring in 1970, on which Dickey Betts emerged as a legitimate songwriting force. The album opens with folksy acoustic guitar strumming on Betts's "Revival," and it delivers a more relaxed, country sound redolent of the song's title. The two lead guitars play an intricate, multi-section melody in close harmony, a defining characteristic of Betts's songwriting.

Betts's other compositional offering is "In Memory of Elizabeth Reed," the centerpiece and longest track on the album. Named after a tombstone inscription in Rose Hill Cemetery where Betts liked to get high and write music, "Elizabeth Reed" features a lilting chord progression partially based on the Miles Davis tune "All Blues," with a sinewy twin lead guitar melody played in close harmony. A second, more intense guitar melody follows, while Duane's dynamic and powerful solo builds the track to a frenzied peak.

Idlewild South also contains Gregg Allman's mellow country-folk tune "Midnight Rider." Tapping into stock American folk imagery such as death and the outlaw, the acoustic guitar and Jaimoe's congas give the entire track a laid-back vibe. Gregg's slightly nasal vocals accentuate the folk feeling, and Duane's guitar solo has a strong country feel. The rest of the album consists of mostly originals, showing off their mastery of many blues-rock grooves and effects.

Tom Dowd, who produced *Idlewild South*, was simultaneously working on Eric Clapton's new album. Duane met Clapton and the two shared an undeniable musical chemistry, so Clapton used Allman as a second guitarist on the album that would become *Layla and Assorted Other Love Songs*. Duane invented the opening seven-note guitar lick of "Layla," one of the most recognizable riffs in rock history. The long coda of "Layla" features soaring slide guitar work from Allman as well as his uncanny imitation of bird song at the end.

Idlewild South rose to number 38 on the *Billboard* 200 chart, yet the band felt that their true magic was in the transcendent improvisations of live performance. The band recorded a three-night stand at the Fillmore East in March 1971, and the resulting album, *At Fillmore East*, captures "for the first time the full, raw power of the band" (Poe 2006, 178). It stands as one of the great live albums in rock history.

Duane's slide guitar comes out screaming to open the album with "Statesboro Blues," showing how far he had advanced his idiosyncratic slide guitar technique. The band offers a slower blues number with the T-Bone Walker ballad "Stormy Monday," where Gregg's vocals thrive in the live setting with more emotion and power than either previous studio recording. With its fast shuffle beat, "You Don't Love Me" is another blues cover, a strong statement from the band about their roots and influences, featuring two virtuoso showcases for Duane's slide guitar where the rest of the band drops out.

The remainder of the album features Allman Brothers Band originals that had grown into monsters in the live setting. Betts offers an impressive solo, showing how much he had improved as a lead guitarist after nearly two years of constant touring, on the 13-minute "In Memory of Elizabeth Reed." Because the song operates within the melodic language of modal jazz rather than the blues, Duane's final solo is very different from his work on "You Don't Love Me," but perhaps even more mesmerizing. He builds to two separate peaks, with a sense of phrasing and line that demonstrate how intuitively he understood the instrument.

The final track, "Whipping Post," stretches out to almost 23 minutes, with a long, trippy breakdown in the middle that slows to an impassioned crawl before Oakley urges the song back to full speed. Allman and Betts each take multiple solos while the rhythm section drives the jam harder than anything else on the album. It is the definitive version of their dark epic and conveys a sense of urgency and intensity that matches the band's gothic aura.

At Fillmore East was released in July of 1971 and reached number 13 on the *Billboard* 200. While nearly continuous touring had led the band to tremendous musical achievements, it had also taken a toll, as much of the band was using hard drugs, including cocaine and heroin. The band came off the road in October of 1971 to recharge and detox, but instead they encountered horrible tragedy.

On October 29, Duane crashed his motorcycle in Macon. Although he was rushed to the hospital, his injuries proved too severe. His death was an all-encompassing shock to the entire Allman Brothers system. Duane had been the leader of the band but also the figurehead of the entire brotherhood of crew and friends who lived in Macon. Trucks later remarked that "there was never any thought of not continuing," likening themselves to apostles to carry on Duane's religion (Poe 2006, 215). Gregg was the most devastated and his drug use escalated to numb the pain; Duane had been a father figure to whom Gregg looked for guidance and leadership.

Eat a Peach, "dedicated to a brother" and released in February of 1972, demonstrated that the Allman Brothers Band could not only survive but also thrive without Duane Allman. Side A consists of songs recorded without Duane, a statement of the group's ability to soldier on. "Ain't Wastin' Time No More" reveals Dickey Betts to be a highly capable slide guitar player. "Melissa" was Duane's favorite of the songs Gregg wrote and takes on the role of elegy here. Gregg's singing is more affectionate than soulful, and Betts steps into Duane's role of playing call and response to Gregg's vocal lines. Betts also uses his volume knob to create swells that recall Duane's slide playing.

The album continues with leftover live tracks from the Fillmore East recordings. "Mountain Jam" is based loosely on a folk melody by Donovan called "There Is a Mountain." The version on *Eat a Peach* is over 33 minutes long and takes up two entire sides of the double album. The opening features a beautiful section of Duane, Betts, and Oakley all playing contrapuntal melodies. The Donovan melody appears sporadically throughout the track, acting as a brief way station along the improvisational journey.

A slow, spacey section features Duane's bird calls, and the middle of the track is a long drum solo, oscillating between Trucks's frenzy of rock drumming and Jaimoe's more subtle jazzy explorations. Oakley gets a long solo, and after the entire band rejoins, Duane turns the jam into a reverential, hymn-like rendition of "Will the Circle Be Unbroken," a song that was sung at his own funeral. "One Way Out" is another blues cover that gets a complete Allmans makeover and crackles with live energy, featuring Betts and Duane trading licks above a particularly bold, chugging rhythm section.

The album closes with studio songs recorded prior to Duane's death. The highlight is "Blue Sky," the first studio track to feature Dickey Betts as lead singer. With his vocal twang matched by Duane's countrified slide work, the song sounds more like a country song than anything the band had previously done. Yet the guitar solo, bass playing, and interlocking drumming is unmistakably Allmans.

At Fillmore East had started the Allmans on a new road of fame and renown, and *Eat a Peach* would launch them even further. It peaked at number four on the *Billboard* 200 while three singles cracked the Hot 100, and led to bigger gigs and paydays. After a 1972 tour as a five-piece unit, the band headed back to the studio that autumn, and called on former Hour Glass member Johnny Sandlin to produce a new album.

Sandlin brought in 19-year-old pianist Chuck Leavell (born Charles Alfred Leavell, April 28, 1952) to play on Gregg Allman's solo project, but Leavell soon found himself jamming in the studio with the Allman Brothers Band. Since replacing Duane with another guitarist seemed out of the question, the band added a pianist to play the double melodies along with Betts. Leavell blended into the veteran crew effortlessly and soon joined as an official sixth member.

Recording on *Brothers and Sisters* began in October 1972, but on November 11, after recording two tracks, tragedy improbably struck again. Berry Oakley crashed his motorcycle a few blocks from where Duane's accident occurred just over a year before and died at age 24. The band auditioned new bass players and decided on Lamar Williams (born January 14, 1949, died January 21, 1983), an old friend and bandmate of Jaimoe's, whose soul pedigree is more groove oriented and less thundering than Oakley.

In July 1973, the Allmans co-headlined a 600,000-person concert in Watkins Glen, New York, featuring the Dead and the Band. Riding that success, *Brothers and Sisters* came out a week later. The sound of the band had fundamentally changed following the deaths of Allman and Oakley: Leavell's playing altered the already complex rhythmic drive, and he took a prominent role as a blues soloist. Betts emerged as a true lead guitarist, and on the up-tempo rock opener "Wasted Words," it is clear that a year on the road without Duane had greatly improved Betts's slide guitar playing.

Betts continued to write songs with a strong country flavor, and "Ramblin' Man," which "typified the macho, go-it-alone ethos of Southern rock" (Cullen 1995, 124), is perhaps his finest. He used studio overdubs and a session guitarist to perform the twin melody lines, and alternates descending triplet melodies with a simple three-note riff that acts as the song's tag line. It is also Berry Oakley's last recorded track. "Jessica" is the album's longest track, another Dickey Betts instrumental that exudes a laid-back, up-tempo, folk groove. Betts perfectly meshes his country and western sensibilities with the hippie vibe of the early Allmans while Leavell delivers a defining piano solo.

By September, *Brothers and Sisters* was the number one album in the United States, and "Ramblin' Man" was a hit single, reaching number two on the singles charts. Stadium gigs followed, some of the first of any U.S. rock band, and the band appeared on the cover of *Rolling Stone*. Although they enjoyed unprecedented success, their personal lives were falling apart. Substance abuse escalated and the band began to drift apart socially. Gregg released a dark and brooding solo album in late 1973, *Laid Back*, containing all of the melancholy that he suppressed on the previous two Allman Brothers albums. Most telling is the hit reworking of "Midnight Rider," which opens ominously with a new minor-key melody.

The Allmans staged a highly successful stadium tour in the summer of 1974, and in the wake of their tremendous success, a new wave of Southern rock bands grew to prominence. The major labels who previously would not have touched the Allmans were now promoting the Charlie Daniels Band, ZZ Top, and Lynyrd Skynyrd, while Capricorn introduced the Marshall Tucker Band.

By 1975, the personal deterioration of the Allman Brothers Band had infested the musical and professional side. Allman and Betts regularly missed recording dates, and Allman became a tabloid side show when he married superstar Cher that summer. In 1976, Allman was at the center of a major drug trial, testifying against his friend, employee, and drug supplier, Scooter Herring. After Herring was found guilty, the rest of the group viewed Gregg as a traitor to the brotherhood and announced that they could not, and would not, continue to play with him, effectively breaking up the band.

Capricorn released *Wipe the Windows Check the Oil Dollar Gas* later that year, a live album culled from performances over the previous three years. The new album did demonstrate the positive contributions of Williams and Leavell, and Jaimoe later admitted "it's a damn fine record, especially in terms of what Lamar, Chuck and I were doing" (Poe 2006, 237). The three later formed Sea Level and released three albums in the late 1970s. Gregg released another solo album while Betts formed a new band, Great Southern. The band's profile remained high thanks to Georgia native Jimmy Carter's love of the band and their public support for his 1976 presidential campaign (Gingerich and Hale 1996, 885).

Gregg's marriage to Cher ended in 1977, and he returned to Macon to attempt an Allman Brothers Band reunion. After reassessing the Scooter Herring trial, Betts, Trucks, and Jaimoe began seriously considering such a move. Leavell and Williams decided to remain with Sea Level, so Betts recruited Great Southern members Dan Toler and David Goldflies on guitar and bass.

The Allman Brothers Band released *Enlightened Rogues* in 1979, featuring two lead guitars for the first time since Duane's death. The album reflects Betts's role as bandleader as well as changing trends of

Southern rock over the decade. The boogie shuffle of the hit single, "Crazy Love," sounds like it could be a Lynyrd Skynyrd tune. Yet the energy and chemistry of *Brothers and Sisters* is apparent on solid tracks like "Blind Love," or "Just Ain't Easy." The album peaked at number nine.

Tours followed, but this time the band was undermined by financial problems, with a variety of lawsuits between band members, Capricorn, and their new CD distributor, PolyGram. The band's new recording label, Arista, wanted to match popular tastes for new wave and disco with synthesizers and electronic drums. The resulting *Reach for the Sky* from 1980 was disastrous. Amid Jaimoe's requests for a financial audit of the band's expenses, he was fired, and Gregg's drug and alcohol abuse returned. The band broke up again in early 1982, although Gregg found solo success with his 1986 album *I'm No Angel*, whose title track topped the rock charts and cracked the Hot 100.

In 1989, PolyGram released a four-disc box set retrospective titled *Dreams*. Featuring not only tracks by the Allman Brothers Band but also recordings from the Allman Joys, the 31st of February, Hour Glass, and Duane Allman solo material, the album generated significant buzz around the band and helped to wash away the bad taste of the Allmans' most recent decade. In 1989, the Allman Brothers Band once again hit the road.

The band wanted to avoid the pitfalls of their previous reunion and Arista albums, which meant adding new blood and signing with Epic Records with the understanding that the band would have complete artistic control in the studio. To emulate the classic two-guitar sound, Betts brought in one of his guitarists from his solo tours, Warren Haynes (born April 6, 1960). Haynes was a tremendous technical talent whose could also play slide guitar. After extensive bass auditions, the band settled on Allen Woody (born Douglas Allen Woody, October 3, 1955, died August 25, 2000).

The Allmans released *Seven Turns* in 1990 to positive reviews, restoring the band's reputation and topping the rock charts with the single "Good Clean Fun."

Salsa percussionist Marc Quiñones (born December 29, 1963) joined the lineup, and the band released *Where It All Begins* in 1994. It was the most successful and best of their early 1990s studio albums, containing Haynes's gospel-blues number "Soulshine," his best songwriting contribution to the Allman Brothers canon. In 1995, the band was inducted into the Rock and Roll Hall of Fame.

After Woody and Haynes departed to form Gov't Mule, the band added former Aquarium Rescue Unit bassist Oteil Burbridge (born August 24, 1964), whose highly melodic style was closer to Oakley than any previous bassist. Butch Trucks's nephew Derek Trucks (born June 8, 1979) was a child slide guitar prodigy and had played with the Allmans while still a teenager. In 1999, he officially joined the band.

Major personnel changes came in 2000, when Betts was fired from the band because of lackluster playing. When Woody died suddenly the same year, Haynes returned to the lineup, establishing the seven-piece group that remains the core Allman Brothers Band at present. *Hittin' the Note*, released in 2003, is a strong studio effort, and Gregg called the album "the band's best . . . since *Eat a Peach*" (Poe 2006, 249).

Starting in 1989, the Allman Brothers Band have played every year at the Beacon Theater on Manhattan's Upper West Side. Growing into an annual March residency of over a dozen shows, the Beacon Theater run is the centerpiece of the band's performing year and often features a variety of special guests. On their 40th anniversary in 2009, the band dedicated the Beacon shows to the memory of Duane Allman, inviting many of the musicians with whom he played (from Eric Clapton to members of the Grateful Dead) to join them onstage (Light 2009, C1).

Along with the Grateful Dead, the Allmans were an important model for the modern jam band. The successful Georgia jam band Widespread Panic is a direct descendent of the Allmans sound and spirit, while Phish used to cover Allman Brothers songs in their earlier touring days. After a series of hiatuses and personnel changes throughout the 1970s, 1980s, and 1990s, the Allman Brothers Band remains a popular touring act among both older rock fans and younger jam band fans, while their hit singles are mainstays of classic rock radio. However, in mid-2014 the Allman's future was put in question as Warren Haynes and Derreck Trucks announced their departure from the band to pursue their own music projects.

Jacob A. Cohen

Selected Discography

The Allman Brothers Band, ATCO Records SD 33–308, 1969.

Idlewild South, Capricorn Records CPN 0197, 1970.

At Fillmore East, Capricorn Records SD 2–802, 1971.

Eat a Peach, Capricorn Records 2CP 0102, 1972.

Brothers and Sisters, Capricorn Records CP 0111, 1973.

Wipe the Windows, Check the Oil, Dollar Gas, Capricorn Records 2CX 0177, 1976.

Enlightened Rogues, Capricorn Records CPN 0218, 1979.

Dreams, Polydor AA8394172, 1989.

Seven Turns, Epic Records E 46144, 1990.

Where It All Begins, Epic Records EK 64232, 1994.

Hittin' the Note, Sanctuary Records 06076–84599–2, 2003.

References

Bangs, Lester. Review of *The Allman Brothers Band*. *Rolling Stone* 52, (February 21, 1970): 52.

Crowe, Cameron. "The Allman Brothers Story." *Rolling Stone* 149, (December 6, 1973): 46–54.

Cullen, Jim. *The Civil War in Popular Culture: A Reusable Past*. Washington, DC: Smithsonian Institution Press, 1995.

Freeman, Scott. *Midnight Riders: The Story of the Allman Brothers Band*. Boston: Little, Brown and Company, 1995.

Gingerich, John, and Grace Elizabeth Hale. "Consuming Politics: The Material Culture of Georgia Campaigns and Conventions, 1840–1976." *The Georgia Historical Quarterly* 80, no. 4 (1996): 873–87.

Graham, Bill, and Robert Greenfield. *Bill Graham Presents: My Life inside Rock and Out*. New York: Doubleday, 1992.

Light, Alan. "A Tradition for 20 Years: Allman Band at the Beacon." *New York Times*, 2009, C1.

Poe, Randy. *Skydog: The Duane Allman Story*. San Francisco: Backbeat Books, 2006.

B

Bad Company (1973–Present)

Bad Company is one of the most highly acclaimed hard rock bands to emerge from England in the past 50 years. Classifying Bad Company's sound is tricky as they have been described as heavy metal, hard rock, and blues-based rock and roll—the fact of the matter is that they played in all of these styles. The band has enjoyed an enormous fan base and a long run of hit records. Additionally, the band has left "an indelible stamp on rock 'n' roll with a straight-ahead, no-frills musical approach that has resulted in the creation of some of the most timeless rock anthems ever" (badcompany.com 2014).

The group formed in 1973 when Paul Rodgers's (born Paul Bernard Rodgers, December 17, 1949; vocals) band Free fell apart. Rodgers met the guitarist from Mott the Hoople, Mick Ralphs (born Michael Geoffrey Ralphs, March 13, 1944; guitar, vocals), and after they played together, the pair decided to form a new band. To that end, Ralphs quit Mott the Hoople and teamed up with Rodgers. They recruited Boz Burrell (born Raymond Burrell, January 1, 1946, died September 21, 2006; bass, guitar, vocals) from King Crimson to play bass and drummer Simon Kirke (born Simon Frederick St. George Kirke), whom Rodgers knew from Free. With this, the band Bad Company was formed as a quasi-supergroup. Ralphs enlisted Led Zeppelin manager Peter Grant to help run the band, and with that, Bad Company was the first band signed to Zeppelin's Swan Song imprint (badcompany.com 2014). At first, the record label was not keen to accept the band's name, but eventually Rodgers's persistence won the day.

In less than a year, the band was already a success. Their eponymous first album, *Bad Company,* was released in 1974 and is now considered a hard rock classic. The eight songs on the album comprise several of the band's most well-known and beloved hits, including "Movin' On," "Can't Get Enough," and "Bad Company." The songs included were written by various members of the group, but Rodgers and Ralphs were emerging as the main songwriters. An interesting inclusion was the Mott the Hoople cover "Ready for Love." The recording of the album was also unique in that it was done using a mobile studio—all the rage in the early 1970s. Led Zeppelin had a mobile unit set up at Headley Grange. The style of playing on *Bad Company* was an early encapsulation of what was to come with the band. The band's sound was defined by a stripped-down approach to rock and blues with slight country influences. The album went on to reach the top of the *Billboard* 200 charts and has since been certified five-time platinum by the Record Industry Association of America.

Of the early sound of the band, Rodgers has said, "We were influenced by people like Jimi Hendrix, Cream, and to a certain extent, the Beatles" (badcompany.com 2014). After the release of their first album, the band toured the United Kingdom and the United States. The band's willingness to jump straight out on tour helped push the sales of the album in the United States and moved it all the way up the charts. The band's rock and blues style coupled with their onstage presence made them immediately attractive to live-show audiences. The audience's enthusiasm also translated to FM radio play, with several of the songs from the debut album going into regular radio rotation.

Bad Company has long played a potent combination of heavy metal, hard rock, and blues-based rock and roll. From left to right: Boz Burrell, Mick Ralphs, Simon Kirke, and Paul Rodgers formed Bad Company in 1973 as one of the first supergroups, with members coming from Free, Mott the Hoople, and King Crimson. (Photo by Gems/Redferns)

On the heels of the success of the first album, which had already gone gold by the time the band returned to England after the U.S. leg of the tour, they were ready to go back to the studio to make another record. In 1975, Bad Company issued their second album called *Straight Shooter*. The album contained several songs that went on to become Bad Company standards and instant hits, including "Feel Like Makin' Love," "Shooting Star," and "Good Lovin' Gone Bad." Of note, the song "Shooting Star" was a fictitious account of a rock star who had died young. It was inspired by the deaths of Jimi Hendrix, Janis Joplin, and Jim Morrison.

Again the band enjoyed the Midas touch, and the album shot up the charts. *Straight Shooter*'s mix of hard rock, blues, and country (with just a hint of

soul in the vocals) made the album an international success. The songwriting credits on the album were spread between Rodgers, Ralphs, and Kirke. The release went to number three on the U.S. *Billboard* 200 charts and made it to the same position on the charts in the United Kingdom and Canada. The backing of Peter Grant, Led Zeppelin, and the Swan Song imprint certainly assisted the band in their early success. The strength of the songwriting and performing ability alone would not have allowed Bad Company to rocket to the top of the charts so quickly had it not been for the established management plan they benefited from with Grant (badcompany.com 2014).

The band again struck while the iron was hot and released their third album in January of 1976. *Run with the Pack* was recorded using the Rolling Stones Mobile Truck in September of 1975 and mixed by Jimi Hendrix veteran Eddie Kramer. The album was fueled by the band's cover of the Coasters classic "Youngblood" and went on to be the group's third consecutive platinum-selling release. The album reached number five on the charts in the United States and the United Kingdom on the strength of songs like "Silver, Blue & Gold" and "Run with the Pack."

As was true in the past, the songwriter credits on the album were spread between Ralphs and Rodgers with Burrell and Kirke weighing in on the song "Honey Child." As Rodgers made clear, "I always thought it was important for the group to have more than one writer" (badcompany.com 2014). Critics of the album described its sound as the Bad Company formula, but what they missed was that the formula was very effective. "It is impossible to refute the merits of the album opener 'Live For The Music' with its cutting three-chord riff and a tugging backbeat. . . . Bad Company levels the overblown art rock of the 70s with a simple 4/4 kick to the gut" (*Encyclopedia of Popular Music* 2008). This straightforwardness was tempered by ballads such as "Silver, Blue & Gold," which highlighted the range of Rodgers's voice.

Burnin' Sky was recorded in France at Chateau d'Horouville in the summer of 1976. The release of the album was delayed until March of 1977 to avoid competing with their still-charting previous album *Run with the Pack*. Compared with the previous three releases, *Burning' Sky* was a relative disappointment. The album topped out at number 15 on the U.S. charts, which was a respectable showing for most bands. Without the strength of a truly stand-out single, the album went gold (as had all three previous albums) but did not have the unprecedented success of its precursors. The title track did chart, but only in the 78th position, and this was not at all up to the band's previous levels of success. Perhaps it was on this fourth album that the Bad Company formula had run its course. The album contained "plenty of those patented ominous midtempo rockers, but nothing you'd want to add to the set list" (Ruhlmann, Allmusic.com, 2014).

In the wake of the relative disappointment of *Burnin' Sky,* Bad Company regrouped and went into Ridge Farm Studio in Surrey, England, in late 1978. Named *Desolation Angels* after the novel by the same name by Jack Kerouac, this fifth studio album found the group back at maximum potency. On the strength of singles such as "Rock 'n' Roll Fantasy," "Gone, Gone, Gone," and "Oh Atlanta," the album shot up the charts and topped out at number three in the United States. Rodgers said of "Rock 'n' Roll Fantasy," "I wanted to write an anthem which expressed my feelings about everything in rock 'n' roll . . . I wanted to cover the spectrum, particularly that rock 'n' roll was a magical illusion of color, sound and light" (bad company.com 2014). With the foundation on that simple concept, the album ended up going double platinum. The song "Oh Atlanta" became the opening music for the Nashville Network's 1993 broadcast of the Motorcraft 500, and "Gone, Gone, Gone" became a standard on the airwaves.

The amazing success of *Desolation Angels* took its toll on Rodgers. He was the only member of the band with children and felt like the band was consuming his life. "I needed to get my feet on solid ground and spend some time watching my children grow" (badcompany.com 2014). Regardless, the band went back to the studio and recorded their sixth album. Just like the previous release, the album was recorded at Ridge Farm Studio in Surrey, England. The recording sessions took place in the spring of 1981 under the watchful eyes of Max Norman. The sessions were difficult, as the group did not have the stabilizing factor of their manager Peter Grant with them in the studio. Grant had temporarily disappeared from the music business in the wake of Led Zeppelin drummer John Bonham's death on September 25, 1980. Without Grant in the studio, tempers ran high and were exacerbated by Rodgers's growing fatigue with the band's schedule.

While the band should have been riding high and ready to capitalize on the success of "Rock 'n' Roll Fantasy," they instead took three years to release their sixth album. *Rough Diamonds* was released in August of 1982 to relatively mixed reviews. The album lacked a stand-out single, with its biggest hit being "Electricland" penned by Rodgers. "Painted Face" was popular on the radio for a time, but neither single was able to push the record to the band's previous heights. The album topped out at a disappointing number 26 on the *Billboard* charts and was their worst-selling album to date. Without being able to crack the top 25 in the United States or the United Kingdom, the album did not even go gold. In the wake of the album's poor performance, Paul Rodgers left Bad Company to spend more time with his family. Ralphs has said of the split, "Looking back, we stopped at the right time . . . Paul wanted a break and truthfully we all needed to stop. Bad Company had become bigger than us all and to continue would have destroyed someone or something" (badcompany.com 2014).

So, for a few years, there was no Bad Company. After a period of rest, Ralphs and Kirke resurrected Bad Company in 1986. At that time, they tried to entice Rodgers back into the fold, but he was already forming the supergroup the Firm with Jimmy Page of Led Zeppelin fame. There was some consternation about a Bad Company without Rodgers, who felt that Ralphs and Kirke should move on with their own band and new songs, the same way Rodgers did.

Regardless, in 1986, Bad Company released their seventh album, called *Fame and Fortune*. The musicians on the album were Ralphs (guitar) and Kirke (drums), with new front man Brian Howe (born Brian

Anthony Howe, July 22, 1953; vocals), who had worked with Ted Nugent and session ace Steve Price (born Steven Price, birthdate unknown; bass). As the band's association with the Swan Song imprint was no longer intact, this album was the first released through the Atlantic Records label. As a means of "updating" the Bad Company sound, the band also included a keyboard player on this album. Gregg Dechert had previously worked with the band Uriah Heep and the Dream Academy and supplied the keyboard parts for *Fame and Fortune*. Radio-friendly singles from the album included "This Love," "If I'm Sleeping," and "Long Walk." While the album was considered enjoyable by the mid-1980s audience, there were no true stand-out singles and the album did not chart.

The band's second release on Atlantic was *Dangerous Age* and again included Howe on vocals and Price on bass. The album was released in 1988 and featured songs written by Howe and songwriter Terry Thomas. Filled with radio-friendly songs, the singles "Shake It Up," "One Night," "No Smoke without a Fire," and the title track all enjoyed significant air time. Although fairly satisfying, nothing on *Dangerous Age* had significant staying power, and the songs largely fell quickly into obscurity.

Holy Water was the band's ninth studio album and their third with Howe at the helm. The album was recorded in 1989 and was an example of late 1980s album-oriented rock (AOR). Although engaging, the material on *Holy Water* was formulaic, with the band working to approximate their own late 1970s sound. Radio-friendly songs included "Boys Cry Tough," "Walk through Fire," and the title track. All were written by Howe, again with the assistance of Thomas. "Holy Water" clocked in at 89 on the singles chart, and "Walk through the Fire" made it all the way to 28.

The stand-out single on the album was "If You Needed Somebody," which eventually charted at number two in the United States. Stylistically, the band missed its original marks, as *Holy Water*'s sound was watered down with reverb, which did not prevent it from charting at number 40 and eventually

achieving platinum status. Of note, Price did not play on this record. He was replaced by bassist Felix Kirsh. Kirsh was a studio player, so the band recruited Paul Cullen for the subsequent tour. Ralphs was also unable to make the *Holy Water* tour for family-related reasons and was replaced by Geoff Whitehorn. Even with all of these machinations, the *Holy Water* tour with support from the band Damn Yankees was one of the top-five grossing concert tours of 1991.

In the aftermath of the *Holy Water* tour, Howe was rumored to want a more significant stake in the band's financial future. Discussions ensued that Steve Walsh, of Kansas fame, would step in, but Atlantic Records liked the band with Howe as the singer. As such, a deal was met and Howe remained in Bad Company. In September 1992, the band issued *Here Comes Trouble*, again on the ATCO subsidiary of Atlantic Records. The band's 10th album was a pretty straightforward shot of hard rock and seemed to put the 1980s AOR era in the past. The album contained 11 songs penned by Howe and Thomas and managed to have some chart success. Interestingly, for this release the band was really just the trio of Howe, Ralphs, and Kirke, with a series of session musicians filling in the gaps. Also present on the album, but not really part of the band, were Felix Kirsh (bass), Dave Colwell (guitar), Rick Wills (bass), and Luke Antonello (saxophone).

On the strength of a couple of solid singles, *Here Comes Trouble* did reasonably well. The song "How About That" topped the charts at 38, and "This Could Be the One" managed to make it to 87. The album went gold, and the band again toured in support. As part of the *Here Comes Trouble* tour, the band cut a live album called *What You Hear Is What You Get: The Best of Bad Company*, which was released in 1993. The live album captured some of the best material from the Rodgers and Howe phases of the band.

After the tour and the release of the live album, Brian Howe left Bad Company. He stated at the time that his departure was a matter of self-preservation. He simply felt he was the only one contributing to the band and that the two remaining original members (Ralphs and Kirke) were riding the coattails of the band's reputation. The next singer for Bad Company was Robert Hart (born November 1, 1958; vocals). Ralphs and Kirke approached the singer who was then affiliated with the band the Distance, and a job offer was made. Hart accepted, and he officially became the band's third singer. Hart's voice has been described as similar to Rodgers's, and he quickly won over the band's fans in the United Kingdom and the United States. With Hart in the group, Bad Company went back in the studio and recorded another new album.

Company of Strangers was the band's 11th album and their first with Hart as the singer. The album was released in 1995 and contained 13 original songs written by Hart, Kirke, Ralphs, and several others. For this recording, the band also enlisted the assistance of Rick Wills on bass and Dave Colwell on guitar. Although Hart was meant to sound like Rodgers, the album that resulted from his inclusion in the band was fairly generic. The album was "another generic installment from the reunited Bad Company [still minus Rodgers]. While the music is certainly accomplished, and the musicians are tasteful professionals, very little on the album is noteworthy . . . there are no memorable melodies or hooks" (Erlewine, 0.com, 2014). In support of the new album, the band again took to the road for a tour with Bon Jovi.

In 1996, Bad Company with Hart at the helm released another album. The band's 12th was called *Stories Told and Untold* and contained an interesting mixture of material. The album contained 14 songs. Some were new and some were Bad Company classics that the band had rerecorded with Hart as lead vocalist. Hart, Ralphs, and Kirke were again supported by Colwell and Wills. The band's reimagining of "Can't Get Enough" was quite good, but the purist fans saw the album for what it was—an attempt to recapture past glory.

When Peter Grant died in 1995, the original four members of Bad Company reconvened at the funeral. Although meeting under unfortunate circumstances, the group was finally in the same place at the same time and discussion turned to the endless desire of the fans for the original four to re-form. Nothing came of

this immediately, but in 1998 Rodgers and Kirke came together to discuss putting out a compilation album. This discussion led to further meetings that included Burrell. Rodgers ended up suggesting that four new songs be added to the compilation of greatest hits. The songs were "Hammer of Love," "Tracking Down a Runaway," "Hey, Hey," and "Ain't It Good." The four original members of the band got together in the studio and tracked the four new songs. The collection of 28 greatest hits plus the four additional songs was released on Elektra Records as *The Original Bad Company Anthology* in March of 1999.

The original members then mounted a tour in support of the anthology, which included David Lee Roth as the opening act. The tour covered the United States with 30 tour dates through the summer of 1999. The tour drew sellout crowds and did much to spur the sales of the new compilation. In the wake of the tour, Rodgers again teamed up with Kirke in 2001 to tour with Bad Company minus Ralphs and Burrell. The tour led to the recording of a new live album and DVD called *Merchants of Cool*, which was released on the Sanctuary Records imprint in 2002. More recently, Rodgers toured with the remaining members of the band Queen in 2005. The collective musicians played some Bad Company songs, and the band was referred to as Queen + Paul Rodgers.

Any further chances of a Bad Company reunion with all four original members were dashed when Boz Burrell died of a heart attack on September 21, 2006. In 2008, it was announced that the remaining three members of Bad Company would perform a one-off show in Florida. The band was joined by Howard Leese of the band Heart and bassist Lynn Sorenson. In this performance, which was subsequently released as a DVD, Rodgers dedicated "Gone, Gone, Gone" to Burrell. In March of 2013, Bad Company and Lynyrd Skynyrd announced a co-headlining tour to commemorate 40 years of music making. For the purposes of these shows, Todd Ronning, from Rodgers's solo band, took over on bass, and second guitarist Howard Leese again joined the group. A second coming of this Bad Company and Lynyrd Skynyrd tour was announced for the summer of 2014. Opening for the July dates of the 2014 tour was Steve Rodgers, Paul's son.

Bad Company's legacy is still being written, but their longevity and influence are unmistakable. Many of their songs have been covered, with recent examples being Five Finger Death Punch's version of "Bad Company" and Kid Rock's version of "Feel Like Makin' Love." Artists who have gone on record as having been directly influenced by Bad Company include guitarist Joe Bonamassa, Van Halen, Tesla, Juliana Hatfield, Alison Krauss, Goldfinger, Dread Zeppelin, and Tori Amos. Clearly, the classic rock of Bad Company has had a deep impact and far-reaching influence that will only continue.

David V. Moskowitz

Selected Discography

Bad Company, Swan Song TP 8501, 1974.

Straight Shooter, Swan Song CS 8502, 1975.

Run with the Pack, Swan Song SS 8415, 1976.

Burnin' Sky, Swan Song SS 8500, 1977.

Desolation Angels, Swan Song SS 8506, 1979.

Rough Diamonds, Swan Song SS 59419, 1982.

Fame and Fortune, Atlantic 781 684–1, 1986.

Dangerous Age, Atlantic 81884–1, 1988.

Holy Water, ATCO/Atlantic Records 7 91371–2, 1990.

Here Comes Trouble, ATCO/Atlantic 91759–2, 1992.

Company of Strangers, EastWest Records 7559–61808–2, 1995.

Stories Told & Untold, EastWest Records 61976–2, 1996.

In Concert: Merchants of Cool, Sanctuary SMRCD157, 2002.

References

Bad Company Official Website. 2010. "Biography." Accessed June 2014. www.badcompany.com/bio.html.

Covers Project Official Website. 2015. Accessed June 2014. www.coversproject.com/artist/bad%20company.

Discogs Official Website. 2015. "Bad Company Discography." Accessed June 2014. www.discogs.com/artist/261941-Bad-Company-3, 2014.

Erlewine, Stephen. "Bad Company-*Company of Strangers*," *All Music Guide*, Rovi Corporation, 2014.

Larkin, Colin, ed. "Bad Company: *Run with the Pack.*" *Encyclopedia of Popular Music*. Oxford Music Online, 2008.

Ruhlmann, William. "Bad Company: *Burnin' Sky*," *All Music Guide,* Rovi Corporation, 2014.

The Band (1963–1976)

Few groups in rock's history are as paradoxical as the Band, the mostly Canadian quintet that created some of the most archetypal American rock ever written. At once deeply private and highly public, chameleonic and straightforward, pastel impressionist and sepia-toned, antebellum Southern and art colony Northern, the Band produced rock pushing the timbral boundaries and lyrical topics of rock music while firmly riveting the genre to its country and blues roots.

The Band was composed of guitarist Robbie Robertson (born Jaime Robert Klegerman, July 5, 1943; guitar), bassist Rick Danko (born Richard Clare Danko, December 19, 1943, died December 10, 1999; bass), drummer Levon Helm (born Mark Levon Helm, May 26, 1940, died April 19, 2012; vocals/drums), keyboardist Garth Hudson (born Eric Garth Hudson, August 2, 1937; keyboard instruments/trumpet/saxophone), and multi-instrumentalist Richard Manuel (born Richard George Manuel, April 3, 1944, died March 4, 1986; multi-instrumentalist). Levon Helm hailed from Marvell, Arkansas, a small town near the Mississippi River, while the other four members hailed from cities in southern Ontario: Hudson from London, Danko from Simcoe, Manuel from Stratford, and Robertson from Toronto, born to a Jewish father and Mohawk mother. All five members grew up on a steady diet of country music and rockabilly. Across from the Mississippi Delta, Helm's family lived in a blues-rich area where "a bunch of fiddles and mandolins and a whole lot of moonshine whiskey was the focal point of family life" (Hoskyns 1993, 24). The renowned bluesman Sonny Boy Williamson lived in Helena, just down the road. The music of Nashville and Memphis was prominent in the Helm household. In the days before radio station watt restrictions, WLAC (Nashville, TN-based country music radio station with nighttime R&B shows that reached 23 states and 3 Canadian

Composed of Arkansas-born singer/drummer Levon Helm and a quintet of Canadian transplants, the Band had a legendary career. In the mid-1960s, the Band (at the time known as the Hawks) backed Bob Dylan and went on to work with him through the rest of the decade. The Band's own original work has become iconic, and their influence on southern rock, country rock, and the jam band sound is undeniable. (Photo by Gijsbert Hanekroot/Redferns)

provinces) also reached up to Ontario's Southern Crescent, allowing the quartet of Ontarians to grow up with a steady diet of American country music.

Soon after graduating from high school in 1958, Levon Helm joined the band of local rockabilly artist Ronnie Hawkins and the Hawks. Hawkins was trying to imitate the success of Sun Records legends like Elvis Presley and Carl Perkins, but he found that rock and roll was eroding his interest in rockabilly. Eager to find a performing niche, Hawkins discovered that rockabilly was still popular in Toronto. He and his band, including young Levon, traveled north of the border. Over the next few years, the original Hawks became homesick and left for Arkansas, to be replaced

by Robertson, Danko, Manuel, and Hudson, in that order. The core players that would become the Band were all part of the Hawks by 1961. Hudson, in particular, was an important acquisition for the group. Hudson had studied music at the University of Western Ontario, and as Helm recalled, "nobody could play like Garth anywhere. He could play horns, he could play keyboards, he could play anything and play it better than anybody you knew" (Bowman 2005, 14). He gave lessons to the other Hawks and greatly increased the band's musicianship.

In 1963, the backing members were tired of the rockabilly repertoire and seceded, becoming Levon and the Hawks. After saxophonist Jerry Penfound and singer Bruce Bruno departed, the quintet was formed, becoming simply the Hawks. They became known around Toronto for their exceptional live shows, but they wanted to move past being merely a local cover band. In 1965, they reached a record contract with Atco, a subsidiary of Atlantic Records, and landed a gig south of the border at a club in Somers Point, New Jersey. Their singles and live show were noticed by Albert Grossman, Bob Dylan's manager. Dylan asked Robertson and Helm to join him for a show at Forest Hills. Soon, the whole band was in tow as Dylan's backing band.

The invitation from Dylan, an established superstar, was the big break the Hawks had been waiting for. Little did the Hawks know, though, what lay in store. Earlier that summer, Dylan had controversially performed "folk-rock" songs on electric guitar at the Newport Folk Festival. He had just released the visionary *Bringing It All Back Home,* whose first side featured rock songs replete with electric guitar, bass, and drums, and he was writing the surrealist masterpieces that would comprise *Highway 61 Revisited.* Dylan's albums joined the lyrical gravitas of folk with the energy of rock and roll, effectively birthing serious, critical rock music. The Hawks were marshaled to help deliver Dylan's new rock gospel to the world. However, folk purists lambasted Dylan for his supposed betrayal of traditional music, with one fan memorably calling him Judas. The Hawks were forced to transition from small clubs to large arenas filled with people spitting bile at them. While the atmosphere would have cowed lesser artists, Dylan's vengeful attitude rubbed off on the Hawks, who performed his songs with spiteful aggression. In addition, Dylan was a very different bandleader than Hawkins. Hawkins was a consummate professional with prompt rehearsal schedules, precise arrangements, and preplanned concert lists. Dylan, on the other hand, was more erratic and intuitive, going by gut feeling and spontaneous intervention rather than concrete arrangement. While Dylan was difficult to deal with at first, the Hawks soon found that Dylan allowed their own creative juices to flow.

The collaboration between Dylan and the Hawks reached full flower over the following two years. After

Blonde on Blonde, Dylan retreated to Woodstock, a small artist colony town in the Catskill Mountains north of New York City. He was injured in a motorcycle accident in August 1966 and stayed away from the public spotlight until releasing *John Wesley Harding* in late 1967. He had retained the Hawks, minus Levon Helm, who had retreated home to Arkansas, and moved them up to a house called Big Pink near Woodstock. Finally freed from the need to gig around, Dylan and the Hawks spent 1966 and 1967 writing, recording, and experimenting with new sounds. While the public speculated about Dylan's public disappearance, he and the Hawks were writing rock music light-years ahead of its time.

The collaboration was pure magic. Dylan had also been a rock and roll and rockabilly fan before becoming the unwitting prophet of folk music, and the Hawks returned him to his rockabilly and country roots. Dylan had allowed the Hawks to explore new sounds and timbres and brought a new poetic dimension to their lyrics. Robbie Robertson recalled that "we went in with a sense of humor. It was all a goof. We were playing with absolute freedom; we weren't doing anything we thought anybody else would ever hear, as long as we lived. But what started in that basement, what came out of it . . . came out of this little conspiracy, of us amusing ourselves. Killing time" (quoted in Marcus 1995, xiv). The sextet recorded more than a hundred different songs, both covers and new material.

Fourteen of the tracks that Dylan and the Hawks recorded were pressed for their friends and unofficially called the Basement Tapes. The tracks quickly made the rounds in the music industry. Songs were covered by a wide range of artists, including the Byrds' country-rock version of "You Ain't Goin' Nowhere," Manfred Mann's sprightly, saccharine rendition of the drawling "Quinn the Eskimo," and a triumphal take on "Million Dollar Bash" by British folk group Fairport Convention. In 1969, a bootleg LP titled *Great White Wonder* circulated 24 tracks, and by the early 1970s most of the recorded tracks were readily available. In 1975, 24 tracks were formally released by Capitol as *The Basement Tapes.*

The Basement Tapes demonstrated Dylan and the Hawks' simultaneously stream-of-consciousness and disciplined sound, effortlessly tiptoeing the line between experimentalism and craft. The Hawks' use of keyboards and lazy vocal harmonies combined with Dylan's new lyrics to bring a new dimension to rock music. Unlike the psychedelic craze of the same year, *The Basement Tapes* sounded new precisely because the songs refracted the dirty Southern roots of rock through the introspection of folk. The songs retain Dylan's gift for melody and the Hawks' tight cohesion, but spin out inscrutable lyrics and keyboard-drenched grooves that sound like the totality of mid-century American popular music spun in a blender.

"Yazoo Street Scandal," a hard, funky number about a fictional Southern red-light district, manages to rock hard and "take it slow and easy," just like "Lo and Behold." "Please Mrs. Henry" features country licks and an organ piping like a train whistle under Dylan's lazy delivery. The blues were especially prominent, showing up in myriad guises: straightforward, electric, and drunken in "Odds and Ends," salaciously understated in "Apple Suckling Tree," and rambling in "Orange Juice (Blues for Breakfast)." A number of tracks, like "Million Dollar Bash," "Yea, Heavy, and a Bottle of Bread," "Please Mrs. Henry," and "Quinn the Eskimo" have refrains that sound like inside joke sing-alongs, but their weirdness and catchiness make them charismatic rather than cloying. "Katie's Been Gone" heralds the Hawks' penchant for ballads like "Lonesome Suzie," while "Bessie Smith," a Hawks original, brightly celebrates the famous blues singer, portending the group's sound on *The Band* and *Stage Fright*.

During the 1960s, though, the public had little knowledge of what Dylan had been doing in Woodstock. The first taste of these new experimental songs was in 1968, on *Music from Big Pink,* a curious album by a group enigmatically called the Band. In August 1967, Levon Helm had rejoined the Hawks in West Saugerties. The Hawks bounced around some new names, including the Crackers, ultimately settling on the Band. They had been known as the band

that Dylan had been performing with, but the moniker's simplicity was perfect for the group. It at once signaled their collaborative power, their desired anonymity, and also their confidence—after all, they were *the* band. Listeners picking up the record had little clue about who the Band was. The album featured a surrealist painting on the front, a picture of five guys in turn-of-the-century suits, a family reunion photo, and a big pink house on the back cover. That cover painting, painted by Bob Dylan, features a bizarre mélange of musicians—a pianist playing an upright while being held up behind the piano, a Native American playing an acoustic bass sprouting little winglike nibs, a drummer in a derby hat playing a marching band bass drum, and a Shankar-looking sitarist with a crockpot on his head, all under the watchful eye of an intruding elephant. The Band performed the first new Dylan compositions released since *Blonde on Blonde,* "This Wheel's on Fire" (cowritten with Richard Manuel), "I Shall Be Released," and "Tears of Rage" (cowritten with Rick Danko).

Music from Big Pink, named after the house where the Band and Dylan enjoyed their bohemian vacation, showcased the Band at its most wildly experimental, but also a highly disciplined band with an incredibly positive synergy between group members. The band insisted on performing live while playing in a circle to maintain the interpersonal connection crucial to their sound. The group's focus on timbre, aided by band members' multi-instrumental talents and Hudson's innovative keyboard playing, led to far-out sounds unheard on rock albums. "Tears of Rage," the opener, featured Robertson's soulful vocals over a Rhodes-organ dirge, a pinched chorus over an almost stop-time jaunt, and horn moans straight out of a New Orleans funeral procession. Garth Hudson opened "Chest Fever" with a keyboard blast riffing Bach's famous *Toccata and Fugue in D minor,* which somehow moves effortlessly into some of the funkiest verse grooves penned in the decade. (During shows later in the decade, Hudson expanded this section to many minutes, creating a stand-alone improvisatory piece called "The Genetic Method.") The finale, "I Shall Be Released," featured a gorgeous falsetto solo over an ethereal plunking piano and guitar accompaniment, a song matched in tenderness by the lovely ballad "Lonesome Suzie." The lyrics blended Southern folklore, poetry, social commentary, and inside jokes. "The Weight," the most straight-ahead song, was a story about an odyssey through small-town life underpinned by Helm's steady backbeat. "We Can Talk" featured some seemingly nonsense lyrics traded between Helm and Robertson that still managed to cut across social differences between North and South.

Released with minimal fanfare and without an accompanying tour, *Music from Big Pink* sold relatively poorly, only reaching number 30 on the *Billboard* charts. The first single, "The Weight," did not even make it to the top 50. However, the album was in heavy rotation among rock cognoscenti. Al Kooper, who played with Dylan, Robertson, and Helm in that fateful Forest Hills gig, lauded the album in *Rolling Stone*, calling it "*my* album for 1968. *Music from Big Pink* is an event and should be treated as one" (Kooper 1968). Despite the initial commercial failure of "The Weight," the song's performance at Woodstock and inclusion in the landmark film *Easy Rider* propelled it to legend status. In 2006, the influential website *Pitchfork* named the song the 13th best of the 1960s, writing that its combination of country rock and biblical pathos was "capable of raising the spirits of even the damnedest drunks yet still complex enough to arouse even the most spiritually confounded" (Fennessey 2006). The group had done little to dispel the shroud of mystery surrounding them, refusing to grant interviews after *Music from Big Pink*. The Band's private nature, combined with building critical acclaim, led to eager anticipation for the quintet's sophomore effort.

Their follow-up album, *The Band*, was recorded in Sammy Davis's pool house in Los Angeles. The group turned it into their own studio, baffling the walls and boarding up the windows. Just as in Big Pink, the quintet lived together in the house, bouncing ideas off one another and maintaining the playful spirit of their first album. The result mimicked this change in architecture—the avant-garde rock and celebrity hoi polloi of Hollywood was kept at bay, as the Band fostered its own unique, unified blend of Southern genres. The group had always been uncomfortable with countercultural psychedelia—*Music from Big Pink* showed the band with their families to stress their devotion to tradition. While a *Time* magazine cover hailed *The Band* the first "country rock" album, the moniker did not do justice to the Band's sound. The result was not just country, but soul, blues, ragtime, Dixieland jazz, country and rock, a cohesive gumbo owing more to the musical world of tiny Marvell, Arkansas, than sprawling Los Angeles. Levon Helm recalled that "the title we had for the record was *Harvest,* because we were reaping this music from seeds that had been planted many years before we'd even been born. But we could have called it *America* as well, because this music was right out of the air. We were saying, *Listen! You can't ignore this*" (Helm 1993, 189).

The album's two most famous tracks come straight out of the South. "The Night They Drove Old Dixie Down" told the story of Virgil Caine, a Confederate soldier trying to return to normalcy after losing in the Civil War. Robbie Robertson described the song as taking the loser's point of view. Rather than revisionist patriotism, however, Robertson tried to depict the "beautiful sadness" of "Americana land," discussing domestic life, simple jobs ("chopping wood" and "the Danville Railroad"), with a tinge of pained nostalgia (Bowman 42). Along with perhaps his finest vocal performance, Levon Helm also offered masterful drumming, including the military rolls in the chorus. "Up on Cripple Creek," on the other side, was the jaunty story about a truck driver's mistress on the road. The song was one of the funkiest the group recorded, led by Danko's bass, Robertson's guitar licks, and Helm's Southern drawl. The chorus contained the group's catchiest hook underneath Hudson's sparkling Rhodes organ. Like the lyrics, the Band's groove was unpretentious, straightforward, dirty, and sexy.

The rest of the album was infused with the music and lyrics of the South. "Rockin' Chair" and "When You Awake" hark back to Southern roots, singing about "old Ver-ginny," "Ragtime Willie," and "my grandpa's knee," while "King Harvest" was a slightly menacing soul number about farm life. "Rag Mama

Rag" was a skewed impression of Dixieland jazz, replete with funky tuba bassline, Jelly Roll Morton–inflected piano melodies, and fiddle hook processed to sound straight out of a dusty 78. Funky Stax horns punctuated "Across the Great Divide," while Rich Danko's warm baritone on "Whispering Pines" was matched by a warm piano and wandering organ. *The Band* managed to evoke the War of Northern Aggression and the communal art colony of Big Pink at the same time, making it one of the most successful rock albums—let alone "Southern" or "country"—ever written.

The Band firmly entrenched the group as superstars. The album reached the top 10, and "Up on Cripple Creek" peaked at number 25, the Band's best-selling single. They played at the legendary Woodstock Festival—held just down the street from Big Pink—made the cover of *Time* magazine, and even appeared on the *Ed Sullivan Show*. Despite the Band's excellent technical chops, the group was uncomfortable with its newfound fame. In songwriting and recording, the quintet's success lay in evoking loose, informal nights of domestic music making among friends, not the bombastic productions of big rock stages. With their new success came money and drugs, and their increasing age (most band members were hovering around 30) brought marriage and children. Their years of communal living had produced some of the most magical rock of the late 1960s, but their collaborative spirit would slowly recede over the next decade.

The Band's third album was *Stage Fright,* a name hinting at the quintet's discomfort with the spotlight. The group wanted to record the album as a live concert in the Woodstock Playhouse, but town members, leery after the zaniness of the Woodstock Festival, denied the request. The band then used the playhouse as their recording studio, importing English producer Todd Rundgren to work the dials. As their first album living separately, and with Rundgren preferring a slicker mix than their usual shambling group recording, the album lacked some of the cohesiveness and strangeness that defined their first two efforts. However, the songwriting on *Stage Fright* matched the

previous album in its refraction of Americana. "The Shape I'm In" was a punchy blues number, the "W.S. Walcott Medicine Show" was a delightfully funky take on vaudeville, and "Stage Fright" featured a tender yet muscular vocal by Rick Danko. The album peaked at number five on the *Billboard* album charts, higher than the first two albums, but critical reviews were mixed.

Their following album, *Cahoots,* was recorded near Woodstock as well. The album's highlights were the joyous Dylan cover "When I Paint My Masterpiece," in which Dylan's lyric of hopeful love in bright New Orleans basked in accordion and effervescent drumming, and "Life Is a Carnival," a funky white soul cut that featured a horn line produced by Allan Touissant, producer of legendary soul artists like Dr. John, Chris Kenner, and B.J. Thomas. Van Morrison added guest vocals on the hard-rocking "4% Pantomime," and the album closed with the warm, nostalgic gospel of "The River Hymn." However, the album lacked the gravitas of the previous three recordings. It reached the top 20 but was soon out of the charts. With a slow decline in their commercial fortunes, the band turned away from recording new material for four years, an eternity by early 1970s standards.

During the first years of the 1970s, the Band garnered a reputation as an exceptional live band. Their performance at the Woodstock Festival, their tight performance on the *Ed Sullivan Show*, and their performance with Bob Dylan at the 1971 Isle of Wight Festival returned the band to their gigging roots. The Band's next two albums turned toward live performance. *Rock of Ages* was a double album recording highlights from a four-day stint at New York's Academy of Music from December 28 to 31, 1971. For these shows, Robertson collaborated with Touissant to add a horn section. The results, from the warmth it added to the tender "The Night They Drove Old Dixie Down" to the funk of "Caledonia Mission," accentuated the quintet's interest in timbre. Hudson also expanded "The Genetic Method" from the initial 30-second opening to a pastiche of styles and melodies, including "Auld Lang Syne" on New Year's Eve, that lasted more than seven minutes. The album reached the top 10 in 1972, outselling their previous two records and returning the Band to the critical spotlight. The quintet followed up *Rock of Ages* with *Moondog Matinee* (1973), which offered a complementary return to the Band's roots as a rockabilly cover band. The cover featured a 1950s cinema matinee reading, "The Band Remembers the Hawks." The group revived their set lists from their Hawks days, playing 1950s and 1960s covers. Despite the group's live verve, the album flopped upon its release.

The Band shot to stardom again with their 1974 tour with Bob Dylan. After the underground success of *The Basement Tapes,* as well as the subsequent reconsideration and canonization of Dylan's 1960s rock experiments, their joint tour was massively popular. As Rob Bowman wryly noted, "it is high irony that in 1966 these same six musicians had been mercilessly booed at virtually every show they played, while in 1974, playing basically the same music, both the audience and the media acted as though this were the Second Coming" (Bowman 2005, 72). The Band recorded another album with Dylan, *Planet Waves,* which featured one of Dylan's most enduring songs, "Forever Young," and released another live album, *Before the Flood.* The tour's success led to the official release of *The Basement Tapes* and helped reinvigorate Dylan's own career, with the masterful *Blood on the Tracks* and *Desire* catapulting the singer back into the critical spotlight.

While Dylan's career reemerged, the Band's studio career remained in slow ebb. In 1975, the band released *Northern Lights—Southern Cross,* their first album of originals since *Cahoots.* The album featured some songs ranking as the Band's best, like the funky "Forbidden Fruit" and the Touissant-inflected horn licks of "Ophelia." Returning to the pathos of "The Night They Drove Old Dixie Down," "Acadian Driftwood" again explored the losing side of war, this time the forced migrations of French settlers from the Atlantic Maritime provinces during the French and Indian War. The song showed the Band returning to their Canadian roots, featuring Hudson on accordion and even some French lyrics in the coda. As biographer Barney Hoskyns wrote, "It was as if Robbie

[Robertson] had finally lived outside Canada for long enough to see it through the same romantic lens he'd used to view the American South a decade before" (Hoskyns 1993, 318). Like the album's studio predecessors, though, the album failed to sell well. The band realized their original spark was missing, and after nearly a decade and a half together, they were all moving in different directions. Due to contractual obligations more than anything else, the group released *Islands* in 1977. The indifferent songwriting, save for the blues shuffle of "The Saga of Pepote Rouge," was matched by apathy on the part of the buying public.

However, the quintet did not want to simply go out with a whimper. Rather, keeping in line with their strong belief in tradition and community, they decided on the going-out party to beat all others: a final three-hour concert, which they called "The Last Waltz." The concert was held at San Francisco's Winterland Ballroom, the site of their first show as the Band back in 1969, featuring the group's roots and fellow 1970s artists. The Band alternated between energetic versions of their hits ("The Night They Drove Old Dixie Down," "Stage Fright," "Ophelia") and, recalling their Hawks origins, playing backing band for idols and friends.

The Band opened by playing Bo Diddley's "Who Do You Love" with Ronnie Hawkins, who had first brought them all together in Toronto back in the early 1960s. They performed with Muddy Waters ("Mannish Boy") and Dr. John ("Such a Night"), matching the blues and funk power of the legendary performers. They warmly performed 1970s rock standards like Neil Young's "Helpless" and Van Morrison's "Caravan," and underpinned singer-songwriters from Neil Diamond's "Dry Your Eyes" to Joni Mitchell's labyrinthine "Coyote." They played a suite of songs with Bob Dylan, including "Forever Young" and "Baby Let Me Follow You Down," a Reverend Gary Davis and Eric von Schmidt song from his debut album. The Staples turned "The Weight" into a soulful classic, while their version of "Evangeline" with Emmylou Harris demonstrated the Band's country talents. For the climax of the performance, everyone came back to the stage, including Ringo Starr and the Rolling Stones' Ron Wood, for a moving rendition of the triumphal, hopeful "I Shall Be Released" from the Band and Dylan's days at Big Pink. The song proved a fitting farewell to the group. The live, three-LP album entered the top 20, and a movie about the concert, *The Last Waltz,* directed by Martin Scorsese, became wildly popular in 1978.

Unlike many "farewell" concerts, "The Last Waltz" was the last time the quintet appeared together on stage. Band members attempted solo careers, but never approached the success of the original group. The Band returned in the 1980s without Robertson, but was nowhere near as successful as before. Haunted by personal demons and drug addictions, Richard Manuel committed suicide while on tour with the reunited group in 1986. In 1999, Rick Danko succumbed to heart failure brought on by years of drug and alcohol abuse, and Levon Helm died of cancer in 2012. His last album before his death, *Dirt Farmer,* was probably the most successful solo album by a Band member, winning a Grammy for Best Traditional Album.

The range of groups influenced by the Band is almost too large to mention. On one end, the group's tight rhythmic groove and lyrics celebrating Southern life helped give rise to Southern rock, country rock, and jam band artists from the Allman Brothers and Kid Rock to Ryan Adams and Wilco. On the other, a number of college and indie bands have tried to replicate the magic of the Band's Catskills sabbatical with Dylan, trying to harness the wild energy of communal living into songwriting inspiration. As Al Kooper wrote about *Music from Big Pink,* "This album was recorded in approximately two weeks. There are people who will work their lives away in vain and not touch it." That does not mean that numerous groups in the Band's wake have not valiantly tried to capture their elusive spark.

David K. Blake

Selected Discography

Music from Big Pink. Capitol SKAO 2955, 1968.

The Band. Capitol STAO 132, 1969.

Stage Fright. Capitol SW 425, 1970.

Cahoots. Capitol SMAS 651, 1971.

Rock of Ages: The Band in Concert. Capitol SABB 11045, 1972.

Moondog Matinee. Capitol SW 11214, 1973.

Before the Flood (Bob Dylan). Asylum AB 201, 1974.

Planet Waves (Bob Dylan). Asylum 7E-1003, 1974.

The Basement Tapes (with Bob Dylan). Columbia C2 33862, 1975.

Northern Lights—Southern Cross. Capitol ST-11440, 1975.

Islands. Capitol SO 11602, 1977.

The Last Waltz. Warner Brothers 3WS 3146, 1978.

The Band: A Musical History. Capitol Records CCAP77 409–6, 2005.

References

Bowman, Rob. Liner notes to *The Band: A Musical History*. Hollywood, CA: Capitol Records, 2005.

Fennessey, Sean. "The Band: The Weight." *Pitchfork Media*. Accessed August 2006. pitchfork.com/features/staff-lists/6405-the-200-greatest-songs-of-the-1960s.

Helm, Levon, and Stephen Davis. *This Wheel's on Fire: Levon Helm and the Story of the Band*. New York: W. Morrow, 1993.

Hoskyns, Barney. *Across the Great Divide: The Band and America*. New York: Hyperion, 1993.

Marcus, Greil. *Invisible Republic: Bob Dylan's Basement Tapes*. New York: H. Holt & Company, 1995.

The Beach Boys (1961–Present)

Widely acknowledged as the United States' most beloved rock group, the Beach Boys helped to mold an image of a mythical California lifestyle of surf, attractive and happy surfing-proficient young people, cruising in the latest cool hotrod cars, and carefree endless summer days. Beneath the surface, the story of the band was one of physical and emotional abuse, infighting, drug and alcohol abuse and addiction, mental illness, acrimonious business battles, media controversies, and lawsuits. Through it all, the Beach Boys became the most commercially successful, best-loved U.S. rock band of them all, largely as a result of the songwriting, musical vision, and production of Brian Wilson (born Brian Douglas Wilson,

June 20, 1942; vocals/bass), and nearly perpetual concertizing. Despite the fact that the Beach Boys' most commercially successful, influential, and productive period was between 1962 and 1966, despite the fact that Brian Wilson had all but dropped out of the group by the late 1960s (he subsequently returned), despite the premature deaths of Wilson's brothers, band members Dennis Wilson (born Dennis Carl Wilson, December 4, 1944, died December 28, 1983; drums) and Carl Wilson (born Carl Dean Wilson, December 21, 1946, died February 6, 1998; guitar), and despite numerous lawsuits and near breakups, the Beach Boys live on and in 2012 released their 50th-anniversary album, *That's Why God Made the Radio,* a collection of new material that was the band's highest-charting album in over 35 years.

The story of the Beach Boys began with brother and sister Murry Gage Wilson and Emily Wilson

Widely acknowledged as one of America's most beloved rock groups, the Beach Boys popularized West Coast rock and roll with images of the beach, surf, and cruising. Here, the Beach Boys perform on the *TAMI Show* in 1964. (Photo by Michael Ochs Archives/Getty Images)

moving with their family to Los Angeles, California, in the early 1920s. In time, Murry married Audree Korthof, and Emily married Edwin Love. These unions produced brothers Brian, Dennis, and Carl Wilson, and their cousin, Michael Love (born Michael Edward Love, March 15, 1941; vocals/saxophone), the four who became the core of the early Beach Boys. Although Murry Wilson was employed as a blue-collar worker, he enjoyed minor success in the music industry during the 1940s and 1950s, and one of his songs, "Two-Step Side-Step," was recorded by several performers and performed by bandleader Lawrence Welk on network television. By the late 1950s, however, music in the Wilson and Love households went far beyond one minor hit written by Murry. Inspired by vocal harmony groups such as the Four Freshmen and the Hi-Lo's, the Wilson brothers, Mike Love, and various other relatives and school friends harmonized, generally under the direction of Brian Wilson. Ultimately, one of the defining features of the early Beach Boys' sound was this combination of elaborate male vocal harmony developed from the 1950s a-cappella groups and early 20th-century barbershop quartet style with Chuck Berry–style rock and roll.

The teen years of the Wilson brothers were not entirely happy: they suffered emotional and physical abuse at the hands of their father. In fact, Brian Wilson's autobiography left open the prospect that a beating at the hands of his father may have caused him to become deaf in one ear (Wilson with Gold 1991, 20). In any case, Murry Wilson pushed and goaded his sons, and when he later became the Beach Boys' first manager and their music publisher, he continued his iron rule.

As teenagers, the Wilson brothers learned to play the piano, and Carl became a proficient Chuck Berry–influenced rock and roll guitarist. Brian Wilson wrote songs, composed vocal harmony arrangements, and played piano and bass guitar. A couple of Brian's pre–Beach Boys songs were recorded, but without much commercial success. His real start as a commercially successful writer, and the real start of the Beach Boys as a band, came out of Dennis Wilson's fascination with surfing. The middle Wilson sibling urged his older

brother to write a song about the sport, which in 1961 was quite popular along the southern California coast. Mike Love (vocals), Carl Wilson (guitar), Brian Wilson (drums), and Brian's folk-singing high school and community college classmate, Alan Jardine (Alan Charles Jardine, September 3, 1942; guitar), took Brian and Mike's collaboration, "Surfin'," to a recording studio owned by music publishers Hite and Dorinda Morgan. The Morgans were favorably impressed with the song, and eventually through their contacts at Candix Records, they helped Murry Wilson secure a recording contract for the Beach Boys (the name chosen after Kenny and the Cadets, Carl and the Passions, and the Pendletones all fell through). By this time, the group consisted of Carl Wilson (lead guitar and vocals), Brian Wilson (bass guitar and vocals), Mike Love (vocals and occasional percussion and saxophone), Al Jardine (rhythm guitar and vocals), and Dennis Wilson (drums and vocals).

After the late 1961 release of "Surfin'" on both the Candix and X labels, the song became a regional hit in southern California. Although "Surfin'" entered the national charts, it did not establish the Beach Boys nationally. Murry Wilson continued to shop demo recordings of the group around, especially following financial problems at Candix (which was out of business before the end of 1962), and the band started playing its first professional live gigs. Al Jardine left the Beach Boys before they broke nationally and was replaced on rhythm guitar by David Marks. Marks played on the group's first major singles and first several albums, but left the group in 1963, following a disagreement with Murry Wilson. The demo of the Brian Wilson/Mike Love collaboration "Surfin' Safari" came to the attention of Capitol Records' Nick Venet. Capitol signed the group and recorded the Beach Boys performing "Surfin' Safari," and the Wilson/Love/Gary Usher song "409" in June 1962. The single charted in August 1962, with "Surfin' Safari" making it to number 14. The B-side also charted, making it only as high as number 76; however, "409" was an important track because it broadened the Beach Boys' subject matter beyond the limits of surfing. In fact, some of the Beach Boys' best-remembered songs of 1962–1964 were about automobiles.

In sharp contrast to "409," Wilson and Usher also wrote "The Lonely Sea" and "In My Room," two 1963 introspective ballads that featured Wilson's falsetto lead vocal. In fact, the early up-tempo car and surfing songs tended to feature Mike Love's gritty baritone lead, and the Beach Boys' ballads tended to feature Brian Wilson's falsetto. In addition to collaborating with Mike Love and Gary Usher, Wilson formed a highly successful, albeit brief, partnership with disc jockey Roger Christian. Wilson and Christian authored the 1963 hit "Shut Down" and the 1964 hit "Don't Worry Baby."

Capitol released the Beach Boys' first album, *Surfin' Safari*, on October 1, 1962. Although the album largely revolved around the successful singles, "Surfin' Safari," "Ten Little Indians," and "Surfin'," it was notable for its high number of group-composed (Brian Wilson and his collaborators) songs. In fact, of the 12 tracks only three were covers. The band's second album, the March 1963 Capitol release *Surfin' U.S.A.*, included several surf-style instrumentals, "The Lonely Sea," "Shut Down," and the highly successful title track. "Surfin' U.S.A.," although initially credited to Brian Wilson, was little more than a remake of Chuck Berry's "Sweet Little Sixteen" with Wilson's lyrics naming famous surfing beaches. After successful litigation, Berry received co-authorship credit for the song. Despite the slight pall that continues to hang over the song, it was a number-three hit for the Beach Boys, and perhaps one of the band's best straight-ahead rock and roll performances ever. "Surfin' U.S.A." also established the Beach Boys as the United States' leading surf band, as well as definers of a California lifestyle that especially appealed to young people outside of coastal California.

The band's other 1963 albums have not aged well and suffered from a thinness of material. Al Jardine returned to the Beach Boys in 1963, and David Marks left the band shortly thereafter. Although Marks had proven to be an important counterpart to Carl Wilson on guitar, especially in the development of the Beach Boys' surf-style sound, Jardine was a significantly stronger singer. With Jardine's return, Brian Wilson's vocal arrangements could now consistently stress four-part harmony that could be reproduced live.

The year 1964 will always be known for the British Invasion; however, it was in the wake of Beatlemania and the British Invasion that the Beach Boys enjoyed their first number-one single, "I Get Around." The success of the single proved that the band could compete with the British pop groups and represented the start of an unofficial friendly competition between Brian Wilson as a composer and arranger and the Beatles, principally Paul McCartney. In October 1964, Capitol released *The Beach Boys Concert,* an album that suffered from less-than-optimal audio quality, but nonetheless a collection that was amazingly successful from a commercial standpoint: it became the first live album ever to make it to number one on the pop charts.

In part because he was uncomfortable on stage, in part because of his deafness in one ear, Brian Wilson withdrew from touring with the Beach Boys following a panic attack on tour in late 1964. Because the Beach Boys were one of the most prolific touring acts of the time, a road replacement for Brian Wilson had to be found. Session musician Glen Campbell played that role from late 1964 into 1965. In 1965, however, Bruce Johnston (born Benjamin Baldwin, July 27, 1942; vocals) joined the Beach Boys on a more permanent basis, and Campbell began his ascent to what eventually became country-pop superstardom. Interestingly, although Johnston was a regular member of the touring band and played and sang on singles and albums beginning with "California Girls," he did not appear in album cover photos of the Beach Boys until the 1968 album *Friends*.

The year 1964 concluded with the release of *The Beach Boys' Christmas Album,* still regarded as one of the best holiday albums of the rock era. The album contained the hit single "Little Saint Nick" and was one of the rare 1960s Beach Boys albums that included orchestral backings for the group that were not arranged by Brian Wilson.

After Wilson withdrew from touring, it was widely reported that he remained in the Los Angeles area to compose and arrange songs for the Beach Boys.

What was not as widely known at the time was that Wilson as a producer scored and recorded instrumental backing tracks for Beach Boys releases using the elite of the elite of Los Angeles studio musicians, the so-called Wrecking Crew. Musicians such as drummer Hal Blaine, guitarist and bass guitarist Carol Kaye, guitarists Glen Campbell and Tommy Tedesco, and others provided much of the instrumental work on tracks such as "Help Me, Rhonda," "Good Vibrations," the bulk of *Pet Sounds,* and other mid-1960s Beach Boys singles and albums. Between 1965 and late 1967, the only member of the Beach Boys other than Brian Wilson himself who regularly contributed his instrumental skills to the group's recordings was guitarist Carl Wilson.

For the first several years of their existence, the Beach Boys primarily were a singles band; most of the band's pre-1965 albums contained several less-than-stellar tracks that easily could be labeled "filler." That situation changed dramatically with Brian Wilson's arranging and production work on the highly acclaimed 1965 album *Today!* Although the album contained hit single material, such as "When I Grow Up (To Be a Man)," "Dance, Dance, Dance," "Do You Wanna Dance?" and an early version of the soon-to-be hit "Help Me, Rhonda," it was organized in such a way as to explore moods that extended from song to song. In other words, more than anything that Wilson had produced before, *Today!* was a coherent work and not just a collection of stand-alone songs. The ballads on the second side of the album, too, were more introspective than previous Beach Boys songs. *Today!* firmly established the Beach Boys as album artists and was ranked at number 271 on *Rolling Stone*'s list of the 500 Greatest Albums of All Time (*Rolling Stone,* "The 500 Greatest Albums of All Time," 2012). The follow-up, *Summer Days (And Summer Nights!!),* although not as consistent, contained the hit "California Girls" and the new, highly successful single version of "Help Me, Rhonda." *Summer Days* was also the first Beach Boys album on which Bruce Johnston performed.

Because he originally was more interested in folk music than rock and roll, Al Jardine was knowledgeable about folk material that might have been unfamiliar to other members of the Beach Boys. In 1965, Jardine suggested to Brian Wilson that the group record the folk song "Sloop John B," a tune that had been recorded by several folk revival musicians and that had been a hit in the late 1950s for the Kingston Trio. Wilson's arrangement of the piece developed from the summer of 1965 to the recording of the final vocal tracks on December 22, 1965 (Leaf, Liner notes for *Pet Sounds,* 1990), and the finished piece contained an unusual and elaborate a cappella vocal section that was completely unlike anything in the pop music of the day. Capitol issued the single of "Sloop John B" in March 1966; it became a top 10 hit and remains one of the Beach Boys' best-remembered recordings of the period.

While it can be said that *Summer Days (And Summer Nights!!)* represented the Beach Boys' return to their earlier focus on a mythical California lifestyle of never-ending fun in the sun, Brian Wilson returned to the introspective style of the second side of *Today!* for what turned out to be the Beach Boys' greatest album, *Pet Sounds.* The album contained the hit single "Sloop John B"; however, Wilson recorded most of the instrumental tracks and overdubbed himself singing a majority of the vocal lines in early 1966 after "Sloop John B" had already been completed. Wilson frequently has stated that he was inspired by the Beatles' *Rubber Soul,* and in fact, a friendly rivalry of sorts developed between Wilson and the Beatles' Paul McCartney. *Rubber Soul* itself had been inspired at least in part by the Beach Boys' *Today!*; *Rubber Soul* inspired *Pet Sounds*; and in turn *Pet Sounds* ultimately influenced some aspects of the Beatles' *Sgt. Pepper's Lonely Hearts Club Band.*

Brian Wilson's use of unusual instrumental tone colors (e.g., sleigh bells, theremin, bass harmonica, heavily reverbed percussion effects, and so on), the relative lack of danceable, beat-oriented rock songs, and Tony Asher and Wilson's introspective and at times melancholy lyrics might have accounted for the somewhat cool commercial reception that *Pet Sounds* received. Critics, however, remain highly impressed with the album. For example, in describing why they ranked *Pet Sounds* number two on their list of the 500 Greatest Albums of All Time, the editors of *Rolling Stone* wrote, "With its vivid orchestration, lyrical ambition, elegant pacing and thematic coherence, *Pet Sounds* invented—and in some sense perfected—the idea that an album could be more than the sum of its parts. When [Brian] Wilson sang, 'Wouldn't it be nice if we were older?' on the magnificent opener, he wasn't just imagining a love that could evolve past high school; he was suggesting a new grown-up identity for rock & roll music itself" (*Rolling Stone*, "The 500 Greatest Albums of All Time," 2012).

The culmination of Brian Wilson's work as a composer, arranger, and producer came with the highly complex 1966 recording and number-one hit single "Good Vibrations." The piece has been recognized by virtually every pop music critic as one of the most important compositions and recordings of the entire rock era. The editors of *Rolling Stone*, for example, ranked "Good Vibrations" at number six on their list of the 500 Greatest Songs of All Time (*Rolling Stone*, "The 500 Greatest Songs of All Time," 2012).

The relatively lackluster commercial acceptance of *Pet Sounds* as well as a realization that the popular music world was changing quite rapidly by late 1966 and early 1967 created a crisis of confidence for Brian Wilson. During that period, Wilson collaborated with lyricist Van Dyke Parks on a wide-ranging collection of highly impressionistic pop songs, highly repetitive chant-like compositions, brief nonsensical child-like pieces, and barbershop-inspired vocalizations, all of which were to be included on the Beach Boys' *SMiLE* album. In terms of its stylistic diversity and freedom from the constraints of traditional pop song structure, the compositions, arrangements, and productions of *SMiLE* would have moved well beyond the songs of *Pet Sounds*. Despite plans by Capitol to release *SMiLE* well before summer 1967 (when the Beatles' *Sgt. Pepper's Lonely Hearts Club Band* appeared), Wilson shelved the project. Wilson also decided that the band should pull out of a planned performance at the Monterey International Pop Music Festival because he was afraid that the Beach Boys' performance would pale in comparison to the new psychedelic hard rock bands that were emerging at the time.

In 2004, Brian Wilson's dream of seeing his *SMiLE* project available to the world finally came to fruition. Wilson, supported by various instrumentalists and vocalists, performed the world premiere of the work at London's Royal Festival Hall on February 20, 2004. Subsequently, a studio recording of Wilson and lyricist Van Dyke Parks's 16 songs (a 17th piece, a brief medley of oldies "Old Master Painter" and "You Are My Sunshine," is also part of *SMiLE*) was issued by Nonesuch, a label more closely associated with classical music than with pop. Insofar as a number of the songs had found their way onto the Beach Boys' albums *Smiley Smile* and *Surf's Up*, it is interesting to compare the 2004 arrangements with those released between 1967 and 1971. The most notable difference was that the 2004 version of "Good Vibrations" used the original Tony Asher lyrics, exorcizing some of Mike Love's contributions to the text. Seven years after the success of Brian Wilson's Beach Boy–less rendition of *SMiLE*, Capitol Records released several editions of recordings from the original 1966–1967 *SMiLE* sessions. The Capitol releases do not necessarily represent exactly what *SMiLE* might have sounded like had Wilson not shelved the project in spring 1967; however, the arrangements and production generally do not vary significantly from Wilson's 2004 version, given the differences in recording technology between 1967 and 2004.

In place of *SMiLE*, the Beach Boys released *Smiley Smile* in 1967. The album was not commercially successful and, although it contained several tracks that were to have been released on *SMiLE*, the substitute album was, as Carl Wilson put it, "a bunt, instead of a grand slam" (Stebbins 2011, 87). Be that as it may, the track "Heroes and Villains" was one of Brian Wilson's most complex arrangements; there were strong hints of Wilson's "Heroes and Villains" vocal arrangements and rhapsodic structure in the later well-known Queen song "Bohemian Rhapsody." Continuing the Beach Boys' descent from popularity as recording artists, the 1968 album *Friends* made it only as high as number 126 on the U.S. charts.

Cowriters Mike Love and Brian Wilson turned nostalgic for the 1968 hit song "Do It Again." The single was the Beach Boys' last top 20 release in the United States until 1976. Part of the song's appeal may have come from the fact that, in the year in which Dr. Martin Luther King Jr. and Robert Kennedy were assassinated and in which antiwar protests outside the Democratic National Convention turned violent (and were captured on national television), the music and lyrics reflected the innocence of the prewar early 1960s. Regardless, as was the case with many mid-1960s and late-1960s releases, "Do It Again" was more commercially successful in the United Kingdom than it was at home: the single made it to number one on the British charts.

Generally, the Beach Boys' late 1960s and early 1970s albums and post–"Do It Again" singles did not fare particularly well from a commercial standpoint. Brian Wilson gradually withdrew from writing and studio work, and in his place Carl Wilson became a more musically dominant figure. Ironically, the post–*Smiley Smile* albums were more rock-band oriented than anything the Beach Boys had produced in several years, with a lesser reliance on studio musicians.

One of the few high points of the period was the relatively positive critical reception of the 1970 album *Sunflower*. This album represented the emergence of Dennis Wilson and Bruce Johnston as strong songwriters and the reestablishment of the Beach Boys as a vocal harmony–focused band. Although the album topped out at number 151 on the U.S. charts and number 29 in the United Kingdom, it appeared at number 380 on the 2003 *Rolling Stone* list of the 500 Greatest Albums of All Time (it has not appeared on subsequent editions of the list). *All Music Guide* critic John Bush wrote, "*Sunflower* was also a remarkably cohesive album, something not seen from the Beach Boys since *Pet Sounds*. As with that album, *Sunflower* earned critical raves in Britain but was virtually ignored in America" (Bush, "*Sunflower,*" 2012).

The late 1960s and the early 1970s were turbulent years in the United States, especially with widespread dissatisfaction over the ongoing war in Vietnam, various countercultural lifestyles, radicalization of politics, and the like. The Beach Boys made scarce commentary on the situation, aside from Carl

Wilson's refusal to serve in the military as a conscientious objector. In the wake of the emergence of the environmental movement in 1970 and the shootings of students at Kent State University and Jackson State University in May 1970, the Beach Boys included several socially relevant songs on the 1971 album *Surf's Up*. Unfortunately, the album's lyrical themes are so wide ranging that the social commentary tended to get somewhat lost, and the year 1971 was late enough in the counterculture era that "Student Demonstration Time" and "A Day in the Life of a Tree" seem like a case of too little, too late. The highlights of *Surf's Up* were the title track and "'Til I Die." Brian Wilson and Van Dyke Parks's "Surf's Up" dated from the *SMiLE* period, but was given a fleshed-out arrangement and production for the album that bore its name. "'Til I Die," with words and music by Wilson alone, although not fully accepted by the entire group when Wilson first shared it with them, is now recognized as one of its composer's most deeply personal statements about the sense of disconnectedness with other people and the world around him that he felt at the time.

Bruce Johnston left the Beach Boys in 1972. Because of Johnston's departure and a hand injury that made it impossible for Dennis Wilson to play the drums for a period of time, the band reshuffled its studio and live lineup, adding the South African musicians Ricky Fataar (drums) and Blondie Chaplin (vocals and guitar). Fataar and Chaplin were full-time members of the band only for a short time, but contributed as singers, players, producers, and songwriters to the albums *Carl and the Passions "So Tough"* and *Holland*. Most notable was Chaplin's lead vocal on the *Holland* track "Sail On, Sailor." Bruce Johnston returned to the band in 1978 and remained one of the group's stalwarts.

The Beach Boys continued to release new material through the rest of the 1970s and the 1980s; however, most of the band's impact was as a touring unit that focused on hits from their heyday. In fact, the group's most successful album of the mid-1970s was *Endless Summer,* a double album of hits from the 1960s. The 1976 album *15 Big Ones* generated more interest in the band, and it represented the return of Brian Wilson as an active producer and member of the studio and touring lineup. Ultimately, the "Brian's Back" campaign that the band's management undertook was not entirely successful; it would still be years before Wilson was mentally, emotionally, and physically fit enough to participate in live performance as an equal with his bandmates.

The early 1980s were especially turbulent for the band. Carl Wilson left the Beach Boys in 1981–1982 to pursue a solo career; however, lack of success in doing so soon brought him back to the band. In 1983, Dennis Wilson married Shawn Marie Love—allegedly the illegitimate daughter of Mike Love (Gaines 1995, 9). Tensions were so high between cousins Mike Love and Dennis Wilson that each obtained a restraining order against the other (Gaines 1995, 10). The same year, the Beach Boys fired Dennis Wilson because of his unreliability and bizarre onstage behavior fueled by alcohol abuse. Shortly thereafter, on December 28, 1983, Dennis Wilson, the former surfer who was the impetus for the band forming back in 1961, accidentally drowned while diving.

Throughout the 1980s the Beach Boys were beloved as a nostalgia act and widely acknowledged as the United States' rock band. This was demonstrated through the widespread ridicule that U.S. Secretary of the Interior James Watt received when he banned the Beach Boys from performing at a scheduled July 4, 1983, concert on the Mall in Washington, D.C. Despite America's love of the group as a concert act and the continuing popularity of their 1962–1966 work, it took the 1988 song "Kokomo," as featured in the soundtrack of the film *Cocktail,* to bring the Beach Boys back to the top of the charts. Because Brian Wilson and Mike Love were at odds with each other, Wilson did not participate in the writing, production, or performance of the number-one hit—the singular commercial success for the longstanding band that contained no contribution from their onetime leader.

Carl Wilson lost a year-long battle with lung cancer in early 1998. Although Wilson was diagnosed in early 1997 and was receiving treatments, he continued to tour and performed with the Beach Boys until his death. In the wake of Carl Wilson's passing, Al

Jardine left the touring lineup of the band in 1998. Jardine put together his own band and in 2008 was sued by Mike Love for including the words "Beach Boys" in the band's name. Unfortunately, that was not the only legal action between various members of the Beach Boys in the first decade of the 21st century. Three years earlier, Love had sued Brian Wilson for including the name of the band and Love's image in promotional materials for *Brian Wilson Presents SMiLE.*

In 2011, the Beach Boys put aside their personal, musical, professional, and legal differences and announced a world tour for 2012 that would include Brian Wilson, Mike Love, David Marks, Bruce Johnston, and Al Jardine, as well as other supporting musicians. The band also reunited to perform at the 2012 Grammy Awards, the first time that the Beach Boys had ever performed at the Grammys. The quintet also released the 2012 album *That's Why God Made the Radio,* the Beach Boys' highest-charting album since 1965. While most of the tracks reflect nostalgically on the California myth that the Beach Boys in large part created a half century before, the album concluded with "Summer's Gone," a song that effectively suggests that the myth is over.

Over the course of their half-century-long career the Beach Boys have sold millions and millions of records, placed 11 of their nearly 35 noncompilation albums in the *Billboard* Top 10, placed over 30 songs in the *Billboard* Top 40, and remain a top concert attraction that continues to transcend pop music trends. More importantly, the Beach Boys still are widely recognized as America's best-loved rock band. Because of their extraordinary commercial success, the artistic successes of Brian Wilson's compositions, arrangements, and productions (particularly of 1964–1966), and how the band has continued to define the carefree California lifestyle of the pre-psychedelic, precounterculture 1960s for audiences that span several generations, the Beach Boys have been the recipients of numerous prestigious awards since the late 1980s.

The band was elected to the Rock and Roll Hall of Fame in 1988, in the same class as the Beatles. The

Hall's biography of the Beach Boys states, "Among rock and roll groups of the Sixties, the California quintet place second only to the Beatles in terms of their overall impact on the top 40. They were the Fab Four's most serious competitors on a creative level, too" ("The Beach Boys Biography," 2012). Unfortunately, however, the Beach Boys' induction might best be remembered less for Brian Wilson's humble acceptance speech than for Mike Love's lengthy tirade against his peers from other groups (Wilson, Wilson, Love, 2012). The Recording Academy's National Trustees presented the Beach Boys with the 2001 Grammy Lifetime Achievement Award. Brian Wilson was a 2002 inductee into the National Academy of Popular Music's Songwriters Hall of Fame. Finally, *Rolling Stone* ranks the Beach Boys at number 12 on the magazine's list of the 100 Greatest Artists of All Time. Lindsey Buckingham, guitarist with Fleetwood Mac, is quoted on the magazine's website as saying, "The Beach Boys showed the way, and not just to California. Sure, they may have sold the California Dream to a lot of people, but for me, it was Brian Wilson showing how far you might have to go in order to make your own musical dream come true" (Buckingham 2012).

James E. Perone

Selected Discography

Note: Although the Beach Boys' albums during their most productive and influential period were released on vinyl, the following discography includes only CD releases and reissues. For reissues, the original release date is included parenthetically.

Surfin' Safari (1962)/*Surfin' U.S.A.* (1963), Capitol 31517, 2000.

Little Deuce Coupe (1963), *All Summer Long* (1964), Capitol 72435–31516–2–0, 2001.

The Beach Boys' Christmas Album (1964), Capitol 95084, 2001.

Today! (1965)/*Summer Days (And Summer Nights!!)* (1965), Capitol 31639, 2001.

Pet Sounds (1966), Capitol, 48421, 1990.

The SMiLE Sessions (recorded 1966–1967; unreleased), Capitol 766324 (Deluxe 2-CD version), 2011.

Smiley Smile (1967)/*Wild Honey* (1967), Capitol 31862, 1990.

Sunflower (1970), *Surf's Up* (1971), Capitol 25692, 2000.

Carl and the Passions, "So Tough" (1972), *Holland* (1973), Capitol 72435–25694–2–7, 2000.

The Beach Boys in Concert (1973), EMI Music Distribution 70549, 2008.

15 Big Ones (1976)/*Love You* (1977), Capitol 27945, 2000.

Good Timin': Live at Knebworth, England 1980 (1980), Eagle 30532, 2012. Note: This reissue also includes a DVD from the concert.

Brian Wilson Presents SMiLE, Nonesuch 79846–2, 2004. Note: This is a Brian Wilson solo recording of material composed in 1966–1967 that includes no participation from other members of the Beach Boys.

That's Why God Made the Radio, Capitol 509996–02824–2–2, 2012.

References

Buckingham, Lindsey. "The 100 Greatest Artists of All Time: No. 12, The Beach Boys." *Rolling Stone* online edition, http://www.rollingstone.com/music/lists/100-greatestartists-of-all-time-19691231/the-beach-boys-19691231, *Rolling Stone,* 2012.

Gaines, Steven. *Heroes and Villains: The True Story of the Beach Boys.* Cambridge, MA: Da Capo, 1995. Originally published in hardback: New York: New American Library, 1986.

Lambert, Philip. *Inside the Music of Brian Wilson: The Songs, Sounds and Influences of the Beach Boys' Founding Genius.* New York: Continuum, 2007.

Leaf, David. *The Beach Boys.* Philadelphia: Courage Books, 1985.

Leaf, David. Liner notes for *Pet Sounds,* CD, Capitol 48421, 1990a.

Leaf, David. Liner notes for *Surfin' Safari/Surfin' U.S.A.,* CD, Capitol 31517, 1990b.

Love, Mike. *Mike Love—The Beach Boys Official Website,* http://mikelove.com, 2012.

Marsh, Dave. *The Heart of Rock & Soul: The 1001 Greatest Singles Ever Made.* New York: Da Capo Press, 1999.

Rolling Stone. "The 500 Greatest Albums of All Time: No. 2, The Beach Boys, *Pet Sounds.*" *Rolling Stone* online edition, http://www.rollingstone.com/music/lists/500greatest-albums-of-all-time-20120531/the-beach-boys-pet-sounds19691231#ixzz20XKf7NzH, *Rolling Stone,* 2012.

Rolling Stone. "The 500 Greatest Songs of All Time: No. 6, The Beach Boys, 'Good Vibrations.'" *Rolling Stone* online edition, http://www.rollingstone.com/music/lists/the500-greatest-songs-of-all-time-20110407/the-beach-boys-good-vibrations-19691231, *Rolling Stone,* 2012.

Stebbins, Jon. *The Beach Boys FAQ: All That's Left to Know about America's Band.* Milwaukee, WI: Backbeat Books, 2011.

Unterberger, Richie. "*Pet Sounds.*" *All Music Guide,* http://www.allmusic.com/album/pet-sounds-mw0000398074, Rovi Corporation, 2012.

White, Timothy. *The Nearest Faraway Place: Brian Wilson, the Beach Boys, and the Southern California Experience.* New York: Henry Holt, 1996.

Will, George F. "The Beach Boys Still Get Around," *The Washington Post* online edition, Wilson, Brian. *Brian Wilson Official Website,* http://brianwilson.com, 2012.

Wilson, Brian, with Todd Gold. *Wouldn't It Be Nice: My Own Story.* New York: HarperCollins, 1991.

Wilson, Brian, Carl Wilson, and Mike Love. "Rock & Roll Hall of Fame Acceptance Speeches," http://www.youtube.com/watch?v=oZSAQX2uuUY, 2012.

The Beastie Boys (1979–Present)

The Beastie Boys are one of hip-hop's most innovative and adaptable groups. They have blended hip-hop with punk, dub, instrumental rock, and alternative music, while maintaining the music's integrity by keeping hip-hop at the core of their style. They have gone from the hard rock and Budweiser-driven *Licensed to Ill* to speaking out against misogyny in lyrics. They have moved from New York to Los Angeles and back again, and started their own record label and magazine. They discovered LL Cool J, made out with Madonna (reportedly), and organized a series of concerts in support of Tibet. With *Licensed to Ill,* they built a new sound from Run-DMC's merger of rap and hard rock that would become a blueprint for future

rap-rock acts such as Limp Bizkit, Korn, and Linkin Park, but they abandoned this sound to consistently experiment with new forms of music.

The Beastie Boys' music career began in 1979, when 14-year-old singer Michael Diamond (aka Mike D, born November 20, 1965; vocals/drums) formed a hard-core punk group called the Young Aborigines with guitarist John Berry and drummer Kate Schnellenbach. In 1979, they made their first recorded appearance with a hard-core track on the compilation cassette called *New York Trash.* In 1981, bassist Adam Yauch (aka MCA, born Adam Nathanial Yauch, August 15, 1964, died May 4, 2012; vocals/bass) joined the group, which was then renamed B.E.A.S.T.I.E. Boys; the name was an acronym for Boys Entering Anarchistic States Through Internal Excellence. They played their first show on Yauch's 17th birthday. The original lineup released one album in 1982, *Pollywog Stew,* on the independent New York punk label Ratcage. They were also featured on the Ratcage compilation *New York Trash.* While Diamond and Yauch founded the group, the third member of the lineup for which the Beastie Boys are known was Adam Horovitz (aka Ad-Rock, born Adam Keefe Horovitz, October 31, 1966; vocals/guitar), whose punk roots served the Beastie Boys well in bringing a distinct energy to hip-hop, a fusion of punk chaos, rock excess, and hip-hop lyricism.

As teenagers in the music scene in New York City in the early 1980s, the Beastie Boys were exposed to the tail end of punk's heyday, as well as the new sounds of Grandmaster Flash, Afrika Bambaataa, and Kool Herc. Their position on the border of these two music movements allowed the Beastie Boys to create a distinctive sound, borrowing and adapting the sounds and styles they liked from both punk and hip-hop. The Beastie Boys met Rick Rubin, a white producer who was making hip-hop records in his dorm room at New York University and the future cofounder of Def Jam Records. Rubin worked initially as part of the Beastie Boys' stage show, as DJ Double R, but he soon left the turntables to work primarily in the production booth. In the studio, Rubin's production proved key to defining the Beastie Boys' sound and influential to the future of hip-hop.

The triple threat of (from left to right) Adam "MCA" Yauch, Mike "D" Diamond, and Adam "Ad-Rock" Horovitz made the Beastie Boys the first major white hip-hop success story. The Beastie Boys' success has been attested to by 10 Grammy Awards, eight MTV Video Music Awards, and induction into the Rock and Roll Hall of Fame in 2012. (Photo by Pam Springsteen/Corbis)

In 1984, Def Jam released the Beasties' *Rock Hard.* This extended-play record featured the first Beastie Boys songs that could be classified as true hip-hop. Their vocal styles had developed in the direction of their mentors Run-DMC, but Ad-Rock, Mike D, and MCA, as Horovitz, Diamond, and Yauch now called themselves, added their own touches. They adopted Run-DMC's manner of rapping hard, shouting or spitting each line so that each word sounded crisp and distinct, rather than delivering the smoother, almost singsong vocals of earlier MCs from Sugarhill Gang, Curtis Blow, and the Furious Five.

Ad-Rock, Mike D, and MCA grew up in New York City, but their first full-length album in 1986, *Licensed to Ill,* brought rap to the suburbs. With lyrics about not wanting to go to school, being caught smoking, and having porno magazines confiscated by parents, the Beastie Boys tapped into a widening hip-hop audience whose experiences were far removed from the crime-ridden New York City streets depicted in songs like the Furious Five's "The Message." The Beasties also took hip-hop uptown with help from Rick Rubin, Russell Simmons, and Run-DMC. In fact, the *Licensed to Ill* track "Slow and Low" was a Run-DMC song that the group had chosen to leave off their *King of Rock* album.

A younger market was buying hip-hop records, and the Beastie Boys' material caught the ears of the kids. The Beastie Boys rhymed about high school, the prom, and dealing with parents, as well as becoming rap stars. They made their music accessible to a new audience. Part of *Licensed to Ill*'s appeal came from a mix of teen-focused subject matter and shock value. The Beastie Boys rhymed about getting busted for smoking and being told to turn down their loud music, but they also boasted about carrying weapons and smoking angel dust.

Lyrically, *Licensed to Ill* was a precursor to gangsta rap. The older, wiser Beastie Boys may not want credit for their contributions to the development of gangsta style, but *Licensed to Ill* was one of the first albums to promote gun play, drug use, and cartoonish violence to listeners in the mainstream. If the gangsta style was characterized by its macho pose, its depictions of everyday acts of violence, and using women, money, and guns as status symbols, then *Licensed to Ill* was a gangsta rap record. The mix of violent and silly lyrics on *Licensed to Ill* made listeners question how literally to take the Beastie Boys. They talked about smoking angel dust, sniffing glue, packing 0.22 automatics, and shooting people at parties, as well as high school pranks like giving people swirlies and breaking into someone's locker to smash his glasses. In the Beasties' lyrics, these stories came off as fantasy, even as they rhymed about shooting people and taking hard-core drugs.

Listeners must remember, though, that *Licensed to Ill* was toned down before its release. The version of *Licensed to Ill* that made it to record stores had been changed significantly. Even with these omissions, *Licensed to Ill* depicted an adolescent male fantasy world, somewhere between punk rock's energy and fraternity films like *Animal House,* somewhere between arena rock's excess and punk's playfulness. As gangsta rap became hip-hop's biggest-selling subgenre, the artists became concerned with the lifestyle promoted in lyrics. Yet the Beasties have talked openly about their construction of personas on *Licensed to Ill.* As MCA says in the *Sounds of Science* liner notes, though, with their success they slowly became the characters they played: drunken, prank-playing frat boys. While they changed their personas on *Paul's Boutique,* they retained some of the elements of *Licensed to Ill.* Ultimately, though, they began a pattern of change and evolution, both in terms of music and persona.

The Beastie Boys split with Def Jam in 1988. They then signed with Capitol Records and began working on their second album, *Paul's Boutique.* It would be very difficult to make the album today, with digital music sampling regulations more clearly defined. In the late 1980s the music business faced a series of lawsuits between artists, labels, and publishing companies, all centering on hip-hop's invention of digital sampling. Sampling is the process by which hip-hop producers extract pieces of existing records and then reassemble them into a new hip-hop song. With the help of the Dust Brothers, the Beastie Boys built the music on *Paul's Boutique* from layers of samples from classic songs mixed with a variety of beats. Sample sources were as varied as Curtis Mayfield's "Superfly" and Sly Stones' "Loose Booty" to Loggins and Messina's "Your Mama Don't Dance" and the Ramones' "Lucy Is a Headbanger."

Visually, the cover and liner notes for *Paul's Boutique* were something in themselves. The 12-inch record folded out to 5 feet of insert panels including all the lyrics from the album. This artistic direction was taken further in the impressionistic music video for the song "Shadrach." Artists worked from film of a Beastie Boys performance and created frame-by-frame oil paintings, which were then animated for the music video. The video for "Looking Down the Barrel of a Gun" was filmed with a fish-eye lens and an infrared camera, both of which the Beastie Boys used in future videos.

Today, *Paul's Boutique* is considered a hip-hop classic, but its initial sales were disappointing. The album took hip-hop music places it had not gone before. The release of *Paul's Boutique* the same year as De La Soul's *3 Feet High and Rising* made 1989 a turning point for hip-hop. The Beastie Boys have said that De La Soul beat them to the punch by releasing their innovative album in the months before *Paul's Boutique,* but the competition between these groups has been friendly. The Beastie Boys would later invite De La Soul to perform at their 1996 and 1997 Tibetan Freedom Concerts, and Mike D and Ad-Rock would guest star on De La Soul's "Squat" on their 2003 album *AOI: Bionix.*

Check Your Head was the first major-label album in which the Beastie Boys took control of their own musical production, recording it in their G-Son Studios (Atwater Village, California) and taking hip-hop in yet another direction as they returned to the live instrumentation of their punk rock origins. They were influenced by Dutch group Urban Dance Squad to return to their instruments. The Beastie Boys did not turn their backs on traditional hip-hop production, but instead merged it with punk, funk, and rock to create a unique new Beastie Boys sound. Partially responsible for the new sound was Mario Caldato Jr., who had helped in the production of *Paul's Boutique* and returned to engineer and collaborate on this record (he would remain in this role on future releases). The Beastie Boys further enhanced their lineup with keyboardist Money Mark Nishita (born Mark Ramos-Nishita; keyboard instruments), whom they had originally hired to build cabinets for their recording studio. Mark's work was best heard on "Gratitude." He would remain with the group through their next album, *Ill Communication,* release a solo album on the Beastie Boys' Grand Royal label (active from 1992 to 2001), and open for the Beastie Boys during some of their *Hello Nasty* tour in 1998. As a testament to the Beastie Boys' ever-increasing fame, the Grand Royal Label spawned *Grand Royal Magazine,* which printed intermittently from 1993 to 2000.

Check Your Head was the first Beastie Boys release to bear the label Grand Royal and could be called the Beastie Boys' comeback album. With the 1992 release of "Smells Like Teen Spirit," Nirvana had given birth to the alternative rock era, bringing a new, punk-influenced style to MTV and the radio. The Beastie Boys were primed to tap into this new market as well. Glen Friedman, famous for his skateboarding photography, shot the cover for *Check Your* *Head,* and the Beastie Boys further emphasized their connections with skateboard and snowboard culture in lyrics. Adam Yauch became an avid snowboarder, and a snowboarding trip to Asia would ultimately lead him to his interest in Buddhism and the plight of Tibet.

If *Check Your Head* suggested that the Beastie Boys were moving away from their hip-hop roots, a listen to 1994's *Ill Communication* appeared to confirm this transition. While the album opens with "Sure Shot," an energetic track driven by a doctored flute sample and peppered with the Beastie Boys' trademark mix of cultural references, the mood shifts quickly to punk on track two, "Tough Guy," and track 16, "Heart Attack Man," a mock tribute to Beastie Boys associate and music journalist Bob Mack. Subsequent tracks were devoted to a violin-driven instrumental, an instrumental tribute to hip-hop photographer Ricky Powell, and Tibetan-inspired songs. Out of the album's 20 tracks, only nine are hip-hop songs. This formula, however, would not let the Beastie Boys lose their fan base.

The Beastie Boys' concerts had always been known for their energy. In 1994, they joined Lollapalooza, the annual concert founded by Jane's Addiction singer Perry Farrell, that was known to include one or two hip-hop acts within a roster of primarily alternative rock groups. The Beastie Boys shared a bill with Green Day, L7, the Breeders, the Boredoms, George Clinton's P-Funk All Stars, Nick Cave, A Tribe Called Quest, and Smashing Pumpkins, who took Nirvana's place after they backed out shortly before Kurt Cobain's suicide in April of 1994.

The Beastie Boys have long demonstrated their dedication to correcting the misogynist images they put forth on *Licensed to Ill,* where songs like "Girls" suggested that women were only useful for washing dishes, cleaning bathrooms, and having sex. They worked to revise this message in the Lollapalooza 1994 tour booklet, where the Beastie Boys urged their male fans to respect their female fans' right to have a good time without being harassed.

In 1998 *Hello Nasty* introduced Michael "Mix Master Mike" Schwartz (born January 16, 1970; turntables) to the lineup and continued the Beastie Boys' connections with both the old and the new that have made them so adaptable. With the addition of Mix Master Mike, *Hello Nasty* sold over 500,000 units in its first week and went straight to number one in the United States, the United Kingdom, Germany, Australia, the Netherlands, New Zealand, and Sweden. Here, the Beastie Boys devoted new songs to correcting their earlier treatment of women in lyrics and went back to playing *Licensed to Ill* songs, often changing the lyrics. After *Hello Nasty,* they released *Sounds of Science: The Beastie Boys Anthology,* which featured a picture of the Beastie Boys dressed as old men. They wrote extensive liner notes themselves, telling the history of the songs and offering a behind-the-scenes glimpse at their lives in the studio and on the road. *Hello Nasty* marked the final Tibetan Freedom Concert (in 2001) and the end of the Grand Royal era. The Grand Royal label folded and the magazine stopped production.

The Beastie Boys' 2005 album *To the 5 Boroughs,* marked a return to their roots as their first all–hip-hop album since *Paul's Boutique.* There were no punk songs, no dub, and no guest stars, just the three Beastie Boys and Mix Master Mike. They continued the New York focus of *Hello Nasty* on *To the 5 Boroughs,* which was the Beastie Boys' most political recording, with "An Open Letter to NYC" addressing the September 11, 2001, terrorist attacks and other songs containing anti-Bush sentiment (Hess 2012). In fact, the Beasties organized and headlined the New Yorkers against Violence Concert of October 2001. The proceeds from this concert went to fund the New York Women's Foundation Disaster Relief Fund and the New York Association for New Americans. *To the 5 Boroughs* was distinctly political and also quite personal as the Beastie Boys did all of the production themselves.

By this point, the Beastie Boys had secured their place in hip-hop by constantly reinventing the music while at the same time never neglecting the forms on which hip-hop music was founded: rhymes, turntables, and beats. Their unique and eclectic blend of hip-hop and other forms of music, their humor, and their energetic live performances have earned them the respect of hip-hop luminaries and fans alike.

The much-anticipated next release, *The Mix-Up,* contained only instrumental tracks and earned the Beasties a Grammy Award. Considered an oddity by many fans and critics, the all-instrumental *The Mix-Up* was neither a step forward nor backward for the group. Instead, it was a complete departure from the standard Beasties fare. "It's the Beasties' first all-instrumental record, grounded in soul-jazz, a sound they've been mining since *Check Your Head* (arguably, even *Paul's Boutique* had elements of the sound in its samples), as they peppered their albums and B-sides with lazy, hazy funk jams" (Erlewine 2012).

The Mix-Up contained 12 tracks and was created by the Beastie Boys with the assistance of Mix Master Mike. Track titles included esoteric names such as "14th St. Break" and "Electric Worm." The eighth song on the album was titled "Rat Cage" in a seeming homage to the label that released the group's first two EPs.

The *Mix Up* was designed as a specific project, so it holds together better, and it's also decidedly less knowing in its references than the cleverly kitschy *In Sound from Way Out.* This is a fusion of sounds—cool organs, elastic guitars, loping bass lines, rolling rhythms—where all of the elements are integrated together, turning into a style that's recognizable as uniquely, undeniably the Beastie Boys, even if they don't utter a word on this record. (Erlewine 2012)

Even without lyrics, *The Mix-Up* scored the Beastie Boys a 2008 Grammy in the Best Pop Instrumental Album category.

At the 2009 Bonnaroo Festival, the Beastie Boys previewed some material from the upcoming album they were calling *Hot Sauce Committee,* including "Too Many Rappers." The album was scheduled for release in September of 2009 and an international tour was planned. During the run-up to the release and tour, the Beastie Boys announced that Yauch had been diagnosed with cancer. The prognosis was that he would likely recover from cancer of his parotid gland and a lymph node. However, the group cancelled their forthcoming tour, as well as their appearance at Lollapalooza and the Osheaga Festival.

Yauch's bout with cancer also cancelled the release of *Hot Sauce Committee Part One*. Yauch underwent a successful course of treatment that included surgery and radiation, and the band went back to work on the unreleased material. After a two-year delay, the Beasties announced that they were going to release a new album in 2011. The resulting album was titled *Hot Sauce Committee Part Two* and included the majority of the material originally slated for the unreleased *Part One,* excluding a *Part One* track called "Bundt Cake."

In the wake of Yauch's cancer recovery, the Beastie Boys released *Hot Sauce Committee Part Two* and seemingly suffered no negative consequences for having used some material that was as much as two years old. This album saw the Beasties return to their tried-and-true formula of layered vocals and rhythms with emphasis on analog synthesizer sounds. Where *To the 5 Boroughs* was a more serious record with measured response to the tragedy of 9-11, *Hot Sauce Committee Part Two* harkened back to the free-wheeling days of *Paul's Boutique* and *Check Your Head*. In addition to the Beastie Boys and Mix Master Mike, this album was released with guest artist appearances from Nasir Bin Olu Dara (aka Nas) on "Too Many Rappers" and Santi White (aka Santigold) on "Don't Play No Game That I Can't Win." Additionally, Money Mark and Mix Master Mike appeared on keyboards and turntables, respectively.

The Beasties constructed instrumental material on this album by recording themselves in the studio and then crafting samples from the recorded material. The group then layered their live instruments and lyrics over the samples in the studio. The album contained 16 tracks and a strong mix of old-school rhyming and cultural references, some reference to their hard-core roots, and an updated hip-hop sound. The best example of their updated approach was the opening track "Make Some Noise." Here the Beastie Boys took their own song "(You Gotta) Fight for Your Right to Party," from *Licensed to Ill* and used it as a jumping-off point

with a twist by changing the lyric to "Party for Your Right to Fight."

The reception to this single was strong as it appeared in the popular video game *Madden NFL 12*, and the Beasties followed it up with both a regular-length and extended video, both directed by Yauch. The group again referenced "(You Gotta) Fight for Your Right to Party" by crafting the video as a sequel. In the new video, the Beasties created a twist as they replaced themselves with popular actors Seth Rogen (as Mike D), Danny McBride (as MCA), and Elijah Wood (as Ad-Rock). The regular-length video included a series of cameo appearances from other popular culture figures such as Ted Danson, Zach Galifianakis, Orlando Bloom, Jack Black, Will Ferrell, John C. Reilly, and several others. The extended-length video was titled *Fight for Your Right Revisited* and again featured Wood, McBride, and Rogen. However, for the full-length version, the three end up in a break-dance battle with their future selves as played by John C. Reilly (as Mike D), Jack Black (as MCA), and Will Ferrell (as Ad-Rock). Again cameos abound, with the addition of Amy Poehler, Mary Steenburgen, Alicia Silverstone, Laura Dern, and others, in addition to those previously mentioned.

Hot Sauce Committee Part Two debuted at number two on the *Billboard 200*. Additionally, the singles "Too Many Rappers," "Make Some Noise," and "Don't Play No Game That I Can't Win" all charted. The album's reception was solid, and most consider it the Beasties' return to their best form. Critics have described the album as having received universal acclaim, and it received favorable reviews in the majority of the music media.

The Beastie Boys began recording early enough to maintain a connection to old school hip-hop, and their early connections with the Def Jam label and the artists Run-DMC, Public Enemy, and Biz Markie, as well as their later connections with Native Tongues groups A Tribe Called Quest and De La Soul, lend another level to their importance. When MTV awarded the Beastie Boys the coveted Video Vanguard Award, which honors an artist's lifetime contributions to music video innovation, they had Public Enemy's Chuck D present the honor.

In hip-hop, where artists acknowledge their predecessors and influences in lyrics, the Beastie Boys' name is kept alive. *Licensed to Ill* has remained a commercial dynamo since its 1986 release, but in the late 1990s a rash of hip-hop samples solidified the album's place as a classic. Several of these samples came from one song, "The New Style," from *Licensed to Ill*. In 1995, the Pharcyde released the song "Drop," which took its title from the Ad-Rock vocal sample from "The New Style" that the Pharcyde turned into their song's hook. The "Drop" video was filmed in reverse motion, and two Beastie Boys appeared in the video, with Mike D riding a bicycle backward down the street and Ad-Rock posing for the camera. Dilated People also sampled Ad-Rock's "Mmmm . . . Drop" and referenced the Beastie Boys in "Another Sound Mission" from their album *20/20*. Tha Alkoholics used this same sample from "The New Style" on *Firewater* (2006), and Redman recorded a cover of "The New Style" (renaming it "Beet Drop") for his 1998 album *Doc's Da Name*. Redman's cover stripped the original to its final verse (the same verse sampled by Dilated Peoples, Tha Alkaholiks, and the Pharcyde), which Ad-Rock begins by screaming, "Let me clear my throat." DJ Kool borrowed this line for his 1997 single "Let Me Clear My Throat." Ad-Rock's "New Style" verse, via its popularity in samples, has become one of the Beastie Boys' most famous. They even sampled it themselves on "Intergalactic." The popularity of this line and Ad-Rock's recognizable voice solidified the Beastie Boys' position in hip-hop circles.

There are further Beastie Boys allusions in many other contemporary hip-hop songs, such as Lil' Kim's "Hold It Now," which incorporates music and lyrics from the Beastie Boys' "Paul Revere" and "Hold It Now, Hit It," and samples MCA's vocals. Lyrical references to the Beastie Boys extend to Eminem, who mentioned Mike D in lyrics and spoke openly about his admiration for the Beastie Boys. Kid Rock, whose career was given a boost by a spread in the Beastie Boys' (B-Boys') *Grand Royal Magazine,* also spoke openly about their influence and importance to his

work. Within the new wave of 1990s white rap and rap-rock acts acknowledging their debt to the Beastie Boys, Insane Clown Posse (ICP) owed them the greatest debt, as ICP's vocal styles were developed by imitating Ad-Rock's nasal delivery. Although white groups like Young Black Teenagers and Lords of Brooklyn had certainly borrowed B-Boy vocal styles before, ICP not only did not acknowledge the influence, but also dissed the Beastie Boys in their lyrics.

Even with their detractors, the Beastie Boys will always have a place in hip-hop history. In 2006, Yauch, under the name of Nathanial Hornblower, produced a film called *Awesome: I Fuckin' Shot That!* He handed out 50 Hi-8 and digital video cameras to fans at a 2004 Beastie Boys concert at Madison Square Garden, and compiled the footage into a feature-length film in order to capture the concert experience from the fans' perspective. MCA, Ad-Rock, and Mike D performed in old-school green track suits and baseball caps with their rap names lettered across the front. They performed songs from each of their albums, from *Licensed to Ill* through *To the 5 Boroughs,* and Mix Master Mike switched LPs and changed the beat at least once per song, prompting the B-Boys to rhyme over a mixture of old-school break beats like "Apache" and "900 Number" (aka "Ed Lover's Theme") and contemporary singles such as Jay-Z's "Dirt Off Your Shoulders" and Fabolous's "Breathe." Darryl "DMC" McDaniels was in the crowd, and Doug E. Fresh joined the Beastie Boys onstage to perform "Time to Get Ill." Even while emphasizing their old-school connections, the Beastie Boys have always looked forward into the future (Hess 2007).

Another indication of the Beastie Boys' overall influence and importance are all of the accolades their music has received. *Licensed to Ill, Ill Communication, Hello Nasty,* and *To the 5 Boroughs* all reached the top of the *Billboard* chart. *Rolling Stone* has ranked the Beastie Boys number 77 in its list of the top 100 bands of all time and listed "Sabotage" the 475th song on their 500 Greatest Songs of All Time list. The Beasties have been nominated for 10 Grammy Awards and won three. They have also been nominated for eight MTV Video Music Awards and won three. Additionally, they were inducted into the Rock and Roll

Hall of Fame with the 2012 class. With a 30-year career and having sold over 22 million albums in the United States and over 40 million albums worldwide, the Beastie Boys' position in hip-hop history is firmly established. Tragically, the future of the Beastie Boys was cast into uncertainty when Adam Yauch lost his battle with cancer on May 4, 2012, at age 47. As of 2014, the remaining members of the Beastie Boys are on record as saying that they will not perform under the band name out of respect for Yauch.

Mickey Hess and David V. Moskowitz

Selected Discography

Pollywog Stew (EP), Ratcage Records MOTR 21, 1982.

Cooky Puss (EP), Ratcage Records MOTR 26, 1983.

Rock Hard (EP), Def Jam DJ 002, 1985.

Licensed to Ill, Def Jam BFC 40238, 1986.

Paul's Boutique, Capitol CDP 79174322, 1989.

Check Your Head, Grand Royal CDP 7989382, 1992.

Ill Communication, Grand Royal C 274238285992, 1994.

Hello Nasty, Grand Royal C 1724383771615, 1998.

To the 5 Boroughs, Capitol C 1724358457117, 2004.

The Mix Up, Capitol 094639408511, 2007.

Hot Sauce Committee Part Two, Capitol 5099968804312, 2011.

References

Christgau, Robert. *Grown Up All Wrong: 75 Great Rock and Pop Artists from Vaudeville to Techno*. Cambridge, MA: Harvard University Press, 1998.

Erlewine, Stephen Thomas. "Beastie Boys." *All Music Guide*. Rovi Corporation, 2012.

Hess, Mickey. "Beastie Boys." *Pop Culture Universe: Icons, Idols, Ideas*. Santa Barbara, CA: ABC-CLIO, 2012.

Hess, Mickey. "Beastie Boys." In *Icons of Hip Hop: An Encyclopedia of the Movement, Music, and Culture*. Westport, CT: Greenwood Press, 2007.

Hess, Mickey. "Hip Hop Realness and the White Performer." *Critical Studies in Media Communication*, 22.5 (2005): 372–389.

Leroy, Dan. *The Beastie Boys' Paul's Boutique*. New York: Continuum, 2006.

Light, Alan. *The Skills to Pay the Bills: The Story of the Beastie Boys*. New York: Three Rivers Press, 2006.

Smith, Chris. "Beastie Boys: *Licensed to Ill* (1986)." *Pop Culture Universe: Icons, Idols, Ideas*. Santa Barbara, CA: ABC-CLIO, 2012.

Smith, Chris. *100 Albums that Changed Popular Music: A Reference Guide*. Westport, CT: Greenwood Press, 2007.

Zwickel, Jonathan. *Beastie Boys: A Musical Biography*. Westport, CT: Greenwood Press, 2010.

The Beatles (1957–1970)

The Beatles are not only the best-selling band in the history of rock, they are also the most important and experimental band. They revolutionized the sound and style of popular music, impacting every artist that followed, and expanded the very boundaries of the genre. Over the course of their seven-year recording history, the Beatles redefined the possibilities of the recording studio, elevated the album to an art form, and established the British claim to a part of rock's legacy.

In October 1954, "Rock Around the Clock" by Bill Haley and His Comets launched Britain's love affair with rock and roll. However, before rock had established a solid presence in the country, "The Rock Island Line" by Lonnie Donegan launched a craze for skiffle: a distinctly British amalgamation of American folk music, country blues, and Dixieland jazz. It shared many of the rhythmic characteristics of rock and roll, but it seemed less complicated and more readily accessible than the U.S. import. The music not only dislodged most rock and roll from the charts, it also generated an explosion of amateur skiffle groups.

John Lennon (born John Winston Lennon, October 9, 1940, died December 8, 1980; guitar, vocals) was one of thousands of teens seduced by skiffle. He was already a fan of country blues and trad jazz. He wanted to learn guitar after hearing an Elvis Presley record, but Donegan made it seem like he could actually do so. His mother Julia, who played the ukulele, bought him a guitar and taught him the basics, and later that year he formed the Quarrymen.

British rock and roll band the Beatles (from left to right): John Lennon, Ringo Starr (front), Paul McCartney (back), and George Harrison. The "Fab Four" revolutionized the sound of popular music worldwide. Additionally, the group remains one of the best-selling acts of all time, continuing to gain new fans decades after the group disbanded. (Photo by David Farrell/Redferns)

In June 1957, the Quarrymen were performing at St. Peter's Church Hall in Woolton, and their mixture of rock and roll and skiffle impressed Paul McCartney (born James Paul McCartney, June 18, 1942; guitar, bass, vocals, keyboards) enough that he introduced himself after the set. McCartney grew up in a musical family, and he absorbed the music of the English dance hall, popular music, and traditional jazz in his youth. He briefly studied piano and trumpet, but when he discovered rock and roll he traded them for a guitar.

He and Lennon promptly hit it off, and McCartney was invited to join the Quarrymen in October.

McCartney introduced Lennon to George Harrison (born February 25, 1943, died November 29, 2001; guitar, vocals), a classmate from the Liverpool Institute. Harrison was a fan of American country music and jazz, but fell for rock and roll when he heard Elvis Presley's "Heartbreak Hotel," and promptly acquired a guitar and formed a skiffle group. In March 1958, he auditioned for the Quarrymen, but

Lennon felt that Harrison, who was only 14 at the time, was too young to join. Nonetheless, Harrison filled in on guitar occasionally, and was admitted to their ranks just before his 15th birthday.

By the beginning of 1959, most of the Quarrymen had left the group. The three guitarists shifted their focus to rock and roll and performed as Johnny and the Moondogs until January 1960, when Lennon recruited an art school friend, guitarist Stu Sutcliffe (born Stuart Fergusson Victor Sutcliffe, June 23, 1940, died April 10, 1962; bass), to join the group on bass. A name change was in order; they performed as the Silver Beetles (after Buddy Holly and the Crickets) before settling on the Beatles in August 1960.

The Beatles played gigs wherever they could get them, many at the Cavern Club in Liverpool. The owner of the Cavern had a friend who booked acts into clubs in Hamburg; through this connection the group secured residencies at clubs in the city's red-light district. There the boys were required to play seven to eight hours a night, six days a week; as a result they mastered a great deal of material by artists like Elvis Presley, Buddy Holly, the Everly Brothers, and Little Richard. They also learned to fake their way through requests, modifying songs they knew into approximations of those they did not. During the Hamburg years the personnel of the group shifted; Sutcliffe was fired, as McCartney, who had never played bass, figured he could do just as well. The Beatles performed without a drummer until adding Pete Best (born Randolph Peter Best, November 24, 1941; percussion) to the lineup.

Lennon and McCartney began writing songs together fairly early in the band's existence. While originally this caused problems—English record executives were not used to new groups bringing their own material into the studio—in short order it became standard operating procedure, and groups that could not provide their own songs were considered a liability.

In June 1962, the Beatles auditioned for Decca Records and were rejected, but the Beatles' manager, Brian Epstein, tried again. He took a tape of the audition to George Martin, a classical musician and head of EMI's fading Parliament label. Martin was not entirely sold on the group, but he liked Lennon and McCartney's vocals, and after an audition signed the Beatles, with one condition: he wanted to replace Pete Best.

By their first recording session on September 4, the Beatles had a new drummer: Ringo Starr (born Richard Starkey, July 7, 1940; percussion, vocals). Starr began drumming at age 14 and soon began performing professionally. He was conversant in many styles, including American Western music (he chose his stage name because it sounded "cowboyish" [Spitz, 324]), swing jazz, and blues. He started playing skiffle before joining the pop group Rory and the Hurricanes. The band was on the same bill as the Beatles in Hamburg, and he had filled in for Best at a Beatles gig that February, and was thus a natural choice as a permanent replacement. their first single, "Love Me Do," released in October, featured studio drummer Andy White; Starr was relegated to auxiliary percussion. The record slowly crept into the charts, peaking at number 17.

The group rushed back to the studio to record a follow-up. "Please Please Me" was a concentration of the band's early sound: a catchy tune with well-wrought, three-part vocal harmonies, guitar lines in octaves, forceful drumming, and a dramatic bass line. It was also radically different than anything on the pop charts, combining elements of the Everly Brothers, Buddy Holly, and Roy Orbison in a uniquely British way. Upon hearing the playback, George Martin announced, "Gentlemen, you've just made your first number one record" (Spitz, 360). He was right. Suddenly, British rock and roll was a reality, and the Beatles were the next big thing.

EMI yanked the group off of a tour to record the Beatles' first album. The 10 tracks of *Please Please Me* were recorded in a single, daylong marathon. Half of the tracks were covers that the Beatles had been playing for years; the others were originals, including their recent singles. The standout among the former was the Isley Brothers' "Twist and Shout," recorded in a single take; the raw, nearly screamed vocals destroyed John Lennon's voice, but the energetic performance remains an early Beatles masterpiece. The originals included "I Saw Her Standing There," a Chuck Berry–influenced rocker, and the lilting pop tune "Do You Want to Know a Secret."

After the album's release, the Beatles continued to tour ceaselessly, and Britain began to experience the first flush of Beatlemania. Lines for their appearances streamed around the block, and girls mobbed the band and screamed at the mention of their name. Their next singles, "From Me to You" and "She Loves You," vaulted into the top 10, ultimately topping all of the British charts. Both featured a contrasting bridge section, which McCartney dubbed the "middle eight," in a contrasting key, which became a common Beatles form, and the falsetto shout that was now indelibly associated with the band.

In fall 1963 the Beatles managed to slip into the studio to complete a second album, *With the Beatles*. It included six covers and eight Lennon/McCartney originals, including "It Won't Be Long," the swinging "All My Loving," and "I Wanna Be Your Man," featuring a lead vocal by Ringo, a double-time chorus, and reverb-laden guitars. Mobs of teenagers scooped up the disc as soon as it hit record stores, and it quickly became the best-selling British album of the year. However, their first album, released in America as *Introducing the Beatles,* did not make much of an impression. As Brian Epstein was pushing the group toward an American tour, this represented a problem.

In 1963, no British band had ever had a successful tour of the United States. The Beatles told Epstein that they refused to go to the United States until they had a chart-topping record. "I Want to Hold Your Hand," a Buddy Holly-esque composition that also borrowed Little Richard's falsetto shout, tight Everly Brothers harmonies, and peppy Motown handclaps, did the trick. Released in November 1963 in Britain, the song sold more than a million copies in advance orders alone and kicked Beatlemania into high gear.

After American news networks ran stories on the Beatles phenomenon in mid-November, the group began to get radio airplay. When Capitol Records released "I Want to Hold Your Hand" on December 26, with "I Saw Her Standing There" as the B-side, the response was immediate: 750,000 copies were sold in the first three days, and 10,000 copies were sold each hour in New York City. The single began its 15-week chart run in January 1964 and reached the number-one spot a month later.

America was already calling. The television impresario Ed Sullivan happened to arrive in London in October 1963 on the same day the Beatles returned from a Swedish tour and witnessed an instance of Beatlemania firsthand. He had not heard of the group but quickly booked them for three appearances on his show, and promoter Sid Bernstein was offering the band two shows at Carnegie Hall, where no rock group had ever been allowed to play. Moreover, Brian Epstein had just interested United Artists in making a feature film starring the group.

After a brief tour of Paris, the Beatles arrived in the United States in February 1964 to find that Beatlemania was in full swing. The group's charm and wit quickly won over the assembled crowd of reporters. Their first appearance on the *Ed Sullivan Show* was watched by a record 74 million viewers, and their concert appearances were received with hysteria. *Meet the Beatles!* (the American version of *With the Beatles*) jumped to the top of the *Billboard* charts, and their singles occupied 14 spots in the top 100. They returned to London as conquering heroes.

Three days later the Beatles convened in Abbey Road Studios to begin work on the soundtrack for their upcoming film. The standouts were the poignant "And I Love Her," the title track, which opens (as does the film) with a strident altered chord of nebulous modality; "Can't Buy Me Love," a rare Beatles 12-bar blues, albeit with more complex harmonies; "You Can't Do That," the group's take on Marvin Gaye; and the beautiful duet "If I Fell," where McCartney and Lennon's vocals are so intertwined that it is all but impossible to tell which was singing what part.

In March and April the group filmed *A Hard Day's Night*: a black-and-white "documentary" of a few days in the life of a Beatle. The script, by Alun Owen, was fast-paced and energetic, and played on the band's natural camaraderie and wit. The quirky film received rave reviews.

The Beatles then set off on a world tour—and discovered that Beatlemania was now everywhere. Thousands lined their motorcade routes, and 200,000 fans greeted them when the band returned to Liverpool for a screening of *Hard Day's Night.*

When they returned to America, they encountered pandemonium. Shrieking fans drowned out the band, and in a number of cities there were near riots. When the band arrived in New York City, journalist Al Aronowitz introduced the Beatles to Bob Dylan. Dylan's comment to John Lennon that the Fab Four's songs were not really about anything and lacked depth had a significant effect on both Lennon and McCartney.

The start of the Beatles' shift to a new kind of songwriting can be heard on *Beatles for Sale,* hurriedly recorded after the tour. Exhausted from touring, Lennon and McCartney had not written enough songs, so the album includes six covers, many old concert favorites. However, the originals display nascent experimentation. "I'm a Loser" was Lennon's first composition that dealt with his own emotions; it also featured an ametric introduction and a more complex melody than his previous efforts; the early Lennon/McCartney tune "I'll Follow the Sun"; the gentle bossa nova "No Reply," a painful song of rejection; and "I Feel Fine," a riff-driven number prefaced by a startling burst of feedback that was unprecedented on record.

After a short tour and a brief hiatus, the band headed back to the studio to record the soundtrack album for their next film, *Help!* The film, shot in February and March 1965, was a patchwork of comedic bits tied to a silly script, but the soundtrack demonstrated the continuing evolution of the Beatles' craft. The songs were in many ways responses to Dylan's charge; the boy-meets-girl lyrics of the early period were replaced by material that was more reflective, abstract, and poetic. The music was also different; it was more harmonically complex, and it employed a broader palette of tone colors. "You've Got to Hide Your Love Away" was a direct homage to Dylan, as evidenced by the simple, strummed acoustic accompaniment and introspective lyrics. The title track, a

jaunty blast of R&B with rhythmically displaced harmonies; "I've Just Seen a Face," an up-tempo blast of country-and-western with Simon and Garfunkel–influenced fills; "Ticket to Ride," a Roy Orbinson-esque song with unusually heavy lyrics, metrically complicated drumming, and a double-time outro; and McCartney's "Yesterday." After several attempted arrangements, it was decided that he would perform the song as a solo, with an overdubbed string quartet. "Yesterday" was fresh and inventive, with a gorgeous melody, timeless lyrics, and complex chord changes. It also changed contemporary notions of what a rock song could be and expanded the possibilities for the genre.

In October, the Beatles began work on their next album; even before Lennon and McCartney started writing, they knew the record would be unlike their previous efforts. Musically and artistically, the group was wholly committed to experimentation. For its time, *Rubber Soul* was unprecedented, filled with unconventional songs and timbral diversity. It was also conceived as an album, rather than a collection of singles. The change was facilitated by George Martin, who became more involved in the creative process.

Many of the arrangements on *Rubber Soul* were partly or entirely acoustic: "Norwegian Wood," a slow waltz that alternated two simple musical phrases, was shaped almost entirely by instrumentation and texture, particularly Harrison's newly acquired sitar; "Nowhere Man," a critique of social isolation, the lyrics reinforced by an a-cappella introduction, treble-laden guitars, and modal orientation; "Michelle," one of McCartney's oldest songs, highlights delicate finger-picked 12-string guitar and understated harmonies; "In My Life," with its soulful melody and unusual timbres, including a harpsichord solo, has the same multivalent quality. They are contrasted by harder-edged songs: the funky "The Word," with George Martin on harmonium; "Drive My Car," the Beatles' homage to Stax, driven by Paul's bass line, lifted from Otis Redding's "Respect"; and Ringo's countrified "What Goes On," built on a pair of syncopated riffs.

The significance of the album was immediately evident to critics and their fellow musicians; Steve Winwood recalled that the album "broke everything open" (Spitz, 595). The Beatles' new commitment to the album as a wholly conceived entity created a dilemma; they were contractually obligated to deliver four singles per year, but they were no longer interested in creating album tracks specifically for the singles market. As a result, the group began to write stand-alone singles: the first was the double A-side "We Can Work It Out"/"Day Tripper" in October 1965, followed by "Paperback Writer." As the Beatles had dramatically reduced their live appearances, they created short promotional films to promote the records: the first music videos.

Under the influence of its new status as the pop kingdom of the world, London was transforming into a place where cutting-edge fashion, art, and music combined to create the most happening place on earth. Drugs, too, were becoming more common. LSD was at that time legal, and the hipster set in London employed the drug for its consciousness-expanding properties. Lennon and Harrison were surreptitiously given the drug at a dinner party. Thereafter both explored Buddhism and meditation, Harrison studied Indian music, and John Lennon's lyrics became more impressionistic and philosophical. McCartney, meanwhile, devoted himself to studying modern art and avant-garde classical music. All came together on the group's next album.

While *Rubber Soul* was a quantum leap forward, with *Revolver* the Beatles became pioneers of the recording studio. The group was now confident enough to request unconventional effects in the studio, and recording engineer Geoff Emerick rose to every challenge and found ways to realize even the most outlandish ideas.

The most technically advanced track was "Tomorrow Never Knows," with lyrics taken directly from the *Tibetan Book of the Dead*. The song, built on a single chord, was the most heavily produced Beatles effort to date. A Leslie speaker from a Hammond organ and backtracking (George Harrison's guitar solo was recorded backward) were employed to replicate the psychedelic experience, and artificial double tracking (ADT) overlaid Lennon's voice with a duplicate at a slightly different pitch. "I'm Only Sleeping," used ADT and varispeed to slow down the track, creating subtle alterations of timbre, and contained simultaneous backward guitar solos; "She Said, She Said" employed many of the same techniques. Other unconventional tracks include "Eleanor Rigby," its dark subject matter of loneliness and detachment reflected in its lack of harmonic drive, repetitive melody, and string octet accompaniment; and the goofy children's song "Yellow Submarine" involved dozens of sound effects, a hearty unison chorus, and a brass band lifted from an old record.

By 1966 the Beatles had been touring, with only short respites, for nearly four years. After a final world tour they announced their retirement from the road to focus on making records. The band's increased attention to sophisticated production reached its full potential with *Sgt. Pepper's Lonely Hearts Club Band*—a concept album based on the conceit of an alter ego for the Beatles. The album began with a whimsical tune that introduced Sgt. Pepper's Lonely Hearts Club Band, and ended with its reprise. The songs defined the fictional space in which the alternate Beatles existed. The album included even more extensive manipulation of sounds and tracks than did *Revolver*. "Lucy in the Sky with Diamonds" was a split meter arrangement; the verse is in 6/8 and the refrain in common time. The vocals of the verse were overdubbed at two different speeds, to create a psychedelic effect, and the bass and guitars were recorded through a Leslie speaker; to create contrast, few effects were added to the chorus. Harrison's "Within You Without You" was based on a song by Ravi Shankar; he was the only Beatle to play on the track; anonymous musicians contributed the additional Indian instrumental parts and overdubbed strings. "A Day in the Life" was the only song to stand outside the album's conceptual frame. The beginning and end were written by Lennon. Most of the lyrics were taken directly from contemporary newspaper stories, a surrealistic "automatic writing technique" of which Lennon was greatly enamored. A completely different song by Paul McCartney comprised the center section. For the avant-garde "apocalyptic" section at the end an orchestra was hired to play from the lowest note on their instruments to the highest over the course of 24 bars; the climax was a crashing piano chord that ended with a long sustain, and two-second tape loop of spoken gibberish which, on a manual turntable, repeated until the needle was removed.

Other, less technically innovative standouts were "When I'm Sixty-Four," McCartney's affectionate tribute to English dance-hall tunes, and the soulful "With a Little Help from My Friends." The album was capped by its innovative packaging, which included all of the lyrics (the first time it had been done) and a cover featuring a collage of waxwork dummies, photographs, and the Beatles in their alternate personae. *Sgt. Pepper's* is widely considered the best album of all time; it won four Grammy Awards in 1968 and topped the charts for six months. It was also their first album released on their new label, Apple Records.

Their psychedelic phase continued with the film *Magical Mystery Tour*. The loosely scripted film was a nonsensical disaster that was justifiably panned; however, the soundtrack contains some excellent songs, including the previously stand-alone, double A-side single "Penny Lane," McCartney's dance-hall influenced, true-to-life travelogue of his hometown, and "Strawberry Fields Forever," a lovely, poignant reminiscence of Lennon's childhood that incorporated myriad effects, mellotron, backtracked cymbals, as well as strings and horns; the track required 45 hours in the studio. Other standouts were the psychedelic "I Am the Walrus," "Hello Goodbye," and "All You Need Is Love," previously performed for a live, worldwide broadcast. In 1968, the Beatles embarked on a more successful film venture, the visually inventive cartoon *Yellow Submarine*; however, save for the soundtrack, the band was barely involved; actors imitated the band members.

Sgt. Pepper and *Magical Mystery Tour* seemed to have exhausted the band's experimental tendencies; moreover, fractures were developing within the band. Lennon began to resent McCartney's increasing dominance of the band's artistic path; to be fair, Lennon was using drugs heavily and was distracted by his romance with avant-garde artist Yoko Ono. Harrison was artistically restless and felt his ideas were not respected,

and for the first time the Beatles had trouble agreeing, particularly on the glut of songs they had composed since the *Magical Mystery Tour*, some of which was spent studying with the Maharishi Mahesh Yogi in India.

Lennon and McCartney had been writing together less frequently for several years, but their collaborations ceased almost entirely. The Beatles began writing songs independently and bringing them to the studio. Stylistically, the material was diverse and increasingly looked back to their past musical influences. Their new approach was evident on *The Beatles,* colloquially known as the *White Album,* the group's only double album. "Rocky Raccoon" was a folk rock/country hybrid, delivered in a broad Western twang; "Honey Pie" was an obvious tribute to the English dance hall, with an introduction engineered to sound like an old radio; "Yer Blues" was an R&B tribute; and "Back in the U.S.S.R." was a tip of the hat to Chuck Berry. Standouts were the rockabilly flavored "Revolution No. 1," one of Lennon's most enduring songs; "Blackbird," built on a fragment of a Bach boureé; "While My Guitar Gently Weeps," with a stunning guitar solo by Eric Clapton; the doo-wop takeoff "Happiness Is a Warm Gun," another mixed meter arrangement; and the hard-rocking "Helter Skelter." However, not all of the songs met the high standards now expected of the Beatles, and for the first time in a long time, reviews were mixed. Nonetheless, the album quickly jumped to the top of the charts on both sides of the Atlantic.

Yoko was not only in the studio for much of the recording sessions, but she also began inserting herself into the process, critiquing songs and offering advice; this further exacerbated the tensions within the group. They came together to record a single, "Hey Jude," McCartney's anthemic, hopeful message to Lennon's son Julian. However, the subject's father had grown bored with the Beatles and determined to leave the group. He was talked down; the band entertained the idea of performing live again and began rehearsals in Twickenham Studios in London; a film crew was engaged to capture the rehearsals for a possible documentary. A week later, Harrison stormed out. To placate him, the concert was abandoned, and the Beatles decamped to a new studio to record *Let It Be*. The situation was still tense, so Harrison brought

Billy Preston, an American keyboardist, into the studio; his presence seemed to stabilize the situation—for a time. When another peak of frustration happened, the Beatles stumbled on a brilliant solution to their desire to play live; they took their equipment to the roof of Apple Records and performed an impromptu concert.

Let It Be reflected the chaos of the circumstances of its recording. There were a few gems: the early Beatles track "One After 909," which captured some of the joy of the band's early days; the lovely, Ray Charles–influenced ballad "Long and Winding Road"; "Across the Universe," Sanskrit chorus inspired by their time in India; the reverent title track; and "Get Back," a straight-up blast of R&B with Preston featured on keyboards. Most of the tracks were lesser efforts, but under the circumstances, a complete album was about all anyone could hope for. After the disc was completed, it was sent to American producer Phil Spector for polishing. His extensive overdubs were so controversial that, in 2003, the original version of the album was released with the title *Let It Be . . . Naked*. Nonetheless, the album won the Academy Award for Best Song Soundtrack in 1970 when the film from Twickenham was released as a feature.

The last thing that would be expected from a band barely hanging together was another album. However, the Beatles' dissatisfaction with *Let It Be* chafed, and it seems none wanted to end things on such a low note; they resolved to make a new and better album. Although none of them were positive it would be their last, but all felt that it was. The result, *Abbey Road,* was one of the band's best discs. The medley on the second side of the album, comprising short songs mostly conceived during the *White Album* sessions, was captivating; opening with "You Never Give Me Your Money," an expression of frustration with the Beatles' management; a set of quirky Lennon character sketches, "Sun King," "Mean Mr. Mustard," and "Polythene Pam"; and a quartet of McCartney contributions: "She Came In Through the Bathroom Window," "Golden Slumbers," derived from a 17th-century poem, and "Carry that Weight," a reprise of "You Never Give Me Your Money," and "The End," which included Starr's

only drum solo in the Beatles' catalog. Other standouts were the hard-rocking blues sendup "Come Together," Harrison's luminous and optimistic "Here Comes the Sun," the beautiful ballad "Something," and "I Want You (She's So Heavy)," a surprisingly progressive rock turn employing white noise, a Moog synthesizer, and complex structure. It would be the last track the Beatles ever recorded.

Prior to the album's release, John Lennon gave the band his final notice. All seemed to accept that the fractures in the band were irreparable, and after 14 years, the Beatles called it quits. Their influence, though, endures. All rock bands, of any style, have been influenced by the Beatles in some fashion, even if indirectly. The band remains one of the best-selling acts of all time, and gains fans from each new generation.

Roberta Freund Schwartz

Selected Discography

Meet the Beatles UK: Parlophone PMC 1202 (mono), PCS 3042 (stereo); US, as *Introducing the Beatles*: Vee-Jay VJLP 1062, 1963 (UK)/1964 (US).

A Hard Day's Night UK: Parlophone PMC 1230 (mono)/ PCS 3058 (stereo); US: United Artists UA 6366 (mono)/UAS 6366 (stereo), 1964.

Help! UK: Parlophone PMC 1255 (mono)/PCS 3071 (stereo); US: Capitol MAS-2386 (mono)/SMAS-2386 (stereo), 1965.

Rubber Soul UK: Parlophone PMC 1267 (mono)/PCS 3075 (stereo); US: Capitol T-2442 (mono)/ST-2442 (stereo), 1965.

Revolver UK: Parlophone PMC 7009 (mono)/PCS 7009 (stereo); US: Capitol T-2576 (mono)/ ST-2576 (stereo), 1966.

Sgt. Pepper's Lonely Hearts Club Band UK: Parlophone PMC 7027 (mono)/PCS 7027 (stereo); US: Capitol MAS-2653 (mono)/SMAS-2653 (stereo), 1967.

The Beatles (the White Album) UK: Apple PMC 7067–7068 (mono)/PCS 7067–7068 (stereo); US: Apple SWBO-101, 1968.

Abbey Road UK: Apple PCS 7088; US: Apple SO-383, 1969.

Let It Be UK: Apple PCS 7096; US: Apple AR-34001, 1970.

Magical Mystery Tour UK: Parlophone PCTC 255, 1976; US: Capitol MAL-2835 (mono)/SMAL-2835 (stereo), 1967.

References

The Beatles Bible. www.beatlesbible.com.

Emerick, Geoff. *Here, There, and Everywhere.* New York: Gotham, 2007.

Everett, Walter. *The Beatles as Musicians: Revolver through the Anthology.* New York: Oxford University Press, 1999.

Everett, Walter. *The Beatles as Musicians: The Quarry Men [sic] through Rubber Soul.* New York: Oxford University Press, 2001.

Norman, Philip. *Shout! The Beatles and Their Generation.* New York: Fireside, 1981.

Spitz, Bob. *The Beatles: The Biography.* New York: Little Brown and Co., 2005.

Womack, Kenneth, ed. *The Cambridge Companion to the Beatles.* Cambridge, MA: Cambridge University Press, 2009.

Big Brother and the Holding Company with Janis Joplin (1966–1970)

Although there had been female rock artists since the 1950s, the first full-fledged female rock star was Janis Joplin (born Janis Lyn Joplin, January 13, 1943, died October 4, 1970; vocals). Her performance with Big Brother and the Holding Company at the Monterey Pop Festival in June 1967 thrust the provincial San Francisco band into the national spotlight. As quickly as Joplin soared to the top, so too did she fall, dying from a heroin overdose in October 1970. Joplin's life was full of contradictions: she was accused of appropriating black musical styles but had a reverential love of the classic blues (especially singer Bessie Smith); she became a feminist icon but never subscribed to any dogma of the sort; she did not conform to contemporary standards of beauty yet became a sex symbol and her tough, assertive outward persona betrayed the sensitive and vulnerable girl inside. Above all, her music exhibited a raw and passionate outpouring of power and charisma, fusing the blues, country, and folk with the frenetic energy of the late 1960s San Francisco rock, and presenting one of the most individual and recognizable singing voices in rock history.

Joplin grew up in Port Arthur, Texas. She was unpopular in her image-conscious high school as much because of weight and acne problems as her intellectualism and lack of conformity to social norms. Janis would later emphasize this crisis of belonging in many interviews, letting it shape her personality as an outsider always trying to be cool and to fit in. She told critic Nat Hentoff that "Texas is O.K. . . . but it's not for outrageous people, and I was always outrageous" (Brackett 2009, 246), and she described Port Arthur as a "drag, a big drag" (Echols 1999, 14).

Joplin found solace with a group of boys who were equally put off by the lack of culture in Port Arthur. Styling themselves as beatniks, Joplin became one of the guys, a rarity in the male-dominated beatnik worldview (Johnson 1983). While she often presented an outward persona as a tough, hard-drinking party girl, she would confide in her friends her occasional desire for domesticity (Echols 1999, 36). Later in her career, reporters expressed shock at her private, offstage vulnerability and insecurity (Jackson 2005, 220). Her identity as an iconoclastic loner became a repeating theme throughout her life: she was a woman in a male-dominated rock scene, she was sexually curious in a predominantly heterosexual culture, she was a heavy drinker in a world of psychedelics, and she was a blues musician in a folk-rock culture.

In high school Joplin became enamored with folk music, discovering her voice by imitating the folk singer Odetta. Janis idolized the blues singer Leadbelly, later admitting, "It was Leadbelly first. I knew what it was all about from the very front. I was right into the blues" (Brackett 2009, 246). Listeners such as Joplin, Bob Dylan, and Joan Baez, who felt like outsiders from their own mainstream white culture, found authenticity in Leadbelly's suffering and marginalized black experience.

Joplin enrolled at the University of Texas in Austin in 1962, where she began to sing and play the autoharp, performing with two male friends as the Waller Creek Boys. While she sometimes sang in the popular

Janis Joplin with Big Brother and the Holding Company at the Monterey Pop Festival in San Francisco in June 1967. The group's appearance at Monterey vaulted them into the rock and roll spotlight. Their meteoric rise rested on the alternately tough and sweet vocals of Janis Joplin. (Photo by Michael Ochs Archives/Getty Images)

folk style of Joan Baez and Judy Collins, it was the blues singer Bessie Smith who most captivated her. Joplin also began to get regular gigs and draw a crowd at Threadgill's, a roadhouse honky-tonk that featured mostly country and bluegrass. A home recording made in December 1962 offers a glimpse into the early Joplin sound at this time (*Janis,* 1993). Singing a self-penned blues tune, "What Good Can Drinkin' Do," she belts out a traditional 12-bar blues with a thin, nasal grittiness that seems more concentrated on affect than melody.

In January 1963, Chet Helms, a fellow Texan who had moved to San Francisco, heard Joplin sing in Austin. He sensed that she would be a big hit in

San Francisco, which he felt was "stuck in a pop-folk sound, yearning for authenticity" (Joplin 1992, 131). Joplin hitchhiked to San Francisco and inserted herself into the folk music scene in the beatnik North Beach neighborhood, where all the cool and eccentric castoffs from mainstream society hung out.

Janis was immediately recognized for her talent and performed widely in the Bay Area's enclaves of post-Beat folkies. Joplin's style, modeled after Bessie Smith, was a marked difference from other female singers in the Bay Area folk scene, who were modeled on Joan Baez and Judy Collins. A bootleg recording from 1964 known as the *Typewriter Tape* reveals Joplin already sporting her deep, raspy voice and sounding like a black blues singer, running through blues standards with Jorma Kaukonen, a future member of the Jefferson Airplane, on guitar (tracks from this session appear on *Janis,* 1993). Compared to her Austin recording from 1962, Joplin's sense of melody was more nuanced, and she allows moments of sweetness.

Although Janis had cultivated a party girl identity in Austin, she escalated her drinking and drug use in San Francisco, becoming addicted to amphetamines. Her substance abuse was part of her brash and rough exterior, an identity that concealed the vulnerable young woman underneath, but she was also motivated by her desire to experience the suffering required to sing the blues. One North Beach acquaintance noted that "somewhere deep inside she felt you had to experience everything you could to be a real singer" (Echols 1999, 78). Ravaged by drugs, Joplin returned home to Port Arthur in May of 1965.

While Joplin spent the next year trying to stay sober in Texas, the San Francisco music world was changing rapidly, refocusing on the Haight district. The easy commute to nearby San Francisco State University lent the area an intellectual bohemianism, with many students living in big, old Victorian houses.

Chet Helms was wandering the Haight in the summer of 1965 when he heard Peter Albin (born June 6, 1944; bass guitar, guitar, vocals) playing guitar in a run-down Victorian at 1090 Page Street. Helms promptly walked in and introduced himself. Around the same time, Sam Andrew (born Sam Houston Andrew III, December 18, 1941; guitar) also heard Albin's playing as he walked by, and went into 1090 Page to introduce himself. Albin had played bluegrass in various peninsula folk scenes, while Andrew had played rock and blues in bands growing up as an army brat in Okinawa. Sensing something magical, Helms began to organize weekly jam sessions in the basement of 1090 Page, charging 50 cents for admission. Featuring Albin on bass and Andrew on guitar, along with Chuck Jones on drums, these underground concerts were the precursors to the ballroom rock-and-roll dances that would soon come to dominate the city's musical scene.

James Gurley (born James Martin Gurley, December 22, 1939, died December 20, 2009; guitar) was a Detroit transplant who lived in a nearby communal house. Helms thought that Gurley would complement his new enterprise at Page Street, and brought the guitarist to meet Andrew and Albin, where the three instantly clicked. Gurley had taught himself guitar listening to old Lightnin' Hopkins blues records, but became obsessed with the eruptive power of John Coltrane. His style was an amalgamation of blues and progressive jazz; his solos were torrents of melodic ideas building to ecstatic peaks in the style of Coltrane's *A Love Supreme.*

The fledgling band dubbed itself Big Brother and the Holding Company. Helms, the mastermind behind the entire operation, became their manager. At their first public performance in December 1965, they played an instrumental and mostly improvised set of noisy music led by Gurley's rapid finger-picked playing.

As 1966 began, a number of bands emerged that had formed, much like Big Brother, as serendipitous meetings of like-minded folk and blues musicians influenced by the Beatles, Bob Dylan's new electric music, and psychedelic drugs. These groups, including the Jefferson Airplane, the Grateful Dead, and the Great Society, formed the core of San Francisco's nascent rock movement. Great Society guitarist Darby Slick recalls Big Brother from their first gigs: "[they] played with aggression and with an extremely treble sound" (Slick 1991, 88).

Big Brother played the Trips Festival at Longshoreman's Hall, January 22, 1966. Their participation in this seminal LSD-soaked party indicated their eminent position within the growing scene. Following the success of the Trips Festival, both Helms and impresario Bill Graham began to book weekly concerts at their Avalon and Fillmore ballrooms, respectively; Big Brother was a mainstay at both venues.

Albin soon met David Getz (born January 24, 1940; drums), whose jazz interests ranged from Ellington to the avant-garde Ornette Coleman. Getz attended a show at the Fillmore in February and was transfixed by Gurley, who had now transitioned to electric guitar. Chuck Jones was a weak drummer whose amphetamine habit was cause enough for concern among the band. When Getz dropped by a band rehearsal to jam, "it was so intense nobody could stop" (Echols 1999, 126), and Getz immediately replaced Jones on drums.

At the time, Albin sang the lion's share of vocals, but singing was clearly Big Brother's weakest department. The band toyed with the idea of a female singer, inspired by the Airplane's Signe Tole Anderson and Great Society's Grace Slick. Chet Helms immediately thought of his old friend Janis Joplin, whom Albin and Gurley remembered from her North Beach days.

Helms lured Joplin back to San Francisco to audition for his new band in June 1966. Her first rehearsal was met with enthusiasm and excitement, and within a week, she was singing in her first gig with Big Brother and the Holding Company at the Avalon Ballroom. A concert recording made on July 28, 1966, at California Hall (released as *The Lost Tapes,* 2008) captures the early Big Brother sound. The band's catalog contained blues, R&B, and early rock classics, such as the Little Richard tune "Oh, My Soul," Howlin' Wolf's "Moanin' at Midnight," and the song that would become one of Joplin's staples, Big Mama Thornton's "Ball and Chain." Yet their treatments were unique; like many of their Bay Area brethren, Big Brother had a frenetic energy and a slightly sloppy sound. San Francisco rock music was a far cry from the polished rock and roll of the 1950s or early Beatles records.

Joplin shared lead vocal duties with Albin, and on the 1966 concert recording she is a member of Big Brother rather than its star front woman. Still, she elevates their songs with her acute understanding of blues singing and how to adapt it for the high volume and tempo of rock and roll. The band retained some of their psychedelic, pre-Janis sound, evident in their take on Edvard Grieg's "In the Hall of the Mountain King." Gurley builds large arcs of sound from distortion and feedback noise, alongside his blisteringly fast soloing inspired by modal jazz and Indian ragas. The band builds a few peaks in this manner over the course of nearly seven minutes. However, with Joplin's

arrival, the band decided to cut down on the longer improvisations and make their music more song oriented (Echols 1999, 135).

For their first out-of-town engagement, Big Brother landed a four-week gig in Chicago. Yet the wild rock by five white hippies from San Francisco fell on cold ears in the home of electric, urban blues, where Muddy Waters or Buddy Guy were playing just down the street. Big Brother was stranded in Chicago when the club refused to pay them due to poor ticket sales. Bobby Shad of Mainstream Records came to their rescue, and the band signed a shady record contract as their only option.

Mainstream's Chicago engineers, unaccustomed to rock bands, would not record the band at their usual volume, meaning that the group's signature distorted live sound was absent on the album. Joplin's vocals were double tracked, although the effect occasionally is a distraction. It was still the energy and power of their live performance that drew praise, and that is nowhere on this album.

As such, *Big Brother and the Holding Company* sounds at times like a parody of the early San Francisco sound. Two Joplin-led tracks, "Bye, Bye Baby" and "Down on Me," are the best offerings on this album, with the band playing solidly behind Joplin's strident vocals. "All Is Loneliness," with its drone and three-part vocal harmony, sounds like a poor imitation of the Beatles' "Tomorrow Never Knows," while Albin's "Light Is Faster Than Sound" is sloppy and melodically uninteresting. Joplin sang background vocals on some songs, but her gravelly timbre blended poorly with her bandmates.

Back in San Francisco, national attention was focused on hippies and the Haight, and Big Brother was at the center of it all. In January 1967, they played the Human Be-In in Golden Gate Park, a daylong celebration of community, music, and psychedelics that arguably launched the Summer of Love media frenzy. Joplin began wearing makeup and met Linda Gravenites, who began sewing sexy costumes for Janis rather than the unflattering draped clothing and ponchos that were popular among hippie women.

Photographer Bob Seidemann shot Janis naked in early 1967, barely covered with beads. The photo became a hot-selling poster, and Janis became the first hippie pin-up girl.

In June of 1967, the Monterey International Pop Festival, one of the first rock festivals, took place just south of the Bay Area. It launched the American careers of Jimi Hendrix and the Who, and exposed Otis Redding to mainstream white audiences for the first time. But it was Janis and Big Brother who stole the show. Joplin's towering presence and in-your-face attitude, coupled with a perceived authenticity and emotional transparency, stunned the crowd. Her rendition of "Ball and Chain"—a performance later released on the retrospective *Janis* (1993)—transfixed the crowd. For her first verse, Janis sang with a tenderness and hushed quality, breaking out on the chorus into more frantic high-pitched singing. The grit, strain, and sheer volume of Joplin's voice enhanced the song's raw emotion, while Gurley's soloing matched her unrestrained power. Janis endeared herself to the crowd and critics with "an individuality of expression which suggests a personal experience of the immediacy of rejection" (Whiteley 2000, 54).

Jazz critic Phil Elwood commented, "She is the best white blues singer I have ever heard," and journalist Michael Lydon praised the rest of the band as well, writing that "the group behind [Joplin] drove her and fed from her, building the total volume sound that has become a San Francisco trademark" (Lydon 2003, 28). Robert Christgau wrote that Joplin "may be the best rock singer since Ray Charles" as "she rocked and stomped and threatened any moment to break the microphone, or swallow it" (Christgau 2000, 24). Historian Buzzy Jackson wrote that Joplin's voice and body "added up to a vision of emotional energy that nearly blinded the unsuspecting audience member" (Jackson 2005, 219).

Monterey changed the course of Big Brother's career, as newfound media attention and success relegated Big Brother to the role of Joplin's backing band while she catapulted into superstardom. Mainstream finally released the band's self-titled LP, hoping to capitalize on their newfound recognition. The band hired Bob Dylan's former New York manager, Albert Grossman, and flew to New York in February of 1968 to sign a contract with Columbia Records. Their East Coast debut at the Anderson Theater was a rousing success, garnering a rave review in the *New York Times*. As a harbinger of the growing strain between Joplin and her bandmates, the *Times* review featured a photo of only Joplin. Unable to cope with the growing spotlight, both Gurley and Joplin took to heroin.

Grossman brought on producer John Simon to handle Big Brother's first Columbia album. Simon felt that the band lacked polish and precision, and believed that a live album could explain these deficiencies. A remote recording truck was set up outside a Detroit concert, but the band's performance was subpar and Simon deemed it unusable.

Instead, Simon replicated the effect of a live performance in the studio. A stage was created with risers, the band set up a public addressing (PA) system rather than use headphones to hear itself, and Simon spliced in recorded crowd noise, even leading off the album with Bill Graham's introduction of the band. As a result, *Cheap Thrills* has the ambience and energy of a live album, even though only "Ball and Chain" was actually recorded in concert.

The biggest hit on *Cheap Thrills* was the Erma Franklin song "Piece of My Heart," which reached number 12 on the singles charts and remains a mainstay of classic rock radio. The song began with raucous guitar work from Andrew, rapid bass notes, and Joplin's semi-shouted exhortations to "come on," inviting the listener into the song. Her verse vocal was some of her sexiest and most seductive singing, and her ecstatic scream just before the last chorus provides an emotional exclamation point.

Gershwin's "Summertime" was another of the album's gems. Sam Andrew lifted his opening guitar riff from a J.S. Bach prelude, giving the entire track a Baroque flavor that was popular in psychedelic rock (Hicks 1999), and Joplin sang with a restraint and delicacy seldom matched in her output. Gurley and Andrew traded and interwove solos, which was their finest instrumental work on the album. Joplin returned to her folk-blues roots with the acoustic "Turtle Blues," featuring Simon on piano and revealing Janis's insecurities when she sang, "I guess I'm just like a turtle/That's hidin' underneath its horny shell."

Cheap Thrills went platinum within a month of its August 1968 release and spent eight weeks as the number-one album in the country. Yet by the end of August, Joplin announced her intention to leave Big Brother and the Holding Company following their fall tour. The band was often disparaged by both critics and other musicians for their musical inadequacies, often in influential hip publications such as *Rolling Stone* and the *L.A. Free Press,* and Grossman believed that Big Brother was holding Joplin back. Yet personal tensions and drug addictions within the band likely had as much to do with the split as anything external.

Joplin wasted no time forming a new band, retaining only Sam Andrew from Big Brother. She made her solo debut at a Memphis revue concert hosted by the legendary soul label Stax/Volt in December 1968. Janis's new band included keyboards and horns, and she hoped to transition from psychedelic rock toward soul, R&B, and blues. Yet the Memphis gig was mediocre, as Joplin's band lacked the refinement and precision of the Stax/Volt groups on the bill. Ralph Gleason, the *San Francisco Chronicle* critic who was an early Joplin supporter, stated that "her new band is a drag" (Selvin 1994, 216). The band embarked on a long European tour where they finally meshed and, freed from American fans who felt bitter about the Big Brother split, Janis felt embraced and delivered knockout performances.

In June 1969, Joplin began recording her first solo album, but there were many problems. The band had been a rotating door of personnel since its inception, which is one reason they never gelled. Additionally, the horns often competed with Joplin's voice, leading one biographer to write that on this album, we find "Janis at her screechiest" (Echols 1999, 246). With many members themselves on heroin, the Kozmic Blues Band, as they became known, was undisciplined and under-rehearsed.

I Got Dem Ol' Kozmic Blues Again Mama! was released in the fall and sold well despite mixed critical response. Saxophonist Snooky Flowers claimed the rock press trashed the album because soul was, at the time, dominated by black artists, yet Joplin's band was mostly white. She would later tell reporter David Dalton that this band "didn't get me off" (Dalton 1991, 89), as they often lagged behind or overpowered her.

Meanwhile, Getz and Albin toured with Country Joe and the Fish during the spring of 1969. Gurley, devastated after the death of his wife from a heroin overdose, returned to San Francisco and reunited with his former bandmates, switching to bass guitar while Albin took up lead guitar. Joplin fired Andrew from the Kozmic Blues Band at the end of the summer. Upon his return to San Francisco, Big Brother reunited featuring Nick Gravenites on vocals.

Joplin's heroin addiction was spiraling out of control by the end of 1969. Lackluster performances at Woodstock in August and throughout the fall with the Kosmic Blues Band fueled her depression and anxiety. She fired the band after the tour ended and began a methadone treatment at the urging of her manager. As 1970 began, Joplin started to rebuild her career. She assembled a new band herself, calling them the Full Tilt Boogie Band, made up of more disciplined players who were interested in being the backup band she needed to succeed. Additionally, she debuted a song penned by a new country music songwriter, Kris Kristofferson, called "Me and Bobby McGee." It revealed Joplin's ability to tap into her Texas rock and country roots, and would eventually become her biggest hit.

Joplin spent the spring and summer touring with the Full Tilt Boogie Band, delivering knockout performances and regaining critical favor, and even sat in with the reformed Big Brother for a few nights at the Fillmore. The summer culminated with the Festival Express, a series of festival appearances across Canada where the musicians traveled together by train. Featuring the Band, the Grateful Dead, and many others, the highlight of this week of concerts was the constant music-making that took place in informal jam sessions on the train, preserved on film and released in 2004 as *Festival Express*. Her onstage performance of "Cry Baby" with the Full Tilt Boogie Band was magnetic and suggested a partial return to her early successes.

Joplin entered the studio in the fall of 1970 with producer Paul Rothschild, ready to record her Full Tilt Boogie tracks. She named the album *Pearl,* a name she had recently adopted for her brash and sassy alter ego. During the recording of *Pearl,* Joplin began to use heroin again.

Janis, who had always lived without abandon, died of a heroin overdose in the early morning of October 4, 1970. The song she was supposed to record that evening, "Buried Alive in the Blues," appeared on *Pearl* as an instrumental track. After her death, *Pearl* was released in January 1971 and became her biggest hit album, providing Joplin with her only number-one single, "Me and Bobby McGee." The song was a large cumulative form with a gradually thickening texture (Spicer 2004), and acoustic guitar strumming and pedal steel guitar hint at her folk and country roots.

Perhaps the track's greatest asset was Janis's hushed and tender "la da da"s following the second chorus. Her ability to crescendo with power and emotion served her well, her clear voice taking on more of her signature grittiness as she moved higher in pitch. Finally she burst out, the drums in a double-time rock beat, rapping about how she "did the best I can." While Joplin always tried to vocalize her emotions, the intimate singing style combined with her well-publicized personal sorrows transformed the song into something approaching autobiography. Especially following her death, the lyric "Freedom's just another word for nothing left to lose" resonated as a testament to Joplin's wild and excessive life that longed for loving stability.

Joplin's voice sounded clear and healthy on *Pearl,* showing considerably more control and polish than she had even on *Cheap Thrills,* and better balance between Joplin and her backing band on tracks like the soul number "My Baby." In a spontaneous moment of humor and sincerity, the album's tiny masterpiece was the a-cappella performance of "Mercedes Benz,"

a tongue-in-cheek materialistic plea that ended with Janis giggling, "That's it!"

Big Brother and the Holding Company released "two undistinguished albums" (Selvin 1994, 339) without Joplin, *Be a Brother* (1970) and *How Hard It Is* (1971). The band split in 1972, but reunited in 1987, touring actively for the next decade. In 1997, old tensions resurfaced and Gurley left the band. He died in 2009, but Andrew, Getz, and Albin continue to play together as Big Brother to the present day.

Janis's image and legacy suffered in the immediate decades following her death. Part of this may have been because the James Dean ideal of living fast and dying young "seemed less acceptable in a woman than a man" (Reynolds and Press 1995, 272). Others believed that "her lack of restraint, her palpable vulnerability" were undesirable qualities (Echols 1999, 309) and that her "overwhelming aura was powerlessness" (Reynolds and Press 1995, 271).

In the critical commentary following Joplin's death, a variety of social topics often seemed to eclipse discussions of her music. Race was a contentious topic throughout her career. Joplin's sister claimed that Janis confided in a friend: "I wish I were black because black people have more emotion" (Joplin 1992, 109), while others claim that Janis "had no pretensions of wanting to be black herself, or of needing to be black to sing the blues" (Jackson 2005, 207). Jazz critic Nat Hentoff wrote approvingly of her ability to "[sing] the blues out of black influences but [she] developed her own sound and phrasing" (Brackett 2009, 246). Her idolization of Bessie Smith, which led to Joplin funding the installation of the blues legend's gravestone, was seen alternately as appropriation, adulation, or imitation.

Sexuality and feminism also frequently appear in various discussions of Janis's life and music. Bill Graham maintains that Joplin "aroused desire but was not the object of that desire" (Graham and Greenfield 1992, 204), a situation that hurt her deeply. Others sexualized her unconventional beauty only through her music. Writing in the *Village Voice* after Monterey, Richard Goldstein admitted that "to hear Janis sing 'Ball and Chain' just once is to have been laid, lovingly and well"

(Echols 1999, 168). Joplin often publicly equated her singing with sex, and her vulgarity in doing so distanced her from conventional norms of femininity. Sexual toughness is natural for male rock stars, but because Janis is a woman, her aggressiveness relays "a sense of the unnatural and the deviant" (Whiteley 2000, 66).

The past few decades have seen a revisionist history for both Joplin and Big Brother. Big Brother's in-your-face, sloppy sound once seemed amateurish, but following the do-it-yourself ethos of punk and underground rock, Big Brother comes off as authentic. Additionally, time has allowed Janis to become a role model for female singers who celebrate her solidarity in the boys club of rock, her ability to command a crowd, and her willingness to lose herself in her music. Melissa Etheridge and Stevie Nicks are among the singers who have cited Janis as a major influence, and it is hard to imagine powerful, R&B-styled white singers such as Amy Winehouse, Adele, or Merrill Garbus of tUnE-yArDs succeeding without Joplin as a precedent.

Jacob A. Cohen

Selected Discography
Big Brother and the Holding Company:
Big Brother & the Holding Company, Mainstream Records S/6099, 1967.

Cheap Thrills, Columbia Records KCS 9700, 1968.

Be a Brother, Columbia Records C 30222, 1970.

How Hard It Is, Columbia Records C 30738, 1971.

The Lost Tapes, Airline Records AR-CD-0214, 2008.

Janis Joplin with Big Brother and the Holding Company:
Live at Winterland '68, Columbia CK 64869, 1998.

Janis Joplin:
I Got Dem Ol' Kozmic Blues Again Mama!, Columbia Records KCS 9913, 1969.

Pearl, Columbia Records KC 30322, 1971.

In Concert, Columbia Records C2X 31160, 1972.

Janis (3 CD compilation), Columbia Records C3K 48845, 1993.

References
Brackett, David, ed. *The Pop, Rock, and Soul Reader: Histories and Debates.* 2nd ed. New York: Oxford University Press, 2009.

Christgau, Robert. *Any Old Way You Choose It Rock and Other Pop Music, 1967–1973.* Expanded ed. New York: Cooper Square Press, 2000.

Echols, Alice. *Scars of Sweet Paradise: The Life and Times of Janis Joplin.* New York: Metropolitan Books, 1999.

Graham, Bill, and Robert Greenfield. *Bill Graham Presents: My Life Inside Rock and Out.* New York: Doubleday, 1992.

Hicks, Michael. *Sixties Rock: Garage, Psychedelic, and Other Satisfactions.* Urbana: University of Illinois Press, 1999.

Jackson, Buzzy. *A Bad Woman Feeling Good: Blues and the Women Who Sing Them.* New York: Norton, 2005.

Johnson, Joyce. *Minor Characters: A Young Woman's Coming of Age in the Beat Generation.* New York: Washington Square Press, 1983.

Joplin, Laura. *Love, Janis.* New York: Villard Books, 1992.

Lydon, Michael. *Flashbacks: Eyewitness Accounts of the Rock Revolution, 1964–1974.* New York: Routledge, 2003.

Selvin, Joel. *Summer of Love: The Inside Story of LSD, Rock & Roll, Free Love, and High Times in the Wild West.* New York: Dutton, 1994.

Slick, Darby. *Don't You Want Somebody to Love: Reflections on the San Francisco Sound.* Berkeley, CA: SLG Books, 1991.

Smeaton, Bob, dir. *Festival Express.* New Line Home Entertainment N7573, 2004.

Spicer, Mark. "(Ac)Cumulative Form in Pop-Rock Music." *Twentieth-Century Music* 1, no. 1 (2004): 29–64.

Whiteley, Sheila. *Women and Popular Music: Sexuality, Identity, and Subjectivity.* London: Routledge, 2000.

Bill Haley and His Comets (1946–1980)

Bill Haley and His Comets were one of the first famous rock and roll bands at the dawning of the rock and roll era. Haley has long been discussed as one of the first real rock and roll stars. Further, some credit him and the Comets as the "first" rock and roll band. Haley and His Comets certainly did much in the style's infancy to make it popular, acceptable, and part of the American landscape. Haley and His Comets sold millions of albums and left an indelible mark on the American popular music landscape. The story of Haley and His Comets' rise is now the stuff of legend (some consider Haley the true King of Rock and Roll, instead of Elvis Presley), and their musical impact continues to be felt around the world. Haley brought the rock and roll style to the world stage and fused country, rhythm and blues, and a steady backbeat rhythm into the roots of rock.

Bill Haley (born William John Clifton Haley, July 6, 1925, died February 9, 1981; vocals, guitar) was born in Highland Park, Michigan, and was blind in one eye from birth. Although a shy youth, Haley developed an early love of music. His first style of choice was country music, and by age 14 he was a solid singer and guitarist. At age 14 he quit school to pursue his music dreams, playing in a host of country bands. His first taste of success came in 1944 when he joined the band the Downhomers. With this band, Haley made his first appearance on record and continued to hone his skills as a singer, guitarist, and country yodeler (Eder, Allmusic.com, 2014). Haley's early approach was similar to one of the fathers of country music, singer/guitarist/yodeler Jimmie Rodgers.

In 1946, Haley left the Downhomers and formed his own band called the Four Aces of Western Swing. In the mid-1940s, Hank Williams Sr. was popularizing the Western Swing style and radio shows such as *Louisiana Hayride* were carrying the style to an ever-growing audience. The Four Aces included Haley, Johnny Grande (born January 14, 1930, died June 3, 2006; keyboard), Al Rex (born Albert Piccirilli, July 13, 1928; bass), and

Bill Haley and His Comets were one of the first famous rock and roll bands who had success in the United States and the United Kingdom. Here the band rehearses at the Dominion Theatre in London on February 6, 1957, where they opened their British tour. The Comets included accordion player Johnny Grande, bassist Al Rex, and saxophonist Rudy Pompilli. (Bettmann/Corbis)

Billy Williamson (born February 9, 1925, died March 22, 1996; steel guitar). Ultimately, this group of four would coalesce into the Comets. The Four Aces of Western Swing managed to get a record deal with Jack Howard and James Meyers's Cowboy Records label. The group released their first record in 1949, the single "Candy Kisses." By the end of the 1940s, the group had changed their name to the Saddlemen and began switching labels—including a stint on the fledgling Atlantic Records, which was founded in 1947 by Ahmet Ertegun. In 1951, the Saddlemen found a home on Holiday Records and released their version of Jackie Brenston's song "Rocket 88." Incredibly, this cover version went on to be regarded by many as the first "real" rock and roll song (Eder, Allmusic.com, 2014). This statement continues to cause quite a bit of conflict among rock and roll historians, many of whom do not consider rock and roll's birth to have taken place until the mid-1950s.

Haley and the Saddlemen did notice that their breed of up-tempo rhythm and blues got a more enthusiastic response from their ever-younger live audience than did their country tunes. David Miller, the head of Holiday Records, began a new imprint called Essex Records, and it was for this new label that Haley and the Saddlemen released the single "Rock the Joint." The song was successful enough that the band toured in support, and along the way played a sold-out show in Cleveland, Ohio. These events created the perfect storm as Cleveland DJ Alan Freed picked up on the Saddlemen song and began calling its style rock and roll. With this, the Saddlemen helped usher in the sound that went on to take over the world in the following decade. It should be mentioned that this account is not universally agreed on and some say that Freed was referring to several other songs.

With the success of "Rock the Joint," Bill Haley and the Saddlemen again changed their name. In a play on words associated with Halley's Comet, the band became Bill Haley and His Comets in 1952. The change in name also marked a change in branding. The band put aside their traditional cowboy garb and replaced it with what they thought was more contemporary clothing. They also revamped their stage show

and added more slick choreography. The band went on to play a long list of high school dances to build buzz for their new name and image.

The early 1950s found Haley and His Comets becoming ever more popular. With songs such as "Rockin' Chair on the Moon" and "Crazy, Man, Crazy," the group was blazing a musical trail. The latter song was written and recorded by Haley in April of 1953 and peaked at number 12 on the *Billboard* charts. By the mid-1950s, the band's relationship with Miller and his Essex imprint was strained. Miller was heavy-handed in the songs he choose for the group to record, and those that he did have them record were not achieving the level of success the band was aspiring to. As a result, the band moved over to Decca Records with the assistance of producer Milt Gabler (Eder, Allmusic.com, 2014). This move proved to be extremely beneficial, as it was under Gabler's tutelage that the band released the song "Rock Around the Clock."

The Decca single "Rock Around the Clock" shot up the charts. Although Haley and His Comets did not write the song—it was written by Max Freedman and James Myers—they did put their stylistic stamp on the recording. The single eventually went to number one in the United States and the United Kingdom. The song was a rebellious anthem of the mid-1950s and captured the imagination of the baby boom generation. On the heels of this success Gabler had Haley and His Comets record the single "Shake, Rattle, and Roll." Although the song had already been released by Big Joe Turner, the version by Haley and His Comets broke the band into the mainstream. The single sold over a million copies in late 1954 and through 1955 (Eder, Allmusic.com, 2014). With this, "Rock Around the Clock" was released and used during the credits of the hit movie *Blackboard Jungle*. In its second coming, "Rock Around the Clock" camped out at number one for eight weeks and went on to sell 25 million copies worldwide.

The popularity that Haley and His Comets had achieved by the mid-1950s made it possible for them to release an album of material that had not been previously released as singles. In March of 1956, the band recorded the material for *Rock and Roll Stage Show* with Milt Gabler serving as producer; was the band's first release that was conceived of as a unit—not a collection of singles. The album was released on the Decca Records imprint in August of 1956 and contained 12 songs, most of which featured Haley as the main songwriter. Of note, by this point the band membership had changed on several key instruments. Haley was still responsible for vocals and rhythm guitar. Billy Williamson played steel guitar and sang backup vocals, Johnny Grande played piano and accordion, and Al Rex played bass. To this was added Franny Beecher (born Francis Beecher, September 29, 1921, died February 24, 2014; lead guitar), Ralph Jones supplying the drum parts, and Rudy Pompilli appearing on tenor sax (born Rudolph Clement Pompilli, April 16, 1924, died February 5, 1976; tenor saxophone).

Although Haley was the quintessential front man, the material on this album often featured other members of the band. "Goofin' Around" and "Blue Comet Blues" were features for guitarist Beecher. "A Rockin' Little Tune" put the spotlight on Johnny Grande's accordion playing, and Billy Williamson sang lead vocals on "Hide and Seek." Williamson, Rex, and Beecher formed a vocal trio for "Hey Then, There Now" and "Tonight's the Night." Of note, Haley sang a version of Gabler's song "Choo Choo Ch'Boogie," which would go on to be a huge hit for Louis Jordan. Several songs from the album were chart successes, with "Ruby's Rock" reaching number 34 on the *Billboard* charts and "Rockin' Thru the Rye" cracking the top 40 on the Cashbox charts. The album as a whole went to the number-one slot on the U.K. album charts in 1956 and contained "killer vocal performances . . . [and] hot guitar noodles . . . [with] a rocking beat" (Eder, Allmusic.com, 2014).

In the wake of the success of the *Rock 'n' Roll Stage Show,* Haley and His Comets were featured in a movie called *Rock Around the Clock.* The film was directed by Fred Sears and also included Alan Freed, the Platters, and Freddie Bell and the Bellboys. The movie was released on March 21, 1956, and was distributed by Columbia Pictures. Haley and His Comets

appeared lip-synching nine performances, which made him a "split-curled star here and abroad. His celebrity was particularly long-lived in Britain, where he came to be regarded as rock and roll royalty" (www .rockhall.com 2014). The movie was conceived as a vehicle to capitalize on Haley and His Comets' success, which it effectively did. The release was the first such rock and roll musical film, but it ushered in countless others. Sears quickly released another film featuring Haley and His Comets. Released in December 1956, *Don't Knock the Rock* again focused on Haley's music, but this time in the company of Little Richard and Dave Appell and the Applejacks. Due in part to its hasty creation and release, *Don't Knock the Rock* was not as successful as the previous release. Although this second movie was not as successful for Haley and His Comets, it did serve to introduce Little Richard to a larger (and predominantly white) audience.

The years 1955 and 1956 were hectic for Haley and His Comets. In addition to an album and two movies, the band also appeared on *Texaco Star Theater* with Milton Berle, and on August 7, 1955, they became the first rock and roll band to appear on the *Ed Sullivan Show.* The year 1957 saw the release of Haley and His Comets' second album, called *Rockin' the Oldies.* The release was again produced by Milt Gabler for the Decca imprint. The record comprised rock and roll style updates of 12 of the band's previously released songs. Standout singles included "The Dipsy Doodle" and "See You Later Alligator." Rudy Pompilli was not able to appear on the release and was replaced by Frankie Scott.

On the heels of this release, Bill Haley and His Comets made two appearances on Dick Clark's hit television show *American Bandstand.* The first show aired on October 28, 1957, and the second came on November 27 of the same year. Although riding a wave of popularity, the late 1950s found the rock and roll landscape becoming increasingly crowded. In 1956, Elvis moved from Sam Phillips's Sun Records to RCA, and with this he gained national distribution and an exploding fan base. Little Richard was emerging as a force to be reckoned with, as was Jerry Lee Lewis. The Everly Brothers released their first full-length record in 1958 and were regulars on the radio. Buddy Holly was also emerging as a significant musical force poised to carry the rock and roll style into the 1960s. Holly and the Crickets were also on the Decca Records label by early 1956 and were topping the charts by the end of 1957—a run that only ended with Holly's death in a plane crash on February 3, 1959.

Haley and His Comets spent part of 1957 touring the United Kingdom, where they continued to enjoy superstar status. They were mobbed by fans and played sold-out venues. The group spent the end of the year doing more touring, which took them to Australia. With this, Bill Haley and His Comets were the first rock and roll band to mount a successful world tour and thereby carried the new American popular style to the rest of the world.

Back in the United States in 1958, Haley launched his own record imprint called Clymax. This action took him away from creating his own music, as he now needed to cultivate a stable of groups to sign to the label. Initially successful, Haley essentially used members of the Comets as paid session players for band artists such as cowgirl country singer Sally Starr and the rockabilly band the Matys Brothers. Under Haley's direction, both of these artists released successful material—in the case of the Matys Brothers, Haley even cowrote their single "Crazy Street."

Also in 1958, Haley and His Comets released *Rockin' Around the World*. Just as before, the album contained 12 tracks, was produced by Milt Gabler, and was issued on the Decca imprint. Recorded at the end of 1957, the album came out on March 17, 1958. The album was the second of Haley and His Comets' themed records. The first, *Rockin' the Oldies,* was composed of rock and roll versions of the Comets' back catalogue. *Rockin' Around the World* was a collection of familiar folk songs reimagined in the rock and roll style. Some of the titles seem pretty contrived in retrospect. For example, "Waltzing Matilda" became "Rockin' Matilda" and "London Bridge" became "Piccadilly Rock." The band's membership was stable for this release, with Pompilli back on tenor saxophone. The only change was the addition of a second guitar player named Joe Olivier. The experiment of remaking folk songs in the rock style was not a significant success, and the album did not yield any hit singles.

Haley and His Comets went straight back to the studio to finish the trilogy of themed albums for Decca. The third installment was recorded in the summer of 1958 and released January 5, 1959. The theme of this release was girls' names, and all of the songs included a name in the title, such as "Whoa Mabel!" Again produced by Gabler and containing 12 tracks, this album was more successful than its predecessor. The song "Skinny Minny" was a hit single and went to 22 on the *Billboard* charts. "Lean Jean" also charted, and the album was considered a success. That having been said, by the late 1950s it was clear that Haley and His Comets were not as popular as they once had been. Haley put part of the blame for this on the band's Decca affiliation, and in 1959 the group left the label and moved to Warner Bros. Records.

With the Warner Bros. deal in place, Haley and His Comets released their next record in 1960. This first Warner Bros. release, produced by George Avakian, appeared as an effort by the band's new label to resuscitate the band's popularity. The release contained 12 songs and the standard retinue of Comets, with one change: Al Rappa appeared on bass for this record. Sessions for the record took place in January and the album was issued in April of 1960. The songs on the album were all "cover" versions, but the band had recorded three of the songs during the Decca era. A significant difference between this record and those that preceded it was that *Bill Haley and His Comets* was released in stereo, not mono. The album included Comet standards "Rock Around the Clock," "Crazy, Man, Crazy," and "Shake, Rattle, and Roll." To this were added songs such as the Carl Perkins hit "Blue Suede Shoes" and "Whole Lotta Shakin' Goin On."

Haley and His Comets recorded their second Warner Bros. Records album in the early part of 1960 and released it that summer. Titled *Haley's Juke Box: Songs of the Bill Haley Generation,* the album was again produced by George Avakian. The band lineup was the same as it had been on the previous release, as the two albums were culled from the same recording sessions. The 12 songs contained on the album were country music classics by songwriters such as Hank Williams Sr. and Melvin Endsley. The album was not a success and received little promotional support from the label. In the wake of this release, Haley and His Comets' contract with Warner Bros. Records ended and the band was not resigned.

After the end of the relationship with Warner Bros. Records, Haley and His Comets never again signed with a major label. In 1961–1962, Haley made an interesting move and signed with the Mexican label Orfeon. This led to the recording of the single "Twist Español," which was a surprise hit for the band. The song captured the twist dance craze popularized in the United States by Chubby Checker's 1960 version of the Hank Ballard song "The Twist." With this, Haley and His Comets brought the twist to Latin America. They parlayed that success with a second single called "Florida Twist," which was a huge hit. Haley recognized the potential in the Latin American audience, and he and the band released a series of Spanish-tinged songs, which continued to sell well south of the border. Haley could also sing in Spanish, and the Latin American audience enjoyed the Comets' instruments, thus the band enjoyed a period of prosperity in that market for the first half of the 1960s. Haley and His Comets released a series of records on Orfeon and their subsidiary Dimsa between 1963 and 1966.

By the end of the 1960s, Bill Haley and His Comets were considered an oldies band and their popularity in the United States was on a steady decline. Never one to leave a potential market untapped, Haley and His Comets returned to Europe—a longtime stronghold of their fans. They signed with Sonet Records in Sweden and released *Just Rock and Roll Music* in 1973. The album was also released in the United States with the title *Travelin' Band* under the Janus imprint. For this release, the band played a series of covers, including "Pink Eyed Pussycat" and "Me and Bobby McGee." Several other Sonet releases followed, including *On Stage* (1977) and *Everyone Can Rock and Roll* (1979). As a harbinger of things to come, Haley was sent reeling in 1976 when his longtime saxophone player Rudy Pompilli died of cancer.

By the end of the 1970s, Haley and His Comets had just about run their course. A highlight was a performance for Queen Elizabeth II during the band's second European tour. In early 1980, the band toured South Africa, but Haley's health was failing. Shortly thereafter, it was reported that Haley had a brain tumor. He spent the last year of his life touring intermittently. His final show came in the summer of 1980. The band had a fall tour of Germany and subsequent recording session booked, but Haley's health was too fragile. Haley was at his home in Harlingen, Texas, on February 9, 1981, when he died in his sleep of an apparent heart attack. Bill Haley was 55 years old (rockhall.com 2014). After Haley's death, various incarnations of the Comets continued to tour. Some have had more credible membership than others, but without Haley these groups are pale imitators.

The musical legacy of Bill Haley and His Comets is simultaneously momentous and difficult to define. Because the group emerged as the rock and roll era was beginning, they have often been heralded as one of the most significant contributors to the fledgling style. However, it is very difficult to pin down whether or not they performed the first "rock and roll" song. Their legacy is much more definable. In 1987, Bill Haley was inducted into the Rock and Roll Hall of Fame. In 2012, the Comets were also inducted. The group was inducted into the Rockabilly Hall of Fame and they were also inducted into Hollywood's Rockwalk.

In 2007, a Bill Haley museum was opened in Munich, Germany, and there are numerous tribute bands still active, such as Bill Haley's New Comets. Haley's son Bill Jr. now has his own version of the Comets and does a "Rock and Roll History Show" in which he performs his father's greatest hits. Bill Haley Jr. and the Comets continue to book shows through 2015.

The musical legacy left by Haley and His Comets clearly continues to this day. The band ranked among the best in the first generation of rock and roll artists emerging in the mid-1950s, and their impact continues to be felt even beyond the tribute bands. The band's music has been covered by numerous artists who range widely in style. Wanda Jackson covered "Rip It Up," the Isley Brothers covered "Rock Around the Clock," as has Tiny Tim. "Skinny Minnie" has been covered by bands from Gerry and the Pacemakers to Louis Prima to the Hillbilly Voodoo Dolls. Imitation is the highest form of flattery, but in creating a cover version of a song it is also an indication of musical influence and impact—both of which are abundant with Bill Haley and His Comets.

Beyond tribute bands and cover versions, many musicians have discussed the influence of Haley and His Comets on their music. John Lennon of the Beatles noted that the first rock and roll music he heard was from the Comets and that it made such an impression on him that he set about imitating it. Paul McCartney reportedly felt a tingle up his spine when he first saw Bill Haley and His Comets on television. Graham Nash still has His Comets ticket stub from the show he attended in Manchester in February of 1957. Roger Waters of Pink Floyd credits hearing Bill Haley as a life-changing musical event. With this, the sound/style/influence of Bill Haley and His Comets continues to be heard (history.com 2014).

David V. Moskowitz

Selected Discography

Note: There are several dozen Bill Haley and His Comets releases from several countries.

Rock 'N Roll Stage Show, Decca DL 8345, 1956.

Rocking the Oldies, Decca DL 8569, 1957.

Rockin' Around the World, Decca DL 8692, 1958.

Bill Haley's Chicks, Decca DL 8821, 1959.

Bill Haley and His Comets, Warner Bros. Records W 1378, 1960.

Bill Haley's Jukebox, Warner Bros Records WB 26175, 1960.

Just Rock and Roll Music, Sonet 623, 1973.

References

Covers Project Official Website. 2015. Accessed June 2014. www.coversproject.com/artist/bill%20haley.

Discogs Official Website. 2015. "Bill Haley and His Comets Discography," www.discogs.com/artist/2828 97-Bill-Haley-And-His-Comets. Accessed 2014.

Eder, Bruce. "Bill Haley and His Comets," *All Music Guide.* Rovi Corporation, 2014.

Larkin, Colin, ed. "Bill Haley and His Comet—*Rock 'n Roll Stage Show.*" *Encyclopedia of Popular Music.* Oxford Music Online, 2008.

Rock and Roll Hall of Fame Official Website. 2014. "Bill Haley Biography." Accessed June 2014. rockhall.com/inductees/bill-haley.

Black Sabbath (1968–Present)

Black Sabbath is one of the earliest and most influential heavy metal bands. Their lyrics are often dark themed and their music is often riff based, blues driven, and heavy. The original lineup included Ozzy Osbourne (born John Osbourne, December 3, 1948; vocals), Tony Iommi (born Frank Anthony Iommi, February 19, 1948; guitar), Geezer Butler (born Terence Butler, July 17, 1949; bass), and Bill Ward (born William Ward, May 5, 1948; drums). Their second album *Paranoid* included three of their most well-known songs: "Iron Man," "Paranoid," and "War Pigs." Commercial success continued but diminished by the end of the 1970s. Rainbow front man Ronnie James Dio (born Ronald James Padavona, July 10, 1942, died May 16, 2010; vocals) replaced Ozzy in 1979. Sabbath recorded two studio albums with Dio, but he left the band in 1982, returning briefly from 1991 to 1992 to record a third. In the 1980s, while Ozzy and Dio had success as solo artists, Black Sabbath was a revolving door of musicians. In fact, Iommi is the only member to appear on all Black Sabbath albums. The original lineup reunited in 1997 and did several tours, but they did not record a full-length album. When Dio returned once again in 2006, Sabbath recorded and toured under the name "Heaven and Hell," in reference to their 1980 release of the same name. Dio died in 2010, and Black Sabbath announced a reunion of the original lineup in 2011. Black Sabbath's first studio album since 1995 was released June 10, 2013.

Black Sabbath was formed in 1968 in Aston (Birmingham), England, as the Polka Tulk Blues Band, later renamed Earth. Before forming Polka Tulk, Iommi and Ward were in a band called Mythology, and Ozzy and Geezer were in a band called Rare Breed. Iommi and Ward responded to a posting at a music store that read, "OZZY ZIG NEEDS GIG," and eventually the two pairs of musicians joined forces. Iommi, for a brief time in December 1968, joined Jethro Tull, but he returned to Earth after only two weeks. Another band touring in England was also named Earth, which led to confusion among audiences, venues, and booking agents. Iommi observed, from lines formed at a nearby movie theater, that people pay money to be scared, so in 1969, Earth began to write darker, frightening lyrics and music. Geezer titled one of their songs after *Black Sabbath,* the 1963 horror film starring Boris Karloff. In reaction to the Earth booking incident and their new lyrical and musical direction, they changed the name of the band to Black Sabbath.

Several musical aspects contribute to Sabbath's heaviness. Iommi plays through heavy distortion and with "palm-muting" on the strings. Much to the chagrin of producers and engineers of the 1970s, Geezer occasionally used distortion as well. Geezer's bass lines follow the guitar riffs to add weight and heaviness to them. For additional thickness on certain notes, Geezer will play a different note than Iommi, in harmony (e.g., the opening riff on "Under the Sun"), or he will bend the string, putting him slightly out of tune with Iommi's chord, thus creating a dissonant, hence thick, sound.

Two significant contributors to their doomy sound are their detuned strings and Iommi's use of "power" chords. These began merely as practical solutions for Iommi; he wears thimble-like caps on two of his fingers because of a factory injury in 1965 that cut the ends off of them. This incident was especially unfortunate because it was the fretting hand, not the picking one that was injured. By loosening the strings slightly, thus lowering the pitch, it became easier for Iommi to overcome the handicap. There are many Sabbath songs that have tuned-down guitars; Iommi says it creates a "bigger, heavier sound" with "more depth to it" (Iommi 2011). When Iommi and Geezer take advantage of these low pitches unavailable on the standard-tuned guitar, it sounds especially sinister

Black Sabbath was one of the most famous and notorious early heavy metal bands. The band (from left to right): Bill Ward, Ozzy Osbourne, Tony Iommi, and Geezer Butler, in 1975. The group's influence is difficult to overstate as the list of bands that note Black Sabbath's sound as an influence is huge and the band has sold over 75 million records worldwide. (Photo by Gems/Redferns)

(e.g., "Children of the Grave"). Partially due to his injury, Iommi played dyads (two-note chords), eventually referred to as "power" chords. He was credited by rock musicians as being the "master of the riff" who developed and popularized the use of the power chord. This became a regular part of his playing style, one that also included three- and four-note chords and impressive guitar solos, leading the listener to believe that this injury was no handicap to Iommi at all. Another important contributor to their heaviness is the "hard and aggressive" style of drumming that Ward described as "centered on rage" (Cope 2010).

A cover of the American band Crow's "Evil Woman" was released as Sabbath's first single, and they signed with Vertigo (UK) and with Warner Bros. Records (U.S.) in January 1970. "Evil Woman" appeared on their first album, *Black Sabbath* (1970), but was replaced by "Wicked World" on the U.S. release. Both versions of the album included a cover of "Warning" by the Aynsley Dunbar Retaliation (Dunbar joined the Mothers of Invention in 1970). The song "Black Sabbath" featured dark lyrics, a slow, brooding tempo, and the interval of a tritone, the "devil's interval." The lyrics in the song "N.I.B." were told from the point of view of Lucifer, and the song "The Wizard" had elements of mysticism.

The music on this album was overtly blues based, but it did not follow the typical 12-bar form: the songs were presented in a more complex, medley-like format with many tempo and key changes. Iommi provided heavy guitar riffs, and Geezer's bass lines drove the band. Ward's drumming style ranged from uptempo jazz on "Wicked World" to the doomy tom-tom work on "Black Sabbath." The introduction to "N.I.B.," aptly titled "Bassically," was a bass solo played by Geezer through a wah-wah pedal and eventually with distortion, two effects not normally used by bass guitarists.

Vertigo's decision to print an inverted crucifix in the gatefold of the album cover (this was not in Warner Bros. Records' U.S. release, nor was the inclusion the band's decision) caused the public to assume the band were Satanists. Occultists attended Sabbath's earliest concerts, and according to Iommi, the head witch of England attended their performances and invited them to their meetings (Baker 2002). Although the band distanced itself from, and even denied, being associated with Satanism, they were continually accused of such. According to Geezer, the band's primary lyricist, the lyrics were "never advocating Satanism. It was warning people against evil" (McIver 2006). Ozzy explained, "We never took the black magic stuff seriously . . . we just liked how theatrical it was" (Osbourne 2009). This reputation made booking gigs difficult for many years. Ward says, "Not many people would want us in their clubs. In fact, it was very difficult to find anybody that would accept us . . . We got banned from many places: Deep South, parts of Texas absolutely refused to have us there" (Mortimer 1998). There were protests from the Church that led to concert cancellations in Glens Falls (New York) on Good

Friday of 1986, San Luis Potosí (Mexico) in 1989, and many other cities on other tours.

Paranoid, their second album, was released in the United Kingdom in 1970. The title track, composed in less than 30 minutes, became Sabbath's most popular song. The title of the album was originally *War Pigs,* named after the opening track on the album, but, according to Ozzy, was changed by Vertigo because they realized the commercial potential of the song "Paranoid" and of an album named after it. Some accounts claim that it was changed by the record label because of the song's antiwar lyrics to show sensitivity toward Vietnam War supporters. "War Pigs" was not a political song originally; it was about a black mass, but the lyrics were significantly rewritten for the album. Even after the album's release, Ozzy sometimes incorporated earlier versions of the lyrics in live performances (e.g., the "Paris 1970" concert). The album contained the heavy metal classics "Electric Funeral" and "Iron Man," both featuring slow, heavy riffs with a contrasting fast section. Not all of Sabbath's music was dark and heavy: "Planet Caravan," for example, was very mellow and featured smooth-processed vocals, clean guitar, piano, and bongos.

Sabbath released their third album, *Master of Reality,* in 1971. Continuing the antiwar sentiment of "War Pigs," "Children of the Grave" was this album's political song. *Paranoid* and *Master of Reality* have drug-themed songs: "Hand of Doom" from *Paranoid* was about heroin, and "Sweet Leaf" from *Master of Reality* was about marijuana. Similar to "Planet Caravan," "Solitude" was the mellow track, a fine example of Ozzy's versatility in vocal style. In contrast to the doomy lyrics of "Black Sabbath," "After Forever" was quite Christian, or as Geezer describes it, "pro-God." *Master of Reality* was the first album on which Iommi and Geezer detuned the strings three half-steps. This allowed them to bend the strings further and to create a lower, darker sound.

Their fourth album, *Vol. 4,* was recorded in Los Angeles in 1972. It was originally titled after the song "Snowblind," but it was renamed *Black Sabbath Vol. 4* because the record company objected to having a drug reference in the title. Around the time of the making of

Vol. 4, the band members began heavy drug use. The riffs that opened "Cornucopia" and "Under the Sun" were some of the heaviest Sabbath ever wrote, contributed to in part by the detuning of the guitar strings. The album contained a soft ballad called "Changes" and an acoustic instrumental titled "Laguna Sunrise." Sabbath began to experiment with different sounds on *Vol. 4,* such as the orchestra on "Laguna Sunrise" and the mellotron on "Changes."

Sabbath's next four albums were more experimental and included elements of progressive rock. In fact, Yes and Gentle Giant toured with them in 1972, and Sabbath befriended Frank Zappa in 1974. *Sabbath Bloody Sabbath* (1973) used an orchestra (on "Spiral Architect"), and it was their first album to use keyboards extensively (including an appearance by Yes's Rick Wakeman). A chamber choir was used throughout the textless "Supertzar" from *Sabotage* (1975), which had a marching rhythm in the rarely used 9/4 meter. Because Sabbath began to use more keyboards and orchestral sounds on their albums, keyboardist Jezz Woodruffe (born Gerald Woodruffe, 1951; keyboard) joined the band for the Sabotage tour. His synthesizer work on *Technical Ecstasy* (1976), especially on "Backstreet Kids," was reminiscent of American progressive rock bands such as Styx and Kansas.

Interestingly, some of the opening bands during Black Sabbath's 1975–1977 tours were non-metal bands Boston, Journey, and Kansas. Keyboards played a prominent role in *Never Say Die!* (1978), especially Don Airey's (born Donald Airey, June 21, 1948; keyboard) performances on "Johnny Blade" and the prog-rock/jazz-fusion song "Air Dance." Keyboardist Geoff Nicholls (born February 29, 1948) joined the band in 1979 and remained with them as a studio and touring musician until 2004. *Technical Ecstasy* and *Never Say Die!* also flirted with a more straightforward American rock sound: "Rock 'n' Roll Doctor" and the Boston-like introduction to "Over to You" were but two examples. Despite these experiments, Sabbath retained their heavy metal style. Two riffs from the title track of *Sabbath Bloody Sabbath* are particularly heavy and require detuning of the

strings. The main riff to "Symptom of the Universe" from *Sabotage* is considered by many to be one of the heaviest riffs ever written; like the song "Black Sabbath," it featured the interval of the tritone.

The song "Killing Yourself to Live" from *Sabbath Bloody Sabbath* made reference to their continued alcohol and drug abuse, a problem that plagued the band for years. This severely affected their productivity, and it worsened to the point where Ozzy was asked to leave the band on April 27, 1979. Ozzy had actually left the band for a short time in 1977—he was temporarily replaced by Dave Walker (of Fleetwood Mac)—but he returned within days of the *Never Say Die!* recording sessions. Ozzy was not the only lead singer on *Technical Ecstasy* and *Never Say Die!;* Ward sang "It's Alright" and "Swinging the Chain," as Ozzy refused to sing the latter. In fact, he refused to sing any song written with Walker, and he rejected many of the lyrics that Geezer had written for the album. Furthermore, Ozzy was displeased with the band's musical direction.

In 1979, Ronnie James Dio replaced Ozzy as lead vocalist. This began a temporary resurgence in popularity, exemplified by two successful studio albums: *Heaven and Hell* (1980) and *Mob Rules* (1981). "Paranoid" was rereleased as a single in September 1980, which presumably contributed to the success of those albums by regenerating interest in the band. Sharon Arden—who would later become, ironically, Ozzy's wife—introduced Dio to Iommi, suggesting they work on a separate project. Geezer was Sabbath's lyricist when Ozzy was in the band, but Dio wrote the lyrics for these two albums. Similar to his work in Rainbow, Dio's lyrics were sometimes neo-medieval, quite a departure from Geezer's lyrical style. Through frequent use in live performances, Dio popularized the "metal horns," the devilish hand sign that has since become associated with heavy metal music.

During the 1980 tour for *Heaven and Hell,* Ward left the band. He said, "It was intolerable for me to get on a stage without Osbourne, and I drank very, very heavily . . . My health was worsening with alcoholism, and I couldn't believe in that [lineup of] Sabbath" (Mortimer 1998). He was replaced by American drummer Vinny Appice (born Vincent Appice, September 3, 1957) for the remainder of the tour, and they recorded *Mob Rules*. The song "The Mob Rules" was written for the cult classic animated film *Heavy Metal* (1981). Several concerts from the 1981–1982 tour were recorded for their next release, *Live Evil* (1982). According to Dio, "the engineer who was doing [*Live Evil*] was drinking a lot, and he would tell Tony and Geezer that Vinny and I were going into the studio and turning up the drums and the vocals." Iommi banned Dio from the studio, the "final straw," so Dio left (Mortimer 1998). Dio began a successful solo career, taking Appice with him. They recorded several albums, including *Holy Diver, The Last in Line,* and *Sacred Heart.*

With Ozzy and Dio gone in 1983, the band recruited Ian Gillan (born August 19, 1945; vocals) of Deep Purple to record the band's 11th studio album, *Born Again* (1983). Gillan's style was quite different from Ozzy's and Dio's. It was defined by his high-pitched "heavy metal scream" (e.g., during the introduction to "Trashed"). The chilling, pulseless instrumental "Stonehenge" served as an introduction to "Disturbing the Priest." The music for the latter was particularly dark, angular, and dissonant; the opening riff even hinted at atonality. Ward returned to Sabbath to record this album. He had been sober for several months around the time of the recording, but the idea of touring again without Ozzy turned him back to drinking, and he quit the band for a second time. Electric Light Orchestra drummer Bev Bevan filled in for the tour. The stage set for this tour included reproductions of Stonehenge from which a dwarf dressed as the red-demon baby from the album cover jumped. This was parodied in the 1984 mockumentary *This Is Spinal Tap.*

After the *Born Again* tour, Gillan returned to Deep Purple, Bevan began the ELO II project, and Geezer left to form the Geezer Butler Band. Iommi began work on a solo album in 1985, but due to record company pressure, it was released as *Black Sabbath featuring Tony Iommi.* When the original lineup reunited for a Live Aid concert in 1985, they were billed as "Black Sabbath featuring Ozzy Osbourne."

Seventh Star (1986) included Nicholls, Glenn Hughes (born August 21, 1952; vocals) of Deep Purple, bassists Dave Spitz (born February 22, 1958) and Gordon Copley (of Lita Ford's band), and Eric Singer (born Eric Mensinger, May 12, 1958; drummer for Lita Ford). Although Iommi's blues-influenced guitar solos ground the band in the classic Sabbath style, this release had the sound of 1980s-era metal: for instance, the power ballad "No Stranger to Love" was sandwiched by two up-tempo metal songs, "In for the Kill" and "Turn to Stone." Hughes was fired during the first week of the tour and was replaced with Ray Gillen (born Raymond Gillen, May 12, 1959, died December 3, 1993), a singer who had recently worked with ex-Rainbow drummer Bobby Rondinelli, for the remainder of the tour.

Bob Daisley (born Robert Daisley, February 13, 1950; bassist for Rainbow and Ozzy) replaced Spitz and began work on *The Eternal Idol* (1987) with Iommi, Gillen, Singer, and Nicholls. On the album sleeve, however, Spitz was credited for Daisley's performance. Gillen quit the band and was replaced with Tony Martin (born Anthony Martin Harford, April 19, 1957). Using the existing melodies and vocal phrasing, Martin rerecorded Gillen's vocal tracks in only eight days, as there was pressure to complete the album. "The Shining" was the single, a song that appeared in subsequent Martin-era set lists. The title track was reminiscent of "Megalomania" from *Sabotage* and "Black Sabbath," particularly the alternation of soft and loud dynamics, slow tempo, and dark lyrics. The band played several concerts in South Africa, which caused a controversy because of the apartheid laws still in effect at the time. The European tour was very short, just 13 performances, and a U.S. tour never happened. Drummer Terry Chimes (of the Clash) and bassist Jo Burt performed with Iommi, Martin, and Nicholls for these dates.

No longer with Vertigo and Warner Bros. Records, Sabbath signed a contract with I.R.S. in 1988. They began work on *Headless Cross* (1989) with a lineup that included drummer Cozy Powell (born Colin Flooks, December 29, 1947, died April 5, 1998; of Rainbow and ELP), Laurence Cottle (born

December 16, 1961; bass), and a guest appearance by guitarist Brian May (of Queen). Unlike the sessions for *The Eternal Idol,* Martin was able to compose his own melodies for this album. Powell's straightforward rock drumming greatly differed from Ward's semi-improvisational style, which, paired with Martin's vocal style, helped give this album a 1980s power rock sound. Cottle was hired as a session musician, so Neil Murray (born Phillip Neil Murray, August 27, 1950) of Whitesnake played bass on the tour. I.R.S. did a poor job promoting and distributing the album, and thus, about 75 percent of the U.S. dates (about one-third of the entire tour) were cancelled.

The Iommi/Martin/Murray/Nicholls/Powell lineup recorded two albums, *Tyr* (1990) and *Forbidden* (1995). The former was stylistically and sonically similar to *Headless Cross,* but lyrically, it was quite different. "Satan," "Devil," or "Lucifer" was mentioned in almost every song on *Headless Cross,* and *Tyr* had song titles such as "The Battle Of Tyr," "Odin's Court," and "Valhalla." Powell's drumming on *Tyr* was just as, if not more, powerful than his work on *Headless Cross. Tyr,* like *Seventh Star,* contained a power ballad: "Feels Good to Me." On the suggestion of I.R.S., *Forbidden* was produced by Body Count guitarist Ernie C. It did not have the rap-rock sound one might expect, with the sole exception of "Illusion of Power," which had a spoken-word part performed by rapper Ice-T. *Forbidden* certainly had elements of earlier Sabbath, such as the "Megalomania"-like riff of "Can't Get Close Enough to You" and the "Zero the Hero"–like riff of "Get a Grip."

In 1991, Dio, Geezer, and Appice rejoined Sabbath, and the band wrote, recorded, and released *Dehumanizer* (1992). Dio and Geezer agreed to abandon the "dungeons and dragons and rainbow stuff" and write lyrics with more current themes. The music was much heavier than *Mob Rules*; the riffs for "After All (The Dead)" and "Buried Alive" were particularly dark. Geezer's and Appice's performances were especially aggressive and inventive: the introduction to "Master of Insanity," in an unusual 14/8 meter, is but one example. For the final two concerts of the

tour, Sabbath was the warm-up band for Ozzy Osbourne. Dio refused to be an opening act and to share the stage with Ozzy, so he quit the band. Rob Halford (of Judas Priest) filled in as lead vocalist for these dates. Ozzy and Ward performed with Sabbath on the final night of that tour, the first time the original lineup had played together since the 1985 Live Aid concert.

Dio and Appice returned in 2006, and the band recorded three new songs for a compilation titled *Black Sabbath: The Dio Years* (2007). To avoid confusion among audiences about the lineup, the band toured under the name Heaven and Hell. They released *Live from Radio City Music Hall* in 2007 and a studio album, *The Devil You Know*, in 2009. This marked the band's first studio album in 14 years—that is, of course, if one considered Heaven and Hell to be Black Sabbath. Taking into consideration that they released three songs as Black Sabbath in 2007, that the lineup was the same as it was on *Mob Rules* and *Dehumanizer*, and that the album's sound was distinctively Black Sabbath, *The Devil You Know* was Sabbath's 19th full-length studio release.

Between *Dehumanizer* and *Forbidden*, Sabbath released *Cross Purposes* (1994). Once Appice left with Dio for the second time, Martin returned, and Bobby Rondinelli (born Robert Rondinelli, July 27, 1955; drummer for Rainbow) joined the band for the album and tour. With Geezer back in the lineup and contributing to the songwriting, this album had elements of *Dehumanizer* and pre-1984 Sabbath. *Cross Purposes— Live*, recorded during the 1994 tour, was released in 1995 only a few months before *Forbidden*. Rondinelli left the band near the end of the tour and was temporarily replaced by Ward. Rondinelli rejoined the band, replacing Powell during the 1995 *Forbidden* tour.

"The OzzFest '97," was a tour which, of numerous hard rock and metal bands, included Black Sabbath with Ozzy, Iommi, Geezer, and drummer Mike Bordin (of Faith No More). Ward played two concerts with the band later that year, and they subsequently released a live album, *Reunion* (1998), with two new studio tracks: "Psycho Man" and "Selling My Soul." These were the first new songs recorded by this lineup since 1978. They toured in 1998, but Ward suffered a heart attack, and Appice filled in. All four original members (i.e., Ozzy, Geezer, Iommi, Ward) toured in 1999, 2001, 2004, and 2005. In 2001, they wrote songs for an album that never came to fruition, although "Scary Dreams" appeared in their touring set list that year. It was announced on November 11, 2011, that the original lineup would record their first full-length album since 1978. Ward announced on his website that due to an "unsignable" contract, he would not be taking part in the 2012 concert dates. In January 2012, it was announced that Iommi was diagnosed with cancer. On June 20, 2013, Black Sabbath released its 19th studio album titled *13*. Following the release, the band launched a successful tour. A 20th album has been planned and a final tour (called The End) is planned through 2016.

Of all the Sabbath alumni, Ozzy has had the most success as a solo artist: 10 successful studio albums over 30 years, numerous tours, and the hit TV show *The Osbournes*. Ozzy employed several Sabbath alumni in his band, including Geezer, Daisley, Airey, and Rick Wakeman and his son Adam Wakeman (Adam played on Sabbath's 2004 and 2005 tours). Dio had much success as a solo artist, but to a lesser extent though by no means less significant. In fact, he is considered to be one of the best metal singers to have ever lived. Iommi has released three solo albums, two of which featured Glenn Hughes. *Iommi* (2000) included appearances from Ozzy, Ward, Cottle, Brian May, Billy Corgan (of Smashing Pumpkins), Dave Grohl (of Nirvana and Foo Fighters), Matt Cameron (of Pearl Jam and Soundgarden), Phil Anselmo (of Pantera), and many others. Geezer has released three solo albums as g//z/r, later Geezer and GZR. The music was extremely heavy, often bordering on industrial metal and thrash metal. Ward released two solo albums; *Ward One: Along the Way* (1990) included guest appearances by Jack Bruce (of Cream), Zakk Wylde (of Ozzy), and three Sabbath alumni (Ozzy, Singer, and Copley).

Martin is the unsung hero of Sabbath, having recorded five studio albums and appeared on five tours with them, yet he has received little recognition. Martin has been part of several projects, including two solo

albums, the first of which included Brian May and Sabbath alumni Murray, Cottle, and Nicholls. Gillan's solo work came *before* his time with Sabbath, but he returned to Deep Purple immediately after the *Born Again* tour. After being fired from Sabbath, Hughes had a prolific recording career as a solo and guest artist, including the two aforementioned Iommi solo releases. After Gillen and Singer left Sabbath, they formed Badlands with guitarist Jake E. Lee (of Ozzy). Gillen died in 1993 from AIDS-related illnesses. Appice's career was primarily with Dio and Black Sabbath/Heaven and Hell, but he has been involved with several other projects.

Black Sabbath's influence on heavy metal music cannot be overstated. Any successful metal band of the last 30 years would cite them as an influence. There have been many Sabbath tribute albums, some of which included contributions from very significant artists. The two *Nativity in Black* albums (1994 and 2000) consisted entirely of Ozzy-era songs with performances by bands such as Biohazard, Faith No More, Godsmack, Megadeth, Pantera, Primus, Sepultura, Slayer, Soulfly, System of a Down, Type O Negative, Ugly Kid Joe, White Zombie, and included appearances by Ozzy, Ward, Geezer, Bruce Dickinson (Iron Maiden), Rob Halford (Judas Priest), Al Jourgensen (Ministry), and even Busta Rhymes. *Evil Lives* was a tribute album with Vince Neil (Mötley Crüe) singing "Paranoid," and *Tribute to Black Sabbath: Eternal Masters* included Cannibal Corpse's cover of "Zero the Hero." Numerous covers of Sabbath songs have been recorded or performed live by bands such as Anthrax, Metallica, Frank Zappa, Green Day, the Bad Plus, the Flaming Lips, and too many others to mention. Other artists (Beastie Boys, Eminem, Ice-T, Sir Mix-a-Lot, and Soundgarden, to list only a few) have sampled Sabbath in their own work or used Sabbath's songs with new lyrics.

Sabbath's music has made many appearances in popular culture. For instance, Beavis and Butthead (of the animated MTV show) chanted the guitar riffs to "Iron Man" and "Electric Funeral." In one episode, they watched the 1970 music video of "Iron Man," and Butthead humorously mistook the

21-year-old Ozzy as being "Ozzy's son" instead of the 40-year-old Ozzy with whom he was familiar.

Sabbath has sold over 75 million records worldwide, of which 16 million were sales in the United States certified by the RIAA. *Paranoid,* the band's best-selling release, went four times platinum (U.S.) in 1995, and by the time of this writing, it is likely that it has sold over five million copies in the United States alone. It is estimated that *Paranoid* has sold over 16 million copies worldwide. *Master of Reality* and their "greatest hits collection" *We Sold Our Soul for Rock 'n' Roll* (1976) went double platinum (U.S.) in 2001 and 2000, respectively. *Black Sabbath, Heaven and Hell, Reunion, Sabbath Bloody Sabbath,* and *Vol. 4* went platinum (U.S.), and *Mob Rules, Never Say Die!, Sabotage,* and *Technical Ecstasy* went gold (U.S.).

Aside from the negative criticism from the press in their earliest years, Black Sabbath has earned much respect and accolades from musicians, fans, and the press throughout their career. Sabbath won a Grammy in 2000 for their performance of "Iron Man" on *Reunion* and were inducted into the Rock and Roll Hall of Fame in 2006. During the induction speech, Lars Ulrich (of Metallica) summed up Sabbath's place in rock history: "Black Sabbath is, and always will be, synonymous with the term 'heavy metal.'"

Nolan Stolz

Selected Discography

Black Sabbath, Vertigo (UK), VO 6 and Warner Bros. Records (US) WS 1871, 1970.

Masters of Reality, Warner Bros. Records BS 2562, 1971.

Paranoid, Warner Bros. Records WS 1887, 1971.

Black Sabbath Vol. 4, Warner Bros. Records BS 2602, 1972.

Sabbath Bloody Sabbath, Warner Bros. Records BS 2695, 1974.

Sabotage, Warner Bros. Records BS 2822, 1975.

Technical Ecstasy, Warner Bros. Records BS 2969, 1976.

Never Say Die!, Warner Bros. Records BSK 3186, 1978.

Heaven and Hell, Warner Bros. Records BSK 3372, 1980.

Mob Rules, Warner Bros. Records BSK 3605, 1981.

Born Again, Warner Bros. Records 1–23978, 1983.

Seventh Star, Warner Bros. Records 1–25337, 1986.

The Eternal Idol, Warner Bros. Records 9 25548–1, 1987.

Headless Cross, I.R.S. IRS-82002, 1989.

Tyr, I.R.S. X2 13049, 1990.

Dehumanizer, Reprise Records 9 26965–2, 1992.

Cross Purposes, I.R.S. 07777 13222 2 8, 1994.

Forbidden, I.R.S. 72438 30620 27, 1995.

Reunion, Epic E2K-69115, 1998.

The Dio Years, Rhino R2 116668, 2007.

The Devil You Know (as Heaven and Hell), Rhino R2 518862, 2009.

References

Cope, Andrew L. *Black Sabbath and the Rise of Heavy Metal Music.* Burlington, VT: Ashgate 2010.

Iommi, Tony, and T.J. Lammers. *Iron Man: My Journey through Heaven and Hell with Black Sabbath.* Cambridge, MA: Da Capo Press, 2011.

McIver, Joel. *Sabbath Bloody Sabbath.* London: Omnibus Press, 2006.

Mortimer, Sarah. "Sabbath Bloody Sabbath," episode 2 of *Rock Family Trees* Series 2. TV Series. Directed by Sarah Mortimer. London: BBC, 1998.

Osbourne, Ozzy, and Chris Ayres. *I Am Ozzy.* New York: Grand Central Publishing, 2010.

Wilkinson, Paul. *Rat Salad: Black Sabbath, the Classic Years, 1969–1975.* New York: Thomas Dunne Books/ St. Martin's Press, 2007.

Blind Faith (1969)

The term "supergroup" was invented to describe Blind Faith, the short-lived collaboration between Eric Clapton (born Eric Patrick Clapton, March 30, 1945; guitar/vocals) and Steve Winwood, two of the most respected musicians in Britain. The band, which included Ginger Baker on drums and Ric Grech on bass, was one of the most successful of the late 1960s, though they were only together seven months. Ultimately a victim of unrealistic expectations and the expansion of concert business in the late 1960s, Blind Faith's brief tenure yielded an album that has endured as one of most beloved of the period,

The first true rock and roll "supergroup." Blind Faith rose from the ashes of Cream, Traffic, Family, and the Spencer Davis Group. Here the group poses for a portrait in 1969. From left to right: Steve Winwood, Ric Grech, Ginger Baker, and Eric Clapton. (Photo by Michael Ochs Archives/Getty Images)

and remains a standout in both the Winwood and Clapton catalogs.

By 1964 Eric Clapton was already considered the finest young blues-influenced guitarist in Britain. As his devotion to the genre grew, he became more estranged from his band, the Yardbirds, whose other members aspired to popular success. After the band scored a hit single with the pop tune "For Your Love," Clapton quit. A few weeks later, after reading an interview in which the young guitarist claimed that "for me to face myself I have to play what I believe is pure and sincere and uncorrupted music" (Sanford 1999, 48), John Mayall invited Clapton to join the Bluesbreakers, which was considered the most serious of all British blues bands.

In the spring of 1966, they recorded several singles for the Immediate and Purdah labels, produced by studio guitarist Jimmy Page (who would, a month later, join the Yardbirds). One track, "Telephone Blues," contained the first truly significant blues rock guitar solo. It also hinted at a new British take on the blues, one that would reach a more articulate fulfillment on

Blues Breakers: John Mayall with Eric Clapton. The album—widely considered the seminal testament of blues rock—proved to have an enormous impact on the British blues scene, as it was the first music by a native group to truly explore the modern blues idiom: fluid solos and fills using string bending, distortion, clipped phrases, and fills.

Clapton's extended solos on Johnny Otis's "Double Crossing Time" and Freddie King's "Hideaway" may have been familiar to blues aficionados, many of whom commented on his facility within the idiom, but to the uninitiated they were unprecedented. Even the sound of his guitar was revolutionary. Clapton was the first British player to adopt the heavy Gibson Les Paul with humbucker pickups, the preferred model of Freddie King and Howlin' Wolf's guitarist, Hubert Sumlin. When run through a reverb-inducing Marshall, the Les Paul created a loud, aggressive sound with a substantial bottom end. Attempting to replicate the sound achieved by modern Chicago blues players, Clapton insisted on turning his amplifier up all the way to create maximum distortion and sustain and allowing the sound to bleed into the microphones. The resulting color and presence led virtually all other blues-influenced guitarists in the country to adopt a similar setup.

Clapton soon became known for his extended guitar solos, which at the time were a novelty in rock and roll. His playing was regarded as so amazing that graffiti proclaiming "Clapton is God" began appearing on walls around London. However, Clapton soon grew dissatisfied with the Bluesbreakers; he felt that Mayall's arrangements were too structured and the rest of the band was not at his level. He was thus amenable when Ginger Baker (born Peter Edward Baker, August 19, 1939; drums), the drummer for the Graham Bond Organization, approached him with a proposition.

Baker, like many of his colleagues in the R&B scene, came from a jazz background. He fell hard for the music of Dizzy Gillespie and played trumpet in the Air Training Corps band, though he had always been interested in drumming. He recalled, "I used to get the kids at school dancing by banging rhythms on the school desk! They kept on at me to sit in with this band. The band wasn't very keen, but in the end I sat in and played the bollocks off their drummer . . . I heard one of the band turn round and say: 'Christ, we've got a drummer' and I thought, 'Hello, this is something I can do'" (jackbruce.com).

Within a year he dropped out of school and took a job as the drummer of the Storyville Jazz Men; the members turned him on to the percussionists Baby Dodds, Buddy Rich, and Max Roach, who became his primary inspiration. Roach was the first to shift timekeeping from the snare drum to the bass drum and ride cymbals, a flexible style that left space for a drummer to add fills, play irregular accents, and create polyrhythmic lines within the kit.

Baker left the Storyville Jazz Men in 1958, but his unorthodox style made finding steady work difficult; he took on freelance tour dates and played with a number of jazz groups, many including Dick Heckstall-Smith (born Richard Malden Heckstall-Smith, September 16, 1934, died December 17, 2004; tenor saxophone). When the saxophonist was invited to sit in with Blues Incorporated he brought Baker along, and the drummer was asked to replace Charlie Watts when he left in late 1962 to join the Rolling Stones. In this new forum Baker's drumming style quickly got noticed, and he became an influence on Keith Moon, Mitch Mitchell, and other British R&B drummers.

Baker, Bruce, Heckstall-Smith, and Graham Bond (born Graham John Clifton Bond, October 28, 1937, died May 8, 1974; alto saxophone/organ), who also played with Blues Incorporated, formed an organ trio in January 1963. They started playing the intervals of Blues Incorporated gigs then split off to form the Graham Bond Organization. The group toured throughout the country and even backed a number of visiting American blues and soul singers. They recorded a handful of singles and even two albums, *The Sound of '65* and *There's a Bond Between Us*, but they never found mainstream chart success.

Baker remained with Graham Bond through the first part of 1966. Dissatisfied with his situation, he proposed the idea of forming a band to Eric Clapton, who agreed, but on the condition that Jack

Bruce play bass. Despite the significant personal animosity between Baker and Bruce, an agreement was reached and Cream was born.

The band was originally conceived of as a blues trio informed by the modern Chicago blues of Buddy Guy and Jimi Hendrix, who was familiar with the cutting-edge experimentation of Earl Hooker and Robert Nighthawk. Jack Bruce recalled "sitting in a London coffee bar with Eric Clapton, when we first formed Cream, and telling him, 'I want us to take the language of the blues and develop it a step further'" (Jisi). In an interview with Chris Welch the trio discussed their potential approach. Clapton directly addressed the potential problems of an all-star trio: "Most people have formed the impression of us as three solo musicians clashing with each other. We want to cancel that idea and be a group that plays together."

After the band's debut at the National Jazz and Blues Festival in Windsor, where a lack of sufficient material necessitated the extension of every song in their still rather short set list, Cream focused on jazz-like extended improvisation, employing the riff-based blues as a flexible structure that could accommodate a fusion of stylistic elements.

The band also prioritized instrumental virtuosity: Clapton contributed long, liquid blues-based solos colored by wah-wah pedal, feedback, and distortion; Bruce added incredibly active bass lines, often in counterpoint to Clapton's guitar. While common in American soul music, such lines were rare in British rock, and the innovation made Bruce the most prominent bassist of his day. When added to Baker's polyrhythmic jazz drumming style, the results were explosive. Cream was at its best live, sometimes working through 10-, 15-, and even 20-minute improvisatory explorations of each song's possibilities.

It was widely expected that the band would immediately rush into the studio and record an album, but instead, Cream played live dates for nine months, in small clubs, large theaters, and festivals before their first album, *Fresh Cream,* was released. The tracks were an almost equal mixture of originals and blues arrangements, drawn from their live set list. In some ways, their approach was typical of British blues rock

bands, but there were significant differences. There was extensive interplay among the musicians, rather than a rigid adherence to the prescribed instrumental roles in Chicago blues. This was facilitated by Ginger Baker's drumming style, which allowed Clapton and Bruce to either play in unison or counterpoint, and his fills articulated the secondary rhythm that was ordinarily covered by bass or rhythm guitar, allowing all three musicians to participate in a dynamic conversation.

The band also liberally applied aspects of psychedelic rock to their blues covers. While this was not unprecedented in contemporary blues, it was nonetheless unfamiliar to most British rock fans at the time. This new hybrid of Chicago blues, British pop, and psychedelic rock would eventually be dubbed hard rock.

Cream made a quick tour of the United States in March 1967, but the band established its international reputation on their return trip in May. Their five-night tenure at the Fillmore West in San Francisco established Clapton's reputation as one of the best guitarists in rock and lifted Cream into the realm of rock superstardom.

The group's second album, *Disraeli Gears* (1967), was more overtly psychedelic than its predecessor. This was partly a reflection of the times—*Sgt. Pepper's Lonely Hearts Club Band* was released that June—but the style was also an ideal vehicle for Clapton's surrealistic interests and Pete Brown's latter-day beat poetry. The album opened with two of Cream's most enduring tracks: "Strange Brew" and "Sunshine of Your Love." The latter was anchored by a bottom-heavy guitar and bass riff wedded to a standard blues progression, a technique inspired by models like Howlin' Wolf's "Spoonful," and extensively adopted by hard rock and heavy metal bands in the late 1960s and early 1970s.

Cream launched a new tour of the United States in February 1968. The group was in such demand that they commanded an unprecedented $20,000 guarantee from venues plus a share of the gate, and tickets sold out so quickly that the tour was extended by a month so that new dates could be added.

Before the tour, the band returned to the Atlantic studios in New York to record tracks for *Wheels of Fire,* Cream's most experimental album. Classical and folk influences were evident, and the band experimented with tempo changes, complex chord progressions, and mixed meters, as well as studio and post production. In order to capture the energy and virtuosity of Cream onstage, *Wheels of Fire* was expanded into a two-disc set: one recorded in the studio and another of the band in concert. Critics praised the album, which firmly established that Cream was more than just a blues band and had the potential to explore myriad stylistic directions. It was a commercial success as well; the album hit number one on both sides of the Atlantic and was the first double album to be awarded platinum status.

However, just after *Wheels of Fire* was released in Britain, and prior to its American debut, Baker, Bruce, and Clapton announced that Cream was splitting up, ostensibly because the members were moving in too many different directions artistically. The guitarist told interviewers that what he really wanted to do was "good, funky songs" like those on the Band's debut album, *Music from the Big Pink.* He soon discovered that Steve Winwood (born Stephen Lawrence Winwood, May 12, 1948; vocals, keyboards), who had recently left the band Traffic, was interested in a potential collaboration. The pair met when he and Clapton recorded together in a pickup group arranged by producer Joe Boyd and Manfred Mann vocalist Paul Jones (born Paul Pond, February 24, 1942; vocals, harmonica) in 1966.

Winwood was the infant prodigy of the British R&B scene. He took up drums, piano, and guitar at a young age, first performing with his father and older brother Muff (born Mervyn Winwood, August 15, 1943; bass) in the Ron Atkinson Band at the age of eight. In 1959, the brothers formed their own group, Johnny Star and the Planets, with 11-year-old Steve singing and playing lead guitar. In 1963, they reorganized as the Muff Woody jazz band and started playing gigs on weekends.

When the British R&B craze swept through Birmingham, the Muff Woody band started adding blues numbers to their set lists, and shortly thereafter they met guitarist Spencer Davis (born Spencer Davis Nelson Davies, July 17, 1939; guitar, harmonica). Discovering they had common interests, they agreed to join forces with Davis and drummer Pete York (born August 15, 1942; drums) to form the Rhythm and Blues Quartette.

The group quickly gained a reputation as one of the best R&B bands in the area. London-based promoter and impresario Chris Blackwell, who ran the small independent label Island Records, saw the group in Birmingham and was suitably impressed; he offered them a contract and signed on as their manager and producer. At this time they changed their name to the Spencer Davis Group.

Blackwell hustled his new band into the studio, where they recorded a cover version of John Lee Hooker's "Dimples." The single sold well in the British Midlands, and their follow-up, "I Can't Stand It," scraped into the bottom of the top 40. By this point it was already clear that the star of the quartet was Steve Winwood, whose soulful, nuanced vocals drew immediate comparisons to Ray Charles. After several more R&B covers, the Spencer Davis Group hit with "Keep on Runnin'," which went to number one on the British pop charts, as did the follow-up, "Somebody Help Me."

Blackwell, tired of paying royalties, encouraged the band to start writing its own material. Though they still relied heavily on covers, Winwood emerged as the band's most able lyricist and composer. His first attempt was "Gimme Some Lovin'," which featured his new Hammond B-3 organ, one of the first in England. The novel sound of the instrument and Winwood's virtuosic vocals propelled the track to number two on the American charts. Winwood's vocal abilities, in combination with his accomplished keyboard skills and writing talents, led Al Kooper to dub him "Superfreak," as it seemed inhuman to him for so much musical ability to have surfaced in one young Englishman.

By this time Winwood had begun to chafe at the limits of the Spencer Davis Group. Looking to expand into more experimental territory, he began playing after-hours jam sessions at the Elbow Room Club in Birmingham, and early in 1967 he announced that he and his brother were leaving the group. Steve united with Jim Capaldi (born Nicola James Capaldi, August 2, 1944, died January 28, 2005; drums, vocals), Dave Mason (born David Thomas Mason, May 10, 1946; guitar), and multi-instrumentalist Chris Wood (born Christopher Gordon Blandford Wood, June 24, 1944, died July 12, 1983; tenor saxophone, flute, keyboards), veterans of the Birmingham R&B scene, to form Traffic.

Capaldi, Winwood, Mason, and Wood had common roots in the Midlands music scene, but rather than pick up from their blues- and soul-based jams at the Elbow Room, they decamped to Winwood's rural cottage for six months to talk through their ideas about music, listen to as many styles of music as possible, and begin building a repertoire.

Traffic's first album, *Mr. Fantasy*—issued in the United States as *Heaven Is in Your Mind*—bore the stamp of Indian music, a potent force in British popular music at the time, and contained songs influenced by English folk, psychedelic pop, soul, jazz, and comic dance-hall numbers including improvisational flights of fancy. The influence of the Beatles' recent albums, particularly *Sgt. Pepper's Lonely Hearts Club Band,* was evident, though the band's sound was in no way derivative. *Mr. Fantasy* was a hit in England, but the disc did not do well overseas.

Even before the album was released, Dave Mason, who was uncomfortable with the group's collaborative approach to songwriting, resigned. Traffic decided to continue as a trio, which suited the band's collaborative approach, which was based on improvisation and extended soloing.

While Traffic was on tour in the United States they began working on their second album at the Record Plant in New York. By chance, they ran into Dave Mason, who was visiting his friend Gram Parsons. They persuaded their former colleague to rejoin the band; as Mason recalls, the band was struggling to come up with enough material for the album and needed his songwriting ability. He ended up contributing five numbers to the 10-track album, including "Feelin' All Right," later a top-40 hit for Joe Cocker.

Traffic (1968), like *Mr. Fantasy,* demonstrated the band's wide variety of influences. Mason's five tracks reflect his interest in country rock; even "Feelin' All Right" in its original format sounds like hillbilly soul. Winwood and Capaldi's songs were keyboard based, looser in structure, and heavily influenced by soul, folk, and jazz. The psychedelic rock and Indian influences of their first album were greatly diminished, and there was far less postproduction, a philosophical decision of the group to capture a more organic interplay between the band's members. Many of the numbers were difficult to classify stylistically without using the term "progressive," a fusion of expanded song structures, jazz-based improvisation with prominent roles for winds, and complex chord changes, a style that would mark much of the band's later work.

In February 1969, much to the surprise of the other members of Traffic, Steve Winwood tendered his own resignation, feeling that he needed to explore different musical avenues with a variety of musicians.

Clapton visited Winwood at his remote cabin; the pair played guitar, listened to records, and discovered a musical rapport that presaged a musical partnership. Both started writing material and discussed forming a band. They were still debating potential collaborators when Ginger Baker heard about the collaboration and dropped by to jam.

The press quickly caught wind of the project, and even before the rumors were confirmed, the as-yet unnamed band was deluged with offers, with booking agents offering immense guarantees against the gate, amid widespread speculation that this would be the best rock band ever. At that point Clapton began referring to the outfit as Blind Faith, and the name stuck. Cream's former manager, Robert Stigwood, who saw the new band (which he dubbed a supergroup) as a substitute for the departed trio, encouraged them to record and tour, and committed them to make their debut at Hyde Park on June 7, 1969.

To do so, Blind Faith needed a bassist. Clapton reached out to Ric Grech (born Richard Roman Grech, November 1, 1946, died March 27, 1990; bass), the bassist for the Family, who had jammed with the Bluesbreakers during Clapton's tenure. Grech started out playing violin in the school orchestra and even performed with the Leicester Youth Orchestra in his teens. He later started to experiment with the guitar, joined a local band (the Berkeley Squares) and took up the bass. In 1965, he joined the Farinas, a British R&B band. The band briefly changed its name to the Roaring Sixties and in 1967 became the Family. The group recorded a single that performed well enough to secure a contract with Reprise Records.

Their 1968 debut album, *Music in a Doll's House,* was an amalgam of blues rock, folk, jazz, and classical music with vestigial traits of acid rock–droning, fuzztone guitars, and electronic effects mixed with strings, horns, and acoustic guitar, often cloaked in a wash of echo and phased vocals. The album failed to capture the popular imagination, but the Family developed a devoted underground following.

Grech was interested in the project but was faced with a conundrum; he was committed to an impending tour of the United States with the Family. He agreed to stay with the band until a replacement could be found, but at their first American performance at the Fillmore East Grech seemed disoriented and played poorly. There was no way to know if this was musical sabotage on Grech's part, but he was immediately given leave to return to England. The release of Blind Faith's first—and, as it turned out, only—album, was held so that Grech could cover the bass parts.

Even though the album was complete, the band had not had much time to cohere as a group or find their own direction and sound before their debut concert in Hyde Park, in front of an audience of between 100,000 and 150,000. The crowd was delighted but the band was panned by reviewers, who felt that their material was weak and that they did not play particularly well. Clapton was stung by the criticism—by some reports, he was ready to abandon Blind Faith immediately, but Stigwood convinced the band that they should embark on a tour of the United States after a short warm-up run through Scandinavia.

Their eponymous album was released in Britain in late July and in the United States in August. The disc was released by Polydor in England and Atlantic in the United States, as were Cream's two final albums, but it was produced by Jimmy Miller, who had worked with

Traffic; his participation was "by arrangement with Robert Stigwood and Chris Blackwell" (Blind Faith, 1969). Controversy immediately arose over the cover, a photograph of a naked, prepubescent girl holding a toy spaceship that many perceived as phallic. Some stores in America refused to stock the album and a new cover, a sepia-toned photograph of the band, was rushed into production. The controversy did nothing to hamper sales; the album sold a million copies on preorders alone and raced to number one in both Britain and the United States. Surprisingly, it also reached number 40 on the American R&B charts, an unusually strong showing for a British band. However, given the high expectations for the group, critics generally found the album disappointing. None panned the disc, which even most negative reviewers admitted was pleasing and contained some beautiful songs, but they found nothing particularly original or spectacular; surely, they mused, Clapton and Winwood could have done better.

In fact, the album captured some of the best aspects of both Traffic and Cream: extended, jazz-based exploration of thematic material, virtuosic solo work, dynamic interplay between all members of the group, facilitated by Baker's bop-influenced drum work, polyphonic and polymetric lines, and tight, Everly Brothers–style vocal harmonies. Despite the variety of the songs, there was a certain timbral uniformity to the work, and the absence of overdubbing and psychedelic tropes made the work seem less experimental than the previous albums of either group.

The album was dominated by Winwood, who wrote the majority of the tracks, sang lead and played standout guitar, keyboards, and bass. Clapton took on a much reduced role, but his stated intent to be just one of the group was already impossible, given his prodigious abilities and unique, coloristic style. That the songs sound like neither group—though it is closer in sound to Traffic's previous outing than to Cream's oeuvre—was a testament to the collaborative ability of the personalities involved.

Blind Faith contains only six tracks, though both the opening number, "Had to Cry Today," and the closer, "Do What You Like," were expansive tracks. The former, a blues-based soul tune, featured extended interludes between the verses, including a virtuoso guitar duet by Winwood and Clapton, whose delicate polyphonic interplay was a high point of the album. "Do What You Like," written by Ginger Baker, was intended as a receptacle for extended solos by each of the band's members. While Clapton normally decried this sort of number as indulgent, Baker's solo was truly thrilling and stood as a fine testament to his abilities as a drummer. "Well, All Right," a cover of a Buddy Holly song, was often dismissed as a throwaway number, but Winwood played some exceptionally fine piano, and the arrangement successfully updated the original. As he did with "Crossroads," Clapton molded a single figure from the accompaniment into a propulsive riff that drove the song, and the delivery reframed Holly's intimate love song as an expansive declaration of the generational ethos of peace and love.

Clapton's contribution as a songwriter, "Presence of the Lord," has proved an enduring standout from the album, an unorthodox gospel tune whose verses frame a muscular wah-wah guitar solo that is still regarded as one of the guitar god's most captivating moments on record. "Can't Find My Way Home" was an acoustic piece that spotlighted Winwood's blue-eyed soul vocals, its captivating melody supported by surprisingly delicate fingerpicking by a very restrained Eric Clapton. "Sea of Joy," the most Traffic-esque piece on the album, was an atmospheric number that has remained in the Winwood repertoire for decades. However, the most notable element was the expansive violin solo contributed by Ric Grech.

The following tour of the United States was dominated by concerts of enormous scale, as Stigwood was determined—perhaps justifiably so—to capitalize on the new supergroup before something went awry. Cream played to large and enthusiastic crowds of adoring fans that, on more than one occasion, turned violent. Their American debut at Madison Square Garden ended in a 45-minute-long riot in which Winwood's keyboard was destroyed. The problems that had plagued the Hyde Park gig persisted; the eight-day tour of Scandinavia had not made any significant difference in the band's ability to play together. The

crowds, however, were still adulatory; Winwood famously speculated they could have gone on stage and farted and gotten a similar response.

Ultimately, the inability of the band to cohere live—which might have been avoided if they had more time to rehearse before embarking on a major tour—created friction between the members of the group, who were also unhappy playing stadium shows. Winwood, in particular, felt control of the band had been superseded by managers and financial interests. All were disappointed in their performances, and Blind Faith drifted apart. While Stigwood arranged rehearsals for a new album, rumors of a breakup began to circulate, which Eric Clapton confirmed in September. Grech, Winwood, and Baker went on to form a new supergroup, Ginger Baker's Air Force, with Denny Laine from the Moody Blues and Chris Wood from Traffic. Clapton, after a brief tour with Delaney and Bonnie and Friends, recorded his first solo album.

Although it did not endure for long and its influence on rock was not as profound as that of Cream and Traffic, the two groups from which it arose, Blind Faith created a template for one-off collaborations between rock musicians, exemplified by Derek and the Dominoes, the Traveling Wilburys, Oysterhead, the Firm, and Them Crooked Vultures. The potential popularity of a supergroup of such magnitude also initiated the era of arena rock, where huge stadium shows came to replace more frequent club dates as a touring model.

Roberta Freund Schwartz

Selected Discography
Blind Faith, Polydor 583 059 US ATCO 33 304, 1969.

References

Baker, Ginger, and Ginette Baker. *Hellraiser, The Autobiography of the World's Greatest Drummer*. London: John Blake, 2009.

Cott Jonathan. "Traffic–Interview." *Rolling Stone* 32 (May 3, 1969), 16–20.

Dalton, David. "Traffic: Who Knows What Tomorrow May Bring." *Rolling Stone* 32 (May 3, 1969), 14–15.

Kooper, Al. "TrafficTrafficTraffic." *Rolling Stone* 9 (April 27, 1968): 12.

Mayall, John. Liner notes to *As It All Began: The Best of John Mayall and the Bluesbreakers 1964–69* [Decca D121768], 1997.

McStravick, Summer, and John Roos. *Blues-Rock Explosion*. Mission Viejo, CA: Old Goat Publishing, 2001.

Ruhlmann, William. "Traffic." *All Music Guide*. Rovi Corporation, 2012.

Sanford, Christopher. *Clapton: Edge of Darkness*. Updated ed. NY: Da Capo, 1999.

Schumacher, Michael. *Crossroads: The Life and Music of Eric Clapton*. NY: Hyperion, 1995.

Schwartz, Roberta Freund. *How Britain Got the Blues: The Transmission and Reception of American Blues Style in the British Isles*. Burlington, VT: Ashgate, 2007.

Steve Winwood Official Website. 2015. "Steve Winwood Biography." Accessed July 2013. www.stevewinwood.com/biography.

Bob Marley and the Wailers (1962–1981)

Bob Marley and the Wailers were the seminal reggae band. They are known throughout the world and are generally credited as the creators of what would be known as roots reggae—the most active Jamaican popular music style of the 1970s and early 1980s. Marley himself is widely regarded as the first Third World superstar, and together with his bandmates, he blazed a musical trail that is still pertinent and influential in the new millennium.

Bob Marley (born Robert Nesta Marley, February 6, 1945, died May 11, 1981; lead vocals, guitar) was born in the rural Jamaican parish of St. Ann. Bob's mother was a 19-year-old Jamaican named Cedella Malcolm, and his father was a white Jamaican, "born in the parish of Clarendon, enlisted in the British army," named Captain Norval Sinclair Marley (Stephens 1998, 254). Their child was named Robert after Captain Marley's brother and was given the name Nesta by his father, but without any explanation as to its origin. Bob began life on his maternal grandfather's farm.

Bob's musical development began in the West Kingston ghetto that became known as Trenchtown. Living on Second Street in Trenchtown, Bob began to make musical connections that affected the rest

of his life. Another family that shared Bob's tenement yard was the Livingstons. One of their children, Bunny (born Neville O'Riley Livingston, April 23, 1947; vocals, percussion) quickly became Bob's closest friend. Together the boys handcrafted makeshift musical instruments out of anything they could find. They fashioned a guitar out of copper wire, a sardine can, and a piece of bamboo and began to sing together. In 1960, Bob and Bunny took the first step toward what would become their singing group, the Wailers.

Trenchtown, although a ghetto, provided Bob with his much-needed teacher in the form of Joe Higgs. Higgs had been part of the "pre-ska singing duo Higgs and Wilson, whose first record—'Manny O'—was produced by the fledgling Kingston recording mogul Edward Seaga in 1960 . . . Joe Higgs resided on Third Street, around the corner from Bob and Bunny's

Bob Marley and the Wailers in Jamaica in 1972. From left to right: Earl Lindo, Bob Marley, Carlton Barrett, Peter Tosh, and Aston "Family Man" Barrett. Together this group forged the classic roots reggae sound, which remains popular decades later. (Photo by Michael Ochs Archives/Getty Image)

Second Street yard" (Davis 1990, 31). Higgs's yard was always filled with aspiring vocalists interested in learning the art of singing. Possessing perfect pitch and an acute sense of close vocal harmony, Higgs not only taught interested parties his secrets but also did so without thought of payment. Although love songs were most popular in Jamaica at this time, Higgs preferred to write on the taboo subjects of Rastafarianism and smoking ganja (marijuana). With Higgs, Bob and Bunny were not just taught close harmony but also were influenced by the lyrics of his new songs. Further, in Higgs's tenement yard classroom, Bob and Bunny met a tall, slightly older ghetto youth who would become the third member of their trio. Peter Tosh (born Winston Hubert McIntosh, October 19, 1944, died September 11, 1987; vocals, guitar) in Grange Hill, Westmoreland, possessed the only other factory-made guitar in the yard besides Higgs's.

With the Bob, Bunny, and Peter union established, the three formed a vocal group called the Teenagers, which also included two female singers (Beverly Kelso and Cherry Smith) and another ghetto youth named Junior Braithwaite. Livingston sang high harmony in a natural falsetto, Marley sang tenor, and Tosh provided the harmonic base with his low baritone voice. The group sang covers of songs by Sam Cooke, Ray Charles, Jerry Butler, and the Impressions.

By 1961, Marley had begun writing his own songs and was looking for a recording studio. He approached the Chinese entrepreneur Leslie Kong (died 1971), who owned a recording studio called Beverley's, and was promptly turned away. The Jamaican recording industry had only started in the 1950s, but already there were several studios. Ken Khouri (Pioneer Record Company), Duke Reid (Treasure Island Studios), and Clement Dodd (Studio One) also had fledgling studios but were quick to discourage anyone who did not fit the mold of the new ska singers.

After being turned away at Beverley's, Marley went back to work in the welding shop. His coworker at the welding shop, Desmond Dekker, had auditioned for Leslie Kong and was then able to record his song "Honor Your Mother and Father," which went on to become a hit on the island. Dekker took Marley back to Beverley's in early 1962 to meet Kong's latest

sensation: a 14-year-old singer named Jimmy Cliff (born James Chambers, April 1, 1948; vocals). Once Cliff heard Marley sing, he immediately took him in and introduced him to Leslie Kong.

Marley sang a couple of ska-inflected spirituals and then his own song "Judge Not," all without accompaniment. Kong liked what he heard, and within a few days Marley had recorded "Judge Not" on the Beverley's label, in addition to two other ska songs, "Terror" and "One Cup of Coffee." A month later Bob Marley's first record, a 45-rpm single of "Judge Not," was released in Jamaica on the Beverley's label. Unfortunately, because he was unknown, Marley received no radio airplay and few record sales. Kong then released "One Cup of Coffee" and "Terror" as singles, with the same result. Marley had his first records at age 16, but his proceeds from his first big break only totaled 20 pounds sterling.

In the West Kingston ghetto one's friends were extremely important for safety, shared food, and frequently for social and business connections. Marley's close friends included those in the group in addition to Vincent Ford, a ghetto youth named Georgie, and Alvin Patterson (born Francisco Willie, December 20, 1930; percussion). Patterson, also known as Willie, Pep, Franseeco, or Seeco, and a Rastafarian hand drummer in the Afro-Jamaican *burru* tradition, coached Marley's group on the intricacies of rhythm. Further, Patterson had connections in the Jamaican record industry, one of which was Clement "Sir Coxsone" Dodd. Dodd owned Sir Coxsone's Downbeat sound system and was preparing to open his own recording facility. In August of 1963, Patterson took Marley's group to Dodd's new studio on Brendtford Road and got them an audition.

Dodd knew the Jamaican music business and had saved enough money by the early 1960s to open his own studio. In early 1963, Dodd's new studio opened on the north edge of Trenchtown at 13 Brentford Road. Called the Jamaican Recording and Publishing Company Limited, but better known as Studio One, Dodd's new studio was primitive, with only one-track recording capability. Regardless of its lack of refinement, Studio One "quickly became the creative center of the Jamaican recording business as well as the laboratory where Jamaican ska, rock steady, and reggae music were researched and developed" (Davis 1990, 41).

Patterson had built Marley's band up to Dodd, and he was aware of, if unimpressed by, Marley's singles released by Kong. At the audition, Marley's band (which alternately went by the names the Teenagers or the Wailing Rudeboys, although Dodd recalled their using the name the Juveniles) played one original song of Bob's and three covers of songs by the Impressions. After this performance, Dodd told the group to return to Studio One on Thursday to record the song. For the Studio One recordings, the band needed to decide on a name, and they settled on "the Wailers, in part because of all the people they had read about in the Bible (particularly in Jeremiah 9) who were 'wailing for their freedom'" (Steffens 1998, 255).

Released on Dodd's Downbeat label in the final weeks of 1963, "Simmer Down" came out in time for the Christmas market rush. By January, the song had reached number one on the Jamaican Broadcasting Company charts and held that spot for the next two months. Without consultation, Dodd had released the single with the name of the group changed to the Wailing Wailers. But regardless of the group's name, they were immediate stars.

In the wake of the success of "Simmer Down," the Wailing Wailers began to record regularly at Studio One. Dodd even invited Marley to stay in a small shed in the back of the studio, knowing that the aspiring young singer was living in squalor. In 1964 and 1965, two more hits quickly followed "Simmer Down" but were much different in character. "It Hurts to Be Alone" was "a slow, plaintive ballad with a brilliant, penetrating lead vocals sung by Junior Braithwaite, who sounded almost exactly like Anthony Gourdine (of Little Anthony and the Imperials)" (Davis 1990, 45). "Lonesome Feeling," written by Marley and Livingston, was composed as a follow-up to "It Hurts to Be Alone" and again dealt with the emotions of loneliness and despair.

"Despite recording over one hundred songs for Coxsone, and having five of the top ten songs on the Jamaican charts at the same time, the Wailers were not seeing any financial rewards for their efforts" (Steffens

1998, 255). Dodd had brokered a deal to send dozens of Wailers hits to England for rerelease. Even with their successes, the Wailers remained poor and uncompensated for their music. When "Bend Down Low" became a hit and Dodd again refused to pay the band its proper share, the Wailers broke their contract.

With their contract with Dodd terminated, the Wailers started their own record label, Wailin' Soul Records (which also appears on some singles as Wail'n Soul'm or Wail'n'Soul). Bob said of this experience, "I thought I wasn't going to work for anyone again, so we split Coxsone to form Wail'n'Soul. But I don't know anything about business and I got caught again. 'Bend Down Low' was number one in Jamaica but they were pressing and selling it in a black market type of business" (McCann 1994, 13). Early releases from the new label included "Selassie Is the Chapel," in which Bob asserted his Rastafarian faith, and "This Man Is Back," which announced Bob's return from America. Sonny Til and the Orioles set "Selassie Is the Chapel" to the tune of "Crying in the Chapel," and it was Bob's first song dealing with Rastafarianism.

In the studio, the Wailers employed the producer Clancy Eccles, and at first their new label seemed to be a success. The early releases included the 45-rpm single "Nice Time," with "Hypocrite" on the B-side, and an early version of Bob and Rita's (Alpharita Constantia Marley nee Anderson, born July 25, 1946) love song, "Stir It Up." Unfortunately, the Wailers did not have the business experience or connections to last in the Jamaican recording industry. The existing labels conspired against them, and their products lacked radio play to boost sales, promotions, and distribution. The label folded at the end of 1967 when they were informed that the stamping machine that actually made the records had broken and production halted.

The closing of Wailin' Soul Records foreshadowed the difficulties that the Wailers had in 1968. Tosh was arrested for taking part in a street demonstration against the white-supremacist government that had been founded in Rhodesia, Africa, and Marley and Livingston were both jailed for ganja possession. Marley served a month long sentence, during which he contemplated his captivity and further identified himself with the captive sufferers in the Bible and in slavery. Livingston had been caught with a large enough quantity of ganja that he was jailed for a year in the General Penitentiary. Later in his sentence he was moved to a work camp called Richmond Farm. These events effectively stopped any progress that the Wailers had been making musically. Marley spent the year that Livingston was incarcerated playing soccer and "listening intently to the Jimi Hendrix Experience and the new funk modes of Sly and the Family Stone [whom the Wailers would eventually tour with] and working on songs" (Davis 1990, 72). Although Marley was struggling in 1968, he was overjoyed when Rita gave birth to his first son that year. David Marley, the newest member of the ever-growing Marley family, was nicknamed Ziggy early in his life and is known by that name today.

Next, Marley, Livingston, and Tosh worked in the back room of Lee "Scratch" Perry's Upsetter Records shop at the corner of Beeston Street and Luke Lane. Perry spent long hours with the Wailers trying to completely remake the basic Wailer sound and altering almost all facets of their music. Marley's vocals were changed to make them rougher, more urgent, and raw. Further, the use of horns was completely dropped and any sign of Kong's smooth production style was removed. The lead instrument was now the bass, whose rhythms were augmented by offbeat chops on electric guitar. The product was a reinvigorated Wailers sound that was more driven, in the vein of the Rudeboy days.

Backing the Wailers for these sessions was Perry's studio band, called the Upsetters. The core of the Upsetters was one of Jamaica's most famous rhythm sections, the Barrett Brothers. Aston, called "Family Man" or "Fams" (born Aston Francis Barrett, November 22, 1946; bass), played bass in a driving melodic manner that provided both a rhythmic and melodic anchor for the Wailers. His counterpart and younger brother Carlton, called "Carlie" (born Carlton Lloyd Barrett, December 17, 1950, died April 17, 1987; drums), had an innate sense of time, and together the Barrett Brothers became the driving force behind the Wailers.

The Wailers' core group of Bob, Bunny, and Peter now included the Barrett brothers but lacked

a keyboard player. Tyrone Downie (born May 20, 1956; keyboard), a 15-year-old who had played in the Young Professionals (the Barretts' club band formed while Bob was in Sweden), was recruited to fill the open position. The first track that Downie played on with the Wailers was the new song "Lick Samba." Engineered by Lee Perry and produced by Bob, Downie's performance on "Lick Samba" cemented his place in the band. In the early summer of 1971, the Wailers and Perry recorded and released "Trench Town Rock," a true reggae standard that not only galvanized ghetto residents but also sent the Wailers to the top of the Jamaican charts for the next five months.

The year 1971 found Bob and the Wailers in England in support of Johnny Nash. Unfortunately, the Nash project fell apart and the group was abandoned in England with no money, no work, and no means of getting back to Jamaica. Bob did the only thing that he knew to do, and in December 1971 he went to the Basing Street Studios of Island Records to see its owner, Chris Blackwell. Shortly after their meeting, Blackwell advanced the Wailers 8,000 pounds to return to Jamaica and begin recording their first album for Island Records. Once back in Jamaica, with the money and support of Blackwell, the Wailers' attitudes improved dramatically. Bob could afford to bring Rita and their children back from Delaware, and everyone was happy to be reunited. Tuff Gong Records was moved to Beeston Street and Chancery Lane, and the Wailers began rehearsing songs for their new album.

There followed a run of nine successful releases on the Island Records label. Along the way, Marley launched his own label called Tuff Gong, which became a subsidiary of Island. The first Island release was 1972's *Catch a Fire,* which comprised nine tracks and effectively introduced the Wailers to the world. In the postproduction stage, Blackwell added his own flavor to the mix by slightly accelerating the tempo of all the tracks to appeal to a greater rock-and-roll crossover audience.

The *Catch a Fire* release was truly unique in that it was the first ever full-length reggae album released in the United States. The album itself came in a cardboard sleeve that was cut to look like a Zippo lighter, which, when opened, exposed the picture of a flame, behind which was the record. In the United States, where reggae was still regarded as alien and unapproachable, *Catch a Fire* did not initially sell well.

The Wailers' lineup changed after they held auditions for a new keyboard player. The Wailers hired a keyboardist named Earl "Wire" Lindo (born January 7, 1953; keyboard). Lindo was well known on the island for his playing in the band the Now Generation. He took the place of the young Tyrone Downie, who had opted to stay in Jamaica through the tour and work in the resorts on the North Coast. When Lindo agreed to join the Wailers on tour, he took a leave of absence from the Now Generation until they got back together for their next album.

The first official Wailers tour began in April 1973 when the group arrived in London for the three-month British leg. Once in London, the group was amazed to find a Wailers album called *African Herbsman* available in local record stores. Released on the Trojan label, *African Herbsman* contained the best tracks from the Wailers' sessions with Lee Perry; however, the Wailers themselves knew nothing about it.

Released in October 1973, the Wailers' second album was called *Burnin'*. The album revealed a more organic roots sound than its overly produced predecessor, *Catch a Fire*. The tracks on the new album covered a mixture of topics that ranged from the political protest sentiment of "Burnin' and Lootin'" to direct Rastafarian content in "Rasta Man Chant." The cover art was a depiction of the heads of the six core Wailers (Bob, Peter, Bunny, Lindo, and the Barrett Brothers) burned into the side of a wooden box. *Burnin'* was released just six months after *Catch a Fire* and was indicative of Bob's prolific song-writing ability.

Back in the studio, Bob went to work on the tracks that would become *Natty Dread*. Work progressed recording new versions of "Bend Down Low" and "Lively Up Yourself." Several new militant songs were also recorded, including "So Jah Seh" and "Revolution." Bob and Carlie Barrett collaborated in the studio to write "Them Belly Full," and a demo of

"Am-A-Do (Do It to Your Bad Self)" was recorded but not released. The group had a continuing problem finding a keyboard player. Bernard "Touter" Harvey (keyboard, born in Jamaica) was frequently used in the studio but was considered too young to go on tour, and Downie was a full-time member of the house band at the Kingston Sheraton, the Caribs. Because of this situation, "Family Man" stepped in to cover the keyboard parts on the recordings of "Road Block" and "Bend Down Low."

Bob and Family Man took the *Natty Dread* master tapes to London in August 1974 so that Chris Blackwell could supervise the mixing. While working in London, Bob and Family Man found the man that would become the next Wailers guitarist, Al Anderson (born Albert Anderson, 1950; guitar). Anderson was a young, black rock guitarist who had played in bands that copied Jimi Hendrix and Jeff Beck.

In January of 1975, the original Wailers officially broke up due to Bunny's refusal to tour and Peter's disgust at the secondary role he was forced to take in the band. While Peter was angry with Bob because he felt that Bob did not support him musically, Bunny still treated Bob as a brother. Bunny had long been aware that Bob's songs of protest did not fit with his own songs of religious activism and brotherhood. Always philosophical, Bunny approached the end of the Wailers as an opportunity to produce even more music, not as a negative breakup. Bunny's idea was soon realized as Bob and the Wailers continued to release new music, Peter started his own label (called Intel-Diplo, short for Intelligent Diplomat) and began releasing singles in Jamaica, and Bunny began work on his album *Blackheart Man,* which Island released in 1976.

In early 1975, the new Bob Marley and the Wailers made their official debut as the opener for a Jackson 5 concert in Kingston. Bob was now able to officially assume his natural role as the front man for the band and stood at center stage singing, dancing, and playing rhythm guitar. Rita, Judy, and Marcia (the I-Threes) provided vocal support and the trademark Wailers three-part harmony. The I-Threes included Bob's wife Rita (born Alpharita Constantia

Anderson, July 25, 1946, vocals), Judy Mowatt (born 1952; vocals), and Marcia Griffiths (born Marcia Llyneth Griffiths, November 23, 1949; vocals). The Barrett brothers continued to provide the reggae rhythms on drum and bass, and Al Anderson took over the role of lead guitarist.

In early February 1975, the third Island Records Bob Marley and the Wailers album, *Knotty Dread,* was released. The title was taken from a single that was released several months earlier by Tuff Gong. However, when the album came out the title had been altered by Island to *Natty Dread.* This caused Bob some reflection on the control that the label exerted over his music; however, he remained stoic about the label's influence. The horn section returned on some tracks on *Natty Dread,* with well-placed punches to add weight to the ends of certain phrases.

The album began with Bob letting out an enthusiastic *Yoruba* look-out call that seemed to herald a new beginning for Bob Marley and the Wailers. This call led directly into a rousing version of "Lively Up Yourself." Eight more tracks followed, including "No Woman, No Cry," "Them Belly Full," "Rebel Music," "So Jah Seh," "Natty Dread," "Bend Down Low," "Talkin' Blues," and "Revolution." The general sentiment of the album was a militant Rastafarianism that culminated in the last two songs.

Completing the Wailers' entourage for a tour in support of *Natty Dread* were Don Taylor (the band's new manager), equipment manager Dave Harper, and Jamaican-born disc jockey and road manager Tony Garnett. Bob also appointed Garnett master of ceremonies, sent on stage to warm up the audience and introduce the Wailers at each show. The tour generated a great deal of media attention, and everywhere the Wailers went they were hounded by the press.

With the completion of the North American tour, the Wailers flew to London on July 16, 1975, for a four-date British tour in support of *Natty Dread.* The dates were set for performances at the Odeon in Birmingham, the Hard Rock in Manchester, and two shows were sold out for the Lyceum in London. Although Bob was nervous about the shows, having learned on arrival at Heathrow Airport that *Natty Dread* was no longer on the British charts, he

rehearsed the band vigorously and the British leg was a success. Chris Blackwell was in attendance at the first of the Lyceum shows and took particular notice when the crowd erupted with emotion at the opening chords of the fifth song, "No Woman, No Cry." Blackwell decided to record the second show, on July 18, 1975, and this recording turned into the *Live!* album that was released in November 1975.

The year 1976 marked the beginning of Bob's career as the first Third World superstar. He was in demand for concerts and interviews, and his records received advanced orders for the first time. *Rolling Stone* magazine voted Bob Marley and the Wailers "Band of the Year," and Bob appeared on the cover of *Rolling Stone* issue 219, photographed by Annie Leibovitz.

The sessions for the next album, called *Rastaman Vibration,* continued and plans were being made for another summer tour of America and Europe. However, the Wailers' lineup was about to change again when Al Anderson decided to leave the group to play with Peter Tosh. The Wailers lost another member to Tosh when Lee Jaffe informed Bob that he was departing. Jaffe cited dissatisfaction with the end of the previous summer's North American tour as his reason for leaving. The end result was that the Wailers, without Bob and the Barretts, were the backing band and Jaffe was the coproducer for Tosh's new album *Legalize It.*

These new developments left Bob with several important vacancies to fill in the Wailers' organization. Earl "Chinna" Smith (aka Earl Flute, born August 6, 1955; guitar), a well-known reggae session player and leader of his own band, Soul Syndicate, soon replaced Anderson. However, Smith opted to fill the rhythm-guitar role, which left the job of lead guitarist open. Chris Blackwell came to the aid of the Wailers in finding the appropriate lead-guitar player. Blackwell had an American black-rock power trio called White Lightning signed to Island Records. The leader of the band was a 23-year-old professional blues guitarist from Gary, Indiana, named Don Kinsey (born Donald Kinsey, May 12, 1953; guitar). Don Taylor called Kinsey in March 1976 and invited him to come to Miami where the Wailers were mixing their new album at Criteria Studios.

The Wailers released their fifth Island Records album, *Rastaman Vibration,* in May of 1976. The album jacket was simulated burlap and depicted Bob, with long dreadlocks, looking contemplative in army fatigues. The album included two parenthetical statements as well; the first was "This album jacket is great for cleaning herb." The second was the Blessing of Joseph from the Old Testament.

Upon release, the album climbed to number eight on the America pop charts and was the top-selling record of Bob's life. The *Rastaman Vibration* tour was the most successful yet and further cemented the Wailers' international reputation.

It was at this time that Bob set into motion his plan to play a concert to thank Jamaica for the support that he and the Wailers had received over the past decade. His plan was to stage a free concert in Kingston's National Heroes Park as a gesture of gratitude. The concert had a theme—"Smile Jamaica"—and was meant to reduce the friction between the warring factions active on the island. The timetable made it appear that all the performers at the "Smile Jamaica" concert were endorsing Manley. The anticipated large audience would then be expected to usher in another term for Manley and his socialist regime. As a result of this perceived political affiliation, which was never real, there was an attempt made on Bob's life by the supporters of the opposing political party. On December 3, 1976, two carloads of gunmen snuck into the yard at 56 Hope Road, where Bob and the Wailers were rehearsing, and opened fire.

At that moment, Bob and several others were in the kitchen. Eight shots were fired into the kitchen, two of which were wild and ricocheted around the room. Five of the bullets hit Don Taylor. The last bullet hit Bob, grazing his chest and lodging in the bicep of his left arm.

Remarkably, no one was mortally wounded during the shooting. Bob, Rita, Lewis Simpson, and Don Taylor were all loaded into cars and taken to the hospital. The police arrived 10 minutes later and secured the area. The injured parties were taken to the hospital where Bob was bandaged around the chest for a chipped sternum, a bullet still lodged in his left arm. Rita received treatment for the bullet fragment that had lodged between her scalp and skull. Don Taylor, who had been the most seriously wounded, needed a life-saving surgery to repair his numerous wounds. Despite their injuries, Bob Marley and the Wailers still played the concert, which is arguably one of the most significant moments in Bob's career. After the concert, Bob decamped to Nassau to recover.

In early 1977, the Wailers were again in the market for a guitar player, and Bob was thinking about trying to entice Al Anderson to return from Peter Tosh's band. Bob talked about this with Chris Blackwell, who brought up a young, black blues guitarist named Junior Marvin (born Donald Hanson Marvin Kerr Richards, Jr., 1949; guitar). In the ensuing sessions, in the winter of 1977, the Wailers recorded more than 20 songs. The earlier recordings produced the next album, called *Exodus: Movement of Jah People.* The other 10 songs from the session were released in 1978 as the album called *Kaya.* Although products of the same recording session, *Exodus* and *Kaya* were very different in character, the former being much more militant in character than the latter. Beyond this, the material on *Exodus* also marked a change in the basic Wailers groove. The fifth song and title track of the album had a more militant drumming style that was popularized by Jamaican studio player Sly Dunbar.

April 1977 was spent rehearsing for the impending tour of the United States and Europe to support the release of *Exodus.* The *Exodus* tour began in May with the first show in Paris just a month after the album had been released. After the European leg of the tour, Bob had a little break that he spent by traveling to Delaware and resting in the comfort of his mother's house. During the American leg of the tour, the Jamaican Peace Concert was announced. The Wailers' lineup was altered again by the return of two old members. Al Anderson was brought back into the band to augment Junior Marvin's guitar playing. Also, Earl "Wire" Lindo returned and was welcomed back into the ranks by everyone, including his replacement Tyrone Downie. The Peace Concert was held at Kingston's National Stadium on Saturday, April 22,

1978. The Wailers then embarked on the Japanese leg of the tour, which was successful even though a reggae band had never played in this part of the world. Next, the Wailers traveled to New Zealand and Bob was greeted by a dozen female Maoris, whom he greatly enjoyed meeting.

After the *Kaya* tour ended, Bob and the Wailers set about recording and mixing the tracks for the new album. For this, Chris Blackwell brought in a new producer to assist in giving the record international appeal; his name was Alex Sadkin. With Sadkin's assistance, the new record was released in the summer of 1979, under the title *Survival* (the working title had been *Black Survival*).

After the release of *Survival*, the song "Zimbabwe" became an African nationalist anthem. Several musicians on the African continent covered it, and it sold well around the country. Bob had been adopted several years earlier by the guerrilla fighters of Zimbabwe's Patriotic Front, and the group was uplifted and fortified by the song. The tour in support of *Survival* began in North America in October 1979, when the Wailers played at Harlem's Apollo Theater. The tour spanned the United States and the Caribbean.

Bob and his management spent the rest of 1979 planning the Wailers' schedule for the new year. Their band had scheduled a short visit to Africa early in the year, then a return to London to record the 10th album on Island Records, to be called *Uprising*. They then launched another extensive tour that kept Bob away from Jamaica during the next general election. In addition to the standard tour destinations, the Wailers also played a concert in the newly established nation of Zimbabwe on April 17, 1980.

During the U.S. leg of the tour, all in attendance began to notice that Bob's voice seemed hoarse. While on a morning jog in New York's Central Park, Bob suffered a seizure, which caused him to seek medical attention. Upon a complete workup, it was discovered that Bob had a large cancerous brain tumor. He was advised to go into treatment immediately. Instead, on September 23, 1980, Bob Marley and the Wailers played their last concert at Pittsburgh's Stanley Theater. Bob sought a variety of treatments, including a series of unconventional treatments in Germany. Regardless of the various treatments, Bob died at approximately 11:45 A.M. on Monday, May 11, 1981.

In the wake of Bob's death, there could be no more Bob Marley and the Wailers. However, there would still be a great deal of music. In 1983, Tuff Gong International and Island Records released *Confrontation,* a posthumous collection of Bob Marley and the Wailers material spanning the final decade of his life. Island Records released one of Bob's most famous albums, titled *Legend,* in 1984 with the subtitle "The Best of Bob Marley and the Wailers." In the years since Bob's death, there has been an astonishing number of posthumous releases. "New" releases surface yearly in the United States and England, and the inevitable bootlegs of live shows are too numerous to list in the discography of this study. Obscure releases and poorly produced collections come out regularly and attest to the continued interest in Bob's music even now. Also common are box sets that intend to compile tracks from certain portions of Bob's career. The most important and authentic of these is *Bob Marley: Songs of Freedom,* released by Tuff Gong and Island Records.

The influence of Bob Marley and the Wailers is difficult to overstate, as they are generally credited with bringing reggae music to the world. Obvious influences are found in bands from the Clash to the Police to the Fugees to Rihanna. Further, his legacy is inescapable, as evidenced by his numerous honors. During his life, Bob Marley and the Wailers were named *Rolling Stone* Band of the Year in 1976. Their album *Exodus* was named Album of the Century by *Time* magazine. The BBC named their song "One Love" the Song of the Millennium, and their album *Catch a Fire* was inducted into the Grammy Hall of Fame in 2010.

David V. Moskowitz

Selected Discography
African Herbsman, Trojan TRLS 62, 1973.
Burnin', Island ILPS 9256, 1973.
Catch a Fire, Island ILPS 9241, 1973.

Natty Dread, Island ILPS 9281, 1974.

Live!, Island ILPS 9376, 1975.

Rastaman Vibration, Island/Tuff Gong ILPS 9383, 1976.

Exodus, Island/Tuff Gong ILPS 9498, 1977.

Babylon by Bus, Island/Tuff Gong ILPS, 1978.

Kaya, Island/Tuff Gong ILPS 9517, 1978.

Survival, Island/Tuff Gong ILPS 9542, 1979.

Uprising, Island/Tuff Gong ILPS 9596, 1980.

Confrontation, Island/Tuff Gong I2 46207, 1983.

References

Davis, Steven. *Bob Marley.* Rochester, VT: Schenkman Books, 1990.

Moskowitz, David. *Bob Marley: A Biography.* Santa Barbara, CA: Greenwood Press, 2007.

Moskowitz, David. *The Words and Music of Bob Marley.* Santa Barbara, CA: Praeger Publishers, 2007.

Steffens, Roger. "Bob Marley: Rasta Warrior," in *The Rastafari Reader: Chant Down Babylon.* Philadelphia: Temple University Press, 1998.

Bon Jovi (1983–Present)

Bon Jovi is a hard rock band that formed in the early 1980s. They rode the tide of the so-called hair metal style that was a spin-off of 1980s heavy metal. The style was characterized by a combination of hard rock, punk rock, and pop-inflected hooks and catchy guitar riffs. The groups in the hair metal style tended toward the use of vocal harmonies and the power ballad. The style was not just about the music, the bands also tended to be composed entirely of long-haired men who wore makeup and clothing denim, leather, and spandex; another aspect of the style was that it was popularized on MTV during its infancy. Hair metal bands included Poison, Bon Jovi, Night Ranger, Mötley Crüe, Quiet Riot, Ratt, and several others. Of any of these bands, Bon Jovi was the only one able to evolve with the changing music styles since 1980. As the 1980s turned to the 1990s, grunge became the predominant style of American popular music, and with this many of the early hair metal bands faded into the sunset. Bon Jovi continued on and continued to create music that maintained an aging audience while simultaneously drawing in the next generation of listeners.

Bon Jovi the band was named for its lead singer Jon Bon Jovi (born John Francis Bongiovi, March 2, 1962; vocals, guitar). In 1983, Bon Jovi surrounded himself with four other musicians, and they cofounded the band. The other members of Bon Jovi were Richie Sambora (born Richard Stephen Sambora, July 11, 1959; guitar), David Bryan (born David Rashbaum, February 7, 1962; keyboards), Tico Torres (born Hector Samuel Juan Torres, October 7, 1953; drums), and Alec Such (born Alexander John Such, November 14, 1951; bass).

The band began forming while Bongiovi was still in high school. He and Bryan met at Sayreville High School where they joined an eight-piece rhythm and blues band called Atlantic City Express (*Encyclopedia of Popular Music* 2008). Bryan decamped to New York to study at the Juilliard Music School, and Bongiovi followed him to the city. Bongiovi had an in at the Power Plant recording studios as his cousin Tony was a well-known producer (Vanilla Fudge, Dr. John, John McLaughlin, Jimi Hendrix). Bongiovi managed to land a job at the Power Plant where he toiled away in obscurity for two years before convincing Billy Squire to help him produce a demo tape. Bongiovi sent his demo to several record companies without success. One song that he recorded, called "Runaway," got some local radio play and appeared on a local artist compilation. The studio musicians who backed Bongiovi on "Runaway" included Tim Pierce (guitar), Roy Bittan (keyboard), Frankie LaRocka (drums), and Hugh McDonald (bass).

As "Runaway" got progressively more air play Bongiovi realized he needed his own band if he was going to continue. He reunited with Bryan and managed to enlist experienced players Sambora (who had toured with Joe Cocker) and Alec Such and Tico Torres, both of whom had experience from playing in the band Phantom Opera. In late 1983, the band Bon Jovi (Jon changed the spelling of his last name) was playing local showcases when they caught the attention of Derek Schulman, who was an A&R representative

Bon Jovi backstage before a performance at the Rosemont Horizon, in Rosemont, Illinois, on May 20, 1984. Pictured are (from left to right): David Bryan, Tico Torres, Jon Bon Jovi, Alec John Such, and Richie Sambora. Together, the members of Bon Jovi rode the tide of "hair metal" through the 1980s. The band then successfully transformed themselves to stay relevant in the new millennium, racking up Grammy, Billboard, and American Music Awards. (Photo by Paul Natkin/ Getty Images)

for Mercury/PolyGram Records. Schulman signed the group to a deal and gave them a support slot on tour behind Eddie Money and ZZ Top (*Encyclopedia of Popular Music* 2008).

The band's sound, coupled with their looks (especially Jon's), attracted immediate attention. In 1984, the band released their first album on the Mercury imprint. The eponymously titled *Bon Jovi* included "Runaway" and "Get Ready." The album was released on January 21, 1984, under the management of Doc McGhee and peaked at 43 on the *Billboard* Top 200. When the album was released, "Runaway" was already a nominal success, and combining it with the other tracks on the album served as a solid introduction for fans. Ultimately, "Runaway" reached the top 40 on the *Billboard* Hot 100. The songs on the album had a consistent hard rock style, passionate playing, and solid melodies delivered through Bon Jovi's distinct vocal range. The album established "the foundation for the band's career, which reached its apex several years later with that very same combination of pop melody and arena-sized ambition" (Mathew, Allmusic.com, 2014).

The success of the first record led to a headlining tour and additional touring as support to the Scorpions, Whitesnake, and Kiss. All of this exposure created buzz for the band's second album, released the following year. *7800 Degrees Fahrenheit* was the band's second studio album and was recorded at the beginning of 1985. The album was released on March 27, 1985, and was named after the melting point of rock. Stylistically, the album was not far from the keyboard-fueled material on their first record and hit-making bands such as Journey. The album produced three singles: "In and Out of Love," "Only Lonely," and the ballad "Silent Night." The arena rock-ready sound pushed the singles up the chart. "In and Out of Love" and "Only Lonely" both charted on *Billboard*'s Hot 100. The album itself charted in several countries, went to number 37 on the *Billboard* charts, and was eventually certified platinum by the Recording Industry Association of America. In the summer of 1985, the band launched a tour that lasted for six months. They toured the United States, Japan, and Europe. Along the way they also appeared in the first Farm Aid concert. With this album and subsequent tour, Bon Jovi was poised to take over the airwaves, and its pumps were primed for the next record.

Slippery When Wet was released in August of 1986 and went on to be the highest-selling rock album of 1987 (*Encyclopedia of Popular Music* 2008). The album was recorded in the first half of 1986 in Little Mountain Sound Studios in Vancouver, British Columbia, and it was issued again by Mercury Records. On the strength of the singles "You Give Love a Bad Name," "Livin' on a Prayer," and "Wanted Dead or Alive" the record soared up the charts around the world and went to number one in the United States. The strength of the songwriting on the album was due, in part, to Desmond Child. Child was a hired gun who collaborated with the band on several songs. The band again went on the road in support of the album. This time, they spent months on tour in the United States and Europe. Along the way, the band played the Monsters of Rock festival in August 1987 in England, where they were joined on stage by members of Kiss, Twisted Sister, and Iron Maiden for a performance of the song "We're an American Band" (*Encyclopedia of Popular Music* 2008).

Ultimately, *Slippery When Wet* was Bon Jovi's biggest commercial success and has been certified 12 times platinum—that is 12 million copies sold—by the Recording Industry Association of America.

Riding high off the success of their third album, it seemed that Bon Jovi could not be stopped. In an attempt to amplify their popularity, the band released *New Jersey* in September 1988. On the strength of the singles "Bad Medicine" and "I'll Be There for You," the band again had a huge success on their hands. It seemed that *Slippery When Wet*'s formula was a winner, and this fourth album was only slightly less successful than its predecessor. It went on to sell five million copies, and both of the singles went to number one on the *Billboard* charts. The *New Jersey* tour lasted for 18 months and left the band at the peak of their popularity, but they were also drained. The high point of the tour was a bit of a homecoming. On June 11, 1989, the band sold out Giants Stadium in New Jersey. All along, Bon Jovi had also been releasing videos for their singles, and they enjoyed a period of major popularity on MTV through the mid-1980s. After the tour in support of *New Jersey* ended, the band was too exhausted to return to the studio and instead went on hiatus, which lasted through 1990 and 1991.

In an attempt to rekindle the band's enthusiasm for the studio, the group fired their management and launched Bon Jovi Management Company in 1991. The break and reorganizing worked, and the band went back to the studio at the beginning of 1992. In January, the group returned to Little Mountain Studios and enlisted the production skills of Bob Rock. The product of these sessions was the November 1992 release *Keep the Faith*. The time off and management change had resulted in a change in sound for the band as well. The early 1990s saw the dawning of the grunge era, and by the end of 1991 Nirvana had released *Nevermind* and Pearl Jam had issued *10*. The members of Bon Jovi sensed the changing tides in American popular music, and the style of the new record was much more hard rock than hair metal. They moved away from the pomp-and-circumstance of their material from the 1980s and instead adopted a more piano-driven, epic rock sound.

The result of these changes was a markedly different sound on *Keep the Faith.* The obvious concern was that the band's fans would not make the change with them. These fears were put to rest once the album was issued. On the strength of five singles, the album went up the charts, peaking at number five on the *Billboard* Top 200; it made it to number one in the United Kingdom and Australia. The band released "Keep the Faith," "Bed of Roses," "In These Arms," "I'll Sleep When I'm Dead," "I Believe," and "Dry County" as singles. The first three all went in the charts and spurred the album on to great heights. The band actually released the single "Keep the Faith" a month before the album was issued to prime the pumps in the wake of the hiatus. The album went on to be certified platinum in 10 countries, including going twice platinum in the United States. Bon Jovi again followed the release with a world tour, which included countries they had not previously visited.

On the heels of their renewed success, the band released their first greatest hits compilation in 1994. Called *Cross Road,* the album also included two new songs: "Always" and "Someday I'll Be Saturday Night." The single "Always" went on to be the group's highest-selling song to date and spent 10 months inside the top 10 on the American charts. *Cross Road* went on to be one of the band's most successful albums, having sold over 21 million units around the world. Even as the band was reaping the success of reinventing itself, Alec Such left the band. Some reports have him getting fired, while others state that he left of his own will or simply retired. Regardless, the band needed a bass player. The slot was unofficially filled by Hugh McDonald (born Hugh John McDonald, December 28, 1950), who had supplied the bass line on the single "Runaway."

With McDonald in the group, Bon Jovi went back in the studio in 1995 and released *These Days* in June. Interestingly, the cover photo of the album only shows the original four members of the band—minus McDonald. The general spirit of the album was darker than any of the band's usual fare. Produced by Peter Collins, the album was written primarily by Bon Jovi and Sambora with additional contributions from the band's old hit maker Desmond Child. Even with the less euphoric lyrical content, the album was a success. It produced the singles "This Ain't a Love Song," "Something for the Pain," "Lie to Me," "These Days," and "Hey God"—four of which landed inside the top 10 on the charts. On the strength of these songs, the album went up the charts around the world. It replaced Michael Jackson's *HIStory* album at number one in the United Kingdom and made it to number nine on the *Billboard* charts in the United States. As was the band's pattern, they toured in support of the record and visited over 40 countries. Of note, on the *These Days* tour the band sold out Wembley Stadium in London for three consecutive nights.

The band again took a break after the tour. Instead of recoiling in exhaustion, this time apart was purposely taken to rest, recharge, and enjoy the fruits of their labors. In 1999, Bon Jovi re-formed to work on their next record. *Crush* was the group's seventh studio album and was released on Island Records in June of 2000. Always able to produce solid singles, the products of this album were not different. "It's My Life," "Say It Isn't So," and "Thank You for Loving Me" were all released as singles and pushed the album up the charts around the world. It spent 51 weeks on the *Billboard* charts and went on to sell in excess of two million U.S. copies. Additionally, it was certified gold or platinum in over a dozen countries. The true standout single on the album was "It's My Life." Written by Bon Jovi, Sambora, and Max Martin, the song has several of the band's stock elements. Sambora used the talk box effect on his guitar, and the lyrics spoke of the fearlessness of their fictional couple Tommy and Gina—who first appeared in "Livin' on a Prayer." Just as the latter song had earned the group fans in 1986, the new single introduced the group to a whole new generation of fans in the new millennium. The album was also nominated for two Grammy Awards and the band again toured in support of their latest record.

Bounce followed *Crush* when it was released on October 8, 2002. Just like the previous album, *Bounce* was produced by Bon Jovi, Sambora, and Luke Ebbin. Created in the wake of the September 11th terrorist attacks, the album contained several songs that were the band's response to the disaster in New York. The single "Everyday" was the band's response to the attacks and rang with defiance and themes of independence.

The album was another success for the band, though it was not a massive hit like several of its predecessors. Regardless, it was certified gold or platinum in a dozen countries and charted inside the top 10 around the world. It was the band's highest debut to date at number two on the *Billboard* charts. The band supported the album with another international tour. Following the tour, the band went into the studio to record acoustic versions of many of their hits. These were used on the 2003 release *This Left Feels Right.* The songs were also released as a DVD in 2004.

Have a Nice Day was the band's ninth studio album and was recorded over several months in late 2004 and early 2005. Outpacing *Bounce, Have a Nice Day* debuted at number one around the world and was a smash hit for the band. The singles "Have a Nice Day," "Who Says You Can't Go Home," "Welcome to Wherever You Are," and "I Want to Be Loved" were all chart successes and helped the album to go triple platinum in the United States. The album was produced by John Shanks and exhibited Bon Jovi pushing his vocal limits further than he had on the previous two albums. Stylistically, the sound on the album was harder and heavier than the previous two releases. Lyrically, Bon Jovi wrote more protesting and defiant lyrics, which made it clear that he was dissatisfied about the state of the world at the time. This was amplified with his recasting of Bob Dylan's song "Chimes of Freedom" as "Bells of Freedom" (Erlewine, Allmusic.com, 2014). The *Have a Nice Day* tour spanned the end of 2005 and the beginning of 2006. During the tour, the band played to over two million fans around the world.

Following the *Have a Nice Day* tour, the band went in the studio to create their 10th album, called *Lost Highway*. This new album again marked a change for the band. Bon Jovi had released a version of "Who Says You Can't Go Home" with Jennifer Nettles from the country group Sugarland, and the experience influenced the sound on *Lost Highway*.

The album represented the group's attempt to create crossover success between rock and radio-ready country. The album contained duets with LeAnn Rimes and Big & Rich and some fiddle and steel guitar playing, but these were just the clothes covering Bon Jovi's usual arena rock anthems (Erlewine, Allmusic .com, 2014). The album was again produced by John Shanks and was another commercial success for the band. The release debuted at number one on the *Billboard* charts and was nominated for a Grammy. It was another example of Bon Jovi's international appeal as it was on the charts around the world, and although not everyone was convinced by the group's quasi-country turn, plenty of fans went along for the ride. In the summer of 2007, the band played a series of concerts in support of the album and was overwhelmed by the fan response. As a result they launched the *Lost Highway* world tour through the end of 2007 and beginning of 2008.

The *Lost Highway* tour was a huge commercial success and went around the world. It was ranked by *Billboard* as the highest-grossing tour of 2008 and played to over two million people. Even with this success, the band did not make a serious change in style to modern country. Instead, they returned to rock and roll with their 11th studio album called *The Circle*. The album was Bon Jovi's response to the economic downturn in the American economy in 2009. "Explicit references to the broken state of blue-collar America pile up throughout *The Circle,* but instead of setting these wannabe working man anthems to the kind of Springsteen-esque rock that's their trademark, Bon Jovi, with the assistance of producer John Shanks, have decided to make their own version of a U2 album, apparently because no other sound sounds as serious as U2" (Erlewine, Allmusic.com, 2014).

The band launched a successful tour in support of *The Circle,* which capitalized on their stadium-sized audiences. The American leg sold out successive shows in multiple locations and the European leg included a 12-night run at London's O2 Arena. All of this touring revenue again pushed Bon Jovi to the top of *Billboard*'s annual top 25 concert tours of 2010.

On the heels of the success of the *The Circle* tour, the band went back in the studio to work on their 12th studio record. *What About Now* stuck to the band's award-winning formula. The album was recorded with John Shanks as the producer over the first half of 2012. The group released the record on March 8, 2013, and it was their third recording in a row to debut at number one on the *Billboard* Top 200 chart. In between *The Circle* and *What About Now,* the band had toured throughout 2013 on the Because We Can Tour, and during this tour they built buzz for the new record. Although the album was disparaged by critics as being more of the same, it still charted in two dozen countries and went on to sell over a million copies.

Through all of this, the band has maintained a remarkably stable membership and has defied critics by continually building its fan base. Bon Jovi was able to do this with a mixture of solid live performances, band charisma, and careful attention to the changing tastes of its listeners. Although the group started out as a hair metal outfit, they moved relatively seamlessly through hard rock, pop rock, and arena rock. Their song lyrics have increasingly taken on more "adult" themes, but this has corresponded to concerns of their core fans.

As Bon Jovi blazed a trail of success through the 1980s, 1990s, and the beginning of the new millennium, they also racked up a long list of awards and honors. They have been nominated for six American Music Awards and won two, they have been nominated for four *Billboard* Music Awards and won one. They have also been nominated for nine Grammy Awards and won one for the country version of "Who Says You Can't Go Home" with Jennifer Nettles from Sugarland in the Best Country Collaboration with Vocals category. The list goes on and the band will surely continue adding to it as time goes on.

Bon Jovi has gone on record as being influenced by bands such as the Rolling Stones, Van Halen, the Beatles, Tom Petty and the Heartbreakers, Aerosmith, and fellow New Jersey native Bruce Springsteen. Additionally, their influences are found in the bands they have chosen to cover, such as Thin Lizzy, Willie Nelson, Elvis Presley, the Boomtown Rats, Elton John, and Neil Young, in addition to those already listed. Their influence on subsequent bands can also be discovered through those who have chosen to cover Bon Jovi. The list of bands who have covered Bon Jovi is long, but it includes Hinder, Jani Lane, the Slackers, Dream Theater, Goldfinger, Northern Kings, Chris Daughtry, Atreyu, and many others.

The future of the band is a bit uncertain. Guitarist Richie Sambora left the group for "personal reasons" in the middle of the Because We Can Tour. He was replaced by Phil X, who is a well-known Los Angeles session guitarist and who is already affiliated with several other bands. Rumors have swirled that Sambora quit or was fired—neither of these have been substantiated. Sambora has enjoyed significant solo artist success in his time away from the band. Regardless of Sambora's status, Bon Jovi shows no signs of letting up and will continue into the future.

David V. Moskowitz

Selected Discography

Bon Jovi, Mercury 814 982–2, 1984.

7800 Degrees Fahrenheit, Mercury 422–824509–1, 1985.

Slippery When Wet, Mercury 830 264–2, 1986.

New Jersey, Mercury 836 345–2, 1988.

Keep the Faith, Mercury 5140197–1, 1992.

These Days, Mercury 5280248–2, 1995.

Crush, Island/Mercury 12042474, 2000.

One Wild Night: Live 1985–2001, Island/Mercury 5480865–2, 2001.

Bounce, Island 440 063 055–2, 2002.

This Left Feels Right, Island B000154002, 2003.

Have a Nice Day, Island B0005533–72, 2005.

Lost Highway, Island B0008902–02, 2007.

The Circle, Island B0013700–02, 2009.

What About Now, Mercury 3729825, 2013.

References

Bon Jovi Offical Website. 2014. "Biography." Accessed June 2014. www.bonjovi.com/.

Bon Jovi Official Website. 2015. "Music." Accessed June 2014. www.bonjovi.com/music.

Bowler, Dave, and Brayn Dray. *Bon Jovi: Runaway.* Oxon, UK: Boxtree, 1995.

Covers Project Official Website. 2015. "Bon Jovi." Accessed June 2014. www.coversproject.com/artist/bon%20jovi/.

Discogs Official Website. 2015. "Bon Jovi Discography." Accessed June 2014. www.discogs.com/Bon-Jovi-Bon-Jovi/master/66782.

Erlewine, Stephen. "Bon Jovi—*Have a Nice Day*," *All Music Guide*. Rovi Corporation, 2014.

Erlewine, Stephen. "Bon Jovi—*The Circle*," *All Music Guide*. Rovi Corporation, 2014.

Iahn, Buddy. "Richie Sambora Candidly Discusses His Future with Bon Jovi and as a Solo Artist." www.musicuniverse, Clapham Junction, London: Atolma Productions Company, 2014.

Larkin, Colin, ed. "Bon Jovi." *Encyclopedia of Popular Music*. Oxford Music Online, 2008.

Mathew, Leslie. "Bon Jovi—*Bon Jovi*," *All Music Guide*. Rovi Corporation, 2014.

Bruce Springsteen and the E Street Band (1971–Present)

Bruce Springsteen and the E Street Band have long been a fixture of American popular music. "The Boss," as Springsteen is known, and his collection of sidemen have carved a distinct and historic path through rock and roll. They have played a style of music that "brought together all of the exuberance of 1950s rock and the thoughtfulness of 1960s rock, molded into a 1970s rock style" (Ruhlmann, Allmusic.com, 2014). Springsteen and the band have continued to update their sound, and some of their most popular music came in the 1980s. By this point they had begun producing a more arena-sized sound and played large venue shows. Along the way, Springsteen and the E Street Band became the arbiters of all things American in rock and roll music. They consistently spoke to the American working class with themes including working in the steel mills/blue-collar industry, returning from foreign wars, and carving out a unique American identity. Now considered part of the American popular music landscape, Bruce Springsteen and the E Street Band show no signs of slowing down with continual new music.

Bruce Springsteen (born Bruce Frederick Springsteen, September 23, 1949; vocals, guitar, harmonica) grew up in New Jersey and cut his teeth as a rock and roll guitarist on the Jersey shore. As a teenager, Springsteen played in a series of bands that ranged in style from garage rock to power trio blues rock—much of which can be heard in his subsequent material. Bands of note that Springsteen played with include the Castiles, Steel Mill, Dr. Zoom and the Sonic Boom, and the Bruce Springsteen Band. This was followed by a period in New York during which Springsteen plied the singer/songwriter folkie trade.

In 1972, Columbia Records came knocking and offered Springsteen a solo artist deal. Instead, Springsteen brought a group of his New Jersey musical associates into the studio, and together they recorded *Greetings from Asbury Park, N.J.* in the summer of 1972. Without yet having the name, the group of backing musicians would form the core of the E Street Band.

The band that appeared with Springsteen on this first studio album included Clarence "Big Man" Clemons (born Clarence Anicholas Clemons Jr., January 11, 1942, died June 18, 2011; saxophone, vocals), Vini "Mad Dog" Lopez (born Vincent Lopez, 1949; drums), David Sancious (born November 30, 1953; keyboard, guitar), and Garry Tallent (born Garry Wayne Tallent, October 27, 1949; bass). Several of these men stuck with Springsteen through the intervening 40-year period and still play with him on stage today.

The album that resulted from this first in-studio experience was released January 5, 1973, to critical acclaim. The issue with this first release was that although it was given approval from the critics, it sold slowly, with only 25,000 copies sold in 1973. In the course of recording the album, Springsteen and representatives from Columbia knocked heads. Springsteen preferred to work with the band, while the label wanted more of a solo sound. The ultimate opinion fell to Clive Davis, then president of Columbia, who said he did not hear a single. In response Springsteen

Bruce Springsteen and the E Street Band perform live on stage at the Carlton Theatre in Red Bank, New Jersey, during the *Born to Run* tour on October 11, 1975. From left to right: Clarence Clemons (1942–2011), Bruce Springsteen, Steven Van Zandt, and Garry Tallent. The storied career of the band includes 20 Grammy Awards, two Emmy Awards, and induction into the Rock and Roll Hall of Fame in 2014. (Photo by Fin Costello/Redferns)

wrote and recorded "Blinded by the Light" and "Spirit in the Night." Interestingly, these songs did not immediately chart for Springsteen, but Manfred Mann's Earth Band ended up with a number-one hit with their version of "Blinded by the Light."

The style of the songs that were released on the first record were quite Bob Dylan-esque with a more up-tempo vocal delivery and saxophone parts. Springsteen's "street scenes could be haunted and tragic, as they were in 'Lost in the Flood,' but they were still imbued with romanticism and a youthful energy. [The album] painted a portrait of teenagers cocksure of themselves, yet bowled over by their discovery of the world" (Ruhlmann, Allmusic.com, 2014). Although not a big commercial success, the first record's strength earned Springsteen and the boys an opportunity to make a second record.

In the summer of 1973, they went back in the studio and recorded *The Wild, the Innocent, and the E Street Shuffle* for Columbia. Released on September 11, 1973, the band's second record again included Clemons, Sancious, Tallent, and Lopez. To this was added Danny Federici (born Daniel Paul Federici, January 23, 1950, died April 17, 2008; organ, keyboard). The album again received rave reviews from the critics, but experienced little commercial success. Many of the songs on the album would go on to be standout singles for Springsteen and the E Street Band in later years, including "Incident of 57th Street" and "Rosalita (Come Out Tonight)." Springsteen himself described the album as a half and half album—half the songs were about New Jersey and half were about Springsteen's time spent in New York.

This record also introduced the audience to the whole concept of the "E Street." The band used to rehearse at Sancious's mother's house, which was on the corner of E Street and 10th Avenue in Belmar, New Jersey—thus the E Street Band, "E Street Shuffle," and "Tenth Avenue Freeze-Out." Regardless of the lack of commercial success experienced by the first two albums when they were released in 1973, they have both gone on to platinum status in the intervening period, and William Ruhlmann described the second record as "one of the greatest albums in the history of rock and roll" (Ruhlmann, Allmusic.com, 2014). The album introduced Springsteen's listeners to some characters he went on to write about multiple times, including Sandy, Rosalita, hoodlums, and fortune tellers (brucespringsteen.net 2014).

With the relatively flat sales of his first two studio albums, Springsteen needed a commercial success for his next release. With the assistance of Jon Landau and the E Street Band, Springsteen built *Born to Run* from the summer of 1974 to the summer of 1975. The album was released on August 25, 1975, and was the smash commercial hit that Springsteen and the E Street Band so badly needed to stay in good favor with Columbia. The album peaked at number three on the *Billboard* charts and would eventually sell over six million copies. The album's sales were spurred by the strength of the singles "Born to Run" and "Tenth Avenue Freeze-Out," though "Jungleland" and "Thunder Road" went on to become successful singles and fan favorites.

The E Street Band was a slightly different collective for this record, but this lineup would coalesce and stay with Springsteen for years. Alterations to the players previously listed included Roy Bittan (born July 2, 1949; keyboards) and Max Weinberg (born April 13, 1951; drums), and Stevie Van Zandt (born Steven Van Zandt, November 22, 1950; guitar, arrangements). Bittan, Weinberg, and Van Zandt became standard members of the E Street Band just as the group found their stride and blew up on the national stage. In the week it was released, *Born to Run* charted at number 84 on *Billboard* and spent the next several weeks on the charts. An interesting aspect of

Born to Run was that it simultaneously marked the start of the band as a commercially successful, major earners for the label, while the lyrics of the album were speaking from a more grown-up perspective—essentially the move from late teenage to young adult years.

In the wake of the success of *Born to Run*, the label's promotion machine went into high gear. Springsteen appeared on the covers of both *Newsweek* and *Time* magazine and he and the E Street Band launched an enormous, nearly year-long, tour. After all of the pomp and circumstance, the band returned to the studio, again with Landau, for the end of 1977 and the beginning of 1978. The product of this period was the June 1978 release *Darkness on the Edge of Town*. Though the band spent the period from 1975 to 1978 touring and ultimately recording, there was also a lingering legal battle that had been raging between them and their former manager, Mike Appel. The suit was finally settled and the band got directly back to work in the studio.

The tone of this release was slightly less euphoric than its predecessor, but the album still received overwhelmingly positive reviews. The standout singles, including "Prove It All Night," "The Promised Land," and "Badlands," helped enhance the album's early reviews. The critical acclaim continued for this record for some time. *Rolling Stone* ranked it number 150 on their list of the greatest albums of all time and it went on to be certified three times platinum by the Recording Industry Association of America. In addition to a slightly darker tone, the album also marked a change in Springsteen's vocal delivery. Previously, he was verbose and filled each line with piles of lyrics—here, the lyrics are more sparse and lean. In the wake of the release and initial success of *Darkness on the Edge of Town,* the band toured. The 1978 tour marked the beginning of the band's now legendary reputation for long concerts.

By the end of 1978, the music community at large recognized Springsteen's strength as a songwriter and his songs were in increasing demand from other artists. A solid example of this was Patti Smith's 1978 version of Springsteen's song "Because the Night."

October of 1970 saw the release of the band's biggest gamble so far, the double-album *The River*. As described by Ruhlmann, "imbedded within the double-disc running time of *The River* is a single-disc album that follows up on the themes and sound of *Darkness on the Edge of Town*—wide-screen, mid-tempo rock and stories of the disillusionment of working-class life and the conflicts within families" (Ruhlmann, Allmusic.com, 2014). The singles "Hungry Heart," "The River," and "Independence Day" made it clear that Springsteen's knack for epic storytelling was intact and the band lineup was the same as on the previous release. *The River* charted in over a dozen countries and ended up being certified platinum, or multi-platinum, in five countries.

In a move that left many scratching their heads, Springsteen retreated from his own success, and his next album was a complete about-face. *Nebraska* was a solo acoustic album recorded in January of 1982 and released in September of the same year. Here the singer/songwriter continued to address the themes of blue-collar challenges, perceived outsider status, and criminals of a variety of sorts. The material for the album was recorded by Springsteen with a four-track cassette recorder in his New Jersey bedroom. The songs on the album, such as "Nebraska," "Johnny 99," and "Atlantic City," were some of his "most enduring works, raw, haunted, acoustic" (brucespringsteen.net 2014). Upon its release, the album received rave reviews, charted internationally, and went gold or platinum in several countries.

While the move to release a solo album seemed like a dangerous game of career Russian roulette, Springsteen and the E Street Band quickly re-formed and went back in the studio to record one of their most stellar albums yet, *Born in the U.S.A.* The band's seventh studio album, this release was equal parts commercial success and critical darling. The album yielded seven top 10 singles and turned the band into international superstars (specifically, Springsteen himself). The "title track is self-described as one of his best songs" (brucespringsteen.net 2014).

Born in the U.S.A. was the band's most commercially accessible album, as attested to by the fact that it sold over 15 million copies. "It stayed in the UK charts for two-and-a-half-years, in the country of origin it stayed even longer" (*Encyclopedia of Popular Music* 2008). The standout singles on the album were the title track, "Cover Me," "I'm on Fire," "No Surrender," "I'm Goin' Down," "Dancing in the Dark," and "My Hometown." All of these solid songs pushed the album's sales over 30 million worldwide. The band also launched a two-year tour in support of the album. The tour was an enormous commercial success and helped turn "Born in the U.S.A." into a patriotic anthem. The album ended up being rated 86th on *Rolling Stone*'s greatest albums of all time.

The next release from the band was a greatest hits collection. Called *Live 1975–85,* the album collected 40 songs and was a compendium of successful live recordings from the E Street Band's first decade. Released in November of 1986, the album included live favorites that had not been previously released, like "Fire" and "Because the Night" (bruce springsteen.net).

The next album was called *Tunnel of Love* and included a new member of the E Street Band. Steve Van Zandt had departed the group to pursue other interests and was replaced by Nils Lofgren (born Nils Hilmer Lofgren, June 21, 1951; guitar). Lofgren had long honed his skills as a member of Neil Young's band for *After the Gold Rush* and *Tonight's the Night,* in addition to being a member of Crazy Horse for a time. Strangely, the album was recorded with members of the E Street Band, but it was not billed as an "E Street Band Record." The members of the band were used sparingly and all 12 songs on the record can be viewed as personal statements about Springsteen's own life.

The new guitarist notwithstanding, *Tunnel of Love* was a departure for the band. The album focused on the confusion and disenchantment associated with lost love. Springsteen had married actress Julianne Phillips in the wake of the *Born in the U.S.A.* tour and their relationship quickly deteriorated. Released in October of 1987, the album featured five singles: "Brilliant Disguise," "Tunnel of Love," "One Step Up," "Tougher Than the Rest," and "Spare Parts." "Brilliant Disguise" was an indictment of relationship issues with the basic message that it was impossible to really know someone. Although an abrupt about-face from previous records, the album sold well, charted worldwide, and went platinum or gold in a dozen countries. The album was followed by the *Tunnel of Love* express tour of the United States and Europe. The 1990s were a period of change for Springsteen. He dissolved the E Street Band, finalized his divorce, made his relationship with backup singer Patti Scialfa public, and then married her in 1991.

Musically, the 1990s were a tumultuous time for Springsteen. He had moved to Los Angeles and this, coupled with the abandonment of the E Street Band, brought accusations of selling out. The albums released in the 1990s were *Human Touch* (1992), *Lucky Town* (released on the same day as *Human Touch* in 1992), and *The Ghost of Tom Joad* (1995). The backing band for these records actually included some E Street Band alumni—specifically the keyboard players Roy Bittan, Danny Federici, and David Sancious. *Human Touch* peaked at number two on the *Billboard* Top 200, *Lucky Town* made it to number three, and *Ghost of Tom Joad* made it to number 11. These albums were accompanied by the customary touring throughout the first half of the decade. The material on these records was solid, sold well, and kept Springsteen's music in the fans' ears—that having been said, it is generally accepted that this was not his best work.

In 1999, Springsteen (without the E Street Band) was inducted into the Rock and Roll Hall of Fame by Bono of U2. Also in that year Springsteen reunited the E Street Band, with Patti Scialfa (born Vivienne Patricia Scialfa, July 29, 1953; vocals) now a member, and undertook a tour that lasted for over a year. The "new and improved" E Street Band included both Lofgren and Van Zandt on guitars (*Encyclopedia of Popular Music* 2008). The final dates of this tour ran into mid-2000 and resulted in another live record called *Bruce Springsteen and the E Street Band: Live in New York City.*

The year 2002 brought the first E Street Band studio album since *Born in the U.S.A.* (an 18-year period) called *The Rising*. This album was produced by legendary producer Brendan O'Brien and reflected on the September 11th terrorist attacks. The album was a "critical and commercial knockout . . . [and] is widely considered Springsteen's response to 9/11. But it's also true that its core themes—faith, hope, loss and the creation of strength from each—were at heart a continuation of the work he'd begun decades before" (brucespringsteen.net 2014). The album was released on July 30, 2002, and produced three singles: "The Rising," "Lonesome Day," and "Waitin' on a Sunny Day." The album's title track went on to earn a Grammy and the album itself won the Grammy for Best Rock Album of 2003. Unlike its three predecessors, *The Rising* was a darling of the critics and a commercial success, going to number one in the United States, the United Kingdom, and Canada.

With all of the new momentum built behind the re-formed E Street Band and the success of *The Rising,* the band joined the 2004 Vote for Change tour alongside John Mellencamp, the Dixie Chicks, Pearl Jam, R.E.M., the Dave Matthews Band, and many others. The purpose of the concert was to add Democratic Party support to swing states. After this tour, Springsteen went back in the studio without the E Street Band again. He released *Devils and Dust* in April of 2005 as the third of his "folk" albums to date—along with *Nebraska* and *The Ghost of Tom Joad*. The album was Springsteen's first number-one debut without the E Street Band in the fold. *Devils and Dust* went on to garner five Grammy Award nominations and won for Best Solo Rock Vocal.

The themes of the lyrics on the title track deal with the human ramifications of the Iraq War. Other songs from the album were known to have been written as long as a decade prior. The ensuing tour found Springsteen on stage alone performing in relatively small venues for the onetime stadium master. Following the tour, Springsteen took an opportunity to pay homage to one of his influences—folk music legend Pete Seeger. Springsteen's admiration of Seeger resulted in the April 25, 2006, release of *We Shall Overcome: The Seeger Sessions*. The album was again made without the E Street Band, and instead employed a collection of 18 lesser-known musicians who went on to be referred to as the Sessions Band. The album marked Springsteen's first album of cover songs and the style of playing contained on the album was a mix of "rock, folk, Dixieland, ragtime, gospel, French Quarter, honky-tonk, blues" (brucespringsteen.net 2014). With this, Springsteen had recorded two albums in a row without the E Street Band, both of which were not in the rock and roll style.

September 25, 2007, saw the return of the E Street Band on Springsteen's 15th studio album called *Magic*. The return of the band was again marked by the production of Brendan O'Brien and Studio in Atlanta, Georgia, continuing the sessions that produced the album and took place at Southern Tracks Recording Studio in Atlanta, Georgia, over the spring of 2007. The style of playing on the album was a return to the heavier full band sound and more straight-ahead rock and roll than Springsteen had produced in a while. "*Magic* debuted at #1 on the *Billboard* album chart, and singles 'Radio Nowhere' and 'Girls in Their Summer Clothes' each won Grammys for Best Rock Song" (brucespringsteen.net). In general, the album was reviewed favorably and it charted in several dozen countries. The band toured in support of the new record without Danny Federici, who was in the process of being treated for cancer. Federici lost his battle with cancer and died on March 20, 2008. He was replaced on the tour by Charles Giordano—who is now described as an E Street Band adjunct.

The end of the decade found Springsteen and the E Street Band moving forward again. The band played in support of Barack Obama's presidential campaign, where they premiered the song "Working on a Dream." Ultimately, Springsteen appeared and performed with Pete Seeger at the Obama inauguration in a rousing version of Woody Guthrie's "This Land Is Your Land." Amid all this, Springsteen and the E Street Band played the halftime show of Super Bowl XLIII.

Working on a Dream was released as the band's next studio album on January 27, 2009. The album showcased some of Federici's last work with the band, and his son Jason also played on the song "The Last Carnival"—the song was written to pay tribute

to Danny Federici's life and times with the E Street Band. Stylistically the album was the most diverse in recent Springsteen memory and was also more optimistic in tone than many other recent releases. The album debuted at number one on the *Billboard* list and shot up the charts around the world. It eventually charted at number one in more than a dozen countries. Oddly, the critics were quite disappointed by this effort, claiming that the stylistic diversity amounted to a confusing hodgepodge. Once again proving the critics wrong, the album went gold or platinum in 13 countries.

Released in the fall of 2010, *The Promise* was a collection of "unreleased tracks from the 1977–1978 recording sessions including long-missed studio versions of such live standards as 'Because the Night,' 'Fire,' and Springsteen's most celebrated outtake, 'The Promise'" (brucespringsteen.net 2014). In addition, the band released a series of other records in this year, including *The Promise: The Darkness on the Edge of Town Story,* a six-CD box set of tracks from the period between *Born to Run* and *Darkness on the Edge of Town.* They also released *London Calling: Live in Hyde Park,* which was the recording of the June 29, 2009, show that captured the strength of the E Street Band on the *Working on a Dream* tour. In the middle of 2011, the E Street Band took a major loss when Clarence Clemons died of complications from a stroke.

The year 2012 saw the release of 11 new E Street Band songs released on March 5, 2012. Clemons was recorded with the band for a pair of songs during the sessions that created this album, so *Wrecking Ball* was the last song that included the legendary saxophone player. Ultimately, Clemons was replaced by his nephew Jake Clemons, who has continued to work with the band. On the strength of songs such as "We Take Care of Our Own" and "Rocky Ground," the album was named the best album of 2012 by *Rolling Stone* magazine. The basic theme of the lyrics on this release cast Springsteen in the roll of "shouldering the burden of telling the stories of the downtrodden in the new millennium, a class whose numbers increase by the year" (Erlewine, Allmusic.com, 2014).

As described by long-time band manager Landau, "Bruce has dug as deep as he can to come up with this vision of modern life . . . the writing is some of the best of his career, and both veteran fans and those who are new to Bruce will find much to love on *Wrecking Ball*" (brucespringsteen.net 2014). The album fared well with the critics and fans alike as it debuted at number one in 16 countries, including the United States and the United Kingdom. It went on to gold or platinum status in a dozen countries. In support of the album, the group again toured with great success. The tour lasted until September 2013 and was enormously successful. In April of 2014, Springsteen had the honor of inducting the past and present members of the E Street Band into the Rock and Roll Hall of Fame.

On January 14, 2014, the band released *High Hopes*. It was the 11th number-one debut for Springsteen and put him at the top of the list of number-one debuts behind only the Beatles and Jay-Z. The E Street Band included guest member Tommy Morello (Rage against the Machine) for this album. The record itself was a collection of previously unreleased material culled from recording sessions in New Jersey, Los Angeles, Atlanta, Australia, and New York City. Also released in 2014 was *American Beauty*. As Springsteen described it, it was "a collection of songs I cut at home." The four-song EP was released on 12-inch vinyl and contained four unused songs form the *High Hopes* sessions. With all of the recent releases, it is clear that—although a few members have been lost along the way—Bruce Springsteen and the E Street Band continue on relentlessly.

With a career of such great length, diversity, and critical acclaim, the legacy of Bruce Springsteen and the E Street Band is significant. Springsteen and the band have won 20 Grammy Awards, were inducted into the Rock and Roll Hall of Fame, won two Emmy Awards, repeatedly charted at number one around the world, and have several songs and albums ranked within the *Rolling Stone* Top 500 lists.

In addition, Springsteen received the Kennedy Center Honor in 2009.

Songs by Springsteen and the E Street Band have been covered by dozens of bands, from 10,000 Maniacs to Manfred Mann's Earth Band to the Gaslight Anthem. Beyond cover versions, a long list of bands have credited Bruce Springsteen and the E Street Band's breed of Americana as an influence, including Arcade Fire, Badly Drawn Boy, Bon Jovi, Drive By Truckers, Foo Fighters, the Gaslight Anthem, the Hold Steady, the Killers, and Kings of Leon, only to name a few.

David V. Moskowitz

Selected Discography

Greetings from Asbury Park, N.J., Columbia KC 32432, 1973.

The Wild, the Innocent & the E Street Shuffle, Columbia KC 31903, 1973.

Born to Run, Columbia PC 33795, 1975.

Darkness on the Edge of Town, Columbia LC 35318, 1978.

The River, Columbia PC2 36854, 1980.

Nebraska, Columbia QC 38358, 1982.

Born in the U.S.A., Columbia QC 38653, 1984.

Tunnel of Love, Columbia CK 40999, 1987.

Human Touch, Columbia CK 53000, 1992.

Lucky Town, Columbia CK 53001, 1992.

The Ghost of Tom Joad, Columbia CK 67484, 1995.

The Rising, Columbia CK 86600, 2002.

Devils & Dust, Columbia C2 93900, 2005.

We Shall Overcome: The Seeger Sessions, Columbia 82876 88231 2, 2006.

Magic, Columbia 88697 17060 2, 2007.

Working on a Dream, Columbia 88697 41355 2, 2009.

Wrecking Ball, Columbia 88691 94254 2, 2012.

High Hopes, Columbia 88843215462, 2014.

References

Bruce Springsteen Official Website. 2015. "Biography." Accessed June 2014. brucespringsteen.net/category/the-band.

Covers Project Official Website. 2015. "Bruce Springsteen and the E Street Band." Accessed 2014. www.cover sproject.com/artist/bruce%20springsteen/.

Discogs Official Website. 2015. "Bruce Springsteen and the E Street Band." Accessed 2014. www.discogs.com/artist/219986-Bruce-Springsteen.

Erlewine, Stephen. "Bruce Springsteen and the E Street Band—*Wrecking Ball*," *All Music Guide,* Rovi Corporation, 2014.

Larkin, Colin, ed. "Bruce Springsteen." *Encyclopedia of Popular Music*. Oxford Music Online, 2008.

Ruhlmann, William. "Bruce Springsteen and the E Street Band," *All Music Guide,* Rovi Corporation, 2014.

Ruhlmann, William. "Bruce Springsteen and the E Street Band—*Greetings from Asbury Park, N.J.*," *All Music Guide,* Rovi Corporation, 2014.

Ruhlmann, William. "Bruce Springsteen and the E Street Band—*The River*," *All Music Guide*, Rovi Corporation, 2014.

Ruhlmann, William. "Bruce Springsteen and the E Street Band—*The Wild, the Innocent and the E Street Shuffle, N.J.*," *All Music Guide*, Rovi Corporation, 2014.

Buddy Holly and the Crickets (1955–Present)

With the Crickets and as a solo artist, Buddy Holly (born September 7, 1936, died February 3, 1959; vocals, guitar) enjoyed the briefest of careers, but his fame continues more than a half-century after his death. It can be argued that Holly influenced the future course of rock music to a greater extent than possibly any other musician of the 1950s. The classic four-piece lineup of the Crickets was not the first self-contained rock band with two guitarists, a bassist, and a drummer that recorded largely their own material; however, for many developing young rock and roll musicians of the late 1950s, the Crickets symbolized the self-contained, four-piece paradigm better than any other band. To a large extent, the importance of Buddy Holly and the Crickets derived in large part from the fact that the band wrote much of its own material. The importance of Buddy Holly and the Crickets in this regard is confirmed by music critic Dave

Marsh, who wrote, "The first modern rock band: self-contained for both playing and singing, wrote its own songs and featured the basic two guitars-bass-drums lineup. . . . This [the single 'That'll Be the Day'] is the one where they prove they really were the Beatles' granddaddies" (Marsh 1999, 29).

After Holly left the Crickets in late 1958 and moved to New York, his former bandmates, drummer Jerry Ivan Allison (born 1939) and bassist Joe B. Mauldin (born 1940), teamed with guitarist Sonny Curtis (born 1937) and several other singers and guitarists to keep the Crickets alive. Although the Crickets remained active to some extent into the 1980s and have reemerged from time to time up to the present, their most important post-Holly music was recorded before the middle of the 1960s. And, although the Crickets' greatest commercial success and influence was a result of their recordings with Buddy Holly, the post-Holly Crickets enjoyed a 1962 top 10 hit in the United Kingdom with "Don't Ever Change," and in the process continued to influence British Invasion bands—the Crickets' version of the song was covered in a nearly identical arrangement by the Beatles on a 1963 BBC broadcast. In addition, the unusual chromatic harmonies and use of the subtonic chord in some of the compositions of Holly and Crickets, as well as Jerry Allison's drum style on the Crickets' first post-Holly recordings anticipated what would become defining features of the work of the Beatles and other British Invasion bands.

Charles Hardin "Buddy" Holley (the correct spelling of his family name) was born on September 7, 1936, in Lubbock, Texas, into a family in which amateur music-making was a regular part of everyday life. Buddy, as he was known from his childhood, took violin and piano lessons, but his real desire was to learn to play the guitar. After Buddy rejected the steel guitar his mother gave him, because he wanted a guitar like his older brother played, Holley's mother purchased a regular, Spanish-style instrument for the youngster. Eventually, Holley learned to play bluegrass-style guitar, mandolin, and four-string banjo.

During his high school years, Holley performed country/bluegrass music in duo settings, sometimes

Buddy Holly and the Crickets (from left to right): Joe B. Mauldin, Buddy Holly (with Fender Stratocaster guitar), and Jerry Allison pose for a group shot on the set of the BBC television show *Off the Record* during their UK tour, on March 25, 1958. The popularity and impact of Holly and the Crickets is attested to by their induction into the Rock and Roll Hall of Fame in the inaugural class in 1986. (Photo by John Rodgers/Redferns)

with schoolmate Jack Neal, but more importantly with Bob Montgomery, with whom Holley wrote a number of songs. Both duos secured weekly radio programs on KDAV, which is purported to have been America's first full-time country music station (Norman 1996, 47). Sometimes Holley, Neal, and Montgomery performed together in the community and on radio, at times adding steel guitarist/bassist Don Guess, bassist Larry Welborn, guitarist Sonny Curtis, and other musicians.

Together, the teenaged Holley and Sonny Curtis increasingly listened to and studied the rockabilly and R&B music that could be found on late-night radio broadcasts. It was in 1955 that Holley and Curtis began working with drummer Jerry Allison (drums generally were not used in traditional country music) and first heard Elvis Presley when he performed in Lubbock. Later that year, Holley and his band worked as an opening act for Presley in the Lubbock area. Holley, Curtis, Allison, and Welborn made the musical move from country to rockabilly; however, Bob Montgomery remained true to his country music roots and ceased performing with Holley and the other musicians, although he did continue to write songs from time to time and remained friends with Holley and the others. On the strength of recordings that the musicians cut at KDAV, Buddy Holley secured a contract with Decca Records. Interestingly, the contract that Decca prepared for Holley misspelled his family name as Holly. Holly continued to use the truncated version of his name throughout the rest of his career, even after his contract with Decca expired.

When Holly, Curtis, and Guess (Jerry Allison did not make this first trip to Nashville)—who called themselves the Two-Tones for the brightly colored stage outfits they wore—arrived in Nashville for their first recording session in early 1956, they were in for a rude awakening. Producer Owen Bradley informed Holly that he could not sing and play guitar simultaneously in the studio the way he did in live performances, so Sonny Curtis had to handle the guitar chores by himself. Unbeknownst in advance to the trio from Lubbock, Bradley also arranged for studio musicians to play drums and bass on the session. Ultimately, Holly recorded several sessions for Decca in Nashville throughout 1956, but the singles that the company released under the moniker Buddy Holly and the Three Tunes were unsuccessful. For the most part, the arrangements and performances fell into the mold of the rockabilly of Elvis Presley's early releases on Sun Records. In fact, some of the tracks, which have been reissued on the BR Records double-CD collection *The Singles* + and on MCA's *The Buddy Holly Collection,* found Holly seemingly intentionally imitating Presley, especially in the vocal style he uses on the cover of the risqué R&B tune "Midnight Shift," and on the Sonny Curtis composition "Rock Around with Ollie Vee." Because of the lack of success of Holly's 1956 singles, Decca did not renew Holly's contract when it expired in early 1957. This created an unanticipated problem for Holly later that year, because although expired, under the contract's terms Holly was not permitted to rerecord any of the songs

that he had first cut with Owen Bradley in Nashville for a period of five years.

Throughout 1956 and into early 1957, the musicians with whom Buddy Holly worked and recorded on a regular basis were in a state of flux. Sonny Curtis left the fold when Holly informed the group that he, Holly, would handle both the lead vocals and the lead-guitar part in the future. Although they did know of the relationship at the time, Niki Sullivan, a somewhat distant relative of Holly's, came on board as the rhythm guitarist. For a variety of reasons, bassists Don Guess and Larry Welborn gave way to the less musically experienced Joe B. Mauldin. Mauldin, despite his relative lack of experience on bass, proved to be a better fit in the Crickets than his predecessors, especially in the showmanship he employed on stage.

Before Mauldin replaced Larry Welborn, however, Holly, Allison, Welborn, and Sullivan began recording new material with producer, studio owner, and music publisher Norman Petty in Clovis, New Mexico. One of the pieces that the quartet recorded with Petty was "That'll Be the Day," a song that Holly originally had cut during his time at Decca. The Decca version of the song had not been released, and the version that Holly and company recorded in Clovis was in a better key for Holly's voice. Because of the constraints imposed by Holly's old Decca contract, Petty and his four young charges had to come up with a way of disguising Holly's involvement with the recording. So, the foursome was christened "the Crickets."

Norman Petty pitched the early recordings he had produced of the Crickets to contacts he had in New York, including the general manager of the publishing firm Southern Music, Murray Deutch. In turn, Deutch brought the recordings to the attention of Coral Records executive Bob Thiele. In his autobiography, Thiele wrote, "I was never as confident in my life anything would be a hit record as I was about 'That'll Be the Day'" (Thiele and Golden 1995, 53). However, Thiele received little if any support at Coral, because rockabilly and rock and roll were so far removed from the middle-of-the-road pop music associated with the label. Ironically, Coral was a subsidiary of Decca, the label that earlier had rejected Holly. Thiele ultimately released "That'll Be the Day" on Decca's R&B-oriented label, Brunswick.

Bob Thiele was so convinced of the commercial potential of Buddy Holly and the Crickets that he contracted with the Crickets (including Holly) on Brunswick, but with Holly as a solo artist on Coral. This enabled Thiele to release group singles and Buddy Holly solo singles. It also enabled Thiele to release both harder-rocking and more ballad-oriented material from the same artists on the most stylistically appropriate labels. While this might have allowed more material to reach the public than would otherwise have been possible, it also caused confusion. Specifically, the Crickets' material that Thiele released on Brunswick all clearly featured Buddy Holly singing lead vocals, often on songs that were at least in part credited to Holly as a songwriter, and with Holly playing lead (and sometimes the only) guitar. Conversely, the majority of the songs released on Coral under Holly's name found him accompanied by the other three Crickets.

After its release, "That'll Be the Day" took an unusually long time to become the commercial success and iconic Holly track that it has since become. Before the single broke on the national charts, Holly and his colleagues recorded numerous tracks with Norman Petty still acting as an independent producer. The professional relationship between Holly, the rest of the Crickets, and Petty was complicated. Petty signed Holly to a songwriting contract with his publishing company, but Petty doled out songwriting credits to Holly, Allison, and Mauldin on what in retrospect appears to have been a random basis. What decidedly was not random was the fact that Petty's name was attached to compositions that were written by Holly alone, or by Holly in collaboration with others. Although this was common practice for producers in the 1950s, it is one of the factors that later caused enormous financial headaches for Buddy Holly and may have been at least indirectly responsible for Holly's decision to undertake his final concert tour. Additional future difficulties arose when Allison, Mauldin, and Sullivan—but not Holly—signed a management contract with Petty. Although Holly's absence from the contract appears to have been a direct result of the early 1957 attempts to disguise Holly's involvement with the Crickets, the absence of Holly's name on the management contract caused additional business difficulties near the end of the singer's life.

The convoluted nature of the Holly/Petty/Crickets relationship was further complicated by the fact that recording at Petty's Clovis, New Mexico, studio allowed Holly and the Crickets (with occasional keyboard contributions from either Norman Petty, or his talented keyboardist wife, Vi) to experiment in the recording studio absent the limitations of a time clock or some of the other rules and standards of big-city, record label–run studios. As *All Music Guide* critic Bruce Eder put it, because the group and Petty enjoyed unprecedented freedom in the studio, they were able to create records "that didn't sound like anyone else's, anywhere" (Eder, "Buddy Holly," 2012). The working relationship, then, could be described as bimodal: it offered Holly and the Crickets significant artistic advantages, but also serious long-term disadvantages.

"That'll Be the Day" ultimately became Buddy Holly and the Crickets' highest-charting hit, making it into the top three on *Billboard*'s Best Sellers in Stores chart, Pop Singles chart, R&B chart, and Top 100 chart. The song opened with a turn-around guitar lick that previously had been used in numerous blues songs. Holly presented himself as a cocky character, countering his lover's threats to leave him by explaining to her just how smitten with him she truly was. One of the most notable features of the recording, however, was Holly's guitar solo, which straddled the line between rhythm and lead guitar, all the while referencing licks that Holly adapted from the blues songs that he and Sonny Curtis had listened to and studied just a couple of years before. The fact that Holly straddled the line between rhythm and lead guitar in his solo is notable, because it made his electric guitar style stand out from the typical single-line, more melodically oriented solos of the day. Also notable was Holly's use of the solid-body Fender Stratocaster, the jangling, bright tone of which contrasted with the tone color of the hollow-bodied guitars of other 1950s lead players such as Scotty Moore (Elvis Presley's original lead guitarist), Eddie Cochran, and Chuck Berry. In fact, it can easily be argued that Buddy Holly was the first great proponent of the solid-bodied electric guitar in rock and roll, as well as the first of a long line of iconic rock Stratocaster players.

Another early Petty-produced recording, "Words of Love," was released under Holly's name in June 1957. Although not nearly as commercially successful as Holly and the Crickets' most popular work, this track, which featured Holly playing the only guitar part (Altman and McKaie 1993), was one of the first examples of double-tracked vocals on a rock and roll record—Holly sang both parts of the duet texture. Holly's guitar part anticipates the riff-based rock style that was particularly popular in 1964 and 1965.

On the strength of the growing popularity of "That'll Be the Day," from July to September 1957 the Crickets performed in numerous venues around the United States. Easily the most famous of the band's performances were their August appearances at Baltimore's Royal Theater, Washington's Howard Theater, and New York's Apollo Theater, all traditionally predominantly black venues. Although the late 1950s were a time period of racial tension in the United States, and white acts were few and far between at these venues, audiences received Buddy Holly and the Crickets warmly.

The group's next major release was "Peggy Sue," a single credited to Holly as a solo artist. From the record's opening, "Peggy Sue" sounded unlike any other release of the time. In particular, Jerry Allison's drum playing dominated. Norman Petty used the studio console and his homemade echo chamber to manipulate the paradiddles that Allison performed on a single drum in such a way that the figure constantly changed volume and tone color. Rock critic Dave Marsh described the result as "the biggest drum beats in rock and roll history" and highlighted the percussion effect as an important part of the reason for the iconic status of the recording (Marsh 1999, 82).

One of the aspects of Buddy Holly's writing that distinguished his songs from other rock and roll compositions of the era was the use of subtle harmonic shifts and chromatic harmonies borrowed from the parallel minor key. In the third verse of "Peggy Sue," for example, Holly incorporated an F major chord in this A major piece on the repetitions of the word "pretty." This was the only time that the harmony appeared in the song, and its unusual nature created a striking effect. It should be noted that this sort of unexpected harmonic motion to chords from outside the key marked the work of British rock bands such as Johnny Kidd and the Pirates, the Beatles, and Mod-style bands such as the Kinks and the Who as British rock developed between 1959 and 1964.

Niki Sullivan left the Crickets shortly after a December 1957 appearance on the *Ed Sullivan Show*. Rather than replace the guitarist, the Crickets continued as a trio, still supplemented from time to time on recordings by either Norman Petty or Vi Petty on keyboards and by backing vocal groups. January 25, 1958, found the Crickets recording in New York City with Bob Thiele producing the session. Although not producing, Norman Petty was in the studio and contributed the distinctive piano part on "Rave On," a composition credited to Sonny West, Bill Tilghman, and Petty. It is worth noting that although Buddy Holly was and remains most closely associated with songs he wrote or cowrote, his interpretations of "Rave On" and "Oh, Boy!" (also credited to West, Tilghman, and Petty) and "It Doesn't Matter Anymore" (Paul Anka) remain the songs' definitive versions.

It was not just the biggest-selling songs of Buddy Holly and the Crickets that exerted influence over future rock artists. One of the most forward-looking songs the group ever recorded was "Well . . . All Right," which was certainly not a major hit. However, the introspective lyrics and the intimate acoustic guitar–based texture anticipated the folk-revival-inspired work of British Invasion bands such as the Beatles and the Rolling Stones by about seven years. The song's extensive use of the subtonic chord and the modal mixture of the tonic major and Mixolydian scales also anticipated the harmonic vocabulary of the Mod representatives of the British Invasion (e.g., the Who and the Kinks). Although the song's lyrics included a dated and high school–ish reference to "going steady," the oscillations between the tonic and subtonic chord, the introspective lyrics that oscillate between resignation and resolve, and the acoustic guitar–based texture also would not have sounded out of date even a decade-and-a-half later sung by a 1970s singer–songwriter such as Gordon Lightfoot.

During March 1958, Buddy Holly and the Crickets undertook a month long concert tour of Britain. The importance of this tour on what would later be called British Invasion rock cannot be overstated. Thousands of British youths—whether they be members of the bands that opened for the Crickets, audience members, or viewers of the Crickets' appearance on the television program *Sunday Night at the London Palladium*—connected with Holly in a way that exceeded that of any other American rock and roll star. Holly's music exhibited a connection to the simple skiffle music that was in fashion in Britain at the time, he looked more like a regular person than an inaccessible heartthrob, and he—unlike Elvis Presley (who never in his entire career performed in the United Kingdom)—actually toured the country. And, if the original incarnation of the Crickets proved that the ideal standard rock band of the future consisted of two guitars, bass, and drums, then the truncated spring 1958 edition of the band proved the viability of what would later be called the power trio (e.g., Cream and the Jimi Hendrix Experience).

Tommy Allsup joined Holly and the Crickets as lead guitarist in summer 1958. Allsup was the one holdover from the Crickets who backed Holly on his ill-fated concert tour of early 1959. He also played from time to time in the post-Holly Crickets. Allsup's principal contribution to Buddy Holly and the Crickets' recordings of late 1958 was to bring a more melodically based style to the guitar solos on tracks such as "Heartbeat" and "It's So Easy." This was, however, something of a mixed blessing: while Allsup brought more technical virtuosity to the band, Allsup's style made Holly's last recordings with the group more conventional sounding than earlier releases that had featured Holly's idiosyncratic chord-based soloing style.

After his 1958 marriage to Maria Elena Santiago, Holly broke from the Crickets and Norman Petty and moved to New York City. Beginning in October 1958, Holly recorded several ballads accompanied by strings, including Paul Anka's "It Doesn't Matter Anymore," Boudleaux and Felice Bryant's "Raining in My Heart," and his own "True Love Ways." During late 1958 and early 1959, Holly and his attorneys were locked in a battle over royalties with Norman Petty. Because of this, accounts were frozen that might otherwise have been payable to Holly. The lack of income—in part exacerbated by the immense cost of Buddy and Maria Elena Holly's New York apartment—appears to have been one of the factors that resulted in Holly agreeing to perform as part of the Winter Dance Party tour in January and February 1959.

The tour began on January 23, 1959, in Milwaukee, Wisconsin. From the start, this tour, which included Holly, J.P. "The Big Bopper" Richardson, Dion and the Belmonts, and Ritchie Valens, was filled with problems: there were numerous breakdowns of the original tour bus and its replacements; Holly's drummer, Carl Bunch, was hospitalized with frostbite; and the fact that the performances were scheduled in the order in which they had been booked (instead of in a manner that emphasized efficiency of travel) resulted in significantly lengthier-than-necessary travel from venue to venue.

Because of continuing problems with a malfunctioning heater on the tour bus and a desire to reach Moorhead, Minnesota, early so as to tend to laundry and other tour details, Holly booked a charter airplane from Mason City, Iowa, for departure following a performance in nearby Storm Lake. The plane's passengers, Holly, J.P. Richardson, Ritchie Valens, and the pilot—Roger Peterson—all perished when the aircraft crashed within minutes of takeoff on February 3, 1959.

Despite the fact that the last studio recordings of Holly suggest that he was in the process of turning away from rock and roll to become a middle-of-the-road crooner, unbeknownst to the public there was evidence to the contrary. During the time Holly lived in New York, he made a number of practice recordings on a professional-quality tape machine that he had in his apartment. Although Holly sang on these recordings accompanied solely by his acoustic guitar, the quality of the tapes and the performances were strong enough that several of the songs were overdubbed with additional instruments and backing vocals and resulted in brand new posthumous Buddy Holly releases. While Holly fans are divided on the authenticity and quality of these releases, three of them are of particular significance within Holly's canon as a songwriter.

The best-known of the supplemented practice tape releases, "Peggy Sue Got Married," exists in two versions: (1) a 1959 production by Jack Hansen that replicated the sound of the Crickets, and (2) a 1963 version produced by Norman Petty that hinted at the then-popular surf music genre. The Hansen version resulted in a fairly successful single in the United Kingdom, where it made it to number 17 on the *New Music Express* charts. Although it is dismissed by some fans, "Peggy Sue Got Married" is a rhetorically significant Buddy Holly song. By wrapping up his character's relationship with Peggy Sue, Holly (whether intentionally or not) tied together his entire songwriting output up to January 1959. In doing so, he effectively staked a claim to all of those previous songs with disputed authorship credit and songwriting royalties.

The B-side to the Hansen-produced version of "Peggy Sue Got Married," "Crying, Waiting, Hoping," also enjoyed popularity in the United Kingdom. It was one of the covers that the Beatles included in the repertoire they performed for their unsuccessful January 1, 1962, audition for Decca Records and that they later recorded for an August 1963 broadcast of their weekly BBC radio program, *Pop Go the Beatles*. On both recordings, lead singer George Harrison hinted at some of Holly's vocal mannerisms, and his lead guitar solo was a near note-by-note copy of the studio guitarist on the Hansen-produced track.

After Buddy Holly left the Crickets, Jerry Allison and Joe B. Mauldin resumed performing and recording with guitarist–songwriter Sonny Curtis. The Crickets also added Earl Sinks as lead vocalist. Still signed with Norman Petty as producer and manager,

this four-man lineup of the Crickets—augmented with Vi Petty on piano and the Roses on backing vocals—recorded two sides, Vi Petty's "Someone, Someone" and the Buddy Holly/Bob Montgomery composition "Love's Made a Fool of You," at Petty's studio in late 1958. The Crickets recorded additional tracks with producer Jack Hansen in New York City for what would become their *In Style with the Crickets* album. The album included Sonny Curtis's song "I Fought the Law," which, along with "Love's Made a Fool of You," became hits for the Bobby Fuller Four in 1966, suggesting the continuing commercial viability of Buddy Holly and the Crickets' style of rock and roll into the dawn of the psychedelic era.

The lineup of the Crickets fluctuated considerably after 1960, with several different singers handling the lead vocals, including David Box, who later perished in a plane crash. By 1963, the Crickets consisted of Jerry Allison, Sonny Curtis, Jerry Naylor (vocals), and Glen D. Hardin (piano). Although this incarnation of the Crickets was largely ignored in the United States, the band enjoyed two moderate hits in the United Kingdom, including "Don't Ever Change," a song from the Brill Building songwriting team of Gerry Goffin and Carole King. Interestingly, the Beatles included a near copy of the Crickets' rendition of "Don't Ever Change" in their live repertoire at the time and in an August 1963 BBC radio broadcast. A cover version by the British group Brian Poole and the Tremeloes was also a nearly exact copy of the Crickets' version.

To a large extent, since the mid-1960s the Crickets have been active only sporadically, and then largely as a nostalgia band. However, in 1988, Paul McCartney produced "T-Shirt," a single by the Crickets of the time, Joe B. Mauldin, Jerry Allison, and Gordon Payne. The single enjoyed some sales success and led to an album by the same name. *T-Shirt,* the album, contained a number of songs penned by members of the group, which made reference to the Crickets' earlier days and the continuing specter and influence of Buddy Holly in their lives.

It is no accident that British researchers, writers, and musicians have produced some of the best and most thorough biographies and scholarly studies of Buddy Holly and the Crickets—Holly as a singer–guitarist–songwriter exerted more influence and the Crickets enjoyed far more commercial success in Britain than in the United States. Holly biographer Spencer Leigh quoted Justin Hayward, the guitarist, primary lead singer, and primary songwriter of the Moody Blues, as saying, "In the fifties the BBC rarely played 'pop' music, records were the only way to hear it . . . Our records were our whole lives, and Buddy's are still my favourites" (Leigh 2009, 185). George Harrison of the Beatles identified the music that exerted the greatest influence on his musical circle by saying, "Elvis, Little Richard and Buddy Holly influenced us very much, and to this day theirs is my favourite rock 'n' roll music" (The Beatles 2000, 27). Holly biographers John Goldrosen and John Beecher detailed the influence of Holly and the Crickets on John Lennon and Paul McCartney as songwriters, and on the performance styles and approaches to vocal harmony of British Invasion acts Peter and Gordon, Billy J. Kramer and the Dakotas, the Searchers, and Freddy and the Dreamers (Goldrosen and Beecher 1996, 158–160).

The magnitude of the impact of Buddy Holly and the Crickets on the United Kingdom is further suggested by the fact that while only three Holly and/or Crickets singles ever made it into the *Billboard* Top 10 in the United States, in the United Kingdom, eight singles made it into the top 10 in the trade magazine *New Musical Express,* including two posthumous releases that were issued in 1963 at the height of Beatlemania.

Buddy Holly was inducted into the Rock and Roll Hall of Fame as part of its inaugural class in 1986. Jerry Allison, Joe B. Mauldin, Sonny Curtis, and Niki Sullivan were inducted into the Rock and Roll Hall of Fame as the Crickets in 2012.

James E. Perone

Selected Discography

Buddy Holly and the Crickets, *The Buddy Holly Collection* (1954–1959), MCA MCAD2–10883, 1993.

Buddy Holly and the Crickets, *The Singles +* (1956–1959), BR Music BS 8126–2, 2001.

Buddy Holly and the Crickets, *The Chirping Crickets* (1957), Decca B0001686–02, 2004.

Buddy Holly and the Crickets, *The Chirping Crickets* (1957)/*Buddy Holly* (1958) BGO Records, CD517, 2001. (Note: This "two-for" CD release also includes Bobby Vee's album *I Remember Buddy Holly.*)

The Crickets, *Bobby Vee Meets the Crickets* (1962), BGO Records CD413, 1998.

The Crickets, *Something Old, Something New, Something Blue, Something Else!* (1963).

BGO Records CD242, 1994.

The Crickets, *T-Shirt* (1988), Epic EK 44446, 1988.

References

Beatles, The. *Anthology*. San Francisco: Chronicle Books, 2000.

Eder, Bruce. "Buddy Holly." *All Music Guide,* http://www.allmusic.com/artist/buddyholly-mn0000538677, Rovi Corporation, 2012.

Eder, Bruce. "The Crickets." *All Music Guide,* http://www.allmusic.com/artist/thecrickets-mn0000785648, Rovi Corporation, 2012.

Eder, Bruce. *"Something Old, Something New." All Music Guide,* http://www.allmusic.com/album/something-old-something-new-mw0000199186, Rovi Corporation, 2012.

Goldrosen, John, and John Beecher. *Remembering Buddy: The Definitive Biography*. London: Omnibus, 1996.

Ingman, John. Liner notes for *Still in Style*, CD, Bear Family Records BCD 15599, 1992.

Lehmer, Larry. *The Day the Music Died: The Last Tour of Buddy Holly, the Big Bopper and Ritchie Valens*. New York: Schirmer, 1997.

Leigh, Spencer. *Everyday: Getting Closer to Buddy Holly*. London: SAF Publishing, 2009.

Leigh, Spencer. "Oh Boy: Why Buddy Holly Still Matters," *The Independent* (January 23, 2009), http://www.independent.co.uk/arts-entertainment/music/features/ohboy-whybuddy-holly-still-matters-today-1501271.html.

Marsh, Dave. *The Heart of Rock & Soul: The 1001 Greatest Singles Ever Made*. New York: Da Capo Press, 1999.

McCartney, Paul, et al. *The Real Buddy Holly Story*. DVD D7190. West Long Branch, NJ: White Star, 2004.

Norman, Philip. *Rave On: The Biography of Buddy Holly*. New York: Simon & Schuster, 1996.

Ruhlmann, William. "The 'Chirping' Crickets." *All Music Guide*, http://www.allmusic.com/album/the-chirping-crickets-mw0000198212, Rovi Corporation, 2012.

Thiele, Bob, and Bob Golden. *What a Wonderful World: A Lifetime of Recordings*. New York: Oxford University Press, 1995.

Unterberger, Richie. "In Style with the Crickets." *All Music Guide*, http://www.allmusic.com/album/in-style-with-the-crickets-mw0000838560, Rovi Corporation, 2012.

Buffalo Springfield (1966–1969; 2010–2011)

The foundation for Buffalo Springfield can be found in Greenwich Village with the Au Go Go Singers, a nine-piece house band for the famous Café au Go Go, which both Stephen Stills (born January 3, 1945; vocals, guitar) and Richie Furay (born Paul Richard Furay, May 9, 1944; vocals, guitar) were members of. Neil Young (born November 12, 1945) and Stills first crossed paths at the Fourth Dimension, a coffee house and folk music club in Fort William, Ontario, while Stills was touring with an offshoot of the Au Go Go Singers called the Company. Young's band, the Squires (or Neil Young and the Squires) was opening for the Company, and the meeting of Young and Stills made an impression on both parties.

The Squires were having a hard time, living in the local YMCA, and Young and a guitarist friend, Terry Erickson, hatched a plan to get out of town. They hit the road with their friend Bob Clark and two members of the band the Bonnvilles. Five hundred miles into the trip, near Blind River, Ontario, Young's 1948 Buick hearse, "Mort," broke down, literally dropping its transmission out onto the highway. Clark and the members of the Bonnvilles headed back to Fort William while Young and Erickson rode together on a Honda motorcycle to Ontario.

In Ontario, Young played around as a solo act and worked his way into the local music scene. Early in 1966 he met the bassist Bruce Palmer, who convinced Young to join his band the Mynah Birds. Fronted by Ricky James Matthews (aka Rick James), the Mynah Birds were set to record an album for Motown when Matthews was arrested for being AWOL from the U.S. Navy. Shortly after the record, the deal fell through, Young picked up a 1953 Pontiac hearse, which he dubbed "Mort Two," and he, Palmer, and four other friends set out for Los Angeles to track down Stephen Stills.

The Company had also broken up after their tour in 1965 and Stills made his way to the West Coast where he worked as a studio musician and auditioned for various groups, including an unsuccessful audition for the Monkees. Barry Friedman encouraged Stills to form a band and he subsequently invited former Au Go Go Singers member Richie Furay and the Squires bassist Ken Koblun (born May 7, 1946) to join him, and both men obliged.

Young and Palmer, now in Los Angeles, spent days looking for Stills to no avail and were about to head out to San Francisco. Furay and Stills were sitting in traffic on Sunset Boulevard when Furay turned to brush a fly off his arm and happened to catch a glimpse of a black hearse with Ontario plates driving in the other direction. Stills and Furay knew that it had to be Young in the hearse, and they quickly made an illegal U-turn and chased Young and Palmer down. The four men soon realized they were bonded in their ambition to form a band.

Barry Friedman put the travelers up in his house and they began rehearsing. The name "Buffalo Springfield" came from a Buffalo-Springfield Roller Co. steamroller that was parked in front of Friedman's house. With the name and the four members, all they were missing was a drummer. Enter Dewey Martin (born Walter Dwayne Midkiff, September 30, 1940, died January 31, 2009). Martin, a native Canadian, already had a reputation as a professional musician, having toured with Patsy Cline, Faron Young, and Roy Orbison. After a stint with the rock/bluegrass fusion group the Dillards, Martin was ready for work when he caught wind of a band in need of a drummer. Martin called Stills, who promptly invited him over for an audition, and Buffalo Springfield was in business. Within 10 days of forming and with the help of

American supergroup Buffalo Springfield had a brief but extremely significant career that helped establish a uniquely American sound that persists today. The group, pictured here in the 1960s, was (from left to right): Rich Furay, Dewey Martin, Bruce Palmer, Stephen Stills, and Neil Young. (Photo by GAB Archive/Redferns)

Friedman, the band was out on the road on a Southern California tour opening for the Byrds, one of the biggest bands of the time.

After the tour the Byrds' Chris Hillman convinced the owner of the Whisky a Go Go, a prominent Los Angeles venue, to audition the band. Following the audition they essentially became the house band at the Whisky from May 2 to June 18, 1966. During this run the band attracted a lot of attention and the offers started coming in. Friedman had passed management of the band to his neighbor and Los Angeles lighting engineer, Richard "Dickie" Davis, who navigated the offers and ultimately placed the band with Sonny and Cher's management team, Charlie Greene and Brian Stone. Bruce Palmer once said of Greene and Stone that they "were the sleaziest, most underhanded, back-stabbing motherfuckers in the business. They were the best" (Greenfield 199).

Barry Friedman had produced some demo recordings of the band at Capitol Records, and Greene and Stone were able to get Ahmet Ertegun of Atlantic Records to Los Angeles to listen to the demos. Ertegun saw something special in the band and he knew that there were other record companies after the up-and-coming act, but as Ertegun put it, "It wasn't over money—it was over 'Who's going to understand our music.' And they finally believed in me" (McDonough 166).

Buffalo Springfield signed a contract with Greene and Stone that officially placed them with Greene and Stone's label, York/Pala Records, who then leased the band to Atlantic's subsidiary label, Atco. The publishing deal gave 37.5 percent of the rights to Atlantic and the same to another Greene and Stone company, Ten East, leaving the band with 25 percent to split six ways with Richard Davis, taking a share as a subsidiary member. Greene and Stone then set the band up with equipment, apartments, and expense accounts and convinced the band to let them produce their record.

The band was off to an amazing start, and one more true believer stepped up to help out—John Hartmann, an agent for America's longest-running talent agency, William Morris. With Hartmann's help, the band, still with no record, was booked as an opening act for the Rolling Stones at the Hollywood Bowl and also arranged six appearances on the *Hollywood Palace* TV variety show.

Even with all of their success so early on, not all was well in the Buffalo Springfield camp. Waitresses from the Whisky recall screaming matches between Stills and Young, usually over musical nuances. Young was also feeling suppressed because Greene and Stone found his voice too odd and wanted other band members to sing his songs; they did not even want Neil to sing harmonies. As things became more difficult, Stills tried to control the group, which instantly backfired with the rebellious Young and Palmer.

Around this time Young had a run-in with local law enforcement that ended with Young being assaulted and jailed. Although Young believes there is no link between the events, shortly after he was arrested and beaten he began to suffer epileptic seizures quite frequently, often onstage. This gave Young anxiety, especially when other members of the band began accusing him of faking the seizures for attention.

Young's medical problems came to a head in the summer of 1966 when he had to be taken to the hospital. He ended up staying for 10 days, in which time they performed a battery of tests culminating with the torturous pneumoencephalogram, a procedure invented in 1919 in which one is strapped to a chair and has their cerebrospinal fluid drained and replaced by air in order to view the structure of the brain more clearly in an x-ray. The MRI has since replaced the procedure. The doctors never found out what was wrong, told him not to use LSD (which he never had), and sent him home with a prescription of Dilantin and Valium to curb the occurrence of seizures.

Various drug habits were another source of rising tension in the band. Dewey Martin, an already high-strung person, was using amphetamines, causing him to get on everyone's nerves. Along with the uppers he also had a substantial drinking problem, even though alcohol was a very unhip substance to abuse at the time. For his part, Palmer was ingesting psychedelics as quickly as anyone gave them to him, leading to multiple car accidents and growing distance between himself and the band.

The problems continued once the band went into Gold Star Studio to begin recording, reportedly due to Greene and Stone's lack of talent as producers. Their first single, Neil Young's "Nowadays Clancy Can't Even Sing," sung by Furay, peaked at number 25 in Los Angeles but was hardly heard outside of town. The band ultimately left Gold Star's four-track studio and moved the sessions to Columbia's new eight-track studio B. Once the album was complete, the band took it to a friend's house with a great stereo, dropped the needle, and were devastated; they thought it sounded terrible. Regardless of what the band wanted, the record, *Buffalo Springfield,* was pressed and released in November of 1966 and ultimately provided the group a loyal following and critical acclaim in the new rock press.

Shortly after the initial release of the album, and with sales not living up to expectations, the band was sharing new songs with Ertegun when Stills offered up "For What It's Worth." Ertegun told the band that they needed to record it immediately. As soon as the track was ready they pulled "Baby Don't Scold Me" off of the original album (Atco SD 33–200) and pressed a second version (Atco SD 33–200A) with the new track in the lead position.

Reportedly written in 15 minutes while on psychedelics, "For What It's Worth" was Stills's reaction to riots that were taking place around Pandora's Box on Sunset Strip, the location that became ground zero for the clashing hippie youth and Los Angeles police. One of the great successes of the song is that the lyric is essentially a description of what Stills observed; this topical nature makes this "protest" song palatable by not bludgeoning the listener with an overtly anti-establishment message. The song caught on quickly and became the anthem for the 1960s protest movement. Even hearing the first few bars of "For What It's Worth" today immediately conjures images of the idealistic hippie youth standing toe-to-toe with the boys in blue.

With the help of the new single, *Buffalo Springfield* made its way to number 80 on the *Billboard* 200 charts and "For What It's Worth" broke into the top 10 at number seven on *Billboard*'s Hot 100. Finally the band had a hit single, an absolute necessity for any band that was to be successful at the time.

Other gems on *Buffalo Springfield* include two of Young's offerings, "Flying on the Ground Is Wrong," and "Nowadays Clancy Can't Even Sing" essentially *the* original Buffalo Springfield song. Young wrote the song soon after meeting Stills for the first time. Young taught it to Furay in New York and Furay then took it to Stills when the duo met in Los Angeles. Once Young and Palmer made it to California and the band got going, it was in the repertoire right away. The song illustrates Young's impressionistic lyricism and showcases the band's early talent at arranging within the band. The lyrics of "Nowadays Clancy Can't Even Sing" touch on feelings of insecurity and rejection, with constant time changes giving the feel of tension and release associated with it.

As the album and single were starting to chart, the band headed out to New York to play the Upper West Side club Ondines. Ertegun said of the gigs, "There was no band I ever heard that had the electricity of that group. That was the most exciting group I've ever seen, bar none." But tempers were flaring

within the band and there was even a physical altercation between Palmer and Stills over the volume of the bass at one of the shows. The trip came to an end with Bruce Palmer getting arrested for possession of marijuana, which ultimately got him deported to Canada. Before he was sent away the band was able to get into Atlantic's New York studio to record Young's tune "Mr. Soul." This track was recorded the way the band wanted to be heard—live.

Greene and Stone were credited with producing the song, but it would be the last time they got a production credit with Buffalo Springfield. Tensions were so high between the band and their management that Greene and Stone were only tenuously involved until later in 1967 when they finally had to settle the contract legally.

With Palmer in Canada the band went through a series of stand-in bassists, including Young's former Squires bandmate Ken Koblun (born May 7, 1946), whom they hired to go out on their first tour. The band was sent out on a package tour with some 1950s acts and the Seeds, who alternated closing the nights with Buffalo Springfield. After a few unsuccessful California dates the tour moved into New Mexico and Texas where Buffalo Springfield ditched out over a financial dispute.

Buffalo Springfield was due for another single, and Stills wanted his new song "Bluebird" to take the A-side. Young, however, wanted the newly cut "Mr. Soul," but Young lost this battle, which became a factor in Young suddenly quitting the band in the spring of 1967. The rest of the band tried to convince Young to stick around through the Monterey International Pop Festival, but Young didn't show up and David Crosby sat in with the band. Young did, however, play a date in Los Angeles with Buffalo Springfield, this time with Crosby sitting in for Furay who couldn't make the gig.

The band was on the verge of another break when Young left with an invitation to play the Johnny Carson show. The date was booked, along with some East Coast dates, but just before the band was leaving Young stopped all communication with the other members. Buffalo Springfield was stunted right as they were on the verge of breaking out. The band was forced to replace Young and found a willing party in the guitarist, Doug Hastings.

Young was down when he left. Buffalo Springfield was making him self-conscious of his voice and songs, but he found an ally and friend in producer Jack Nitzsche (born Bernard Alfred Nitzsche, April 22, 1937, died August 25, 2000), Phil Spector's right-hand man. The two began working together to produce solo recordings for Young. This partnership produced one beautiful recording, "Expecting to Fly," a lush yet subdued bit of early psychedelic music, which Nitzsche masterfully filled out with a beautiful string section. "Expecting to Fly" made its way onto *Buffalo Springfield Again* following Young's reunion with the band.

Buffalo Springfield was working on their second album when Young left the band. By that time the recording sessions had already become significantly different from the live-style recording of "Mr. Soul," with only one or two members in the studio at a time. This was partly attributable to the recording style of the biggest new record on the scene, *Sgt. Pepper's Lonely Hearts Club Band*. This made it easier to continue progress on the project when not everyone could be available at the same time; on the other hand it took away from the live feel of the recordings, which can be so important to a band that stands out in live performance.

Young's return to the band was just as abrupt as his departure. He had made big plans with his new friends Nitzsche and Denny Bruce to move to England. They were so serious Nitzsche had even sold his house. However, in true Neil Young style, shortly before their departure the three men were driving home from breakfast when "Mr. Soul" came on the radio. The DJ, B. Mitchell Reid, said dramatically, "When Neil was with 'em, baby" (McDonough 221). At that moment something flipped for Young and he wanted to be back in Buffalo Springfield. Young returned to the band and humbly asked to rejoin. The band obliged and kicked out Doug Hastings.

When Young returned to Buffalo Springfield he brought with him his newly recorded track "Expecting to Fly." "Broken Arrow," another Young composition, further exemplified the influence of *Sgt. Pepper.* The

song incorporated every trick in the book: self-quotes, crowd noises, horns, strings, a jazz quartet, constant time changes, and cryptic lyrics, all combined in a six-minute overture that simply oozed Beatles influence. Whether one views the track as a success or a self-indulgent, overworked hodgepodge of a song, it is, without doubt, an ambitious piece on the part of Young and Buffalo Springfield. It is interesting that "Broken Arrow," the most psychedelic song on the album, was written by the member who had never even tried LSD; it was purely musical psychedelia.

Buffalo Springfield Again was released in October 1967. This time the band remained in control of the majority of the decisions related to the album, even controlling the cover art, an Eve Babitz collage piece. *Buffalo Springfield Again* features 10 tracks, three each from Young and Furay, and four from Stills, and is the band's most ambitious studio effort.

The standout tracks of the album include Young's "Mr. Soul" and the aforementioned "Expecting to Fly," and Stills's "Bluebird" and "Rock and Roll Woman." "Bluebird" is a beautiful earthy song that showcases the guitar work of Stills and Young, which helped make the song an exciting staple of their live shows. It is also a clear and fitting precursor to Stills' work with Crosby, Stills, and Nash, especially his masterful "Suite: Judy Blue Eyes." "Rock and Roll Woman" is a wonderful illustration of Stills' brand of folk rock featuring a rolling vocal backdrop, again reminiscent of his later work with Crosby, Stills, and Nash, and very tasteful guitar work.

Furay, who had not contributed any original compositions to the debut album, offered up one memorable composition to *Buffalo Springfield Again* with "A Child's Claim to Fame," a country-rock tune with a Dobro hook by James Burton. The song also foreshadowed Furay's post-Springfield work with the rock-country band Poco.

Following the release of *Buffalo Springfield Again* the band hit the road with the Beach Boys and Strawberry Alarm Clock and released three singles; unfortunately, none of them took off. Things began to decline once again. Tensions between Stills and Young spawned an altercation in a dressing room that Dewey Martin had to break up. Bruce Palmer also had another run-in with the law when he was pulled over driving without a license with an open bottle of booze and an underage girl who was carrying marijuana. While he was out on bail he was arrested again and quickly sent back to Canada, and Jim Messina, who had worked with the band as an engineer on *Buffalo Springfield Again*, was brought in to substitute. The band also lost their manager, Richard Davis, after he and Martin had a fight following a concert in Fresno.

Fragmented and lacking guidance, Messina tried to get the band back into the studio but could never get the entire band there at the same time; in Young's words, the whole thing was "pieced together by Jim Messina because neither Stills nor I gave a shit" (McDonough 226). Another tour saw chaos in Jacksonville, Florida. With Young's mother and brother, Rassy and Bob, in attendance, Dewey Martin jumped into the audience and local law enforcement shut the concert down and drove the band out of town. Shortly thereafter, Martin Luther King Jr. was assassinated and the tour was canceled, leaving the band with a sizable debt.

The next disaster struck on March 20 when the band was back in California. Stills had moved to a house in Topanga Canyon, and the band was partying with Eric Clapton when one of the neighbors called in a noise complaint. Dewey Martin had just left when he saw the police driving up the canyon. Everyone in the house was arrested except Stills, who had managed to escape out a window. Stills, for his part, ran to a neighbor's house and called Ahmet Ertegun to get legal assistance. The bust made the papers, perhaps because Clapton was already fairly famous, but the lawyers sorted things out quickly and everyone got off with simple disturbing the peace charges—everyone, that is, except for the band's tour manager, Chris Sarns, who was charged with possession of marijuana and was assessed a $300 fine and three years of probation.

Shortly following the bust, the band had a gig at the Long Beach Arena on May 5, 1968; it proved to be their last. When they returned, the band called a meeting with Ahmet Ertegun and announced their breakup. Ertegun was devastated. In the breakup Stills stayed on with Atlantic, but Young was released to Warner Brothers, where he has been ever since. Furay also stayed on with Atlantic until Crosby, Stills, and Nash formed. Poco, Furay's new endeavor, was traded to Epic Records in order to get Graham Nash over to Atlantic.

The final Buffalo Springfield album, *Last Time Around,* was released postmortem in August of 1968. The album featured only two songs by Young, though he also got a cowriting credit with Furay on "It's So Hard to Wait." Five of the 12 tracks go to Stills, Furay contributed three numbers (including "It's So Hard to Wait) and cowrote one song with Micki Callen, and Jim Messina contributed one. The album does have its gems, including Young's plaintive, country-tinged "I Am a Child," Stills's "Pretty Girl Why," and Furay's "Kind Woman." Each individual artist's offerings make sense when you consider their individual directions after Buffalo Springfield, but all in all the album failed to capture the band as a unit and lacked the continuity that makes a great record.

In addition to the group's studio albums there have been multiple "Best Of" releases over the years, the first of which, *Retrospective: The Best of Buffalo Springfield,* was issued by Atco in 1969. More recently a box set titled *Box Set,* in keeping with the lack of creativity in the band's studio albums, was released in 2001. This release features over 30 previously unreleased outtakes, demos, and alternate mixes, along with many of the released versions, on four CDs. For some reason this set is not comprehensive, as there are known unreleased recordings that did not make the set. There are also some songs from the albums that were oddly omitted from the collection.

The band recently made some live appearances, but the deaths of Bruce Palmer in 2004 and Dewey Martin in 2009 made a reunion of the original lineup impossible. In 2010, Stills, Young, and Furay reunited to play the annual Bridge School Benefit Concert organized by Young in Mountain View, California. Bassist Rick Rosas and drummer Joe Vitale joined the trio for a string of dates in 2011 in California and made an appearance at the Bonnaroo Music and Arts Festival in Manchester, Tennessee.

In an interview backstage at Bonnaroo, Furay spoke of plans to do a 30-date tour in 2012; however, this tour was sidelined by Young as he was working on a new album with his longtime band Crazy Horse.

The influence of Buffalo Springfield can be directly traced by the bands that its former members created. Stills, Young, and Furay all had successful solo careers with varying degrees of commercial success, and Young is the standout in this regard with some 37 albums to his credit over a span of six decades. Stills went on to help form the hugely popular Crosby, Stills, and Nash, which was joined at times by Young. In the later 1960s Furay created the rock-country fusion act Poco and went on to work with the Souther Hillman Furay Band. Al Perkins, the pedal steel player for the Souther Hillman Furay Band, introduced Furay to Christianity during this time and his later work with the Richie Furay Band reflects his religious beliefs.

Buffalo Springfield was among the first-generation "Americana" bands to gain commercial popularity, and with that distinction there are a number of acts that followed in their footsteps. The Eagles, Creedence Clearwater Revival, and the Flying Burrito Brothers are of this lineage. More recent acts in this regard include bands like Uncle Tupelo, Ryan Adams, and My Morning Jacket. Additionally, the group's direct influence lived on in the careers of Stills, Furay, and Young, CSNY, Poco, Loggins and Messina, the Eagles, Jackson Browne, and Americana music in general.

It is somewhat amazing that Buffalo Springfield was able to have such a lasting impact considering their short and tumultuous career. It seems they were prone to stunting their own growth every time a major opportunity presented itself. It leaves one to imagine the influence the band could have had if they had been able to gel as a group and fully exploit their various opportunities.

Joshua Rieck

Selected Discography
Buffalo Springfield, Atco, SD 33–200-A, 1967.

Buffalo Springfield Again, Atco, SD 33–226, 1967.

Last Time Around, Atco, SD 33–256, 1968.

Retrospective—The Best of Buffalo Springfield, Atco, SD 33–283, 1968.

Box Set, Rhino Records, R2 74324, 2001.

References
Furay, Richie, and Michael Roberts. *Pickin' Up the Pieces: The Heart and Soul of Country Rock Pioneer Richie Furay.* Colorado Springs, CO: Waterbrook Press, 2006.

Greenfield, Robert. *The Last Sultan, The Life and Times of Ahmet Ertegun.* New York: Simon and Schuster, 2011.

Kubernik, Harvey. *Canyon of Dreams.* New York: Sterling Publishing Co., Inc., 2009.

McDonough, Jimmy. *Shakey: Neil young's Biography.* New York: Random House, 2002.

The Rock and Roll Hall of Fame. All Inductees: Alphabetically. www.rockhall.com.

Unterberg, Richie. "Buffalo Springfield." *All Music Guide.* Rovi Corporation, 2012.

Young, Neil. *Waging Heavy Peace.* New York: Blue Rider Press, 2012.

The Byrds (1964–1973)

In a decade marked by rapid innovation increasing rock and roll's breadth and reach, the Byrds were at the forefront of new musical frontiers. The group pioneered the incorporation of folk, jazz, Indian, country, and blues into rock music. Their music ranges from electronic psychedelia to 1950s Nashville covers, but the Byrds' sound is unmistakable. Led by the sparkling timbre of Roger McGuinn's 12-string Rickenbacker guitar, smooth vocal harmonies, and a gift for simple, catchy melodies, the Byrds remain among the most recognizable 1960s artists today.

The Byrds' lineup originally consisted of lead singer and guitarist Roger McGuinn (born Jim McGuinn, July 13, 1942; guitar, vocals), singer and guitarist David Crosby (born August 14, 1941; vocals, guitar), singer and tambourine man Gene Clark (born Harold Eugene Clark, November 17, 1944, died May 24, 1991; singer), bassist Chris Hillman (born December 4, 1944; bass, mandolin, guitar), and drummer Michael Clarke (born Michael James Dick, June 3, 1946, died December 19, 1993; drums).

British supergroup the Byrds pioneered the incorporation of folk, jazz, country, and the blues in their rock and roll sound. The group, pictured here in 1970, had enormous impact on the power-pop of the 1970s and the new wave/alternative music of the 1980s. (Photo by Michael Ochs Archives/Getty Images)

The band came from a variety of backgrounds: McGuinn hailed from the Chicago suburbs, Clark from the rural central Missouri town of Tipton, and Clarke from Spokane, Washington. Both Hillman and Crosby were born in Los Angeles, Crosby into a wealthy Hollywood family. Both McGuinn and Clark got their start in the music industry fresh out of high school as part of pop-folk groups during the early 1960s folk revival. McGuinn had played banjo for the Limeliters and the Chad Mitchell Trio. He was briefly hired as a songwriter for Bobby Darin, and he played banjo and guitar on Judy Collins's 1963 album *Judy Collins III*. That experience introduced McGuinn to two of the Byrds' iconic early folk covers, "The Bells of Rhymney" and "Turn! Turn! Turn!" Clark had been discovered playing folk music in clubs in Kansas City and joined the New Christy Minstrels as banjo player;

he was featured on two albums. Despite Crosby's privilege, he was a rebellious child who, like Bob Dylan, left home for Greenwich Village. He eventually wound around the country before becoming part of Les Baxter's Balladeers, a group that accompanied TV personality Jack Linkletter around the country.

As the folk revival died down during 1963 and 1964, one event changed all three of their musical paths—Beatlemania. Suddenly, each wanted to move past the slowly stultifying restrictions of folk music and combine folk music with the Beatles' fresh rock backbeat. McGuinn and Clark met one another in Los Angeles and started gigging around as a duo. They had had a passing acquaintance with Crosby through his work with the Balladeers and another folk duo with San Francisco musician Dino Valenti. As the story goes, McGuinn and Clark were practicing together after a show when Crosby joined them. When the three voices harmonized together, the result was pure magic. The three decided to form a group called the Jet Set, with McGuinn and Clark on guitar and Crosby on bass. Crosby was connected with manager Jim Dickson, who provided the group with a recording studio and rehearsal space. In order to fully replicate the Beatles, though, they needed a drummer. The group soon recruited Clarke, who with his tall, handsome features and hippie long hair, looked more the part of a rock drummer than played it. In fact, his first drum set with the Jet Set was made of cardboard boxes! With regular performance space and connections in the music industry, the Byrds soon got their first break, receiving a contract from Elektra and money from a wealthy Los Angeles businesswoman to purchase new instruments. Those funds allowed Clarke to get a real Ludwig drum set, the same as Ringo Starr, but most importantly, McGuinn also purchased the instrument that would come to define the Byrds' sound, a 12-string Rickenbacker electric guitar.

The recording session resulted in a single, "It Won't Be Long/Please Let Me Love You," released under the British-sounding name The Beefeaters. The single did not go anywhere on the charts, and the foursome soon realized the limitations of their current configuration. Clark could not play guitar and sing at the same time, and Crosby was a limited bass guitarist. Crosby moved to guitar, while Clark moved to backup singer and tambourine player. The band's manager, Jim Dickson, asked Chris Hillman, a bluegrass musician who played mandolin for the Hillmen, to play bass. Though the group's first single made little chart impact, it had attracted the attention of a very influential 11-year-old: Michelle Davis, Miles Davis's young daughter, who thought the group sounded like the Beatles. Miles Davis urged his record label, Columbia (also the home of Bob Dylan), to sign the new group, and the contract became official in November 1964. With the quintet signed to a major label, both Dickson and Columbia agreed the Jet Set needed to change their name. McGuinn, keeping with the

aviation theme, suggested the Birds after a song by Valenti. Since "bird" was British slang for "girl," the group decided to alter the spelling. A quick substitution of i for y, and the Byrds were born.

The Byrds' first single was a cover of Bob Dylan's "Mr. Tambourine Man." Dylan initially recorded the song with a rock band for his *Another Side of Bob Dylan* album in 1964, but shelved it. (Ironically, it was released as an acoustic track on *Bringing It All Back Home,* the album on which Dylan notoriously "went electric.") Dickson acquired a copy, and the Byrds began recording it in 1964. Columbia was eager to cross-market artists, and Peter, Paul, and Mary were successful with their cover of Dylan's "Blowin' in the Wind" the previous year, making "Mr. Tambourine Man" a natural choice for the band's first single. One slight problem remained, though: the Byrds had three wonderful singers, but the group was simply not yet talented enough for a major label contract. The Byrds' first recording session in January 1965 thus featured CBS studio musicians, with only McGuinn playing his signature Rickenbacker guitar. The results were fantastic; McGuinn's opening guitar line, followed by the tight harmonies of McGuinn, Clark, and Crosby, arguably best epitomized the Byrds' sound. However, the gap between the exceptional studio ingenuity of the Byrds and their average-at-best live concerts would haunt them throughout their career.

During early 1965, the band began performing nightly at Ciro's Le Disc, a nightclub on the Sunset Strip, in Hollywood. Though their live show was uneven, the band's novel mixture of folk with rock made them the hip band for young actors such as Peter Fonda and Jack Nicholson and the town's many beatniks and hippies. Assisting the Byrds' coolness was their unusual stage presence. The band traded the short hair and button-down shirts of the folk revival for Beatles mops, blue jeans, turtlenecks, and blazers. McGuinn began sporting glasses with small, square lenses, while Crosby draped himself in a green suede cape. The band made no pretense toward ingratiating themselves with the audience, maintaining a detached cool, which added an air of mystery. Most importantly for the band's credibility, Bob Dylan came to Ciro's and dug their rock versions of his songs, even briefly joining them on stage one night. "Mr. Tambourine Man" was released in April 1965, a month after Dylan's own version. The song shot to the top of both the U.S. and U.K. charts, and "folk-rock" became the craze of 1965.

With the rapid success of their debut single, the Byrds rushed to cobble together an album, also titled *Mr. Tambourine Man*. The album continued in the vein of their first single, combining folk and rock with the band's trademark Rickenbacker jangles and vocal harmonies. Folk songs dominated the album; *Mr. Tambourine Man* featured four Dylan covers, including the title track, "Spanish Harlem Incident," "Chimes of Freedom," and "All I Really Want to Do," as well as "The Bells of Rhymney," a song about a Welsh miners' strike popularized by Pete Seeger and Judy Collins. Not content to be merely a cover band, the Byrds also included four originals written by Gene Clark, the band's most prolific songwriter. The breezy, up-tempo "I'll Feel a Whole Lot Better" and brooding "I Knew I'd Want You" were original contributions to the new folk-rock style. Beginning a trend of whimsical final songs, *Mr. Tambourine Man* closed with "We'll Meet Again," the Vera Lynn torch song ironically played over the apocalyptic end of Stanley Kubrick's *Dr. Strangelove*.

The album was a top 10 success in both the United States and United Kingdom, and the Byrds spent the summer touring across America. Their flight, however, was not without its turbulence. Their second single, "All I Really Want to Do," was released simultaneously with two other Dylan covers, including Cher's version of "All I Really Want to Do." While the Byrds' version reached number four in Britain, it barely scraped the bottom of the U.S. Top 40, even getting outsold by Cher. Troubles continued in August, when the band embarked on a British tour. Right before they left, the American press was crowning the Byrds "America's Answer to the Beatles." Much like the Beatles took the United States by storm in early 1964, the Byrds were expected to do the same in

Britain. However, the young Byrds were not nearly as polished as the Hamburg-tested Beatles, and their cool Los Angeles demeanor went over poorly with the British press. Though the band tanked in the press, they became close with the hip British Invasion groups, including the Rolling Stones, the Who, and even the Beatles. The Fab Four visited the Byrds in Los Angeles, and George Harrison later used the riff of "The Bells of Rhymney" for his "If I Needed Someone" on *Rubber Soul*.

The Byrds' British tour did not go according to plan, but the group's third single, "Turn! Turn! Turn!," rocketed them back to the top of the U.S. charts. The single was a rock version of a setting of Ecclesiastes 3:1–8 popularized by Pete Seeger. The use of biblical texts was considered potentially controversial, but the final line, "a time for peace/I swear it's not too late," dovetailed with anti-Vietnam and Civil Rights movements. The subsequent album, *Turn! Turn! Turn!,* followed their first album by combining Dylan covers, "The Times They Are a-Changin'" and the then-unreleased "Lay Down Your Weary Tune" with Gene Clark's originals, including the breezy "It Won't Be Wrong" and "Set You Free This Time." The band became more politically engaged, especially in McGuinn's poignant adaptation of the folk song "He Was a Friend of Mine" in memory of recently assassinated President John F. Kennedy. However, just like "We'll Meet Again" on *Mr. Tambourine Man,* the album closed with a whimsical cover, this time the Stephen Foster standard "Oh Susannah." Released in December 1965, *Turn! Turn! Turn!* reached the top 20 in both the United States and the United Kingdom. While 1965 made the Byrds the king of folk rock, the following year would see the band expanding into new musical terrains, led by David Crosby.

Crosby was a fan of avant-garde jazz legend John Coltrane and Indian sitarist Ravi Shankar. When the Beatles visited the Byrds in 1965, he introduced George Harrison to Shankar's music. Harrison, of course, subsequently purchased a sitar, using it on "Norwegian Wood (This Bird Has Flown)" on the Beatles' *Rubber Soul*. During their U.S. tour in late

1965, Crosby played Coltrane's *Africa/Brass* and *Impressions* and Shankar's records repeatedly on the band's tour van. The Byrds' immersion into jazz and Indian music resulted in their following landmark single, "Eight Miles High"/"Why." For "Eight Miles High," McGuinn attempted to emulate Coltrane's saxophone playing in his guitar solos. The opening riff quotes the first four notes of his "India," the first track from *Impressions,* and the guitar breaks attempt to capture some of Coltrane's musical gestures. "Why" turns to Shankar's music, especially in the lengthy guitar solo, in which the band drones on one harmony like a Shankar raga while McGuinn filters his guitar to sound like a sitar.

Released in March 1966, "Eight Miles High" was rising into the top 20 in the *Billboard* charts when the song was censured by the Gavin Report for potential drug references. The lyrics ostensibly describe the euphoria of a transcontinental flight to London, changing the "six miles high" of usual commercial traffic to eight. However, in the LSD- and marijuana-fueled days of the mid-1960s, other meanings of the word "high" could be implied. The Byrds vehemently denied it—Roger McGuinn famously stated, "We could have called the song 'Forty-Two Thousand Two Hundred and Forty Feet,' but somehow this didn't seem to be a very commercial song title"—but the song was blacklisted by many radio stations" (Hjort 2008, 93–94). Despite the song's controversy, the single placed the Byrds at the vanguard of what critics called "raga-rock," the incorporation of Indian influences in rock music. The Beatles continued to sing the Byrds' praises, and later in the year the band played seminal rock and jazz clubs like Los Angeles's Whisky a Go Go and New York's Village Voice theater.

The Byrds would do so, however, without their most prolific songwriter, Gene Clark. The band was about to take off to New York City when Clark was struck with a severe fear of flying. He could not stay on the plane and insisted the Byrds leave without him. (Ironically, the Byrds were performing to promote their "Eight Miles High" single.) Clark had written all the originals on their first two albums. With Clark gone, the band veered away from his bouncy

folk-rock tracks to new, experimental music fueled by Crosby's jazz and Indian influences and Hillman's bluegrass background. These diverse influences fused into their most diffuse album, *Fifth Dimension.* The title of *Fifth Dimension,* like "Eight Miles High," could be an oblique reference to drugs, but McGuinn insisted that the "fifth dimension is the threshold of scientific knowledge" (Rogan 1990, 70). This concept backed the lyrics of the title track, "5D," which contained lines like "my two-dimensional boundaries are gone." "Eight Miles High" remained the album's highlight, but tracks like the jaunty "Mr. Spaceman," the sitar-like guitar punches and light hearted existential puzzlement of "What's Happening!?!?," Crosby's first recorded song, and the funky "I See You," demonstrated the band moving in exciting new directions. Even their folk songs, "Wild Mountain Thyme" and "John Riley," incorporated lush, majestic orchestral strings. Other highlights included an up-tempo version of "Hey Joe," which the Jimi Hendrix Experience would use for their legendary debut single the following year; the haunting "I Come and Stand at Every Door," a dirge about the wandering spirit of a child killed in the Hiroshima bombing; and "Satisfied Mind," which heralds the group's first foray into country music.

In a year marked by experimentation and expansion of what rock music could be (*Revolver, Pet Sounds, Blonde on Blonde*), *Fifth Dimension* showed the band at the forefront of rock's development. The marked change in musical direction in the Byrds' third album proved less commercially successful than their predecessors, only barely scraping the bottom of the U.S. Top 20. However, the album prepared the group for perhaps their two most important albums, *Younger Than Yesterday* and *The Notorious Byrd Brothers.* In these albums, the experimentation of *Fifth Dimension* cohered into a unique sound blending psychedelia, country, jazz, soul, and Indian music, while retaining McGuinn's signature Rickenbacker jangles.

Younger Than Yesterday was titled after the lone Dylan cover on the album, *My Back Pages,* whose refrain goes, "Oh but I was so much older then/I'm younger than that now." Unlike the band's previous albums, which split covers and originals roughly equally, *Younger Than Yesterday* only has one cover, "My Back Pages." The rest of the tracks show Crosby, Hillman, and McGuinn developing their own unique songwriting voices. McGuinn's "CTA-102" was a bright, whimsical tune named after the first discovered quasar, mixing jaunty melodies and space themes in the vein of "Mr. Spaceman." "So You Want to Be a Rock and Roll Star," written by Hillman and McGuinn, offered a satiric jab at music industry machinations. The song notably opened with a recording of screaming fans from their England tour, marking one of the first uses of "found sound" in rock music. Hillman's contributions, including "Have You Seen Her Face" and "The Girl Who Has No Name," were strong originals with winsome melodies and a steady, up-tempo beat, while the shuffle rhythm and close harmonies of "Time Between" betrayed his bluegrass background. David Crosby's tracks were perhaps the most radically divergent and most psychedelic. "Renaissance Fair" invoked the sensations of a fair Crosby attended, using a chant-like melody, descriptive lyrics, and possible references to hallucinating. "Mind Gardens" similarly featured a droning melody and lyrics comparing the mind with a garden. The song interestingly quoted Shakespeare's *Hamlet,* "the slings and arrows of outrageous fortune" in Hamlet's famous "To Be or Not to Be" soliloquy.

Younger Than Yesterday found the group's songwriting becoming stronger, but despite catchy singles like "So You Want to Be a Rock and Roll Star" and "Have You Seen Her Face," the album sold even worse than *Fifth Dimension.* Not even "My Back Pages," an attempt to capitalize on the success of their earlier Dylan covers, mustered the success of the previous year. The Byrds were again plagued by international touring woes; a return tour to England, Sweden, and Italy was poorly received. The band was also suffering from internal frictions, mostly due to David Crosby's increasingly rebellious behavior. During the 1967 Monterey Pop Festival, he accused the Warren Report of covering up a conspiracy about John F. Kennedy's assassination. He also began hanging out with Graham Nash of the Hollies and Stephen Stills of

Buffalo Springfield, even performing with the latter group during the Monterey Folk Festival to the consternation of the rest of the Byrds. Crosby began recording songs singlehandedly, including "Lady Friend" and "Triad," without the rest of the band's participation. Midway through recording *The Notorious Byrd Brothers,* tensions reached a boiling point, and Crosby was summarily fired from the group. Initially, Gene Clark returned to fill his spot, and he even contributed the album's tender "Get to You." Clark's fear of flying soon reared its head, though, and within a month he was gone, this time for good. Soon after Crosby left the group, Michael Clarke also decided he had enough, leaving shortly after the album was finished.

The Notorious Byrd Brothers, released in January 1968, culminated the musical experimentation of their previous two albums, despite the extensive turmoil during its recording. Crosby's selections, "Draft Morning," "Tribal Gathering," and "Dolphin's Smile," merged psychedelic lyrics with studio experimentation. "Draft Morning," a song describing a man's feelings on the eve of his enlistment to Vietnam, featured wild phasing in the choruses and a delightfully skewed rendition of an army reveille in the coda. "Tribal Gathering" depicted a be-in Crosby attended in San Francisco earlier in 1967, featuring funky, syncopated verses and a haunting, chant-like melody. "Dolphin's Smile" used a Moog synthesizer to mimic the chirping of a dolphin, marking one of the first uses of the Moog in a pop album. McGuinn's songs bookended the album with not-so-subtle connections between expanded horizons and drug use. "Artificial Energy" was a paean to amphetamines featuring phased and flanged guitars and surrealist lyrics. "Space Odyssey" featured Moog sound effects to mimic a space voyage. Chris Hillman's "Natural Harmony" and "Change Is Now" ratchet up the psychedelic meter on his *Younger Than Yesterday* contributions, while "Old John Robertson" merges country and rock with a strange, almost Baroque-like interlude.

Perhaps the most affecting tracks on the album, though, were two covers of songs written by Carole King and Gerry Goffin. King and Goffin achieved fame writing girl group hits like Little Eva's "Locomotion" and the Shirelles' "Will You Still Love Me Tomorrow," but began combining their melodic gifts with deeper lyrics, as evidenced in the Monkees' hit "Pleasant Valley Sunday." "Goin' Back," the album's first single, was a touching piece of nostalgia with a country-rock backing that resembled the simpler folk rock of their first albums. "Wasn't Born to Follow" likewise weaves a tale of rugged individualism, which the Byrds placed under a clopping shuffle beat. Like in "Old John Robertson," the middle explodes the song in flanges and phases over an obsessively repeated harmony. As Ric Menck rhapsodized, "the band locks into a one-chord drone that pounds with the intensity of a ferocious garage rock band, and McGuinn explodes into a searing guitar solo that lifts the track up into the heavens. . . . Suddenly there we are, riding in the clouds with God" (Menck 2005, 104). The power of this track led director Terry Southern to use it in his groundbreaking 1969 film *Easy Rider* as the soundtrack to Wyatt (Peter Fonda) and Billy's (Dennis Hopper) majestic, pot-laced motorcycle ride through scenic Rocky Mountain roads. Despite these varied influences, *The Notorious Byrd Brothers* seamlessly flowed from track to track. Famed rock critic Jon Landau lauded the band's "ability to assimilate everything that they touch" in a *Rolling Stone* review (Njort 2008, 158).

While *The Notorious Byrd Brothers* arguably marked the band's peak, it also heralded the most tumultuous period of the band's career. With the five original members now down to two, McGuinn filled the group with two country musicians, drummer Kevin Kelley and singer/guitarist Gram Parsons. Parsons had recently formed the International Submarine Band, whose *Safe at Home* was considered the first country-rock album. The addition of Parsons, combined with Hillman's bluegrass background, marked the beginning of the third phase of the Byrds—as a full-fledged country-rock band. Their first album in this vein was *Sweetheart of the Rodeo,* an album full of lap steel twang, close harmonies, moanin' honky-tonk lyrics, fiddle lines, and shuffle rhythms. The cover featured a cowgirl in 19th-century attire framed by pictures of cowboys and horses. While the band's

previous two albums featured new, experimental originals, *Sweetheart* featured almost exclusively covers. The band continued to pull from its folk music background, turning two then-unreleased Dylan songs, "You Ain't Goin' Nowhere" and "Nothing Was Delivered" into country romps. "Pretty Boy Floyd," a Woody Guthrie song about a generous outlaw, featured bluegrass banjo picking and Chris Hillman's mandolin frailing. The Byrds performed a wide assortment of country standards, including Merle Haggard's "Life in Prison," the Louvin Brothers' "The Christian Life," and Cindy Walker's "Blue Canadian Rockies." The only originals on the record were two Gram Parsons tracks, "Hickory Wind," a gorgeous reminiscence of South Carolina's lush hickory forests, and the futuristic "One Hundred Years from Now."

Sweetheart of the Rodeo is considered today one of the most influential country rock albums of the 1960s. As reviewer Mark Deming wrote, "At a time when most rock fans viewed country as a musical L'il Abner routine, the Byrds dared to declare that C&W could be hip, cool, and heartfelt" (Deming n.d.). However, it was the least successful of the band's albums to date, reaching only number 77 in the U.S. *Billboard* charts. Neither of the album's two singles, "You Ain't Goin' Nowhere" and "I Am a Pilgrim," reached the top 40. Like *The Notorious Byrd Brothers,* the album was marred by controversy. McGuinn had originally intended the album to be a revue of 20th-century musical genres, but Parsons's and Hillman's slavish devotion to country shelved the idea. Yet, due to a contract dispute with Parsons's previous record label over his departure from the International Submarine Band, the Byrds were forced to remove his vocals from the album. While Parsons's Southern twang was a perfect match for the album's lap steel and Rickenbackers, McGuinn's emulations, awkwardly heard in "The Christian Life," paled in comparison. Lastly, Parsons and McGuinn fought for control of the band. By the time *Sweetheart of the Rodeo* was released, Parsons was no longer a Byrd.

The Byrds' tours were similarly tumultuous. The band performed at country music's most prestigious venue, Nashville's Grand Ole Opry, but they were caught between the rock crowd, who thought country music was too square, and the country crowd, who thought the Byrds' psychedelic background made them interlopers on their turf. The band also briefly toured South Africa, but they became ensnarled in apartheid politics and the tour ended in a disaster. By the end of 1968, Chris Hillman and Kevin Kelley had departed, leaving Roger McGuinn as the only remaining Byrd from the band's founding just four years earlier.

Drummer Gene Parsons, guitarist Clarence White, and bassist John York joined the band in the wake of *Sweetheart of the Rodeo.* The following album, 1969's *Dr. Byrds and Mr. Hyde*, retained the country influence of the previous two albums but with a harder rock edge. The band opened with another Dylan cover, a fuzzed-out version of "Wheels on Fire" (which was also heard on the Band's *Music from Big Pink*), and offered some political satire in "Drug Store Truck Drivin' Man." The group flashed their tender, lyrical side on "Old Blue" and "Your Gentle Way of Loving Me." With the changes in the band, though, *Dr. Byrds and Mr. Hyde* continued the band's commercial decline.

After the album, York left to be replaced by bassist Skip Battin. The new quartet, the most stable lineup in the Byrds' history, interestingly marked a 180-degree turn from the band's beginning. The earlier Byrds were excellent on record but barely passable on stage, while the new Byrds were an excellent touring group with lackluster albums. This was evidenced in *Untitled,* a double album pairing an inspiring live disc of the band's greatest hits with mediocre country rock on the other side. However, the album featured the stately "Chestnut Mare," which returned the band to chart success in the United Kingdom. Their wholly studio albums, *Ballad of Easy Rider* (1969), *Byrdmaniax* (1971), and *Farther Along* (1971) failed to make much commercial impact. In 1973, McGuinn and Crosby made amends, and the original five members returned to the studio to create a new album. The re-formed group tried to harness the magic of their first few albums, but old

tensions reared their ugly heads, and the resulting album, *Byrds,* was poorly received. As the original Byrds disbanded again, the touring group also slowly dissolved. By the end of 1973, Roger McGuinn officially retired the Byrds name and embarked on a solo career.

Though the band's albums had a slow commercial decline from their opening folk-rock salvo, the Byrds have endured as one of the most influential groups of the 1960s. The band's interests in folk, psychedelia, and country presaged their incorporation by many subsequent 1960s groups. It is difficult to imagine Woodstock or the Haight-Ashbury Summer of Love without the Byrds' influence in the 1960s (Unterberger 2002). The band's Rickenbacker guitar sound found new life in 1970s power-pop groups like Big Star, 1980s new wave/alternative music artists such as R.E.M. and the Bangles, and early 2000s indie bands like the Olivia Tremor Control and the Apples in Stereo. Byrds members also enjoyed incredible success after their departures. Crosby joined with Stephen Stills of Buffalo Springfield and Graham Nash of the Hollies to form the folk-rock supergroup Crosby, Stills, and Nash (which occasionally included Neil Young as well). Gram Parsons and Hillman formed the Flying Burrito Brothers, whose debut album, *The Gilded Palace of Sin,* is a landmark of 1960s country rock. Parsons also released two influential solo albums, *G.P.* and *Grievous Angel*, before his untimely death in 1973 from drug abuse. The band was deservedly elected into the Rock and Roll Hall of Fame in 1991. Just like classical music has its three Bs—Bach, Beethoven, and Brahms—the Byrds sit ensconced next to the Beatles and the Beach Boys as the "Killer B's" of the 1960s.

David K. Blake

Selected Discography

Mr. Tambourine Man. Columbia CS 9172, 1965.

Turn! Turn! Turn! Columbia CS 9254, 1965.

Fifth Dimension. Columbia CS 9349, 1966.

Younger Than Yesterday. Columbia CS 9442, 1967.

The Notorious Byrd Brothers. Columbia CS 9575, 1968.

Sweetheart of the Rodeo. Columbia CS 9670, 1968.

Ballad of Easy Rider. Columbia CS 9942, 1969.

Dr. Byrds and Mr. Hyde. Columbia CS 9755, 1969.

(Untitled). Columbia G30127, 1970.

Byrdmaniax. Columbia KC30640, 1971.

Farther Along. Columbia KC 31050, 1971.

Byrds. Asylum SD 5058, 1973.

References

Deming, Mark. "Sweetheart of the Rodeo." *All Music Guide*. Rovi Corporation. 2014.

Hjort, Christopher. *So You Want to Be a Rock 'N' Roll Star: The Byrds Day-By-Day 1965–1973*. London: Jawbone Press, 2008.

Menck, Ric. *The Notorious Byrd Brothers*. New York: Continuum, 2007.

Rogan, Johnny. *Timeless Flight: The Definitive Biography of the Byrds*. Brentwood, UK: Square One Books, 1990.

Rogan, Johnny. *Requiem for the Timeless, Volume 1*. Bury St. Edmunds, UK: R. House, 2012.

Unterberger, Richie. *Turn! Turn! Turn! The '60s Folk Rock Revolution*. San Francisco: Backbeat Books, 2002.

C

Captain Beefheart and His Magic Band (1965–1982)

Captain Beefheart and His Magic Band (1965–1982) pushed past the boundaries of rock music, inventing a radical kind of popular music that, to this day, continues to surprise and astonish. The music has become a touchstone for total musical freedom. It was punk well before punk and entirely unpopular popular music. Musicologist David Sanjek commented on the band's most important album, "Most people never heard of it and if they did listen to it, they wouldn't want to listen to it again" (Sanjek 2012). The band, however, was and is immensely influential on generations of edgy, arty musicians. Of the band's 13 studio albums, *Trout Mask Replica* (1969) is by far the most well known and is often included in surveys of the most influential rock albums of all time.

The story of Captain Beefheart and His Magic Band is fascinating in and of itself. It is laden with myths and tall tales created by an impossibly strong-willed painter and sculptor, Don Van Vliet (aka Captain Beefheart, born Don Glen Vliet, February 18, 1941, died December 17, 2010; vocals, harmonica, saxophone), who could not read or write notated music and yet conceived complicated musical pieces. He claimed that he remembered his own birth, went a year and half without sleep, could foretell when a phone would ring, and possessed three-and-a-half-inch ears. Vliet created his persona as a *sui generis* (unique) genius. Critic Ben Thompson (2001) stated, "It would not be an exaggeration to call Beefheart the most mythical figure in all popular music," and rock historian Greil Marcus (2011) described Van Vliet as a trickster figure (Marcus 2011).

To support his self-mythologizing, Van Vliet deliberately did not give credit to the members of the Magic Band as musicians as well as creative contributors. Every band member was known by their band name, assigned by Van Vliet. The Magic Band had its own fraught history, and not surprisingly, the band went through significant and complicated personnel changes. Some members went on to acclaim as solo artists—for example, Ry Cooder (born Ryland Peter Cooder, March 15, 1947; guitar). However, two of the most important and long-lived members of the band, Bill Harkleroad (aka Zoot Horn Rollo, born Bill Harklewood, December 12, 1948; guitar) and John French (aka Drumbo, born John Stephen French, September 29, 1948; drums, vocals, guitar), were known chiefly only by Beefheart fans. A significant number of Magic Band members were members of Frank Zappa's Mothers of Invention. This was not coincidental: Van Vliet sporadically worked with Zappa, his high school friend.

The band's first few albums were of their time, a combination of blues and psychedelia popular in the mid- to late 1960s, and music industry promoters thought they could make the band huge rock stars. However, between Van Vliet's curmudgeonly and paranoid personality and the increasingly difficult music, it became apparent that the band would never become massively commercially successful. By 1969, the year *Trout Mask Replica* was recorded, the band had transitioned to a totally avant-garde sound. Critically acclaimed, the album landed the band on the cover of *Rolling Stone* in May 1970. The subsequent album, *Lick My Decals Off, Baby,* also traveled in the same musical territory. Subsequent albums grew

American musician, singer, songwriter, artist, and poet Captain Beefheart (Don Van Vliet), on the right, and his Magic Band pose for a portrait in Topanga, California, on February 26, 1969. Together with the Magic Band, Captain Beefheart released radical music that remains influential to this day and contained punk music elements before punk existed. (Photo by Ed Caraeff/Getty Images)

increasingly more commercial, but the music only returned, in part, to its edgy aesthetic in its last six years.

Van Vliet had a multi-octave vocal range, but his growly, deepest blues voice (similar to that of blues musician Howlin' Wolf) is often described as the signature of the band's sound. The music was often based in the blues, both Delta and urban, frequently featuring slide guitar and Van Vliet on harmonica. Free jazz, rock, minimalist classical music, and spoken word are other key elements of the music. For the most part, the sound fits no genre or category in popular music. Many critics and scholars of Beefheart allude to art movements including Dada and Surrealism, as well as the pure spontaneity of Abstract Expressionism (which heavily influenced Van Vliet's own painting) (Courier 2007). Of all rock bands, Captain Beefheart aligned the most closely with the

visual arts. Lyrically, as well as musically, absurdism was combined with primitivism. The early 20th-century Dadaists created sound poetry, and Van Vliet's lyrics break with standard lyrical conventions of logic. The influence of jazz poetry from the 1950s was also found in the half-sung, half-spoken, or entirely spoken vocals. Thematically, a common lyrical thread was nature and ecology. Van Vliet gravitated to animals specifically because they were not humans. However, the line of separation was fairly thin: Van Vliet's lyrical universe was populated by strange, hybrid creatures such as Ant Man Bee.

A child prodigy sculptor, Don Van Vliet was born in Glendale, California, and grew up in the Mohave Desert of California. A fan of rhythm and blues, he loved Muddy Waters, Jimmy Reed, John Lee Hooker, and Bo Diddley as well as free jazz, including Ornette Coleman and Cecil Taylor. He went to high school in Lancaster, California, where he befriended Frank Zappa. Zappa became an important figure at critical junctures in the history of the band and Van Vliet's career. In 1964, the two moved to Cucamonga, California, and formed a band called the Soots, but the project floundered and Beefheart went home to Lancaster while Zappa went on to Los Angeles and formed the Mothers of Invention. On his return to Lancaster, Van Vliet took on the stage name of Captain Beefheart. The name came from a film that he and Zappa never made, *Captain Beefheart Meets the Grunt People.*

The first Magic Band, formed by guitarist Alex St. Clair (born Alexis Clair Snouffer, September 14, 1941, died January 5, 2006; guitar), a high school friend of Frank Zappa, played covers of rhythm and blues songs and became a very popular live band. Van Vliet was with the band largely from its inception. A & M Records signed the band in 1964 and released a single, a cover of Bo Diddley's hit, "Diddy Wah Diddy." The single sold enough for A & M to commission the band to record its first album, but the record company did not like the music and rejected the album. Some tracks were released in 1984 as *The Legendary A & M Sessions.* St. Clair also played on the band's first official album, *Safe as Milk,* as well as the subsequent album, *Strictly Personal.* Longtime

Magic Band member John French played drums. *Safe as Milk* (1967) opened up with the pronouncement, "I was born in the desert . . . came on up from New Orleans." A mixture of reworked older material and new songs, *Safe as Milk* was heavily based in psychedelic blues and features outstanding slide guitar playing by Ry Cooder. Cooder, fed up with Van Vliet, abruptly quit the band, precipitating a cancellation of their gig at the historic Monterey Pop Festival. Some of the theremin-accented rock and pop-oriented songs sound of their time (the 1967 "Summer of Love"), but others incorporate unexpected time changes or feature spoken vocals. "Electricity," the standout song on the album, was later covered by Sonic Youth.

At this relatively early stage of his musical career, Van Vliet had the opportunity to hear jazz musician Rahsaan Roland Kirk perform. Kirk was an audacious player of not only the saxophone but other brass and woodwind instruments and would sometimes play multiple instruments simultaneously. Van Vliet was awestruck and inspired—he and Kirk eventually became lifelong friends. The *Mirror Man Sessions* (some material was recorded for an aborted double album titled *It Comes to You in a Brown Paper Wrapper*) were originally recorded in 1967/8 on the Buddah label and released in 1971 as *Mirror Man*. The songs were lengthy, psychedelic blues jams. "Tarotplane," an intense blues song, takes its title and some of its lyrics from Robert Johnson's classic blues song "Terraplane Blues." "Kandy Korn" was typical of how the recording marked a transition toward the more sophisticated fare of *Trout Mask Replica*. As Buddah Records shifted to bubblegum pop, they dropped the band from its label.

Full-blown acid rock with an ample dose of blues, *Strictly Personal* (1968) marks the band's transition from the semi-commercial to the out-and-out noncommercial. Drug references were explicit in songs such as "Ah Feel Like Ahcid." The blues infuse the album but were also satirized as well. Jeff Cotton (aka Antennae Jimmy Semens, born Jeffrey Ralph Cotton, May 31, 1949; guitar) joined the band on guitar and stayed on through *Trout Mask Replica*. Producer and record label owner Bob Krasnow remixed the tracks to create a more psychedelic sound. Van Vliet was outraged, claiming that changes were made without his consent. Accordingly, the next album, *Trout Mask Replica,* produced by Frank Zappa for Zappa's Straight Recordings, provided Van Vliet complete control of the recording process. In the same year, Zappa provided Van Vliet with the opportunity to sing "Willie the Pimp" on Zappa's *Hot Rats* (1969).

Trout Mask Replica (1969) was by far the most influential and critically acclaimed Captain Beefheart album. However, the album's greatness came at a high cost. *Trout Mask Replica* took over a year to compose and record under extreme conditions. The band lived and worked in an isolated cabin in Woodland Hills, outside of Los Angeles. Van Vliet kept his young band of talented musicians in a state of fear and dependency. John French needed countless hours to transcribe the parts for the band. Van Vliet, unable to read or write music, had complex musical ideas in his head, and no means to easily communicate them, and acted out his frustration. At times Van Vliet used a piano to explain his musical ideas, but he continued to use unorthodox means to communicate with French (and subsequent Magic Band members), including whistling or singing as well as cryptic, surreal verbal descriptions of the sounds he wanted—for example: "Make it like Fred Astaire dangling through a tea cup; like BBs on the plate; babies flying over the mountains." Jeff Cotton was often responsible for transcribing Van Vliet's lyrics and spoken word output. Original Magic Band members Jerry Handley (bass) and St. Clair (guitar) left the band to be replaced, respectively, by Mark Boston (aka Rockette Morton, born 1949; bass, guitar) and 19-year-old Bill Harklewood. When the album was released, French was not even listed as a band member. A spiteful Van Vliet removed French's name in response to French leaving the band. Van Vliet would tell the media that the Magic Band were musical novices, an ironic twist.

A double album with 28 relatively short tracks (at this time, many rock bands were venturing toward longer songs), *Trout Mask Replica* had its own avant-garde technique. Some of the album was recorded at the cabin—Zappa approached the recording in the manner of an anthropological field recording. Van Vliet, however, wanted to record in a studio, so the album was a mix of both styles of recording. The music was created with some improvisation but then endlessly rehearsed, recorded, and performed without variation. Richly varied stylistically, and loaded with surprises, the album deserves its fame. Rhythms change unexpectedly; often, the drumming is totally freed up from traditional timekeeping. Musical themes shift constantly with little repetition. Although the musicians often do not seem to be playing together, the music still coheres. In 1991 Van Vliet explained the album as "trying to break up the mind in many different directions, causing them not to be able to fixate" (Barnes 2002).

An exciting element of *Trout Mask Replica* can be found in "Orange Claw Hammer," a song featuring unaccompanied vocals based on field hollers and sea shanties. The clicking of the tape recorder being paused was deliberately left intact in this piece, and when Van Vliet stumbled at the beginning, he just started over again, leaving the mistake intact. Van Vliet engaged his cousin Victor "The Mascara Snake" Hayden (bass clarinet) in a bizarre patter: "A squid eating dough in a polyethylene bag is fast 'n' bulbous. Got me?" Snatches of conversation between songs and a phone conversation enhanced the experience of the album as lived and alive.

Some studio vocals were recorded somewhat out of sync with the band. Van Vliet refused to wear headphones and would sing to the leakage of the recording coming through the panes of glass from the control room. *Trout Mask Replica* required repeated listening to appreciate. Many fans of the album found it offputting if not cacophonous on first listening (Chusid 2000). The album was not successful in terms of sales. Zappa promoted the album with his roster of oddball performers on Bizarre/Straight, and Van Vliet was deeply displeased to be labeled a freak. Friction between Zappa and Van Vliet intensified.

The successor to *Trout Mask Replica, Lick My Decals Off, Baby* (1970), was also lauded. With the critical success of *Trout Mask Replica*, the band landed with Warner Bros. Jeff Cotton left the band and Artie Tripp (aka Ed Marimba, born Arthur Dyer Tripp III, September 10, 1944; marimba, drums, percussion), a member of Frank Zappa's band the Mothers of Invention, joined the band. Tripp played marimba to great effect, especially on "Woe-Is-Uh-Me-Bop." The band moved to Laurel Canyon. They recorded *Lick My Decals* in a standard manner, with multiple takes of songs. The group was now known as Captain Beefheart and the Magic Band. Many of the songs were more straightforward and rock-oriented with a more prominent bass. That said, the music itself was just as complex as before, if not more so. Some songs were about sex, such as "Neon Meate Dream of a Octafish." Other songs (e.g., "Petrified Forest") touched on ecological disaster. The album ranged widely from Bill Harklewood's beautiful guitar piece to the punkish double saxophones on "Flash Gordon's Ape." Van Vliet rated *Lick My Decals Off, Baby* as his favorite of his albums.

Soon after the release of *Lick My Decals Off, Baby*, another member of the Mothers of Invention joined the Magic Band: guitarist Elliot Ingber (aka Winged Eel Fingerling, born August 24, 1941; guitar). *The Spotlight Kid* (1972) sought a more commercial sound and a broader audience. The pace was slower and the songs were bluesier (although not standard 12-bar blues). Some critics found the lyrics less humorous and more ominous. "Click Clack," a train song, was the standout track on the album. Critical reception of the album was fairly positive and the album was commercially successful without being a hit.

Van Vliet had his first art exhibit in London in 1972. He married his wife Jan in 1969 and at this stage of his career, Van Vliet stated repeatedly that his intention was to create music for women. In *Clear Spot* (1972), the songs were more melodic and the rhythms much more groove-oriented. "Big-Eyed Beans from Venus," was critically regarded as the best cut on the album, particularly for its outstanding guitar work and its lyrics. This complex, big song harkened back to *Trout Mask Replica*. Harklewood, Ingber, and Tripp stayed with the band. Mark Boston moved from bass over to guitar with the addition of Mothers of Invention bassist Roy Estrada.

After *Clear Spot*'s disappointing sales, Van Vliet left Warner Bros., moving to Virgin Records, and hired new managers. The two ensuing albums, according to most critics and fans, represent the nadir of Van Vliet and the band's career. *Unconditionally Guaranteed* (1974) deepened Van Vliet's efforts at commercialism. A few critics felt the album worked well as a pop album. More notably, after years of poverty, and with disgust at the results of *Unconditionally Guaranteed,* the Magic Band quit before going on tour. This devastated Van Vliet.

For *Bluejeans & Moonbeams* (1974), a pickup band of studio musicians were brought on board. Critically dismissed as the weakest album, *Bluejeans & Moonbeams* had some charming songs, particularly "Observatory Crest," which featured Van Vliet's melodious singing. However, the album had a generally sanitized, Southern California rock sound and was a commercial failure. Van Vliet was at a professional low point. He apologized to Frank Zappa, asking to work with him again. The result was documented in the live album *Bongo Fury* (Discreet, 1975). Van Vliet contributed "Sam with the Showing Scalp Flat Top" and "Man with the Woman Head." Yet again, the collaboration ended in rancor. Van Vliet, while on stage but not performing, would sketch Zappa, infuriating Zappa.

During this difficult period, a teenage fan, Moris Tepper (born Jeff Moris Tepper; guitar) became Van Vliet's friend and next door neighbor. After the *Bongo Fury* tour, Van Vliet re-formed the Magic Band and John French rejoined the band not only on drums but also guitar. Bruce Fowler (aka Fossil, born Bruce Lambourne Fowler, July 10, 1947; trombone) and Jimmy Carl Black (aka India Ink, born James Carl Inkanish Jr., February 1, 1938, died November 1, 2008; drums), both formerly with Frank Zappa, joined the band, and Elliot Ingber returned on guitar. The band toured successfully. By 1975, Black left the band and French moved back over to drums, with Denny Walley (also previously with Mothers of Invention) on guitar. The original Magic Band (Tripp, Harklewood, and Boston)

formed a group called Mallard. With the support of Ian Anderson from Jethro Tull, they released one self-named album in 1976 on Virgin. Van Vliet was outraged and badmouthed Mallard in the media.

Despite the considerable friction between Zappa and Van Vliet, Zappa became the executive producer of the next album, *Bat Chain Puller* (1976). Moris Tepper joined the band on guitar. This album returned, in part, to the more avant-garde territory of earlier Beefheart. Stylistically, the album was extremely diverse. John French played an exquisite solo guitar piece. "Brick Bats," featuring Van Vliet on saxophone, was punkish. "The Floppy Boot Stomp," was classic psychedelic Americana. After the album was completed, Thomas quit the band and joined Mallard. Eric Drew Feldman (born April 16, 1955; keyboards, bass) was brought into the band. Unfortunately, due to legal problems involving Zappa and his manager, the album was not issued for sale. In 2012, Zappa's estate released the original album.

After French decamped yet again, Robert Williams, a new drummer, joined the band in 1977. Bruce Fowler returned on trombone. Getting a deal with Warner Bros., Van Vliet decided to, in part, rerecord *Bat Chain Puller*. Many of the other songs were unused on earlier albums, but there were four entirely new songs. The resulting album, *Shiny Beast (Bat Chain Puller)* (1978), was not as edgy and exciting as its unreleased predecessor, but it was a critical success and stood on its own merits. The album, for the first time, included extensive artwork from Van Vliet. Van Vliet loved the album. Unfortunately, due to more legal problems, the album was not actually released until 1980.

Gary Lucas (born June 20, 1952; guitar) was a guest guitar player on the next-to-last Captain Beefheart album, *Doc at the Radar Station* (1980), and he and his wife took on managerial duties for the band. About half of the material on the album was repurposed from earlier material including *Bat Chain Puller*. Most of the same personnel from *Shiny Beast (Bat Chain Puller)* were on *Doc at the Radar Station*. John French rejoined the band for this album. "Ashtray Heart" shared some common aesthetics with the contemporaneous No Wave sound in

New York City. Lucas rearranged and performed "Flavor Bud Living." In the post-punk era, the album was very well received: it was selected as one of 1980's 10 best albums by the *New York Times*, and the band performed on *Saturday Night Live*.

The band toured on a receptive new wave/post-punk circuit. French quit the band again and Rick Snyder, another Beefheart fan, was brought in on bass. However, U.K. distribution by Virgin fell apart, leaving the band to perform in cities without the album available. Drummer Robert Williams also left the band after what ended up as the Magic Band's final concert performance in Huntington Beach, California, in January 1981. Van Vliet decided to stop touring but returned to the studio for one final album.

Ice Cream for Crow (1982) was the band's last album, and like its immediate predecessors, used some repurposed older material. "Hey, Garland, I Dig Your Tweed Coat," sported intense surrealistic spoken word and chaotic instrumentals. Cliff Martinez (born February 5, 1954; drums), who played with punk bands, joined the band. Lucas performed his arrangement of Van Vliet's previously unrecorded "Evening Bell," a solo guitar piece. Van Vliet wanted some of the cuts from the original *Bat Chain Puller* to be included on the album, but Zappa balked, refused to cooperate, and a confrontation ensued. Critical reaction was fairly positive but not as warm as that for *Doc at the Radar Station*. After *Ice Cream for Crow* was released, Van Vliet was persuaded to make a video for the title cut, a very catchy tune featuring Gary Lucas on slide guitar. This early rock video was shot in the desert and featured Joshua trees, tumbleweeds, Van Vliet's paintings, and an exuberant performance by the band. It allowed the viewer to get a sense of Van Vliet as a physical being, grinning and flapping his arms in his imitation of a crow.

Van Vliet appeared on David Letterman in the early 1980s. Online clips reveal that Van Vliet persisted in his outrageous claims and self-mythologizing. Virgin still had an option on another album, and bizarrely, tried to induce Van Vliet and the band to appear in *Grizzly II*, a horror film about a killer bear. This was the final straw after years of disappointing

earnings. Van Vliet decided to end the band in order to focus on being a full-time painter.

Van Vliet abandoned the name "Captain Beefheart" and went on to have a lucrative and satisfying career as a painter, exhibiting widely. His painting style was heavily influenced by Abstract Expressionist Franz Kline. Beefheart fan Julian Schnabel helped introduce Van Vliet to the New York and German art scenes and gain gallery representation. Soon thereafter, Van Vliet was able to buy land and build a house in Northern California. He and his wife Jan remained there until his death from complications related to multiple sclerosis in 2010.

Most of the Magic Band members continued to perform and record. French and Harklewood published memoirs about their experiences, and French recorded *O Solo Drumbo* (1998). Gary Lucas has had a successful career as a band leader, solo artist, and collaborator with many rock and jazz luminaries. Eric Drew Feldman played with the Pixies as well as Frank Black, Pere Ubu, and P.J. (Polly) Harvey. Cliff Martinez drummed for the Red Hot Chili Peppers and now is a prominent film music composer. Moris Tepper performed both as a solo and supporting artist. Art Tripp rejoined the Mothers of Invention. More recently, the Magic Band, with French, Lucas, Walley, Williams, and Boston, occasionally re-form to perform. Gary Lucas puts together Captain Beefheart symposiums, where he lectures, shows video footage, and performs.

Critical reception of the band has played an important role in its historical significance. British deejay John Peel, who was based in California in the 1960s, was a champion of the early Magic Band and cited *Trout Mask Replica* as his favorite album. The band also toured England extensively, contributing to its impact on the British punk and post-punk era. Critic Lester Bangs, who continues to be hugely influential in contemporary rock journalism, was a big supporter of the band. *Rolling Stone* currently lists *Trout Mask Replica* as number 66 in their Top 500 Greatest Albums of All Time; in 1987, *Rolling Stone* listed it as number 33 in their Top 100 Best Rock albums issue, calling it "rock's most visionary album." The band's enduring popularity in Great Britain has not only *Trout*

Mask Replica but also *Clear Spot* and *Safe as Milk* on listings of best albums of all time. Two tribute albums featuring well-known bands were released: *Fast 'n' Bulbous—A Tribute to Captain Beefheart* (1988) and *Neon Meate Dream of a Octafish* (2003). *Trout Mask Replica* was inducted into the Library of Congress's National Recording Registry in 2010.

Notable covers of Captain Beefheart songs include the White Stripes EP *Party of Special Things to Do* (2000), a three-song tribute covering "Ashtray Heart," "China Pig," and "Party of Special Things to Do." Early covers included the Tubes recording "My Head Is My Only House Unless It Rains" (1977). Magazine recorded "I Love You, You Big Dummy" in 1978, and Coati Mundi and Rubén Blades did their own version of Shiny Beast *(Bat Chain Puller)*'s "Hot Dog Mambo" in 1983. More recently, Joan Osborne covered "(His) Eyes Are a Blue Million Miles," the Kills included a cover of "Dropout Boogie" on their debut *Black Rooster* EP (2002), and the Black Keys released a cover of "I'm Glad" in 2008.

Captain Beefheart and the Magic Band's sound often is less apparent in the many bands that cite Beefheart as a major influence. In 1978 Devo's Mark Mothersbaugh cited *Trout Mask Replica* as inspiring an underground movement of people. Beefheart inspired the guitar playing of the Fall's Craig Scanlon "just in a liberating way; I wouldn't dare to try to copy him" (Barnes 2002). Other punk and postpunk performers and bands citing Beefheart include Joe Strummer of the Clash, John Lydon of the Sex Pistols and Public Image Limited, the Gang of Four, the B-52s, and XTC. Industrial music pioneers Genesis P-Orridge of Throbbing Gristle and Psychic TV, and Z'EV, can also be counted as influenced by the band.

Some postpunk bands that clearly incorporated some of Beefheart's musical innovations directly into their music include the Minutemen, Pere Ubu, the Residents, and the Birthday Party. Tom Waits's 1983 *Swordfishtrombones* represented a shift in Waits's work as a direct outcome of his hearing Beefheart. Black Francis of the Pixies references *The Spotlight Kid* as one of the albums he listened to regularly when first writing songs. Guitarist John Frusciante of the Red

Hot Chili Peppers cites the band as a prominent influence on their 1991 album *Blood Sugar Sex Magik*. Other bands referencing the Beefheart sound include the Henry Cow/Art Bears/Slapp Happy group of bands, Half Japanese, Sun City Girls, Thinking Fellers, and U.S. Maple, Deerhoof, and Olivia Tremor Control. P. J. (Polly) Harvey was a fan and became friends with Van Vliet. She taught herself guitar by playing along to Beefheart albums. Pavement's 1999 song "Ground Beef Heart," was influenced by *Lick My Decals Off, Baby*. Beck included "Safe as Milk" and "Ella Guru" in his 2009 Planned Obsolescence series of mash-ups. Captain Beefheart and the Magic Band continue to live on, inspiring future generations of rock experimenters as well as new listeners who now have access to the entire body of the band's recorded work.

Monica Berger

Selected Discography

Safe as Milk, Buddah Records, BDS-5063, 1967.

Strictly Personal, Blue Thumb, BTS 1, 1968.

Trout Mask Replica, Straight, STS 1053, 1969.

Lick My Decals Off, Baby, Straight/Reprise, RS 6420, 1970.

Mirror Man, Buddah, BDS 5077, recorded 1967, released 1971.

The Spotlight Kid, Reprise, MS 2050, 1972.

Clear Spot, Reprise, MS 2115, 1972.

Bluejeans & Moonbeams, Mercury, SRM-1–1018, 1974.

Unconditionally Guaranteed, Mercury, SRM-1–709, 1974.

Shiny Beast (Bat Chain Puller), Warner Brothers, BSK 3256, 1978.

Doc at the Radar Station, Virgin, VA 13148, 1980.

Ice Cream for Crow, Virgin/Epic, ARE 3827, 1982.

The Legendary A & M Sessions, A & M, SP 12510, recorded 1965, released 1984.

Bat Chain Puller, Vaulternative Records, VR2012–1, recorded 1976 by Frank Zappa, released 2012.

References

Bangs, Lester. "He's Alive, But So Is Paint. Are You?" *Village Voice,* October 1980.

Barnes, Mike. *Captain Beefheart: The Biography.* New York: Cooper Square Press, 2002.

Captain Beefheart Official Website. 2013. "Life." Accessed January 2014. www.beefheart.com/life/.

Chusid, Irwin. *Songs in the Key of Z: The Curious World of Outsider Music*. Chicago: Chicago Review Press, 2000.

Courrier, Kevin. *Trout Mask Replica*. 33 1/3. New York: Continuum, 2007.

Harkleroad, Bill, and Billy James. *Lunar Notes: Zoot Horn Rollo's Captain Beefheart Experience*. Wembley, UK: SAF Publishing, 1998.

Marcus, Greil. "Captain Beefheart (1941–2010)." *Artforum* 49 (8) (2011): 57.

Sanjek, Dave. "Life in the Fast and Bulbous Lane: Captain Beefheart (1941–2010)." *Popular Music and Society* 35 (2) (2012): 301–13.

Thompson, Ben. "Captain Beefheart." In *Ways of Hearing: A User's Guide to the Pop Psyche, from Elvis to Eminem*, 98–107. London: Orion, 2001.

The Cars (1977–1988, Original Group; The New Cars, 2005–2007; Without Ben Orr, 2011–2012)

In the late 1970s, rock music had splintered into punk, new wave, and mainstream. The Cars were one of the few bands who transcended these boundaries. Boston-based rock journalist Brett Milano remarked on this when writing the liner notes for a 1995 Cars retrospective album: "During the late '70s and early '80s, most rock fans were split into two camps, with hardly any common ground. Either you listened to 'punk' bands like the Clash, Talking Heads, and the Cars, or you were into 'mainstream' bands like Aerosmith, Queen, and the Cars" (Verna, 58). With the success of their first album in 1978, critics decided that the Cars were more "new wave" than punk, although this may have been a distinction without a difference; as Cleveland rock journalist Anastasia Pantsios famously said, "The term 'new wave' was invented to dignify what was previously called 'punk rock'" ("New Wave," F26).

Still, finding a concise way to describe the Cars was important for journalists and reviewers; despite the fact that the band had gained a local following by playing at a dirty and grungy club called "The Rat," which was known for punk rock, most critics agreed the band fit better into the "new wave" category, along with bands like Blondie and Talking Heads; some critics also noted the influence of the art rock band Roxy Music (Morse, 17). But while many of the bands with whom the Cars were compared only attracted a cult following, the Cars consistently appealed to listeners of both top 40 and album rock, as well as to viewers of MTV, who loved their music videos. As the producer of a Cars tribute album observed in 2003, the Cars were important to rock music because they were the first to "[make] New Wave safe for the Heartland" (Guarino, 5). In fact, at the height of their popularity, rock critics were calling the Cars "the first new wave supergroup" (Johnson C8). Reviewers said their songs were "infectious" (Oppel, "The Cars' Performance," 10) and praised their "quirky pop hooks, techno-synth sensibility and sparse but punchy guitar leads" (Dickinson, 4E). The Cars' first two albums sold six million copies worldwide, and by the mid-1980s, they had become known as "one of rock's most dependably popular bands" (Pareles, C20). Even after they broke up in 1988, their influence continued to be heard in bands like the Killers, as well as Weezer and the Strokes (Rosen 2011).

The two men who founded what ultimately became the Cars were Ric Ocasek (born Richard Otcasek, March 23, 1949; vocals) and Benjamin "Ben" Orr (born Benjamin Orzechowski, September 8, 1947, died October 3, 2000; bass, vocals). They began working and performing together in Columbus, Ohio, circa 1970. Orr had grown up in Parma, a suburb of Cleveland, and gained local fame when he was still in high school: in 1964, he joined a popular band called the Grasshoppers, who made several records and even got some local airplay (Adams, 51; Scott, 34). Because his last name was so long, he jokingly called himself Benny "Eleven Letters" (St. John, 29) before finally shortening it to Orr sometime in the mid-1970s (Fricke, "The Return," 52). Ocasek was born in Baltimore but moved to the Cleveland area when he was in high school. His father worked for NASA, and from a young age, Ric was fascinated by all things related to engineering and electronics (Fricke, "Workaholic," E8). A self-identified loner, he briefly attended

The Cars pose for a portrait in Memphis, Tennessee, on July 5, 1979. The group spearheaded the new wave/post punk sound and remains relevant today even without new music. (Photo by Ebet Roberts/Redferns)

college, but dropped out to pursue his other interest—music (Ladd, B1). He began a small booking agency in Columbus, Ohio, handling local bands. He also reconnected with Benjamin Orr, who was in Columbus too, and also was booking bands; Orr and Ocasek had first become friends in Cleveland when Orr's band was performing regularly on WEWS-TV and Ocasek got in touch with him. They wrote some songs together, but nothing came of it at that time (Scott 1986, 40). Now, however, Orr and Ocasek decided the time was right to move away from booking bands and do some performing. Working as a duo, they played clubs in East Lansing and Ann Arbor, Michigan, and New York City's Greenwich Village before moving to Boston (Rees and Crampton, 87). By 1972, they had formed a trio (guitarist Jas Goodkind was the third member) called Milkwood. They played folk music and recorded one album, *How's the Weather*. A session musician named Greg Hawkes (born October 22, 1952; keyboards) played keyboards and saxophone on it, and he would later become the keyboard player for the Cars. But Milkwood was not successful, so Orr and Ocasek moved on to form another band, Cap'n Swing. This band played jazz rock, and among its members was guitarist Elliot Easton (born Elliot Shapiro, December 18, 1953; guitar), a graduate of Boston's Berklee College of Music (Papineau, H-13). But while Cap'n Swing achieved some local popularity in the Boston area, the band was not offered a recording contract, and it broke up (Romanowski and George-Warren, 154). By 1976, Orr and Ocasek decided to try one more time to find the right combination that would lead them to success. Elliot Easton stayed on, and they asked Greg Hawkes to rejoin them. In addition, they added drummer David Robinson (born April 2, 1949; drums), who had been a member of another popular local band, the Modern Lovers. With Orr, Ocasek,

Easton, Hawkes, and Robinson, the new band took shape, and its new name was the Cars.

There are several stories about how that name was chosen, although Ric Ocasek has always credited Robinson with coming up with it. In one explanation, Robinson chose the Cars because of the automobile's importance in popular culture. "A car is one of the American staples. You jump into the car, and close the door . . . and drive through the environment while you listen to music, completely in your own privacy" (Robinson, 18). Another explanation involved a conversation held in Ocasek's car. Robinson said he thought the name would work because it was "simple, futuristic [and] familiar . . . We talked about a chrome-trimmed stage, and calling our future greatest hits album *Used Cars*" (Isaacs, 6). In either case, the band decided to go with the name, much to the delight of newspaper headline writers, who would soon offer playful headlines like "Cars Travel a Smooth Road" and "The Cars Take Off Fast in the Record Derby."

Meanwhile, Ocasek, Orr, and the rest of the band began to rehearse, practicing in the basement of the home where Ocasek was living (Romanowski and George-Warren, 154). The Cars did their first live performance as part of a show at an Air Force base in New Hampshire on New Year's Eve 1976. They also began making a demo tape that they could send to radio stations; not many stations played unsigned bands, but Ocasek and Orr hoped someone would take a chance on the Cars. In Boston at that time, the dominant album-rock radio station was WBCN-FM, and fortunately for the Cars, one of their announcers, Maxanne Satori, was impressed by what she heard. Maxanne had a reputation for championing bands she liked: she had gotten behind Aerosmith and helped to make them popular, and now she began to play the Cars' tape on a regular basis (Alan, 109). She especially liked the song "Just What I Needed," and so did WBCN's listeners; it was not long before the Cars were getting played at another Boston album-rocker, WCOZ-FM, with equally positive results. In addition to getting airplay in Boston in early 1977, the Cars were performing at the Rat (formerly the Rathskeller). It was a nightclub that often gave up-and-coming rock

bands a start, but it was not known for its aesthetics—one writer said it was "as attractive as its name," referring to its threadbare and grimy rugs, and rooms that were small, crowded, smoky, and littered with gum wrappers and cigarette butts (Daniels, 12). As it had for other local bands, the Rat proved very hospitable for the Cars, and helped them to develop such a devoted following that they set an attendance record at the club ("Big Contract," 13). The band was also able to find a manager: Fred Lewis was experienced, and he knew both the music industry and the local rock scene. He had been the manager for the J. Geils Band in their early years, and he had also worked as a record promoter. Lewis was able to get the Cars added as the opening act for a sold-out Bob Seger concert at the Music Hall in Boston (Robinson, 18); they sufficiently impressed an important local concert promoter, which led to additional opportunities: the Cars opened for Bryan Ferry and J. Geils in June 1977, and for Robin Trower in October (Morse, 17). By October of 1977, the band had a recording contract with Elektra Records, and in February 1978, they began recording their first album in London, England; it was produced by Roy Thomas Baker (well known for his work with Queen) (Isaacs, 6).

The buzz about the Cars was growing as fans eagerly awaited their first album, which was scheduled for release in early June. A few weeks prior to that, the song "Just What I Needed," already a favorite with album-rock stations, was released as the first single, and it began to get airplay on top 40 stations almost immediately. *Boston Herald-American* critic Bill Adler described the Cars as "masters of popcraft—well-managed [and] well-recorded" and he wondered if the band would become "the Next Big Thing" to come out of Boston (Adler, 36). The Cars certainly seemed ready for success in 1978. They sold out six shows at Boston's Paradise Theatre, a venue that held 600 people (Isaacs, 6). They also played larger arenas: in early June, they performed in front of 4,000 rock fans at the Cape Cod Coliseum, on a bill with the Charlie Daniels Band and Southside Johnny; although most of the fans were there to see the other bands, the Cars' short set was well received. Thomas Sabulis, a *Boston Globe* correspondent, used adjectives like "cosmopolitan," "articulate," and "versatile" to describe the Cars, and he too shared Bill Adler's sentiment that they might be the next local band to achieve the kind of success that the rock band Boston did (Sabulis, 21). The Cars also made a trip to perform in Cleveland, which was a homecoming for Orr and Ocasek. John Gorman, program director of influential album-rock station WMMS-FM, praised the Cars, calling them "the best new rock band on the scene" (Scott "Agora Kicks," 30). And by year's end, they had made their first trip to Europe, performing in Brussels, Paris, Hamburg, Amsterdam, and London (Morse, "The Cars Spin," 11). Music critics were also enthusiastic about the Cars' debut album: typical of the comments were those of the *Boston Globe*'s Steve Morse, who lauded the Cars' creativity and musicianship (he said David Robinson's drumming was "exquisite"), as well as noting that while the band was influenced by Roxy Music and Queen, the Cars did not sound like an imitation of some other band. Morse also said the songs were so good that the album might go gold, or even platinum, in album sales (Morse, 8). And several months later, when the *Globe*'s entertainment section, "Calendar," named the annual "Best of Boston" choices, the Cars were selected as "best rock group." The *Globe*'s critics also said the Cars' first album could well be the best debut rock album of the year. *Rolling Stone* magazine's readers seemed to agree: the Cars placed at the top of the annual Readers Poll in the Best New Artist category ("Springsteen Wins," 30).

Although the band had been founded by Ric Ocasek and Benjamin Orr, it was Ocasek who quickly became the dominant figure in the Cars. He was the band's rhythm guitarist, he often sang lead vocals, and he wrote nearly all of the songs the band performed. Ocasek was a unique figure on stage: tall and thin, with jet black hair, usually dressed in black. He always wore sunglasses, and whether performing or being interviewed, he often seemed aloof (Arar, E8). One critic described him as "a cross between Frank Zappa and the Fonz" (Oppel, 10) and another compared him with Lou Reed (Thomas, F23). Ocasek also became known for the degree of control he had over everything the band did. In fact, he sometimes had to

refute stories that he was a tyrant. As he told one reporter, "I do want things my way, but I do try to be fair." And he also acknowledged that "I know what the songs should sound like and we work until they sound that way" (Hunt, 5). Of course, as the reporter noted, such total control was a recipe for resentment from the other band members. In the Cars' early years, it did not seem to be a problem, as the band members were enjoying the success they had worked so long to achieve; if there was any dissension, it did not come up in interviews at that time. But years later, it became obvious that there had been resentment, and it contributed to the band's breakup. After all, as drummer David Robinson said in 2011, being in the Cars had always been about "us helping Ric in what he wanted to do." And guitarist Elliot Easton concurred, saying that since Ric was the songwriter, and the Cars were known for the great songs they performed, "it was only natural that he would be the sun around which the other planets revolve" (Robinson and Easton quoted in Fricke, 50).

The Cars' first album produced three singles: "Just What I Needed," which reached number 27 nationally on the pop charts; "My Best Friend's Girl," which got to number 35; and "Good Times Roll," which reached number 41. But while none of these songs was a big top 40 hit, they all got considerable airplay at both pop stations and album rock stations, and created even more interest in what the Cars would do next. Their second album, *Candy-O,* was released in June 1979; it featured the band's first top 15 hit single, "Let's Go," which reached number 14. As with "Just What I Needed," the vocals in "Let's Go" were sung by Benjamin Orr. The catchy hook (rhythmic hand claps and the chant "Let's Go!") contributed to the airplay the song received on top 40 radio. But the Cars' third album, *Panorama,* was not as successful on the pop charts, although like everything the band released, it received a lot of airplay. Critical reaction was mixed. While many reviewers spoke positively of it, others spoke of a certain sameness to the material (Baldridge, 16B). Many noted it relied more on synthesizers and did not sound as much like a rock album, the way their debut album did (Marsh, 22); and even those who liked the album said they did not hear a hit single (Catlin, "Few Real," 11). This turned out to be an astute observation, as no song from the album reached the top 30 on the pop charts, at a time when top 40 radio could still help bands to sell records. But Ric Ocasek had mixed feelings about top 40 when critics praised the band's next album, *Shake It Up,* by saying it was "more pop" than either *Panorama* or *Candy-O.* Ocasek was not amused. He told a rock reviewer that the band had never intended to make a pop album—it had just happened that way. "You never know how an album will come out when you first go into the studio to begin work on it" (quoted in Oppel, "The Cars Turn," 1C).

But it was not just any studio where the band recorded *Shake It Up.* In 1981, Ocasek had bought the former Intermedia Studio, located in the Back Bay section of Boston (Romanowski and George-Warren, 155). Intermedia had a good reputation, having been used by Aerosmith, Jonathan Edwards, and Livingston Taylor. Ocasek upgraded and modernized the equipment, and renamed the studio "Syncro Sound." It was there that the Cars recorded their new album, which was once again produced by Roy Thomas Baker. Being in the studio was something Ocasek much preferred to touring. In fact, he was realistic about his lack of charisma on stage: "I'm basically a writer, and to me, the most fun I have is when the song is finished . . . Iggy Pop, Bruce Springsteen—they're great showmen. I'm not, and I'm not going to pretend that I am" (Simon, M6). The studio also gave Ocasek a chance to do something else he had come to enjoy—producing other artists. And whether the album turned out very mass-appeal by accident or by design, *Shake It Up* brought them back to top 40 prominence. The title song, with its dance-pop style, became their highest-charting single, rising to number four on the *Billboard* Hot 100 in early 1982. As for critical response to the album, one Midwestern reviewer gave it four out of five stars and praised it for being much more mass-appeal, and much more fun to listen to, than its predecessor (Catlin, "Cars New Fun," 19). One critic even said this was their best album yet (Oppel, "Pop Records," 6C). But other critics were not impressed.

One found the album "downright silly" ("A Critical Guide," 4), and Boston-based critic Steve Morse dismissed it as "banal," with trite lyrics, lacking in creativity. In fact, he said this was "the first bad record they've done" ("Geils Accelerates," 1981). But the fans seemed to have no problem with "Shake It Up": it became a favorite party song, as well as another best seller for the Cars. In fact, by some estimates, their albums had now sold about 18 million copies worldwide (Van Matre, E6).

In early 1982, Ocasek decided to record and produce his first solo album. *Beatitude,* which came out late that year, was released on Geffen Records; it featured guest performances by Jules Shear and Stephen Hague (of Jules and the Polar Bears), and the Cars' Greg Hawkes played keyboards. (Ocasek was not the only band member to do his own album. Hawkes also recorded one—a primarily instrumental work called *Niagara Falls,* which came out in 1983.) For Ocasek to do a solo project in the midst of the Cars' success was not surprising: he was known as a workaholic, and he rarely slowed down. It was a trait that he would admit years later had caused serious problems in his first two marriages (Fricke "The Return," 52). When not touring with the Cars, he was producing at Syncro Sound, or writing and rehearsing new songs. Other members of the band had side projects too. For example, David Robinson's passion was graphic arts: he designed the T-shirts and backstage passes for the Cars' upcoming tour, he codesigned the band's stage setting, and he was involved with creating the band's last two album covers (Pantsios, "The Cars Buys," 38). And like Ocasek, Robinson was also producing some local artists, as was Elliot Easton (Johnson, C8).

The Cars' next album was "Heartbeat City," and it came out in 1984; the band used a new producer, Mutt Lange, known for his work with AC/DC and Foreigner. The album's first single, "You Might Think," was another big hit with both top 40 and album rock, and it was also a very popular music video. MTV had launched on cable in August 1981, and since then, many rock groups found that the right music video could enhance their career and sell more copies of their albums. The Cars took their quirky style and applied it to the video for "You Might Think," which featured Ocasek's inscrutable face, sunglasses and all, popping up unexpectedly in various places (in a lipstick case, on a clock, on the body of a fly, in a periscope, just to name a few) as he sang of his love for the beautiful girl, who seemed unable to get away from him. The video was so well received that at the first annual MTV Video Music Awards, it was named "Video of the Year." Their next single release, "Magic," did not do as well on the charts, reaching number 12, but its music video once again showed the Cars at their creative best, including a scene in which Ocasek appears to walk on water (Ladd, B1). Their third single, "Drive," earned the band their most successful hit—number three on the pop charts. A beautiful ballad, the song was also played by Adult Contemporary stations. But once again, it was the music video that attracted attention, due in large part to the presence of model and actress Paulina Porizkova. She and Ocasek played an arguing couple in the video, and she later admitted that she fell in love with him almost immediately. It was an unlikely relationship: she was a beautiful model and he was an aloof and less-than-handsome rock star—plus, he was married. He eventually ended up divorcing his wife and married Porizkova in 1989.

It seemed the Cars could do no wrong: they had hit songs, hit videos, and legions of fans. In 1985, they released a Greatest Hits album, which contained the top 10 single "Tonight She Comes." But despite their fame, all was not well with the band, due in large part to Ocasek's controlling nature and individual band members becoming tired of doing everything his way. There had been rumors before, but by 1985, some rock journalists were beginning to see signs that band members were not getting along. Ocasek, never known for being tactful, was quoted in an interview as saying that he alone did 95 percent of the work in the band; this did not make the other members happy, although they tried to downplay their reaction (Katz, 35). Meanwhile, instead of recording their next album, the band took another of its hiatuses. Elliot Easton put out a solo album, *Change No Change,* and several other members seemed ready to do some solo work as well. Even Ocasek said he wanted to make music that was different from what the Cars had been doing (Spotnitz, 35).

The Cars' cofounder Benjamin Orr released his solo album, *The Lace,* in October 1986; all the songs on it were cowritten by Orr and his then-girlfriend Diane Grey Page; they acknowledged that some of the songs had been inspired by their relationship (Von Matre, "Another Solo," 3). There was a party held at Syncro Sound in October to celebrate the new album, but Orr had not recorded the album there: much of it was recorded in England. Then in December, with no warning and no explanation, it was announced that Syncro Sound was closing (Morse, "Cars Recording," 26). Meanwhile, Ocasek had released his second solo album, *This Side of Paradise,* and it too was not recorded at Syncro Sound. In 1987, the Cars put out their sixth album, *Door to Door.* It would be their last, although nobody knew that at the time; in fact, the Cars told reporters they were excited to have completed the album and were eager to get back on the road to tour in support of it (Morse, "Cars Getting," B24). But something was different: perhaps new wave was no longer considered fresh and interesting, or perhaps the album was not as strong as some of their earlier work, but *Door to Door* was not anywhere nearly as successful as previous Cars albums. It yielded no top 20 hits, and the crowds coming to see the band were smaller than they had been, even in Boston and Providence (Sullivan, 61; Morse, "Cars Come Home," 79). By early 1988, the Cars had announced they were breaking up after 10 years together.

The individual members of the Cars continued to pursue solo careers, with Ocasek remaining as prolific as ever, recording two more albums of his own music and producing a number of bands, including Weezer's debut album. But Boston was no longer Ocasek's primary residence. He and his wife Paulina had moved to New York City (Katz, 49). By this time, Benjamin Orr was not on speaking terms with his former friend Ric Ocasek; creative differences during their years with the Cars, exacerbated by Orr's problems with alcohol, took their toll. Eventually, Orr moved to Vermont, quit drinking, and formed a new band. But his life (and the perpetual hope of fans for a Cars reunion) was cut short when he died of pancreatic cancer in 2000, at age 53. Before he died, he and Ocasek had made peace with each other (Fricke, "The Return," 51). In 1995, Rhino Records, in conjunction with Elektra Traditions, released a 40-track double-set retrospective of the Cars' career; in addition to their hits, it included some rare B-sides and several previously unreleased tunes (Sullivan, 61; Dickinson, 4E). And then, in 2005, former Cars members Greg Hawkes and Elliot Easton teamed up with Todd Rundgren to tour as the "New Cars." Initially, critics were skeptical as to whether Rundgren could fit in with a band that played Cars songs. But somehow, the New Cars managed to do a good enough job to win over a number of the fans who came to see them; in addition to Cars hits, Rundgren also sang some new material, putting his own stamp on the collaboration (Korbelik, 5). The New Cars also put out a live album before going their separate ways. But then in 2011, something surprising occurred: Greg Hawkes got a phone call from Ric Ocasek with an invitation to restart the Cars. Hawkes admitted to being apprehensive about getting back together after 23 years, especially given how the band's interactions had become acrimonious during the tail end of their time as the Cars, but he decided to take a chance (Krewen, E9). It turned out to be a good decision: Ocasek had some new material, and the time that the members had spent away from him allowed old wounds to heal. In May 2011, the remaining members of the Cars put out *Move Like This,* a short but impressive set (only 37 minutes of music) that brought back memories of the band at their best. Said one critic, "Despite a two-decade gap in their discography, the reunited members of The Cars don't sound as if they've missed a beat" (Mansfield, 4D).

Although the reunited Cars have not produced any other albums since then, critics and fans who remember them fondly, hope there will still be more music released in the future. In the 10 years the original members were together, they left their mark on pop music. As Boston-based critic Sarah Rodman said after the Cars got back together, "Why is this band not in the Rock and Roll Hall of Fame? Such new wave contemporaries as Blondie and Talking Heads have been enshrined there, but the Cars no longer seem to share the same hipster patina. We hear them on the radio constantly. Do we simply take them for granted? We shouldn't" ("The Band Revs," N1).

Donna L. Halper

Selected Discography

The Cars, Elektra 6E-135, 1978.

Candy-O, Elektra 5E-507, 1979.

Panorama, Elektra 5E-514, 1980.

Shake It Up, Elektra 5E-567, 1981.

Door-to-Door, Elektra 9600747–1, 1987.

Heartbeat City, Elektra 60296–1, 1987.

Move Like This, Hear Music HRM-32872–02, 2011.

References

"A Critical Guide to the Top-40 Albums." *New Orleans Times-Picayune,* December 18, 1981, 4.

Adler, Bill. "Peter Brown Tops Pop's Something-for-All Program." *Boston Herald-American,* June 16, 1978, 36.

Arar, Yardena. "Wry Superstar Ric Ocasek Steers the Cars." *Portland Oregonian,* September 21, 1979, E8.

Baldridge, Anne. "Fans Welcome the Cars to Baton Rouge." *Baton Rouge Advocate,* October 19, 1980, 16B.

"Bests of Boston." *Boston Globe,* Calendar Section, September 14, 1978, 16.

"Big Contract for Hub Rock Band." *Boston Globe,* October 22, 1977, 13.

Catlin, Roger. "Cars: New Fun with Synthesizer-Based Rock." *Omaha World-Herald,* December 8, 1981, 19.

Catlin, Roger. "Few Real Surprises, No Lulls Found in Cars' Third Album." *Omaha World-Herald,* August 26, 1980, 11.

Daniels, Dennis. "Cars Join Rat Race, Win with Punk Score." *Boston Herald-American,* September 13, 1977, 12.

Dickinson, Chris. "Cars Revisited at Quirky Best." *St. Louis Post–Dispatch,* November 24, 1995, 4E.

Fricke, David, "The Return of the Cars." *Rolling Stone,* June 9, 2011, 50–53.

Fricke, David. "Workaholic Ric Ocasek Freaks Out at Vacationtime." *Omaha (NE) World-Herald,* March 21, 1982, E8.

Hunt, Dennis. "Not a Dictator, Says Cars' Driver." *New Orleans Times-Picayune,* October 17, 1980, 5.

Isaacs, James. "Cars' Sound Immaculate, Streamlined." *Walla Walla (WA) Union-Bulletin,* September 8, 1978, 6.

Johnson, Dean. "Hard-Driving Cars Keep Boston on Rock Map." *Boston Herald,* June 10, 1984, C8.

Katz, Larry. "Cars Guitarist Drives Alone." *Boston Herald,* March 3, 1985, pp. 29, 35.

Katz, Larry. "Cars' Ocasek Still Driven." *Boston Herald,* September 5, 1991, 49.

Korbelik, Jeff. "Rundgren, New Cars Rock State Fair's Open-air Auditorium." *Lincoln (NE) Journal Star,* August 31, 2007, 5.

Krewen, Nick. "Cars Idling No More: 23-year Layoff Ends with Surprisingly Fresh Album, and Short Tour." *Toronto Star,* May 20, 2011, E9.

Ladd, Susan. "Leader of the Cars Knows How to Crank Out Video Hits." *Greensboro (NC) News & Record,* July 13, 1984, B1.

Mansfield, Brian. "The Cars' Next 'Move': Is That All They Can Do?" *USA Today,* May 10, 2011, 4D.

Marsh, Dave. "Cars' Hooks Are Intact, But Rhythm Is Altered." Omaha *World-Herald,* October 31, 1980, 22.

Milano, Brett. *Sounds of Our Town: A History of Boston Rock and Roll.* Beverly, MA: Commonwealth Editions, 2007.

Morse, Steve. "Cars Come Home for Garden Party." *Boston Globe,* November 10, 1987, 79.

Morse, Steve. "Cars Getting Set to Hit the Road." *Boston Globe,* August 23, 1987, B24.

Morse, Steve. "The Cars on the Road to Success." *Boston Globe,* January 12, 1978, Calendar, 17.

Morse, Steve. "Cars' Recording Studio Closes." *Boston Globe,* December 23, 1986, 26.

Morse, Steve. "The Cars Spin Home." *Boston Globe,* December 7, 1978, 10–11.

Morse, Steve. "Geils Accelerates, While the Cars Stall." *Boston Globe,* 29 Nov 1981, n.p.

Oppel, Pete. "The Cars' Performance Proves Group Is Vintage." *Dallas Morning News,* June 25, 1979, 10.

Oppel, Pete. "The Cars Turn Pop Accident into a Smash." *Dallas Morning News,* February 22, 1982, 1–5.

Oppel, Pete. "Pop Records." *Dallas Morning News,* January 10, 1982, 6C.

Pantsios, Anastasia. "The Cars Buys Own Parking Space." *Cleveland Plain Dealer,* February 5, 1982, 38.

Pantsios, Anastasia. "New Wave Bands Play Own Music, Promote Selves." *Cleveland Plain Dealer,* July 8, 1977, F26.

Papineau, Lou. "Easton on His Own: The Cars' Lead Guitarist Wheels Out." *Providence Journal-Bulletin,* May 5, 1985, H-13.

Rees, Dafydd, and Luke Crampton. *Rock's Movers and Shakers,* revised edition. New York: *Billboard* Books, 1991.

Robinson, Lisa. "The Cars: Revving Up." *Springfield (MA) Union,* August 17, 1978, 18.

Rodman, Sarah. "The Band Revs Up for a Reunion with a New Album, and It's Just What We Needed." *Boston Globe,* May 8, 2011, N.1.

Rodman, Sarah. "The Cars: A Drive-By History." *Boston Globe,* May 8, 2011, N4.

Romanowski, Patricia, and Holly George-Warren, eds. *The* Rolling Stone *Encyclopedia of Rock & Roll,* revised edition. New York: Fireside, 1995.

Scott, Jane. "Agora Kicks Off Rock-Ettes, Quiz." *Cleveland Plain Dealer,* July 14, 1978, Friday Magazine, 30.

Scott, Jane. "Cars Are Roaring Back; Blossom Is a Sell-Out." *Cleveland Plain Dealer,* August 7, 1984, C.

Scott, Jane. "Meet the Men with Green Feet." *Cleveland Plain Dealer,* January 30, 1965, 34.

Simon, James. "Cars Reluctantly Hit Road to Push Hot Album." *Trenton (NJ) Evening Times,* May 28, 1982, 6.

Smith, Laura C. "My Husband the Car." *Entertainment Weekly,* August 18, 1995, 68.

Spotnitz, Frank. "Bumpy Road for the Cars." *Boston Herald,* March 3, 1985, 29–35.

"Springsteen Wins 3 in Poll by Rolling Stone." *Cleveland Plain Dealer,* December 8, 1978, Friday Magazine, 30.

St. John, Tracy. "Ben Orr Is Still in the Driver's Seat." *Cleveland Plain Dealer,* November 1, 1985, Friday Magazine, 29.

Sullivan, Jim. "Up on Blocks: The Cars Box Set Recalls Glory Days of the New Wave Superstars." *Boston Globe,* November 10, 1995, 61.

Thomas, Mike. "Cars Ran Smoothly, But Lowe Never Got in Gear." *San Diego Union,* March 11, 1982, F23.

Von Matre, Lynn. "Another Solo Act for Cars." *Chicago Tribune,* December 30, 1986, p. 3.

Von Matre, Lynn. "Ric Ocasek: Trying Not to Change the Model of His Cars." *San Diego Union,* February 28, 1982, E6.

The Clash (1976–1983)

Originating in the British pub-rock scene of the early 1970s, the Clash was a band that formed in 1976 as part of the first wave of British punk. The band's 1977 eponymous release was one of a handful of seminal punk albums released in the purported "year that punk exploded," and the popular music scholar Dave Laing has argued that *The Clash* helped to define the British punk sound alongside such 1977 releases as the Damned's *Damned, Damned, Damned,* the Jam's *In the City,* the Sex Pistols' *Never Mind the Bollocks,* the Stranglers' *Rattus Novegicus,* and the Vibrators' *Pure Mania* (Laing 1985). The Clash's variant of punk was marked by the use of reggae, invoked by the band as a sonic signifier of the "other," and by its unapologetic critique of the government, the police, the media, the monarchy, and any person or institution that held authority and wielded power against the oppressed.

The significance of the band to a musical scene like punk that sought to resist the demands of the marketplace was echoed in a sentiment expressed when

Often described as "the only band that mattered," the British band the Clash appear here in a promotional portrait from 1983. From left to right: Paul Simonon, Mick Jones, Pete Howard, and Joe Strummer (1952–2002). The group was inducted into the Rock and Roll Hall of Fame in 2003 and *Rolling Stone Magazine* ranked them as the 28th most influential band in the history of popular music. (Photo by Epic Records/Hulton Archive/Getty Images)

the band secured a lucrative recording contract with a major label in January 1977, in spite of their stated objections to any type of authority. In his seminal punk fanzine, *Sniffin' Glue,* Mark Perry lamented that "punk died the day that the Clash signed to CBS." The extent to which the Clash became absorbed into mainstream culture, for which it represented "punk" to the mainstream listener, was reflected by their induction into the Rock and Roll Hall of Fame in 2003 (an honor extended to, but curtly and crudely rejected by, their punk peers the Sex Pistols in 2006).

The Clash emerged out of a pub-rock band formed by future Clash member Joe Strummer (born John Graham Mellor, August 21, 1952, died December 22, 2002; vocals, guitar) in 1974 and named after the flat in London's Maida Vale neighborhood where the band members purportedly squatted, located at 101 Walterton Road. Fronted by Strummer, the 101-ers was a rockabilly outfit that covered such tunes as Chuck Berry's "Maybellene" and Van Morrison's "Gloria" and that released their debut single, "Keys to Your Heart," on the independent Chiswick label in 1976. The band was a local hit, and played a variety of pub venues for two years, until, on April 3, 1976, they found themselves on the same bill with the Sex Pistols, who opened for the 101-ers at the Nashville club in London.

Reflecting back upon that night, Strummer admitted that when he heard the Sex Pistols in performance, "I knew [the 101-ers] were finished, five seconds into their first song and I knew we were like yesterday's papers, I mean we were over" (The Clash, 59). Shortly thereafter, he was approached by the impresario Bernie Rhodes and Mick Jones (born Michael Geoffrey Jones, June 26, 1955; guitar, vocals), the latter of whom played guitar for the band London SS, with the idea for a new band. Strummer agreed and formed the Clash with fellow guitarists Jones and Keith Levene (born Julian Keith Levene, July 18, 1957; multi-instrumentalist)—who later formed Public Image Limited with former Sex Pistol John Lydon—, bassist Paul Simonon (born Paul Gustave Simonon, December 15, 1955; bass), and drummer Terry Chimes (born Terrence Chimes, July 5, 1956; drums). As the force who claims to have put the quintet together, Rhodes became the group's manager.

Only three months after hearing the Sex Pistols for the first time, Strummer and his new band, the Clash, played their first gig, supporting the Sex Pistols at the Black Swan pub in Sheffield on July 4, 1976. The Pistols had already begun to establish themselves as the quintessential punk band, having performed at the now-famous show at Manchester Lesser Free Trade Hall on June 4 in a concert that has since been said to mark the beginning of punk. In comparison to the seasoned Pistols, the Clash was unpolished and admittedly in its rehearsal stage by July, and was purported to have played a short set of songs, some of which were not yet completed. A month later, the band was back in London, where they staged a second concert at their Camden rehearsal studio, Rehearsals Rehearsals, ostensibly to preview a variety of completed material in front of a crowd of invited guests. By the fall of 1976, the band had begun to accumulate a fan base among London punks after important appearances at the Screen on the Green punk festival in Islington on August 29 and the 100 Club London Punk Festival on September 20 (where Siouxsie Sioux performed for the first time, singing a version of the Lord's Prayer with Sid Vicious as her backup drummer).

Between July and November 1976, the band played publicly with increasing regularity in London, appearing at 18 concerts with playlists that included the 101-ers song "Keys to Your Heart" and also such future fan favorites as "I'm so Bored with You" (later recorded as "I'm so Bored with the USA"), "London's Burning," "White Riot," "1977," and "Career Opportunities." With the exception of their cover of the 101-ers' song, each of these songs was later recorded and released on the band's 1977 debut album, *The Clash.* By November 1976, Terry Chimes had decided to leave the band, citing personality conflicts with his bandmates and difficulties with Rhodes. Pat Gilbert explains that "the truth was he couldn't stand Bernie's politburo-esque machinations," and as the band matured, this aspect of Rhodes's personality would eventually prove to be problematic for the others, too (Gilbert, 117).

By December 1976, the Clash had enlisted Rob Harper (born November 28, 1955; drums) as a substitute drummer, and the quartet was scheduled to join the Sex Pistols, the Heartbreakers, and the Damned on the Anarchy in the UK tour. The tour was derailed after the Pistols famously clashed with Bill Grundy during a two-minute interview on Thames Television's *Today* show on December 1. The next day, photos of the band were splashed on the front page of various newspapers, decrying the Pistols, and punk in general, as "the filth and the fury." Fourteen shows out of a total of 21 that comprised the Anarchy tour were canceled in the wake of the Grundy incident, and media coverage of the remaining shows (and their protestors) was intense. From the Clash's perspective, however, Jon Savage notes that "it was a strange situation . . . neither the Clash nor the Heartbreakers had any record-company support. Although they had bread and board through the existing block hotel booking, if they didn't play, they had no money. 'We still had solidarity,' says Joe Strummer, 'but we felt pretty small just then, because the Sex Pistols were front-page news, and we were just nothing, we were at the bottom of the bill'" (Savage, 271). In 2004, a tape surfaced of the Clash's performance at Manchester's Electric Ballroom, as part of the Anarchy Tour, and Gilbert explained that "the tape catches the Clash in their early, clattering glory. The songs were played fractionally slower than on the first album, and 'Protex Blue,' a totem from their earliest days, was reworked as a political song 'about Big Brother' (although the lyrics are indecipherable)" (Gilbert, 130).

Despite the outcome of the Anarchy tour, those who had seen the Clash in performance were impressed by their energy and by the quality of their songs. The band's carefully crafted visual appearance also made an impact on those who observed the Clash. Mining their art-school backgrounds for inspiration, the Clash had adopted a Jackson Pollack inspired look of paint-splattered and stenciled clothing that was described in *Sounds* magazine as "couture bezippered ensembles [that were] so hot that [the reviewer] can't make out which is the bigger plus, the music, the words, or the image" (Goldman 1977). Indeed, the January 1977 issue of *Sounds* magazine, featuring a

photograph of the Clash with its new drummer, Nicholas Bowen "Topper" Headon (born Nicholas Bowen Headon, May 30, 1955; drums), on its front cover, proclaimed the band as their "pick" for the year.

On January 27, 1977, the Clash signed a £100,000 recording contract with CBS Records that purportedly committed the band to five albums. As Joe Strummer argued, "The Pistols had signed to EMI by this time and our signing to CBS gave Punk a credibility in the big, bad old music business" (The Clash, 113). Immensely prolific at the beginning of their recording career, the band released its first album, *The Clash,* on April 8, 1977, packaged in a sleeve that features an iconic grayscale photograph of Strummer, Jones, and Simonon taken by the photographer Kate Simon outside their rehearsal studio and done up to seem as though it had been photocopied and torn from a scrapbook or a poster. As one critic noted about the debut album, "The Clash eschewed the self-destructive ethos [of punk] and instead opted for edgy political songs, catchy slogans, and clothes from a decorator's van" (Dimery, 378). The absence of Headon from the photograph suggests that his position in the band was still in limbo at the time of its recording. Indeed, Terry Chimes (credited as "Tory Crimes") returned to the band to set down the drum tracks as the debut album was recorded in February 1977. Deemed too British in its political focus, the album was not released in the United States until 1979, and even then, the U.S. version of *The Clash* replaced the songs "Cheat," "48 Hours," "Deny," and "Protex Blue" with "Complete Control," "Jail Guitar Doors," "Clash City Rockers," "[White Man] in Hammersmith Palais," and "I Fought the Law." As one observer noted, "the rough, boxy sound [of the album] conjures up a London based entirely around the facts of survival, boredom, compromise and refusal to compromise. The short, sharp songs find a kind of beauty, even while they suggest days of endless grey, and make England 1977 sound like a police state, which it sort of was" (Mulholland, 17).

Although he did not appear on the album, Headon began to tour with the Clash in the spring of 1977. He had been enlisted to replace Chimes because he was a drum prodigy who had already established himself with the progressive rock outfit Mirkwood, which he had joined at the age of 18. With Headon on drums, Mirkwood had opened for a number of big acts, including Supertramp. Headon's entrée into the punk scene had begun with London SS, for whom he played drums for about a week. Headon and the new lineup of the Clash were officially unveiled at a gig at London's Roundhouse club on April 10, 1977, just before the band embarked on the promotional White Riot tour on May 1, 1977. With the Jam, Buzzcocks, the Slits, and Subway Sect as their support, the Clash played 28 concerts throughout the United Kingdom as a warm-up to a five-month European tour that introduced the band in live performance to audiences in France, Belgium, Germany, Austria, and Sweden. Among other things, the band became noted for its unique fashion style, developed by the designer Sebastian Conran exclusively for the Clash. Trousers with zips, D-rings, and military-style map-pockets became trademarks of the band, all of which were paint-splattered in the style of Jackson Pollock or decorated with political slogans or words that hinted at the identity of the band.

As the year 1977 drew to a close, the Clash was playing to bigger audiences in increasingly larger venues across the United Kingdom. By April 1978, for example, the band was slated to headline the open-air Rock-against-Racism (RAR) concert at Victoria Park, London, which had been organized partly in response to remarks made by Eric Clapton at a Birmingham concert in August 1976 that supported Enoch Powell and his "Rivers of Blood" political agenda. The RAR concert was also meant to draw attention to the growing political threat posed by the National Front, which had begun to mount candidates in greater numbers in elections. The concert was a showcase for many punk bands of the time, and the Clash played alongside such acts as the Buzzcocks, X-Ray Spex, the Ruts, Sham 69, and Generation X. Their performance at RAR was documented on the film *Rude Boy*, directed by David Mingay and Jack Hazan.

The year 1978 saw many changes in the band. By early 1978, the band had signed a new producer, Sandy Pearlman, in the hopes of finding a way to break into the U.S. market. Pearlman had made his name as the producer for the Blue Oyster Cult, and the band hoped that his familiarity with American tastes in popular music would help their quest. In the spring, the band's association with Sebastian Conran soured as the band sought to distance itself from its art-school roots in order to cement its working-class credibility. As Gilbert explains, "In Britain, you're prejudged by how you speak and the school you went to . . . Joe [Strummer]'s private-school education was becoming a hot potato; it suggested he was a fraud. His link with Sebastian was further putting the Clash's street-credibility—there's no other phrase for it—in jeopardy" (Gilbert, 180). Sebastian quickly became persona non grata at the Clash's rehearsals and, following his betrayal by the band, has been disinclined to speak about his early association with punk ever since. Finally, in September, Rhodes was sacked after he booked a gig in Harlesden without informing the band, and was then forced to cancel when he discovered that the band was unable to attend.

As one observer noted, "1978 is the pivotal year. The Clash have made it in terms of being on the cover of NME and reaching a wide audience, but what does that mean? Paul [Simonon] seems to enjoy it—he was the most hedonistic of the group . . . but with Mick [Jones], I think he finds it more of a responsibility than he ever imagined" (Gilbert, 202). Despite their professional upheavals, the band released their second album, the "American-friendly" *Give 'Em Enough Rope,* on November 10, 1978. With such new songs as "Safe European Home," "Guns on the Roof," "Last Gang in Town," "All the Young Punks," and "Tommy Gun" now recorded, the band set off to promote the new album on their "Out on Parole" and "Sort It Out" tours in July and October 1979, respectively, both of which took the band to various locales in Britain, Paris, and Belgium. The proceedings from the December 4 concert at London's Music Machine were earmarked for Sid Vicious's legal defense after he was charged with the murder of his girlfriend, Nancy Spungen, in New York's Chelsea Hotel on October 12, 1978. Sid never used the fund because he overdosed on heroin on February 2, 1979, before his trial began.

The band had begun to gain a following in North America, although the first album had yet to be released into the American marketplace. This changed when *Give 'Em Enough Rope* appeared in the States in April 1979. To set the stage for its arrival, the band launched the pre-promotional "Pearl Harbour" tour of North America in the spring, with the journalist Caroline Coon as the band's temporary manager. She successfully oversaw the American tour, for which she managed to secure Bo Diddley as the supporting act, but stepped down at the conclusion of the tour and ceded her managerial position to Blackhill Enterprises, a management company founded in the 1960s by the four original members of Pink Floyd (Syd Barrett, Nick Mason, Roger Waters, and Richard Wright), Peter Jenner, and Andrew King. When the band split with Bernie Rhodes, they also had to give up their studio at Rehearsals Rehearsals, since it was owned by Rhodes, so Blackhill secured a new rehearsal space for the band in Pimlico.

At the end of March 1979, the band went into the Pimlico studio to work on a new set of songs for their third album, *London Calling,* which was recorded through the summer and produced by Bill Price and Guy Stevens. The cover, an ingenious mash-up of the typography that appeared on the cover of Elvis's self-titled debut album and a photograph taken by Pennie Smith of Simonon as he smashed his bass guitar during a concert in New York City, has become one of the iconic photographs of the punk era. In advance of the album's release in Britain on December 14, 1979 (and in the United States a month later), the band launched the pre-promotional "Take the Fifth" North American tour. This generated a wealth of interest in the upcoming album, which entered the British charts at number nine and which peaked at number 27 in the U.S. charts. For some critics, "*London Calling* is regarded . . . as the death of punk rock, owing to its sophistication that steps well beyond the accepted limits of punk amateurism. . . . And yet, despite the competent musicianship and far-reaching influences that earned the Clash categorization as a new-wave band, their music retained all the fury and frustration of punk's most snarling activists, expanding

working-class aggravation beyond London's poorer districts to speak for injustice everywhere" (Smith 154).

Once the album had been released in the United Kingdom, the Clash launched their "Sixteen Tons" tour, which ran in Britain from January 5 to February 27, 1980, and then in the United Stated from March 1–10 (with a final, unadvertised concert at the Roxy Theatre in Hollywood on April 27). The tour was named after a Tennessee Ernie Ford song that the band admired and, now sporting 1950s-style quiffs, the members of the band entered the stage at each gig to the strains of that song. During the brief hiatus from touring between the March and April 1980, the band convened at New York's Electric Ladyland studio to begin work on their fourth studio album, *Sandinista!*

The band also traveled to Jamaica to record in Channel 1 Studios and to Wessex Studios in London to work with their longtime producer Bill Price. Supporting the band on the "Sixteen Tons" tour was Mikey Dread (Michael George Campbell), a Jamaican musician who had been introduced to the band by the London DJ Don Letts. Dread later produced the band's single "Bankrobber" (released on August 8, 1980) and appeared as a backup singer on *Sandinista!* In May, the "Sixteen Tons" tour continued, this time in Europe, and wrapped up in late August with a final concert in Toronto, Canada.

Sandinista!, the band's fourth studio album, was released as a triple-album set in Britain on December 12, 1980 (and appeared one month later in North America). Perhaps reflecting or responding to an increased interest among its contemporaries in world music, the album ranges in style from reggae and ska to calypso, jazz, and even rap. According to Mick Jones, the band's insistence that the album be sold for the cost of a single album riled CBS. He revealed that "they hadn't wanted us to do the 'Two For The Price of One' on *London Calling* and must have been exasperated when we suggested three for *Sandinista!* So we stole the master tapes and held them in a safe place until the negotiations were finished. They agreed it could be a triple album, but we had to take a cut in the royalties on the first couple of hundred thousand copies sold or something. I don't think it got there for ten years or so" (The Clash, 283). The band quickly sank into debt under the weight of *Sandinista!* and, disillusioned with Blackhill, canceled their management contract and reinstated Bernie Rhodes shortly after the release of the album. Rhodes immediately decided to book the band for a series of large-venue performances, both to promote the new album and to attempt to find some financial equilibrium.

The "Mission Impossible" tour began in Barcelona, Spain, on April 27, 1981, and played in 21 arena-style venues across Europe before concluding in Florence, Italy, on May 23. Almost immediately thereafter, the band did a 15-show residency at the Bonds nightclub in New York's Times Square district, where they were supported by Grandmaster Flash, who introduced them to the burgeoning New York hip-hop scene. At the time, Martin Scorsese was filming *The King of Comedy* in New York, and he wanted to hook up with the band for a future project, titled *Gangs of New York*. That project was not realized until 2002, at which point the band had long been broken up. The residency project suited the band because it did not require them to travel. In September 1981, they agreed to another residency at the Theatre Mogador in Paris, where they were joined by supporting acts the Beat and Wah!

At the beginning of 1982, the Clash flew to Japan to begin a tour of the Far East and Pacific Rim, and then spent March and April recording their new album, *Combat Rock,* at New York's Electric Ladyland studio. More experimental than any of their previous albums, *Combat Rock* featured sound collage and spoken-word tracks that enlisted the Beat poet Allen Ginsberg. As Gilbert has noted, "the prevailing musical mood [of *Combat Rock*] is humid funk-reggae. There are echoes of Gil Scott Heron, Tom Waits, Lee Perry, Van Morrison, Perez Prado. The leitmotif of the album soon established itself as Vietnam—and America in moral decline" (Gilbert, 307).

Realistically, the album offered only two radio-friendly tracks, "Should I Stay or Should I Go?" and "Rock the Casbah," but despite this, it peaked at number two shortly after its release in Britain on May 14, 1982, and in the United States, it peaked at number seven. To promote the new album, the band launched the "Casbah Club USA + UK" tour in May 1982 without Topper Headon, whose heroin addiction had begun to affect his ability to play. The band's original drummer, Terry Chimes, was recruited as the drummer. As Joe Strummer later admitted, Headon's departure signaled "the beginning of the end, really. Whatever a group is, it's the chemical mixture of those four people that makes a group work. You can take one away and replace him with whoever you like, or ten men: it's never gonna work" (The Clash, 357).

Further, the band had not taken a break from writing, recording, or touring for five years, and the strain was beginning to show. When the "Combat Rock USA" tour was over, Terry Chimes left the band because of clashes between Strummer and Jones, and was quickly replaced by Pete Howard. *Combat Rock* had given the Clash their biggest-selling album and had been a top 10 hit around the world. In the United States, the band had been invited to support the Who and were booked to headline the U.S. Festival in San Bernadino, California, on May 28, 1983, an event that was organized by Apple cofounder Steve Wozniak. The Clash was on the brink of superstardom, but problems within the ranks meant that it was also on the brink of collapse. The U.S. Festival was Mick Jones's last appearance with the band; he left to form the band Big Audio Dynamite with Don Letts.

Many fans of the Clash view the departure of Jones in 1983 as the end of the Clash. Others are willing to accept that the band continued, albeit in a different configuration, with the absence of two key members. On October 1, 1983, the band placed an advertisement in *Melody Maker* for a guitarist, eventually recruiting Nick Shepphard (born November 28, 1960; guitar)—formerly from Bristol-based punk band the Cortinas—and Vince White (born Gregory Stuart Lee White, April 28, 1960; guitar)—a recent science graduate from University College London—as the new guitarists. Howard agreed to remain with the band as its drummer. The Clash MKII (mark II) played its first set of gigs in California in January 1984, followed by their London debut at the Brixton

Academy in March. As Gilbert noted in his biography of the band, "many people have commented how musically tight the five-man Clash were [but] despite a new anthem proclaiming 'We Are the Clash,' it didn't seem much like the Clash at all. The overriding impression was of something stylized and false" (Gilbert, 347).

Nonetheless, the band embarked on the "Out of Control" tour, which booked almost 80 shows in the United Kingdom, Europe, and North America. By 1985, CBS began to pressure the band for a new album to fulfill their original contract, so the band set to work on what would become their final, and most disastrous, album, *Cut the Crap*. By this point, Rhodes had decided to play a more active role in the creation of the album, which he produced under the pseudonym "Jose Unidos." Marked by musical differences between Strummer and Rhodes, and the mission of the latter to control the direction of the album, *Cut the Crap* was universally viewed as the band's weakest offering and as the death knell of the Clash. In Greil Marcus's view, "*Cut the Crap* seemed to be set in a riot—not the idealized 'White riot/Wanna riot of my own' of the Clash's 1976, not their 'London's Burning with Boredom Now!,' but a far more prosaic affair, tired, too familiar, the everyday bad news of the New Britain," and he concluded that the album "all seems lost in a shoving match between skimpy lyrics and football-match chants of vague slogans" (Marcus, 307–308). By 1986, Strummer and Rhodes had parted ways for good, with the former working briefly with Mick Jones and Big Audio Dynamite before forming the Mescaleros in the mid-1990s. Much to the shock of his many fans, Strummer died unexpectedly on December 22, 2002, of an undiagnosed congenital heart condition. His life and career were subsequently documented by Julian Temple in the 2007 tribute film *Joe Strummer: The Future Is Unwritten*. Rhodes, by contrast, left the music industry entirely to devote his life to a variety of social and humanitarian causes. According to rumor, he is at work on a documentary about his life and career both with the Clash and beyond, although the film has neither a title nor a release date.

Given the enormity of the Clash's legacy, it is almost impossible to summarize their influence on popular music in a mere paragraph. The band's adoption of reggae and ska opened the door for the 2-Tone movement that emerged in Britain in the wake of punk, while their appeal to Jamaican culture also paved the way for U.S. punk bands that cut across racial and cultural divides, like Bad Brains and No Doubt. The political critique that marked the lyrics of the Clash became a template for bands who sought to react to the political and economic climate of their day, like U2 and Green Day, and the unforgiving nature of their critique invited bands like Dead Kennedys, Rancid, and Black Flag to be pointed and direct in their discussions about U.S. politics in the 1980s. In January 2003, the band was inducted into the Rock and Roll Hall of Fame in Cleveland, and three months later, the Grammy Awards paid tribute to the Clash with a concert of their music played by a selection of established artists who cite the band as an influence, including Elvis Costello, Bruce Springsteen and Steven Van Zandt, Dave Grohl (Nirvana), Pete Thomas (Elvis Costello and the Attraction), and Tony Kanal (No Doubt). In 2004, *Rolling Stone* ranked the band as the 28th most influential act in the history of popular music.

Karen Fournier

Selected Discography

The Clash, UK release, CBS Records CBS8200, 1977.

Give 'Em Enough Rope, UK release, CBS Records CBS 82431, 1978.

London Calling, UK release, CBS Records CBS CLASH3, 1979.

Sandinista!, UK release, CBS Records FSLN1, 1980.

Combat Rock, UK release, CBS Records FSLN2, 1982.

Cut the Crap, UK release, CBS Records CBS26601, 1985.

References

The Clash. *The Clash: Strummer, Jones, Simenon, Headon.* New York: Grand Central Publishing, 2008.

D'Ambrosio, Antonio. *Let Fury Have the Hour: The Punk Rock Politics of Joe Strummer.* New York: Nation Books, 2004.

Dimery, Robert. *1001 Albums You Must Hear Before You Die.* New York: Universe, 2005.

Fletcher, Tony. *The Clash: A Complete Guide to Their Music*. London: Omnibus Press, 2005.

Gilbert, Pat. *Passion Is a Fashion: The Real Story of the Clash*. London: Aurum Press, 2005.

Goldman, Vivian. "The Clash Etc. . . . Harlesden's Burning." *Sounds* (March 1977): n.p.

Gray, Marcus. *The Clash: The Return of the Last Gang in Town*, 2nd ed. London: Helter Skelter, 2001.

Gray, Marcus. *Route 19 Revisited: The Clash and London Calling*. London: Random House, 2010.

Green, Johnny. *A Riot of Our Own: Night and Day with the Clash*. New York: Faber and Faber, 1999.

Marcus, Greil. *In The Fascist Bathroom: Punk in Pop Music 1977–1992*. Cambridge, MA: Harvard University Press, 2005.

McNeil, Legs. *Please Kill Me: An Uncensored Oral History of Punk*. New York: Penguin Press, 1997.

Mulholland, Gary. *Fear of Music: The 261 Greatest Albums since Punk and Disco*. London: Orion Books, 2006.

Needs, Kris. *Joe Strummer and the Legend of the Clash*. Medford, NJ: Plexus Publishing, 2005.

O'Hara, Craig. *The Philosophy of Punk: No More Than Noise*. Oakland, CA: AK Press, 2001.

Smith, Chris. *101 Albums That Changed Popular Music*. London: Oxford University Press, 2009.

Cream (1966–1968)

Cream (or the Cream) was rock's first power trio—bass, lead guitar, and drums—and one of the earliest supergroups. Fusing blues and psychedelic rock into a vehicle for extended virtuosic solos and free-form improvisation, the band opened up new possibilities within rock that led to new styles like hard rock and heavy metal. The band's members were all veterans of London's rhythm and blues scene: Eric Clapton (born Eric Patrick Clapton, March 30, 1945; guitar) was the lead guitarist of the Yardbirds; Jack Bruce (born John Simon Asher Bruce, May 14, 1943; bass, vocals, harmonica, keyboard) was a member of Blues Incorporated, Britain's first "R&B" band, the Graham Bond Organization, and Manfred Mann; and Ginger Baker (born Peter Edward Baker, August 19,

1938; drums) was the drummer for the Graham Bond Organization.

By 1964, Clapton was already considered the finest young blues-influenced guitarist in Britain. As his devotion to the genre grew he became more estranged from the Yardbirds, whose other members aspired to popular success. He quit the band because, in lead singer Keith Relf's words, "he loves the blues so much. I suppose he did not like it being played badly by a white shower like us!" ("Clapton Quits Yardbirds"). A few weeks later, after reading an interview where the young guitarist claimed that "for me to face myself I have to play what I believe is pure and sincere and uncorrupted music" (Sanford 1999, 48), John Mayall invited Clapton to join the Bluesbreakers, which was considered the most hard-core and serious of all British blues bands, as he too was "very dedicated and wanted to put the blues on the map and play it right" (Mayall 1997).

In the spring of 1966 Clapton and the Bluesbreakers recorded several singles for the Immediate and Purdah labels, produced by studio guitarist Jimmy Page (who would, a month later, join the Yardbirds). One track, "Telephone Blues," contained the first truly significant blues rock guitar solo. It also hinted at a new British take on the blues, one that would reach a more articulate fulfillment on *Blues Breakers: John Mayall with Eric Clapton*. The album—widely considered the seminal testament of blues rock—would prove to have an enormous impact on the British blues scene, as it was the first music by a native group to truly explore the modern blues idiom: fluid solos and fills using string bending, distortion, clipped phrases, and fills.

Clapton's extended solos on Johnny Otis's "Double Crossing Time" and Freddie King's "Hideaway" may have been familiar to blues aficionados, many of whom commented upon his facility within the idiom, but to the uninitiated they were unprecedented. Even the sound of his guitar was revolutionary. Clapton was the first British player to adopt the heavy Gibson Les Paul with humbucker pickups, the preferred model of Freddie King and Howlin' Wolf's guitarist, Hubert Sumlin. When run through a

The members of the classic power trio Cream (from left to right): Jack Bruce, Ginger Baker, and Eric Clapton at London Airport on their way to Los Angeles on August 20, 1967. Although the group did not play together for long, they had enormous impact through fusing blues and psychedelic rock. Additionally, their extended improvisatory explorations became the new standard for popular music in the late 1960s. (Photo by George Stroud/Express/Getty Images)

reverb-inducing Marshall, the Les Paul created a loud, aggressive sound with a substantial bottom end. Attempting to replicate the sound achieved by modern Chicago blues players, Clapton insisted on turning up his amplifier all the way to create maximum distortion and sustain and allowing the sound to bleed into the microphones. The resulting color and presence led virtually all other blues-influenced guitarists in the country to adopt a similar setup.

Clapton soon became known for his extended guitar solos, which at the time were a novelty in rock

and roll. His playing was regarded as so amazing that graffiti proclaiming "Clapton is God" began appearing on walls around London. However, Clapton soon grew dissatisfied with the Bluesbreakers; he felt that Mayall's arrangements were too structured and the rest of the band was not at his level. He was thus amenable when Ginger Baker, the drummer for the Graham Bond Organization, approached him with a proposition.

Baker, like many of his colleagues in the R&B scene, came from a jazz background. He fell hard for the music of Dizzy Gillespie and played trumpet in the Air Training Corps band, though he had always been interested in drumming. He recalled, "I used to get the kids at school dancing by banging rhythms on the school desk! They kept on at me to sit in with this band. The band wasn't very keen, but in the end I sat in and played the bollocks off their drummer. And that was the first time I'd sat on a kit. I heard one of the band turn round and say: 'Christ, we've got a drummer' and I thought, 'Hello, this is something I can do'" (jackbruce.com).

Within the year he dropped out of school and took a job as the drummer of the Storyville Jazz Men; the members turned him on to the percussionists Baby Dodds, Buddy Rich, and Max Roach, who became his primary inspiration. Roach, along with Kenny Clarke, shifted timekeeping from the snare drum to the bass drum and ride cymbals, a flexible style that left space for a drummer to add fills, play irregular accents, and create polyrhythmic lines within the kit.

Baker left the outfit in 1958, but his unorthodox style made finding steady work difficult; he took on freelance tour dates and played with a number of jazz groups, many including saxophonist Dick Heckstall-Smith (born Richard Malden Heckstall-Smith, September 16, 1934, died December 17, 2004; tenor saxophone). When Heckstall-Smith was playing with Blues Incorporated he brought Baker along; the band was a good fit, and Baker was asked to replace Charlie Watts when he left in late 1962 to join the Rolling Stones. In this new forum Baker's style quickly got noticed—Chris Welch of *Melody Maker* declared him the finest drummer in England—and he influenced Keith Moon, Mitch Mitchell, and other British R&B drummers.

The bass player for Blues Incorporated was Jack Bruce, who, in his youth studied piano, voice, and cello, eventually growing into the upright bass, the instrument he had always wanted to play. At age 15 he was accepted into the Royal Scottish Academy of Music in Glasgow, but left after two years. He developed an interest in modern jazz and blues, which he discovered was not fostered and in fact actively discouraged at the academy. He started playing at jazz clubs throughout England and even toured in Italy for

a time. At a gig in Cambridge he sat in with Heckstall-Smith and Baker; they found his playing sufficiently impressive to invite him to sit in with Blues Incorporated, and he was appointed the group's permanent bassist in May 1962.

Baker, Bruce, and Graham Bond (born Graham John Clifton Bond, October 28, 1937, died May 8, 1974; alto saxophone, organ), another member of Blues Incorporated, formed a trio in January 1963. They started playing the intervals of Blues Incorporated gigs and then split off to form the Graham Bond Organization with Dick Heckstall-Smith. At that time Bruce switched from upright to electric bass. The group played throughout England on the R&B circuit, where their experimentation in jazz/R&B fusion was welcomed, and they backed a number of visiting American blues and soul singers, including Memphis Slim and Marvin Gaye. In 1964, the Graham Bond Organization got a recording contract with Decca Records. They cut a handful of singles and even two albums, *The Sound of '65* and *There's a Bond Between Us,* but they never had mainstream chart success.

Baker (through Bond) fired Bruce from the band in September 1965, ostensibly because his jazz-rooted style was "too busy," but largely because he and Baker had frequent and sometimes violent disagreements, which on several occasions resulted in on-stage brawls. Bruce continued to show up for gigs, believing that Bond would reverse his decision. Baker finally resolved the situation by pulling a knife and threatening to stab the bassist.

Bruce almost immediately secured another job, replacing John McVie (the Mac of Fleetwood Mac) in John Mayall's Bluesbreakers. During his tenure he met and played briefly with Peter Green (another later member of Fleetwood Mac) and Eric Clapton. Bruce's preference for improvising and recomposing parts on stage energized the Bluesbreakers, and he encouraged Clapton to stretch out and explore his full potential on the guitar.

The bassist left the Bluesbreakers in December to join Manfred Mann, a group with several hits under its belt that had far better commercial prospects than the Bluesbreakers. A month later he and Clapton recorded together in a pickup group arranged by Manfred Mann's vocalist, Paul Jones (born Paul Pond, February 24, 1942; vocals, harmonica) and producer Joe Boyd.

Ginger Baker stayed with the Graham Bond Organization until early 1966, but he increasingly felt creatively stifled and frustrated with their lack of commercial success. Eric Clapton soon agreed to Baker's suggestion that they form a new band, but he had one condition: he wanted Jack Bruce to play. Despite Baker's significant personal animosity toward his former bandmate, an agreement was reached, and Cream was born. Early on they considered adding a singer to the group; both Steve Winwood and Paul Jones were approached, but each declined, and ultimately the idea was abandoned, as Bruce was an able vocalist.

As Clapton, Bruce, and Baker were arguably three of the finest musicians in London, the story in *Melody Maker* by Chris Welch—who had been invited to the band's first "unofficial" rehearsal on June 11, 1966—announcing that they were forming a "group's group" generated significant excitement. For the musicians it was also a bit awkward, as none had yet informed their respective bands of their departure.

Cream was originally conceived as a blues trio informed by the modern Chicago blues of Buddy Guy and by Jimi Hendrix, whose use of feedback and distortion was informed by the cutting-edge experimentation of guitarists Earl Hooker and Robert Nighthawk. After seeing Hendrix in London in September 1966, Clapton was awestruck and immediately influenced by the American:

> It opened [me] up a lot because I was still at that time pretty uptight by the fact that we weren't playing 100 percent blues numbers, and to see Jimi play that way I just thought, Wow! That's all right with me. . . . It just opened my mind up to listening to a lot of other things and playing a lot of other things. (Schumacher 1995, 82)

Jack Bruce recalls "sitting in a London coffee bar with Eric Clapton, when we first formed Cream, and telling him, 'I want us to take the language of the blues and develop it a step further'" (Jisi 2005). They were also interested in making some money, something that, despite their lofty reputations, had not yet happened. In an interview with Chris Welch the trio discussed their potential approach. Clapton directly addressed the potential problems of an all-star trio: "Most people have formed the impression of us as three solo musicians clashing with each other. We want to cancel that idea and be a group that plays together" (Schumacher 1995, 76). The band also revealed that their core repertoire would be drawn from the blues; Baker claimed that they were digging into blues going back as far as 1927, which is to say, virtually the earliest recordings of the country blues. The band's set list when they started rehearsing in June 1966 indeed revealed a wide cross-section of blues material: "Crossroads," an arrangement of Robert Johnson's "Crossroad Blues"; Howlin' Wolf's "Spoonful"; "I'm So Glad," by Skip James; "Traintime," by Forrest City Joe Pugh; and two originals: "I Feel Free" and "Toad."

After the band's debut at the National Jazz and Blues Festival in Windsor, where a lack of sufficient material necessitated the extension of every song in their still rather short set list, Cream focused on jazz-like extended improvisation, employing the riff-based blues as a flexible structure that could accommodate a fusion of stylistic elements.

The band also prioritized instrumental virtuosity: Clapton contributed long, liquid blues-based solos colored by wah-wah pedal, feedback, and distortion; Bruce added incredibly active bass lines, often in counterpoint to Clapton's guitar. While common in American soul music, such lines were rare in British rock, and the innovation made Bruce the most prominent bassist of his day. When added to Baker's polyrhythmic jazz drumming style, the results were explosive. Cream was at its best live, sometimes working through 10-, 15-, and even 20-minute improvisatory explorations of each song's possibilities.

It was widely expected that the band would immediately rush into the studio and record an album, but instead, Cream played live dates in small clubs, large theaters, and festivals for nine months. Those close to the group indicated that there was still some disagreement of what kind of band Cream was or would turn out to be. Clapton was reportedly pushing for a Dadaist or surrealistic approach; Baker and Bruce, for once in agreement, wanted to focus more on jazz.

When they did release their first single "Wrapping Paper," it did nothing to clarify their vision. In fact, it was the last thing that anyone had expected from the group: an English dance-hall soft-shoe that, save for the electric guitar, could have been written in the 1930s. Bruce, who wrote the number with British beat poet Pete Brown, admitted that the incongruous number was done in part to shock and surprise people, but also to overcome what all three felt was their largest potential problem: being characterized as just a blues band. While the genre was undoubtedly at the core of the band's identity, they also wanted the freedom to explore any and all potential avenues that piqued their interest. Although the track was odd, it reached number 34 on the British pop charts, the best outing for any of the musicians to date.

Finally, in December 1966, Cream's first album, *Fresh Cream,* was released. The tracks were an almost equal mixture of originals and blues arrangements, drawn from their live set list. The originals were hit and miss. Except for a stinging, extended fuzztone guitar solo, "Sweet Wine" might have been by any number of British pop groups, and "Dreaming" and "Sleepy Time Time" failed to gel. The psychedelic, riff-based "N.S.U." was a solid track, but the clear standout was "I Feel Free," which most clearly pointed toward the mature Cream sound: Clapton and Bruce in tight, Everly-brothers vocal harmonies with the guitar or bass reinforcing the melody line, riff-based guitar erupting into fuzztone heavy fills or solos, an active bass line, and timekeeping duties split between the three musicians.

The album also included "Toad," the first rock drum solo; "From Four 'Till Late," by Robert Johnson, which marked Clapton's debut as a lead vocalist; "Spoonful," "I'm So Glad," "Cat's Squirrel"—listed as a traditional, but by Dr. Isiaah Ross; and a rollicking arrangement of the R&B club favorite, Muddy Waters's "Rollin' and Tumblin'." In some ways, their approach was typical of British blues rock bands: the

tempo was nearly double that of the original and the shuffle rhythms had been hammered into even eighth notes, but the energy and vitality were effectively maintained. However, Cream's approach was also distinctly different. There was extensive interplay among the musicians rather than a rigid adherence to the prescribed instrumental roles in Chicago blues. This was facilitated by Ginger Baker's drumming style, which allowed Clapton and Bruce to either play in unison or counterpoint, and his fills articulated the secondary rhythm that ordinarily would be covered by bass or rhythm guitar, allowing all three musicians to participate in a dynamic conversation.

The band also liberally applied aspects of psychedelic rock to their blues covers. While this was not unprecedented in contemporary blues, it was nonetheless unfamiliar to most British rock fans at the time. This new hybrid of Chicago blues, British pop, and psychedelic rock would eventually be dubbed hard rock.

Eric Clapton's approach to blues arrangements was also novel. His idea was to "take the most obvious things and simplify them. Like my way of doing 'Crossroads' was to take that one musical figure"— the fill that Robert Johnson used to conclude each phrase—"and make that the point, the focal point. Just trying to focus on what the essence of the song was—keeping it simple" (Guralnik 1990, 54). Cream reduced the intricate figure of the original into a propulsive riff that gave their version a relentless drive, a technique they also employed with Skip James's "I'm So Glad."

Eric Clapton was somewhat concerned about the band's novel sound. "I don't believe we'll get over to [the public]. People will always listen with biased ears, look through unbelieving eyes, and with preconceived ideas, remembering what we used to be, and so on. The only way to combat this is to present them with as many facets of your music as possible" (McStravick and Roos 2001, 90).

Cream made a quick tour of the United States in March 1967, but the band established its international reputation on their return trip in May. Their five-night tenure at the Fillmore West in San Francisco established Clapton's reputation as one of the best guitarists in rock and lifted Cream into the realm of rock super-stardom. While the songs were good, what garnered attention were their extended solos and improvisation; some reported that Cream had played only five songs in two hours. Mickey Hart of the Grateful Dead attended one of the shows and openly declared Cream the best band in the world. The reviews were so adulatory that even the mainstream press took notice; *Time* magazine dubbed Cream's tour "the most exciting musical jolt to come out of England since the Beatles and the Rolling Stones" (McStravick and Roos 2001, 91).

Four days before their visas expired, Cream recorded their next album at the Atlantic studios in New York; Ahmet Ertegun, the president of Atlantic records, offered not only the use of the studio but the services of engineer Tom Dowd and producer Felix Pappalardi. *Disraeli Gears*—the title was derived from a roadie's mispronunciation of derailleur, the type of gears commonly found on 10-speed bicycles, as Disraeli, the name of a 19th-century British prime minister—was released in November 1967. Atlantic withheld the album for five months over concerns that the new material, especially the Jack Bruce and Pete Brown numbers, were not "happening." Once Ertegun acquiesced, his fears about the album were definitively allayed. The record shot into the top 10, peaking at number five in Britain and number four in the United States, and it has endured as one of the classic albums of rock.

Disraeli Gears was more overtly psychedelic than its predecessor. This was partly a reflection of the times—*Sgt. Pepper's Lonely Hearts Club Band* was released that June—but the style was also an ideal vehicle for Clapton's surrealistic interests and Pete Brown's latter-day beat poetry. The psychedelic cover was designed by Clapton's roommate Martin Sharp, who also cowrote "Tales of Brave Ulysses," Homer's *Odyssey* on an acid trip. The song marked Clapton's first use of the wah-wah pedal; though the effect was not new, the pedal itself had been invented only a year before and was released publicly in February 1967. "Tales of Brave Ulysses" introduced the effects pedal to the musical world. The song was based on a descending chord progression in D minor

that, according to Clapton, was taken from the Lovin' Spoonfuls single "Summer in the City," and made liberal use of stop time, a device drawn from the Chicago blues. The song was a set pair with "SWLABR" (She Walks Like a Bearded Rainbow), a psychedelic rock classic awash in wah-wah and fuzztone.

The album opens with two of Cream's most enduring tracks: "Strange Brew" and "Sunshine of Your Love." The latter was anchored by a bottom-heavy guitar and bass riff wedded to a standard blues progression, a technique inspired by models like Howlin' Wolf's "Spoonful," and extensively adopted by hard rock and heavy metal bands in the late 1960s and early 1970s. "Strange Brew" represented another approach of British blues rock, a pastiche of elements from several blues rearranged in distinctly new ways and combined with original elements. The song was based on the group's earlier arrangement of the traditional blues "Oh Lawdy Mama" with new lyrics written by Eric Clapton, Felix Pappalardi, and Gail Pappalardi. The bass and rhythm guitar riff were taken from the Buddy Guy and Junior Wells recording "Everything's Gonna Be Alright" and the lead guitar lick from Albert King's "Crosscut Saw." The melody was entirely new, but Clapton's solo was lifted in large measure from King's "Personal Manager."

Cream launched a new tour of the United States in February 1968. The group was in such demand that they commanded an unprecedented $20,000 guarantee from venues, plus a share of the gate, and tickets sold out so quickly that the tour was extended by a month so that new dates could be added.

Before the tour, the band returned to the Atlantic studios in New York to record tracks for *Wheels of Fire,* Cream's most experimental album. Classical and folk influences were evident, and the band experimented with tempo changes, complex chord progressions, and mixed meter, as well as studio and postproduction. *Wheels of Fire* was one of first albums to employ an eight-track tape recorder, an innovation that Tom Dowd had advocated for years. The device made extensive overdubbing possible. On "Politician"—Cream's best original blues—Clapton's rhythm guitar was overlaid with two solo guitar lines in counterpoint; in stereo, the parts aurally shift from right to left, creating the impression of floating. Unlike their previous outings, the group made use of additional instruments. This was exemplified by "Pressed Rat and Wart Hog," Ginger Baker's recitation of an original poem that sounded like a folk tale garbled by centuries of oral transmission. In between the verses are interludes for trumpet and bass. As the track progresses, overdubbed parts weave a complex yet subdued interplay of two bass lines, three guitar parts, trumpet, recorder, and tonette—song flute—the instrument's first and only appearance in rock. "Passing the Time" employed a graceful and haunting introduction for cello, violin, bells, and glockenspiel that at the halfway mark exploded into a jam for guitar, bass, and organ. Such studio and coloristic experimentation stood next to blues covers like Albert King's "Born under a Bad Sign," the venerable "Sittin' On Top of the World," and "White Room," the riff-based sibling of "Sunshine of Your Love."

Felix Pappalardi confronted the problem of capturing the energy and virtuosity of Cream onstage by convincing Ahmet Ertegun to green-light a two-disc set: one recorded in the studio and another of the band in concert. Atlantic had a mobile recording studio shipped to San Francisco, and six shows at the Winterland Ballroom and Fillmore West were taped for possible use. Pappalardi ultimately chose songs that featured each of the members of the band: "Toad" (Baker), "Train Time" (Bruce), and "Crossroads" and "Spoonful" (Clapton).

With the exception of the reviewer for *Rolling Stone,* who felt it was too sloppy, critics praised the album, which firmly established that Cream was more than just a blues band and had the potential to explore myriad stylistic directions. It was a commercial success as well; the album hit number one on both sides of the Atlantic and was the first double album to be awarded platinum status.

However, just after *Wheels of Fire* was released in Britain, and prior to its U.S. debut, Baker, Bruce, and Clapton announced that Cream was splitting up, ostensibly because the members were moving in too many different directions artistically. Eric Clapton

was also stung by a concert review by Jon Landau in *Rolling Stone,* which said that Clapton was "a master of the blues clichés of all the post-WWII blues guitarists . . . Clapton's problem is that while he has vast potential, at this time he isn't fulfilling it. He is a virtuoso at performing other people's ideas" (Landau 1968). However, his "official" reason was that he found the new direction of the band unsatisfactory and wanted to get back to playing experimental blues. "You really get hung up and try to write pop songs or create a pop image. I went through that stage and it was a shame because I was not being true to myself. I am and always will be a blues guitarist" (Sanford 1999, 94). The wording was virtually identical to the statement he gave when leaving the Yardbirds.

In truth, Cream was doomed from the beginning. The key to its success, the tension between the musicians' individual and creative talents, also contained the seeds of its destruction, as did the stress of Clapton being the "star" in a trio of musicians of equal ability. The animosity between Ginger Baker and Jack Bruce also made the combination unsustainable; the two complemented each other as musicians and communicated well in a performance context but were simply unable to coexist for long. Numerous times the pair had to be physically separated, and by Cream's second U.S. tour all three band members not only had separate dressing rooms but also stayed in separate hotels.

Despite their impending split, Cream went on a final U.S. tour in October and November 1968 and played a farewell gig at Royal Albert Hall in London, which was expanded to two concerts when the entire 5,000-seat venue sold out. They even released a final album, *Goodbye,* in March 1969, which combined a trio of unreleased studio tracks with live selections from their last U.S. tour.

The impact of Cream has endured far longer than the band itself; their hybrid of blues and psychedelic rock laid the foundation for hard rock, heavy metal, progressive rock, and most of the "classic" rock of the 1970s. Additionally, their extended improvisatory explorations became de rigueur for any band with ambitions of greatness. In 1993, Cream was inducted into the Rock and Roll Hall of Fame and performed at the ceremony. In 2005, they reunited for a series of concerts, having at last found a sustainable formula: very short tours.

Roberta Freund Schwartz

Selected Discography

Fresh Cream, U.K.: Reaction 593 001 (mono)/594001 (stereo); U.S. Atco 33–206 (mono), SD-33–206 (stereo); 1966.

Disraeli Gears, U.K. Reaction 953 003 (mono)/594 004 (stereo); U.S. Atco 33–323 (mono)/SD-33–323 (stereo); 1967.

Wheels of Fire, U.K. Polydor 582 031/2 (mono)/583 031/2 (stereo); U.S. Atco SD-2–700, 1968.

Goodbye, U.K. Polydor 184 203; U.S. ATCO SD 7001, 1969.

References

Baker, Ginger, and Ginette Baker. *Hellraiser, The Autobiography of the World's Greatest Drummer.* London: John Blake, 2009.

"Clapton Quits Yarbirds, Too Commercial," *Melody Maker,* March 13, 1965, 5.

Guralnick, Peter, "Eric Clapton at the Passion Threshold," *Musician* 136 (1990): 44–56.

Headlam, Dave. "Blues Transformations in the Music of Cream," in John Covach and Graeme M. Boone, eds. *Understanding Rock: Essays in Musical Analysis.* Oxford: Oxford University Press, 1997.

Jisi, Chris. "Cream Rises: After 36 years, Jack Bruce & Co. Whip Up a Heavy Reunion." *Bass Player* 16 (December 2005): 34.

Landau, John. "Cream." *Rolling Stone* 10 (May 11, 1968): 14.

Mayall, John. Liner notes to As *It All Began: The Best of John Mayall and the Bluesbreakers 1964–69.* Decca D121768, 1997.

McStravick, Summer, and John Roos. *Blues-Rock Explosion.* Mission Viejo, CA: Old Goat Publishing, 2001.

Pappalardi, Felix. "How Cream Was Made." *Ginger Baker Press Archive.* www.gingerbaker.com/albums/cream-wheels-of-fire.html.

Sanford, Christopher. *Clapton: Edge of Darkness.* Updated ed. Boston: Da Capo, 1999.

Schumacher, Michael. *Crossroads: The Life and Music of Eric Clapton.* New York: Hyperion, 1995.

Schwartz, Roberta Freund. *How Britain Got the Blues: The Transmission and Reception of American Blues Style in the British Isles.* Aldershot: Ashgate, 2007.

Shapiro, Harry. *Jack Bruce, Composing Himself.* London: Jawbone, 2010.

Creedence Clearwater Revival (1959–1972)

Creedence Clearwater Revival's roots can be found in El Cerrito, California. John Fogerty (born John Cameron Fogerty, May 28, 1945; guitar, vocals) had dreamed of being a musician since his boyhood, fronting an imaginary band called Johnny Corvette and the Corvettes. Some of John's early influences included Ray Charles, Bo Diddley, and Chuck Berry, but it was Carl Perkins that clarified John's choice to become a rock star.

An interest in music came to the Fogerty boys from their mother, who had a bit of a musical background. In the 1950s she used to take the boys to see folk singers at festivals in the Bay Area. At these festivals they saw the likes of Pete Seeger and Ramblin' Jack Elliot among others. Their mother's interest in folk music also meant there was an acoustic guitar around the Fogerty household, which John and Tom shared. Eventually the brothers pitched in together and rented an electric guitar for five dollars a month, and when this guitar no longer suited their needs, John took on a loan (cosigned by his mother Lucille) to purchase a Danelectro Silvertone guitar and amplifier for $80 plus $8 interest, which John paid for with a paper route.

The beginning of Creedence Clearwater Revival dates to 1959 when John finally felt proficient on his guitar and sought out other musicians to play with. He was lucky enough to find two of his fellow Portola Junior High classmates who shared similar interests. The first to join John was Doug "Cosmo" Clifford (born Douglas Ray Clifford, April 24, 1945; drums) who shared John's love for the blues and luckily enough had an interest in the drums. The two boys played together and quickly decided they needed a third player to flesh out the sound. Clifford immediately thought of his good friend Stu Cook (born

Brothers John (seated, right) and Tom Fogerty (seated, center) came together with Doug Clifford (standing) and Stu Cook (left) to form Creedence Clearwater Revival (CCR), pictured here ca. 1970. CCR created a unique blend of blues, rock and roll, and American that stands the test of time and continues to be influential. (Photo by Michael Ochs Archives/Getty Images)

Stuart Alden Cook, April 25, 1945; bass), another admirer of the blues and fellow musician who had taken piano lessons and played trumpet. The three formed the Blue Velvets, playing popular instrumentals on guitar bass and piano at sock hops, parties, carnivals, fairs, and school assemblies.

While the Blue Velvets were honing their skills, John's older brother Tom Fogerty (born Thomas Richard Fogerty, November 9, 1941, died September 6, 1990; guitar) was also making a name for himself on the high school dance circuit with his band the Playboys and later with the locally acclaimed band Spider Webb and the Insects. Tom also sat in with the Blue Velvets on the occasions where the gigs required vocals.

The Blue Velvets started hanging around at the local recording studios and backing up anyone they could. This meant the boys were able to log a significant amount of studio time in their teenage years, including their own debut recording in 1960.

Tom Fogerty also gained recording experience when Spider Webb and the Insects landed a contract with Los Angeles–based Del-Fi Records after the label lost their star, Ritchie Valens. They cut a track titled "Lydia Jane," which was never released, leading to the breakup of the band. After this, Tom asked the Blue Velvets to record a demo with him and subsequently convinced John, Stu, and Doug to let him join their band. This made the group essentially two bands: the Blue Velvets, or Tommy Fogerty and the Blue Velvets, depending on whether or not the gig required vocals.

With Tom's leadership, Tommy Fogerty and the Blue Velvets were able to have a record pressed by a Bay Area record company called Orchestra. The record received some local airplay but did not sell well. A month later Orchestra pressed a second record for the band, which received a fair amount of airplay thanks to Casey Kasem, the program director at KEWB at the time, but again the sales were poor. Orchestra pressed one more record for the band; however, its sales were even worse than the first two and Orchestra dropped the band.

An unlikely break for the band came on the heels of Vince Guaraldi's surprise crossover instrumental hit "Cast Your Fate to the Wind," which inspired a documentary titled *Anatomy of a Hit*. The band happened to see the documentary and recognized the studio. Within the day the band traveled to the studio with instrumental recordings in hand to try to sell to this small Bay Area record company with a national instrumental hit, Fantasy Records.

Up to this point Fantasy Records had primarily been a jazz label releasing albums by Dave Brubeck, Gerry Mulligan, Chet Baker, and many others. The label saw something in the band, likely due to the popularity of emerging rock bands like the Beatles. One of the owners of Fantasy, Max Weiss, took on the Blue Velvets under a management contract. To sound more modern the band changed its name to the Visions.

As part of their initial contract with Fantasy, the band had recorded a two-song demo in a small recording studio outside of the Fantasy office; it took nine months, but Fantasy eventually released the demo. In the interim the British invasion had taken a firm hold on the U.S. market, and in an effort to capitalize on this, Max Weiss took the liberty of changing the band's name to the Golliwogs.

The band hated the name but went along with Weiss's new ideas, even the hokey matching outfits and white afro-styled wigs. In this period they were seeking out a booking agent and approached Scott Longston. "We laughed our asses off when their promo pack came into our office," Longston said before telling the band "that they had a lot of maturing and rehearsing to do before anyone would ever consider them as serious artists" (Bordowitz 1998).

Up to this point the band was still performing in the same arrangement as Tom Fogerty and the Blue Velvets, but there was a change coming. John was very self-conscious about it, but on a trip to Portland where he was gigging with some friends he made the decision that he was going to try to sing. Over the course of a two-week engagement John recorded whole sets of him singing, and then would go home and scrutinize the tapes before going back the next night and doing it all over. When John returned to the Golliwogs the band soon realized that they would have a new direction. Tom was willing to admit it, saying, "I could sing, but he had a sound." With this new revelation, Tom made the switch to rhythm guitar and Stu Cook moved over to electric bass (Werner 1998).

In 1966, both John and Doug were notified that they were wanted for military service. John got into the Army Reserves, and Doug was in the Coast Guard. Both men served six months of active duty, which put the band on hold. John's recollection of his military service was not generally positive; however, it does mark a significant change in his songwriting. The song "Porterville," later recorded for the debut Creedence Clearwater Revival album, was sketched by John while marching during training at Ft. Bragg in North Carolina.

When John and Doug returned from their six months of military duty it was time to make a big push for the band. Stu had just graduated and his father was pushing him to go to law school, but instead Stu told his father that he was going to pursue the band, and he sold the new car that he had received as a graduation present to help with funds. Tom also left his long-term job with the PG&E utility company and cashed in his retirement savings to fund the band. With Stu and Tom's money they started a fund, and John took care of the finances. Everyone was paid $20 per week, and all the band's earnings were put back into the fund.

In 1967, the Weiss brothers were getting ready to sell Fantasy Records and retire. They had been in talks with an East Coast record company to sell their assets. This deal eventually went sour and Saul Zaentz, the longtime director of sales and marketing for Fantasy, rounded up a group of investors to temporarily lease Fantasy with an option to buy.

Luckily, Zaentz was a bit more in tune with what was happening in the San Francisco rock scene than his predecessors and promptly told the Golliwogs it was time for a new name. After two weeks of thinking of nothing else, they came up with Creedence Clearwater Revival. "Creedence" came from a friend of a friend whose name was Credence Nuball; the band liked the Credence part but added the extra "e" to make it more reminiscent of a creed, something to believe in. "Clear water" came from a TV commercial for Olympia beer and related to the band's environmental senses, and "revival" spoke to the resurgence of the band and the revival of their musical values in opposition to the acid-drenched musical sensibility of the Bay Area.

The band played their first gig as Creedence Clearwater Revival on Christmas Eve 1967, and a month later the single of "Porterville" was released under the new name. John used a pen name for his writing credit on this single, this time using T. Spicebush Swallowtail.

Through all of the bands leading up to Creedence Clearwater Revival the group had hardly (if ever) played in San Francisco. Now with their newly found confidence they made the leap and booked a weekly gig at Deno-Carlo in the North Beach neighborhood. Although the band was essentially paid in tips for the gig, it allowed them to play what they wanted and build an audience in San Francisco. One of the occasional audience members was Zaentz, who told them after a show one night that he thought it was time they made an album.

With the prospect of an album at hand the band started woodshedding, as John put it: "I resolved at that point to not be mediocre, I resolved at that point to write real songs" (Bordowitz 1998). The album was tracked as a band, usually two or three takes and the vocals were overdubbed later.

The tracks on Creedence Clearwater Revival's 1968 self-titled debut included some of the covers that the band became best known for, such as Dale Hawkins's "Susie Q" and Screamin' Jay Hawkins's "I Put a Spell On You." Original offerings included Creedence's first single "Porterville" and the last song Tom Fogerty would receive a cowriting credit for, "Walk on the Water," a remake of a previously released single by the Golliwogs titled "Walking on the Water."

The track "Suzie Q," as it was spelled by CCR, was used as a vehicle to craft an arrangement for the band that included a nod to the psychedelic sounds that were so common of the time and place. While John was not particularly interested in being part of that scene, he did recognize the commercial value of adding a few psychedelic touches to the record; this in spite of the fact that John, unlike so many of his peers, was not a drug user.

When the masters were ready, CCR took a copy to one of the local FM radio stations, KSAN, who gave the band a good bit of airtime before the album was released. With this new boost Creedence was able to break into the Avalon and the Fillmore. Shortly thereafter, Bill Drake, a powerful force in the pop radio market, decided he liked "Suzie Q" and got it playing in Chicago on WLS. The song peaked at number 11 on the top 40 charts and the album made it to number 52 on the *Billboard* 200.

To capitalize on their new success the band began touring more, although they could not set out on a major road tour due to John and Doug's obligations to the reserves, which still required them to attend camp one weekend a month. In spite of this, the band started to get around, playing in places as far out as Honolulu and New York and receiving positive reviews as they did so.

As they were playing supporting dates for the debut album, the next album was already in the works.

One of the songs that defines the CCR sound, "Born on the Bayou," had already entered the live repertoire. This song kicked off the "swamp-rock" style for the band. John was working on a few songs all at one time, including "Born on the Bayou," "Proud Mary," and "Keep on Chooglin'," and thought the songs and album would be more powerful if all the songs were interrelated.

John had always been infatuated with the South and the music that came from the region. As he put it in the liner notes to the CCR box set, "All the great records, or the people who made them, somehow came from Memphis or Louisiana or somewhere along the Mississippi River in between." This newly exploited inspiration and association gave the band an identity that elevated them above the fray. Many people, even those in the South, were convinced that the band was from that region, and also that they were African American.

The iconic song "Proud Mary" exploded out of John on a joyous occasion. He had been carrying the title around for some time, just waiting to be able to develop it into something special. The moment came when in 1968 he received his letter for an honorable discharge from the military. "I was so happy," John says, "I ran out onto my little patch of lawn and turned cartwheels. Then I went into my house, picked up my guitar and started strumming. 'Left a good job in the city' and then several good lines came out of me immediately . . . I knew I had written my best song. It vibrated inside me" (Werner 1998).

Still early in 1969 CCR went down to RCA studios in Los Angeles to record their sophomore album *Bayou Country*. Just months after their debut album was released CCR followed with a single of "Proud Mary," with "Born on the Bayou" on the B-side. The singles took off and received worldwide airplay; they earned CCR their first gold record. The full-length album was released in February of 1969.

Around this time John began to impress people with his intuition about the record business, especially with regard to his timing. John believed that a new single should be released as soon as the last one was declining. He exercised this action in March of 1969,

just a month after *Bayou Country*, by heading back into the studio to track two more classic CCR tunes, "Bad Moon Rising" and "Lodi." These two songs became back-to-back hits, with "Bad Moon Rising" hitting number two and "Lodi" peaking at number 52 on the singles charts.

In the spring of 1969, CCR seemed relentless as they began work on another album. *Green River* was recorded at Wally Heider's studio in San Francisco, in much the same way as the previous two albums: simple rhythm tracks and John recording vocals and overdubbing guitar, piano, and additional percussion parts on his own. The band was always well rehearsed before going into the studio, making their productions fast and relatively cheap. Each of the first three albums cost less than $2,000 to make, and *Green River* was recorded in about a week.

The tracks on *Green River* were some of the most personal tunes to date from Fogerty. The title track was based on events from his childhood; the name was even taken from his favorite slushy-lime drink at his local soda fountain. "Wrote a Song for Everyone" was taken from a pure emotional response to a spat between John and his wife; as she walked out of the room with their son, John looked at a blank page and wrote the words, "Wrote a song for everyone and I couldn't even talk to you" (Werner 1999).

In July, with a new album on the way and a string of major concert dates, the band released the single of "Green River" with "Commotion" on the B-side. The tracks quickly climbed the U.S. charts and peaked at number two and number 30, respectively. The band was also making waves in the United Kingdom with "Proud Mary" hitting number eight and "Bad Moon Rising" following in August and reaching number one in England.

Green River was released in late August of 1969 and sold close to a million copies by mid-November. Though they were denied a number-one single in the United States, the album held the number-one position on the charts for three weeks before being dethroned by the Beatles' *Abbey Road*. *Green River* proved the band was not just a one-hit wonder but a group with true staying power.

Just weeks off of their tour CCR began rehearsals to start working on the next album. By fall of 1969 they were back in the studio working on *Willie and the Poor Boys,* their third full-length for the year. As production on the album came to a close, Fantasy released the single "Down on the Corner" backed by "Fortunate Son," the fiery political statement about those of privileged backgrounds being able to get out of military service. These two singles peaked at number three and number 14 respectively.

The album *Willie and the Poor Boys* reached stores just in time for Christmas of 1969, making three albums in one year for CCR, a feat by any standards and all the more notable for the quality of material and the clear musical progression of the band in such a short period.

For good measure the band made one more trip into the studio in 1969 to track their next singles, "Travelin' Band" and "Who'll Stop the Rain." The single was released early in 1970 with "Travelin' Band" again hitting number two and "Who'll Stop the Rain" peaking at number 19. These songs also showed the band stretching out of their comfort zone a bit with the inclusion of saxophone on "Travelin' Band" (played by John on a rented instrument) and harmony vocals from Stu and Tom on "Who'll Stop the Rain."

Over the last year CCR had come to demand a $50,000 guarantee for performances; to put this into perspective, that is the equivalent of $311,421.75 in 2015 dollars. This was the band's primary income due to the terms of their record contract, which only entitled them to a small cut of album sales. The group decided to form a partnership under the name of Gort Functions to be the official management entity.

The formation of Gort Functions was timely as they began preparations for a European tour. While they were planning to leave, their previous singles were peaking, which by John's logic meant it was time to cut new singles. The week before they were to fly to Europe, John wrote "Up Around the Bend" and "Run through the Jungle." The songs were rehearsed and tracked in two days and the band flew out the following Monday to start the European tour.

These two singles showcase the dichotomy in John's songwriting; "Up Around the Bend" was a lighthearted tune about getting away, and "Run through the Jungle" was another politically virulent song that resonated all too clearly for the soldiers in Vietnam. Fogerty says that the song was meant to be metaphorical: society was a jungle, and the line "Two hundred million guns are loaded" was about the ease with which firearms were purchased in the United States. However, he had to be aware of the literal truth of his statements as the song was written.

After the tour the group was back in Wally Heider's studio to cut the remaining tracks for the next album, *Cosmo's Factory.* They had four singles done already and seven more tracks to get down, including four covers. The cover that became the biggest hit for the group had already served Gladys Knight and the Pips and Marvin Gaye well, but now it was CCR's turn to take a stab at "I Heard It Through the Grapevine." They turned the tune into an extended jam, allowing Clifford and Fogerty to play off of each other. An edited version of "I Heard It Through the Grapevine" was released in the mid-1970s and became a minor hit.

Cosmo's Factory also included the closest thing to a love song that CCR had produced to date, called "Long as I Can See the Light," and a whimsical song written for his kids that was taken as an endorsement of the use of drugs, titled "Lookin' Out My Back Door." As perhaps a testament to their fame, Vice President Spiro Agnew spoke out in opposition to the song, though he was sadly mistaken about the meaning.

Cosmo's Factory was CCR's strongest commercial showing, going straight to number one on the charts. John was pushing his musical and vocal abilities with the addition of more instruments, including slide guitar, saxophone, and organ, along with tape effects and layered vocal harmonies.

Despite all of their success, not all was well in the Creedence camp. Though most of the time the band got along, there had been tension since the recording of their debut album as John took control of tracking harmony vocals. Over the previous busy year John had continued to take the reins of the band in all business and musical decisions; he even unilaterally decided that the band would no longer play encores.

The year 1970 saw one more release from CCR, *Pendulum*. The album came out in December and spawned two more top 10 singles with "Have You Ever Seen the Rain?" and "Hey Tonight."

During tracking for *Pendulum,* Tom, deciding he could no longer work with John, quit the band. They were initially going to replace him but instead carried on as a trio. Another shocking change took place in the spring of 1971 when John told Stu and Doug that the band would only be able to continue if they operated as a democracy. John had been resisting this idea for some time, thinking that it could compromise the quality of the material. The new deal John offered was that Doug and Stu would be responsible for writing and singing their own material and that he (John) would only contribute rhythm guitar to their tracks. Cook and Clifford resisted but were basically left with no option as John told them he would leave the band if they did not like it.

With its new arrangement the band went back to the studio and tracked Fogerty's "Sweet Hitch-Hiker" with Stu Cook's "Door to Door" as the B-side. After the singles were out they toured the United States and Europe once again.

What was to be CCR's final album, *Mardi Gras,* was released in April of 1972 and featured songs by all three remaining members of the group. The album was heavily criticized in the press, with an especially severe comment from *Rolling Stone*'s John Landau, who said it was the "worst album I have ever heard by a major rock band." Despite this review the album sold well, reaching number 12 on the album charts (Bordowitz 1998).

With tensions running high the band set out for a two-month tour. Once they returned, the band dissolved because of personal conflict and poor relations with Fantasy due to their dated contract, which left CCR with one of the worst deals in the industry for a major act. The official statement was made in October of 1972.

Following CCR, John was the only member to put together a successful solo career, even though it has been somewhat sporadic. In 1973, he released a solo project called *The Blue Ridge Rangers*, for which he recorded a collection of country and gospel tunes. The Creedence breakup had left Fogerty with a contractual agreement to produce eight more albums for Fantasy; eventually he simply refused to record anything. David Geffen ultimately bought the contract from Fantasy for $1,000,000, after which John produced a new hit album, *Centerfield* (1985).

When Fogerty was touring to support *Centerfield* he refused to play any CCR tunes. He remained dedicated to this until he was convinced by Bob Dylan and George Harrison that if he did not play the tunes everyone would think "Proud Mary" was Tina Turner's song. The prodding worked and John played a set of CCR classics in 1987 at the Palomino Club in Los Angeles, with Dylan and Harrison joining him onstage.

Fogerty was out of the music spotlight from the late 1980s until 1997 when he released a Grammy Award–winning album titled *Blue Moon Swamp*. Including the three solo albums mentioned, Fogerty has released 14 total albums in the post-CCR years. His most recent release is 2012's *Wrote a Song for Everyone,* essentially a greatest hits album featuring current popular bands performing alongside Fogerty. Additional musicians include the Foo Fighters, My Morning Jacket, Keith Urban, Kid Rock, and others. John Fogerty continues to tour and is now performing CCR classics along with the rest of his catalog.

Unfortunately, Tom Fogerty's solo career was not very long or successful. He was able to get the whole original CCR lineup to perform on a single track aptly titled "Joyful Resurrection," though John tracked his parts separately from the rest of the group.

Tom released six solo albums from 1972 to 1984 before he died in 1990 of an AIDS complication. He contracted the disease from a tainted blood transfusion received during a back operation. Prior to his death Tom had recorded an album with Ray Oda, which was released in 1993 and titled *Sidekicks*.

Doug Clifford and Stu Cook continued to work together both musically and as business partners in Factory Productions, a mobile recording service in the San Francisco area. In 1995, they formed Creedence

Clearwater Revisited, playing the songs of CCR with additional musicians. As of 2015, the band remains active and tours intermittently.

The relationship between Fantasy and CCR had been problematic since CCR became popular. When they originally signed their contract it was understood that it would be renegotiated when they had their first hit. That time came and went and the contract remained. Instead, Zaentz convinced John that it was not about how much you make but how much you keep, and he brought the band, through John, into an offshore banking scheme. After the band's breakup, this caused some legal issues, adding one more to a string of legal battles between Fogerty and Zaentz. Fantasy was bought out by Concord Music Group in 2004, bringing Fogerty back to the label for a time. The new owners also made good on Zaentz's earlier promise of a greater percentage of album sales to the remaining CCR members after the buyout.

There has never been an official CCR reunion show. They had all played together on Tom's track, and John, Stu, and Doug played as the Blue Velvets at a high school reunion, but the four were never reunited before Tom's death. When the band was inducted into the Rock and Roll Hall of Fame, John refused to play with the others and instead played solo with an all-star backing band, even though Tom's widow had brought his ashes in hope of a reunion.

Creedence Clearwater Revival was a major force when it came to bringing blues and classic rock and roll back into the mainstream in the 1960s. While the Beatles were pushing production techniques and song forms in new directions and bands like the Grateful Dead were departing on extended jams and creating a counterculture, CCR was creating soulful, radio-friendly hits much like the generation before them. Yes, CCR offered political commentary and, yes, they indulged in the occasional 10-minute jam, but the bulk of their output was Southern-influenced rock as pure as can be. At least as pure as a bunch of boys from San Francisco could muster.

Richie Unterberger lists a wide variety of bands on allmusic.com that have been influenced by Creedence Clearwater Revival. Roots rockers such as John

Mellencamp and Bob Seger stylistically harken back to CCR's sound. The rock and roll element of the music of Los Lobos, along with much of the sprite of early releases by the Kings of Leon (such as "Holy Roller Novocaine" and "Youth and Young Manhood"), can be traced to CCR's influence. Although CCR have not performed as a full band in several decades, their lasting musical presence in the sound of other groups and on television and movies attests to their enduring impact.

Joshua Rieck

Selected Discography
Creedence Clearwater Revival, Fantasy 6049, 1968.

Bayou Country, Fantasy 8387, 1969.

Green River, Fantasy 8393, 1969.

Willy and the Poor Boys, Fantasy 8397, 1969.

Cosmo's Factory, Fantasy 8402, 1970.

Pendulum, Fantasy 8410, 1970.

Mardi Gras, Fantasy 9404, 1972.

References
Borowitz, Hank. *Bad Moon Rising: The Unauthorized History of Creedence Clearwater Revival.* Chicago: Chicago Review Press, 1998.

Creedence Online. History. www. credence-online.net.

Fong-Torres, Ben. "Creedence Clearwater Revival: An American Band." Liner notes to *Creedence Clearwater Revival* Box Set. Berkeley, CA: Fantasy Records, 2001.

Paolo, Alec. "Pre-Creedence: The First Decade." Liner notes to *Creedence Clearwater Revival* Box Set. Berkeley, CA: Fantasy Records, 2001.

Unterberger, Richie, "Creedence Clearwater Revival." *All Music Guide.* Rovi Corporation, 2012.

Werner, Craig. *Up Around the Bend.* New York: Avon Books, Inc., 1998.

Zollo, Paul. *Song-Writers on Song-Writing.* Cincinnati, OH: Da Capo Press, 2003.

Crosby, Stills, Nash, and Young (1968–Present)

Crosby, Stills, Nash, and Young (CSN&Y) is the quintessential American band of the late 1960s and early 1970s. While there may be bands that were more

Crosby, Stills, Nash, and Young had all of the ingredients of a great band: mass appeal, political clout, and an all-star lineup. The group, pictured here on stage during a live performance in 1974, has gone platinum 21 times in the United States, in addition to its members having individually successful careers. (Bettmann/Corbis)

prolific or had a bigger cult following, none surpassed the mass appeal and political clout that CSN&Y was able to garner. The music produced under the CSN&Y (and for that matter the Crosby, Stills, and Nash) names has stayed true to their roots. This is not to say that they lack creativity or diversity. Each member of the group of individuals that make up CSN&Y stretched out through various solo, duo, and collaborative projects with members of many of the finest bands of the era. They went through the ringer of the American music industry, split and re-formed more times than anyone, had the highest highs and the lowest lows imaginable, and somehow seem to come out on top over and over again.

The formation of CSN&Y began with the demise of two other popular American bands, the Byrds and Buffalo Springfield. David Crosby (born David Van

Cortlandt Crosby, August 14, 1941; vocals/guitar) was kicked out of the Byrds in 1967 due to artistic differences within the group. As Crosby related in his autobiography *Long Time Gone,* the exchange went something like this: "You're real difficult to work with." "We don't dig your songs that much and we think we'll do better without you" (Crosby and Gottleib, 1988).

Buffalo Springfield broke up in 1968 over complications involving drug offenses, deportation, and artistic differences, leaving Stephen Stills (born Stephen Arthur Stills, January 3, 1945; vocals/guitar) a free agent. Both Crosby and Stills had known each other previously; they had even performed together at the 1967 Monterey Pop festival shortly after Neil Young (born Neil Percival Young, November 12, 1945;

vocals/guitar) had left Buffalo Springfield. Crosby and Stills had also written a song together (along with Paul Kantner of Jefferson Airplane), a later CSN&Y staple called "Wooden Ships."

Crosby and Stills became good friends and played together obsessively in Laurel Canyon, a particularly artsy Los Angeles neighborhood. After learning a few songs they decided to go into the studio and get their sound on tape. They recorded three demo tracks: "Guinevere," "49 Bye-Byes," and "Long Time Gone." Somehow the Los Angeles disk jockey B. Mitchell Reed got his hands on these tracks and began playing them on the radio under the provocative band name the Frozen Noses, a reference to the members' burgeoning cocaine habits.

The duo sounded great, but they agreed they needed to add another element. Enter Graham Nash (born Graham William Nash, February 2, 1942; vocals), who was a member of the Hollies at the time. The Hollies, thanks to Mama Cass of the Mamas and the Papas, who flew them over to meet a record agent, played in Los Angeles in February 1968. Artistically, Nash had been drifting from the blatant pop of the Hollies and was introducing songs, like the later CSN hits "Marrakesh Express" and "Teach Your Children," that the rest of the band was not into. Crosby and Stills, in the meantime, were talking about, but not believing in, the possibility of stealing Nash to start a new band with the two of them.

The trio of Crosby, Stills, and Nash first sang together in Laurel Canyon to Stills's song "You Don't Have to Cry." All three of them immediately knew the sound that they created was magical. Mama Cass was the middle woman in the whole operation, and she was recruited to approach Nash about leaving the Hollies to join Crosby and Stills. After hearing how they sounded together and feeling somewhat rejected by the Hollies, he agreed. All they needed was management, and they decided on Elliot Roberts (who also managed Joni Mitchell and Neil Young, and was good friends with Crosby) and David Geffen. The clincher for CSN choosing this management team came when they told the band, "Listen, do what you do. Leave the rest to us" (Kubernick 2009).

Crosby, Stills, and Nash intended to be a new kind of group from the outset. Each of the members had come from traditional bands with traditional hierarchical structures; this band was intended to be a group of individuals. They were all to be equals, and any member was free to leave and do solo projects whenever they felt the need. This understood freedom and lack of structure might have been a curse for the group as they subsequently went through many cycles of breakups and reformations.

As the newly formed band was getting ready to record, they set up a meeting with Apple Records who, after hearing the group, decided it was not right for them. This minor setback did not hold them up for long, as they found a champion in Ahmet Ertegun of Atlantic Records, who was a fan from the start and ultimately released every CSN and CSN&Y album of the 20th century.

Crosby, Stills, and Nash had tuned their songs playing in friends' living rooms and prided themselves on being able to perform what would become the album *Crosby, Stills & Nash* cover-to-cover on a couple of acoustic guitars. The album was recorded in Wally Heider's Los Angeles studio beginning in February 1969. The sessions were jubilant and the album came together quickly with the help of only one outside musician, drummer Dallas Taylor (born Dallas Woodrow Taylor Jr., April 7, 1948). This album also set the precedent for later projects, with Stills doing much of the instrumental tracking and logging far more hours in the studio than the other members.

Released in May 1969, *Crosby, Stills & Nash* was a groundbreaking album leading to the band being referred to as the American Beatles in the press. The songs on this album have not held up as well as others, but those that do still work are as solid as the day they were tracked. Among the finest of the 10-track collection was the timeless love song by Stephen Stills, "Suite: Judy Blue Eyes," written for his girlfriend at the time, singer/songwriter Judy Collins. This seven-and-a-half-minute track opened with a short guitar intro then broke straight into the trademark CSN three-part harmonies on the line "It's getting to the point, that I'm no fun anymore." Another timeless gem was

Crosby's slow-burning "Long Time Gone," written about the assassination of Robert Kennedy and setting the stage for later political pieces and activism from the group. Unfortunately, some of the tracks have not held up as gracefully over time. The phony Eastern influence found in "Marrakesh Express" comes off rather hokey today. *Crosby, Stills & Nash* sold very well, topping out at number six on the 1969 *Billboard* 200 chart and setting the stage for superstardom.

It was time to tour in support of the album, which brought up an issue. In the studio, Stills overdubbed many of the parts to create a full rock band. In order to re-create the sound, they needed to add at least two musicians. At first they were going after keyboard player Steve Winwood (born Stephen Lawrence Winwood, May 12, 1948; vocals/keyboards/guitar) of the Spencer Davis Group, Traffic, and Blind Faith; however, he was not interested. After looking for other available players Ahmet Ertegun finally suggested Stills's former Buffalo Springfield bandmate, Neil Young. Considering the breakup of Buffalo Springfield, who had also been on Atlantic Records, and the known tension between Stills and Young, it is interesting that Nash was the skeptical party. After a couple of meetings the group decided it was a good fit. Initially they tried to hire Young as a sideman, but he was not interested—it was full partnership or nothing, and thus Crosby, Stills, Nash, and Young was born.

On joining this "group of individuals," Young did make it clear that he intended to pursue his solo career as well; after all, he had already recorded a solo album (*Neil Young*, 1968) and an album with his backing band Crazy Horse (*Everybody Knows This Is Nowhere*, 1969) since the breakup of Buffalo Springfield. Later on, after leaving the group, Young was often criticized for using the success of CSN&Y to further his solo career. Whatever his intentions, there was no doubt that joining forces with CSN helped make Neil Young a household name.

The maiden voyage for the newly formed CSN&Y was truly trial by fire. They played Chicago's Auditorium Theatre on August 16, 1969, and two days later they performed at the most iconic music festival in American history, the Woodstock Music and Art Fair. After an adventurous trip getting into the festival (involving an airplane, a helicopter, and a hotwired car with Jimi Hendrix as a hood ornament). the band arrived backstage, took the stage at 3:00 in the morning, and won over the many thousands who had congregated there.

At the time of Woodstock, Nash was in a relationship with the singer/songwriter Joni Mitchell, who was scheduled to perform at the festival but was advised by her management to skip it in order to make her scheduled appearance on *The Dick Cavett Show*. As she watched news coverage of the epic event on television, she penned the song *Woodstock,* which became a significant hit for CSN&Y (Zimmer and Diltz 2000).

The band was also part of another major festival that went down in rock and roll history, unfortunately for all the wrong reasons. The Rolling Stones paired up with the Grateful Dead to try to capture the spirit of Woodstock on the West Coast. The show was held at the Altamont Speedway and was called the Altamont Speedway Free Festival. Held on December 6, 1969, the festival was a complete disaster. Some blame the drugs: the marijuana and LSD of Woodstock were traded for speed and heroin; others blame the Hells Angels, who were hired to provide security. The worst imaginable incident took place at Altamont: the murder of 18-year-old Meredith Hunter. Hunter had been thrown back into the crowd after attempting to get on stage, and he (Hunter) subsequently pulled a gun and pointed it in the air. At that point, Hell's Angel member Alan Passaro rushed at Hunter, knocked the gun aside, and attacked him with a knife. Hunter was ultimately beaten and stabbed five times and died on the scene. CSN&Y had performed earlier in the day and were doing a show in Los Angeles the same evening; they subsequently requested that their performance (which they say was among their worst) not be used in the Rolling Stones' film *Gimme Shelter*.

In the midst of the band's 1969 concert dates they took time to record another album. *Déjà Vu* was recorded in the latter half of the year, and the process and vibe could not have been a greater contrast from the first album. Tragedy had struck when Crosby's longtime girlfriend, Christine Hinton, was suddenly killed in a car accident, leaving Crosby absolutely devastated. Along with this tragic loss, Nash and Joni Mitchell had broken up and Stills was no longer with Judy Collins. With the addition of the excesses of the time and the flowering of their individual egos, tension began to rise. During the sessions the group seldom appeared in the studio together. Young was even recording another album with Crazy Horse (*After the Gold Rush*, 1970) at the same time. Stills related in the biographical book *Crosby, Stills & Nash* that the album turned into each of the members recording their own tracks. Stills, as he did on the first album, put in more hours than anyone and estimates that the record took around 800 hours to complete (Zimmer and Diltz 2000).

Despite the issues recording the album, *Déjà Vu* was a major success and one of the most anticipated albums of the era. CSN&Y had begun to be referred to as a supergroup, and *Déjà Vu* was either going to make or break that feeling—it made it. By the album's release in March of 1970, it had already shipped two million copies.

Another collection of 10 songs, the album produced three hit singles, Joni Mitchell's "Woodstock," Nash's "Our House," which was written about the house he and Joni shared in Laurel Canyon, and a countrified version of Nash's "Teach Your Children," with lap steel added by the Grateful Dead's Jerry Garcia. One thing *Déjà Vu* did do very effectively was show the diversity and depth the band was capable of. It nicely illustrated the various songwriting styles of the individual members, from Nash's propensity for feel-good tunes like "Our House" to Young's down-tempo but moving and powerful rock "Helpless," Crosby's tendency to play with meter and rhythm on "Déjà Vu," and Nash's haunting, bluesy acoustic piece "4+20."

As soon as the band finished recording *Déjà Vu* they hit the road on a whirlwind tour of the United States, with three additional European dates, before taking a much-needed break. However, when CSN&Y reunited to support *Déjà Vu*, things got off to a bad start. Bassist Greg Reeves (born circa 1955) was fired just days before the band was to hit the road; the call was made to Calvin "Fuzzy" Samuels who had recently recorded with Stills for his upcoming solo album, *Stephen Stills* (1970). Fuzzy came to Los Angeles as quickly as possible and the band rehearsed as much as they could before the tour began. The first show of the tour was in Denver; the band seemed underrehearsed, except for Stills's songs, which Fuzzy had recently recorded. The second stop was a two-night stand in Chicago, but things got out of hand. The band was fighting over the amount of Stills's material in the show, and Young left the stage in the middle of a song the first night, convinced that drummer, Dallas Taylor, was intentionally messing up his songs. Backstage, Young demanded Taylor be fired, which he was, and shortly thereafter there was no band at all. The next day all of the members flew back to Los Angeles, except Stills, who had already left for sound check and missed the conversation. He found out while he was standing on stage, waiting for the band to arrive, that there would be no show. Stills explained what happened next:

> After that aborted sound check, at one amazing meeting I watched Neil, David Graham, Elliot, and God knows who else smoke an ounce of weed and blow off a seven-million-dollar year, purportedly because I was being a showboat. If a voice of reason could have cleared that fog, we would have realized our full potential and CSN&Y would be mentioned in the same breath with the Beatles and the Stones. . . . So we all lost, right there, that day to indulgence. We lost it all. (Zimmer and Diltz 2000)

Unfortunately, it took a tragedy to get the band back together again. On May 4, 1970, the National Guard shot and killed four students on the campus of Kent State University in Kent, Ohio. Young was with Crosby and Leo Makota, their road manager, in California, when they got news of the shooting; after some discussion Young sat down and wrote the song "Ohio." According to Young, the whole band was in the studio within 24 hours and the song was all over the radio within a week (Young 2010). This recording brought the band back together enough that they headed back out on the road and finished the tour, this time with Johnny Barbata (born April 1, 1945; drums) on drums.

At the end of the 1970 tour, the band took another break from one another. This was an important time in the career of each of the individuals who, between 1970 and 1971, each released successful solo albums. Crosby's *If I Could Only Remember My Name* (1971), Stills's *Stepen Stills* (1970) and *Stephen Stills II* (1971), Nash's *Songs for Beginners* (1971), and Young's *After the Gold Rush* were all very successful releases that ended up high on the charts. Every one of these albums peaked in the top 15 of the *Billboard* 200; the most successful of them was *Stephen Stills*, which topped out at number three. *Stephen Stills II* and *After the Gold Rush* both peaked at number eight.

Regardless of the success of the solo albums, the public, and Atlantic, was hungry for more CSN&Y. The response was the double live album *4 Way Street*, released on April 7, 1971. Created from live recordings of the 1970 summer tour, the album peaked at number one on the *Billboard* 200. In various interviews taken after the release, the band, primarily Stills, was critical of the album. His main problem was that they did not go back and overdub anything on the record. Though there were some out-of-tune harmonies when they were all singing together, the album was successful and, if nothing else, honest. It was structured somewhat like their live show with a combination of band and solo performances.

It would be many years before the quartet's name appeared on an album together again, though not for lack of trying. One instance took place in 1973 when all four members regrouped and headed to Hawaii with the intention of recording an album with the working title *Human Highway*. The sessions initially went well and the group headed back to finish the vocal tracks in California, where the whole project fell apart.

Elliot Roberts managed to get the group back together the following year to take on one of the biggest, most ambitious tours any band had done by that time. The 1974 tour consisted of 32 dates in 25 cities across the United States, with the final show in London at Wembley Stadium. This was the first stadium tour that any band had attempted. There were mixed feelings about this tour on all sides. Critics said it was CSN&Y getting back together for the money,

and members of the band thought they were sacrificing the quality of the concertgoers' experience. Regardless of these critiques, the shows were hugely successful and met with generally good reviews.

Alongside the tour, Atlantic Records wanted another album to release. What they compiled was *So Far* (1974), a greatest hits collection from the first two albums with only two new additions, Young's "Ohio" and Stills's simple but haunting "Find the Cost of Freedom." Remarkably, this album also hit number one on the *Billboard* 200, regardless of the lack of much new material.

After another well-deserved break following the exhausting summer tour, the band met up in California to begin recording another album. It began well with new tracks cut in a matter of days, but it was not long before the fighting began. One evening they were not getting anything accomplished and decided to leave the studio so as to not waste valuable studio time. As they parted ways, Neil said, "Well, see you guys tomorrow." Tomorrow came and went and Neil never came back (Zimmer and Diltz 2000).

This is somewhat characteristic behavior for Young. A similar incident involving Young's temperament took place while he and Stills were touring as the Stills-Young Band. The band was on tour supporting their release *Long May You Run* (1974) when Neil simply left midtour. The band was on its way to Atlanta, and when the rest of the group arrived they all received telegrams from Young. Stills's message read: "Dear Stephen, funny how some things that start spontaneously end that way. Eat a peach. Neil" (Zimmer and Diltz 2000).

Subsequent group albums were few and far between, though CSN has ultimately been more active than CSN&Y. Neil Young, for his part, has created the most sustained, successful, and relevant solo career of any of the individuals. Later CSN albums include the 1977 self-titled *CSN*, released right in the heart of the disco era (*Saturday Night Fever* was also released this same year). Though audibly from another time, it was a very successful album, peaking at number two, right behind Fleetwood Mac's iconic album *Rumours*. "Just a Song Before I Go" became a top 10 single, and songs like "Dark Star," "Shadow Captain," and "Cathedral" all became staples of CSN live shows.

While the process of creating *CSN* was simple and straightforward, the next release, *Daylight Again* (1982), was quite a bit more complicated. As Crosby's drug use was becoming more of a problem, Stills and Nash decided to do a duo album. In order to fill out the harmonies, Stills and Nash brought in long time CSN band member Mike Finnegan (born 1945; keyboard) and added Timothy B. Schmidt (born October 30, 1947; bass), of the Eagles, to the vocal blend. They also brought in Art Garfunkel (born Arthur Ira Garfunkel, November 5, 1941; vocals, guitar) to sing a low harmony on Stills's Civil War ballad "Daylight Again." However, something was missing and the duo decided to bring in Crosby to contribute. He added one song, "Delta," to the album and fit in harmonies wherever he could, often doubling parts or not appearing on a track at all. *Daylight Again* made it into the top 10 and provided tracks like "Southern Cross," and "Wasted on the Way," which were viable singles and more fodder for their live shows.

In the early to mid-1980s, Crosby's drug use became more of an issue, eventually leading to legal problems. It was quite amazing that drug use in the group did not cause more problems earlier on. From the early days of the Frozen Noses recordings it was common knowledge that the members were using marijuana, cocaine, and LSD. But only Crosby really struggled with addiction in a major way. He had begun smoking freebase cocaine in the early 1980s and was arrested in California with cocaine and firearms; shortly after this first offense he was arrested in Texas on similar charges and was ultimately sentenced to five years but was paroled after three. Once he was clear of these charges he cleaned up and wrote the book *Long Time Gone* with his friend Carl Gottlieb, chronicling his struggles.

The trio put out two more albums, *Live It Up* (1990) and *After the Storm* (1994), in the 1990s. Both failed to capture the magic of the early recordings and found the band reaching for material and a relevant sound in the midst of grunge rock, mainstream rap, and 1990s R&B.

CSN&Y were also able to release a couple albums after their heyday, though it took a little longer to get this group back together. In 1988, 18 years since their only other studio effort, CSN&Y released *American Dream*. The album sold marginally well, but it did produce one number-one single on the 1988 Mainstream Rock chart: the Young/Still song "Got It Made." Even though the album was recorded with everyone present in the studio, it comes off more as individual contributions. While some of the songwriting was quite good, much of the album now sounds dated.

Eleven years later the quartet tried once again with the self-produced 1999 release *Looking Forward*. By this time the band was out of their record contract, resulting in a self-produced album released on Young's Reprise Records. The album was not particularly commercially successful, though it was a more successful attempt at capturing the magic of the early releases than its predecessor.

In 2008, Young took the reins in bringing the band back together for the (perhaps misleadingly titled) album *Déjà Vu Live*. While it may sound like this was a live release of the classic CSN&Y album of *Déjà Vu,* it was not. Instead, the album stemmed from the tour arranged by Young in support of his 2006 album *Living with War*. The title comes from the feature-length documentary film titled *Déjà Vu* that Young made about the tour. This collection of 16 songs was unabashedly political.

Most recently CSN released a live album titled *CSN 2012*; this live set was the audio version of a DVD/BluRay of the same name. The two-disc set of nostalgia finds the band sounding surprisingly good.

Throughout this band's long and storied career there have been a great number of side projects between the band members as they ventured out of their fold. Neil Young has maintained a steady relationship with his band Crazy Horse, and the most stable duo arrangement of the group has been Crosby and Nash. Stills has stretched out more than anyone else, constantly forming and re-forming various bands. The most important of Stills's side projects was the short-lived band Manassas, which he formed with Chris Hillman and Al Perkins (of the Flying Burrito Brothers) and a cast of other longtime musical acquaintances. Their 21-track double-LP debut release *Manassas* (1972) made it to number four on the *Billboard* 200.

Perhaps one of the most amazing things about CSN and CSN&Y was their influence on both popular culture and music of the late 1960s and early 1970s, with remarkably little output as a unit. With essentially two albums and a couple of singles they were able to speak for a generation in a way that very few artists have since. The reason for this was a sort of perfect storm of time, place, sound, and message. The counterculture of the late 1960s was ready for peace and harmony, and CSN&Y could give them that; however, they also wanted to rock and roll and party, and they could do that too. California was a hotbed for music and the epicenter of the hippie culture; CSN&Y were smack in the middle of it and provided songs that everyone could relate to and rally behind. There are few songs that capture the feeling of a moment the way "Ohio," "Woodstock," "Long Time Gone," or "For What It's Worth" (though first released by Buffalo Springfield, CSN&Y performed it regularly) were able to.

Crosby, Stills, Nash, and Young have the distinction of all being inducted into the Rock and Roll Hall of Fame on two separate occasions. Crosby, Stills, and Nash were inducted in 1997, while Neil Young was inducted separately in 1995. Each of the members was also inducted for their previous work with the Byrds (1991), Buffalo Springfield (1997), and the Hollies (2010). Along with that remarkable credit, the band was also included on *Rolling Stone*'s 500 Greatest Albums list at number 262 for *Crosby, Stills & Nash* and at number 148 for *Déjà Vu*. The band, under the names of Crosby, Stills, and Nash and Crosby, Stills, Nash, and Young, has gone platinum 29 times in the United States. These distinctions, along with their respective and respectable solo careers, make it no stretch at all to say that Crosby, Stills, Nash, and Young have earned their place in the history of rock music.

As a group and as individuals, CSN&Y has had enormous influence on the American singer/songwriter style. They had a direct impact on artists such as Laura Nyro, Joni Mitchell, and Jackson Browne, and their country rock styling laid the groundwork for the early sound of the Eagles. Additionally, their gritty style of rock has influenced countless artists and styles. Individually, Neil Young has been referred to as the "godfather of grunge," and some credit him for creating the musical environment that spawned Nirvana, Pearl Jam, and others.

Joshua Rieck

Selected Discography

Crosby, Stills & Nash, Atlantic SD 8229, 1969.

Déjà Vu, Atlantic SD 7200, 1970.

4 Way Street, Atlantic SD 2–902, 1971.

CSN, Atlantic SD 19104, 1977.

Daylight Again, Atlantic SD 19360, 1982.

American Dream, Atlantic 7567818882, 1988.

Live It Up, Atlantic 7567821072, 1990.

After the Storm, Atlantic 7567821072, 1994.

Looking Forward, Reprise 9362474362, 1999.

Déjà Vu Live, Reprise 9362498391, 2008.

CSN 2012, CSN Records CSN 4095, 2012.

References

Crosby, David, and Carl Gottlieb. *Long Time Gone: The Autobiography of David Crosby*. New York: Doubleday, 1988.

Kubernik, Harvey. *Canyon of Dreams*. New York: Sterling Publishing Co., Inc., 2009.

McDonough, Jimmy. *Shakey: Neil Young's Biography*. New York: Random House, 2002.

The Rock and Roll Hall of Fame. All Inductees: Alphabetically. www.rockhall.com.

Schinder, Scott, and Andy Schwartz. *Icons of Rock*. Westport, CT: Greenwood Press, 2007.

Verlinde, Jason. "Gale Force: David Crosby Reflects on History and Harmonies." *The Fretboard Journal* 25 (Spring 2012): 43–61.

Young, Neil. *Waging Heavy Peace*. New York: Blue Rider Press, 2012.

Zimmer, Dave, and Henry Diltz. *Crosby, Stills & Nash: The Authorized Biography*. Boston: Da Capo Press, 2000.

The Cure (1976–Present)

Fans of the Cure who argue that the goth scene emerged out of the 1970s British punk movements are likely to point to bands like Joy Division, Siouxsie and the Banshees, Bauhaus, and the Cure as bands that both pioneered the scene and that eventually brought goth into the mainstream by the mid-1980s. For its part, the Cure's particular brand of goth might be said to have been influenced by the suburban environment in which the founding members of the Cure were raised. In the mid-1970s, the town of Crawley was a bedroom community located in the southern reaches of London, near Gatwick Airport, and was marked by nine-to-five work routines that were often bracketed by long commutes into the city. Founding member Robert Smith (born April 21, 1959; vocals, guitar), who has been the only ongoing member of the Cure, has been particularly vocal in his contempt for the suburban routines that he witnessed around him, and was driven to create a different kind of life for himself. He found sympathizers in his classmates Laurence "Lol" Tolhurst (born February 3, 1959; drums, keyboard) and Michael Dempsey (born November 29, 1958; bass), both of whom he met at Crawley's Notre Dame Middle School in the early 1970s.

The school was unique because it invited its students to challenge ideas, to engage in free thinking, and to question authority—for his part, Smith took the school's mandate personally, and is alleged to have

The Cure popularized early goth rock sensibilities in the mid-1980s. The group, pictured here in 1987, was (from left to right): Simon Gallup, Boris Williams, Robert Smith, Porl Thompson, and Laurence Tolhurst. With Smith as the focal point, and only constant member throughout the band's run, the Cure continues to be an active and influential group. (Photo by Dave Hogan/Getty Images)

appeared at least once at the school in a velvet dress, perhaps as a nod to the visual aesthetic of the growing glam movement. His inspiration likely came from David Bowie, whose appearance on the July 6, 1972, episode of *Top of the Pops*, introduced the teenager and his friends to glam rock. Like many teenagers of the time, Smith became fascinated with the glam scene embodied in the music of bands like Sweet, Slade, T. Rex, and Roxy Music, and also with the eye-linered and lipsticked androgyneity of glam's male performers.

The idyllic intellectual atmosphere of Notre Dame was short-lived, however, and at their next school, the conservative St. Wilfrid's Comprehensive, the trio was met with a more controlling environment against which Smith, in particular, rebelled. Seeking an outlet for their frustrations at school, they coalesced into a musical group with Smith on guitar, Dempsey on bass, and Tolhurst on drums. At first, they merely called themselves the Group, then, the Obelisk, and by January 1976, the band had adopted the more menacing name "Malice." Discovering that nobody in the band appeared to be able (or willing) to sing, the trio enlisted the help of Paul ("Porl") Thompson (born Paul Stephen Thomson, November 8, 1957; vocals) as their front man, whom they knew because he happened to be dating Tolhurst's sister at the time. On December 18, 1976, as punk was making itself known on the streets (and in the newspapers) of London, Malice staged its first live punk-inspired performance as part of the Christmas party for the Crawley division of Up-johns, where Smith's father was a manager. The brief gig was an utter fiasco and quickly degenerated into an onstage fight as Tolhurst allegedly grabbed the microphone from Thompson and replaced the singer on Malice's rendition of The Troggs' 1966 garage rock hit "Wild Thing." This would be the first of a string of personality clashes that would mark the interpersonal dynamics of the band throughout its history but which would never entirely derail the band. In January 1977, and despite the clash, the group reconvened under a new name proposed by Tolhurst: "The Easy Cure."

Under the name Malice, the band members had learned to play their instruments by focusing on cover songs. The Easy Cure, by contrast, decided to compose and rehearse its own material, written almost exclusively by Smith, and to distribute demo tapes in the hopes of landing a recording contract. After a string of rejections, the band got an invitation to audition at Hansa Records on May 13, 1977, in response to a talent competition that was advertised in *Melody Maker*. Five days later, the Easy Cure was signed to the label for £1,000, but quickly discovered that Hansa had little interest in their original music and had signed the band in the hopes of creating a teen group that would perform covers.

The band, by contrast, was busily at work on songs that addressed issues, like pedophilia ("See the Children") and existentialism ("Killing an Arab"), that would have proven either uninteresting or offensive to the mainstream teen listener. It seemed clear from the start that Hansa was not the right "fit" for the Easy Cure, and by March 29, 1978, the band left the label with a handful of original recordings for which they managed to secure the rights. In early May, Thompson left the Easy Cure, which subsequently shortened their name to the Cure, now with Robert Smith as its front man. By this time, the band had already begun to cultivate what critics have variously described as a lean, spare, and skeletal sound on a set of songs that they distributed as their demo, comprising "10.15 Saturday Night," "Killing an Arab," "Boys Don't Cry," and "Fire in Cairo."

The demo caught the attention of Chris Parry, an A&R executive at Polydor who had signed the Jam and who had coproduced their first two albums, *In the City* and *This Is the Modern World* (both of which were released in 1977). On August 27, 1978, Parry made arrangements to see the Cure in live performance, attending their gig at the Redhill Laker's Hotel in Surrey and signing the band to his new label, Fiction, on September 13. A week later, the Cure convened in London's Morgan Studios to rerecord their demo tracks and two other songs, "Plastic Passion" and "Three Imaginary Boys," for what would later become their debut album. The remaining tracks of the debut were recorded at Morgan Studios over two more sessions, on October 12, 1978, and January 8–10, 1979.

As the songs' producer, Parry played an enormous role in the creation of the band's first album, released as *Three Imaginary Boys* on May 11, 1979, while Smith and his bandmates played no part in decisions about song selection for the album and its packaging. (For instance, the band's first and most controversial single, "Killing an Arab," was omitted from the album and was released instead as a single in December 1978. Decisions about its omission might have been influenced by the song's misinterpretation as a racist rant by those who had no idea that it was actually created in homage to Albert Camus's *L'Étranger*.) While Smith had hoped to strike a balance between his two prime musical influences at the time, the Buzzcocks (whose angular melodies he hoped to replicate in his own songs) and Siouxsie and the Banshees (whose "wall of sound" he admired), he felt that Parry did not understand his vision and produced an album that fell short of his musical ideal.

Despite Smith's reservations about the album, it was generally well received by critics, peaking at number 44 in the U.K. charts. Moreover, the album brought the Cure to the attention of John Peel, who featured the group on his BBC Radio 1 broadcast of December 11, 1978. (The Cure's "Peel Sessions," recorded a week before the broadcast, were only released for purchase a decade later and feature early versions of the four demo songs that had landed the band their contract with Fiction.) Finally, *Three Imaginary Boys* also put the band in contact with Mike Hedges, the recording engineer who would help to define the band's sound on the next two albums.

The year 1979 also saw the release of the band's second and third singles, "Boys Don't Cry" and "Jumping Someone Else's Train," on June 26 and November 20, respectively. (While neither song appeared on the band's U.K. debut, each was included as a track on the Cure's first U.S. album, *Boys Don't Cry*, released on February 5, 1980. Somewhat different from its U.K. version, the album featured a selection of songs from *Three Imaginary Boys* combined with the band's first three U.K. singles.) "Jumping Someone Else's Train" was significant in the band's history for two reasons. First, it marked Dempsey's

final recording with the band. Citing artistic differences with Smith, Dempsey was replaced by Simon Gallup, who had been the bassist for such punk outfits as Lockjaw and Magspies, both bands that had played live shows with the Easy Cure.

Perhaps to entice Gallup to join the Cure, the band also hired the Magspies's keyboardist, Matthieu Hartley (born February 4, 1960). Second, the single's B-side, "I'm Cold," featured Siouxsie Sioux on backup vocals and forged a connection between the Cure and the Banshees that was strengthened through the fall, when the Cure (with Dempsey still in tow) embarked on tour with the band. The Banshees would come to provide a different kind of creative outlet for Smith at various points in his career. Not only did Siouxsie's goth appearance influence the onstage persona later created by Smith, but also at various times he would be asked to stand in as the band's guitarist (as he was during the 1979 tour following the abrupt departure of the Banshees' John McKay).

Following the completion of the Cure's first major tour, Smith retreated to Crawley, where he began to record home demos of the songs that would comprise the band's next album, *Seventeen Seconds*. These songs were recorded by Smith, Tolhurst, Gallup, and Hartley at London's Morgan Studios between January 13 and January 20, 1980, and engineered by Mike Hedges to create a stark sonic landscape that would be reflected in the artwork chosen by Smith for the album's cover. As one critic noted, "Like the album's cover art, which is little more than an abstract blur, the bleak, minimalist sound of this *Seventeen Seconds*–era Cure is subtly suggestive. The dark, existential motifs that are so much a part of the Cure become more prevalent" in the second album (Dimery, 456).

The album produced the band's first chart single, "A Forest," which reached number 31 shortly after its release on March 28, 1980, and secured a spot for the band on BBC's *Top of the Pops* on April 24. By May, the Cure had departed on a promotional tour of Europe, Australia, and New Zealand, playing over 80 shows in total. The stress of the tour took a toll on the band, and particularly on Hartley, who quit when the band returned from Australia at the end of

August. Undeterred, the band continued without him, touring Eastern Europe until the end of November.

At the beginning of 1981, Smith, Dempsey, and Tolhurst began to plan for their next album, *Faith*, and booked space at Morgan Studios at the beginning of February. As work progressed on the album, both Tolhurst's mother and Smith's grandmother had become gravely ill, and the subject of death became a narrative thread in *Faith* that ran through such songs as "Other Voices," "The Funeral Party," "The Holy Hour," and the album's title track, "Faith." Smith's interest in Mervyn Peake's gothic trilogy, *Gormenghast*, provided themes of melancholia and hopelessness that reinforced the narrative, particularly as this trilogy was referenced in such tracks as "All Cats Are Grey" and "The Drowning Man." One observer suggests that by referencing the novels, Smith "was clearly staking out his spot as top Goth on the block. Smith mightn't have been quite ready to join [Joy Division's] Ian Curtis in taking that final step into the unknown [Curtis had committed suicide on May 20, 1980], so instead he opted to craft an album so low, so heavy-hearted, that it should have come with a warning about being played to those of a nervous and/or fragile persuasion" (Apter, 135).

Faith was released on April 11, 1981, and stood alongside such contemporary albums as Siouxsie and the Banshees' *Juju* (released on June 6), Joy Division's *Still* (released on October 8), and Bauhaus's *Mask* (released on October 19) as works that would come to define the goth scene at the time. To promote the new album, the Cure launched the worldwide "Pictures" tour where, in place of an opening act, Gallup's brother, Ric, was enlisted to create a stark animation for which the Cure composed the instrumental soundtrack *Carnage Visors* (a goth-inspired play on the notion of rose-colored glasses). The tour was interrupted on June 24, when Tolhurst received a call from England to tell him that his mother had died—a call that would precipitate his slow and steady decline into chronic alcoholism, which would plague him through his tenure with the band.

When the tour was over, the band set to work on the album *Pornography*, but since Mike Hedges was already engaged in the recording of Siouxsie and the Banshees' *A Kiss in the Dreamhouse*, he directed the Cure toward Phil Thornalley, the house engineer at London's RAK Records. Just a few months younger than Smith, Thornalley had worked with bands as diverse as Hot Chocolate and Kim Wilde, but had little knowledge of the Cure, having only heard "Killing an Arab" by chance on the radio. Thornalley and Smith developed a strong working relationship over their mutual interest in "found sounds," and they sought to develop a collaboration that would mirror that between Brian Eno and David Byrne, which led to that duo's 1981 album *My Life in the Bush of Ghosts*.

Thornalley and Smith looked to television for their samples and stumbled upon a televised debate on the subject of pornography between the feminist scholar Germaine Greer and the comedian Graham Chapman; they remixed this debate to form the opening of the album's title track. The sample also gave the album its title. The band's most successful enterprise to date, *Pornography* charted at number eight on the U.K. charts. Looking for an image to reflect their music, the Cure launched their promotional tour with what would become their trademark look of "towering hair and bleeding-face make-up [that] exacerbated the impact of the brutal music they were unleashing on the public. This was a freak show" (Apter, 167). In a study of androgynous imagery in the Cure's videos, Thomas Geyrhalter argued that while "the only comparable point of reference [was] Culture Club (in fact, members of the Cure have reputedly been mistaken for Boy George) . . . [t]his visual style and imagery, arguably the standard for goths worldwide, does not seem to be borrowed from any gay subculture or drag tradition; it is its own subculture" (Geyrhalter, 219).

Imagery aside, the tour was also noteworthy for antipathies that erupted between bandmates both off-stage and in performance. By the final show of the tour, on June 11, the band descended into a chaotic mess reminiscent of the final Malice concert when Smith decided that he would play drums while Gallup and Tolhurst retaliated by playing guitar and bass, respectively. The band made its way through a small selection of songs, but the show ultimately devolved into an onstage brawl, after which Gallup quit the band.

With the seeming dissolution of his flagship band, Chris Parry began to worry for the future of his Fiction label, so he convinced Smith and Tolhurst to remain together and to consider a new sound. Both agreed, and Tolhurst began to take keyboard lessons while Smith, fresh from a month's respite in a detox clinic in Wales, penned the upbeat "Let's Go to Bed." Released on November 15, 1982, the song became an instant hit in the United States and Australia and reached number 44 on the U.K. charts. As the band was considering its next step, Smith was invited to join Siouxsie and the Banshees after their guitarist, John McGeogh, departed because of illness, and he toured the United Kingdom with the Banshees through the end of 1982 before leaving for Australia with the band at the beginning of 1983.

After the Banshees' tour was over, Smith and the Banshees' bassist, Steve Severin, collaborated on a project named "The Glove," from which the album titled *Blue Sunshine* (named after a particularly potent form of LSD) emerged in August 1983. Tolhurst, being similarly freed from his commitments to the Cure, assumed his first production role for the eponymous debut album of the band And Also the Trees. However, the Cure continued to exist alongside these side projects. In 1983, Smith and Tolhurst released the single "The Walk," which peaked at number 12 in the U.K. charts. The single also increased the band's profile among American audiences, and the band toured in New York, Toronto, and San Francisco before recording a set of four new tracks, "The Love Cats," "Mr. Pink Eyes," "Speak My Language," and "Hand inside My Mouth," in Paris on August 4, 1983. With Phil Thornalley enlisted to play bass on these recording sessions, the four singles were released to some acclaim, particularly the first of these, which charted at number seven in the United Kingdom. Hardly fresh from this recording session, Smith found himself bouncing between sessions for the Cure's fifth studio album, *The Top* (recorded at London's Garden Studios between December 1982 and January 1984, and released on April 30) and the Banshees' sixth studio album, *Hyæna* (recorded at Pete Townshend's Eel Pie Studios in Twickenham and released on June 8, 1984).

Unlike the trio of goth albums that preceded it, *The Top* provided its listener with an equal balance of introspective numbers (like "Wailing Wall," "Piggy in the Mirror," or "Give Me It") and upbeat tunes (like the album's only single, "The Caterpillar," which reached number 14 on the U.K. singles charts shortly after its release on March 26, 1984). Juggling his commitment to his band on the one hand and to Siouxsie's band on the other, Smith claims to have found the energy to fulfill all of his commitments from a potent brew of hallucinogenic-mushroom tea. Whether or not this is true, the Cure's front man began to descend once again into alcohol and drug abuse, which inevitably triggered a physical collapse that forced him to resign from the Banshees in May 1984, just prior to their departure for an American tour.

Smith was now free to focus exclusively on the Cure, which now comprised Smith, Tolhurst, Thornalley, and a new drummer, Andy Anderson (born Clifford Leon Anderson, January 30, 1951; drums) and, after a summer's respite, the band launched a promotion tour on September 30. By October 17, the rancor that marked the band while on tour surfaced again, and Anderson was asked to leave the band after a violent outburst in which he destroyed a hotel room. He was eventually replaced by Boris Williams (born Boris Peter Bransby Williams, April 24, 1957; drums), who had previously worked with the Thompson Twins and Kim Wilde and who remained with the Cure through 1993. The end of the tour also marked the departure of Thornalley from the band after he realized that he was not up to the physical and emotional demands of touring. Seemingly always in flux, the Cure reconfigured once again in 1985 when former Cure members Simon Gallup and Porl Thompson rejoined the group.

In February 1985, Smith, Tolhurst, Gallup, Thompson, and Williams convened at F2 Studios in London, and later in Angel Studios in Islington, to begin work on their next album, *The Head on the Door*, inviting Dave Allen (who had made his name as the engineer of Human League's 1981 hit album, *Dare*) to coproduce. The album proved to be the band's biggest hit yet, propelled onto the charts principally because of the international success of its two singles "Inbetween Days" (released on July 15, 1985, as the first Cure single to crack the *Billboard* 100 list in the United States when it reached number 99) and "Close to Me" (released on September 9, 1984, reaching number 97 on *Billboard* 100, while peaking at number 13 in the United Kingdom). One observer has noted that the appeal of the album lay in the fact that its songs "were very easy to sing along with, but . . . could also be scrutinized more closely for Smith's ever-changing moods" (Apter, 211). Released on August 26, 1985, *The Head on the Door* consolidated the band's reputation not only in the United States, where it charted at number 59 on the *Billboard* Top 100, but also in Germany, Switzerland, Sweden, and France, where it also climbed the charts. By this time, the Cure was also selling out arenas, and in the promotional tour that ensued, the band sold out shows at Wembley Arena, Manchester Apollo, Birmingham NEC, and New York's Radio City Music Hall.

Riding on his recent chart success, Smith returned to the studio in February 1986 to remix and update the vocals on three early songs (among them "Boys Don't Cry") with a view to shooting a video. The project, which brought the three original Cure members together for the first time since Dempsey's departure in 1979, led to the April 21, 1986, rerelease of the single "Boys Don't Cry (New Voice–Club Mix)" and the release, on May 6, 1986, of the band's 10th-anniversary "greatest hits" album, *Standing on a Beach* (titled *Staring at the Sea* when released as a CD). In the United States, this album sparked some controversy when the American Arab League petitioned Elektra to have "Killing an Arab" removed from the American release. Smith issued an explanation to his American audience, which appeared on a sticker affixed to the album's cover, that described the track as "a song which decries the existence of all prejudice and consequent violence." *Standing on a Beach* quickly became the band's biggest commercial success in the United

States, where it went gold in February 1987. The promotional tour was also documented on video, when the shows held on August 9–10 at the Théâtre antique d'Orange in southern France were filmed and released on VHS as *The Cure in Orange*.

Riding the success of the compilation, the Cure convened in August 1987 at Studio Miraval in the south of France to record their next album, *Kiss Me Kiss Me Kiss Me*, whose cover featured a close-up shot of Smith's painted lips. While the meaning of the image might be interpreted in relation to the title of the album, "Smith explained later that it was more about swallowing people" than it was about any act of affection (Geyrhalter, 219). On April 6, 1987, the band released the album's first single, "Why Can't I Be You?," described as a dance number "powered by some drunken funk guitar" (Apter, 223). The video, which was perhaps the band's most famous, "has the playful atmosphere of a child's carnival or dressing-up party, although being a more bizarre and distorted version. 'Why Can't I Be You'? indeed, the viewer might ask. (Apparently Smith wrote the song when inspired by a fan asking just that question.)" (Geyrhalter, 220). The song climbed to number 54 on the *Billboard* Hot 100, while the album's next charting single, "Just Like Heaven" (released on October 5), reached number 40. The album itself, released on May 25, 1987, credited all five members of the band as equal contributors, despite the fact that Tolhurst's alcohol abuse was beginning to curb his participation in the Cure (a situation to which Smith alludes in the lyrics to the album's penultimate track, "Shiver and Shake"). Like its singles, *Kiss Me Kiss Me Kiss Me* rose rapidly to the top of the charts, peaking at number 35 on the American *Billboard* 100 and at number six on the U.K. Albums Chart.

The release of *Kiss Me Kiss Me Kiss Me* was followed by a now-established routine of press interviews and touring through the remainder of 1987, first through North America (in July and August), and then in Europe (from October to the beginning of December). The rigors of touring took a final toll on Tolhurst, whose drinking had intensified to the point where he was barely able to contribute to the band. By late 1987,

Roger O'Donnell, the former keyboardist for the Psychedelic Furs and the Thompson Twins, had been enlisted to "assist" (more truthfully, to replace) Tolhurst, who simply drank his way through the tour.

During a brief hiatus in 1988, Smith married his longtime partner, Mary Poole, and penned "Lovesong" as a musical gift to her. The song was the first in a series of moody songs that harkened back to the goth days of *Pornography* and that would eventually coalesce into the band's eighth studio album, *Disintegration*, released on May 1, 1989. In spite of the overall "goth" ambience of the album—described by one critic as "doom and gloom-a-go-go"—*Disintegration* proved to be the band's most successful effort to date, charting at number three on the U.K. Albums Chart and at number 12 on the U.S. *Billboard* 100 (Dimery, 621). The singles released from the album fared even better, and "Fascination Street" (released on April 18) and "Lovesong" (released on August 21), climbed to number one on the U.S. Modern Rock chart and number two on the U.S. Hot 100 chart, respectively.

By the time *Disintegration* was finished, however, Tolhurst's alcoholism had to be confronted, and while Smith was reluctant to fire him because of their longstanding friendship, he eventually caved to the demands of the other members of the band. Tolhurst was fired in February 1989, and, embittered, sued the Cure two years later over what he perceived as outstanding royalties and the rights to the band's name (which he had proposed when the band was still called Malice). The court case would distract the band for four years and impeded their productivity in the early 1990s. (There was a four-year gap between the release of the band's 1992 album *Wish* and the 1996 album *Wild Mood Swings*.) Tolhurst's dismissal required another change in the band's lineup, and he was eventually replaced by Perry Bamonte (born Perry Archangelo Bamonte, September 3, 1960), who made his debut in Paris at the Cure's 1991 Bastille Day show.

As a way to shift the focus away from the ongoing trial, the band reconvened to begin their ninth studio album, *Wish*, which marked the band's commercial peak. Released on Smith's 33rd birthday (March 24, 1992), *Wish* charted at number two on the U.S. *Billboard* 100 while two of its singles, "High" (released March 16) and "Friday I'm in Love" (released May 11), both rose to number one on the Modern Rock Tracks chart. The *Wish* tour that spanned April through December 1992 took the band across Europe and the United States on a punishing schedule that finally took its toll on Gallup. Suffering from exhaustion, he was sent home from Milan at the end of October, and the tour limped on without him. When the tour was finally finished, the band decided to take an extended break, interrupted only by the case of *Tolhurst v. Smith* when it was finally heard in the courts through February and March 1994. On September 6, 1994, the final ruling came out in favor of Smith, and Tolhurst moved permanently to Los Angeles.

During the band's hiatus, Porl Thompson was invited to tour with Led Zeppelin while Wilson moved on to work in a band called the Piggle. By the time Smith began to think about the Cure's next album, *Wild Mood Swings*, many of his bandmates were already otherwise engaged, leaving Smith, Bamonte, and Gallup (who rejoined the band at the end of 1994) as the only remaining members. Joined by Jason Cooper (born Jason Toop Cooper, January 31, 1967; drums) on drums (whom they hired through an advertisement placed in *New Musical Express*) and Roger O'Donnell on keyboards, the Cure recorded the songs for the album at an uncharacteristically leisurely pace, laying down five tracks between November 1994 and January 1995, and completing the album between August and December 1995. The album was poorly received, in part because, as Jeff Apter has argued, "the orbit of the musical world had shifted. Acid house and Madchester had blazed briefly then burned out, likewise grunge and the British shoegazers. But Britpop, with Blur, Suede and Oasis as its main banner-wavers, was now in the midst of its second-coming" (Apter, 273). Apter suggests that *Wild Mood Swings* might have been more successful if it had appeared earlier, but that, by the time it was released on April 26, 1996, the audience was looking elsewhere after the release of such albums as Oasis's *Definitely Maybe* (1994), its follow-up *(What's the Story) Morning Glory?* (1995), and Blur's *The Great Escape* (1995).

Following the release of *Wild Mood Swings*, the band's remaining albums appeared less frequently, roughly at four-year intervals. The reason was that, on the one hand, Smith was engaged in other professional activities (e.g., he was invited to play at David Bowie's 50th birthday celebration in January 1997 and was featured on a South Park episode in 1998), while, on the other hand, he began to find more contentment in his family life. The band's next album, *Bloodflowers* (with the lineup of Smith, Gallup, Bamonte, Cooper, and O'Donnell), did not appear until February 14, 2000, and this was followed by *The Cure* (with the same lineup as the previous album) on June 28, 2004, and *4:13 Dream* (featuring Smith, Gallup, Thompson, and Cooper) on October 27, 2008.

Bloodflowers marked a return to the moodier sonic landscapes of *Pornography* and *Disintegration* and was a moderate success (being nominated for a Grammy Award for Best Alternative Album). *The Cure* fared somewhat better on the charts, debuting at number seven in the United States (and at number eight in Britain). The band's most recent album, originally intended as a double album but reduced to a single album when Smith decided to hold the "moodier" songs for a later album, debuted at number 16 on the *Billboard* 100 charts. In spite of the comparatively lackluster sales and chart performances of the band's last four albums, the band continues to hold sway over current bands that look to the Cure as the quintessential goth band. The Cure's influence extends across the popular landscape, as Jeff Apter has noted, "Interpol, My Chemical Romance ... were at the forefront of those who owed a hefty debt to the downbeat moods and heavily lipsticked look of Smith and Co. . . . Even the late Heath Ledger's star turn as The Joker, in the film *Dark Knight,* seemed to be, at least in part, a nod in the direction of the odd, increasingly portly little man from Crawley" whose career with the Cure continues (Apter, 302). On January 13, 2010, Smith announced that the band was working on their new album, which would be a follow-up to *4:13 Dream* comprising the tracks that had been omitted from that album. The album has yet to materialize, and its delay can be explained in large measure by various side ventures that have occupied the band in the past several years (these include a set of concerts in Australia in 2011, various appearances in London, New York, and Los Angeles in early 2012, and a summer festival tour of Europe in 2012). In September 2012, the band was also nominated for induction into the Rock and Roll Hall of Fame.

Karen Fournier

Selected Discography
Studio Albums:
Three Imaginary Boys (UK) Fiction FIX1 2442–163, 1979.

Boys Don't Cry (US) PVC Records PVC7916, 1980.

Pornography (UK) Fiction FIXD 7–2383–639, 1982, (US) A&M, SP-4902, 1982.

The Walk (mini-album) (UK) Fiction/Polydor 8107521, 1983, (US) Sire, 1–23928, 1983.

The Top (UK) Fiction FIXS9, 1984, (US) Sire, 1–25086, 1984.

The Head on the Door (UK) Fiction FIXH11, 1985, (US) Elektra, 9–60435-4, 1985.

Kiss Me Kiss Me Kiss Me (UK) Fiction FIXH13, 1987, (US) Elektra, 60737–1, 1987.

Faith (UK) Fiction/Polydor FIX004 2383–574, 1980, (US) Elektra, 9–60783, 1988.

Seventeen Seconds (UK) Fiction FIX004, 1980, (US) Elektra, 9–60784-2, 1988.

Disintegration (UK) Fiction FIXH14, 1989, (US) Elektra, 60855, 1989.

Wish (UK) Fiction/Polydor FIX20, 1992, (US) Elektra, 61309, 1992.

Paris (UK) Fiction/Polydor FIXH26, 1993, (US) Elektra, 61662, 1993.

Show (UK) Fiction/Polydor FIX25, 1993, (US) Elektra, 61551, 1993.

Wild Mood Swings (UK) Fiction FIXLP28, 1996, (US) Elektra, 71744, 1996.

Bloodflowers (UK) Fiction/Polydor FIX31, 2000, (US) Elektra, 62236, 2000.

The Cure Geffen 654189, 2004.

4:13 Dream Geffen 001091302, 2008.

References

Apter, Jeff. *Never Enough: The Story of the Cure.* London: Omnibus Press, 2005.

Barbarian, Steve Sutherland, and Robert Smith. *Ten Imaginary Years.* London, England: Zomba Books, 1988.

Butler, Daren. *The Cure on Record.* London: Omnibus Press, 1995.

Carman, Richard. *The Cure and Wishful Thinking.* London: Independent Music Press, 2005.

Dimery, Robert. *1001 Albums You Must Hear Before You Die.* London: Universe, 2006.

Geyrhalter, Thomas. "Effeminacy, Camp, and Sexual Subversion in Rock: The Cure and Suede." *Popular Music* 15/2 (1996): 216–24.

Goodlad, Lauren. "Looking for Something Forever Gone: Gothic Masculinity, Androgyny, and Ethics and the Turn of the Millennium." *Cultural Critique* 66 (Spring 2007): 104–26.

Smith, Robert. *The Cure: Songwords 1978–1989.* London: Omnibus Press, 1989.

Thompson, Dave. *In Between Days: An Armchair Guide to the Cure.* London, England: Helter Skelter Press, 2005.

Thompson, Dave, and Jo-Ann Green. *The Cure: A Visual Documentary.* London: Omnibus Press, 1988.

Young, Tricia Henry. "Dancing on Bela Lugosi's Grave: The Politics and Aesthetics of Gothic Club Dance." *Dance Research: The Journal for the Society for Dance Research* 17/1 (1999), 75–97.

D

Dave Matthews Band (1991–Present)

Dave Matthews Band (DMB) has made history by defying expectation, avoiding labels, and giving audiences what they want. Since their inception as a Virginia bar band in 1991, DMB has been a steady presence in the recording industry, on events calendars of major cities, and on the cutting edge of what it means to relate to fans. Despite what is described as a "conspicuous absence of hit singles," DMB has defied odds on earnings and longevity, redefining what is a successful rock band (Vargas 2008). It is indisputable that the music and the social and cultural philosophies of DMB are today an indelible part of American pop culture discourse.

DMB escapes narrow classification, and even "suffers" from a supposed identity crisis. A band that comfortably hops style and genre boundaries, DMB relates best to fans in live settings that support improvisation and spontaneity, as well as the music-making philosophy of its members: that a song does not have to sound the same way twice. With concerts comes high-intensity fan reverberation, where hoards respond to every move. Fans feel intimately connected with the music and with the musicianship, a balance of experimentalism (to satisfy the creative energies of the core musicians' deep talent) and delivery of what listeners crave.

DMB epitomizes ensemble collaboration and equality, so each member's signature talents contribute to the ensemble's bottom line. Dave Matthews is the originator, not the leader, thus the band's name is far from perfect, and Matthews bemoans the "laziness" that resulted in the moniker (Scaggs 2003).

The original roster was rounded out by Carter Beauford (born November 2, 1957; drums), Stefan Lessard (born June 4, 1974; bass), Boyd Tinsley (born May 16, 1964; violin), and LeRoi Moore (born September 7, 1961, died August 19, 2008; saxophone, flute), who was replaced by Jeff Coffin (born August 5, 1965; saxophone) after Moore's untimely death in 2008. Other artists complement recordings and stage shows, and Tim Reynolds (guitar), Rayshawn Ross (trumpeter), and Butch Taylor (keyboard) have become regulars.

Certain statistics place the band in a class all its own: in 1999, DMB boasted the third-highest-grossing tour, surpassed only by Bruce Springsteen and the Rolling Stones (Van Noy 2011). In 2000, DMB was the top-grossing touring rock band in the United States, earning $66 million. As of 2009, Pollstar and *Rolling Stone* listed DMB as the decade's biggest global ticket seller, moving more than 11 million tickets to 547 shows, where no other North American band drew more than 10 million (Waddell 2009). Such enviable statistics accumulated only by commitment to a punishing road schedule (according to DMBalmanac.com, by December 2012 the band had logged 2,211 shows, 75 in 2012 alone) and to unselfishness, accepting paltry payment for double-set shows. Early on, DMB and its management avoided traditional marketing and distribution methods. Matthews related, "Some years are good years for the stadiums, some are good for the amphitheaters. Our management has always been pretty successful at thinking of the fans" (Waddell 2009). Coran Capshaw is that management. A pioneer in "direct-to-fan marketing," Capshaw changed how "fans discover events, buy tickets, and experience live music" (Waddell 2012), banking on

Begun in 1991, Dave Matthews Band has had an unprecedented run of success without the standard hit singles on which most bands rely. Pictured in the early 1990s in Chicago, Illinois, the group derives its longstanding popularity from its unique blend of extended instrumental jams, singalong-friendly vocals, and obsessive touring. (Photo by Paul Natkin/WireImage)

a passionate fan base, where exposure would trump revenue; hence, deals were made with fraternity houses over red-carpet record labels. He first booked the fledgling band at his own club, Trax, and soon had DMB on stage 200 nights a year.

DMB's songs have been heard in almost every country of the world, thanks to tape trading and to the systematic release of sanctioned live recordings. Studio albums factor in as well: the band has cultivated a long-term business relationship with RCA Records, initiated with a progressive deal brokered by Capshaw in 1993. DMB is allowed to negotiate freely outside of the United States, solidifying the ability to distribute live recordings online, and thus to exploit multiple ways of reaching its audience (Newman/Price 2004).

As the band's front man, Matthews (born January 9, 1967; vocals, guitar) is an open, communicative artist. An American citizen since the age of 13

Matthews colorfully expresses his artistic, social, and political ideologies. Everything from details about the songwriting process to his passion for environmental projects is fair game in the existing 15-plus years of interviews, available in publications from *Rolling Stone* to *Acoustic Guitar* and on media like *VH1*, *CBS Sunday Morning*, and *60 Minutes*. Matthews is brash, comfortably bashing the Grammys, the "constant blabbering" of musicians, the lip-syncing trend on American stages, and how often artists mention a God that surely is not "paying attention" ("Dave Matthews Talks about His Career" 2010). Matthews also vents in song lyrics. The politically charged words of the 1998 single "Don't Drink the Water" relate a message that adopts fresh resonance with shifting political and social circumstances, and "Mercy," the first release of the 2012 album *Away from the World*, is an inspiring plea to individual responsibility.

Of the places Matthews calls "home," Charlottesville is most notable, as that is where the band formed, but it was only as an adult that the eclectic town became his destiny. Matthews was born in Johannesburg, South Africa. The family moved to New York when Matthews was two, then in 1974 to England. Matthews's mother, Val, returned the family to Johannesburg after her husband's 1977 death from cancer, to a country that was by then on the edge of civil war. The unrest there left an indelible mark on the singer/songwriter, because even though Matthews's home life was centered in the more isolated northern suburbs, he paid attention to the black youth, claiming an association that helped to make him "color blind" and aware of the gaps between the "haves and have nots" (Docu-Drama, "Driven"). Matthews channeled these cultural and social influences into weighty and reflective song lyrics, many of which echo youthful experiences and his ever-evolving philosophy regarding freedom and passivity.

After high school graduation, Matthews took refuge in New York to avoid compulsory military time. His mother relocated to Virginia, and by 1986, so did Matthews. He began bartending at Miller's, a downtown hotspot that became a "clearinghouse for the talented musicians who would later coalesce to form the

Dave Matthews Band" (Delancey 2001). Fresh social connections put Matthews in contact with musicians already active in town and with a rich cross-section of the deep Charlottesville talent. By 1990, Matthews had been playing guitar for over a decade and was dabbling in songwriting, but he had never played publicly or shared any songs. He approached other musicians with the desire to combine ideas and sounds, with no preconceived notion of what personnel and instruments would work best, admitting that he was most attracted to what came through a player's instrument (Rose interview, 2001). Aside from replacing Moore with Coffin, and the habit of inviting guests for summer road shows, the original ensemble remains intact.

Beauford grew up near Moore in Charlottesville, and they shared a range of musical passions. As house drummer for *BET on Jazz*, Beauford absorbed diverse influences from renowned players like Roy Hargrove and Paquito d'Rivera, which he transferred to DMB, lending to the band's almost exotic appeal. Moore studied at James Madison University, concentrating on tenor sax, but was also proficient on baritone, soprano, and alto, as well as bass clarinet. An engaging lyricist, Moore played percussively but with a versatile and nimble approach to melody, acknowledging influences ranging from John Coltrane to Ben Webster. He, too, remained "at a loss to explain how the . . . sound came together. It was just different, but I . . . knew that there was something there" ("Dave Matthews: Charlie Rose Show Part 1," 2001). Moore succumbed to injuries sustained during a 2008 ATV crash. Fans and band members mourn the loss, but celebrate the musical legacy that lives on in the many recordings.

Coffin joined DMB in 2008 as Moore's replacement. A member of Bela Fleck and the Flecktones since 1997, Coffin is also a solo artist: he has released four records with the Mu'tets. As a prolific studio musician, Coffin's artistry graces hundreds of recordings, and as a clinician he brings to students complex musical influences stemming from studies at the University of North Texas and association with artists like Phish and Branford Marsalis.

The most recognizable cocaptain of any rock band is Boyd Tinsley. Tinsley grew up near Moore and earned a history degree from the University of Virginia. Tinsley started violin in middle school, took years of classical training, and then put the instrument aside. A renewed interest emerged when Tinsley began to explore the improvisatory playing along the lines of Stephan Grapelli. In 1986, Tinsley formed Down Boy Down with rhythm guitarist Harry Faulkner and in the early 1990s fronted the Boyd Tinsley Band. Although busy with regular gigs and tours, Tinsley made time to play on the demo of "Tripping Billies" and soon split his creative energies among multiple ensembles before joining DMB officially in 1992 (Delancey 2001).

Lessard grew up in Charlottesville and began playing with Matthews and company at age 16. Lessard's teacher, John D'earth, recommended the bassist to Matthews after the group had had just a single rehearsal (Colapinto 1996). Lessard exchanged his upright and concert hall ensembles for electric bass and soon abandoned studies at Virginia Commonwealth University to hedge bets by touring with DMB. Lessard channeled lessons from his musical parents, a nomadic upbringing, and exposure to non-Western lifestyles into a specific feel for bass. He inventories reggae as a formative influence, stating, "Reggae was my emphasis outside of jazz, which I viewed as the music to study" (Fox 2005).

Additional talent is called upon for studio work and stage performances. Moore discovered Rayshawn Ross (born January 16, 1979; trumpet), a Virgin Islands–born trumpeter and graduate of Berklee College of Music, who became a standard presence on the road. Ross boasts ties to a number of heavy hitters, including Stevie Wonder and Roy Hargrove. Butch Taylor (born April 13, 1961; keyboards), a Charlottesville native, was the touring keyboardist for DMB from 1998 to 2008, coming to DMB via connections with Beauford, with whom he played in the band Secrets, and Tim Reynolds (born December 15, 1957; guitar). Taylor attended Virginia Commonwealth with Moore and played with DMB for a decade. Taylor's résumé includes work with Tanya Tucker, and for DMB he layered inventive keyboards to contribute to the signature sound. He offered leisurely, mellow sequences across nearly 500 DMB shows, and his playing is particularly prominent on "Crush," "Too Much," "Two Step," and "Ants Marching."

While not on the official roster, guitarist Reynolds is a mainstay of shows and a partner in the acoustic duo, Dave and Tim. The two play bare-bones shows in off-season months, at small venues where tickets are hard to come by; the acoustic sets are replete with intense, communicative improvisations. Reynolds is also featured on DMB studio records like *Crash*, *Big Whiskey and the GrooGrux King*, and *Away from the World*, marking 20 years of collaboration since meeting Matthews in 1990.

Even before Internet technology, DMB members were uniquely available to fans, fostering a valuable closeness. DMB wanted fans to have a complete musical experience at shows and to afterward enjoy access to the music in any format, thus DMB legitimized "bootleg" activity. Fans were always allowed to tape shows, then archive and trade recordings. Capshaw supported this, which meant the music disseminated via cassettes, then CDs, and now digital files (Colapinto 2001). Tapers were even allowed to plug into the soundboard at concerts; Capshaw related, "We figured fans were gonna get the song anyway, so they might as well get a clean copy" (Farley 2001). Most every show was thus captured in all its uniqueness: each taper had different equipment and vantage points. Fans could later critique performances, reconsider sets, and compare song versions. The system buoyed ticket sales: a fan expected to hear well-worn songs, inevitably in a new version at every concert; thus, he was inclined to repeatedly see the band live. Due to the taping phenomenon, DMB songs arrived in a town before the band, even before radio play. When people mouthed the words along with the music, Matthews realized what was happening and in this regard accepted comparison to the Grateful Dead.

New technology enhanced the already sophisticated DMB fan community. The Internet introduced fresh methods for band-to-fan and fan-to-fan contact and advanced new forums that became the clearing house for data related to song lyrics, set lists, and touring dates. The first website was founded in 1996, replacing Minarets, a listserv begun in 1993. Another fan initiative came about in 1998 with the nonprofit Nancies.org, another organized format for accessing set lists, tour dates, and to facilitate trading. (An early 2013 survey of the site indicates the last posts date to 2008.) Antsmarching.org was founded in 2002 to offer interactive set lists; the site expanded to include interviews with DMB members, some as podcasts. The most comprehensive site for DMB tracking remains DMBAlmanac.com. The site, current as of early 2015, provides full song lyrics, venue details (419 cities are listed to date), a "This Day in DMB History" feature, and tour data compiling the average number of songs per show, top openers and closers, and a curious category known as the "Liberation List." The original tape-trading spirit still drives DMB, as band and management align distribution methods with how fans naturally come to their music. DMB was the first band signed with a major label to release a single on Napster ("I Did It"). "Mercy," from the 2012 release *Away from the World*, debuted on late-night television and on MySpace Music months ahead of the full record.

DMB is known for the individuality of its core members, and on this artistic platform the group has built its longevity. Matthews himself is clearly attracted to indigenous African music, and claimed that imitation of it is where his songwriting begins. He sings and plays guitar with a traceable percussiveness, and other African musical commonalities contributed to the developing band's sound, notably an emphasis on participation and a fully realized harmonic palette (which may stem from African choral music traditions). Critics rely on Matthews's declared listening history, reflecting personal interest in African and American music. He digested Abdulah Ibrahim's synthesis of saxophone and keyboard with understated vocals, as well as the inventive sounds of Miriam Makeba and motoric rhythms of Johnny Clegg. Vargas summarizes the musical result as "a diverse sonic blend that is rarely jazz . . . but almost always . . . jazz-inspired" melded with funk, dance, and rock (Vargas 2008).

Matthews also consumed the music of the Beatles, Pink Floyd, Peter Gabriel, and some heavy metal. His introduction to straight-ahead jazz came only via Beauford's fascination with Coltrane, and all of the above contributes to critics' and analysts' confusion: Paul Evans said that DMB is "almost unclassifiable" and that they sound like "four or five groups in one" (Evans 1998). One label with which the industry (if not Matthews and company) seems reasonably comfortable is "jamband." Budnick defines the jamband philosophy as a "penchant for bending and blending established genres," where eclecticism comes to fruition via extended solo and group improvisation. A jamband is best experienced live, by a fan community "hooked" in a personal way (Budnick 2003). There is no prescribed instrumentation, nor melodic and rhythmic formulae, for this umbrella term coined in the late 1990s to describe bands like the Grateful Dead and Phish; the label now extends to describe alternative bands like Widespread Panic and the Stringcheese Incident, but remains only a vague suggestion for defining DMB (Budnick 2003). Some analysts believe the jamband tag stuck simply because of a "guilty by association" factor, since DMB did, early on, open for Phish and for the Dead (Budnick 2003). Matthews himself seems more inclined toward an affinity for jazz, but DMB does fit the jamband aesthetic by realizing definitive versions of songs while playing live. In fact, Lessard admits that "a lot of words and melodies" are "discovered during the tour" (Van Noy 2011).

DMB has released nine studio albums, all anchored in Matthews's songwriting. Matthews originally worked alone, underscoring angular melodies with unexpected metrical patterns, and he admits to pouring parts of himself into the lyrics, so that his "live now, no matter what the cost" attitude is often palpable (Colapinto 1996). The creative process evolved into an open forum among bandmates, and the inaugural compilation, *Remember Two Things*, was released in September 1993 on Bama Rags Records. Matthews later asserted that it was important for the first record to be a compilation of live tracks, to give back to the fans for paying attention all along. This was, though,

a turning point, as the band started to delineate recorded album from "bootleg" tape, and DMB confirmed that officially recorded versions would bring "clarity" to songs already heard on the road during past tours (Van Noy 2011).

DMB's first record deal was inked with RCA just hours after the release of *Remember Two Things*. Three studio records followed, affectionately bound as "The Big Three," each combining new material with recorded versions of familiar road songs. *Under the Table and Dreaming* (1994) was the first effort with British-born producer Steve Lillywhite, who aligned most recognizably with U2, but had also worked with Phish and the Rolling Stones. An advocate for a band's "body of work" rather than the industry trend of a "song-by-song" market, Lillywhite produced DMB's "Big Three" and the 2012 release *Away from the World* (Newman 2006). In one year, *Under the Table* went four times platinum, and by 2010, six times platinum, setting the bar high for subsequent releases.

Lillywhite tended to celebrate DMB's live habits, evidenced by the spontaneous shouts retained on "What Would You Say." The most durable single from the album, "What Would You Say" hit number nine on the *Billboard* 40 and the cut was nominated for a 1997 Grammy for Best Rock Performance by a Duo or Group. A dense commentary on a man's role in his own downfall, the song situates probing questions in a lighthearted dance jam. Lyrics suggest that a person should be intent on "looking in the mirror" before "a lifetime's passed by," echoing a sentiment that would become standard in DMB songs: musing about the fleeting nature of life. The hard-driving duple meter and Moore's dominant saxophone combine for a definitive funk aesthetic against long lyrical lines of guest John Popper's (of Blues Traveler) harmonica.

"Ants Marching" is a staple of most live performances and is considered the band's anthem. It hit number 19 on the *Billboard* 40 and was reincarnated on many live records, including *The Best of What's Around,* Vol. 1. Its theme aligns with "What Would You Say," creating cohesiveness for the record, with lyrics that lament the pace of life and the inability of humans (from the microcosm of a couple to large communities) to connect. In pre-2008 live performances, Moore's barking soprano saxophone was complemented by Ross's playing, and the song always features acrobatic playing by Tinsley and Beauford. "Satellite" was the final single released from *Under the Table and Dreaming* and reached number 34 on the *Billboard* 40. Guitar players remain fascinated by its complex melodic riff and compound meter, which require significant manual dexterity. Even though Matthews has never considered himself a "real" guitarist, saying he "likes the wrong notes" as much as the right notes, the melody did evolve from practice material (Apcynski 2009). The lyrics reflect on the "smallness" of humans.

Crash, the second of the "Big Three," was recorded in April 1996 and hit number two on *Billboard*. Singles like "Tripping Billies" and "Too Much" (nominated in 1997 for Grammy's Best Rock Song) kept the record on the charts for over 100 weeks. Although featuring basic personnel (with Reynolds joining on electric guitar), Lillywhite declared a deliberate style change, claiming a "conscious production decision" to craft something with more of a rock feel (Van Noy 2011). Other singles from the Grammy-nominated album include the flute-driven "Say Goodbye" and hits like "Two Step" and "So Much to Say" (winner of Best Rock Performance by a Duo or Group Grammy). The ballad "Crash into Me," inspired by Matthews's relationship with his wife, Ashley, remains one of DMB's most beloved and recognizable songs to date and was nominated in 1998 for Best Rock Performance by a Duo or Group and for Best Rock Song.

The band was back in the studio at the end of 1997 to work on *Before These Crowded Streets*, again with Lillywhite at the helm. Production moved to California for the creation of mostly new songs. While critics denigrated the record as inaccessible to fans, the collection shot to number one on *Billboard*, selling 500,000 copies in its first week; the record was nominated in 1998 for Grammy's Best Rock Album and went triple platinum by 1999. The trend of inviting outsiders in continued: Reynolds's electric guitar and Bela Fleck's banjo enhanced several songs. John D'earth played trumpet on "Halloween," a song for which he also crafted orchestral arrangements, while Alanis Morissette's vocals graced the first released single, "Don't Drink the Water," a commentary on South African apartheid. (This cut became the most common show opener, so its inclusion across countless live compilations is no surprise.) The Kronos Quartet guested on "The Stone," where Matthews established a guitar ostinato after a strings introduction. Momentum accumulates by means of a motoric pulse colored with syncopation. All gives way to a steadier lyricism for the words, "I was just wondering if you'd come along," imparting the song with a shifting, narrative appeal. "Crush" was the third release from *Before These Crowded Streets*. The lyrics pit otherworldly musings against the grit of human activity, all combined with unexpected polyrhythm and disjunct melodies. A wide range tests Matthews's vocal abilities, while Tinsley's smooth countermelodies banter with the vocals, and the cut earned a Grammy nomination for Best Pop Performance.

An interim followed, but by 2000, DMB was back in the studio, this time in Charlottesville. With the explosion of Internet activity, fans were more involved than ever. "Insider leaks" caused friction and confusion about the musical material, and the band felt stifled under constant expectation and altered perceptions, even though this community connection had been critical to DMB's success. Lessard relates that everyone was "grumpy," working on uncharacteristically "dark" songs, each band member isolated with headphones on, all day for six months in a stuffy studio (Van Noy 2011). Lag time concerned RCA, so the unfinished recording was put on hiatus as DMB began a tour, hoping for renewal in the forum where the band had historically found footing for songs to later record. In October, with prompting from the label, Matthews took the drastic step of moving to California to try and finish the songs and then summon the others. Here Matthews worked with Glen Ballard, a protégé of Quincy Jones, which meant alienating Lillywhite, who graciously stepped aside and shelved the unfinished recordings. (That abandoned compilation was dubbed "The Lillywhite Sessions" and the music found its way to Internet channels by March 2001; certain songs, rerecorded, would become official via the 2002 *Busted Stuff* album.)

Matthews claims that in nine days, 10 new songs came together, via a fresh process that included Matthews on electric guitar. Released in 2001, *Everyday* soared to number one, selling 700,000 copies in the first week. By year's end *Everyday* was triple platinum. The record "ventures in a new direction with a new producer and a fresh sound," and the "songs are shorter and more focused" (Farley 2001). Ballard, who shares song-writing credits for the title track, had convinced Matthews that 20-minute-long improvisations were not "listener-friendly" on a studio CD, and he took the liberty of creating charts for instrumental parts (Fox 2005). Laying down tracks with the full group was more efficient, and what resulted was a polished sound. *Everyday* made DMB more commercially successful than ever before, but die-hard fans complained about the more "radio-ready" sound (Van Noy 2011). Still, the music is characteristically complex, and each song boasts what Ballard called a "density" to the storytelling. Standout singles include "The Space Between," nominated in 2002 for Best Rock Vocal Performance by a Duo or Group. "When the World Ends" is a haunting, suggestive perspective on companionship.

Busted Stuff was the sixth studio album for DMB, and its 2002 release meant a number-one *Billboard* debut. The record was in part realization of the Lillywhite Sessions singles, as nine of the 11 songs came from that creative period (only "Where Are You Going" and "You Never Know" were new material). The band recorded their work in California with producer Stephen Harris, who engineered the original Lillywhite Sessions, with each band member contributing to the song-writing process. "Where Are You Going" earned a Grammy nod for Best Pop Performance by a Duo. In early 2005, DMB began studio work on a new record, hiring producer Mark Batson. Batson had creative ties to the likes of Eminem and 50 Cent and was an artist with whom DMB members shared mutual friends. Clearly a new aesthetic was at hand, and *Stand Up* was built from the ground up, with an experimental spirit. Batson cowrote several singles, working individually with each musician as "songs emerged from the five members listening to one another's riffs" (Scaggs 2005). In terms of song composition, this is the most collaborative album to date: each musician gets composer credit for every song. Some personnel shifts were in order: Tinsley played mandolin, Lessard played guitar, and Matthews played piano, all to serve the new profundity of these collective lyrics.

Batson's experience on R&B and hip-hop projects made sense for DMB at this juncture in their musical journey, and this new artistic relationship bridged aesthetic gaps as DMB persisted in an aggressive avoidance of being definitively categorized. In many ways *Stand Up* departs from the DMB formula; fans noted that the typical dry, acoustic touch was replaced with a richer, more "produced" sound, which one *Rolling Stone* critic panned as less "durable" for live performance (Van Noy 2011). Nonetheless, *Stand Up* became the band's fourth consecutive number-one release and the start of DMB's exposure on iTunes. Although replete with messages related to love, God, death, and sex, political references also abound in this post-2004 election environment. "American Baby" opens with battle sounds, but Matthews claims an optimistic vibe (that of the American "apple pie and lemonade") prevails. "Louisiana Bayou" is flavorful and infectious, while "Old Dirt Hill" nostalgically wanders through childhood memories, colored with Tinsley's violin pizzicato contrasts.

In 2008, the group headed to Piety Street Studio in Seattle, with Rob Cavallo (Green Day, Kid Rock) in place of Batson. DMB had in hand the seeds of a full record, germinated during the summer tour and jam sessions. By now, Taylor had left but Reynolds was more of a fixture, so his electric guitar filled in missing keyboard parts. The resulting record, *Big Whiskey and the GrooGrux King*, became DMB's fifth straight number-one album debut, earning two Grammy nods (Album of the Year and Best Rock Album). As another example of DMB acting on the cutting edge of record distribution, the music was released via Pandora before the CD release, as were videos that chronicled the genesis of this landmark record. Released in June 2009, critics took note of a harder rock sound along with a full-textured band. Easily detectable are New Orleans musical influences, perhaps in homage to the city that was a favorite of the recently deceased Moore (Matthews considered the record an ode to Moore, who passed during the making of the songs for *Big Whiskey*). Still, the more traditional DMB sound seems to have returned, even though Matthews plays some electric guitar and its lyrics impart a certain moody melancholy. The making of this album was a return to the old way of doing things—as a group—and a chance to heal wounds that inevitably result during lengthy working and personal relationships. Tinsley related, "I think when we're at our best, we create things from the ground up, and it has to come from each individual member" ("Scenes from Big Whiskey" 2009). Reynolds, Ross, and Coffin all guest on the record, along with Charlottesville banjo player Danny Barnes, and indeed Moore is present in more ways than one. His licks start and end the record, made possible from snippets of previously recorded material. "Why I Am" references the "GrooGrux King," Moore's nickname, and for "Baby Blue" Matthews revels in a duet with recordings of Moore. "Funny the Way It Is" tells of the human ability to move past suffering, surely a timely message for all involved.

In 20 productive years, DMB has provided ample material for fans, critics, analysts, and imitators. DMB has modeled affection for and accessibility to fans, as well as a sharp focus on making meaningful music. While certainly no band espouses the exact DMB formula, there are traceable lines of influence to and from the band via this inventory: a road-warrior mentality; a jamband philosophy toward live performance; a focus on rhythmic intricacies and improvisation stemming from jazz or blues influences; a grassroots following; and a cooperative process toward the realization of songs.

Numerous bands emerged in the 1990s with similar aims and aesthetic, many of which have enjoyed impressive longevity, if not the same financial success as DMB. Widespread Panic (WP) predated DMB, but in process and production, WP matches up: the members work collectively to successfully "translate their live, improvisational vibe to the studio" (Wilhelm 1997). Blues Traveler, still selling out concerts after 22 years, makes for a logical comparison to DMB. According to harmonica player John Popper, this eclectic ensemble continues to "reconcile the different things we do and cultivate what we're individually good at into something that's bigger than the sum of its parts" (Lastfm 2009). The Disco Biscuits, "born on the jamband circuit" in 1995, are another similar case study. Keyboardist Aron Magner states, "I think our collective musical palette is very diverse . . . a jam band . . . gives you that flexibility to play in whatever style and whatever genre you want" (Levine 2011). Bands that emerged from the college scene, like Moe and Umphrey's McGee, also align with DMB in lengthy onstage improvisations, and O.A.R., a "roots and reggae infused" and "relentless touring" band, boasts a diverse sound that includes saxophone as well as classically trained musicians (keyboardist Mike Paris studied at the Hartt School of Music) (Gennet 2008).

The DMB legacy is gradually being revealed in young artists, like *American Idol* winners Lee DeWyze, who chronicled Matthews's gospel-inspired tendencies in "Hallelujah," and Philip Phillips, who gamely channeled Matthews's sound with his cover of "The Stone." DMB enjoyed some commercial and critical success with their release, *Away from the World* (marked number 29 on *Rolling Stone* magazine's list of 50 Best Albums of 2012), and continue to forge a specific, and likely unexpected, path toward their next frontier, always as a bridge between old and new, linking disparate vocal and instrumental styles across musical categories.

Sarah Tyrrell

Selected Discography

Remember Two Things, Bama Rags Records BAMA001, 1993.

Remember Two Things, RCA 07863 67547–2, 1993.

Under the Table and Dreaming, RCA 07863 66449–2, 1994.

Crash, RCA 07863 66904–2, 1996.

Live at Red Rocks 8.15.95, RCA 07863 67587–2, 1997.

Before These Crowded Streets, RCA 07863 67660–2, 1998.

Everyday, RCA 07863 67988–2, 2000.

The Warehouse 5, Bama Rags Records DMBFAN001, 2000.

Busted Stuff, RCA 07863 68117–2, 2002.

The Central Park Concert, RCA 82876 57501–2, 2003.

Stand Up, RCA 82876 69288–2, 2005.

Big Whiskey and the GrooGrux King, RCA 88697 48712–2, 2009.

Away from the World, RCA 88725–45257–2, 2012.

References

Apczynski, Dan. "King Dave." *Acoustic Guitar* 20.6 (2009): 48–53.

Budnick, Dean. *Jam Bands: North America's Hottest Live Groups.* Toronto: ECW Press, 1998.

Budnick, Dean. *Jam Bands: The Complete Guide to the Players, Music, and Scene.* San Francisco: Backbeat Books, 2003.

Colapinto, John. "The Raging Optimism and Multiple Personalities of Dave Matthews." *Rolling Stone* 749 (12/12/1996): 56+.

Colapinto, John. "The Salvation of Dave Matthews." *Rolling Stone* 864 (3/15/2001): 46–51; 88–89.

Dave Matthews Band. "Scenes from Big Whiskey." Hulu video, 28:58. May 5, 2009. http://www.hulu.com/watch/74995.

"Dave Matthews: Charlie Rose Show—2001 Part 1." Youtube video, 9:52, from a televised *Charlie Rose Show* on February 26, 2001. Posted by "dmbondemand." April 10, 2010. http://www.youtube.com/watch?v=01b6lMz-y94.

"Dave Matthews Talks about His Career." Youtube video, 4:27. December 1, 2010. http://www.youtube.com/watch?v=mZVUEKKiq28&feature=fvwrel.

Delancey, Morgan. *Dave Matthews Band: Step into the Light.* Toronto: ECW Press, 2001.

Evan, Lucy, and Jaclyn Albert. "Deaths." *Billboard* 120 (9/13/2008): 9.

Evans, Paul. "Dave Matthews Band: *Under the Table and Dreaming.*" *Rolling Stone Reviews* (February 1998).

http://www.rollingstone.com/music/albumreviews/under-the-table-dreaming-19980202 (accessed January 31, 2013).

Farley, Christopher John. "And the Band Plays On." *Time* 157.9 (3/5/2001): 70.

Fox, Brian. "Fonzie Plays It Cool: Stefan Lessard Shows His Street Smart with the Dave Matthews Band." *Bass Player* 16.9 (2005): 44–46.

Gennet, Robbie. "Keyboard Revolution: Musical Multi-Tasker Mike Paris Anchors the Exuberant Rock of O.A.R." *Keyboard* 34.8 (2008): 30–31.

Gillan, Marilyn. "Capshaw, Matthews Launch Indie Label." *Billboard* 112.7 (2000): 3.

Jacobs, Justin. "Dispatch Opens Up," *Billboard* 124.29 (2012), 24.

Kafka, Peter. "Musicians." *Forbes* 170.1 (2002): 108–10.

Levine, Mike. "Back-Talk: Q&A Aron Magner." *Electronic Musician* 27.1 (2011): 66.

Meredith, Bill. "Flecktone Jeff Coffin: Constant Change." *Jazztimes* (October 2008).

Newman, Melinda. "Q&A: Steve Lillywhite." *Billboard* 118.14 (2006): 21–25.

Newman, Melinda, and Deborah Evans Price. "Dave Matthews Band Cuts New RCA Deal." *Billboard* 116.10 (2004): 15–17.

Norris, Chris. "Citizen Dave." *Spin* 19.11 (2003): 68–72.

Paoletta, Michael. "Six Questions with Mark Batson." *Billboard* 117.28 (2005): 64.

Rose, Charlie. *An Interview with Dave Matthews.* September 18, 2006. B000IU32HK. DVD.

Scaggs, Austin. "Dave Matthews." *Rolling Stone* 935 (2003): 34.

Scaggs, Austin. "Matthews Mixes It Up." *Rolling Stone* 969 (2005): 39.

Van Noy, Nikki. *So Much to Say: Dave Matthews Band, 20 Years on the Road.* New York: Touchstone, 2011.

Vargas, George. "What Would You Play: The Dave Matthews Band on African Jazz, Improvising for the Masses, the Absurdity of Racism, and Why 'Jam' Is a Dirty Word." *Jazz Times* 38.6 (2008): 66–71.

Waddell, Ray. "The Backstage Team." *Billboard* 119.27 (2007): 40–43.

Waddell, Ray. "It's About the Experience." *Billboard* 123.14 (2011): 20.

Waddell, Ray. "Move the Crowd." *Billboard* 121.51 (2009): 168–72.

Wilhelm, Theo. "Widespread Panic." *Keyboard* 23.7 (1997): 13.

Deep Purple (1968–1976; 1984–Present)

Deep Purple were pioneers of heavy metal and modern hard rock. They began as a psychedelic rock band influenced by the explorations of Jimi Hendrix and Cream, but they also incorporated classical influences into their music. They briefly explored progressive rock, and then turned to a harder sound that influenced bands from Judas Priest to Def Leppard. The band has endured so many personnel changes over the years that fans refer to its various lineups as Mark I–Mark VII. Regardless, over the years the style of Deep Purple has shifted only slightly to reflect new strains of hard rock, though experiments with extended improvisation and classical influence have always been elements of the band's oeuvre.

Deep Purple began in 1968 as a supergroup of sorts, the brainchild of Chris Curtis (born Christopher Crummey, August 26, 1941; drums), the former drummer for the Searchers. He envisioned a group with a quartet of permanent members and a flexible membership that would allow prominent musicians from the British rock community to explore new ideas and collaborate without committing to creating a new band. As members could enter and exit, Curtis called the band Roundabout.

Curtis's first recruit was Jon Lord (born June 9, 1941, died July 16, 2012; keyboards), a classically trained organist and former member of the Artwoods, a band fronted by former Blues Incorporated singer Arthur Wood. Lord had initially planned to become a classical pianist, but his affections turned to rock after hearing "Whole Lotta Shakin' Goin' On." He played in a jazz combo before hooking up with the Don Wilson Quartet, a British R&B group that renamed itself after Wood joined the group. The Artwoods recorded a demo, and shortly thereafter met Johnny Jones, a London-based booking agent who got them a residency at the prestigious 100 Club in London and a contract with Decca Records.

The Artwoods become a popular live act on the British R&B circuit but, despite positive reviews, they failed to make the charts until early 1966, when "I Take What I Want" became a minor hit. Even with no top-40 single, the band and Decca gambled on an album, *Art Gallery,* in November 1966, but the album performed poorly and the label dropped the group. After a few more unsuccessful singles, the Artwoods disbanded; Lord played with a few temporary ensembles before joining Roundabout.

Curtis next approached Ritchie Blackmore (born Richard Hugh Blackmore, April 14, 1945; guitar), a studio guitarist who had played with the Screaming Lord Such and the Savages and Neil Christian and the Crusaders. Blackmore became fascinated with the guitar in his early teens during the skiffle era, traveling into London to look at the instruments in shop windows before finally convincing his parents to buy him his first instrument. Convinced he was destined to be a guitarist, he looked up one of his heroes, guitarist Big Jim Sullivan of the Marty Wilde Band, in the phone book and showed up on his doorstep. Sullivan was not sure of what to make of the precocious youth, but he was supportive and encouraged Blackmore to develop his own style.

Blackwood started his first band, the Dominators, when he was 16. He moved through a series of local groups before getting his big break in the Outlaws, a studio band assembled by British pop producer Joe Meek. After they disbanded he played in a few different groups before his short stint with the Savages (then called Lord Caesar Sutch's Roman Empire) and the Crusaders. Blackwood was playing with a group in Germany when Curtis recruited him for the project.

Curtis tasked Blackmore and Lord with finding a rhythm section. They approached drummer Bobby Clarke, who had played with Marty Wilde in the early 1960s, and bassist Dave Curtiss, who led his own beat combo, the Tremors.

Though it now had its core members, Roundabout had no musical direction, repertoire, or guests who wanted to play with the proposed supergroup. The lack of specificity led Curtiss and Clarke to abandon the project, and even Chris Curtis lost interest. Blackmore and Lord determined to continue and quickly found replacements. Their first choice for a bassist was Nick Simper (born Nicolas John Simper, November 3, 1945; bass), another former member of the Savages. Simper started out in a number of local bands before landing a job in the reboot of the influential group Johnny Kidd and the Pirates, whose 1960 number-one record, "Shakin' All Over" was one of biggest English hits of the early rock and roll era. After Kidd was killed in a car crash in 1966, Simper took over the Pirates and the group carried on until 1967. They then played with the Savages and were called the Flower Pot Men and Their Garden, which included Jon Lord. Thus, he was amenable to joining a group with two former colleagues.

The group then recruited Rod Evans (born January 19, 1947; vocals) and Ian Paice (born Ian Anderson Paice, June 29, 1948; drums) of the band Maze. Paice's father played piano with local dance bands and encouraged his son when he showed interest in the drums; by the time Paice was in his teens he was performing with his father at Saturday night dances. He joined his first group, the Shindigs, in 1964, before moving to another local band, the Horizons, where he met Evans. The group got a recording contract in 1966, but when their first single did not take off, the band changed its style from R&B to psychedelic rock and its name to the Maze. The band was signed to the Reaction label, whose acts included the Who and Cream. The Maze, however, failed to rise to the same level, and Evans and Paice were happy to join whatever Roundabout was to become.

The band was still searching for a direction when Lord discovered Vanilla Fudge, a "heavy" American band that infused the dimensions of classical music into psychedelic and pop rock. The group decided to pursue the same baroque sensibilities, but also incorporate elements of modern jazz, rock and roll, Jimi Hendrix's sonic explorations, and classical music

English hard rock band Deep Purple was on the cutting edge of the birth of heavy metal. Pictured here in 1970, the group has soldiered on through multiple personnel changes, all the while exerting influence on subsequent generations of musicians. Their hit single, "Smoke on the Water," remains a perennial favorite and an enduring heavy metal classic. (Photo by Michael Ochs Archives/Getty Images)

that they summarized as "baroque 'n' roll" (Thompson, 45). Elaborate, extended improvisation emerged as a core characteristic in their earliest gigs. Lord recalled, "We used to swap musical jokes and attacks . . . [Blackmore] would play something and I'd have to see if I could match it. That provided a sense of humor, a sense of tension to the band, a sense of . . . what the hell's going to happen next?" (Thompson, 34). They also decided to rename the group Deep Purple, a 1930s piano piece that was a favorite of Blackmore's grandmother, as well as a popular type of LSD.

Even though Deep Purple had written only a few songs, the American label Tetragrammaton, which was looking for new English talent, signed the band and assigned producer Derek Lawrence to get the group into the studio; their first album, *Shades of Deep*

Purple, was released a few months later. "Hush," a psychedelic cover of a 1967 hit by American singer Billy Joe Royal, driven by an electric guitar riff thickened by Hammond organ, became the group's first single; it failed to move in England but went to number four in the United States. Several tracks exemplify the group's distinctive approach. Their turgid cover of "Hey Joe" included a florid, flamenco introduction, an emphatic bolero rhythm, and arabesques by Lord, punctuated by distorted guitar flourishes. "Help" was a radically slow, minor-mode version of the Beatles hit that opened with electronic effects, sitar-like organ, and delicate guitar, then built to heavy, Wagnerian climax, with Lord layering Baroque ornaments over emphatic drumming and overdriven guitar. "One More Rainy Day" was a psychedelic pop tune that featured organ arpeggios with shifting accents that foreshadowed Lord's future work, and "Mandrake Root" was a dazzling instrumental cut that sounded a bit like Jimi Hendrix's "Foxy Lady." The album performed well in the States, rising to number 24 on the album charts, but British critics found it pretentious, and the disc sold poorly despite a series of high-profile concerts and television appearances.

Even before the band's first American tour, their label pushed Deep Purple to record a second album, *The Book of Taliesyn*. "Kentucky Woman," their next single, was a feisty reworking of a Neil Diamond hit that scraped into the top 40. As the band heard that John Lennon and Paul McCartney liked their version of "Help," they worked up another Beatles cover, "Exposition: We Can Work It Out." The exposition was an extended introduction interspersed with mixed meter organ interludes, sheets of simultaneous arpeggios by Lord and Blackmore, and thunderous percussion that abruptly segued into the Lennon/McCartney tune, which included frequent suspensions of meter; the reverb-laden vocals were the song's least compelling element. Other standouts were "Anthem," a folk/pop hybrid that contained a classically influenced interlude for organ, strings, and guitar that sounded like a Bach fugue; and "Wring That Neck," a funk-influenced, riff-based instrumental that showcased the intricate interplay between Blackmore and Lord.

Once again, the album did better in the United States than in their home country, something the band took very much to heart. They felt they had paid their dues in earlier bands, and if the rewards lay across the Atlantic, so be it. Thus, they focused all of their energies on their upcoming American tour and played few live dates in Britain. Heavy promotion paved the way, and by the time that Deep Purple played their first American dates opening for Cream on their farewell tour, there was significant talk that the band might be the next big British musical export. After they set out on their own, Deep Purple was in such demand that the tour was extended by four weeks.

Tetragrammaton demanded a new hit single immediately, and the group attempted to work up new covers in their own unique style, but none jelled; their musical vision no longer included giving more songs the "Deep Purple treatment," but lay in experimentation and extended collective improvisation (Thompson, 58).

Their eponymous 1969 album reflected this new direction; it was a transitional work that combined proto metal with touches of progressive rock. The disc contained only one cover, Donovan's lovely ballad "Lalena," which was perhaps Rod Evans's best vocal performance; the rest were originals, including "The Painter," a blues-based track dominated by Blackmore's aggressive, fuzztone lead; the percussion-driven "Chasing Shadows"; "April," a 13-minute suite penned by Lord that includes a full orchestral interlude; and "Why Didn't Rosemary," an affectionate look back to London's R&B scene. Tetragrammaton, which was on its last legs, did little to promote the album, and it failed to hit the top 100. Later that year, the label was bought by Warner Bros., which became the band's new American label.

In July 1969, Blackmore, Lord, and Paice decided that they wanted to take the band in a heavier direction, and they felt that Evans's voice did not have the proper heft. They briefly considered Terry Reid (who had passed on an offer to join Led Zeppelin the previous year), then approached Ian Gillan (born August 19, 1945; vocals), the lead singer for Episode Six who had a powerful voice and soaring range. Gillan came from a musical family; his grandfather had been an opera singer. He fell in love with Elvis Presley while in his teens, and in 1964 he joined the Javelins, an R&B band; he then sang with the soul outfit Wainwright's Gentlemen before he was drafted to lead Episode Six. Gillan had been invited to join Roundabout a year earlier, but at that time he felt that his band was poised for mainstream success. Things had not panned out, and when Blackmore and Lord approached Gillan again, he was ready to make the move, though on the condition that Roger Glover (born November 30, 1945; bass), the bassist for Episode Six, be hired as well. The others had some reservations about Simper's ability to play harder rock, so they acquiesced.

The first album of the Mark II lineup was *Concerto for Group and Orchestra*, a three-movement work by Jon Lord that was inspired by Dave Brubeck's *Dialogues for Jazz Combo and Orchestra*. The piece, which was performed with the London Symphony Orchestra, was one of the first collaborations between a rock band and an orchestra. The idea, a concerto with Deep Purple as the featured "soloist" was conceptually sound, and the sections that involve both orchestra and band work quite well. However, the solo sections, particularly those featuring Blackmore, were so stylistically disjunctive that the overall impression was of two separate musical events that periodically interrupt each other. American reviewers panned the album as ineffective and self-indulgent, but the publicity from the event gave the band the boost it needed at home, and *Concerto for Group and Orchestra* became the group's first album to chart in Britain. The album marked a transition in the band's style, though their next album could not have been more different.

Though the style did not yet have a name, *Deep Purple in Rock* was considered one of the founding documents of heavy metal, as well as one of the group's finest albums. It was also Gillan's debut; his powerful vocals largely defined the Mark II version of the band. The standouts are "Speed King," which started with an assault of guitar noise before dissolving into a slower, classically influenced organ solo, then erupted into an assault on a dozen early rock hits; "Child in Time," which contained an extended

virtuoso interlude with Blackmore and Lord dueling for domination; and "Black Night," a swaggering shuffle with Blackmore and Glover locked into the kind of dual guitar–bass riff that dominated heavy metal for the next decade. The album did not sell well in the United States, but it went to number two in Britain and cemented the group's popularity in Europe.

After an American tour, the group dispersed briefly. Ian Gillan sang the role of Judas for the concept album of Andrew Lloyd Weber's *Jesus Christ Superstar*; he would reprise the part in occasional performances and brief tours until the 1990s. Paice, Glover, and Lord went into the studio to record Lord's classically influenced *Gemini Suite,* which became the debut release on the band's newly established label, Purple Records.

The group broadened their stylistic range on their next album, *Fireball.* "Strange Kind of Woman," a top 10 hit, followed the blueprint of *Deep Purple in Rock,* but stood side by side with the country-influenced innuendo of "Anyone's Daughter." "Fools," a progressive rock/metal hybrid, fused delicate, minor-mode organ lines to menacing, growled vocals and an interlude for distorted cello and maracas. "Mule," a psychedelic and Indian-influenced work with mumbled lyrics, sounded like a throwback to 1968 that included extended instrumental improvisations supported by some exceptionally fine and nuanced drum work.

The band saw their supporting tour as a chance to reconnect with American audiences, but after only a handful of dates Gillan fell ill and the band returned to Europe. After he recovered, Deep Purple decamped to Montreaux in Switzerland to record a follow-up album at the Casino, a cavernous club that would be vacant after one final show by Frank Zappa and the Mothers of Invention. During the concert the arena caught on fire and burned to the ground. The incident caused delays but ultimately paid off, as it provided the inspiration for one of the band's biggest hits. The album was hastily recorded in a nearby hotel that had closed for the season.

Machine Head (1972) is an enduring heavy metal classic that included many of Deep Purple's biggest hits: "Smoke on the Water," which introduced the iconic riff that became the first mastered by a generation of hard rock guitarists; "Space Truckin'," an intergalactic, four-on-the-floor boogie driven by a fuzztone riff; and "Highway Star," a blistering slab of metal that featured Gillan at his best, including a no-holds-barred solo duel between Lord and Blackmore that was chaotic and thrilling. *Machine Head* finely reestablished the band in the United States, where it charted at number seven; it went to number one in England. On their subsequent tour, the band achieved a different kind of fame. Deep Purple secured an entry in the *Guinness Book of World Records* as the loudest band in the world when their volume at the Rainbow, in London, was measured at an ear-splitting 117 decibels. They moved on to a tour of Japan in August, which is preserved for posterity on the live album *Made in Japan*, one of the finest live albums of the decade.

By the end of the year the band was exhausted from nearly three years of constant work, and the group began to fracture. Blackmore was particularly upset by Gillan, as he felt the singer's distinctive style was restricting his guitar work. There were also frequent clashes with the band's management, which insisted that Deep Purple continue touring and recording at a breakneck pace.

Who Do We Think We Are (1973) turned out to be the last album of the Mark II lineup. The band was never together in the studio; backing tracks were recorded piecemeal and the vocals were added later. The strain within the band was audible; the tracks were of inconsistent quality and the album lacked the cohesion of their previous efforts. There were some fine songs—the OAR hit "Woman from Tokyo"; the Zeppelin-influenced "Rat Bat Blue," which featured some fine riff work by Glover and Blackmore and a solo by Lord that sounded like a futuristic Bach excerpt; and "Smooth Dancer," a blazing blast of heavy metal that evoked the drive of "Speed King"—but many of the other tracks sounded dispassionate, as though most of the band would have preferred to be elsewhere. Blackmore stated as much in press interviews, opining that the band had advanced musically

as far as it could, and more than once he referred to his involvement in Deep Purple in the past tense.

However, it was Gillan who tendered his resignation in December 1972. Blackmore telegraphed his intent to leave Deep Purple as well; after a lengthy conversation with Lord and Paice he agreed to stay on, but only if Roger Glover was fired. They quickly found a replacement: Glenn Hughes (born August 21, 1952; bass), the vocalist and bass player for the band Trapeze, who was considered one of the finest English bassists of the era. Though Hughes was capable of singing lead vocals, Deep Purple was unwilling to compromise instrumental virtuosity by having him perform double duties, and the search for a singer proved difficult. After soliciting tapes from dozens of interested vocalists, they chose David Coverdale (born September 22, 1951; vocals), a relative unknown who had fronted several bands in northern England.

Coverdale proved an excellent fit, and the new members seemed to rejuvenate the band. The stability injected the band's next album, *Burn,* with some of the fire of *In Rock,* though the band's heavy metal bite was softened appreciably by Coverdale and Hughes's funk and soul orientation. The pair sang dual lead on nearly every track, trading phrases and doubling up on the choruses, though the total rarely equaled the sum of Gillan's vocal power. Nonetheless, *Burn* was a fine album. The title track, based on a syncopated riff from Glenn Miller's "Fascinating Rhythm," came closest to the heights of *Machine Head.* The funk-driven "Sail Away" and the extended blues jam "Mistreated" were standouts; only the closing instrumental feature for Jon Lord, "A 220," failed to deliver.

In contrast, the next Mark III album, 1974's *Stormbringer*, was a lackluster affair. As Coverdale took over more songwriting duties, pre-composed songs that exploited the dual–lead singer format were prioritized over extended explorations of a riff or central idea. There were some good songs—the title track was a gritty and dark outing that presaged goth metal, and the driving "Lady Double Dealer" satisfied—but most were formulaic, and the virtuosic solos that were prominent in the Mark I and II lineups were almost entirely absent.

Both *Burn* and *Stormbringer* reached the top 10 in Britain and the top 20 in the United States, but Blackmore was not happy with the new direction of the band. Expressing a desire to get back to playing blues, he quit Deep Purple in May 1975 and formed Rainbow with Ronnie James Dio. Despite the loss of one of its core members, the rest of the band decided to continue with a new guitarist. After another long round of auditions they selected Tommy Bolin (born Thomas Richard Bolin, August 1, 1951, died December 4, 1976; guitar), formerly of the James Gang.

The new lineup jammed for a few weeks, then set to work recording an album. Hughes and Bolin, both heavily influenced by funk, quickly discovered a rapport, and the kind of collaborative development that had sustained the band in its early years once again came to the fore. However, the resulting songs were somewhat weak. *Come Taste the Band,* the sole album of the Mark IV lineup, was rather homogenous. "Dealer" was a fine hard rock tune driven by aggressive, crunching guitar, but there was little to distinguish it from "Lady Luck," "Drifter," and the other cuts. Only "You Keep on Moving," which was leavened by Motown-influenced harmonies and a soulful organ interlude, and the haunting "Owed to G" broke new ground. However, neither sounded much like Deep Purple. While reviews were kind, it was their worst-performing record in years, and the band was disillusioned. The problem was worse onstage, where Bolin's shortcomings soon became evident. Paice and Lord, who contributed little to *Come Taste the Band*, were not inspired by the new material, and Bolin, Coverdale, and Hughes were bored with nightly repetitions of the band's Mark II catalog. After a series of disastrous gigs in England, the members of Deep Purple, frustrated and exhausted, decided to call it quits.

Even though Deep Purple had dissolved, compilations and live sets were released steadily, keeping the band in the public eye. Fans repeatedly called for the band to reunite, and in 1984 the Mark II lineup came out of retirement with the album *Perfect Strangers* (1984). The album was not a reboot of the classic Deep Purple sound, though a number of tracks—"Nobody's

Home," "Under the Gun," and "A Gypsy's Kiss," with its interlude of traded licks between Blackmore and Lord—would fit comfortably on *Fireball* or *In Rock*. Most of the other tracks bore the stamp of late 1970s and early 1980s hard rock and heavy metal. Blackmore claimed to be aiming for an "'80s version of Machine Head," which updated the band's appeal for the MTV generation (Thompson, 246). It was also the best-selling Deep Purple album in a decade.

The slickly produced *The House of Blue Light*, released in 1987, continued the band's new, more commercial approach. There were a few progressive touches—"Strange Ways" and "The Spanish Archer" contained some of the extended exploration of early Deep Purple—but creative struggles between Gillan and Blackmore resurfaced, and the album had the same desultory quality as *Who Do We Think We Are*. Critics noticed, and though none panned the disc, it was not the reception the band had hoped for. They remained a potent force on stage and played to sold-out audiences in the United States and Europe, though the live album *Nobody's Perfect* (1988) did not reflect the band at its best.

The conflicts that caused the Mark II lineup to fracture in 1973 were not eased by time, and Ian Gillan, highly critical of the band's artistic choices, was fired. Plans for their next studio album were put on hold while Deep Purple searched yet again for a replacement vocalist, ultimately selecting former Rainbow vocalist Joe Lynn Turner (born Joseph Linquito, August 2, 1951; vocals). Not surprisingly, *Slaves and Masters* (1990) sounded more like Rainbow than Deep Purple, and the songwriting was decidedly weak. Gillan rejoined Deep Purple in 1993 for *The Battle Rages On*, which explored the same territory as *Perfect Strangers*: fast, 1980s-style metal with only a few cuts—the title track and "Anya"—that exploited the band's abilities to their fullest.

The subsequent American tour, unsurprisingly, reignited the antipathy within the band, and before its end Ritchie Blackmore abruptly quit Deep Purple. Joe Satriani (born July 15, 1956; guitar) replaced Blackmore for 1994 tours of Japan and Europe. He was soon replaced by Steve Morse (born July 28, 1954;

guitar), the guitarist for the Dixie Dregs and the mid-1980s version of Kansas. Morse brought new influences into the band, and *Purpendicular* (1996), was the band's most stylistically diverse album. "Soon Forgotten" fused post punk and progressive rock; "Rosa's Cantina" opened with a classically influenced solo by Lord, then became a Latin-inspired shuffle and bluesy melody; and "The Aviator" was an acoustic track that evoked Scottish highlands. "Sometimes I Feel Like Screaming" opened with a folk-influenced melody that gradually built to an aggressive peak and ended with an extended guitar solo.

The same diversity was heard on *Abandon* (1998). "No No No" was clearly influenced by hip-hop; "Watching the Sky" sounded like late 1990s nu-metal; "Seventh Heaven" was a psychedelic prog metal wonder, awash in reverb; and "Fingers to the Bone" returned Lord to classically influenced territory. He retired in 2002 and was replaced by Don Airey (born Donald Airey, June 21, 1948; keyboards), a former member of Rainbow who also played with Ozzy Osbourne and Judas Priest. Deep Purple recorded two more studio albums—*Bananas* (2003) and *Rapture of the Deep* (2005)—but has since focused its energies on touring.

In 2012, Deep Purple was nominated for the Rock and Roll Hall of Fame, a reflection of their influence on heavy metal and hard rock, and of their continuing efforts to introduce progressive elements into both styles.

Roberta Freund Schwartz

Selected Discography

Shades of Deep Purple US: Tetragrammaton T102; UK Parlophone PMC 7055 (solo); PCS 7055 (stereo), 1968.

Concerto for Group and Orchestra US: Tetragrammaton T171; UK Harvest SHVL 767, 1969.

Deep Purple in Rock US: Warner Brothers WS 1877; UK: Harvest SHVL 777, 1970.

Fireball US: Warner Brothers BS 2564; UK: Harvest SHVL793, 1971.

Machine Head US: Warner Brothers BS 2607; UK: Purple TPSA 7504, 1972.

Made in Japan US: Warner Brothers 2WS 2710, 1973; UK: Purple TPSP 351, 1972.

Burn US: Warner Brothers W2766; UK: Purple TPS 3505, 1974.

Perfect Strangers US: Mercury 284 003–1 M-1,1984; UK: Polydor POLH 16LP, 1985.

The Battle Rages On BMG/RCA 74321 15420–2, 1993.

Purpendicular BMG 7 4321 33802–2, 1996.

References

Bangs, Lester. Review, "Machine Head." *Rolling Stone* 109 (May 25, 1972), 61.

Christe, Ian. *Sound of the Beast: The Complete Headbanging History of Heavy Metal*. New York: Harper Collins, 2004.

Crowe, Cameron. "Deep Purple: Self-Evaluation Time Again." *Rolling Stone* 137 (June 21, 1973), 26.

Macan, Edward. *Rocking the Classics: English Progressive Rock and the Counterculture*. New York: Oxford University Press, 1997.

McStravick, Summer, and John Roos, eds. *Blues-Rock Explosion: From the Allman Brothers to the Yardbirds*. Mission Viejo, CA: Old Goat Publishing, 2001.

Thompson, Dave. *Smoke on the Water: The Deep Purple Story*. Toronto: ECW Press, 2004.

Zanes, Warren. *Revolutions in Sound: Warner Bros. Records, the First Fifty Years*. San Francisco: Chronicle Books, 2008.

Depeche Mode (1980–Present)

In the wake of British punk, the 1980s were marked by a shift away from guitar-based popular music and toward a synthesized sound that was spearheaded by bands like Kraftwerk, the Normal, Gary Numan, and Thomas Dolby. Depeche Mode was central to the electronic dance music known variously as New Wave, synth-pop, and alternative dance, and since their formation in 1980, they have been cited as influential by bands as diverse as the Pet Shop Boys, Linkin Park, Coldplay, the Crystal Method, and Rammstein (the latter of whom have covered Depeche Mode's "Stripped"). In one of the most recent biographies of the band, Simon Spence argued that the band's formative years in Basildon, a postwar town fabricated largely to house the families of factory workers, shaped the band's interest in synthetic, industrial sounds, and in the samples recorded from their urban environment that marked the band's later musical output. Spence argued that the band members were "lab rats in a truly alien landscape. It was no surprise that when they first made it out of Basildon, the London music press described the group as 'half-Martian'—or that, when they first found their fame, it was as part of a movement called the Futurists" (Spence, 1). That the band continues to grow and consolidate their reputation among a new generation of listeners at the time of this writing is a testament to the endurance of their music.

In 1977, the first incarnation of the band, known as "No Romance in China," comprised Vince Clarke (born Vincent John Martin, July 3, 1960; vocals, synthesizer) and Andy Fletcher (born Andrew John Leonard Fletcher, July 8, 1961; vocals, bass guitar, synthesizer), was formed at St. Nicholas School in Basildon between two friends who had become close because of their common interests in music and religion. Music was central to the fellowship at St. Paul's church in Basildon, where the pair attended weekly service, and Fletcher has suggested that this was where they learned to play music (Miller, 14). Also at St. Nicholas School, fellow student Martin Gore (born Martin Lee Gore, July 23, 1961; vocals, guitar, bass, synthesizer) had formed the band Norman and the Worms with his friend Phil Burdett. Painfully shy as a teenager, Gore hid behind his acoustic (and later electric) guitar while Burdett took the lead as the vocalist. While with the Worms, Gore experimented with songwriting and composed two songs that were later recorded by Depeche Mode: "See You" and "A Photograph of You."

After leaving high school in 1979, both Gore and Fletcher disbanded these early bands and moved to London for work, the former landing a job at Nat-West bank on Fenchurch Street and the latter working around the corner at Sun Life Insurance. While neither enjoyed their jobs, the work provided enough income to feed their growing interest in synthesized music. Within months of starting his job, and inspired by the *Billboard* success of Gary Numan's 1979 hit "Cars"

Depeche Mode helped usher in the synthesizer-heavy pop style of the mid-1980s. The group, pictured here in a studio group portrait, Berlin, July 1984, was (clockwise from top left): Dave Gahan, Alan Wilder, Andrew Fletcher, and Martin Gore. Depeche Mode's styles have included synth-pop and techno, which has allowed it to maintain a career spanning over three decades, selling over 72 million records. (Photo by Michael Putland/Getty Images)

and the Human League's 1979 synth-pop album *Reproduction*, Gore purchased a Yamaha CS5 synthesizer. Fletcher was also intrigued by the move toward the synthesizer in popular music, suggesting that, in the wake of punk, "along came these cheap monophonic synthesizers; it was like a continuation of the punk ethic: you could make new, weird sounds—without guitars" (quoted in Miller, 26). With his new interest in synthesized sounds, Gore joined forces with former classmates Clarke and Fletcher to form a new synth-pop band named Composition of Sound. The trio played three unsuccessful gigs in Basildon before they decided to look for a lead singer. Ultimately, the band settled on Dave Gahan (born David Gahan, May 9, 1962; vocals) as the ideal candidate. Completely different from his future bandmates because of his love of punk bands like the Clash, the Damned, and the Sex Pistols, Gahan held a degree in retail display from the

Southend College of Technology and was in the midst of starting his career. He spent weekends at the London punk clubs and sported a punk "look" that made him a target for street thugs in Basildon but that drew the attention of the members of Composition of Sound. Clarke explained that the band perceived Gahan as a "local fashion accessory" whose flamboyance and extroverted personality suited the role of the front man (Miller, 39). Given his interest in fashion and marketing, Gahan suggested that the band might profit from a catchier name and suggested a phrase that he had seen on the cover of a French fashion magazine, "Depeche Mode" (which translates roughly to "ready-wear").

Under this new moniker, the reconstituted band played their first live concert in May 1980 at St. Nicholas school and followed this up with a gig at a biker club in Southend. Their music was a hit for these very different audiences, and the success inspired Depeche Mode to record a demo tape that landed them a recurring spot at a small but important venue, Crocs Glamour Club in Rayleigh. As Boy George remembered, "Crocs was Southend's premier freak club . . . it drew a mixed crowd, office boys and secretaries. [Vivienne] Westwood pirate hats, rockabillies with high tops and flat tops" (quoted in Malins, 12). Boy George himself would make his first live appearance at Crocs on October 24, 1981, with his band, Culture Club. The recurring Saturday-night gig put the band in contact with Crocs' resident DJ, Stevo Pearce, who invited Depeche Mode to sign to his new record label, the curiously misspelled Some Bizzare Records. (Bizzare later signed such pivotal synth-pop bands as Soft Cell, the The, and Cabaret Voltaire.) Despite the invitation, the band opted for Mute Records in the winter of 1980, prompted by their interest in working with Mute's Daniel Miller, who was an early pioneer of synth-pop and who founded the label as a way to release his own songs, "Warm Leatherette" and "T.V.O.D," which he performed under the band name the Normal. Perhaps as a show of gratitude to Stevo for his interest in the band, Depeche Mode's first recording, the song "Photographic," was produced by Miller and released on Stevo's Some Bizzare Album collection in November 1980.

Less than a year after they formed, the band landed their first major gig at the Rainbow Club in London's Finsbury Park, where they supported Ultravox in the People's Palace Saint Valentine's Ball on February 14, 1981. Five days later, the band released their debut single for Mute, "Dreaming of Me," produced by Daniel Miller at Blackwing Studios. The single charted at number 57, which, according to biographer Jonathan Miller, "was not bad going considering Mute Records lacked the financial clout and distribution of a major label" (Miller, 63). After the release of "Dreaming of Me," the band suddenly found itself in the unique position of being courted by various A&R executives, but they opted to stay with Mute and returned to the studio to record their second single, "New Life," which was released on June 13, 1981. This song became the band's breakthrough hit, charting at number 11 on the U.K. charts and securing a place for the band on Top of the Pops. With every new success, the band upgraded its instruments, so that by 1981, Vince Clarke had replaced his Kawai K100SF with a 1978-vintage Roland Jupiter-4 that could play four notes simultaneously. (This instrument still paled in comparison to the Roland Jupiter-8 that was then in use by Duran Duran.)

By mid-1981, synth-pop had begun to dominate the British charts, and Depeche Mode's "New Life" appeared on the charts with such synth-pop hits as the Human League's "Love Action (I Believe in Love)" (which charted at number three) and Soft Cell's number-one hit, "Tainted Love." Driven by the growing momentum of synth-pop, the band entered the studio in June 1981 to work on what would become their first album, Speak & Spell. At this time, Vince Clarke was the band's principal songwriter, despite Martin Gore's early interest in songwriting, although this was soon to change. Clarke left the band after the release of the album, citing his intense dislike of publicity and media intrusion as the reason for his departure. The first single released from Speak & Spell, "Just Can't Get Enough," appeared on September 7, 1981, climbing to number eight on the U.K. Singles Charts and securing the band their second spot on Top of the Pops. During their performance the band appeared dressed in a kind of "camp S&M" look, and Gore, in a move that would define his appearance for years to come, performed shirtless, in suspenders, and with a candy-floss hairstyle. The single was also the basis for the band's first music video, and the only Depeche Mode video in which Clarke appeared with the band. To promote the album, released on October 5, 1981, Depeche Mode immediately departed for a four-date European tour of Amsterdam, Brussels, and Paris, which concluded with 14 dates in the United Kingdom.

Although Clarke left the band after *Speak & Spell*, he continued to cast his shadow over the band, particularly after forming such competitors as the highly successful synth-pop duo Yazoo (known as Yaz in the United States) with Alison Moyet and, later, the duo Erasure, with Andy Bell. In the short term, his absence was felt by Depeche Mode because they were left without a songwriter, a role that was eventually filled by Martin Gore. With Gore in his new role, the remaining trio returned to Blackwing Studios with Daniel Miller to record the band's fourth single, "See You." Released on January 29, 1982, the single rose to number six on the U.K. Singles Charts, but was overshadowed by the number-two ranking of Yazoo's "Only You" in March. To make matters worse, the April 26 release of Depeche Mode's single, "The Meaning of Love," which peaked at number 12 on the U.K. Singles Charts, was eclipsed by the release of Yazoo's second single, "Don't Go," on May 5, which soared to number three in the United Kingdom and climbed to number one on the U.S. *Billboard* chart.

Reeling from the loss of Clarke, the band issued an anonymous advertisement in *Melody Maker* for his replacement, with the stipulation that the applicant must be under 21. After two auditions, and despite being 22, Alan Wilder (born Alan Charles Wilder, June 1, 1959; synthesizer and drums), a keyboardist from London, was invited to join the band in February 1982, just in time to appear in the video of "See You," directed by Julian Temple, and to join the band on an eight-date, coast-to-coast American tour that began in New York on May 7. While the tour was marked by a variety of technical difficulties,

it was largely successful in expanding the band's American fan base. Encouraged by the tour, the band returned to London to work on their second album, *A Broken Frame*, which was released on September 27, 1982. Although Wilder had been an asset on tour, the band opted to exclude him from the album because, according to him, "they had something to prove to themselves. The three of them didn't want the press to say they'd just roped in a musician to make things easier after Vince [Clarke] left" (Miller, 134). Despite the slight, Wilder opted to stay with the band.

The single that appeared before the album was released, "Leave in Silence," and its instrumental B-side, "Excerpt from: My Secret Garden," were characterized by the darker sonic palette that eventually became a trademark of the band. At the time, however, this change in sound drew sharp criticism in the music press, where the band's attempts to engage with darker emotions were misunderstood by those who thought of the band's output merely as dance music. Further, the band continued to be dogged by comparisons to Yazoo, whose debut album, *Upstairs at Eric's* (released on August 23, a month before *A Broken Frame*), had risen to number two on the U.K. album charts and was praised for its unique merger of synth-pop and American-style R&B.

Undeterred and back in the studio, the band set to work to record their new single, "Get the Balance Right!" at the end of 1982. Released on January 31, 1983, the single performed well and charted at number 13 on the U.K. singles charts, but by the time the band began to work on the next album, *Construction Time Again*, the song was abandoned because it did not reflect the new direction in which the band was headed. Inspired by an Einstürzende Neubauten concert he attended at the time, Gore sought to experiment with industrial sounds and samples on *Construction Time Again*, such as those that were heard in the song whose lyrics gave the album its title, the third track, "Pipeline." By this time, the band's newest member, Allen Wilder, had also begun to compose songs and contributed the tracks "Two Minute Warning," "The Landscape Is Changing," and "Fools" to the new album. In recording the album, the band enlisted the Garden Studios in East London, a spot owned by John Foxx (born Dennis Leigh), formerly of Ultravox. Facing challenges in mixing the album, Daniel Miller decamped to the state-of-the-art Hansa Tonstudios in Berlin, where such albums as David Bowie's *Low* and *Heroes* had previously been recorded and mixed.

While *Construction Time Again* marked a change in the musical direction of the band, the single "Everything Counts," released on July 11, 1983, also suggested that the band was becoming more politically aware. The song served as a comment on the capitalism in Britain and was packaged in a sleeve that featured the image of a worker wielding his sledgehammer. When asked by the *New Musical Express* what the theme of construction was meant to refer to, Alan Wilder was quoted as saying that one needed to build a "whole new ways of thinking" (*NME*, September 10, 1983). Biographer Jonathan Miller has speculated that Wilder's interest in politics might have contributed to the political awareness displayed on the first album on which he was a collaborator (Miller, 170). Regardless of the reason for the band's new political stance, the single was the band's first hit since "See You," peaking at number six on the U.K. singles charts by July 23, where it remained for 11 weeks. To reflect the more industrial sound of their new album, Depeche Mode designed a new stage act for their 1983 Construction Tour, placing the band members on risers and surrounded by an elaborate light show. The British leg of the tour wrapped up in early October, after which the band toured mainland Europe through December. Everything seemed to be looking up for the band, particularly after their old rival, Yazoo, split apart when Vince Clarke decided to take a sabbatical from his collaboration with Alison Moyet in May 1983.

Although Depeche Mode had made progress in the United States, where their fan base had been growing steadily since their 1982 *Broken Frame* tour, it was not until 1984 that the band became a worldwide success. Much of this had to do with the release of the single "People Are People" on March 12, 1984, whose theme of inclusion made it a favorite with LGBT audiences, for whom the song became a kind of anthem.

The single also coincided with the 1984 Summer Olympics in Los Angeles and was used as a commentary on the Eastern Bloc boycott of the Games. Despite the important role it played in the career of Depeche Mode, the song has been dismissed by its writer, Martin Gore, as superficial, and has not been played live in concert since 1988. Nonetheless, to capitalize on the success of the single at the time, the band released the compilation album *People Are People*, available only in North America on the Sire label and featuring a mixture of such recent songs as the title track, "Told You So," and "Pipeline" from *Construction Time Again*, and the B-sides "Now This Is Fun" and "Work Hard." The album rode on the success of the single, appearing for 30 weeks on the U.S. *Billboard* Top 200 Albums Chart.

Despite the dance-like ambience of "People Are People," the album on which the song appeared, *Some Great Reward*, was a further step in the band's experimentation with sampling. In preparation for *Some Great Reward*, the band continued to record outdoor sounds and also frequented Hamleys toy shop in London, where they recorded sounds made by various toy instruments. The album was recorded throughout the summer at Music Works in London, mixed at Hansa in Berlin, and released in the United Kingdom on September 24, 1984. The band's promotional single, "Master and Servant," was released a month earlier and showed that while the band might have abandoned the political tone of their third album, their music continued to explore darker themes, in this case about sexuality and interpersonal relationships. With its sampling of synthesized whip and chain sounds and its overt lyrical references to sado-masochism, the song was banned on some American radio stations, but nonetheless entered the U.S. *Billboard* Hot 100 Chart at number 87. Three days after the release of *Some Great Reward,* the band launched a punishing worldwide tour that began in the United Kingdom and took them through Europe, Canada, the United States, and Japan before returning to Europe in the summer of 1985. By this time, the band had become a worldwide sensation, selling out the 3,500-seat Hollywood Palladium show, slated for March 30, 1985, within

15 minutes and forcing promoters to change the venue for the March 31st show to the 10,000-seat Irvine Meadows Amphitheater.

Despite their newfound financial success, the band returned to work almost immediately after the tour concluded at the end of July and booked themselves into the Genetic Studios, owned by former Human League producer Martin Rushent. Their first effort, the single titled "It's Called a Heart," proved to be a divisive issue between the band and Mute's publicists. Martin Gore argued that the song belied the band's interest in sampling and industrial noise. He claims that "we'd worked diligently to build up recognition for a harder sound, with more depth and maturity, and here was this ultra-poppy number that did nothing for our reputations" (Miller, 205). Instead, the band had hoped to release the single's B-side, "Fly on the Windscreen," but that idea was rejected by Mute publicists because the song began with the word "death" and was therefore too dark in tone for most audiences, in their view.

While "It's Called a Heart" was omitted from the band's next album, *Black Celebration*, "Windscreen" was remixed with new effects (like the sound of a power drill and the voice of Daniel Miller saying, "Over and done with"); it was released as the second track on the album and renamed "Fly on the Windscreen— Final." Featuring samples drawn from such diverse sources as a car ignition, fireworks, and aerosol cans, *Black Celebration* was released on March 17, 1986. As Andy Fletcher later noted regarding producing the album, "We had this theory at the time that every sound must be different, and you must never use the same sound twice" (Miller, 212). In the making of *Black Celebration*, and in its subsequent promotional tour, the band took little time off and the strain was beginning to show, particularly in the studio, where Daniel Miller and the recording engineer Gareth Jones reworked each track multiple times to capture a particular "vibe" on the album.

By the end of production, Miller decided that Depeche Mode was demanding too much of his time, and he opted to redirect his focus to the management of Mute in general, and Vince Clarke's new duo, Erasure, in particular. After the *Black Celebration* promotional tour, which began on March 29, 1986, and ended on August 16, the band also decided to take a break, as Martin Gore moved into a house in London's Maida Vale neighborhood and Dave Gahan and his wife celebrated the arrival of their first child. Alan Wilder, having moved to Hampstead, set up a 16-track home studio and began to experiment with a set of Depeche Mode samples, releasing an album titled *1+2* under the pseudonym Recoil. This work was followed by the album *Hydrology*. Both albums established Wilder as a pioneer in pop electronica. Unfortunately, Wilder had little time to promote either album, since his obligations to Depeche Mode kept him busy as the band planned for their next album, *Music for the Masses*, released on September 28 1987. Having lost Daniel Miller as their producer, the band enlisted David Bascombe, who had just finished recording Peter Gabriel's smash hit *So*.

Music for the Masses was considered the band's most polished album and, according to Robert Dimery, was "the album with which Depeche Mode bade farewell to their embryonic electro-pop and embraced the sound that inspired goth gonks and dance pioneers alike" (Dimrey, 568). The album cemented the band's reputation in America, where the *Music for the Masses* tour was documented in the film *Depeche Mode 101*, produced by Don Allen Pennebaker, who was renowned for his behind-the-scenes documentary about Bob Dylan's 1965 U.K. tour and his film about the 1967 Monterey Rock Festival. Here, the viewer can see the extent to which the band was admired by the enormous audiences who filled every American venue in which they played. Oddly, however, the band failed to receive the same critical acclaim in Britain, where, as Dimrey has argued, they continued to be viewed as "peculiar pop stars."

The American obsession with Depeche Mode continued into the 1990s, when the band's release party for the next album *Violator*, drew 30,000 fans to Wherehouse Records in Los Angeles, five of whom were hospitalized in the crush to see the band. Called "sophisticated but soulful" and "beautifully produced" by Dimrey, the album was produced by Mark "Flood"

Ellis and Alan Wilder, who worked and reworked the sounds and samples on a song that would become the album's first single, "Personal Jesus." Released on August 29, 1989, the success of the single garnered a spot for the band on *Top of the Pops*. The duo was equally attentive to the details on the remaining tracks of the album, which was slow to appear and was eventually released on March 19, 1990. *Violator* entered the *Billboard* Top 100 chart just three weeks after its release, where it remained for 74 weeks, and was the first Depeche Mode album to sell over a million copies in the United States. The band's follow-up album, *Songs of Faith and Devotion* (released on March 22, 1993), was even more successful, soaring to first position on the U.K. and U.S. charts and selling close to a million albums in the United States.

Despite their growing success, the band had rarely taken any time away from their careers, and after the *Devotion* tour of 1993, the strain on the band was beginning to show. Andy Fletcher had already experienced a nervous breakdown, while Gore was battling alcoholism and Gahan had become addicted to heroin. Disillusioned with his bandmates, Alan Wilder left in 1995 and shifted his focus to the Re-coil project that he had begun eight years earlier. By the mid-1990s, the future of Depeche Mode looked grim. However, by 1997, Gahan had cleaned himself up after an overdose, and the trio began to work on their ninth album (and their first as a trio since *A Broken Frame*), *Ultra*, produced by Tim Simenon (who has also worked with Björk, David Bowie, and Massive Attack), was released on April 14, 1997. The rerelease of the album in 2007 was also accompanied by a documentary on the making of *Ultra*, titled *Depeche Mode 95–98 (Oh well, that's the end of the band . . .)*, on which each member of the band reflected on Wilder's departure, Gahan's near-fatal overdose, and his rehabilitation. Despite the obstacles posed by their personal problems, the band has endured, and continues to record and release albums, but at the slower pace of one album every four years. In 2001, the band released *Exciter*, produced by Mark Bell (who had worked with Björk). The album peaked in the ninth position in the U.K. albums charts and eighth position in the U.S. *Billboard* 200, and launched the band's *Exciter* tour.

The 2005 release of *Playing the Angel* fared even better on the charts, debuting at number six in the United Kingdom and number seven in the United States. The band's most recent album to date, 2009's *Sounds of the Universe*, rated better still, climbing to second position on the U.K. charts and to third position in the United States. The album also garnered a nomination for Best Alternative Album at the Fifty-Second Grammy Awards, held on January 31, 2010. Gahan's solo career also took off in the 2000s, and he has released the albums *Paper Monsters* (2003), *Hourglass* (2007), and *The Light the Dead See* (2012). Shortly after its release, *Hourglass* topped the U.S. Top Electronic Albums chart. Martin Gore also recently engaged in solo work, recording a set of 11 covers of songs that were influential in his development as a musician. Released on April 28, 2003, under the title *Counterfeit*, the album ranges from covers of Kurt Weill and Nick Cave to David Bowie and John Lennon. The band returned to the studio to record their 13th album, *Delta Machine*, which was released on March 22, 2013. The *Delta Machine* world tour extended from May 2013 through March 2014.

In a career that now spans over three decades, Depeche Mode is often cited as a central influence in the areas of techno and synth-pop. In recent years, the band has garnered interest among a surprising range of artists, who have covered many of Depeche Mode's more successful singles. Although artists who have covered Depeche Mode songs are far too numerous to list, the more memorable ones include RuPaul (who released a cover of "People Are People" in 2006), Coldplay (who pay tribute to Depeche Mode's "Enjoy the Silence" in the 2008 video for "Viva la Vida"), Hilary Duff (who quotes from "Personal Jesus" in the 2008 song "Reach Out"), Johnny Cash, and Marilyn Manson (both of whom released covers of the song "Personal Jesus" in 2003 and 2004, respectively). Further, the Depeche Mode tribute album titled *For the Masses* was released in 1998 and featured covers by such well-known bands as the Smashing Pumpkins, the Cure, Hooverphonic, and Deftones (among others). While covers provide one measure of the band's influence, one might also look more broadly at the many musical genres (and the bands that mark them) that owe an enormous debt to the brand of techno-pop pioneered by Depeche Mode. Genres that make extensive or exclusive use of electronic instruments, like techno, trip-hop, electronica, big beat, or breakbeat, trace a clear lineage to Depeche Mode, while bands as varied as Hooverphonic, the Killers, Linkin Park, and Pet Shop Boys have cited their interest in the band as formative to their own work. As noted on the gatefold for the collector's edition of the 2007 LP reissue of *Music for the Masses*, the band has sold over 72 million records and played to an audience of over 30 million, and remain "one of the most highly regarded and passionately supported groups in modern music."

Karen Fournier

Selected Discography

Speak and Spell, UK release, Mute Stumm4, 1981, US release, Sire SRK3652, 1981.

A Broken Frame, UK release, Mute Stumm9, 1982, US release, Sire 23751–1, 1982.

Construction Time Again, UK release, Mute Stumm13, 1983, US release, Sire, 23900–1, 1983.

People Are People, US release, Sire 1–25124, 1984.

Some Great Reward, UK release, Mute Stumm19, 1984, US release, Sire 25194–1, 1984.

Black Celebration, UK release, Mute Stumm26, 1986, US release, Sire 9 25429–1, 1986.

Music for the Masses, UK release, Mute Stumm47, 1987, US release, Sire 25614–1, 1987.

101, UK release, Mute Stumm101, 1989, US release, Sire WI-25853, 1989.

Violator, UK release, Mute Stumm64, 1990, US release, Sire 26091–1, 1990.

Songs of Faith and Devotion, UK release, Mute Stumm106, 1993, US release, Sire/Reprise 9–45243–2, 1993.

Ultra, UK release, Mute Stumm148, 1997, US release, Reprise 9–46522–2, 1997.

Exciter, UK release, Mute Stumm190, 2001, US release, Reprise 9–47960–2, 2001.

Playing the Angel, UK release, Mute Stumm260, 2005, US release, Reprise 2–49348, 2005.

Sounds of the Universe, UK release, Mute Stumm300, 2009, US release, Capitol 50999–6–96770, 2009.

References

Blythe, Daniel. *An Encyclopedia of Classic 80s Pop.* London: Alison and Busby Ltd, 2002.

Capuzzo, Guy. "Neo-Riemannian Theory and the Analysis of Pop-Rock Music." *Music Theory Spectrum* 26/2 (Fall 2004): 177–200.

Dimery, Robert, ed. *1001 Albums You Must Hear Before You Die.* New York: Universe, 2005.

Gahan, Dave. *Depeche Mode and the Second Coming.* London: Independent Music Press, 2009.

Kinder, Marsha. "Music Video and the Spectator: Television, Ideology, and Dream." *Film Quarterly* 38/1 (Fall 1984): 2–15.

Malins, Steve. *Depeche Mode: Black Celebration: A Biography.* Innsbruck, Austria: Hannibal Verlag, 2007.

Miller, Jonathan. *Stripped: Depeche Mode.* London: Omnibus Press, 2003.

Rideout, Ernie, Stephen Fortner, and Michael Gallant, eds. *Keyboard Presents the Best of the '80s: The Artists, Instruments, and Techniques of an Era.* Milwaukee, WI: Hal Leonard, 2008.

Rule, Greg. *Electro-Shock! Groundbreakers of Synth Music.* San Francisco: Miller Freeman Books, 1999.

Spence, Simon. *Just Can't Get Enough: The Making of Depeche Mode.* London: Jawbone Press, 2011.

Devo (1973–Present)

Among the many contradictory sayings that Devo adopted as guiding doctrines, perhaps none more aptly sums them up than "The beginning was the end." Devo is a band that seemed to ignite nearly overnight in the public consciousness, only to flame out at what should have been the peak of their career. In true phoenix fashion, the band stunned naysayers by dusting off their iconic red "energy-dome" hats to record their most ferocious record in 2010, perhaps having the last laugh after all by claiming that the

New Wave punk music group Devo pose for a portrait ca. 1979. The synth-pop band was founded on the concept that humankind was on a downward spiral of entropy. Regardless, songs such as "Whip It" have kept them popular for over 30 years. (Photo by Richard Creamer/Michael Ochs Archives/Getty Images)

preceding 30 years only proved their philosophy of de-evolution. And that "perhaps" was only included because if there is one overriding truth about Devo, it is this: truth is a slippery concept, and any seeming fact that might be uttered by one band member is immediately repudiated by another.

The origins of these synth-pop oddballs can be traced back to the shootings at Kent State University on May 4, 1970. According to founding member Jerry Casale (born Gerald Vincent Pizzute, July 28, 1948; vocals, bass, synthesizer), an art major who counted two of the massacred students among his personal friends, the shootings "completely changed me from some kind of free-love, pot-smoking hippie into a very politicized person that had a new agenda, and a new well-founded anger" (Casale 1995). Casale's new anger spilled over into a vengeful mistrust of the media, especially as the story got twisted around and reported as *students* killing National Guardsmen. Associates of Casale's at the time regard the incident as cementing his beliefs, rather than being their origin, and in fact Casale was already peripherally involved with the Kent State University chapter of 1970s campus radicals Students for a Democratic Society. Either way, Casale used the shootings to ramp up the shock value of his artistic output, and Devo certainly became an outgrowth of his efforts.

Casale was friends with many of Akron's disenfranchised artists, but the relationship that fueled the idea of forming a band to explore his philosophies was the one he forged with another Kent State art student, Mark Mothersbaugh (born Mark Allen Mothersbaugh, May 18, 1950; vocals). Mothersbaugh and Casale became friends in 1972 almost as a matter of course: the two were northeast Ohio natives attending the same university and majoring in the same subject. Both were delicious oddities: Mothersbaugh wrote snippets of alternative verse, prose, and lyrics, embellished them with his drawings, and published the whole lot as a quasi-autobiography titled *My Struggle*. Casale was a more overt performance artist who created a masked character called Gorj; towing his costumed accomplice "Pootman" on all fours, the two would crash area art shows and render their inevitably harsh judgments. Casale and Mothersbaugh were also both instrumentalists, and had separately performed with many local bands. The two ultimately enrolled in an experimental art class being offered at Kent state, which, at that time, "had a really progressive faculty . . . bringing most of the interesting young filmmakers, sculptors, and artists from the East Coast" (Dellinger 2003). Two members of this progressive faculty were charged with assembling an arts festival in the spring of 1973, and it was for this event that the musical portion of "project Devo" was born.

The conceptual identity surrounding Devo included many aspects, but perhaps the most overriding one—indeed, the one from which their name is derived—is a philosophy that humankind is on a downward spiral of entropy: de-evolution, instead of evolution. An early use of the term "devolution" comes from an odd pamphlet first published in the mid-1920s titled "Jocko-Homo Heavenbound." This antievolution tract, introduced to the Devo mix by

Mothersbaugh, featured a drawing of a devil with "devolution" emblazoned across his chest; the author went on a 31-page rant of slippery-slope logic, determining that "rudimentary organs prove that equipment not used . . . becomes atrophied. THIS IS NOT EVOLUTION, it is the *opposite*. Show us a species that is *in the making*. Show us how to grow wings where there are none" (Shadduck 1924). Mothersbaugh and Casale applied this concept to society and politics at large; making the case that human beings began in a state of near perfection, and have declined at an accelerating pace: hence, the beginning was the end. Casale, with his Pootman-and-Gorj bit, showed his disdain for modern art he felt was "devolved." For the arts festival, he and Mothersbaugh could add a musical element to their philosophy, merging the visual and the aural for a multimedia barrage of devolvement.

Devo's first concert—performed as a sextet—was set for April 18, 1973. There were stalwarts Casale, on bass, and Mothersbaugh, on electronic keyboards. Jerry's brother Bob (born Robert Casale, July 14, 1952; keyboard, rhythm guitar), soon to be reborn as "Bob2" in Devo, was recruited to play guitar, as was his longtime friend Bob Lewis. Other local Kent musicians filled out the roster on vocals and drums, with an end result that was "calculated to both attract and repel . . . challenge and provoke" (Dellinger, 2003). A full year would pass before Devo performed again, this time as a quartet that included Mark's brother Jim on a bizarre set of electronic drums. Throughout the whole of this period, the band was more concerned with demonstrating a deconstructed (or, devolved) version of what a rock band ought to sound like. Likewise, the members were not necessarily focused on being a "band" at all, merely using the forum of the festivals to promote one version of their artistic vision.

The idea of being a band—in the truest sense of working musicians looking to be paid professionally for what they do—began to solidify throughout 1975. Mark's brother Bob (born Robert Leroy Mothersbaugh, August 11, 1952; guitar) came onboard as the guitar-playing "Bob1," and Mark and Jerry eliminated the need for a lead vocalist by sharing singing duties.

Still, their attempts to break into the music business were thwarted at every turn by executives and industry insiders who simply could not comprehend the electric bleeps and bloops that Devo was trying to pass off as music. This is the beginning of one of the legendary paradoxes about Devo: even while searching for acceptance, the band heaped scorn on those too "devolved" to understand the music. This was a band set on attaining musical success via knocking rock stars off their lofty perches. Matters were not helped by the fact that the group went about at all hours wearing rubber masks, even billing themselves at gigs as their alter egos: Booji Boy (pronounced "boogie"), the Chinaman, Jungle Jim, and so forth.

This erasure of individual identity was a strong undercurrent in the group: much as their contemporaries in KISS, Devo performed in costumes, never street clothes. Unlike KISS, however, who sought to glorify their individuality even while assuming anonymity, Devo wanted to subsume the entire idea of individualism: no matter if the outfit was blue coveralls augmented with hard hats, yellow janitorial suits with 3D specs, or silver lamé jackets with red flowerpot hats, the group was always dressed identically. Even diehard fans during the group's heyday period would have been hard-pressed to accurately name the members in a photo. To maintain their image, Devo went a step further, halting the issuance of any personal information or detail that did not pertain to the concept of the group and its philosophies. Confirming whether or not Devo was intended to be a joke—and if so, if it was even a funny one—was becoming increasingly difficult.

As purveyors of a multimedia artistic assault, Devo was well aware of the power of movies, and in 1976 they produced the short conceptual film *In the Beginning: The Truth About De-evolution*. Part music video, part expressionist art film, *In the Beginning* interlaced segments of quirky dialog and stilted acting with lip-synched performance. Devo entered the movie in juried art festivals, where it was the unlikely first-prize winner of the short film category in the 1977 Ann Arbor Art Festival. The film represented a culmination of Devo's aspirations to combine various veins of art, and they went on to be pioneers in the dawning era of MTV and music videos. Mothersbaugh recalled in 1982 that "the next thing you knew, there were hundreds of bad videos that were blatant copies of Devo's concept film," an influence that would spread over 1980s bands like Human League and A Flock of Seagulls (Bahadur 1982).

By 1977, Devo was being hailed as a legitimate band, and their classic lineup of Casale, Mothersbaugh, and respective brothers Bob2 and Bob1 was cemented with the addition of drummer Alan Myers (birthplace and date unknown). Myers came to the band from a musical tradition deeply rooted in the avant-garde, counting experimental composers Arnold Schoenberg and Edgard Varèse as influences, as well as the eclectic saxophone musings of John Coltrane. Musically the group was moving away from the sort of junkyard electronic noise that Casale favored to a more streamlined quasi-pop based on the superior songwriting strengths of Mothersbaugh, who was quickly becoming the "star" of the group. Main-act gigs in Cleveland were becoming more frequent, and the ascendancy of punk rock swept up Devo and deposited them at high-visibility gigs at landmark New York City clubs CBGB's and Max's Kansas City. While the band maintained a public adherence to their devolved philosophy, some peers questioned this devotion as a publicity stunt designed to attract press: their Cleveland peers in Pere Ubu denounced the devolution "theory" as "vacuous, populist and cynical to a repulsive and unnecessary degree. Devo wanted a career more than anything else" (Dellinger 2003).

With a full slate of material, Devo went shopping for a record deal . . . only to discover that the record companies were about to start an all-out bidding war for what was being deemed the "next big thing."

Devo thus represents a circumstance nearly unique in the music business: a band that had existed for four years, but had comparatively few gigs to their credit, became the focal point of several high-caliber record companies. Sire, Elektra/Asylum, A&M, and Columbia all called to express interest, but when the dust settled Warner Bros. had secured recording rights to the band in the United States, with Island representing them overseas. The band entered the studio with famed producer Brian Eno in tow, and their resultant debut record *Q: Are We Not Men? A: We Are Devo!* emerged in late 1978 as a quirky synthesis of Kraftwerk-style electronic art music and catchy guitar-driven rock. All their earliest material was represented, from the de-volution manifesto "Jocko Homo" (paying homage to the influential Shadduck pamphlet with the lines "they tell us that/we lost our tails/evolving up from lit-tle snails") to the aberrant jab at chromosomal defor-mity that was "Mongoloid." Also present was Devo's soulless cover of the Rolling Stones "(I Can't Get No) Satisfaction," with a downbeat no sane human could hope to find. Reaction to the album was mixed, with praise and barbs often coming from the same source. *Rolling Stone* magazine opined that "it's impossible to tell whether these guys are satirizing robot-like regi-mentation or glorifying it . . . its shriveling, ice-cold absurdism might not define the Seventies as much as jump the gun on the Eighties" (Carson 1978).

A second album, *Duty Now for the Future*, quickly followed in 1979, containing many songs Devo had already been performing live. Sounding much like its predecessor, critics were less enthusiastic about giving the band any benefit of the doubt, with one writer not-ing that "repeated exposure to the band's music only serves to expose its hollowness and the absence of any real emotion" (Morris 1979). This may have been De-vo's point all along, with their nihilistic penchant for a deconstructed blues form combined with a desire both for acceptance and to change the way that audi-ences perceived what counted as acceptable. Casale and Mothersbaugh may have seen themselves as high-brow stylists making art, but the music industry was more interested in *music*: "Devo regurgitates slogans and clichés without thinking much about their mean-ing . . . the group is compelling only to those without the intellectual vigor to penetrate the band's surface pose" (Marsh 1979).

As a testament to the now-extinct power of 1970s-era record companies, it was Devo's third album that finally cemented their cultural significance. Current bands have little choice but to produce a hit their first time out; there are no second chances. In the heyday of A&R people working to foster a band until the music caught on, groups like Devo were given the opportunity to build a fan base and refine their craft. Thus it was Devo's 1980 record that ignited a world wide conflagration. The title track from *Freedom of Choice* maintained the group's devotion to their phi-losophy of societal entropy, implying that people claim to want the freedom to choose when in fact they want the exact opposite. Likewise, "Gates of Steel" brought up devolution again by insisting that "the be-ginning was the end of everything, now/the ape re-gards his tail: he's stuck on it." The sparkling energy of "Girl U Want," rooted in a churning electric guitar ostinato, belied the dark suffering of the boy who des-perately wanted the unattainable girl. But the breakout runaway hit of the pack was the infectious urgency of "Whip It." Reaching number 14 on the *Billboard* charts, the song was wedded to the incongruous video imagery of the band frolicking among cowboys at a barn dance, with every whip crack in the song de-livered visually to a woman whose clothes are slowly stripped away by the lashing. MTV eventually banned the video, misconstruing the group's stated purpose of showing a "mockery of mainstream, narrow-minded misogyny" for the real thing (Dellinger 2003).

Nevertheless, a hit single drives album sales, and *Freedom* rocketed off shelves, achieving gold status within six months of its release. Singer/songwriter Beck commented on the impact the album had on him: "I wasn't sure if they were an army, a gang, or a specialized task force of geological engineers; what-ever they were . . . there was something so satisfying about their regimented chaos" (Dellinger 2003). An intense tour followed, with Devo either electrifying or bewildering audiences in seemingly equal measure. Their stop in Petaluma, California, was recorded and eventually issued in 2005 as *Devo: Live 1980*, and to watch the film now is to be imbued with wonder at their success. There was virtually no stage show at all, aside from a lighting scheme that seemed designed to make the members seem as ugly as possible. Coor-dinated movements among the members recalled the Motown-era synchronization of dance moves á la the Supremes, only as realized by zombies on acid. Mark

Mothersbaugh, now mostly freed from his instrumental duties, jerked across the stage in movements that deliberately eschewed the lead-singer godhood of a Robert Plant or Paul Stanley in favor of a heavily bespectacled look that seemed to resemble an ersatz Buddy Holly. It is no wonder that audiences rarely knew what to make of them: nothing so preposterous could possibly be serious, yet Devo ran through their set with a grim, stone-faced intensity.

Devo were now certifiable stars, but with that stardom came an insistence from Warner Bros. for another hit like "Whip It." The band, still working on devolving what they saw as the self-indulgence of modern rock, moved to eliminate both guitars *and* drums entirely from their next album, *New Traditionalists*. Casale had long felt that such instruments were a detriment to the music Devo desired to make, saying, "It's real limiting to have to use guitars and basses to get at new ideas because the instruments themselves determine musical form . . . in time we'll probably get rid of guitars" (Springer 1979). This shedding of traditional instruments, however, led to extreme dissatisfaction with drummer Alan Myers, who would perform on the subsequent tour but was largely overshadowed in the studio by the use of a Linn drum machine in his place. In spite of the single "Beautiful World" and a ramped-up version of "Working in a Coal Mine" for the *Heavy Metal* soundtrack, Devo had begun to flounder, with at least some of the blame being placed on the utter lack of emotion delivered by the synthesized music.

Oh No! It's Devo was released in late 1982, and the tour that followed featured a multimedia breakthrough of sorts: the band had largely pioneered technology that allowed them to play in synch with video imagery projected onto a screen behind them. The result sometimes worked and sometimes did not, but even when it did, audiences were mostly left scratching their heads. Devo's message, if in fact there ever *was* intended to be a serious message, was now completely passing their audience by. The band's public appearances were also creating confusion, as can be seen in their May 1983 appearance on *Late Night with David Letterman*. Casale attempted to answer Letterman's inquiries about devolution in a serious manner, but Mothersbaugh seemed intent on cracking wise and enjoying himself; at one point, he turned his costume collar upside down to demonstrate how it could be used to hold chips and salsa.

If *Oh No!* bordered on being a commercial flop, its 1984 follow-up record, *Shout*, was an outright disaster. Bowing once again to pressure from Casale to limit what he felt were "obsolete" guitars, the album compounded the soulless aspect of synthesizers with a vocal delivery that was nearly obscured by heavy reverb. This aspect made Devo sound more like *followers* of 1980s-era Brit-pop, rather than originators. The sound was watered-down, computerized Duran Duran, who had already scored big back-to-back hits with *Rio* and *Seven and the Ragged Tiger*. Devo's influence was clear across a broad spectrum of New Wave bands, but by embracing an ideal so far outside the established traditions of rock, they were "trapped in a corner of their own making . . . (without) the conventional 'comeback' devices to rely on" (Dellinger 2003). Truly, then: the beginning was the end, with a band who only seven years earlier had been at the center of a bidding war among record companies now pathetically limping along.

With Myers's dissatisfaction at the use of drum machines leading to his departure, and Bob1's admitted cocaine addiction, the band was breaking apart. Mothersbaugh released a solo album and began a successful new career in film composing, beginning with the music for the otherworldly television show *Pee-wee's Playhouse,* and moving on to do music for the *Rugrats* cartoon, plus nearly 20 feature films in the 1990s alone. Casale stayed peripherally associated with the music world by working as a video director in the later 1980s. When new label Enigma picked the band up in 1988 for the release of *Total Devo*, the end result was not only a washed-out dance record, but also the complete annihilation of the band's career. Mothersbaugh recalled in 2010 that "[Enigma] were our own jetliner, along with 20 other bands, that we all got to ride in to a crash landing almost immediately after we signed with them" (Greene 2010). One more album followed, 1990's *Smooth Noodle Maps,* continuing the now-established trend of anonymous synth-pop. The record-buying public had moved on, and with Enigma first being acquired by Capitol, only to be merged with Restless Records, there was no stable footing—or money—to be of any help to the band. Limited tours for both records saw Devo reduced to playing in clubs, including one old Cleveland haunt where the band had first begun to break on their climb to the top.

And that was pretty much that. Or, it ought to have been, but Devo maintained a limited cultural significance by engaging in one-off performances, buoyed by a two-disc collection titled *Greatest Hits* and *Greatest Misses*. These occasional live cameos reached their apex with a brief stint on the Lollapalooza Tour of 1996, which Devo joined as part of a quasi-reunion tour. More Lollapalooza dates followed in 1997, with the band reaching deep into their back catalog and giving fans everything they wanted, from the yellow janitor suits to the red energy-dome hats. Casale mused, "More people are interested now than were then . . . there's a lot of people that have these fond memories of Devo" (Dellinger 2003). This latent, almost after-the-fact interest in the band led Mothersbaugh to invite the two Bobs to take part in a recording project under the name the Wipeouters, whose 2001 CD *P'Twaaang!!!* featured Devo-styled synthesized surf music.

Devo's reputation and influence were noteworthy among a narrow band of other musical acts, most notably New Wave–inspired artists of the 1980s. After beginning as a theatrical art–music ensemble in the 1970s, Oingo Boingo, under the leadership of Danny Elfman, evolved in the 1980s to spawn several Devo-influenced hits, chiefly "Weird Science," which combined the robotic undercurrents Devo favored with Mothersbaugh's almost melody-less vocal delivery. Like Mothersbaugh as well, Elfman eventually moved into the lucrative sphere of composing music for films and television. Always one to embrace both the ridiculous *and* the theatrical, Weird Al Yankovic released his self-penned parody song "Dare to Be Stupid" in 1985, which, in video form especially, pays homage to the aural and visual style of Devo. And, in 1999,

Barenaked Ladies performed their song "Some Fantastic" solely on keytars, dressed uniformly in Devo-inspired worksuits. Thus, while Devo's odd deference to the concept of devolution might be limited solely to themselves, the sound and style of the group appears in often unexpected ways across generations of later bands.

As the 2000s progressed, a wave of nostalgia began to combine with a societal sense that devolution, as predicted by Devo, might actually have been eerily prescient. The political "hollowing-out" of centrist ideology, the replacement of scripted television drama with eye-rolling "reality" TV, the general sense that "things" were getting worse instead of better . . . a whole host of socio-political attributes were making Devo's once-bizarre philosophy seem normal, even quaint, and certainly right on the money. And so, against all common logic, talk began among band members about the possibility of recording a new album.

A first step was taken to test the musical waters by releasing a single in 2007. "Watch Us Work It" had all the hallmarks of early, classic Devo: still synthesizers, but guitars were now heavily back in the mix, and the needless echo-y reverb of the later 1980s was dismissed in favor of a return to the über-dry sound of the first two albums. The song proved to be a hit, especially when it was used for a series of Dell computer commercials. Although the drum track was sampled from "Super Thing," a song off of Devo's 1981 *New Traditionalists* album, session drummer Josh Freese (born in Orlando, Florida, December 25, 1972), who had already worked on and off with Devo since the late 1990s Lollapalooza gigs, came onboard for the follow-up full-length album. Released by Devo's original label Warner Bros. in 2010, *Something for Everybody* became an unlikely hit for these now–senior citizen band members. Casale, Mothersbaugh, and the two Bobs delivered an album full of urgent intensity, sounding decades younger than their actual years.

Ultimately, *Something* came across as the logical successor to *Freedom of Choice,* as if the intervening 30 years had simply not happened. *Rolling Stone* magazine gave the record 3½ stars in its review, noting that it "[combined] the punk-funk fury of Devo's earliest recordings with synth pop . . . this ninth disc is frantic and wall-to-wall catchy" (Walters 2010). Certainly the Internet era allowed Devo easier access to a willing audience: self-promotion on their official website and Facebook chatter built up a critical mass of interest that then spilled over to the public at large, resulting in the biggest surge of interest in the band since their early 1980s heyday. However, while the band remained a working unit enjoying a fresh burst of popularity, individual artistic endeavors remained, especially the film and television projects of Mothersbaugh who, in addition to wide-ranging scoring contributions, also hosts a "how-to-draw" feature on Nick Jr.'s outlandish TV show *Yo Gabba Gabba!*

This late-era Devo still adheres to the concept of anonymous uniformity, but the effect is gentler now. Professional TV appearances, such as their June 2010 performance on *The Late Show with David Letterman,* still show the band performing in upscale stage costumes, complete with masks; "regular" gigs on the *Something* tour, however, gave the band a chance to relax a little in, say, matching Hawaiian tops or silk-screened T-shirts. The energy domes are still there, though, in red *and* blue, and audiences no longer seem quite so confused about their meaning. Are they otherworldly devices capable of channeling energy to the wearer, or are they simply iconic Devo hats from that great album of the early 1980s? Who cares? The message of devolution, ever present at the core of the band's philosophy, has taken a backseat to a good-time rock show, and the members do not seem particularly bothered by it; they are happy to be back in the spotlight once again at this unlikely late date. Hell, maybe this was all part of the master plan of Casale and company all along; come to think of it, that kind of a plan would be *particularly* Devo.

Scott Harding

Selected Discography

Q: Are We Not Men? A: We Are Devo!, Warner Bros. 521441, 1978.

Freedom of Choice, Warner Bros. 521442, 1980.

DEV-O Live, Warner Bros. MINI 3548, 1981.

New Traditionalists, Warner Bros. BSK 3595, 1981.

Now It Can Be Told: Devo at the Palace, Restless 772755–2, 1989.

Greatest Hits, Warner Bros. 926449–2, 1990.

P'Twaaang!!! (as The Wipeouters), Tone Casualties XOCD 0158, 2001.

Devo Live 1980, Target Video 4442, 2005.

Something for Everybody, Warner Bros. 9362496604, 2010.

Live 1981 Seattle, Booji Boy Records LP-BOOJI-001, 2012.

References

Azerrad, Michael. "Total Devo." *Rolling Stone* 532 (August 11, 1988): 82–83.

Bahadur, Raj. "A Spudboy Speaks His Mind." *Scene* (November 18–24, 1982): 9.

Carson, Tom. "Evolving with Devo: Are We Not Amused?" *Rolling Stone* 279 (November 30, 1978): 63–64.

Dellinger, Jade, and David Giffels. *We Are Devo!* London: SAF Publishing, 2003.

Goldberg, Michael. "Devo: Sixties Idealists or Nazis and Clowns?" *Rolling Stone* 358 (December 10, 1981): 68–70.

Greene, Andy. "Inside Devo's Weird Return." www.rollingstone.com (June 21, 2010).

Maerth, Oscar Kiss. *The Beginning Was the End*. New York: Praeger, 1974.

Marsh, Dave. "Devo Destroyed." *Rolling Stone* 300 (September 20, 1979): 98.

Miller, Debby. "Oh No! It's Devo!" *Rolling Stone* 389 (February 17, 1983): 55.

Morris, Chris. "Devo's New Nuremberg Rally." *Rolling Stone* 299 (September 6, 1979): 68.

Peck, Abe. "Devo: Mutants from Akron." *Rolling Stone* 283 (January 25, 1979): 26–27.

Shadduck, B. H. *Jocko-Homo Heavenbound*, 5th ed. Rogers, OH: Jocko-Homo Publishing Co., 1924.

Springer, Cole, et al. "Devo: Future of Rock or Total Crock?" *Trouser Press* 35 (January 1979): 14–18.

Walters, Barry. "Something for Everybody." *Rolling Stone* 1106 (June 10, 2010): 78.

Willman, Chris. "Devo Comeback Disc Gets Assist from LCD Soundsystem." *Rolling Stone* 1080 (June 11, 2009): 30.

Wolk, Douglas. "Pioneers Who Got Scalped." *Rolling Stone* 842 (June 8, 2000): 120–22.

The Doors (1965–1973)

In addition to the Beatles, the Rolling Stones, and the Who, perhaps no band better personified the spirit of the 1960s better than the Doors (1965–1973).

The band's unique sound (vocals, guitar, drums, keyboards), thought-provoking and controversial lyrics, and thrilling (often chaotic) live performances seemed to channel the spirit of revolution and change expressed by the 1960s counterculture. In fact, because the Doors—particularly their lead singer Jim Morrison—enjoyed dissolving musical, artistic, and cultural barriers, the Doors can also be credited with foreshadowing later punk and alternative movements in the late 1970s and early 1990s, respectively. Like the aforementioned British bands, the Doors conveyed

The Doors, pictured here ca. 1970, created a unique style that combined thought-provoking and controversial lyrics tempered by mesmerizing and improvisatory organ and guitar work. The group was (from left to right): John Densmore, Robby Krieger, Ray Manzarek, and Jim Morrison. Together, the four enjoyed a meteoric rise to fame marked by induction into the Rock and Roll Hall of Fame in 1993. (Photo by Michael Ochs Archives/Getty Images)

a sound that reflected a deep knowledge of and respect for the blues, but also infused an appreciation of contemporaneous jazz artists like John Coltrane and Miles Davis, as well as classical masters Bach and Chopin. Since their debut album in 1967, the Doors have gone on to sell over 100 million copies of their albums worldwide and they put Elektra Records on the map by becoming the first American band to accumulate eight consecutive gold records. Moreover, they continue to enjoy considerable airplay on classic rock radio stations across the country. Finally, contemporary groups such as Aerosmith, Jane's Addiction, Pearl Jam, and Linkin Park all consider the Doors to be an important influence.

The Doors came together when Ray Manzarek (born Raymond Daniel Manzarek Jr., February 12, 1939, died May 20, 2013; keyboards, keyboard bass, vocals) encountered Jim Morrison in 1965 (born James Douglas Morrison, December 8, 1943, died July 3, 1971; lead vocals) on Venice Beach in Venice, California, just weeks after their graduation from UCLA's film department. The two met in classes together where they bonded over music, philosophy, French New Wave cinema, and drugs. Morrison had been writing songs and poetry while living on a mutual friend's rooftop in Venice and sang his "Moonlight Drive" for Manzarek on the beach. Following their chance meeting, the two decided upon a future in rock and roll. Morrison even knew what he wanted to call the band: the Doors, inspired by Aldous Huxley's *The Doors of Perception* (1954), whose title was based on William Blake's observation in *The Marriage of Heaven and Hell* (1790–1793) that, "If the doors of perception were cleansed, everything would appear to man as it is, infinite."

Manzarek had already been playing in a band called Rick and the Ravens with his brothers, Rick and Jim (Morrison had also joined at times), but now they began to fit music to Morrison's new lyrics. Manzarek also knew John Densmore (born John Paul Densmore, December 1, 1944; drums/percussion) from a Maharishi transcendental meditation class and he asked Densmore if he wanted to join the band. The group recorded a demo in September 1965 and

pitched it to local recording studios without success until a local Columbia Records talent scout signed the band to a short-term deal. When Manzarek's brothers quit, leaving the Ravens without a guitarist, Densmore contacted his former Psychedelic Rangers bandmate, Robby Krieger (born Robert Alan Krieger, January 8, 1946; guitar, vocals), to complete what would become the core personnel of the Doors.

Rehearsals began in Manzarek's Venice Beach residence and it quickly became clear that while blues was the basis for the group's sound, each member contributed a distinct musical personality. Manzarek was born on Chicago's South Side, witnessed blues singers on nearby Maxwell Street, and spent his adolescence listening to Muddy Waters, Howlin' Wolf, and John Lee Hooker. His father initially taught him piano and in addition to a fairly standard, "classical" repertoire, he eventually took lessons from a local bandleader where he learned popular and jazz standards. Thus Manzarek's diverse background allowed him—often through a variety of different keyboards—to provide richer and more nuanced accompaniment and improvisation beyond the band's fundamental electric blues sound. John Densmore played drums in his school band and, after sneaking into the myriad jazz clubs in his native Los Angeles and witnessing the most important jazz acts in the 1950s and 1960s, desired to become a jazz drummer. Densmore's jazz sensibilities became a crucial element to the Doors' sound because his ability to fill in the frequent, wide spaces between Morrison's poetic musings was similar to a jazz drummer's communicative "fills" between successive improvisations. Moreover, in order to compensate for the group's lack of a bass player (the band usually brought in a session player for studio dates, but Manzarek played a Fender Rhodes keyboard bass in live performances), Densmore was able to provide an even wider variety of percussive textures. Robby Krieger first learned guitar in an acoustic/folk idiom and later became an accomplished Flamenco player before a Chuck Berry concert convinced him that electric guitar would be his chief instrument. In addition to his experiences (along with Manzarek and

Densmore) in a transcendental meditation group, Krieger also became interested in Indian music (a sound heard, for instance, on "The End") and played both the sarod and sitar. Morrison was enthralled with Krieger's electric slide guitar abilities and had always been interested in blues and country music, yet what he contributed to the group was his brilliant poetry. Through short, esoteric, even absurd verses, often conceived during hallucinogenic trips, Morrison pushed his fellow musicians to play beyond what they thought was possible in the same way that Morrison stretched the boundaries of lyric writing at the time. In return, Morrison's bandmates—because of their ability to improvise effectively—provided a suitable musical context that complemented and enhanced Morrison's poetry.

Eventually, Columbia dropped the band and they were forced to make a name for themselves at parties and other local venues. In order to diversify their material, Morrison also encouraged his colleagues to contribute more lyrics, and Krieger responded most prominently with some of the band's biggest hits, including "Light My Fire," "Love Me Two Times," "Touch Me," and "Love Her Madly." The Doors also tried to secure a regular gig along the Sunset Strip and failed until the owner of the very sparsely attended London Fog hired them as the house band. After consistently weak audience attendance, the London Fog's owner fired the band. Fortunately, a booking agent from the Strip's most important club, Whisky a Go Go, heard the Doors and hired them as the Whisky's house band. There they opened for Buffalo Springfield, Captain Beefheart, the Byrds, and Them (featuring Van Morrison and with whom the Doors collaborated on "Gloria") before becoming a featured band themselves. In May 1966, Jac Holzmann, president of Elektra Records, visited the Whisky and heard the Doors. Initially unimpressed, Holzmann was intrigued by the unique blues sound tinged with classical and jazz influences. Shortly thereafter, Holzmann urged Elektra producer Paul Rothchild to come to Los Angeles and see the band as well. The two agreed that Elektra needed to sign the Doors and offered the band a contract almost immediately.

With a contract in hand the Doors, particularly Morrison, decided to push the envelope even further during subsequent performances at the Whisky. During one particular evening in 1966, the Doors decided to play "The End" in the middle of their set instead of using it as their set closer. For the first time during the song's central improvisational section, Morrison spoke the lyrics. As Manzarek remembers, "It froze the Whisky. I looked out at the audience and . . . no one was dancing. The waitresses had stopped taking drink orders" (The Doors, 61). Morrison then went on to intone the oedipal fantasy sequence for which the song became famous, but his inflammatory lyrics so enraged the Whisky ownership that they fired the band that night.

At the same time the Doors were also working on their eponymous debut album, which was initially scheduled for release in November 1966. However, Elektra waited until January 1967 to release the album in order to put their entire marketing energies behind the Doors rather than mire the band among numerous other year-end releases. The Doors reflects the honing of their sound through rehearsals and live dates at the London Fog and Whisky a Go Go. It also comprises an ideal document of the coalescing of other musical styles around the blues that became one of the Doors' hallmarks. "Break on Through" sounds a clarion call for the counterculture by asking the listener to "break on through to the other side," an idea central to Morrison's worldview. Manzarek's organ solo also displays his fluency in jazz improvisation. Later the band displays its "classical credentials" by covering Kurt Weill's setting of Bertolt Brecht's "Alabama Song." The band's biggest hit, Krieger's "Light My Fire," contains one of the most distinctive openings in rock history, inspired largely by Manzarek's familiarity with the music of Johann Sebastian Bach. The song's central section comprises two extended solos by Krieger and Manzarek indebted to the modal jazz improvisations of John Coltrane and Miles Davis. Finally, much of the spiritual feeling exuded during "The End" comes not only from Morrison's haunting, spoken lyrics, but also the drone–melody–percussion texture integral to Indian classical music. In fact the piece's trajectory from contemplation to frenzy, and back to a state of calm, also permeates much Northern Indian classical music.

Overall *The Doors* was a very successful debut album and has sold almost 13 million copies to date. While the Doors lost their attractive gig at the Whisky, the notoriety garnered from the performance, combined with the exposure gained from the Elektra publicity machine, made them a hot commodity not just at other clubs in Los Angeles, but in important musical venues like the Fillmore in San Francisco and at trendy Greenwich Village clubs in New York City. By the summer of 1967, "Light My Fire" reached number one on the *Billboard* Hot 100, and in September the band appeared on *The Ed Sullivan Show* to perform their hit song when the band famously enraged network executives by singing "Girl we couldn't get much higher" despite being warned that such references to drug use were forbidden on television.

At the same time, the Doors were also working on their second album, *Strange Days*, released in October 1967. Their sophomore LP was a critical success and arguably the one the band itself most appreciated musically and creatively. Despite an eventual platinum certification, the Doors (especially Rothchild) considered the LP a commercial failure. After the success of *The Doors* and their newfound place as one of the most prominent new acts in American rock, the Doors began to experiment more on *Strange Days* from both musical and production perspectives. For instance, Rothchild employed new, eight-track recording and, as Manzarek put it "[used] the studio itself, as an instrument to be played" (The Doors, 96). Krieger's "Love Me Two Times," one of the album's two "hits," sounds rather conventional on the surface, but Manzarek's harpsichord accompaniment provides the song with a unique texture. Inspired by the Beatles' recent audio trickery on *Sgt. Pepper's Lonely Hearts Club Band*, Manzarek's piano line on "Unhappy Girl" is rendered backward. "Horse Lattitudes," one of the more avant-garde songs in the entire Doors catalog, featured Morrison's spoken poem written in high school about a sinking ship forced to offload its cargo of horses, contextualized amidst synthesized winds

blowing, moaning, aleatoric keyboard riffs, and other ambient noises. Finally, the initially funky "When the Music's Over" finds Morrison rhapsodizing poetically, and politically, above Manzarek's pulsating keyboard bass—similar in affect to his narrative in "The End"—and in addition to pleading for the environment, requests on behalf of the counterculture, "We want the world and we want it . . . NOW!"

Following their controversial performance at Whisky a Go Go and their refusal to conform to network protocol on *The Ed Sullivan Show*, the Doors may have made enemies with the corporate establishment but were only further idolized by youths, especially among the hippie movement. In December 1967, this demographic split was even more evident during a performance in New Haven, Connecticut. Before the show Morrison had been mingling with an eager fan in a shower room backstage, and when a policeman—who did not realize his target was Morrison—maced Morrison and his companion, chaos ensued. After order was apparently restored, the show commenced, but during "Back Door Man," Morrison began to recount for the audience what happened, thus further turning the youthful audience against the gathered authority figures. Later, Morrison suggested, "I thought their motto was 'protect and serve.' The fascists!" (The Doors, 111). The police ended the show, forcefully escorted Morrison offstage, and arrested him. While the charges against Morrison were eventually dropped, the band's perception changed following the confrontation. From the corporate perspective, radio stations and record stores began pulling *Strange Days* off the shelves, drastically reducing what should have been stellar sales for such a critically acclaimed album that also exhibited very strong commercial success initially. Youth across the United States were further emboldened to push against what society expected of them, and even though some found answers through the Doors' music, many attended concerts less to experience that music in a live setting, and more to witness what sort of spectacle Morrison might make of himself at the next concert. Regardless, it soon became clear that the Doors were charting a trajectory that was unsustainable in the long term.

As the Doors began work on their third album, *Waiting for the Sun*, in the spring of 1968, the creative process began to diminish, in part due to Morrison's increasing interest in other projects like writing and filmmaking, but more damaging was the singer's further abuse of drugs and alcohol. In fact, Rothchild was forced to conduct many more takes of songs than in previous recording sessions, followed by splicing the usable excerpts, because Morrison was often too inebriated to complete one full take as conceptualized. *Waiting for the Sun* was also a more difficult LP to make because the band could no longer depend on Morrison's cache of songs written before the band's formation in 1965, from which the first two albums derived. Whether as a result of the numerous takes needed to satisfy Rothchild's perfectionist tendencies, or because audiences appreciated the mellower aesthetics throughout the album, *Waiting for the Sun* became the group's only LP to reach number one on the *Billboard* charts and has sold seven million copies since 1968.

While the group put a great deal of energy into making the theatrical antiwar tune "The Unknown Soldier" into their next big hit, the Doors enjoyed much more success with a song that did go back to the band's initial formation: "Hello, I Love You." The album's opening track—which recalls both the Kinks' "All Day and All of the Night" as well as the opening drum riff from Cream's "Sunshine of Your Love"—became the Doors' first number-one single since "Light My Fire." The Doors also continued their stylistic diversity on the LP, evidenced in "We Could Be So Good Together," wherein Manzarek quotes Thelonious Monk's "Straight No Chaser" and "Spanish Caravan," in which Krieger displays his mastery of the flamenco style with some help from Isaac Albeniz's *Leyenda*. Further, the album was supposed to feature what would become one of the band's longest compositions, "Celebration of the Lizard." Yet, the group, especially Morrison, could not produce a coherent take of the 17-minute suite, and released only the dissonant, haunting "Not to Touch the Earth."

The band continued their relentless pace for the remainder of 1968, dividing their creative energies between recording their fourth studio album, *The Soft Parade*, and performing at prestigious venues in Europe and the United States, most notably the Hollywood Bowl in July 1968. Eventually released on CD and VHS formats in 1987, the video footage from the Hollywood Bowl date displays the band at their best, yet only hints at the live spectacle of which the Doors were capable. As "straight" as Morrison played the Hollywood Bowl concert, he pushed the limits of art and free speech in March 1969 at the Dinner Key Auditorium in Miami, Florida. The Doors faced the challenge of playing for an audience of 10,000 in a space that held 6,000; the audience was already riled up when an extremely intoxicated Morrison arrived at the show very late. Before too long, Morrison taunted the audience by calling them "idiots" and "slaves" and questioning, "How long are you going to let them push you around?" Later he invited them to abandon all rules and just to "have fun" with "no limits," suggested visually after Morrison removed his shirt and repeatedly asked the audience if they wanted to see his genitalia. Eventually pandemonium ensued when audience members stormed the stage, causing police and security to forcefully disperse the mob, forcing the band offstage and ending the show. Unlike the New Haven incident, no one was arrested immediately, but charges were eventually levied against Morrison—most seriously, felony allegations of "lewd and lascivious behavior" (specifically, "feigning oral copulation, masturbation, and self-exposure"). While Morrison had been drinking on flights from Phoenix to Miami, and backstage before the show, band members and scholars assert that Morrison was also employing tactics he had seen during performances of the avant-garde, confrontational exploits of the Living Theatre, whose goal was to interrogate society's arbitrary conventions and deconstruct them theatrically (The Doors, 163, 165).

The fallout from the Miami fiasco was severe and almost caused the dissolution of the band entirely. The concert was the first on a 20-city tour, and most of the subsequent venues pulled out almost immediately. In addition, both AM and FM radio stations banned the Doors' music from the airwaves.

Solace emerged in recording *The Soft Parade,* which had been delayed during extensive touring in late 1968–1969. However, because Morrison was granted a "creative sabbatical" after he threatened to leave the band, Krieger contributed much of the album's material. *The Soft Parade* also displayed the Doors experimenting with extensive brass and string arrangements throughout the album. For instance, Krieger's "Tell All the People" opens with a brass riff reminiscent of contemporaneous charts for Blood, Sweat & Tears. His "Touch Me" again includes a punchy brass line softened by strings in the song's bridge. The latter song also became the album's biggest hit, helped in part by Morrison's lip-synched performance on *The Smothers Brothers Comedy Hour.* "The Soft Parade," encapsulated a mini-suite in which Morrison exhorted the listener in the manner of an evangelical preacher, lamented the need for a "Sanctuary," waxed philosophically in the style of Herman's Hermits, and closed out with a bluesy, driving piece that gave the song its title. The song complex that comprised "The Soft Parade" represented an appropriate culmination to an album that many consider the band's most experimental.

The closing of "The Soft Parade" also signaled a return to the band's bluesy roots that would resurface on their next album, *Morrison Hotel* (1970). Clearly *The Soft Parade*'s lackluster sales caused the band to rethink its creative trajectory, because gone were the complex arrangements for winds and brass as well as the experimentalism that had been increasing through their last album. The LP opens with the dynamic, rollicking "Roadhouse Blues" (featuring John Sebastian on harmonica), which makes clear the band's return to the blues. Similar energy resurfaces in "Peace Frog," a song based on Morrison's "Abortion Stories" set to Krieger's funky riff, which also references the 1967 confrontation in New Haven as well as the riots that permeated the 1968 Democratic National Convention in Chicago. The LP also included typically psychedelic tunes like "Waiting for the Sun" and "Spy."

Despite the bad publicity from the Miami concert, Holzmann, Bill Graham, and others encouraged the Doors to participate in Woodstock, but they refused because they typically did not participate in mass festivals in which they were not the headlining act. However, they did perform in the Isle of Wight Festival in August 1970, joining Jimi Hendrix, Miles Davis, and the Who, among many others, and entertained an audience estimated at between 600,000 and 700,000. The Doors' set proved to be rather lackluster, once again because of Morrison's extreme intoxication, and at the time Morrison vowed it would be his last live concert. A few weeks later, amidst reports of Jimi Hendrix's overdose and death, and just before Janis Joplin's similar fate, Morrison was found guilty of public exposure and eventually sentenced to six months in Dade County Jail, a charge Morrison's defense immediately appealed.

Following the sentencing, the Doors set out on another tour, playing dates in Dallas and New Orleans, and after Morrison's onstage breakdown in New Orleans, the remaining dates were canceled and the two performances represented the final times the complete Doors performed together. In the studio the band continued its return to blues-based music on *L.A. Woman,* which proved to be their final studio recording. The resulting LP is arguably the strongest since *The Doors,* but the band recorded the album without the individual largely responsible for their unprecedented string of gold records: Paul Rothchild. Their longtime producer sensed that he was increasingly unable to lead the band through the recording process, believed their material—especially Krieger's "Love Her Madly," the album's biggest hit—unworthy of his time, and grew exhausted of Morrison's erratic studio behavior. Rothchild handed the reins over to his chief engineer, Bruce Botnick, who found giving the band more control over the album's sound was exactly the sort of creative impetus needed to produce their most bluesy album yet. Moreover, including former Elvis Presley bassist, Jerry Scheff, as well as prominent blues rhythm guitarist, Marc Benno, on the recording further solidified the bluesy aesthetics. In addition to "Love Her Madly," both "L.A. Woman" and "Riders on the Storm" have remained favorites of countless Doors fans and staples of classic rock radio to the present day.

While the Doors were in the studio recording *L.A. Woman*, Morrison was already considering a break from singing and moving to Paris during the sabbatical to concentrate on writing poetry. About a month before the album's April 1971 release, Morrison informed his fellow bandmates of his decision to leave for Paris with his "soul mate," Pamela Courson. While Morrison corresponded with the remaining band members about returning in a few months to record and tour, a reunion never occurred because Morrison died on July 3, 1971, of what has officially been called "heart failure." Manzarek, Krieger, and Densmore tried to continue the Doors without Morrison, recording and releasing *Other Voices* later in 1971 and *Full Circle* in July 1972. Early in 1973, the band decided they needed to find a lead singer and considered both Joe Cocker and Paul McCartney, but Morrison's death left a deep void, and the overall chemistry suffered irreparably, resulting in the official dissolution of the Doors. The trio reunited in 1978 to supply music to a series of poems Morrison had recorded before his death, resulting in *An American Prayer*. The venture was a reasonable success and, ironically, gave the Doors their first Grammy nomination: in the "Best Spoken Word" category. The Doors also reunited for their induction into the Rock and Roll Hall of Fame in 1993 as well as for an episode of VH1's Storytellers in 2000. Following Ray Manzarek's death in May 2013, plans for any further collaborations appeared unlikely.

While Morrison died more than 40 years ago, the Doors' music never left circulation, and in many ways their musical legacy has only strengthened over time. In September 1981, *Rolling Stone* placed Morrison on their cover with the provocative tag, "Jim Morrison: He's Hot, He's Sexy, and He's Dead." Inside, *Rolling Stone* reported that sales of the Doors' recordings had either doubled or tripled from 1979 to 1980. One reason for the sudden resurgence in popularity might have been the powerful juxtaposition of "The End" against the horrors of the Vietnam War in the opening scene of Francis Ford Coppola's *Apocalypse Now* (1979). In 1991, Oliver Stone's *The Doors* reintroduced the band to a new generation eagerly

hoping to change the world following the fall of the Berlin Wall and the end of the Cold War. Stone went to great lengths to re-create important concerts and incorporated cameos from Paul Rothchild, John Densmore, and Patricia Kennealy, a writer and one of Morrison's many lovers. Despite many convincing scenes, Stone repeatedly used the band and Morrison's leadership of it as the basis for a cautionary tale against the excesses of drugs and alcohol that hindered rather than enhanced the Doors' music.

More recently, a series of 40th-anniversary reissues of studio and live recordings have done much to capitalize on the Doors' importance to rock history. Further, subsequent musical developments—namely punk and alternative styles—have benefitted directly from the band's extension of the boundaries of what can acceptably be called "rock" music as well as their insightful political commentary found throughout their output. For instance, Pearl Jam was often compared to the Doors, especially in the way that Eddie Vedder performed daring stage acrobatics similar to Morrison's famous tightrope walk. Moreover, parallels have also been drawn between their songwriting talents, and for a time during the mid-1990s, Vedder's increasing alcohol use was compared to Morrison's substance abuse. Such associations were validated further when Vedder introduced and performed with the band during their Rock and Roll Hall of Fame induction in 1993. Later, the electronic music producer Skrillex worked with the remaining Doors members to create "Breakn' a Sweat" (2011), which includes riffs provided by the band members as well as a sampled passage from an interview Morrison gave in which he imagined a time when music would consist of one person, surrounded by machines and tapes, singing and speaking. Both the Crystal Method and Paul Oakenfold have also remixed Doors songs as dance tunes.

This connection between seemingly disparate popular idioms exemplifies the dissolution of rock convention that underpinned the group's formation in 1965. The Doors sought to change the face of music by combining a thorough assimilation of the blues with healthy doses of jazz, classical, non-Western, and performance art sensibilities. Moreover, their ethos of exploration and experimentation has been a model for subsequent rock acts that also faced similar questions about how to change the musical world. In another passage from Blake's *The Marriage of Heaven and Hell*, the author surmised, "The road of excess leads to the palace of wisdom." One could certainly apply this adage to the Doors as a method that led to both wonderful and disastrous results. Regardless, what the Doors discovered along that road is also what has endeared them to generations of fans and cemented their prominent place in rock history.

Anthony Bushard

Selected Discography

The Doors, Elektra EKS-74007, 1967.

Strange Days, Elektra EKS-74014, 1967.

Waiting for the Sun, Elektra EKS-74024, 1968.

The Soft Parade, Elektra EKS-75005, 1969.

Absolutely Live, Elektra EKS-9002, 1970.

Morrison Hotel, Elektra EKS-75007, 1970.

L.A. Woman, Elektra EKS-75011, 1971.

An American Prayer, Elektra 5E 502, 1978.

References

Densmore, John. *Riders on the Storm: My Life with Jim Morrison and the Doors*. New York: Delacorte, 1990.

Didion, Joan. "Waiting for Morrison." In *The Age of Rock: Sounds of the American Cultural Revolution,* edited by Jonathan Eisen, 385–88. New York: Random House, 1969.

Doors, The, and Ben Fong-Torres. *The Doors*. New York: Hyperion, 2006.

Hopkins, Jerry. "Jim Morrison." In *The Rolling Stone Interviews,* 207–33. San Francisco, CA: Straight Arrow Publishers, 1971.

Kuwahara, Yasue. "Apocalypse Now!: Jim Morrison's Vision of America." *Popular Music and Society* 16.2 (Summer 1992): 55–66.

Magistrale, Tony. "Wild Child: Jim Morrison's Poetic Journeys." *Journal of Popular Culture* 26.3 (Winter 1992): 133–44.

Manzarek, Ray. *Light My Fire: My Life with the Doors*. New York: Putnam, 1998.

Marcus, Greil. *The Doors: A Lifetime of Listening to Five Mean Years*. New York: PublicAffairs, 2011.

Shaw, Greg. *The Doors on the Road*. New York: Omnibus, 1997.

E

Eagles (1971–1980; 1994–Present)

The Eagles were one of the most successful rock bands of the 1970s. Originally formed to serve as a backup band for a Linda Ronstadt concert, they went on to create five top-selling albums. Combining intricate, multilayered guitar melodies with consistently strong three-part vocal harmonies, the Eagles are the inspiration for many country, alternative, and rock bands that use some vocal harmonies in their music. Having created such evocative hits as "Hotel California," the legendary album *Desperado*, and other such projects, the band disbanded due to infighting in 1980. In 1994, due to their continued popularity and success, they re-formed the band. They have since released a sixth album and have issued a historical documentary on their glory years. They remain one of the most successful rock acts to this day.

The Eagles were first formed in the spring of 1971 when Linda Ronstadt's manager, John Boylan, recruited Glenn Frey (born Glenn Lewis Frey, November 6, 1948; vocals, guitar, keyboards) and Don Henley (born Donald Hugh Henley, July 22, 1947; vocals, drummer) to work on Ronstadt's eponymously named album, *Linda Ronstadt*. These two musicians had each come from bands that were prominent in the South and Midwest. Don Henley had been part of a band in his native Texas called Shiloh. Under the patronage and support of Kenny Rogers, they had produced a record. The quality of this music led Henley to receive offers to work in Los Angeles.

Glenn Frey came from Michigan, and after college worked as a recording session musician for Bob Seger. Frey then moved to Los Angeles to follow his girlfriend. He took with him his reputation as an accomplished session musician. This allowed him to stand out to producers looking to fill band rosters. And so it was, Glenn Frey was introduced to Don Henley to record music for an entirely different person.

After successfully recording Linda Ronstadt's record, she took them on tour with her to a concert. They were joined on tour by Bernie Leadon (born Bernard Matthew Leadon III, July 19, 1947; multiple guitars and vocals) and Randy Meisner (born Randy Herman Meisner, March 8, 1946; bass and vocals). After a successful show at Disney World, Henley and Frey decided to start a band. They then recruited Meisner and Leadon to join them.

Randy Meisner had already formed a band by the time the Eagles had offered him the position. Poco was another attempt at a Western rock band. When offered the opportunity to play with Henley and Frey, Meisner grabbed it. Meisner not only could play bass, but he had what was described as a very high range for a man. This aided the Eagles in creating beautiful tenor song parts, which Meisner would then sing.

Initially, it was suggested they should call themselves the Eagles; however, Henley insisted on simplicity, and they were simply named Eagles. In 1972, they released their eponymously named first album, *Eagles*. They were signed to Asylum Records and were offered the expertise of Glyn Johns to serve as the band's producer. It was widely thought, at the time of the band's formation, that Meisner and Leadon would prove to be the band members who would lead the group. However, it turned out Frey and Henley were far more dominant. In the period the Eagles were

Known for their vocal harmonies and mix of country, rock, and alternative music sounds, the Eagles are a multigenerational favorite. Pictured here ca. 1974 (from left to right): Bernie Leadon, Glenn Frey, Don Henley, Randy Meisner, and Don Felder. The band's sound changed dramatically when Leadon left and was replaced by Joe Walsh. (Photo by Gems/Redferns)

broken up, it was Henley who was cited when asked if the band would ever regroup. Those two young men were the principal songwriters and organizers of the set lists for concerts. They were and are forces to be reckoned with.

Eagles was recorded in London by Glyn Johns, and the album produced three solid hits. "Take It Easy," "Witchy Woman," and "Peaceful Easy Feeling" evoked a country feel. While some critics decried the album as too slick and professional, Bud Scoppa of *Rolling Stone* suggested it possessed a distinguished country rock roots background, and after Jackson Browne's debut album, it was the best album of 1972 (Brackett and Hoard 2004).

"Take It Easy" was the first signature song of the Eagles. It has been performed in every concert tour. The smooth melody and vocal harmonies featured on the single remain trademarks of the band's sound even now. It has also been featured on every greatest-hits collection the Eagles have released.

The Eagles, at this point, were seasoned road musicians, so after a brief and successful tour, they immediately returned to the studio to produce their second and highly memorable album, *Desperado*. Created as a tribute to the Dalton gang, some of the most legendary outlaws in the Old West, *Desperado* was the last album released by their then label Asylum. In 1973, Asylum merged with Elektra Records, and for the rest of their recording years, Eagles albums would be distributed by Elektra. The album promoted two singles, "Tequila Sunrise" and "Outlaw Man." However, it was the title track and first song on the album, "Desperado," that stood the test of time. Although it was not deemed worthy of being a single, it became a signature song for the Eagles in concert.

After two successful country rock efforts, Henley and Frey wished to move the band more toward hard rock. *On the Border* was the album they created as a hybrid of country and hard rock. Early into the recording, they fired their then producer, Glyn Johns, and brought in Bill Symczyk. They found they needed a slide guitar on at least one track, and Leadon suggested they bring in a longtime friend of his, Don Felder (born Donald William Felder, September 21, 1947; guitarist). They were so impressed with his work they hired him as the fifth member of the band.

On the Border presented three singles. "Already Gone" and "James Dean" were respectable hits, but "Best of My Love" was the first number-one hit on the *Billboard* charts that the Eagles had played.

Following the release of *On the Border*, the Eagles went on to perform in the California Jam. A large festival and rock concert, the California Jam was billed as "The Woodstock of the West." Acts such as Black Sabbath, Emerson, Lake & Palmer, Deep Purple, Rare Earth, and others participated. It was so well attended that ABC televised portions of it during prime time viewing hours.

Upon completing their performance schedule, they went into the studio. In 1975, they released their fourth album, *One of These Nights*. This was their first album to place at the number-one position in the *Billboard* Top 100 charts. It further yielded three top 10 singles. "One of These Nights," "Lyin' Eyes," and "Take It to the Limit" brought the Eagles worldwide acclaim. They had now solidified a hard rock sound and were destined to bring about several more top-rated albums. However, this album was the last they recorded with Bernie Leadon. Unhappy with the direction the band was taking musically, Bernie left after completing *One of These Nights*. He contributed two songs to this album; one of them, "Journey of the

Sorcerer," served as the opening-credit music for the phenomenal radio/TV series *The Hitchhiker's Guide to the Galaxy*.

Leadon was replaced in December 1975 by Joe Walsh (born Joseph Fidler Walsh, November 20, 1947; guitars). Joe Walsh had been part of two prior bands, notably James Gang and Barnstorm. Considered a bit reckless by Don Henley, Walsh proved a potent force that helped the Eagles skyrocket in popularity. However, before they progressed further, the band chose to release their first compilation, *Their Greatest Hits 1971–1975*. The success of this album confirmed the Eagles were progressing ever upward. It cemented the band's reputation as being one of the best American rock bands of the 1970s.

One of These Nights also distinguished itself by being the first album for which the Eagles won a Grammy. "Lyin' Eyes" took the Best Pop Vocal Performance for 1975. They went on to win five more Grammys.

Following *One of These Nights,* the Eagles had to capitalize on their success. As they prepared songs for their fifth album, it became clear they could combine and interchange lead guitar parts between Joe Walsh and Don Felder. This dueling guitar style of solo created the sound for their single greatest hit, "Hotel California."

In December of 1976, *Hotel California* debuted. This was their second number-one album on the *Billboard* chart and featured the singles "New Kid in Town," "Hotel California," and "Life in the Fast Lane." Of these songs, "Hotel California" was the very best song recorded by the Eagles, and it serves as a signature song in concert. In fact, it has become such a staple of their performances, it is often reserved for encores, as the fans fully expect to be delighted each and every time with that classic single.

More to the point, "Hotel California" has enjoyed near continuous radio play, first on rock stations, then on classic rock stations. Its meaning has been seriously disputed, and for a long time, it was thought to be discussing Satanism. Detailing a faded hotel on the Pacific Coast Highway, the song discusses an encounter the band's protagonist experiences one weekend when he checks into the hotel only to learn that he will never be permitted to check out again.

Don Henley, on *60 Minutes,* attempted to clear the air and discussed how the song explores the "dark underbelly of American excess." The 1970s were famed for extreme excess in the studio-recording/major label system of rock music. In exchange for recording albums and touring excessively, bands were privileged to receive money, drugs, and other hedonistic pleasures from the recording labels they belonged to or were courted by. With the single "Hotel California," the band attempted to capture the experience through dark and mysterious lyrics.

Equally of note, however, is the outro guitar solo (outro meaning "at the end"). Joe Walsh and Don Felder weave and combine intricate, Spanish-infused guitar licks and phrases to create one of the most memorable and compelling sequences of guitar solos ever recorded. To this day, "Hotel California" is the most remembered and memorable song in the Eagles' back catalog. Even now, "Hotel California" is an often-requested song at every concert.

Hotel California was such a tremendous accomplishment in 1977 the album netted two Grammy Awards. "New Kid in Town" earned Best Vocal Arrangement. *Hotel California* then earned the most prestigious of Grammys, Record of the Year. This was the only time in the history of the Eagles they won that prestigious honor.

Hotel California generated the need for a huge worldwide tour. They secured Fleetwood Mac as their opening group and toured the entire world, each member being asked to lead the vocals on a "signature song." This "signature song" requirement of the Eagles made them wholly unique. However, it also damaged working relationships. During the 11-month tour, Randy Meisner experienced both ulcers and flu. A consummate professional, Meisner continued to perform despite his illnesses. However, due to his continued illness he tried to not perform his "signature song," "Take It to the Limit." The extreme high notes in that song were not achievable in his condition. This aggravated Glenn Frey, the dominant force in the band next to Don Henley. Frey continually addressed

the issue of Randy Meisner's performing "Take It to the Limit." The summer of 1977 found Frey's aggressive attitude escalating to the point where one evening he and Meisner had a physical altercation.

After that fight, Randy Meisner resolved to leave the Eagles once the tour ended. While Walsh and Felder purportedly pleaded with Meisner not to quit the band, his mind was made up. He no longer tolerated Frey's behavior. On September 20, 1977, Randy Meisner left the band and headed for his home in Nebraska.

Later that year, the band replaced Meisner with Timothy B. Schmit (born Timothy Bruce Schmit, October 30, 1947; bass and vocals). Timothy Schmit had replaced Meisner on his pre-Eagles band, Poco. He was considered by Henley the only legitimate replacement for Meisner, and the decision met no resistance from the rest of the band. Timothy Schmit continued to serve as the Eagles bassist for many years to come. Schmit was by far the most affable member of the band. Even after the breakup to come in 1980, Schmit served as background vocalist for the solo work of other former bandmates. In this regard, Schmit was a wholly original rock and roll musician. No one ever had a serious issue with him.

After hiring Timothy Schmit, the band opted to take time to prepare what was their first original double album. In the late 1970s many concept albums, such as *The Wall*, were being recorded and released. The Eagles wished to be part of that momentum and created an American work that served as a testament to hard rock and country.

However, the recording process was long and arduous. In 1978, while the Eagles were struggling with their upcoming album, Joe Walsh released a solo album *But Seriously, Folks*. This solo album stood as an indicator of what the band members would do once they broke up in 1980.

In 1979, the album *The Long Run* also earned the Eagles what was their fourth, and for many years considered their last, Grammy win. "Heartache Tonight" won Best Vocal Performance. It seemed foreshadowing: a song that discussed heartbreak served as the Grammy Award winner for the Eagles in 1979, right before they began what was their last big promotional push.

Critics found *The Long Run* less impressive than *Hotel California*, but it still became a top-selling album. It presented three top singles, "Heartache Tonight," "The Long Run," and "I Can't Tell You Why." In releasing the album, the Eagles began a long tour. All tours had proven arduous for this band, and this tour, which ran from 1979 to 1980, proved the most painful.

During the tour, the band was asked to perform a concert in support of Senator Alan Cranston's reelection bid. After publicly thanking the band for their efforts on his behalf, Don Felder responded through a mic, "You're welcome—I guess" (*The Times,* 2007). The public ambivalence of Felder's off-handed remark aggravated Glenn Frey. Being an aggressive personality, Glenn Frey rarely forgave a grudge. It was his resentment of Randy Meisner that had forced the bassist out of the band, and he was preparing to confront Felder over this supposed slight.

The confrontation did not occur until July 31, 1980. It has been called the "Long Night at Wrong Beach" (*The Times,* 2007). During this concert at Long Beach, Glenn Frey was determined to pick a fight with Don Felder, and Felder, unlike Meisner, was more than willing to accommodate. As both men tell the story, each of them approached the other and informed him of when they would fight. Frey contended that Felder started it, but it was clear from Felder's account that he was simply reciprocating the bad feelings and animosity he felt directed at him from Glenn Frey. The evening ended backstage with a large altercation of a very physical nature. By the time the parties were separated, all goodwill in the band had evaporated. The Eagles were finished as a band.

They still owed Elektra a live album. To that end, *Eagles Live* was recorded and engineered on both the East and West coasts. After the fight that ended the band, Don Henley and Glenn Frey were unwilling to be in the same state, let alone the same studio space. In November 1980, the live album was finished. It featured a new cover, "Seven Bridges Road," which the band had perfected on the road before breaking up.

A paean to Southern culture and astronomy, "Seven Bridges Road" remained on the radio as a lasting reminder of just how expert the band was at complicated vocal harmonies.

As of 1981, the Eagles had ended their term as one of the most successful bands of the 1970s. In fact, *The Long Run* was considered the last number-one album of that decade. When there was nothing left to do, each of the band members turned to solo careers. However, each former member experienced varying degrees of success.

Joe Walsh recorded nine albums before the Eagles reunited. Many of them were considered less than successful. He proceeded to work with many other bands and generated hits for them.

Glenn Frey, the instigator of the breakup, found success in the 1980s. Of particular note are the songs he contributed to film soundtracks. "The Heat Is On" was a big hit in support of the film *Beverly Hills Cop* (1984). For the television show *Miami Vice* (1984–1990) he contributed the song "You Belong to the City." He would even work on a solo live album, and generally performed widely until the 1994 reunion.

Don Henley enjoyed the most successful solo career. Two of his five albums, *Building the Perfect Beast* and *The End of the Innocence*, capture a nostalgic feeling for bygone days. His first truly popular single, "The Boys of Summer," was quite backward-looking. Even after the Eagles reunited, Henley was still under contract to Warner Music to produce a few more solo albums.

Of all the members of the Eagles, Henley was the most idealistic and political. It has been tallied that he donated $680,000 to Democratic politicians over his lifetime. Further, he worked on the Walden Woods project. The Walden Woods project was founded to protect Henry David Thoreau's historic location, where he wrote and contemplated his philosophies.

Timothy Schmit proceeded to work with all the other Eagles members on solo projects. He provided background vocals for all. He worked on a number of solo albums, but none of them went anywhere. He has two singles of note, "So Much in Love" and "Boys Night Out." Neither broke the top 10 of any chart.

Don Felder worked on film songs as well. He contributed "Heavy Metal (Taking a Ride)" for the film *Heavy Metal* (1981), an animated cult film. This song featured background vocals from former band members Don Henley and Timothy Schmit. He helped the Bee Gees on their 1981 album *The Living Eyes*. He proceeded to serve as a recording artist for many other bands. *The Living Eyes* stood out because it was one of the last Bee Gees albums issued, as disco was approaching the end of its run.

In 1983, Don Felder released his first solo album, *Airborne*. Its first single, "Never Surrender," was a minor hit, having been featured on the soundtrack of *Fast Times at Ridgemont High* (1983). He recently released a second solo album.

In 1993, in support of the Walden Woods project, Don Henley arranged for a tribute album for the Eagles to be released. *Common Thread: The Songs of the Eagles* returned the band to its Southern rock and country roots. All the songs covered are performed by country and Western artists. Most notable was "Take It Easy" covered by Travis Tritt. He requested all the Eagles to appear in his video. There were no objections, and after reacquainting with each other, the Eagles resolved to reunite.

This required a tour, and in 1994, the *Hell Freezes Over* reunion tour launched. It was so named because Don Henley had often stated that the only way the band would reunite was if "Hell freezes over." As it was remarkable in 1994 that the world would once again enjoy the live music of these long-term broken-up musicians, it was deemed the most appropriate name for the tour.

Once again, Don Henley, Don Felder, Glenn Frey, Timothy Schmit, and Joe Walsh toured in support of the Eagles. The name of the live album was the same as the tour. It featured footage from a special MTV concert event they scheduled as part of their reunion tour. From that point forward, the Eagles performed at least two more tours before 2001. There was great interest in the band, and the shows were often sold out. Even as the Eagles raised the ticket prices to astronomical amounts, fans new and old were not deterred from seeking out the concerts that were staged across the world. So, the Eagles remained intact until 2001.

In 1998, in their first year of eligibility, the band was inducted into the Rock and Roll Hall of Fame. All seven members—Don Henley, Glenn Frey, Randy Meisner, Bernie Leadon, Don Felder, Timothy Schmit, and Joe Walsh—performed two songs at the event: "Take It Easy" and "Hotel California." It was considered a great evening.

In 2001, Don Henley and Glenn Frey fired Don Felder. Citing the music equivalent of irreconcilable differences, they let the longtime guitarist go. This resulted in Don Felder issuing two lawsuits against the band. Both are still ongoing and show no sign of being resolved. Don Felder is suing the band for $50 million in damages and claims they did not provide him equal shares while touring between 1994 and 2000. To this day, Don Felder cannot join the rest of the band on stage due to the ongoing lawsuits.

In 2001, the remains of the band—Henley, Walsh, Frey, and Schmit—got together and started work on what would be the seventh studio album. Not since 1979's *The Long Run* had the Eagles considered working on another album. For these older rockers, the recording of the album took a lot more time and energy. In 2007, *Long Road out of Eden* was released. It had three singles, "How Long?," "Busy Being Fabulous," and "Waiting in the Woods." It earned two Grammys: one for "How Long" and the other for an instrumental called "I Dreamed There Was No War." When asked if there would be a follow-up album, the general answer seemed doubtful. Joe Walsh contended the band might have one more album to create. At this time, it seems *Long Road out of Eden* might well be the last new Eagles studio album.

The Long Road also netted the band two further Grammy Awards. In 2008, the Eagles were granted Best Country Performance for their single "How Long?" They started out playing country rock, and as time wore on, it was country music that assisted them in creating their most recent album.

In 2009, the instrumental from *Long Road out of Eden*, titled "I Dreamed There Was No War," earned Best Instrumental Performance. The instrumentals they had included on their albums had always been good compositions, but with this last award, the decision to include an instrumental on every album was vindicated. The Eagles proved their instrumental work was every bit as potent in the Grammys as their vocal performances had been. "I Dreamed There Was No War" and "Journey of the Sorcerer" stand out as the two instrumentals most often referenced from the band's back catalog.

Upon completion of their latest album, the band launched the *Long Road out of Eden* tour. For the next three years, the band covered the globe and reminded the world of the music of one of the most beloved bands of the 1970s. In the 21st century, many bands have found a second act for touring purposes, and the Eagles are no exception.

In 2010, when the tour concluded, the Eagles began to consider their history as a band. In 2012, Alison Ellwood and Alex Gibney created a two-part documentary titled *History of the Eagles*. It was screened at Sundance and ultimately aired on Showtime. At the Sixty-Fifth Primetime Emmy Awards, the film won Outstanding Sound Mixing for Nonfiction Programming.

Spurred on by the success of this documentary, the Eagles decided to do a fresh new tour. For this tour, *The History of the Eagles*, they wished to include every member of the now venerable band. However, Randy Meisner could not participate due to health issues. Also, given the ongoing lawsuit with Don Felder, they could not include him. So with Leadon, Henley, Frey, Schmit, and Walsh, the Eagles began a year-long tour with dates scheduled through the end of July 2015.

The Eagles have been a dominant force in country rock and hard rock. They produced six studio albums, numerous compilation albums, and six number-one albums. As violent as their early history was, it was symptomatic of the time. The 1970s was a decade of great excess, and thus, bad behavior was considered to be the way rock bands would often settle disputes. Even now, Don Felder has two unsettled lawsuits with the rest of the band.

Despite the negative decisions, the Eagles, unlike so many other bands, continue to tour and are productive. Focusing on their joint history as a band, they serve as a positive example of what many bands still

operating could do. The Eagles have been inducted into the Rock and Roll Hall of Fame, have won many Grammys, and have a back catalog of hits that are great songs.

The *History* tour represents a new form of music entertainment. Here the band traces the steps of their career, from their roots in other bands to the time when they were brought together initially to back up Linda Ronstadt. In fact, in tribute to Meisner, they even discuss how Meisner's original band Poco tied into the history of the Eagles; as Timothy Schmit is also from Poco, he has taken over what would have been Meisner's narration.

Beyond their 2015 tour, no one knows what the future holds for the Eagles. They may yet record another album. They may engage in more historical tours. One thing is for sure: their music shall endure. Hits such as "Hotel California," "Take It Easy," and "Desperado" will always have a place, as they are part and parcel of American culture. It is no mistake that country music, as well as rock and hard rock, identify the Eagles as a primary influence. They are genuinely one of the bands that best captured the history of the Old West in their music. If nothing else, the Eagles exist to remind us that country music as a genre includes not only the South, but also the Old West and the Southwest. These are also country music territories. For the five remaining members, while they dabbled in other forms of music, they were all still country boys at heart.

The Eagles have had their greatest impact on country music. Although a hard rock band, Country Music Television listed them as among the Top 40 Men of Country Music. Travis Tritt was heavily influenced by the Eagles, as he not only prepared a song for Common Threads, but even recorded a video to support the tribute album. Lester Flatt and Earl Scruggs both list the Eagles as an influence. Brooks and Dunn and Trisha Yearwood have also been influenced by the Eagles. This would explain the "New Rebel" sound of country music. This is where the country sounds start to sound a bit more like hard rock (Elliot 2004). So the Eagles blend of country and rock lives on in a type of country music.

Benjamin Franz

Selected Discography

Eagles, Asylum B000002GVS, 1972.

Desperado, Asylum B000002GYW, 1973.

On the Border, Elektra B000002GXO, 1974.

One of These Nights, Elektra B000002GXX, 1975.

Hotel California, Elektra B001J1RPFC, 1976.

Their Greatest Hits 1971–1975, Elektra B000002GVS, 1976.

The Long Run, Elektra B000002GWZ, 1979.

Eagles Live, Elektra B000002GXJ, 1980.

Building the Perfect Beast, Geffen B000000OPC, 1984.

The End of the Innocence, Geffen B000000ORB, 1989.

Common Thread: The Songs of the Eagles, Giant B000002L1S, 1993.

Hell Freezes Over, Geffen B000000OU0, 1994.

The Long Run out of Eden, Eagles B000Y179KO, 2008.

References

Elliot, Marc. *To the Limit: The Untold Story of the Eagles.* New York: Da Capo Press, 2004.

Felder, Don, and W. Holden. *Heaven and Hell: My Life in the Eagles (1974–2001).* New York: Wiley and Sons, 2009.

Gilles, Shawn, et al. "Eagles, the." In *Baker's Biographical Dictionary of Popular Musicians since 1990.* Vol. 1. Detroit: Schirmer Reference, 2004, 199–200. Gale Virtual Reference Library.

"How the Eagles Took It to the Limit." *The Times,* London (2007).

Earth, Wind & Fire (1970–2012)

Music of the 1970s—depending on the genre—is described as varied, drug induced, and reeling from the 1960s. Many changes in music happened as the tastes of the country evolved. Subgenres within rock and roll emerged such as punk, rap, heavy metal, fusion, and black pop. Through the din of popular music Earth, Wind & Fire emerged exhibiting all of the characteristics of a multitude of genres. Author Rhonda Baraka summed up what many have said: "Earth, Wind & Fire has been as essential to raising our collective consciousness and quenching our spiritual thirst as the elements themselves are to our very existence."

Baraka continued, "The band . . . has showered the world with its message-drenched, feel-good, thought-provoking lyrics and ultra funky, danceable rhythms. From the colorful, symbol-splattered album covers to the melodic tones of the kalimba, Earth, Wind & Fire is as familiar to us and as much a part of us as earth, wind and fire" (Baraka 2001). Or as Jim Payne stated, "Earth, Wind & Fire was a phenomenon. Musically sophisticated, yet infectious and funky—as-you-wanna-be" (Payne 1996). They managed to combine a diverse set of elements from many genres of music and created something that has resonated with audiences for decades.

Maurice White (born December 19, 1941; vocals, kalimba, percussion) pioneered Earth, Wind & Fire. White was the firstborn in his family and grew up in Memphis, Tennessee, with his grandmother while his father was in medical school in Chicago. His mother lived in Chicago to support his father. By the time he was five years old, White was singing in church. For seven years he was a member of a vocal group called the Rosehill Jubilee. His time with the Jubilee introduced him to the experience of performing on tour. The Rosehill Jubilee enjoyed performing short tours from church to church. In addition, during this time he had the opportunity to see a drum and bugle corps perform. As soon as he saw the drummers in the group he decided to switch to the drums, joined the marching band in his junior high school, and started to study drumming formally (Payne 1996).

Before White could finish high school, his mother moved him to Chicago to live with his parents. Moving to live with his parents should have felt like a homecoming, but instead it felt more like being uprooted. As White stated, "In my last year in high school, my Mom came and got me and took me to Chicago. In going to Chicago, I had to start my career all over" (Payne 1996). The family plan was for him to become a doctor, so once he graduated high school he enrolled in college.

White enrolled at Crane Junior College with the medical field as his goal. However, he found the college big band as soon as he could and began rehearsing and performing with them. In no time he started to get hired as a drummer and performed around Chicago with his college bandmates. According to Maurice, "Eventually I quit medical training and enrolled in the conservatory. I felt that if I was going to be in music, I might as well go ahead on and learn it correctly, so I went off to the Chicago Conservatory of Music for four years" (Payne 1996).

Maurice's big break came in 1962 when he got called to audition as a drummer for Chess Records. He got hired and recorded Betty Everett's "You're No Good." "I was scared to death but I agreed to do it. When I got down to the recording session it turned out to be for Vee-Jay Records—Betty Everett's 'You're No Good.'" From that point forward Maurice was in a band. He worked for Chess Records from 1962 to 1966 as a session drummer. According to Maurice, "I recorded with Muddy Waters, Sonny Boy Williamson, who was a harmonica player, Willie Dixon, Howlin' Wolf, the Dells, Sugar Pie DeSanto, Tony Clarke . . . all the hits with Billy Stewart . . . I recorded with Fontella Bass, 'Rescue Me,' all the hits from the latter part of '62 to '66, I was on 'em" (Payne 1996).

Then in 1966 Maurice joined the Ramsey Lewis Trio. Lewis was a Chess label artist who was extremely popular during the late 1960s. "That was an experience, to go out and play in front of 10,000 people! I was like, oh my God, this is really the big time! . . . Ramsey was my introduction to big time show biz" (Payne 1996). While working with Lewis, Maurice was already sketching out his vision of the band he wanted to lead. He worked with Lewis for three years, recorded 10 albums with him, and according to Lewis:

> One night . . . he said, "I think in a few months I'm gonna be leaving the group. I'm going to form my own group." I said, "What is it—jazz trio or quintet, you got a couple horns or what?" He said, "No, man, I'm gonna form a group that's gonna do magic. We're gonna play R & B, pop, jazz and dance." (DeYoung 2006)

White put together the band with family members and contacts he made as a session drummer for Chess

Musical sophistication was the calling card for the band Earth, Wind & Fire, pictured here ca. 1970. The band stayed musically relevant for several decades due to its ability to change along with the tastes of American popular music. (Photo by GAB Archive/Redferns)

Records in Chicago in 1970. "White was responsible for bringing funk, R&B, jazz, pop and spirituality together in a way that nobody—not even Sly Stone, who'd aimed in the same direction—could have foreseen" (DeYoung 2006). He wanted to make a successful band, but he probably did not anticipate the band would still be performing and recording four decades later. Even though White formed the band, their success was a result of the members' collective dedication and talent. All of the musicians in Earth, Wind & Fire grew up with formal musical training and an understanding of the hard work ethic required for success in the music business.

Maurice had a clear vision of the kind of band he wanted to lead. According to Bob Cavallo, former manager for the band, "I'll never forget my first meeting with Maurice White. He had the most specific vision of any artist I had ever encountered . . . he wanted to incorporate all of the musical influences in his life: R&B, jazz, gospel, blues and rock, occasionally flavored with African or Afro-Cuban accents" (Mitchell 2001). "He was on a plane," recalled Maurice's half-brother Verdine (born July 25, 1951; bass, percussion). "And he sketched it out, a band that would encompass all different types of music" (DeYoung 2006).

In 1970, Maurice quit Ramsey Lewis's band to begin leading his own. They were called the Salty Peppers. The band effectively established the foundation for the beginnings of Earth, Wind & Fire and enjoyed modest success. They recorded the tune "La La Time" in Chicago and it became a regional hit. The tune eventually got picked by Capitol Records for national distribution (DeYoung 2006). White moved the Salty Peppers to Los Angeles, but the band was not successful. The musicians who followed White to Los Angeles quit due to the lack of gigs and returned to Chicago for steady work (DeYoung 2006). Any remaining musicians were let go and Maurice along with his brother Verdine formed another band.

The newly formed and revitalized band signed a contract with Warner Bros. in 1970. The personnel consisted of Ronnie Laws (born October 3, 1950; flute, saxophone), Philip Bailey (May 8, 1951; vocals, conga, percussion), Ralph Johnson (born July 4, 1951; drums, percussion), Larry Dunn (born June 19, 1953; keyboard, synthesizer), Roland Battista (born May 30, 1951, died February 29, 2012; guitar), and Jessica Cleaves (born December 10, 1948; vocals). Maurice derived the band's name from his astrological sign Sagittarius—the lack of water sign (Waller 2001). The first two albums with Warner Bros. were a self-titled debut, *Earth, Wind & Fire* (1971) and *The Need of Love* (1971). The band began to make some progress.

The sound of these two albums incorporated many different styles, some of it unexpected from an R&B-oriented group. The track "Energy" contained free jazz–style improvisations and vocalese. The album was not necessarily a big success, but it was important work for the developing band. Verdine felt the tune "was a breakthrough song for me,

even though it was a ten-minute avant-funk jam" (Jisi 2005). In addition to their own albums they recorded songs for the soundtrack of writer/director Melvin van Peebles's *Sweet Sweetback's Baadasssss Song* (DeYoung 2006).

The band was beginning to enjoy some success, but they were still honing their sound. Ralph Johnson reflected on the formation of Earth, Wind & Fire, "I think there was a lot of social commentary going on within the music—not just our music, but everyone else's. A lot of political change was going on. We were just so young at the time. When we put this thing together, Verdine, Philip and myself were like 20, 21 years old. It was a time of change, a time of transition on a lot of different levels" (Baraka 2001). The transition for Earth, Wind & Fire continued as they continued to tour, performing on college campuses and developing an audience base.

A crucial member of their audience was the influential producer Clive Davis with Columbia Records. According to Verdine, "Maurice and I had heard that Clive was looking for us . . . We had opened up for Dizzy Gillespie at the Bitter End East, and some guy named Chuck said, 'That man's looking for you.' Reese and I thought it was the police, so we started trotting back to the hotel room! And he said, 'No, no, no it's Clive Davis'" (DeYoung 2006). Davis bought Earth, Wind & Fire's contract with Warner Bros. According to Davis, "I'll never forget the Earth, Wind, and Fire audition for me. They were absolutely electrifying and mesmerizing. I just had to sign them and so we, in effect, bought them out of their Warner Bros. contract. They and their music will always be an indelible memory that I will never forget" (Mitchell 2001). Once they were with Columbia their sound as a band began to coalesce and their music began to resonate with the public.

The band's sound was due partly to the addition of Charles Stepney as one of their producers. He was an old acquaintance of Maurice's from his time at Chess Records and became and influential arranger and teacher for the band. He arranged many of the band's wildly successful hits, but also coached the musicians on what they were playing. According to Verdine, the band's relationship with Stepney was akin to what

> Quincy Jones was to Michael Jackson or George Martin to the Beatles. We would go to Chicago, to his basement, and go over the songs. Then we'd go back and record 'em. Then Step would fly out and write the arrangement—or we'd send him the tracks—and then we'd go to the studio and he'd conduct the orchestra. (DeYoung 2006)

The band's relentless and infectious grooves were the primary focus. As guitarist Al McKay stated, "The groove was paramount." Maurice, Al, Verdine, and Larry would record most of the tracks. "It started out, in the studio, with Maurice on drums and me, Verdine and Larry." Maurice hired two very different guitarists. McKay's experience from Motown brought a "commerciality" to the band, while Johnny Graham brought a hard electric blues background (DeYoung 2006). These two guitarists, combined with Verdine's sturdy technique and funk bass lines, with Larry's keyboards, and Maurice's drumming, became an incredible combination. Added to this personnel for live performances was the youngest White brother, Fred, on drums. According to Larry, "He was just laying it down, I'd never really heard a drummer hit that bass drum like that. At the first rehearsal, it wasn't miked, and I could feel the bass drum. I was like 'Man, this cat is serious'" (DeYoung 2006).

The first Columbia album *Last Days and Time* (1973) illustrated the band's transition to their eventual dominance of pop fusion with the principal tunes of the album. The album incorporated interludes between each tune, completely clearing the mind of the previous tune. For example, the first interlude was a solo saxophone playing a free improvisation, and the second interlude was a short stride piano excerpt. The third interlude began with crowd noise and segued into strings with an epic soaring horn line before the ballad "Where Have All the Flowers Gone." Further, the electric kalimba—a modernized traditional African thumb piano—became more prevalent, as in the

tune "Power." The album was successful and created momentum for their second album with Columbia, *Head to the Sky* (1973).

Head to the Sky began with the hit "Evil." Maurice White began the song with the the sound of an explosion which started a stop time introduction. The introduction quickly grew into Maurice's improvising on the kalimba over a Latin-inspired vamp. The album exhibited a balance between funk-groove-oriented pop tunes, ballads, and Miles Davis–inspired fusion. "Zanzibar" began with an unmetered improvised introduction performed by guitar and keyboards. It was purely an instrumental tune spanning over 13 minutes. There are vocals, but they are treated as vocalese lines used as part of the instrumental color rather than for lyric delivery. The tune showed Miles Davis's influence, as much of the tune evoked the albums *Jack Johnson* and *Bitches Brew*. "Zanibar" and the rest of the album showed Earth, Wind & Fire's virtuosic instrumental improvisation, songwriting, and solid arranging.

The third Columbia album, *Open Our Eyes*, officially solidified Earth, Wind & Fire as a force not only in black pop music, but pop music in general. The album sold over a million copies and reached number one on the black album charts (DeYoung 2006). Stepney had a prominent role with the arranging for this album and worked diligently with the band to create as tight of a sound as possible. The most successful single from the album was "Mighty Mighty," which hit number four in R&B and number 20 in pop in March 1974 (DeYoung 2006).

The next album began as a soundtrack for the film directed by Sig Shore called *That's the Way of the World* (1975). The film was unanimously referenced as a flop and did not get released to video until 2007. In the film, Harvey Keitel performed the role of producer for a band, performed by Earth, Wind & Fire. The single from the film, "Shining Star," reached number one on the R&B and pop charts. The single "That's the Way of the World" also reached the top 10 of the R&B and pop charts (DeYoung 2006). Following *That's the Way of the World,* Earth, Wind & Fire became wildly successful.

The band sold more than 30 million albums and won six Grammy Awards, and their world tours were among the hottest of tickets. Six consecutive albums went platinum. The next albums contained an on-slaught of major hits. *Gratitude* (1975) featured new releases such as "Sing a Song" and live recordings of previous hits such as "Power," "Devotion," and "Shining Star." *Spirit* (1976) contained the hits "Getaway" and "Saturday Nite." *All 'N All* (1977) contained the hits "Serpentine Fire," "Fantasy," and "Love's Holiday." Then in 1979, *I Am* produced "After the Love Has Gone," "Boogie Wonderland," and "In the Stone." Their popularity crossed more boundaries as they were featured in Robert Stigood's film *Sgt. Pepper's Lonely Hearts Club Band,* performing "Got to Get You into My Life" (DeYoung 2006).

As Earth, Wind & Fire became successful with record sales and live performances, Maurice was able to work toward his ambitious goal of what he termed "Full Spectrum Music" (DeYoung 2006). Great music was only the beginning for Maurice. According to Johnson, "He wanted to take it up to the next level. He wanted to have a black band that could play all styles of music and at the same time have a great live presentation" (DeYoung 2006). As a result, the Phenix Horns led by Don Myrick and Louis Satterfield joined the band, adding sizzle and virtuosity. Maurice liked the fact that they omitted the letter "o" from the word "Phenix" for its connotation as a living thing rising from the ashes of its ancestors, reborn (DeYoung 2006). To stage "Full Spectrum Music" Maurice needed to hire some help. Instead of stage designers, Maurice turned to magicians for special effects. The effects not only involved raising Dunn's piano eight feet in the air and spinning the instrument as he played, but also "levitating" Verdine horizontally on a wire while he was playing his bass (DeYoung 2006). Eventually they hired Doug Henning and his assistant, David Copperfield, to create an elaborate stage setup using Egyptian symbolism. Further, to make all of this work on stage they hired George Faison as their choreographer. According to Bailey, "We wanted to give the audience more than just an audio concert, we were big fans of Broadway, and we wanted to make the visual effects as spectacular as the music"

(DeYoung 2006). He had even told Ramsey Lewis early on that his band would "fly" on stage.

The most fantastic example of staging illusions was for the tour promoting the *Spirit* album. Maurice's interest in Egyptology became the focus with Henning's designs. Instead of walking out on stage, the band descended in a spaceship onto a giant gold pyramid. The pyramid would rise in the air and split apart, while the band would reappear in astronaut costumes, playing and dancing. Louis Satterfield—the trombonist in the Phenix Horns—would take over on bass for Verdine while Verdine participated in the staged illusions.

After the incredible success of *I Am* in 1979, the band unknowingly began their decline. In 1980, Earth, Wind & Fire recorded *Faces*, and then Al McKay quit. According to him:

> It was just time to get away. Maurice and I were starting to clash pretty bad. It was time to move on—no regrets . . . In the beginning it was a family thing. We all created, and that was it. It was understood that we were a band, and that's the way I'd always thought of it, as our band. We go in and create music together, and everybody shares in the rewards . . . but things work out a little different sometimes. Not to fault anybody, but you just have to be aware of what you're getting into when you get involved in a situation like that, with so many people. (DeYoung 2006)

The collaborative spirit responsible for their rise to popularity and global success dissipated. According to Bailey, "After Al left, it became the Maurice White Show. We just started being sidemen, and it just lost all of the magic of what it was before" (DeYoung 2006).

The next three albums, *Raise!* (1981), *Power-light* (1983), and *Electric Universe* (1983), illustrated a departure from their hard-driving funk-groove-oriented pop tunes to the slick commercial sound of many dance-oriented bands in the 1980s. The hit single "Let's Groove" from *Raise!* remained the only hit from the 1980s albums. The cherished sound of Earth, Wind & Fire is the sound on the albums during their peak in popularity: 1975–1979.

Unofficially, the band broke up in 1983. According to Bailey, "The group broke up. All our stuff was sold, all our costumes . . . some people with tell you, 'oh, we went on a hiatus.' You don't go on a hiatus and sell all your stuff" (DeYoung 2006). The Phenix Horns began their famed tenure with Phil Collins. Bailey also recorded a number-one hit with Phil Collins, titled "Easy Lover."

After four years, Maurice, Verdine, Bailey, and drummer Ralph Johnson managed to come together and reunite Earth, Wind & Fire. Bailey became a co-owner and coleader of the band along with Maurice (DeYoung 2006). To signal the reunion they recorded *Touch the World* (1987) and composed the hit single "System of Survival," which made it to number one on the R&B charts. Other personnel on the album included Andrew Woolfolk (born Andrew Paul Woolfolk II, October 11, 1950; saxophone) and Sheldon Reynolds (dates unknown; guitar, vocals). They found mixed reception during their initial tour promoting the album. According to Bailey:

> To say you're not disappointed would be just lying, really. You're used to going to different cities and selling out three nights in the largest halls, and now we're going in and doing one night in some major markets, and [filling] only half the hall. At the same time, we've done considerably well in some places. We did five nights at Radio City Music Hall in New York, and we sold out in LA, D.C., Atlanta. Those are our bases and you build from there. (Graff 1988)

Earth, Wind & Fire persevered. The arrangement of the group changed as Maurice was diagnosed with Parkinson's disease and quit touring with the band in 1994. White retains ownership of the band name and leases it to Bailey, Johnson, and Verdine (DeYoung 2006). While they continued to perform their hits from the 1970s, they also composed new songs. During the 1990s they collaborated with artists such as Sly Stone and MC Hammer and recorded and released several live albums.

The album *Illumination* (2005) contained tunes reminiscent of their biggest hits and the addition of young hip-hop and R&B artists. The album exhibited many of the musical features that brought Earth, Wind & Fire their popularity in the 1970s. The opening track, "Lovely People," featured Earth, Wind & Fire's characteristic hard-driving funk groove with soaring harmonized vocalese in the chorus, alternating with will.i.am's rapped verses. The ballad "To You," featuring vocalist Brian McKnight, contained borrowed material from their single "Would You Mind" and paralleled Earth, Wind & Fire's other popular ballads, such as the aforementioned, along with "Reasons," and "After the Love Is Gone." The Grammy-nominated single "Show Me the Way" featured Raphael Saadiq, which successfully fused tight horn lines and Verdine's sturdy bass groove with Raphael's powerful singing style. The band was excited about promoting this album. According to Verdine, "To the new generation we're like a new group so they really are taking everything firsthand. [Older fans] have more history [with the group], so you might wonder, 'Does Philip still sing as great? Can Verdine still play as great? Let me check it out.' And then when you check it out you say, 'Wow!'" (Baraka 2005).

Illumination is only one illustration of Earth, Wind & Fire's profound influences on popular music. The collaboration with Raphael Saadiq was momentous for him, as Saadiq has stated on many occasions that Earth, Wind & Fire's album *Gratitude* was a significant album for him. Also, in 2004 the Recording Academy held the first annual Grammy Jam, paying tribute to Earth, Wind & Fire. The event featured many performers, including George Duke, Usher, Kanye West, Jill Scott, Brian McKnight, Yolanda Adams, India.Arie, and Stevie Wonder. Musicians from the 1970s to today perform Earth, Wind & Fire's music. From Maynard Ferguson to contemporary R&B artists, they have embedded Earth, Wind & Fire's music into the fabric of popular music. According to jazz guitarist Pat Metheny:

> The importance of Earth, Wind & Fire to serious musicians is significant. They remain one of the

last massively popular groups that has actively involved themselves in elevating the listening skills of their audience by challenging them and exposing them to some of the more sophisticated possibilities of what the modern song from— and popular music in general—can become at its best. (Baraka 2001)

Metheny also admires the accessibility of Earth, Wind & Fire's music (Baraka 2001). Even though they were always trying to push themselves and their audience, the music remained accessible. The notion of self-motivation and consciousness is a prominent theme in their music, which has resonated with their multigenerational fan base. For R&B singer Raheem DeVaughn, "I'm just trying to continue the vibe they created . . . Their music wasn't just music. It was therapy, food for the soul, with very conscious and self-motivating lyrical content" (Mitchell 2005). DeVaughn used Verdine's bass line from "Can't Hide Love" as the foundation for his single "Guess Who Loves You More" from the album *The Love Experience*.

In addition to musical homages, they have been honored with many awards. In 2000, they were inducted into the Rock and Roll Hall of Fame. In 2005, they received the BET Awards' Lifetime Achievement Award. The hit "Shining Star" was added to the Grammy Hall of Fame in 2008, and in the same year they received honorary degrees from the Arts and Media College at Columbia College Chicago (www .earthwindandfire.com).

Earth, Wind & Fire's ability to remain a relevant band after four decades of recording and performing is impressive. Through their dedication to the music of Earth, Wind & Fire they are enjoying renewed popularity in the United States and abroad. "The original intention was to make great music and, in our little way, to enlighten the world and raise consciousness," stated Verdine. "Playing great music and the passion for the work has kept it together. That's always the common denominator. That's really the glue that holds it together, and it's probably bigger than any of us" (Baraka 2005). According to Grammy-winning songwriter India.Arie, they achieved their goal: "The

spirituality in their music and the symbolism of their album covers are so moving. The chakras, the colors, and the pyramids, I love them for that!" (Mitchell 2001).

Earth, Wind & Fire's discography illustrates many of the changes in American popular music during the 1970s. Studying their recordings by beginning with Maurice's work during the 1950s with Chess Records elucidates the rise of African American musicians as record producers, formally trained session musicians, and global pop stars. A student of American popular music and American history would be remiss to omit Earth, Wind & Fire from their material.

Kevin Fullerton

Selected Discography

Earth, Wind & Fire, Warner Bros. WS 1905, 1971.

The Need of Love, Warner Bros. WS1958, 1971.

Last Days and Time, Columbia KC31702, 1972.

Head to the Sky, Columbia KC32194, 1973.

Open Our Eyes, Columbia KC32712, 1974.

Gratitude, Columbia PG 33694, 1975.

That's the Way of the World, Columbia PC33280, 1975.

Spirit, Columbia PC34241, 1976.

All 'N All, Columbia JC34905, 1977.

I Am, ARC FC35730, 1979.

Faces, ARC KC2 36795, 1980.

Raise!, ARC TC 37548, 1981.

Electric Universe, Columbia QC 38980, 1983.

Powerlight, Columbia TC 38367, 1983.

Touch the World, Columbia FC 40596, 1987.

Heritage, Columbia C 45268, 1990.

Millennium, Reprise 45274–2, 1993.

Greatest Hits Live, Tokyo Japan, Pyramid R2 72621, 1996.

In the Name of Love, Pyramid/Eagle R2 72864, 1997.

Live in Rio 1980 Recording, Kalimba 973001, 2002.

That's the Way of the World: Alive in '75, Columbia/Legacy CK 85805, 2002.

The Promise, Kalimba/Snapper 973002, 2003.

Illumination, Sanctuary Urban 87513, 2005.

Compilations

The Best of Earth, Wind & Fire Vol. 1, ARC FC 35647, 1978.

The Best of Earth, Wind & Fire Vol. II, Columbia CK 45013, 1988.

The Eternal Dance 3-CD Box Set, Columbia C3K 52489, 1992.

Love Songs, Columbia/Legacy CK 90863, 2004.

Videography

In Concert, Pioneer Artists PA-83–039, 1983.

The Eternal Vision, Sony Records SRLM 836, 1992.

Live in Japan '90, Pioneer PILP-1011, 1990.

Live in Japan, Pioneer LDCE ltd. PLMJB 00431, 1992.

1994 World Tour in Japan, King Video KILM-111, 1994.

Live (The Millennium Concert), Polygram Video 800 635 727–3, 1995.

Shining Stars: The Official Story of Earth, Wind & Fire, Evergreen Entertainment, 2001.

The Collection, Columbia 202465 5, 2004.

Live at Montreux 1997, Eagle Vision EREDV663-A, 2004.

Chicago/Earth, Wind & Fire: Live at the Greek Theatre, Image Entertainment IDO345DFDVD, 2005.

References

Baraka, Rhonda. "A Conversation with Verdine White, Philip Bailey and Ralph Johnson." *Billboard—The International Newsweekly of Music, Video and Home Entertainment.* July (2001): 32, 42, 44.

Baraka, Rhonda. "Getting Down with Verdine White." *Billboard—The International Newsweekly of Music, Video and Home Entertainment.* September (2005): 46, 48.

DeYoung, B. "Earth, Wind & Fire: The Way of the World" *Goldmine* August (2006): 14–17, 19.

Earth, Wind & Fire Official Website. 2014. "Timeline." Accessed September 2014. www.earthwindandfire.com/history/biography.

Graff, G. "A Few Words with . . . Earth, Wind & Fire: [2 Star Edition]." *Houston Chronicle* August (1988): 6.

Jisi, C. "Shining Star: Verdine White: His Legendary Bass Style Is Back on Earth, Wind & Fire's Illuminating New CD." *Bass Player* (2005): 16, 34–36, 38–40, 42.

Larkin, Colin, ed. "Earth, Wind and Fire." *Encyclopedia of Popular Music,* 4th ed. *Oxford Music Online.* Oxford: Oxford University Press, 2008.

Mitchell, Gail. "Maurice White" *Billboard—The International Newsweekly of Music, Video and Home Entertainment.* July 14, 2001: 34, 36, 44.

Mitchell, Gail. "Stars: Earth, Wind & Fire." *The International Newsweekly of Music, Video and Home Entertainment.* September (2005): 41, 44.

Mitchell, Justin. "Earth, Wind and Fire's Bailey Generating Some Musical Heat on His Own: [Final Edition]." *Chicago Tribune,* February (1985): 11.

Payne, Jim. "Maurice White." In *Give the Drummer Some!: The Great Drummers of R&B, Funk & Soul,* edited by Harry Weinger. Miami, FL: Warner Bros. Publications, 1996.

"Stars Jam for Earth Wind & Fire." *Billboard.* December (2004): 55.

Waller, Don. "Grooving to 30 Years of Earth, Wind, & Fire," *Billboard—The International Newsweekly of Music, Video and Home Entertainment.* July (2001): 27, 30, 25, 46.

The Everly Brothers (1956–2004)

Although the Everly Brothers had their first hit record in 1957, their impact on popular music is still being felt nearly six decades later; in fact, as the *Rolling Stone Encyclopedia of Rock and Roll* put it, "The Everly Brothers are the most important vocal duo in rock" (*Rolling Stone Encyclopedia,* 317). Their songs, which were a melodic fusion of bluegrass, country and Western, and rock and roll, featured close harmonies and lyrics that touched the listener's heart. The Everly Brothers influenced a wide range of classic rock performers: as one critic said, "When you listen to the Beatles, you're hearing the Everlys. Same goes with the Beach Boys. And Bob Dylan. And the Rolling Stones. And Neil Young. And Crosby, Stills & Nash" (Reed, N5). The Everly Brothers have also been called the forerunners of country rock, and an influence on such 1970s artists as Gram Parsons, Emmylou Harris, the Eagles, and Linda Ronstadt (Morse, D1).

Don and Phil Everly emerged as the most country-sounding group in the first generation of rock and roll in the mid-1950s. Pictured here on *The Ed Sullivan Show* in New York on March 4, 1957, the Everly Brothers were solely responsible for launching the long-popular country-rock sound. (Photo by CBS Photo Archive/Getty Images)

The Everly Brothers, Don (born Isaac Donald Everly, February 1, 1937; guitar, vocals) and Phil (born Phillip Everly, January 19, 1939, died January 3, 2014; guitar, vocals), were born in Chicago, Illinois. Their father Ike was a country and Western guitarist, and their mother Margaret joined with him to form a vocal duo not long after they were married. Ike and Margaret Everly performed throughout the Midwest, and by the mid-1940s, they had their own radio show on KMA in Shenandoah, Iowa. That was where the two brothers got their start as performers, when Phil was six and Don was eight; they had sung with their parents at home and were invited to join

them on the radio (Houston, 11). The listeners reacted positively to "Little Donnie and Baby Boy Phil," as they were then called (Pareles, A22); the show was soon renamed "The Everly Family." But while harmonizing with their parents was enjoyable, the schedule was grueling: the show went on the air at 6 A.M., and throughout much of their childhood, Phil and Don were up early to entertain the radio audience, and then they went off to school (Scott 39). During summer vacation, they performed with their parents at county fairs, square dances, and other local events.

The Everly Family continued to sing on radio through the early 1950s; by this time, they had left Iowa to live in Knoxville, Tennessee, and perform on station WROL. But live country radio shows were dying out, replaced by recorded music. By 1955, even though "The Everly Family" had been popular, Ike and Margaret believed it was time for a change of career. They settled in Nashville, where Ike became a barber, and Margaret became a beautician (Witbeck, H8). Phil and Don, however, were determined to go out on their own and have a music industry career. Thanks to their parents, they had met Chet Atkins, a successful country guitarist and recording star, who later became a producer. Atkins was one of the brothers' first mentors: he was convinced they had a bright future as performers.

Phil and Don began hanging around Nashville recording studios: they had started writing songs, and they hoped to get an audition that would lead to a recording contract. Being the protégés of Chet Atkins helped them to attain both of those goals: several of the songs Don wrote were recorded by other artists, and in 1956, the brothers were signed by Columbia Records (Rhodes, 5E). But their first song, "Keep A-Loving Me," which Don wrote, did not make the charts, and Columbia soon dropped them. Fortunately, they were introduced to Archie Bleyer, a former orchestra leader who owned Cadence Records; he was seeking a new country act and signed the brothers to his label. It seemed the timing was perfect for the Everly Brothers to join them. But Phil and Don did not see themselves as strictly country. In fact, they were soon identified with a hybrid of country and rock known as "Rockabilly" (the name came from a blend of "rock" with "hillbilly").

Archie Bleyer's chief songwriters were a married couple named Felice and Boudleaux Bryant, and Bleyer had a song of theirs he wanted the Everly Brothers to record. It was called "Bye, Bye Love," and although as many as 30 other artists had rejected it, the Everlys decided to take a chance on it. There was nothing to lose: they knew they would be paid at least $64 for the session (Bronson, 28). So with their friend Chet Atkins accompanying them on guitar, and Bleyer producing, they recorded the song. The end result was a huge success in both country and top 40. "Bye, Bye Love" went to number one on the country charts, and reached number two on the pop charts; it went on to sell more than a million copies (Pareles, A22). The Everly Brothers quickly proved they were not just one-hit wonders. By mid-October 1957, they had their first number-one pop hit, "Wake Up Little Susie." Some radio stations found the lyrics too risqée and refused to play it, but despite the controversy, "Wake Up Little Susie" was the Everly Brothers' second million-seller.

Suddenly, the Everly Brothers were in demand. They sang on *The Ed Sullivan Show*, their personal appearances sold out, and radio stations nationwide were deluged with requests for their songs. In fact, a number of stations even flipped over both of their hits and played the B-sides—the emotional ballads "I Wonder If I Care as Much" and "Maybe Tomorrow." And their songs were also charting in other countries; they began to develop an international following in England, Canada, and Australia. Some of the older music critics were not impressed: they dismissed the brothers as temporary sensations, "top sellers of the moment" (Kleiner, 12B). But the Everly Brothers' popularity with top 40 fans continued to grow, undoubtedly helped by Don and Phil's good looks, their lyrics about young love and teenage heartache, and their ability to connect with the audience. Despite the fact that Phil was 18 and Don was 20, they were polished and confident on stage, a by-product of the years they had spent performing with their parents (Larson, 14). They also had a positive image:

they were seen as clean-cut, well-dressed, polite, and not associated with the rebellious side of rock and roll (Pareles, A22).

After their next release, a top 40 version of the Ray Charles rhythm and blues song "This Little Girl of Mine," failed to become a big pop hit, Phil and Don recorded another Felice and Boudleaux Bryant–written ballad, "All I Have to Do Is Dream." By mid-May 1958, it was at the top of both the country and the pop charts. Phil later told reporters that this was one of the most important songs the Everly Brothers ever recorded (Bronson 37); but at the time they first sang it, he and Don probably did not realize the global impact this song, or their other hits, would have. For example, in Liverpool, England, a young man named Paul McCartney was learning to play guitar, trying to imitate the sound of American rock records by Little Richard, Carl Perkins, and Elvis Presley. But while he enjoyed hard-driving rock and roll, it was the music of the Everly Brothers that especially caught his attention. From their songs, he learned that "rock and roll could be performed at a lesser volume, in close, even subtle harmony." In fact, he and a friend attempted to create a vocal duo of their own, one that sounded as much like the Everlys as possible (Norman, 41). Those efforts did not work out, and McCartney went on to join the Quarry Men. One of his bandmates was John Lennon, and the two would sometimes perform American rock songs for the students at the art school where Lennon was studying: among the ones they chose to sing was "All I Have to Do Is Dream" (Everett, 24). Critics have also noted that John and Paul's early Beatles vocal duets, such as "Love, Love Me Do," were modeled after the harmonies of the Everlys (Everett, 76; Riley, 41, 47).

Meanwhile, in Queens, New York, two boyhood friends named Paul Simon and Art Garfunkel made their first record; it was 1957, and they were still in their teens. At that time, they used the pseudonym "Tom and Jerry," and although their song "Hey Schoolgirl" was not a big hit, anyone who listened to it could hear the influence of the Everlys (McCardle, C1). Further evidence of their affection for the Everlys' music can be heard on Simon and Garfunkel's 1970 album *Bridge over Troubled Water,* which contained a cover version of "Bye, Bye Love." Years later, Paul Simon told an interviewer that "[t]here wouldn't have been a Simon and Garfunkel without the Everly Brothers" (Cummings, F9). Even singer-songwriter Bob Dylan, known for being taciturn, said of the Everly Brothers, "We owe these guys everything. They started it all" (Houston, TV11).

Throughout 1958, the Everly Brothers continued turning out hit songs: "Bird Dog," an up-tempo tune with a rockabilly beat, was their next big single. It reached number one on the country charts and number three on the pop charts; and as often happened with their records, the flip side also got considerable airplay—the love song "Devoted to You" became a hit in its own right, reaching number seven on the country charts, and number 10 on the pop charts. In addition to hit singles, Phil and Don also released two albums. Their first, *The Everly Brothers,* contained all of their hits and B-sides up to that point, along with their own versions of rhythm and blues songs like Little Richard's "Keep A-Knockin'" and Ray Charles's "Leave My Woman Alone." Their second paid tribute to their father Ike: *Songs Our Daddy Taught Us* was a departure from their mass-appeal pop songs. It contained traditional country and Western and folk tunes such as "Who's Gonna Shoe Your Pretty Little Feet," "That Silver-Haired Daddy of Mine," and "Barbara Allen." Although *Billboard*'s album reviewer praised it in the December 15, 1958, issue (70), only one song from the album, "I'm Here to Get My Baby out of Jail," got much pop air play, and the album was mainly embraced by country radio stations.

Their final single release in 1958 was "Problems," which reached number two on the pop charts and became their fifth single to sell a million copies (Rees and Crampton, 180). But the song did not do as well on country radio, only reaching number 17, a sign that the brothers had become more identified with top 40 and less with their country roots. After their next two releases failed to get into the top 15 on what was now called the *Billboard* Hot 100 Chart, the Everlys recorded a song that Don had written: "('Til) I Kissed You." As Don later recalled, it was inspired

by a girl named Lillian, whom he met while the brothers were on tour in Australia (Loder 1986). The song went to number eight on the country charts, the last time one of Phil and Don's songs received enough country airplay to get into the top 10. But more importantly, "('Til) I Kissed You" returned the Everlys to pop success, reaching number four in September 1959. Making this song sound even better was the fact that Don and Phil were accompanied by members of the Crickets, the late Buddy Holly's band.

Cadence Records released a *Best of the Everly Brothers* compilation in early 1959; it contained all of their hits up to that point, plus several of the singles and B-sides that had received airplay but never charted well. Fan magazines and newspaper articles stressed how happy the brothers were with their careers ("A Tribute," 14); but behind the scenes, tensions were beginning to emerge. Both brothers felt creatively stifled by Cadence Records, plus they felt they deserved more money, and they decided to leave the label. Their final song for Archie Bleyer was one that neither Felice and Boudleaux Bryant nor the Everly Brothers wrote: "Let It Be Me" was a romantic ballad originally sung in French by Gilbert Bécaud in 1955; an English-language version became a minor hit for Jill Corey in 1957. Phil and Don's melodic harmonies were perfect for this song, and Archie Bleyer sweetened the sound by adding strings—the first Everly Brothers single to use a string section. It was also the first song they recorded in New York City, rather than in Nashville, and it reached number seven on the Hot 100. In February 1960, Don and Phil signed with Warner Bros., receiving a 10-year, $1 million contract (Rees and Crampton, 180).

Both brothers collaborated on writing the first single for their new label: "Cathy's Clown" was influenced by classical composer Ferde Grofé's "Grand Canyon Suite," which gave the brothers the idea for the marching beat on the chorus; the lyrics were also inspired by a girlfriend of Don's named Catherine (Loder 1986). "Cathy's Clown" turned out to be the Everly Brothers' biggest hit, both in the United States and in England: it spent five weeks at number one in the United States and seven weeks at the top of the

British pop charts (Bronson, 68), and it sold eight million copies worldwide. In fact, the British magazine *New Musical Express* named them the world's best vocal group in 1958, 1959, and 1960; American trade publications like *Cashbox* gave them similar honors (Larson, 14). And as further proof of how well known they were, popular folk singers the Kingston Trio mentioned them in one of their songs—a minor hit called "Everglades," written by country songwriter Harlan Howard. The song opened with chords that sounded like the Everly Brothers' hit "Bird Dog," and the joking last line contained the words "Skipping through the trees from the Everlys" (Dean, 99). Meanwhile, their former label, Cadence, released one other song the brothers had recorded while still with that label, "When Will I Be Loved." Written by Phil Everly, and sung in the rockabilly style of several of their other hits, it reached number eight on the *Billboard* charts in the summer of 1960. It was later redone by Linda Ronstadt in 1975; her version made it much more of a rock song, and it became a number-two hit for her. Ronstadt later spoke about listening to the Everly Brothers when she was only 11. Upon hearing "Bye, Bye Love," she was immediately attracted to their sound: "Those voices with traces of Hank Williams's vibrato, the Blue Sky Boys' old-timey duet and the sibling sound that can be achieved only in the presence of similar genetic coding and matching regional accents" (Ronstadt, 16).

The Everly Brothers had their next pop hit with a song that Don wrote, "So Sad (To Watch Good Love Go Bad)"; inspired by the breakup of his marriage to his high school sweetheart, it reached number seven on the *Billboard* charts in October 1960. Don's fans might have known that he was married, a fact mentioned in passing in teen-oriented magazines like *Hit Parader* ("A Tribute," 14); but since divorce was still regarded negatively during the conservative 1950s, it is not surprising that little was said about it. In early 1961, the Everlys had yet another top 10 hit with "Walk Right Back." This song was written by Sonny Curtis, a country guitarist who had once played in a band called the Three Tunes with Buddy Holly, and who later played in Phil and Don's band when they toured; it reached number seven on the pop charts in March; and once again, disc jockeys flipped the song over to play the B-side, "Ebony Eyes," a tragic ballad about a man whose beloved dies in a plane crash. Written by country singer/songwriter John D. Loudermilk, it became a number-eight song for the Everly Brothers. Their final hit of 1961 was also a song they did not write: in fact, it was cowritten by a woman who would eventually go on to great success as a pop singer—Carole King. "Cryin' in the Rain" became a number-six top 40 hit for the Everlys. Meanwhile, they had two new albums. One was called "It's Everly Time," released in 1960 and their first for Warner Bros.; its only hit was "So Sad (To Watch Good Love Go Bad)." Then, in late 1960, they released "A Date with the Everly Brothers." The one hit on this album was "Cathy's Clown," but it contained several other interesting tracks: an early version of the ballad "Love Hurts" (also recorded by Roy Orbison as the B-side to his 1961 hit "Running Scared"); and "So How Come (No One Loves Me)," a rockabilly song, which the Beatles later sang on a 1963 BBC broadcast (McArdle, C1).

In June 1962, the Everly Brothers had what turned out to be their last top 10 hit, "That's Old-Fashioned (That's the Way Love Should Be)," cowritten by Bernie Baum, who was better known for writing pop standards rather than top 40 songs. The lyrics described a traditional approach to courtship and romance which touched a chord with older listeners. the song not only reached number nine on the Hot 100, but it also reached number four on what were then known as the easy listening charts (the kind of softer pop music that would later be known as adult contemporary). Meanwhile, there were several changes in Phil and Don's personal lives. Rather than waiting to be drafted, the brothers joined the Marine Corps Reserves in October 1961, completing boot camp in February 1962; although their songs were still receiving airplay, they were not able to go out on tour or appear on television while they went through 12 weeks of basic training. Also, Don got married again, although the press generally presented it as his first marriage. This time, the wedding got some media attention: Don and his bride, a former actress named Venetia Stevenson, were married in a small ceremony at the chapel of the Naval Training Center in San Diego, with Phil serving as best man. The brothers received permission to perform on *The Ed Sullivan Show* several days later. Dressed in their Marine uniforms, they sang "Crying in the Rain" (Best, B1).

But fans would have been surprised to know that the brothers, who had such a positive public image, had begun to experience tension in their relationship; one reason was the pressure of constant touring and never having time to relax. But another reason was substance abuse. After Phil and Don completed their stint in the Marines and returned to touring, they were taking amphetamines to give them energy. In those days, there was little understanding of the long-term effect of "speed," and Don became addicted. When the Everlys began a tour of Europe in October 1962, Don suddenly collapsed in London and was rushed to the hospital. He was treated and released, but then collapsed a second time, and was once again admitted to a London hospital ("Don Everly," 8). The press reported what they were told by Don's wife: he had a mystery ailment that she thought was food poisoning. But the British tabloids were not convinced and continued to investigate; they soon reported that Don had suffered an overdose of drugs, possibly sleeping pills. His wife and friends insisted he was instead a victim of "physical and nervous exhaustion" ("Singer Don," 54), but Don had to fly home to the United States, leaving Phil to continue without him. Years later, Don admitted that what really happened in London was a suicide attempt by taking an overdose of sleeping pills; but at the time, all anyone knew was that Don did not tour for a while due to an unspecified illness. In reality, he was seeing a therapist and gradually recovering from his addiction (Loder 1986; Morse, D1).

By the time the Everlys were able to tour again, music had changed dramatically. The British invasion began, and suddenly the Everly Brothers were considered part of another era. But they still had a dedicated fan base; and even though they never had another top 10 hit in the United States, some of their records sold well overseas, and they continued to be in demand for live concerts. In 1970, they were invited to host a summer variety program on ABC-TV, filling in for country legend Johnny Cash; among their guests during the 10-week show were Linda Ronstadt, Stevie Wonder, Arlo Guthrie, and Rick Nelson (Witbeck, H8). But like a number of 1950s rock stars, the Everlys had struggled to remain relevant during the 1960s, a decade that featured so many new trends in pop music. Most of their albums did not sell, and some critics believed the brothers had lost their direction. Still, one particular release from this time period has earned critical acclaim—"Roots" came out in 1968, and it was regarded as a forerunner of country rock (Pareles, A22). The *Rolling Stone Album Guide* considered it a companion to the Everlys' 1958 album *Songs Our Daddy Taught Us* and gave it four out of five stars, praising it as a "moving look back at the sources of their own music" (287).

Although Phil and Don's relationship had begun to show strains in the early 1960s, it came apart entirely in 1973. By this time, Don's second marriage had ended (he would remarry a third time in 1975), and so had Phil's first (he remarried in 1972). The brothers were beginning to have very different views about politics and about the Vietnam War (Loder 1986), and constantly touring together was becoming increasingly difficult. At a live performance in mid-July 1973 at Knott's Berry Farm, not far from Los Angeles, Don showed up too drunk to play well, and Phil stormed off the stage, throwing his guitar down in frustration. Don had already told Phil he was fed up with their life as a duo and no longer wanted to be an Everly Brother (Gardner and Gardner, 27). As he later explained to a reporter, "We broke up . . . because we couldn't get along. We had been singing together, and hadn't really been apart, since we were around 6 years old. It kept us immature, in a way, kept us from developing any individuality" (Palmer, C19).

After the Everly Brothers' acrimonious parting of ways, they each pursued solo careers, and solo lives, not even speaking to each other (Blanche, 26). Both wrote songs for other artists, and both recorded solo albums that neither sold well nor received critical praise:

for example, a reviewer called Don's 1974 album *Sunset Towers* "mostly lightweight" (Smith, 7). Each brother also provided background vocals on other performers' records: Don could be heard on Emmylou Harris's 1979 album *Blue Kentucky Gal*, and Phil participated in Warren Zevon's 1976 debut album. But even as they no longer performed, they were not forgotten: longtime fan Paul McCartney not only mentioned them in the chorus of his 1976 hit "Let 'Em In" ("Sister Suzie, Brother John, Martin Luther, Phil and Don"), but when there was talk of an Everly Brothers reunion in 1984, he wrote a song for their new album; "On the Wings of a Nightingale" was not a top 40 hit, but it did get a lot of airplay at adult contemporary stations, reaching number nine on the adult contemporary charts. As for how they got back together after 10 years of not speaking, several of their music industry friends encouraged them periodically, but it was British guitarist Albert Lee, who had been friends with the brothers (and especially with Don) since the early 1960s, who seems to have facilitated the reunion (Graff 2014). After they got back together, Don told a reporter that "I think we both knew we wanted to do it. Words had been passed back and forth through friends. And then I just called Phil up one day and said, 'How ya doin'?' And he said, 'Fine, how you doin'?' And that was it" (Morse, D1). Phil concurred, saying the time away from each other had been necessary and beneficial, but in the end, "we're brothers and we should be together" ("Cable Concert," 38).

The Everly Brothers Reunion Concert took place in September 1983 at Royal Albert Hall in London; it was broadcast on cable TV in January 1984 and also released as a two-disc CD by Passport Records. Phil and Don then released *EB 84*, their first album of new material, later that year. That was followed by two other albums, *Born Yesterday* in 1986, and *Some Hearts* in 1988. In 2003, they went out on tour with Paul Simon and Art Garfunkel, longtime fans of theirs who had endured an acrimonious breakup of their own before eventually reuniting. Simon noted that the Everlys had actually retired from performing but were willing to come out of retirement to join him and Art on the "Old Friends" tour (Simon, 120).

Although the Everlys were never able to return to the pop charts with the kind of success they had in the 1960s, a new generation was discovering their older songs, as baby boomer parents played the duo's classic hits for their children. Billie Joe Armstrong, lead singer for Green Day, recalls, "My mother was an Everly Brothers fan, and I remember her playing their music in the house and hearing songs like 'Bye Bye Love' and 'Wake Up Little Susie'... They were a part of the foundation of rock 'n' roll. You have Chuck Berry and Jerry Lee Lewis and Buddy Holly and Little Richard and Elvis Presley—a lot of those guys are straight rockers. But the Everly Brothers... brought in straight harmony, and that was so important to establish how the future of popular music was going to go" (Armstrong, C3). Armstrong was so impressed with the music of the Everly Brothers that he collaborated with singer/songwriter Norah Jones in late 2013 to make an album called *Foreverly*. It was a 12-set inspired by the Everlys' *Songs Our Daddy Taught Us*.

Further proof that the Everly Brothers have stood the test of time is the honors they have received. They were in the first group of performers inducted into the new Rock and Roll Hall of Fame in 1986; they were also inducted into the Country Music Hall of Fame in 2001. They received a Lifetime Achievement Award at the Grammy Awards in 1998. Phil Everly was inducted into Nashville's Songwriters Hall of Fame in 2001. When Phil died suddenly in January 2014, at age 77, many rock and country musicians offered their tributes. Paul McCartney even stated that Phil was one of his heroes. "I will always love him for giving me some of the sweetest musical memories of my life" (Reed, N5). Looking back on the life and achievements of the Everly Brothers, Phil Gallo of *Billboard* magazine explained their lasting appeal—so many of their songs are timeless, and can be reinterpreted to suit a new generation. "Their best work combined sweetness with urgency, and despite the bulk of their hits coming when they were teens and in their early 20s, the songs and stories [are] often worldly and universal" (Gallo, 8). And Billie Joe Armstrong added, "Those harmonies live on forever" (Pareles, A22).

Donna L. Halper

Selected Discography

The Everly Brothers, Cadence CLP-3003, 1958.

Songs Our Daddy Taught Us, Cadence CLP-3016, 1958.

The Everly Brothers: Their Best, Cadence CLP 3025, 1959.

A Date with the Everly Brothers, Warner Bros. W 1395, 1960.

The Everly Brothers Sing Great Country Hits, Warner Bros. W 1513, 1963.

Roots, Warner Bros. WS 1752, 1968.

The Everly Brothers Reunion Concert, Passport PB 11001, 1983.

EB 84, Mercury 822 431–2, 1984.

Born Yesterday, Mercury 826–142–1, 1986.

References

Anderson, Nancy. "Versatile Phil Everly Presenting New Image." *Dallas Morning News* (August 9, 1976): A17.

Armstrong, Billie Joe. "The Man in Perfect Harmony." *Wall Street Journal* (January 11, 2014): C3.

"A Tribute to the Golden Stars of the Month: The Everly Brothers." *Hit Parader* (August 1958): 14.

Benson, Carl. "Archie Bleyer." In *Encyclopedia of Recorded Sound*, 2nd ed., edited by Fred Hoffman. New York: Routledge, 2005.

Best, Natalie. "Rock 'n' Roll Marine Weds with Brother as Best Man." *San Diego Union* (February 14, 1962): B1.

Blanche, Ed. "Everly 'Laid Back.'" *Springfield (MA) Union* (June 21, 1977): 26.

Bledsoe, Jerry. "Ike and Margaret Everly Don't Like Doing Nothing." *Greensboro (NC) Daily News* (November 29, 1971) B1.

Bronson, Fred. *The Billboard Book of Number 1 Hits,* 5th ed. New York: *Billboard* Books, 2003.

Cummings, Sue. "Seminal Role in Rock 'n' Roll Not Over for the Everly Brothers." *Baton Rouge (LA) State Times Advocate* (October 3, 1986): F9.

Dean, Murray. *Rock and Roll Gold Rush.* New York: Algora Publishing, 2003.

"Don Everly Ill, Taken to Hospital." *San Diego Union* (October 15, 1962): 8.

Everett, Walter. *The Beatles as Musicians: The Quarry Men Through Rubber Soul.* New York: Oxford University Press, 2001.

"Everly Brothers Return." *Cleveland Plain Dealer* (July 5, 1970): 29E.

Paul Friedlander. *Rock and Roll: A Social History.* Boulder, CO: Westview Press, 1996.

Gallo, Phil. "In Memoriam: Phil Everly 1939–2014." *Billboard* (January 18, 2014): 8.

Gardner, Marilyn, and Hy Gardner. "Everly Brothers Too Close for Too Long." *Springfield (MA) Union* (August 24, 1973): 27.

Graff, Gary. "The Everly Brothers 1983 Reunion Concert: Albert Lee on Bringing Phil and Don Together After 10 Years of Not Speaking." *Billboard,* January 4, 2014, online at www.Billboard.com/articles/news/5862261/the-everly-brothers-1983-reunion-concert-albert-lee-phil-don.

Houston, Robert. "Everlys, Ex-Iowans, to Fill in for Cash." *Omaha World-Herald* (June 28, 1970): TV11.

Kleiner, Dick. "Teenagers on the Record Beat." *Corpus Christi (TX) Times* (July 26, 1957): 12B.

Lieberson, Goddard. "Country Sweeps the Country." *New York Times* (July 28, 1957): M13.

Loder, Kurt. "The Everly Brothers: The *Rolling Stone* Interview." *Rolling Stone,* May 8, 1986, online at www.rollingstone.com/music/news/the-rolling-stone-interview-the-everly-brothers-19860508.

Norman, Philip. *Shout: The Beatles in Their Generation.* New York: Fireside Books, 1981.

Palmer, Robert. "The Pop Life: New Record by Everlys." *New York Times* (February 29, 1984): C19.

Pareles, Jon. "Phil Everly, Half of a Pioneer Rock Duo That Inspired Generations, Dies at 74." *New York Time* (January 4, 2014): A22.

Reed, James. "A Legacy of Harmony: The Music of the Everly Brothers Endures and Thrives." *Boston Globe* (January 12, 2014): N5.

Rees, Dafydd, and Luke Crampton. *Rock's Movers and Shakers*. Revised edition. New York: *Billboard* Books, 1991.

Rhodes, Don. "Country Music an Influence on Everly Act." *Augusta (GA) Chronicle and Herald* (September 23, 1979): 5E.

Riley, Tim. *Tell Me Why*. New York: Vintage, 1989.

Rolling Stone Album Guide. Nathan Brackett and Christian David, editors. New York: Fireside, 2004.

Rolling Stone Encyclopedia of Rock. Revised edition. Patricia Romanowski and Holly George-Warren, editors. New York: Fireside, 1995.

Ronstadt, Linda. "Tribute to Phil Everly." *Time* (January 20, 2014): 16.

Scott, Jane. "Phil Everly: 'It's Like New Times.'" *Cleveland Plain Dealer* (July 13, 1984): 39.

"Singer Don Everly Flies to N.Y. Hospital." *Boston Traveler* (October 16, 1962): 54.

Smith, Will. "New Sounds." *Omaha World-Herald* (October 11, 1974): 7.

Witbeck, Charles. "Everly Brothers Surprised." *Richmond (VA) Times-Dispatch* (July 5, 1970): H8.

F

Fleetwood Mac (1967–1995; 1998–Present)

Fleetwood Mac, one of the drivers of the mega-platinum pop rock phenomenon of the 1970s, began its existence quite differently: as a spinoff of John Mayall's Bluesbreakers, the most serious British blues band of its era. Myriad personnel changes radically reshaped the band's sound from British blues rock to West Coast soft rock, though the rhythm section of Mick Fleetwood and John McVie, for whom the band was named, has anchored the band for more than 40 years.

Fleetwood Mac was founded by the gifted blues guitarist Peter Green (born Peter Alan Greenbaum, October 29, 1946; guitar, vocals). He started playing guitar at age 10, and within a few years was playing in a skiffle group. He switched to bass in his late teens and played with a number of British R&B groups. In 1965, Green once again took up guitar, one of the hundreds of British youth influenced by Eric Clapton's work with the Yardbirds. He began attending concerts of the guitar god's new group, the Bluesbreakers, led by John Mayall (born November 23, 1933; guitar) an unorthodox guitarist, vocalist, and keyboard player from Manchester.

Mayall moved to London in 1963 and started assembling musicians for a band. One of the first he recruited was bassist John McVie (born John Graham McVie, November 26, 1945; bass), who anchored Mayall's rhythm section for the majority of the next four years. McVie picked up the guitar in his teens and then switched to bass; when he met Mayall he was playing with a beat group modeled after the Shadows. McVie admitted that he did not know much about blues, but

the older musician gave him some records to study and told him to keep it simple.

Ironically, Green's first gig as a lead guitarist was filling in for Eric Clapton in the Bluesbreakers. Clapton had taken off in August 1965 for an unscheduled holiday, leaving Mayall with a full schedule of club dates. He employed a series of temporary guitarists, but Mayall recalled, "Peter, this cockney kid, keeps coming down to all the gigs and saying, 'Hey, what are you doing with him; I'm much better than he is. Why don't you let me play guitar for you?'" (McStavick and Roos, 180). Mayall relented, and discovered that Green was every bit as good as he claimed. After only a few dates with the band, Clapton returned, and Mayall had to let the disappointed young guitarist go.

Shortly thereafter Green was approached with an offer to join Peter B's Looners, a Stax-soul-influenced group that included drummer Mick Fleetwood (born June 24, 1947; percussion), a veteran of the London R&B scene. In July 1966, Green received a call from John Mayall, offering him the lead guitar spot in the Bluesbreakers, as Eric Clapton had just quit.

The next year the Bluesbreakers released *A Hard Road.* Green proved to be a surprisingly mature guitarist who was heavily influenced by B. B. King and had mastered the American guitarist's expressive vibrato and economic style. The album was hailed on both sides of the Atlantic as a superlative example of white blues.

During sessions for the follow-up, *Crusade,* Mayall fired drummer Aynsley Dunbar and replaced him with Mick Fleetwood, Green's bandmate from the Looners. While they were in the studio, McVie,

Named for the the band's rhythm section (Fleetwood and McVie), Fleetwood Mac, pictured here in 1975, were (from left to right): John McVie, Christine McVie, Stevie Nicks, Mick Fleetwood, and Lindsey Buckingham. Together, these musicians created a unique blend of blues and rock spearheaded by a female vocalist. (Photo by Michael Ochs Archives/ Getty Images)

Green, and Fleetwood also laid down a few tracks, including an instrumental titled "Fleetwood Mac."

Mayall determined that his next album would be an exploration of jazz-blues fusion. Green became disillusioned with the new direction and quit to form a new band with Fleetwood, who had been fired several months earlier. They adopted the name of their recently recorded instrumental, as they were convinced that McVie would eventually break with Mayall to join them. While they waited, they auditioned a number of bassists to fill the spot temporarily, ultimately finding Bob Brunning through an ad in *Melody Maker*.

Though the band had not yet played a single live date, they already had a record contract. Mike Vernon,

the Decca staffer who produced *A Hard Road,* also ran a small blues label with his brother Richard. Blue Horizon was eager to expand its roster, and based on their earlier association with Green, the brothers agreed to record Fleetwood Mac whenever it was ready. Green had determined that the group should include a second guitarist, and Mike Vernon suggested he check out Jeremy Spencer (born Jeremy Cedric Spencer, July 4, 1948; guitar), who was playing with a blues trio in Birmingham. Spencer had fallen for early rock and roll before discovering Elmore James, and had mastered the Chicago blues man's electric slide guitar. Green was taken with his style and conviction, and he was added to Fleetwood Mac's roster.

The group, billed as Peter Green's Fleetwood Mac, made their well-received debut at the Windsor Jazz and Blues Festival on August 13, 1967, and the band quickly became a popular act on the English blues circuit. Less than a month later, they recorded their first single for Blue Horizon; the day it was released, McVie announced that he was leaving the Bluesbreakers to join Fleetwood Mac.

The quartet decamped to the studio to record an album of blues-influenced tracks, with Green and Spencer sharing lead vocal duties. The disc included a version of Mississippi Fred MacDowell's "You Got to Move"; Elmore James's "Shake Your Money-maker," a feature for Spencer; and "Hellhound on My Trail," by Robert Johnson. The majority of the numbers are blues-based originals: the harmonica-driven "Long Grey Mare," inspired by Howlin' Wolf's "Killing Floor"; Spencer's superb "My Baby's Good to Me" and "My Heart Beats Like a Hammer," both retrofits of "Dust My Broom"; and "The World Keeps on Turning," one of Peter Green's best numbers.

The album, *Fleetwood Mac*, leaped up the charts to number four, the highest position a blues-oriented album had attained to date. Pop critics hailed it as one of the best albums of 1968, and Fleetwood Mac was considered Britain's finest blues band until the end of the decade. The album's mainstream success also signaled that the British blues had become an accepted alternative to pop, and record companies began signing new acts at a steady clip.

Four weeks after their debut was released, the band returned to the studio to record *Mr. Wonderful*. The album included keyboard work by Christine Perfect (born July 12, 1943; keyboards, vocals), another Blue Horizon artist. She started playing the piano at age four, focused on the classical repertoire until age 15, and then shifted to rock and boogie-woogie after her brother bought her a book of Fats Domino songs. In art school she met Stan Webb and Andy Silvestre and joined their band, Sounds of Blue, a popular act in the Birmingham area. When Webb and Silvestre started the blues rock outfit Chicken Shack, they brought Perfect on board; she also wrote most of their material. She was also John McVie's fiancée.

Mr. Wonderful was as indebted to the blues as the band's first album, but the material, which was written quickly, was of lesser quality. There were nonetheless some fine songs: Green's "Love That Burns"; "Stop Messin' Round," which featured a horn section; and the 1950s rocker "Evenin' Boogie." Although the album made the top 10 in Britain, it was considered a disappointment after their stellar debut.

After *Mr. Wonderful*, Fleetwood Mac added a third guitarist, Danny Kirwan (born May 13, 1950; guitar). His first professional gig was opening for Fleetwood Mac with his band, Boilerhouse. Green did not think the band was particularly good, but he found Kirwan quite impressive. He tried to help the younger musician put together a trio that would better showcase his talents, but Fleetwood suggested adding him to their roster instead.

Mr. Wonderful was not released in the United States; instead, Blue Horizon issued *English Rose*, which included a handful of new songs, including Kirwan's powerful, B. B. King–styled "Without You" and "Something Inside of Me," as well as the band's British singles. The standouts were "Albatross," with Hawaiian-style guitar and Allman Brothers–influenced harmonies, and "Black Magic Woman," a fusion of blues, rock, and Caribbean music later made famous by Santana.

In 1969, Fleetwood Mac's contract with Blue Horizon expired. Mo Ostin, an executive at Warner Brothers, convinced the group's management to sign with his Reprise label, which would be their home for the next 35 years.

Shortly thereafter, members of Fleetwood Mac traveled to Chicago to record with artists from Chess Records, including Otis Spann, Willie Dixon, and Buddy Guy. The tracks, released as *Blues Jam in Chicago* in 1969, were the band's last pure blues recordings. By the time *Then Play On* was recorded in 1969, the band had branched out in new directions. Kirwan's "Coming Your Way" revisited the style of "Black Magic Woman." "Oh Well Parts 1 & 2," which ran nearly 9 minutes, fused hard rock, flamenco-inspired guitar, recorder, and cello, an unorthodox combination that worked better than it should; it was one of the early band's most compelling tracks. The wistful "My

Dream" and "When You Say" combine folk rock, psychedelia and Beatles-inspired lyricism, and "Rattlesnake Shake" and "Show-Biz Blues" were hillbilly blues. The two instrumental tracks, "Searching for Madge" and "Fighting for Madge," were edited improvisations that demonstrated Green's guitar prowess.

By the end of 1969 Fleetwood Mac had produced an impressive string of top five hits and was outselling both the Beatles and the Rolling Stones. However, an aesthetic split had emerged; Green wanted to pursue the sort of blues-based improvisation pioneered by the Yardbirds and Cream, while the rest of the band wished to continue exploring new musical avenues. The problems were exacerbated by Green's erratic behavior, mental instability, and excessive LSD use. During their European tour in April 1970 Green abruptly quit, claiming that money and stardom were corrupting his relationship with God.

Fleetwood Mac decided to continue as a four-piece ensemble, with Spencer and Kirwan sharing guitar and vocal duties. *Kiln House* (1970) demonstrated the band's stylistic diversity: Spencer's love of rock and roll is reflected in the Elvis Presley–influenced "This Is the Rock," "Buddy's Song," and a rockabilly retrofit of the Fats Waller tune "Hi Ho Silver." The album also contained numbers that were influenced by country music, including "Station Man" and the honky-tonk ballad "Blood on the Floor"; the Beatles-esque "Jewel-Eyed Judy"; and the folk-pop-influenced "Mission Bell." Christine Perfect—now Christine McVie—again contributed keyboard and vocal harmonies. She had stayed with Chicken Shack for two years and sang lead on their biggest hit, "I'd Rather Go Blind," then embarked on a solo career. After one disappointing album she became a permanent member of Fleetwood Mac.

Kiln House did not sell well in England, but it broke the top 100 in the United States, and the band launched an American tour in early 1971. A few hours before a show in Los Angeles, Spencer vanished; when he was located four days (and cancelled dates) later, it was discovered that he had joined the Children of God, a religious cult. Interestingly, the band turned to Green, who replaced Spencer on the tour.

Spencer's departure left Christine McVie and Kirwan as the group's only songwriters, and they began a search for a replacement guitarist who could also contribute material. They settled on Bob Welch (born Robert Lawrence Welch Jr., August 31, 1945, died June 7, 2012; guitar, songwriter), an American who had played with Ivory Hudson and the Harlequins, a popular nightclub act that had recently disbanded. Welch found himself in the unusual position of leading a band that was still searching for a musical identity. The new lineup played club dates for a few months before going into the studio to record *Future Games*. The album was a radical departure from their earlier style; the blues were left behind as Fleetwood Mac wholeheartedly embraced the dominant West Coast fusion of pop, folk, and country music.

Welch's eight-minute title track is the disc's clear standout and a declaration of the band's new ethos: a pop-folk-influenced melody, Beach Boys–influenced vocal harmonies, a subdued rhythm section, and ambiguously mystical lyrics. The song is a blueprint for the entire album; little distinguishes it from "Sands of Time" or "Show Me a Smile," though country influences are present in McVie "Morning Rain" and "Sometimes." Kirwan's psychedelic pop-folk "Woman of a Thousand Years" seemed at odds with the rest of the collection. The reviews were uniformly poor and the album performed abysmally in Britain, but it was embraced by American audiences.

Their follow-up, *Bare Trees*, contained standout tracks by each of the group's three songwriters. Welch's "Sentimental Lady" was an early example of the pop rock style that came to dominate rock in the 1970s, and "Spare Me a Little of Your Love," a lovely tune by McVie, foreshadowed her mature style. Kirwan's contributions were all sterling: the country and blues hybrid "Child of Mine"; "Danny's Chant," a slide guitar riff supporting vocalization that evoked early 1960s Roy Orbison; and the jazz-funk-inspired "Bare Trees." The group seemed to have finally found its stylistic equilibrium; however, it was not to last.

During the recording process Kirwan started to come unglued; he was drinking heavily and alienated everyone else in the band. After a drunken outburst before a concert, Kirwan refused to take the stage and instead stayed in the wings and heckled his bandmates; he was fired days later. With his departure the band's last link to Peter Green was gone, and the psychological effect was surprisingly powerful. Fleetwood Mac entered a "foundering stage" (Graham, 35) defined by constantly shifting membership and doubt about the band's musical identity.

In late 1972, Fleetwood Mac hired two new members: Dave Walker (born David Walker, January 25, 1945; lead vocals, guitar), the former lead singer of blues-rock band Savoy Brown, and guitarist Bob Weston (born Robert Joseph Weston, November 1, 1947, died January 3, 2012; guitar). With little preparation, the band rushed into the studio. On *Penguin*, it was evident that the group lacked direction: McVie's tracks, "Remember Me," "Did You Ever Love Me," and "Dissatisfied," continued the stylistic hybrid under development on *Bare Trees*, but the Motown cover "I'm a Road Runner"; "Derelict," featuring banjo and harmonica; and the instrumental "Caught in the Rain" sounded like tracks by other bands that were mistakenly added to the album.

Walker's hard-edged vocal style was a poor fit for Fleetwood Mac, and he was fired before the band recorded *Mystery to Me* (1973) three months later. The album shared the inconsistency of its predecessor. The standout track, "Hypnotized," was an exploration of the paranormal, with jazz- and Latin-influenced guitar fills and atmospheric electric piano; it is Welch's strongest contribution to the band's repertoire. Many of his other songs were influenced by contemporary soul: "Keep on Going," "The City," and "Somebody," the latter with some fine bass work by McVie. Some tracks just do not work: a psychedelic rockabilly version of the Yardbirds' "For Your Love"; "Forever," an ill-advised mixture of reggae and country; and the breathy "Believe Me"; however, "Why," a soulful ballad sung by McVie with a slide guitar intro by Weston, was stunning.

On their supporting U.S. tour the quintet was finally beginning to cohere when Fleetwood discovered that Weston was having an affair with his wife. The guitarist was summarily sacked and the band abandoned the tour. The group's manager, Clifford Davis, who contractually held the rights to the name Fleetwood Mac, recruited Weston and a new group of musicians and sent them out on the road. The bogus Fleetwood Mac fooled no one, and both fans and the real members of Fleetwood Mac were incensed. The band fired Davis and filed an injunction, and Mick Fleetwood took over the band's management.

Welch convinced Fleetwood that the group should relocate to Los Angeles, where he felt audiences would be more receptive to the band's stylistic exploration. Their first West Coast recording was *Heroes Are Hard to Find* (1974). The blues ran through the album like a touchstone to a more stable past, which was evident in "Bad Loser," the swamp pop title track; "Bermuda Triangle," a Hendrix-influenced sibling to "Hypnotized"; and a bizarre, psychedelic rendition of Elmore James's "Coming Home." The album sounded decidedly unfocused, and it did not sell well.

Welch, exhausted and feeling he had nothing further to contribute, resigned after the album was completed, and Fleetwood Mac was once again looking for a guitarist. While checking out recording studios, Fleetwood heard tracks by the pop folk rock duo Lindsey Buckingham (born Lindsey Adams Buckingham, October 3, 1949; guitar, vocals) and Stevie Nicks (born Stephanie Lynn Nicks, May 26, 1948; vocals). Nicks learned to sing from her grandfather, a failed country singer. She started writing songs on the guitar she received for her 16th birthday, and formed a band, the Changing Times. During her senior year in high school she met Buckingham, who played banjo and guitar. The pair formed a romantic and musical bond and played with Bay Area band Fritz from 1968 to 1972; then they made their way to Los Angeles in search of a record deal. They released *Buckingham Nicks* in 1973. Fleetwood was taken by Buckingham's guitar style, their striking harmonies, and well-written songs. Initially he was interested only in Buckingham, but he refused to join unless Nicks was hired as well. Fleetwood, feeling that destiny was at work, agreed. The new members came bearing gifts: several songs they had been preparing for their next album, which included Nicks's "Rhiannon."

The new chemistry of the group imbued a sense of stability, and the folk-influenced pop rock of Buckingham and Nicks gave focus to the band's stylistic explorations of the previous years. The band retreated to their Malibu compound and started working on material; their first album with the new lineup, *Fleetwood Mac*, was recorded in only 10 days. The disc was stylistically varied, but an overarching pop rock aesthetic provided cohesion. Besides the captivating, quasi-mystical "Rhiannon," "Monday Morning," was reminiscent of James Taylor, with driving rhythm guitar; and with "Over My Head" and "Say You Love Me," McVie's fusion of soft country, folk, and pop rock reached maturity. The album even contained a nod to the original Fleetwood Mac: a revision of Green's "World Keeps Turning." Driven by three top 20 singles and extensive touring, the album went to the top of the charts in the United States and ultimately sold more than five million copies; it also served as a blueprint for California soft rock for the rest of the decade.

The smash success of *Fleetwood Mac* was dwarfed by the band's follow-up, *Rumours*. The album was recorded under unusual circumstances: every member of the band was in the process of a divorce or breakup. Instead of disbanding, they poured their emotional turbulence into songwriting. *Rumours* took almost a year to record, but the end result was both a chronicle of personal dysfunction and one of the most finely wrought pop rock albums to date. Buckingham deserved a large share of credit, taking raw songs of disparate emotional content from himself, McVie, and Nicks and, through arrangements, creating a unified sound. The album spawned four top 10 singles: "Go Your Own Way," "Dreams," "Don't Stop" (later to become the campaign anthem of President Bill Clinton), and "You Make Loving Fun." The disc went platinum in less than a month and stayed at the top of the charts in both Britain and the United States for 31 weeks; it remains one of the best-selling albums in history. In 1977, it won the Grammy for album of the year.

Fleetwood Mac spent most of that year and the next on tour and began working on their next album. Buckingham took control of the project, but instead of capitalizing on their winning formula he drove the group to embrace experimentalism and subvert its own wildly successful brand. The result, *Tusk*, was a sprawling double album that interspersed creative oddities with introspective, country-tinged soft rock ballads that harken back to the Welch era. Only one track, Nicks's "Sara," was stylistically consistent with *Rumours*, but her ethereal vocals, over spare piano and guitar, were gradually buried in overdubbed harmonies and echo. The influence of punk and New Wave was evident on many of the tracks, particularly "What Makes You Think You're the One," and "Not That Funny." "The Ledge" and "Save Me a Place" sounded like low-budget country folk demos, and "That's Enough for Me" was a bluegrass and hard rock fusion driven by banjo and toy piano. All pale in comparison to the gloriously weird title track, which opened with computer-generated noise, sotto-voce chanting, and nonsensical vocal interjections; this was followed by a full-throated chorus accompanied by the University of South California (USC) marching band and interrupted at midpoint by a rare Mick Fleetwood drum solo over a tape collage.

Critics hated the album—*Mojo* called it "one of the greatest career sabotage albums of all time" (Brackett, 135)—yet it rose to number four in the United States and both "Sara" and "Tusk" were top 10 singles. In hindsight, it was one of the strongest albums of the classic lineup. The group followed with *Fleetwood Mac Live*, a double album chronicling the band's 1980 tour. The disc proved that, regardless of their stylistic direction, the band was a force to be reckoned with on stage.

Afterward, the members went their own ways and worked on solo projects. The runaway success of Nicks's *Bella Donna* (1981), which went quadruple platinum, led many to question the future of Fleetwood Mac, but in 1982 they released *Mirage*, the true sequel to *Rumours*, which made up for a lack of substance with radio-friendly accessibility. The band's 1977 style was updated with touches of country, New Wave, and 1980s pop, and was greeted with enthusiasm by fans. It shot to number one and spawned three hits: the Nicks classic "Gypsy," "Hold Me," and "Love in Store."

Seemingly drained by the effort of reviving their brand, Fleetwood Mac went on hiatus until 1985, when they came together for a new album. Complicated by personal matters and Nicks's cocaine addiction, *Tango in the Night* was not completed until 1987. While there were touches of the classic Mac sound, it had been updated for the 1980s: electric keyboard and synthesizer permeated nearly every song, effects were added to the percussion, and the bass was buried in the mix so deeply that its presence was more assumed than heard. Buckingham, again serving as producer, achieved a small miracle by taking the fragments that Nicks was able to contribute and inserting them into songs that she never recorded. Fleetwood and John McVie were similarly disengaged; most of their parts were overdubbed. Buckingham contributed many of the songs, and they were the strongest cuts. "Big Love," "Tango in the Night," and "Isn't It Midnight" all hit the top 20, but the number-one singles from the disc—"Everywhere" and "Little Lies," perfect gems of 1980s pop—were penned by Christine McVie. The album was wildly popular, and Fleetwood Mac seemed ready to resume its place at the top of the pop rock hierarchy.

However, Buckingham, frustrated by the travails of *Tango in the Night,* refused to tour behind the album. After an acrimonious row with his bandmates, he left Fleetwood Mac. As before, the band found replacements: Billy Burnette (born William Beau Burnette III, May 8, 1953; guitar) and Rick Vito (born Richard Vito, October 13, 1949; guitar). They performed on the *Tango in the Night* tour and joined the group for the 1990 album *Behind the Mask*, a lackluster effort. The songs were generally weak and the production ineffectual, though two tracks broke the top 10. The two new members were dismissed after the album, and both Christine McVie and Nicks indicated that while they would remain with the band, they would no longer tour.

The classic lineup reunited briefly in 1993 to perform at President Clinton's first Inaugural Ball, but dispersed immediately afterward, and Nicks announced her departure from the band several months later.

Fleetwood and John McVie once again found themselves in need of new members and reached out to Dave Mason (born David Thomas Mason, May 10, 1946; guitar), the cofounder of Traffic, and Bekka Bramlett (born Rebekkah Ruth Lazone Bramlett, April 19, 1968; singer), the daughter of Delanie and Bonnie Bramlett, the core members of Derek and the Dominoes. Despite their excellent pedigrees, their first and only album, *Time*, was considered a bad album even by die-hard fans; it sounded like a desperate attempt to keep the band's name alive. After a tour playing to nostalgia audiences, Fleetwood Mac dissolved.

The *Rumours* lineup, reunited in 1998 for a filmed studio concert for MTV, released one album called *The Dance*; later that year, Fleetwood Mac was inducted into the Rock and Roll Hall of Fame. After the performance, Christine McVie announced her retirement and returned to England. The rest of the group went back to their solo projects, but when Buckingham was working on an album in the late 1990s he asked McVie and Fleetwood to serve as his rhythm section. He ultimately decided that the project was, for all intents and purposes, a Fleetwood Mac album; all that was needed was Stevie Nicks. In 2003, they released their final album, *Say You Will*. The disc, with nine songs each by Buckingham and Nicks, has some of the eccentricity of Tusk: "Murrow Turns Over in His Grave," with its robotic, spoken word chorus; "Illume (9/11)," a virtual recitation over electronic percussion; and the country-folk-bluegrass workouts "Miranda" and "Red Rover." The album closed with Buckingham's "Say Goodbye" and Nicks's "Goodbye Baby," their apparent final farewell. Since 2003, Fleetwood Mac has devoted its energies to touring.

From their first album, which established that blues rock was still a viable commodity, to the pop rock standard bearer *Rumours* and the wildly experimental *Tusk*, Fleetwood Mac has musically influenced bands as diverse as Blues Traveler, Matchbox Twenty, and Hootie and the Blowfish. Their two female singer/songwriters also paved the way for female-led bands like 10,000 Maniacs, Rilo Kelly, the Cranberries, and No Doubt.

Roberta Freund Schwartz

Selected Discography

Peter Green's Fleetwood Mac. UK: Blue Horizon 7–63200; US: Epic BN26402, 1968.

Mr. Wonderful. UK: Blue Horizon 7–63205; US: as *English Rose,* Epic BN26446, 1968.

Then Play On. UK: Reprise RSLP 9000; US: Reprise RS6368, 1969.

Bare Trees. US: Reprise MS2080; UK: Reprise K44181, 1972.

Fleetwood Mac. US: Reprise MS2225; UK: Reprise K54043, 1975.

Rumours. US: Warner Brothers BSK3010; UK: Warner Brothers K56344, 1977.

Tusk. US: Warner Brothers 2HS 3350; UK: Warner Brothers K66088, 1979.

Mirage. US: Warner Brothers W1 23607; UK: K56952, 1982.

Tango in the Night. Warne Brothers 92547 1–2, 1987.

References

Brackett, Donald. *Fleetwood Mac: 40 Years of Creative Chaos*. Westport, CN: Praeger, 2007.

Brunning, Bob. *The Blues in Britain: History 1950s to the Present*. London: Blandford, 1995.

Fleetwood, Mick, with Stephen Davis. *My Twenty-Five Years with Fleetwood Mac*. New York: Hyperion, 1992.

Graham, Samuel. *Fleetwood Mac: The Authorized History*. Washington, DC: Warner Brothers Publications, 1978.

Illingworth, David. Review of "I Believe My Time Ain't Long" b/w "Rambling Pony" [CBS 3051] by Fleetwood Mac. *Jazz Journal* 20/12 (December 1967): 32.

Mayall, John. Liner notes to *As It All Began: The Best of John Mayall and the Bluesbreakers 1964–69* [Decca D121768], 1997.

McStravick, Summer, and John Roos, eds. *Blues-Rock Explosion*. Mission Viejo, CA: Old Goat Publishing, 2001.

Schwartz, Roberta Freund. *How Britain Got the Blues: The Transmission and Reception of American Blues Style in the British Isles*. Aldershot: Ashgate, 2007.

Zanes, Warren. *Revolutions in Sound: Warner Bros. Records, the First Fifty Years*. San Francisco: Chronicle Books, 2008.

Frank Zappa and the Mothers of Invention (1965–1976)

The Mothers of Invention were an experimental band led by composer-guitarist Frank Zappa. They are difficult to categorize in any particular style of music, as they fused and juxtaposed several styles of music, including rock, jazz, doo-wop, and avant-garde classical. Frank Zappa, who described himself as a composer who plays the guitar, was the band's leader and primary composer/songwriter. His lyrics were satirical, comical, bizarre, and sexual (ranging from subtle to overt). His music was often very complicated due to its dissonant harmonies, complex rhythms, unusual time signatures, tempo changes, and multiple sections within songs. The Mothers of Invention released several albums, studio and live recordings. The Mothers broke up temporarily in 1969, but were re-formed in 1970 with a new lineup. By 1975, the new version of the Mothers had released six albums, including the soundtrack to Zappa's film *200 Motels*. The name "The Mothers" was dropped in 1976, and subsequent releases were branded simply "Frank Zappa." *Ahead of Their Time* was released in 1993 as Frank Zappa and the Mothers of Invention, but it was recorded in 1968 when the Mothers name was still in use. Musicians from various Mothers lineups appeared on Zappa's releases before and after 1976, blurring the line between what should be considered Mothers or Zappa's band.

Frank Zappa (born December 21, 1940, died December 4, 1993; guitar and vocals) moved to California in 1950. He began playing drums at age 12, and at age 13 became enamored with the avant-garde music of composer Edgard Varèse. As a teenager he composed 12-tone works, and in 1959, he was asked to compose a film score for a low-budget movie, *Run Home Slow*. Although he started playing guitar at age 18, he did not have an electric guitar until age 21. In 1963, Zappa appeared on *The Steve Allen Show,* where he played a bicycle as a musical instrument; he blew through the handlebars and used drumsticks and a bass bow on the spokes. Allen, Zappa, and the TV-show band improvised along with a prerecorded tape part. This performance was an early example of the avant-garde experimentalism, that was an important element of Zappa's music.

Zappa invested some of the money that he earned from *Run Home Slow* by purchasing a studio in Cucamonga, California, which he called "Studio Z." There he recorded with Don Van Vliet (aka Captain Beefheart, born Don Glen Vliet, January 15, 1941, died December 17, 2010; vocals, harmonica), Ray Collins (born November 19, 1936; vocals), Jim Sherwood (aka Motorhead, born Euclid James Sherwood, May 8, 1942, died December 25, 2011; saxophone, vocals), and others. Zappa formed the Soots with Beefheart in 1963; their recording of "I Was a Teenage Malt-Shop" (1964) was particularly dissonant, a precursor to the genre now known as noise rock.

In 1965, Zappa joined a rhythm and blues cover band called the Soul Giants. The band consisted of Collins, Roy Estrada (born April 17, 1943; bass), Jimmy Carl Black (born James Inckanish Jr., February 1, 1938, died November 1, 2008; drums), and David Coronado (saxophone). Zappa's intent was to perform original music, specifically his own, so Coronado left. Once the Soul Giants began to perform Zappa's music, they changed their name to the Mothers (in 1963, Zappa started a trio called the Muthers).

By the end of 1965, they had developed a following within the Los Angeles "freak" scene. Vito Paulekas and Carl Franzoni, two Los Angeles freaks, wore strange outfits and danced oddly at early Mothers concerts; it became a spectacle, and the band gained a following and much publicity. The Mothers song "Hungry Freaks Daddy" was dedicated to Franzoni. Herb Cohen began working as the band's manger in October 1965, and by March of the next year, the Mothers had a record deal with Verve. The record label objected to "The Mothers" as the band name and insisted it be changed ("Mothers" was short for "motherfuckers," a colloquialism used by musicians that meant "skilled musicians"). Thus, the album was released as *Freak Out!* by the Mothers of Invention in 1966.

Frank Zappa and the Mothers of Invention. Frank Zappa (center) poses for a group portrait with the Mothers of Invention (clockwise from far left): Ian Underwood, Bunk Gardner, Euclid James "Motorhead" Sherwood, Roy Estrada, Jimmy Carl Black, Art Tripp, and Don Preston, on the set of the German TV show *Beat-Club* in Bremen, Germany, on October 6, 1968. With Zappa, these men and a revolving cast of others delivered Zappa's satire-drenched songs to the masses for over a decade. (Photo by K & K Ulf Kruger OHG/Redferns)

Freak Out! (1966) was ambitious in terms of length and instrumentation. It was a double album, and, at the time of recording, no "pop" artist had released such a lengthy work. The album involved a studio orchestra, which Frank conducted. The music was not simple, even by professional orchestral musicians' standards. Frank brought in nearly 100 freaks from the Los Angeles scene to record on the album; they played percussion instruments and chanted whatever they wanted. The music on the album, like most of Zappa's output, was stylistically diverse. The opening track, "Hungry Freaks Daddy," began, in many ways, like the Rolling Stones' "(I Can't Get No)

Satisfaction." "Go Cry on Somebody Else's Shoulder" was the first of many 1950s R&B and doo-wop songs the Mothers recorded (Collins had a background in doo-wop singing). The third song, "Who Are the Brain Police?," featured bizarre, dissonant vocals; Zappa said it had a "Varèsian aroma" (quoted in Slaven 2003, 79). Mallet percussion appeared several times on the album, which, although unusual for a rock band, was a regular part of Zappa's instrumentation. The second movement of "Help, I'm a Rock" was titled "In Memoriam Edgar Varèse," dedicated to Zappa's lifelong idol. On side four was "Ritual Dance of the Child-Killer," a reference to Igor Stravinsky's ballet *Rite of Spring*.

There were several additions to the Mothers in 1966. Elliot Ingber (born August 24, 1941; guitar) joined the band shortly before *Freak Out!,* but he was fired for drug use after the album's release (Zappa was very antidrug). Bunk Gardner (born John Leon Gaunerra, May 2, 1933; saxophone) joined, as did Billy Mundi (born Antonio Salas, September 25, 1942; drums). Motorhead worked as the band's roadie, but he sang and played saxophone in the band occasionally. Perhaps the most significant addition to the Mothers in 1966 was Don Preston (born Donald Ward Preston, September 21, 1932; keyboards), who had worked with jazz greats such as Elvin Jones, Charlie Hayden, and Carla Bley.

Like *Freak Out!,* the Mothers' second release, *Absolutely Free* (1967), began with a reference to another band's song. The three-chord 1950s song "Louie, Louie" was played with intentional "wrong" notes at the beginning of "Plastic People." The melody for "Louie, Louie" appeared in "Son of Suzy Creamcheese," but it was re-harmonized in an odd, Zappaesque fashion, a fine example of his style and use of quotation. One of Zappa's most important contributions to rock music was his use of unusual meters. Instead of the 4/4 meter of "Louie, Louie," he alternated 4/4 with the rarely used 9/8 (e.g., "Suzy, you were such a sweetie, yeah, yeah, yeah!"). He placed the trite, ordinary early 1960s rock-ism *"yeah, yeah, yeah"* in an out-of-the-ordinary meter. Although not common to rock music, "unusual" meters were commonplace in

the music of Stravinsky, whom Zappa admired and often quoted. For example, he quoted the beginning of Stravinsky's ballet *Petroushka* in "Status Back Baby," and the "Ritual Action of the Ancestors" from *Rite of Spring* was quoted at the opening of "Amnesia Vivace."

The sixth song on the album was titled "Invocation & Ritual Dance of the Young Pumpkin," another clear reference to *Rite*. "America Drinks and Goes Home" parodied the cocktail jazz that Zappa had to play in the early 1960s in order to make a living. The highlight of the album was the multisectional "Brown Shoes Don't Make It." It included a greasy-blues shuffle, a performance by jazz trumpeter Don Ellis, 1920s-style cabaret music, New Orleans jazz, and a string quartet that provided some eerie, atonal accompaniment. Zappa's music was truly multi- and polystylistic—even yodeling appeared on the album (on "Call Any Vegetable").

Before *Absolutely Free* was released, the band headed to New York City for a series of gigs in the East Village. By May 1967, performances were billed as "*Absolutely Free*: A Musical by Frank Zappa with the Mothers of Invention." Audiences were intrigued by the stage antics and the audience participation. For instance, Collins would take a hand puppet and massage a three-and-a-half-foot-tall stuffed giraffe that sprayed the audience with whipped cream out of its backside. Zappa was well aware that most of his audience did not know how to listen to music actively and was more interested in the theatrical elements of the Mothers' concerts than their music.

Ian Underwood (born May 22, 1939; woodwinds and piano) joined the band around the time the Mothers recorded their third album, *We're Only in It for the Money* (1968; sometimes referred to as *WOIIFTM*). With Motorhead officially joining the band, the woodwind section expanded to three performers. The album's inner sleeve (which became the album cover on later releases) parodied the cover of the Beatles' *Sgt. Pepper*, a recent release at the time. The album's lyrics satirized the flower-power, hippie, psychedelic subculture of the time. The song "Flower Punk," for instance, included the lyric "Hey punk, where you going with that flower in your hand? Well, I'm goin' up to Frisco to join a psychedelic band." This parodied the song "Hey Joe," made famous by Jimi Hendrix: "Hey Joe, where you going with that gun in your hand? I'm going down to shoot my old lady; you know, I caught her messing around with another man." Zappa had much respect for Hendrix, and he even invited Hendrix to "sit in" with his band one night as Zappa listened from the audience. Some of the lyrics on the album were censored; some words were removed from the recording, some were in the recording but omitted from the album sleeve, and others were disguised. Although a partially censored version was released in 1972, an uncensored version was not released until 1985 on Zappa's own label Barking Pumpkin.

Like much of Zappa's work, *WOIIFTM* had various time signatures and several style parodies, such as the Tin Pan Alley send-up in "Bow Tie Daddy." "What's the Ugliest Part of Your Body?" began as a straightforward doo-wop song, but a verse in 7/8 meter followed. There was a 7/8 section in the eighth track, "Absolutely Free." "Flower Punk" was not a straight-ahead 4/4 song like "Hey Joe"; the meter alternated between 5/8 and 7/8. Perhaps a nod to Varèse, "Nasal Retentive Calliope Music" was a piece of musique concrete, which was interrupted by surf-rock. "The Chrome Plated Megaphone of Destiny" was similar to "Nasal" in that it used various unusual sounds, but it was unique due to its use of several woodwind instruments, atonal piano, and recorded laughter.

Zappa called the Mothers' fourth album, *Cruising with Ruben & the Jets* (1968), an "experiment in cliché collages" whose songs were "careful conglomerates of archetypical clichés" (quoted in Miles 2004, 172–73). The quirkiness normally associated with Zappa's music was particularly subtle on this album; it was a doo-wop album that paid a parodic tribute to 1950s R&B. Although he did not sing on *WOIIFTM*, Collins returned to the band for *Cruising*. Billy Mundi left the band and was replaced by Arthur Tripp (born Arthur Dyer Tripp III, September 10, 1944; drums). Chad Wackerman played drums on the Barking Pumpkin remix released in 1985, and bassists Jay Anderson and Arthur Barrow provided overdubs. It seemed, perhaps, a Mothers album would be incomplete without

a Stravinsky reference, and as Zappa has pointed out, the "ooh-wee-ooh" background vocal at the end of "Fountain of Love" used the melody of the bassoon solo at the beginning of *Rite of Spring*.

Although *Uncle Meat* (1969; recorded from October 1967 to February 1968) was released as the Mothers' fourth album, some of the recordings actually predated *Cruising* (which was recorded December 1967 through February 1968). The lineup included three drummers (Black, Mundi, and Tripp), as some recordings were made before Mundi had left the band. Tripp and Ruth Komanoff (born May 23, 1946, later Ruth Underwood; mallet percussion) played mallet percussion on the album. Prior to joining the band, Ruth studied classical percussion at Ithaca College and at the Juilliard School, and Tripp had played with the Cincinnati Symphony Orchestra. *Uncle Meat* was a story album conceived as a soundtrack for a film that was never completed. The album was mostly instrumental, and the vocals were both sung and spoken. For instance, the track "Ian Underwood Whips It Out" opened with Ian speaking about how he became a member of the Mothers.

The album opened with "Uncle Meat: Main Title Theme," its melody played on mallet percussion. "The Uncle Meat Variations," from side three, was mostly instrumental, and the "Uncle Meat" theme played several times. One of the more well-known works from the album was "A Pound for a Brown on the Bus." The song appeared on several other Zappa releases as "A Pound for a Brown (on the Bus)," or simply "Pound for a Brown." In the middle of side two was "Prelude to King Kong," an instrumental track with the horn section playing free jazz over a fast 5/8 pattern in the bass and drums (similar to the 5/8 pattern for Ian's solo in "Whips It Out"). Side four was "King Kong," a jazz-rock work with solos by Preston, Motorhead, Bunk, and Ian. *Uncle Meat* was completed in the spring of 1968 around the time when the band moved back to Los Angeles and when *WOIIFTM* was released.

On October 25, 1968, the Mothers recorded a live concert with members of the BBC Symphony Orchestra. The first half of the performance was a collection of Zappa's "classical" chamber pieces woven together by a narrative. These formed a musical play that he later titled *Progress?* It opened with "Prologue" (which was later titled "Bogus Pomp"). "Agency Man" contained some very sophisticated, and difficult, music played by the orchestra. The play closed with "Epilogue," which recalled music from the end of "Agency Man." The second half of the concert consisted of nine songs from the Mothers' repertoire, such as "King Kong," "Pound for a Brown," and "Harry, You're a Beast." The recording of this concert was not released until 1993 on Barking Pumpkin as *Ahead of Their Time*.

Zappa and Cohen formed Bizarre Records in October 1968 because Verve did not renew their contract. *Cruising with Ruben & the Jets* was released on Verve at the end of 1968, and *Uncle Meat* was released on Bizarre in April 1969. Lowell George (born April 13, 1945, died June 29, 1979; guitar and harmonica) and Bunk's brother Buzz Gardner (born Charles Guanerra, 1931, died February 1, 2004; trumpet) joined the band in November 1968 and appeared on the Mothers' sixth release, *Burnt Weeny Sandwich* (1970).

Burnt Weeny Sandwich was a collection of instrumental songs sandwiched between two doo-wop covers: "WPLJ" (1955) by the 4 Deuces and "Valarie" (1960) by Jackie and the Starlites. The fourth track, "Theme from Burnt Weeny Sandwich," was included on the soundtrack for Zappa's 18-minute film *Burnt Weeny Sandwich* (1969). No other song from *Burnt Weeny Sandwich* (the album) appeared in the film; however, the soundtrack contained several songs from *Uncle Meat*. "Igor's Boogie" (in two short "phases") was another reference to Igor Stravinsky. "Holiday in Berlin" contained material from Zappa's score for the film *The World's Greatest Sinner* (1962). "Holiday" appeared briefly on the *Ahead of Their Time* concert as well. Zappa reworked the song and added lyrics for *200 Motels* (1971). "Little House I Used to Live In" was the album's 18-minute centerpiece. It began with an atonal piano solo by Ian, followed by a jazz-rock fusion section and a lengthy solo by Don Harris (aka Sugarcane, born June 18, 1938, died November 30, 1999; violin).

The Mothers' seventh release, *Weasels Ripped My Flesh* (1970), was a collection of studio and live performances recorded from 1968 to 1969. The lineup was the same as it had been on *Burnt*, but with the addition of Collins (he had left and rejoined the band on several occasions). Zappa was not modest in letting his audiences know about the rhythmical complexity of his music. For instance, in "Toads of the Short Forest," Zappa said, "At this very moment on stage we have drummer 'A' playing in [the time signature of] 7/8, drummer 'B' playing in 3/4, the bass playing in 3/4, the organ playing in 5/8, the tambourine playing in 3/4, and the alto sax blowing his nose." "Prelude to the Afternoon of a Sexually Aroused Gas Mask" was a reference to Claude Debussy's orchestral work *Prelude to the Afternoon of a Faun*, and "Eric Dolphy Memorial Barbecue" was a tribute to the jazz great who had died in 1964.

Zappa broke up the Mothers in 1969 before *Burnt* and *Weasels* were released. It had become a financial burden to pay the band to rehearse and tour, and he had recorded enough material to release. From 1967 to 1970, Zappa composed the music for his film *200 Motels*. A concert of that music played by the Mothers and the Los Angeles Philharmonic (Zubin Mehta, conducting) took place on May 15, 1970. In preparation for the concert, Zappa temporarily re-formed the Mothers, albeit with a slightly different lineup, to play several concerts. The lineup included Collins, Ian, Motorhead, Mundi, and Preston, with Aynsley Dunbar (born January 10, 1946; drums) and Jeff Simmons (born May 1979; bass). Two former vocalists of the Turtles, Howard Kaylan (born June 22, 1947) and Mark Volman (born April 29, 1947), attended the concert, and they soon joined the Mothers. For contractual reasons, Volman and Kaylan went by "Flo & Eddie," respectively. They appeared on Zappa's third solo album, *Chunga's Revenge* (1970), as did George Duke (born January 12, 1946; keyboards) and four members of the Mothers (Dunbar, Ian, Sugarcane, Simmons). Zappa used members from the *Chunga* lineup, as well as the original and new Mothers, for *200 Motels*.

In the months between the filming and release of *200 Motels*, the Mothers played two concerts at the Fillmore East in New York. The new lineup consisted of Dunbar, Flo, and Eddie, Ian, Preston, Zappa, Jim

Pons (born March 14, 1943; bass, vocals), and Bob Harris (died July 6, 1993; keyboard, vocals; not to be confused with the Bob Harris that played in Zappa's band in 1980). Recordings from these concerts were released in August 1971 as the Mothers: *Fillmore East—June 1971*. It was the first time "of Invention" was dropped from the band name on an album cover. However, "Starring the Mothers of Invention" was written on the album cover of *200 Motels* released two months later. With the addition of Flo and Eddie, this album was far more vocal-oriented than *Burnt* and *Weasels*. There were only two instrumental tracks, "Lonesome Electric Turkey" and "Peaches en Regalia." The latter appeared on Zappa's second solo album, *Hot Rats* (1970), and has been performed and recorded by many other bands (partly due to its inclusion in the *Real Book*, which gigging jazz musicians have been using since the 1970s).

Recordings from an August 7, 1971, Mothers concert were released as *Just Another Band from L.A.* in March 1972. The lineup was the same as it was on *Fillmore*, but without Bob Harris. Two of the album's five songs appeared on earlier albums: "Dog Breath" was a shortened version of *Uncle Meat*'s "Dog Breath, in the Year of the Plague," and "Call Any Vegetable" from *Freak Out!* was extended and reworked. The album's opener was "Billy the Mountain," a 24-minute story-song whose bizarre and absurd storyline was told through narration and singing. This story was about Billy (a mountain who lives in Southern California) and Ethel (a tree who grows from Billy's shoulder), who leave for a vacation to New York by way of Las Vegas. Like many Zappa songs, "Billy the Mountain" had numerous references to Southern California (e.g., the "Jack in the Box on Glenoaks" in Glendale).

December 4, 1971, was the date of the "Smoke on the Water" incident. During the encore of the Mothers' concert at the Montreux Casino on Lake Geneva in Switzerland, an audience member fired a flare gun. It set fire to the balcony, and the Casino burned down. The band's equipment was destroyed. Deep Purple, an early hard rock/heavy metal band, was in the audience. This event was the inspiration for Purple's hit song "Smoke on the Water"; a line from the first verse

was, "Frank Zappa and the Mothers were at the best place around, but some stupid with a flare gun burned the place to the ground."

Six days later in London, Zappa was attacked by an audience member; he punched Zappa and pushed him into the orchestra pit 15 feet below. Zappa suffered head injuries, a broken rib, a broken leg, and a crushed larynx (which, according to Zappa, lowered his voice by the interval of a third). Confined to a wheelchair for several months, Zappa focused on composition, recording, and producing instead of touring. Recordings from that concert, and other performances in 1971, were released in 1992 on *Playground Psychotics*.

In the spring of 1972, Zappa recorded his fourth solo album, *Waka/Jawaka*, a jazz-fusion record with performances by Zappa, Mothers alumni (Duke, Dunbar, Preston, Simmons), and several others. At the time of the *Waka/Jawaka* sessions, Zappa recorded *The Grand Wazoo*, a jazz-fusion big band album released in July. On the original LP release, the band was labeled as the Mothers, even though Ian and Ruth Underwood were the only ones who returned (Ruth Komanoff had married Ian by this time). The 20-piece electric big band toured for two weeks in September billed as Mothers of Invention/Hot Rats/Grand Wazoo. From October through December, a 10-piece version of the band toured under the name Petit Wazoo.

In February 1973, Zappa began a tour with three new musicians in the lineup: Tom Fowler (born June 10, 1951; bass), Ralph Humphrey (born May 11, 1944; drums), and Jean-Luc Ponty (born September 29, 1942; violin). The five returning Mothers were Duke, Ian and Ruth Underwood, Sal Marquez (trumpet, played on *The Grand Wazoo*), and Bruce Fowler (born July 10, 1947; trombone, played on *The Grand Wazoo* tour). This lineup, with an uncredited guest appearance by Tina Turner, recorded *Over-Nite Sensation* (1973) after the first leg of the 1973 tour. It was their highest-charting (number 32 on *Billboard*) album since *WOIIFTM* (number 30) and the only Mothers release to receive Recording Industry Association of America (RIAA) certification (gold in 1976). With some exceptions, like "Zomby Woof" and "Montana," the music was primarily straightforward (and certainly more commercial), and even funky at times thanks to Duke's clavinet work. Some of the songs' lyrics were overtly sexual, such as "Dinah-Moe Humm" and the zoophilic "Dirty Love." Jean-Luc Ponty quit the band after the album but before the Roxy concerts. In Ponty's words:

It was a very interesting experience at the beginning, because Zappa took out all the very complex instrumental music that he had stashed in his desk for a long time, since it was too sophisticated for the previous members of the Mothers. He had written music that was very influenced by Stravinsky, so he wanted to put together a group of excellent instrumentalists. But the public lost interest quickly, and he had to go back to satire and more commercial rock. That wasn't what I wanted to do, so I left after only seven months. (quoted in Miles 2004, 239)

By December, Napolean Murphy Brock (aka Napi, born April 23, 1943; saxophone and flute) and Chester Thompson (born December 11, 1948; drums) joined the band. Recordings from six concerts at the Roxy in Hollywood, California, were released in July 1974 as a double album, Zappa/Mothers' *Roxy & Elsewhere* ("Elsewhere" refers to concerts and overdubs recorded at locations other than the Roxy club). "Echidna's Arf (Of You)" and "Don't You Ever Wash That Thing?" were two difficult-to-play instrumental songs that showcased the talents of the band. Before Zappa counted off the last song on the album, "Be-Bop Tango," he told the audience that "this is a hard one to play." In 1976, Thompson was hired as the live drummer for Genesis partly due to his performance on this album, particularly for his ability to play alongside another drummer (Humphrey), a requisite skill for the Genesis job because Phil Collins played drums with Thompson during instrumental sections. Recordings from this lineup's (excluding Bruce and Humphrey) September 1974 concert in Finland were released in 1988 on Barking Pumpkin as *You Can't Do That on Stage Anymore, Vol. 2*. Bizarre Records dissolved in 1973 when their contract with Warner Bros. expired,

so *Roxy* was released on Zappa's and Cohen's newly formed label, DiscReet.

Branded as Frank Zappa and the Mothers of Invention on the album cover, *One Size Fits All* (1975) was considered Zappa's "progressive rock" album, but there were many blues and jazz-fusion elements present as well. *Bongo Fury* (1975) negated the assumption that Zappa's move toward progressive rock by way of jazz fusion was the direction in which he was headed. Lowe (2006) described *Bongo Fury* as "far from the progressive rock he had been playing as he could get and back to the roots that he became attached to as a kid in Southern California." It featured Captain Beefheart on vocals and harmonica, and, surprisingly, included two songs written by Beefheart. DiscReet's branding of the album's band name as "Frank Zappa/Captain Beefheart/The Mothers" duly suggested that the album was not purely Zappa. Terry Bozzio, the virtuoso drummer who played with Zappa for many years afterward, replaced Thompson for this record.

The Mothers of Invention ceased to exist in May 1976 after Zappa fired Cohen, accusing him of stealing from DiscReet. The resulting lawsuit prevented Zappa from using the name "Mothers of Invention," so subsequent releases were branded as "Frank Zappa" or simply "Zappa." Many of the same musicians who were on Zappa's solo records were on Mothers releases, so the lines between what should be retroactively classified as Frank Zappa solo, Mothers of Invention, or Frank Zappa and the Mothers (of Invention) are blurry.

In 1980, Walley defined the latter distinction concisely: "Before [the breakup of] 1969, there was the Mothers of Invention, afterward there was Frank Zappa and the Mothers of Invention." Zappa defined the distinction between a Zappa album and a Mothers release as "whether or not the group that's on it is actually a touring Mother unit," without any mention of the lawsuit. Perhaps *Zoot Allures* (1976) would have been another Zappa/Mothers release. After all, Estrada played on it, and he had not played any Zappa solo effort before, only Mothers albums. *Studio Tan* (1978) and *Sleep Dirt* (1979) included recordings of

Duke, Thompson, Ruth Underwood, and Bruce and Tom Fowler from 1974. These albums included post-1976 sessions and overdubs, so it would be difficult to classify these as Mothers releases in their completed form.

After 1976, Zappa had a successful career with numerous releases and live performances. He used ex-Mothers and many other fine musicians, most notably Adrian Belew and Steve Vai. Zappa remixed, over-dubbed, reedited, and/or rerecorded Mothers albums and released them on various labels, such as Barking Pumpkin and Rykodisc. There are many live and studio recordings of the Mothers that have been released since 1976, including recordings that originated as bootlegs.

Zappa died on December 4, 1993, from cancer. He was inducted into the Rock and Roll Hall of Fame in 1995, and he won three Grammys (including the Lifetime Achievement Award in 1997). There are several "ghost" bands that perform his music, such as Zappa Plays Zappa (fronted by Zappa's son, Dweezil), Grandmothers of Invention (including Brock, Preston, and others), and Project/Object (featuring Zappa alum Ike Wills). Zappa has sold over 60 million albums worldwide, a number spread among nearly 100 Mothers and solo releases.

The influence of Frank Zappa and the Mothers of Invention ranges widely. In some cases, Zappa's musical aesthetic has influenced other musicians. In other cases, musicians and nonmusicians discuss how they were influenced by his way of thinking. Many notable artists came under Zappa's influence, both during and after the Mothers of Invention period. Some of those who have gone on record include Cedric Bixler-Zavala (The Mars Volta), Les Claypool (Primus), Alice Cooper, Jon Fishman (Phish), Aaron Freeman (aka Gene Ween of Ween), John Frusciante (Red Hot Chili Peppers), Mike Portnoy (Dream Theater), and Derek Shulman (Gentle Giant). Portnoy cited Zappa as his biggest inspiration when he dedicated Dream Theater's 1994 album *Awake* to him. Comedian–parodist–musician Weird Al Yankovic's "Genius in France" from *Poodle Hat* (2003) was a style parody and homage to Zappa; the song's title referenced Zappa's "In France," and the album's title referenced Zappa's recurring poodle theme.

Nolan Stolz

Selected Discography

Freak Out! (as the Mothers of Invention), Verve V6–5005–2, 1966.

Absolutely Free (as the Mothers of Invention), Verve V6–5013, 1967.

We're Only in It for the Money (as the Mothers of Invention), Verve V6–5045, 1968.

Cruising with Ruben & the Jets (as the Mothers of Invention), Verve V6 5055–X, 1968.

Uncle Meat (as the Mothers of Invention), Bizarre 2MS 2024, 1969.

Burnt Weeny Sandwich (as the Mothers of Invention), Bizarre RS 6370, 1970.

Weasels Ripped My Flesh (as the Mothers of Invention), Bizarre MS 2028, 1970.

Chunga's Revenge (as Frank Zappa), Bizarre MS 2030, 1970.

Fillmore East—June 1971 (as the Mothers), Bizarre MS 2042, 1971.

200 Motels (starring the Mothers of Invention), United Artists Records UAS-9956, 1971.

Just Another Band from L.A. (as the Mothers), Bizarre MS 2075, 1972.

The Grand Wazoo (as the Mothers), Bizarre MS 2093, 1972.

Over-Nite Sensation (as the Mothers), DiscReet MS 2149, 1973.

Roxy & Elsewhere (as Zappa/Mothers), DiscReet 2DS 2202, 1974.

One Size Fits All (as Frank Zappa and the Mothers of Invention), DiscReet DS 2216, 1975.

Bongo Fury (as Frank Zappa/Captain Beefheart/The Mothers), DiscReet DS 2234, 1975.

You Can't Do That on Stage Anymore, Vol. 2: The Helsinki Concert (as Frank Zappa), Barking Pumpkin BPR 74217, 1988.

Playground Psychotics (as Frank Zappa, the Mothers of Invention), Barking Pumpkin D2 74244, 1992.

Ahead of Their Time, Barking Pumpkin D2 74246, 1993.

References

James, Billy. *Necessity Is . . .: The Early Years of Frank Zappa and the Mothers of Invention*. London: SAF Publishing, 2005.

Kostelanetz, Richard, and John Rocco, eds. *The Frank Zappa Companion: Four Decades of Commentary*. New York: Schirmer Books, 1997.

Lowe, Kelly Fisher. *The Words and Music of Frank Zappa*. Westport, CT: Praeger, 2006.

Miles, Barry. *Zappa*. New York: Grove Press, 2004.

Slaven, Neil. *Electric Don Quixote*. New York: Omnibus Press, 2003.

Verfaillie, Jurgen. "Kill Ugly Radio." Last modified January 28, 2012, http://www.killuglyradio.com.

Walley, David. *No Commercial Potential: The Saga of Frank Zappa, Then and Now*. New York: E. P. Dutton, 1980.

Watson, Ben. *Frank Zappa: The Negative Dialectics of Poodle Play*. New York: St. Martin's Press, 1993.

Zappa, Frank, and Peter Occhiogrosso. *The Real Frank Zappa Book*. New York: Poseidon Press 1989.

Zappa, Frank, and Steve Rosen. *Frank Zappa: The Classic Interviews*. CD. Chrome Dreams, CTS2007, 2004.

G

Genesis (1967–2007)

Genesis was a band formed in 1967 in England. The classic (1971–1975) lineup consisted of Tony Banks (born Anthony Banks, March 27, 1950; keyboards), Phil Collins (born Philip Collins, January 30, 1951; drums and vocals), Peter Gabriel (born February 13, 1950; vocals and flute), Steve Hackett (born Stephen Hackett, February 12, 1950; guitar), and Mike Rutherford (born Michael Rutherford, October 2, 1950; bass and guitar). After Gabriel departed in 1974, Collins assumed the role of front man. Many divide the band's output into two periods (Gabriel era and Collins era), but musically, that distinction was arguably less important. The band's first two albums could be described as formative: the first pop rock, the second more experimental. Their progressive rock era began and ended with the arrival and departure of Hackett (1971–1977), including the two albums after Gabriel's departure. The compositions of that period had roots in Western art music, especially in respect to harmony, meter, and long forms. Their choice of instruments contributed to their 1970s sound, including keyboards such as Mellotron, ARP ProSoloist, Hammond organ and RMI Electra piano—sometimes through effects pedals, Rickenbacker bass, Moog Taurus bass pedals, six- and 12-string guitars, and a large drum set including concert (i.e., single-headed) toms.

Although some of the material on their first post-Hackett album (*. . . And Then There Were Three . . .*) was progressive rock, it included the first of 13 Genesis songs that appeared on *Billboard*'s Adult Contemporary chart. The subsequent albums with Collins as lead vocalist had multiple charting singles.

The style change was not sudden, and the albums from 1978 to 1981 may be understood as transitional. With the development of synthesizers, drum machines, and sampling, Genesis's sound changed throughout the 1980s and 1990s. Their live shows were known as being visually spectacular: Gabriel donned elaborate costumes, and, in the 1980s, they pioneered the earliest computer-programmed lighting systems to create impressive and massive light shows. Genesis has sold over 21 million albums in the United States (certified by the RIAA, four of which were multi-platinum) and over six million albums in the United Kingdom (certified by BPI). Although sales of less than 40 million albums have been certified worldwide, Dodd estimated Genesis's total worldwide album sales at 150 million (Dodd 2007).

Banks and Gabriel met at boarding school in 1963. It was there they met Chris Stewart (born 1951; drums), and the three played in a band called Garden Wall. Rutherford entered the school in 1964, and Anthony Phillips (born December 23, 1951; guitar) entered the following spring; they played in a band called the Anon. In 1966, Phillips joined the Garden Wall for a concert at the school. Banks, Gabriel, Phillips, Rutherford, and Stewart came together as a band in January 1967 and signed with pop producer Jonathan King's publishing company. Originally a guitarist, Rutherford began to play bass in the fall of 1967.

King liked the simplicity of the band's earliest songs. When they sent King eight new additional songs he did not like them, and they were never released. Banks explained, "As we went on, the music got more involved" (Fielder 1984). To appease King's musical taste in order to keep their relationship with

Progressive rock band Genesis in 1973. From left to right: Tony Banks, Phil Collins, Mike Rutherford, Steve Hackett, and Peter Gabriel. With or without Gabriel (who left in 1974), Genesis delivered music with wide-ranging style from straight-ahead pop to deeply experimental prog. (Photo by Michael Ochs Archives/Getty Images)

him, they wrote "The Silent Sun" in a pseudo-early–Bee Gees style, a group they knew King liked. To Phillips, it seemed like a real compromise. Around this time, King suggested "Genesis" for the band's name. Recorded in December 1967, "The Silent Sun" was released as Genesis's first single in February 1968. Shortly after recording their second single, "A Winter's Tale," Stewart was put out of the band. Phillips said Stewart lacked dedication, so he was replaced by John Silver (born 1950), who recorded the remaining tracks for their first album, *From Genesis to Revelation*, in the summer of 1968. The album was released in March of 1969, and Genesis wrote new material

during the following summer. After the band recorded a few demos in August, Silver quit the band in order to attend college in the United States.

Genesis replaced Silver with John Mayhew (born March 27, 1947, died March 26, 2009), and they played their first professional gig in September of 1969. Starting that fall, the band lived in a cottage in Wotton (a small village 30 miles southwest of London) for several months, during which they rehearsed, wrote music, and performed live on occasion. John Anthony (of the progressive label Charisma Records) heard Genesis perform during their March/April 1970 residency at Ronnie Scott's, in London. As a result of positive reports from John Anthony, Tony Stratton-Smith, who founded Charisma, signed the band to his label. Charisma's philosophy was different from King's: release an album without singles and have the band tour in order to build a following. Charisma was a much better fit for Genesis because their music was quickly becoming more experimental, complex, and album-oriented, not necessarily intended for radio.

In June/July 1970, with John Anthony producing, Genesis recorded their second album, *Trespass*. Although comparable in total duration to their first album, *Trespass* had only six songs. With the exception of "Dusk" (which was written before their stint at the cottage), the songs were fairly long, about seven to nine minutes. The 12-string guitar, played by Phillips and Rutherford, was an important part of Genesis's sound at the time. Shortly after completing *Trespass,* Phillips left the band and Mayhew was asked to leave. Banks recalled, "We felt that John Mayhew was not quite right for us, and that we could get a better drummer" (Gallo 1980). Phillips quit because he became "paralytically nervous" before performances and developed bronchial pneumonia.

Phil Collins saw an advertisement placed by Stratton-Smith in *Melody Maker* seeking a drummer sensitive to acoustic music. Collins saw Stratton-Smith at a Yes concert and Stratton-Smith encouraged him to audition for Genesis. That night, Collins arranged an audition for Yes, because he was aware that their drummer Bill Bruford was leaving the band. Collins never did audition for Yes, but he successfully auditioned for Genesis. Coincidentally, Bruford joined Genesis for the 1976 tour when Collins assumed the role of front man. Genesis replaced Anthony Phillips with guitarist Mick Barnard for only two months, meanwhile seeking a more permanent replacement. They responded to an advertisement placed by Steve Hackett in *Melody Maker* and encouraged Hackett to check out the band. Gabriel invited Hackett to listen to *Trespass* and to see the band live. He was impressed, auditioned for them, and joined Genesis in January of 1971.

Recorded in August 1971, *Nursery Cryme* was released in November. Charisma did not promote it as much as they did *Trespass*, and it was unsuccessful in

England at first; however, the album charted at number four in Italy. With the arrival of Collins and Hackett, the band ventured into a progressive rock style, incorporating elements of Western art music. The February 1973 tour program listed Collins's musical influences as the Beatles, Yes, and Mahavishnu Orchestra; Hackett's favorite composers were listed as Satie, Albinoni, Scarlatti, and Bach; and Banks's favorite composers were Shostakovich and Mahler.

The band explored interesting chord progressions and key modulations, odd phrase lengths, and dynamics ranging from a whisper to a loud rock band. Gabriel played flute on occasion; Banks provided classically influenced piano, Mellotron, and rock-style Hammond organ; Rutherford's fast and melodic bass lines cut through the texture; and Collins's drum work was intricate, delicate, and powerful. Hackett played understated solos and provided interesting textures (e.g., the staccato palm muting on "The Musical Box" sounding like *pizzicato* violins). He used a technique in which the picking hand taps on the fretboard; called "tapping," this technique is often incorrectly attributed to Eddie Van Halen as its inventor. Lyrically, the songs were in the narrative form, telling bizarre (perhaps absurd) stories. Gabriel delivered his vocals very dramatically by using a wide range of dynamics and timbres, like character voices.

Released in October 1972, *Foxtrot* opened with "Watcher of the Skies." Banks's Mellotron solo consisted of unusual, modulating harmonies, showing his affinity for late 19th-century harmonic practices. The song's syncopated 6/4 (4/4 + 2/4) groove was driven by Rutherford's Rickenbacker bass slightly "ahead" of the beat. Before the closing instrumental sections, Genesis demonstrated their ability to play in extreme dynamic contrast with complete control by alternating phrases *pianissimo* to *fortissimo*. The album's centerpiece was the 23-minute multisectional "Supper's Ready." The song opened with their signature 12-string guitar sound, but it intensified with the entrance of Collins's drums and Banks's Hammond organ in the second part. The sixth part, "Apocalypse in 9/8," employed the unusual time signature of 9/4 for the verse, and an unusual grouping of 9/8 (3+2+4) for the following instrumental section. Parts of Banks's organ solo were polymetric, for he played in 4/4 over the underlying 9/8 pattern. An example of their bizarre lyrics can be found in the song's fifth part: "the frog was a prince, the prince was a brick, the brick was an egg, the egg was a bird." *Foxtrot* reached number 12 in the United Kingdom, but they were still largely unknown in the United States. To promote the album overseas, Charisma and their U.S. distributor, Buddha, booked them for one night at Philharmonic Hall (later, Avery Fisher Hall) at Lincoln Center in New York on December 13, 1972. In March and April, they returned to the United States to embark on their first American tour.

Gabriel's stage presence was as dramatic as the music. As the band prepared for songs, he told surreal tales as long, elaborate introductions. In May 1972, Gabriel shaved only a part of the front of his head (a very strange haircut by anyone's standards) and wore thick black eye makeup. During the instrumental section of "The Musical Box" at a September 1972 performance in Dublin, Gabriel left the stage and returned in a red dress and a fox head (referencing the cover of their then-forthcoming album *Foxtrot*). For later performances of "The Musical Box," Gabriel wore an old man mask to depict one of the story's characters. He wore a "Britannia" costume for "Dancing with the Moonlit Knight," and wore multiple costumes during "Supper's Ready" (e.g., the flower head). For their February 1973 show at the Rainbow Theatre in London, Gabriel wore fluorescent eye makeup, which glowed under the black lights, a cape, and large bat wings attached to his head. His appearance and behavior on stage caught the attention of the press.

Failing to reach Charisma's deadline for another album, the band released *Genesis Live* in July 1973. It was offered at a budget price and stocked in department chain stores in order to reach a greater audience. The sales tactic was successful; the album reached number nine in the United Kingdom. Released in October, *Selling England by the Pound* (hereafter *SEBTP*) reached number three in the United Kingdom. *SEBTP* had the elements of progressive rock

found on *Foxtrot*, but to a greater extent. For instance, the classically influenced piano solo opening to "Firth of Fifth" had Romantic harmonies, but with complex meters like 13/16, 15/16, 21/16, and others. Banks started using the ARP ProSoloist, which became an important part of Genesis's sound; the synthesizer solos on "Firth of Fifth" and "Cinema Show" were but two examples. "I Know What I Like (In Your Wardrobe)" was more radio-friendly than the other songs on the LP; released as a single, it reached number 23 in the United Kingdom.

Genesis toured until the beginning of May 1974, at which point *Nursery Cryme* entered the U.K. charts for one week; they were beginning to build an audience. After the tour, Gabriel took time away to be with his wife. Meanwhile, in his absence, the rest of the band wrote the music for the next album, *The Lamb Lies Down on Broadway*, a concept album. Gabriel joined them mid-summer, and in August, they started recording. By September, with the band having already recorded much of the material, Gabriel still had not completed the lyrics and vocal melodies. *Lamb* was released as a double album on November 18, two days before they started a tour. Rather than performing a variety of songs, the band played the album from start to finish, staging it in the manner of a rock opera. This led to a confused audience because the album had just been released, leaving little time to familiarize themselves with the new material. The tour was scheduled to begin October 29, but Hackett injured his hand, and the band was forced to postpone. Meanwhile, Rutherford worked with Anthony Phillips on a side project, one that would eventually be released as a Phillips solo album, *The Geese and the Ghost*.

The album's opener and title track introduced the story's protagonist, Rael. Gabriel wore jeans, a leather jacket, and heavy makeup to portray the character in concert. For "The Colony of Slippermen," Gabriel wore a full-body costume to portray the deformed, lumpy Slipperman character. Gabriel varied his vocal timbre and sang in different registers and in dynamic contrast, like he had done with the character voices on earlier albums. Harmonically, the music was quite inventive, particularly the progressions in the title track and "Hairless Heart." The band continued to show interest in atypical meter: for instance, the heavy, powerful 7/8 through most of "Back in N.Y.C." or the smooth metric modulation from 6/8 to 3/4 in "In the Cage." The album included impressive performances by all, from the avant-garde improvisatory passages in "The Waiting Room" to their tightly arranged compositions. The songs "The Colony of Slippermen: The Raven," "Riding the Scree" and "In the Cage" included three of Banks's most famous synthesizer solos.

During the tour, Gabriel announced to the band that he would be leaving. He explained, "I was beginning to dislike myself for doing what I was doing . . . I was sick of rock, the business, and everything about it" (Fielder 1984). Gabriel stayed on for the remainder of the tour, which concluded in May 1975. With Gabriel gone, Rutherford continued work on *The Geese and the Ghost* with Phillips, and Hackett worked on a solo album, *Voyage of the Acolyte*, which included performances by Rutherford, Collins, and others.

Genesis auditioned about 20 singers, and as Rutherford recalled, Collins would sing the song to the person auditioning and often sounded better than the prospective singer. Collins had been singing background vocals in the studio and in concert, and was the lead singer on "For Absent Friends" from *Nursery Cryme* and "More Fool Me" on *SEBTP*. Genesis brought in Mick Strickland to record vocals for "Squonk," but they were not pleased with the results. When the band came into the studio the next day, Collins recorded vocals for the song, and the band approved. Collins sang the remaining songs on *Trick of the Tail* (1976), and, thus, became the new voice of Genesis.

Compositionally, *Trick of the Tail* was not unlike their previous four studio releases. Four of the five band members remained, so the material (especially the instrumental aspects of the music) was quite similar and sounded like a natural, logical continuation of their musical direction. Like Gabriel assumedly would have, Collins sang in character voices for "Robbery, Assault and Battery." That song, like so many from their progressive rock era, employed

unusual time signatures (e.g., 7/4 in the introduction, 13/8 in its instrumental section, etc.). "Ripples" incorporated chords and progressions that, although classically influenced and derived, had unconventional and inventive resolutions. Rutherford's bass lines remained melodic, as heard on the title track and others. Collins's drumming, especially on "Dance on a Volcano," was fast, tight, intricate, and complex, drawing influence from jazz–rock fusion. The album's closer, "Los Endos," incorporated key themes from various songs not as a medley, but as a dramatic finale.

For the purpose of live performance, Genesis decided that Collins would front the band and hire a second drummer. Collins had been working with Brand X, a jazz–rock fusion outfit with Bill Bruford (Yes; King Crimson), and Bruford offered to join the band for the tour. The audience's reception to Collins as lead singer was positive, owing partly to the fact that they recruited from within.

After the tour, the band returned to the studio in October 1976 to record *Wind & Wuthering*. Banks considered it to be the band's most complex and harmonically extreme album. Musically complex indeed, it included several progressive rock masterpieces: "Eleventh Earl of Mar," "All in a Mouse's Night," "One for the Vine" (with its oddly phrased instrumental middle section), and "Unquiet Slumbers for the Sleepers . . . / . . . In That Quiet Earth." The latter was a two-part instrumental prog-rock workout that led directly into the grandiose rock ballad "Afterglow." "Blood on the Rooftops" demonstrated Hackett's fluency on the classical guitar. "Wot Gorilla?" was a prog-rock/jazz-fusion instrumental, into which Collins incorporated the primary drum pattern from Weather Report's "Nubian Sundance" (1974). The album also included a pop ballad, "Your Own Special Way," Genesis's first obvious departure from its progressive style and toward pop music.

Bruford declined to return for the 1977 tour, so the band searched for another drummer. Collins was impressed with Chester Thompson's (born December 11, 1948) drumming on the Zappa/Mothers album *Roxy & Elsewhere* (1974). The album demonstrated Thompson's ability to play alongside another drummer, a requisite skill for the Genesis job because Collins also played during instrumental sections. The tour included several nights in Brazil, the band's first performances outside of Europe and North America. In May, amidst the 1977 tour, Genesis released a three-song EP called *Spot the Pigeon*, consisting of selections from the *Wind & Wuthering* sessions that were not included on the LP.

Recordings from concerts in June 1977 (plus "Cinema Show" from their 1976 tour) were released as a double-live album, *Seconds Out*, in October. During the mixing of the album, Hackett quit for multiple reasons. He was disappointed with the lack of his material being used for the albums. The band voted on what material to use, and, apparently, his contributions were not considered to be as strong as others. Genesis was not in favor of Hackett working on a solo album, even though they had rejected much of his material. On leaving Genesis, Hackett said, "I just didn't think there were enough risks being taken with the form or the content of the songs" (Stump 1997). He was "interested in instrumental music and the balance was shifting more to songs, to simplifying . . . The wackiness was being toned down, maybe in search of a new audience" (Bowler 1992).

As they did after the departure of Gabriel, Genesis recruited from within to fill the guitar vacancy. Rutherford took over guitar and bass duties for all subsequent releases; after all, he started as a guitarist, switching to bass in the earliest days of the band. The aptly titled *. . . And Then There Were Three . . .* (1978) began a musical change for the band. The album closed with their first widely successful single, "Follow You, Follow Me" (number 23 on the U.S. charts). The album, however, retained much of the band's progressive rock style: for example, Collins's drumming and Banks's solo in "The Lady Lies," the instrumental introduction to "Burning Rope," and the asymmetrical meter in "Down and Out." "Many Too Many" was a pop-oriented tune, but it had multiple key changes, symphonic-like textures, and unconventional harmonic progressions.

At first, Rutherford was not sure if he wanted a bassist/guitarist or a guitarist who could play bass for the tour. He invited Weather Report bassist Alfonso Johnson to join the band, but because guitar duties were also expected, Johnson declined and suggested Daryl Stuermer (born November 27, 1952; guitarist for jazz–rock fusion artists Sweetbottom and Jean-Luc Ponty). Stuermer was hired to play Rutherford's bass work on the post-Hackett albums and Hackett's guitar parts. The tour ended in Japan, the band's first performances in Asia.

After the 1978 tour, the band went on hiatus, during which Banks and Rutherford worked on solo albums. At the end of 1979, Banks, Collins, and Rutherford returned to the studio to record *Duke* (1980); Stuermer and Thompson were only hired as touring musicians and did not appear on the band's studio releases. *Duke* had a more commercial sound (e.g., the drum machine on "Duchess"), but still had elements of progressive rock (e.g., like the 13/4 meter in "Turn It On Again," Banks's keyboard work in "Duke's Travels," and Collins's drumming in "Duke's End"). *Duke*, which peaked at number 11 in the United States, contained two U.S.-charting singles: "Misunderstanding" at number 14 and "Turn It On Again" at number 58. The latter was described by the band as "deceptively simple," and to them, it felt more natural in 13/4 than a more common meter. In fact, when Rutherford wrote the riff, he thought it was in 4, but Collins informed him that it was in 13. They called it a "very unlikely single," but it worked because it "sounds simple" (Bowler 1992).

Rutherford considered their next album *Abacab* (1981) the point at which they stylistically "broke from their past," their "only conscious change" (Maylam 2007). Collins's solo album *Face Value* (also released in 1981) had an even simpler sound than *Abacab*, but the parallels between the two albums were quite audibly evident (for comparison, the early drum machine sounds on "Man on the Corner"). The title track, as straightforward and radio friendly as it may have been, had several clever moments stylistically related to their past. In the chorus, Banks played a nondiatonic organ melody phrased in groups of three against the 4/4 meter. The bridge modulated back into the key of the verse via a guitar/organ unison line, played in a classic prog-rock manner. *Abacab*, which peaked at number seven in the United States, had three U.S.-charting singles: "Abacab," "No Reply at All," and "Man on the Corner."

Recordings from the 1981 tour appeared on the first three sides of *Three Sides Live* (1982), and the fourth side consisted of three songs left over from the *Abacab* sessions (songs that also appeared on their 1981 EP *3×3*) and two songs left over from the *Duke* sessions. "Paperlate," which peaked at number 32 in the United States, featured the "horn" section from Earth, Wind & Fire. A video of performances from the same tour was released as *Three Sides Live* on VHS in 1982. As may be seen on the VHS, Genesis became known for their impressive light shows. The *Duke* tour included a light show with 367 lights, of which 80 were airplane landing lights. The lighting for the *Abacab* tour was the most sophisticated of its time, with computer-programmed movable lights from Vari-Lite, a new company in which the band invested. Their 1983/1984 tour outdid *Abacab*'s, with nearly four times as many Vari-Lites used.

By the summer of 1982, Gabriel had released three solo albums and was working on a fourth. His solo work was very experimental and art rock, unlike Genesis's new direction, and he incorporated elements of World Music. Gabriel put on the first WOMAD (World of Music, Arts and Dance) festival in July 1982, which became a financial disaster. In order to raise funds for WOMAD, Genesis did a one-off reunion show in October (Banks, Collins, Gabriel, Hackett, and Rutherford, with Stuermer and Thompson).

After concentrating on solo efforts in 1982, Banks, Collins, and Rutherford came together in 1983 to write the next album as a group effort (i.e., no individual song credits). The eponymously titled *Genesis* (1983), which peaked at number nine in the United States, contained four U.S.-charting hits: "Mama," "Illegal Alien," "Taking It All Too Hard," and "That's All." Peaking at number six, the latter was their highest-charting single before 1986. "Mama" included eerie synths, Collins's percussive laughs, and heavily gated drums that overpowered the soft electronic

drums of the first part of the song. The album was not entirely pop driven; it included "Home by the Sea/Second Home by the Sea," an 11-minute work in two parts. The second part was a pseudo–progressive rock keyboard-laden instrumental, until it recalled the third verse of "Home by the Sea" at the end.

After completing the "Mama" tour to support *Genesis*, the band members took a break to work on their own projects. Banks worked on music for two films and released *Soundtracks* in 1986. Rutherford started a band called Mike + The Mechanics, and they released an album in 1985, which included three charting singles. Collins released his third solo album, *No Jacket Required* (1985), which included four charting singles, including two at number one: "One More Night" and "Sussudio." Genesis's success in the early 1980s certainly helped their solo efforts, and vice versa.

Invisible Touch (1986) outcharted *Genesis*, as it included the band's five highest-charting hits in the United States: "Invisible Touch" (number one), "Tonight, Tonight, Tonight" (number three), "In Too Deep" (number three), "Throwing It All Away" (number four), and "Land of Confusion" (number four). The album was the band's highest-charting (number three) and their best-selling (six times platinum) in the United States. The title track was up-tempo and radio-friendly, its chorus/hook consisting of only four different pitches. "In Too Deep" was a pop ballad, and "Land of Confusion" was a 1980s protest song. "Tonight, Tonight, Tonight" contained slow, long keyboard textures filled with electronic percussion and drums. It had a symphonic-like texture underneath the vocal melody, lacking a strong backbeat from the drums. With synthesizers and electronic drums at the fore and the absence of an active bass line, it lacked the typical rock band role as accompaniment. At nearly nine minutes in duration, the song was very long for a radio hit of its time. Like *Genesis, Invisible Touch* did not consist entirely of pop songs. "The Brazilian" was an instrumental featuring electric percussion and synthesizers. Like "Home by the Sea/Second Home by the Sea," "Domino" was in two parts and about 11 minutes in duration. Its second part had interesting chord progressions over a pedal "D" almost entirely throughout. Pedal point has been a "trademark" of Genesis's music since the early 1970s. "The Brazilian" and "Domino" were not merely "album tracks"; they were a regular part of the band's touring set list. Booked at stadiums and other large venues, the *Invisible Touch* tour was one of the world's top concert draws that year, totaling over three million in ticket sales. The tour included Europe, North America, Japan, and their first performances in Australia and New Zealand.

After the conclusion of the 1987 tour, Genesis took another band hiatus. Rutherford released his second Mike + The Mechanics album, *Living Years* (1988), whose title track charted at number one in the United States and was nominated for Grammy's Song of the Year Award in 1990. Collins released his fourth studio album, *. . . But Seriously* (1989), which included four U.S.-charting hits, including the number-one hit "Another Day in Paradise," his second Grammy nomination (1991). By 1990, Genesis had sold over 10 million albums in the United States, with *Invisible Touch* already at three times platinum. *And Then There Were Three* and *Duke* were certified platinum in 1988, *Abacab* was certified two times platinum in 1988, and their four releases from 1973 to 1976 were certified gold in 1990.

Their 1991 album *We Can't Dance* was a successful follow-up, reaching number four in the United States, with five charting singles. Collins stated that "I Can't Dance," a single that peaked at number seven, was recorded in only a few hours, its lyrics written in only 30 minutes, and its melody written in less than 10 minutes. They did not want the song to sound "over-rehearsed" or "overwritten." Banks said that they wanted to keep their music simple, rather than take a "small idea and make it massive," like they did in the past (Yukich 2002). The pop ballad "Hold On My Heart" peaked at number 12 and at number one on *Billboard*'s Adult Contemporary chart. With 13 songs having appeared on the Adult Contemporary chart, it was evident that the album-oriented, progressive rock Genesis had become giants of pop and adult contemporary music.

By the end of the *We Can't Dance* tour in November 1992, *Genesis* and *We Can't Dance* had gone three times platinum, and *Invisible Touch* went five times platinum. Collins recorded a fifth solo album in 1993 and made his departure from Genesis publicly known in March 1996. Vocalist Ray Wilson (born Raymond Wilson, September 8, 1968) and drummers Nick D'Virgilio (born November 12, 1968; of the progressive rock band Spock's Beard) and Nir Zidkyahu (born November 5, 1967) were brought in to replace Collins on the next Genesis album, *. . . Calling All Stations . . .* (1997). Although the album reached number two in the U.K. charts, it only reached number 54 in the United States. None of its three U.K.-charting singles entered the U.S. charts. Although the band toured for five months throughout Europe, the United States and Canada dates were cancelled. Thompson and Stuermer did not return for the tour; their positions were filled by Zidkyahu and Anthony Drennan, respectively.

Banks, Collins, Gabriel, Hackett, and Rutherford reunited in 1999 to record a new version of "The Carpet Crawlers" from their 1974 album *The Lamb Lies Down on Broadway*. It was released as "The Carpet Crawlers 1999" on *Turn It On Again: The Hits*, a "greatest hits" collection. With no tour to support the release, the band remained inactive until 2006, when they announced a reunion tour that employed Banks, Collins, Rutherford, Stuermer, and Thompson.

There are no known plans for Genesis to tour or record another album. If they tour, it is unlikely that Collins will play drums, because he had neck surgery in 2009 and has had great difficulty playing drums since (although in 2010 he released an album on which he played drums). When Genesis was inducted into the Rock and Roll Hall of Fame in 2010, they did not perform (Phish performed two Genesis songs instead). Although Genesis is no longer active, fans can hear their music performed live. Hackett continues to tour with a set list that includes music from his time with the band. His *Genesis Revisited* (1996) and *Genesis Revisited II* (2012) consisted of new versions of Genesis classics. Of the 52 Genesis tribute bands listed on their official website, arguably the most important is the Musical Box, a group that re-creates, in extreme detail, various tours from the 1970s. Hackett and Collins have performed with them in concert, and in Collins's words, "they played that stuff better than we ever did" (Collins 2005). Their most ambitious project was the re-creation of the tour for *The Lamb Lies Down on Broadway*, a staging complete with costumes, vintage musical instruments, and the original visual slides (the latter provided by Genesis). Officially licensed from Genesis and Gabriel, the Musical Box has performed the rock opera many times from 2000 to 2006, reviving it for another tour lasting from 2011 to 2013.

Nolan Stolz

Selected Discography

From Genesis to Revelation, London Records PS 643, 1969.

Trespass, Charisma CAS 1020, 1970.

Nursery Cryme, Charisma CAS 1052, 1971.

Foxtrot, Charisma, CAS 1058, 1972.

Selling England by the Pound, Charisma CAS 1074, 1973.

Genesis Live, Charisma CLASS 1, 1973 (UK); CAS 1666, 1974 (US).

The Lamb Lies Down on Broadway, ATCO Records SD 2–401, 1974.

A Trick of the Tail, ATCO Records SD 36–129, 1976.

Wind & Wuthering, ATCO Records SD 38–100, 1976.

Seconds Out, Atlantic SD 2–9002, 1977.

Spot the Pigeon, Atlantic EP 1800, 1977.

. . . And There Was Three . . . , Atlantic SD 19173, 1978.

Duke, Atlantic SD 16014, 1980.

Abacab, Atlantic SD 19313, 1981.

Three Sides Live, Atlantic SD 2–2000, 1982.

Genesis, Atlantic 80116–1, 1983.

Invisible Touch, Atlantic 81641–1-E, 1986.

We Can't Dance, Atlantic 7 82344–2, 1991.

. . . Calling All Stations . . . , Atlantic 83037–2, 1997.

Turn It On Again: The Hits, Atlantic 83244–2, 1999.

References

Banks, Tony, et al. *Genesis: Chapter and Verse.* Edited by Philip Dodd. New York: Thomas Dunne Books/St. Martin's Griffin, 2007.

Bowler, Dave, and Brian Dray. *Genesis: A Biography.* London: Sidgwick and Jackson, 1992.

Collins, Phil. "The Phil Collins Forum: Messages from Phil." www.philcollins.co.uk/ posted March 9, 2005.

Fielder, Hugh. *The Book of Genesis.* London: Omnibus Press, 1984.

Gallo, Armando. *Genesis: I Know What I Like.* Los Angeles: DIY Press, 1980.

Holm-Hudson, Kevin. "A Study of Maximally Smooth Voice Leading in the Mid-1970s Music of Genesis." In *Sounding Out Pop: Analytical Essays in Popular Music,* edited by Mark Spicer and John Covach, 99–123. Ann Arbor: University of Michigan Press, 2010.

Holm-Hudson, Kevin. *Genesis and the Lamb Lies Down on Broadway.* Burlington, VT: Ashgate, 2008.

Koss, Michael Paul. "From Prog to Pop: Progressive Rock Elements in the Pop-Rock Music of Genesis, 1978–91." Ph.D. diss., University of Arizona, 2011.

Maylam, Tony, et al. Interviews in *Genesis 1976–1982.* DVD. Directed by Tony Maylam et al. Burbank, CA: Atlantic/Rhino, 2007.

Miller, May. *Genesis: A History.* VHS. Directed by May Miller. New York: Polygram Records, 1991.

Russell, Paul. *Genesis: Play Me My Song, A Live Guide, 1969–1975.* London: SAF Publishing, 2004.

Spicer, Mark. "Large-Scale Strategy and Compositional Design in the Early Music of Genesis." In *Expression in Pop-Rock Music: A Collection of Critical and Analytical Essays,* edited by Walter Everett, 77–111. New York: Garland, 2000.

Stump, Paul. *The Music's All That Matters: A History of Progressive Rock.* London: Quartet Books, 1997.

Yukich, James. Interviews in *Genesis: The Way We Walk–Live in Concert.* DVD. Directed by James Yukich. B [S.l.]: Pioneer Entertainment, 2002.

Yukich, James. Interviews in *Genesis: Live at Wembley Stadium.* DVD. Directed by James Yukich. Burbank, CA: Virgin Records, 2003.

The Grateful Dead (1965–1995)

The Grateful Dead were at the heart of the blossoming San Francisco psychedelic rock scene in the 1960s, while during the 1970s, 1980s, and 1990s, they served as the unofficial flag bearers for the remnants of hippie

Credited as the heart of the San Francisco psychedelic rock movement of the late 1960s, the Grateful Dead (pictured here in the mid-1960s) were the flag bearers of hippie culture. Their innovations in song structure and live performance style helped create the still popular jamband scene. (Photo by Michael Ochs Archives/Getty Images)

identity. Their music, which survives not only in dozens of studio albums but also in thousands of live concert recordings, blends rock, folk, blues, funk, bluegrass, jazz, and country music with a unique improvisational approach that stands as one of the most dynamic and individualistic musical styles in rock history. Grateful Dead fans make up one of the most devoted subcultures in music, the Deadheads, whose lifestyle has filtered down to influence the modern jamband scene. Throughout their long career, the band was at the forefront of innovations in sound design and in-house business practices (Barnes 2011). As rock impresario Bill Graham often said: "They're not the best at what

they do, they're the only ones who do what they do" (Graham and Greenfield 1992, 423).

The main figure in the band's history was Jerry Garcia (born Jerome John Garcia, August 1, 1942, died August 9, 1995; lead guitar, vocals). In the early 1960s, Garcia became a fixture in the burgeoning Bay Area folk and bluegrass scene centered in Palo Alto, which included Joan Baez, David Crosby, Jorma Kaukonen, and later Janis Joplin.

In January 1964, Garcia formed Mother McCree's Uptown Jug Champions, featuring future Grateful Dead members Bob Weir (born Robert Hall Weir, October 16, 1947; rhythm guitar, vocals) and Ron

"Pigpen" McKernan (born Ronald Charles Mc-Kernan, September 8, 1945, died March 8, 1973; vocals, keyboards, harmonica). Inspired by the Rolling Stones' revival of classic American Blues, Pigpen encouraged the band to become an electric blues outfit in 1965. The new band, dubbed the Warlocks, needed a drummer, so Garcia and Pigpen asked their friend Bill Kreutzmann (born William Kreutzmann, May 7, 1946; drums) to join the group. After a few gigs, Phil Lesh (born Phillip Chapman Lesh, March 15, 1940; bass guitar, vocals) replaced the band's original bassist, even though Lesh had never played the instrument before. The band changed its name to the Grateful Dead in November 1965.

Defining the Grateful Dead's sound was difficult partially because the band members' varied musical backgrounds mirrored the group's pluralistic inclusion of many American musical traditions. Garcia was an aficionado of bluegrass and folk, and an avid consumer of electric blues. Weir's teenage interests lay mainly in folk and rock, while Kreutzmann listened to jazz, rock, and played in R&B bands. Pigpen, the son of an R&B radio disc jockey, was steeped in traditional blues, while Lesh was grounded in classical music, played jazz trumpet, and later became a student of avant-garde classical composition.

The Warlocks learned to play together as a band during long, multinight stands at Bay Area nightclubs, developing a group mindset and learning to stretch out rhythm and blues standards via John Coltrane–inspired improvisation. In late 1965, the Grateful Dead experienced another exercise in group improvisation and communication, as they became the house band for Ken Kesey's LSD-fueled parties called "acid tests." Intellectual descendants of the Beats, Kesey and his group of friends, the psychedelic, bohemian jesters known as the Merry Pranksters, would be immortalized in Tom Wolfe's stylized account of their escapades, *The Electric Kool-Aid Acid Test* (1968).

The acid tests of 1965 and 1966 were experiments in "uncontrolled anarchy" (Lesh 2005, 68), where the goal was an expansion of consciousness and achievement of a communal mentality. Weirdness was encouraged and expected. Band historian Dennis

McNally noted that "the glory of an acid test for the Dead was that it wasn't a show and they weren't the night's entertainment. *Everybody* was the show, and Lord knew everybody was entertaining" (McNally 2002, 114). Lesh recalled that "while high we were able to go very far out musically but still come back to some kind of recognizable space or song structure" (Lesh 2005, 66), a pattern that would repeat itself in the best Grateful Dead jams in the ensuing decades. Although LSD and other psychedelics played a role in the Dead's musical development (except for Pigpen, who stuck to alcohol), they were merely one part of the band's education in musical communication.

In the fall of 1966, the members of the Dead moved into a communal house at 710 Ashbury Street in San Francisco, near the intersection of Haight Street. The Haight was becoming a geographical and philosophical continuation of the acid test ethos. Many of the city's most visible hippie institutions settled in or began in the Haight, including the radical political theater of the San Francisco Mime Troupe, the anarchist activist group the Diggers, and bands such as Jefferson Airplane.

On January 14, 1967, the Dead participated in one of the watershed moments of the San Francisco psychedelic scene, the Human Be-In at Golden Gate Park. Over 20,000 people assembled for a combination concert, speaking event, and celebration of life, psychedelic drugs, and positive attitudes. Ralph Gleason, a *San Francisco Chronicle* writer and an important early advocate for the Dead, wrote that it was "the greatest non-specific mass meeting in years, perhaps ever" (McNally 2002, 180). However, the event would spark a media storm of interest in hippiedom and the Haight-Ashbury. By the so-called Summer of Love in 1967, when tens of thousands of young people flooded the neighborhood, naïve innocence deteriorated into opportunism, hard drugs, and crime. The Dead often played for free that summer as a kind of community service for the overcrowded neighborhood.

For their first ever rock act, Warner Bros. Records signed the Grateful Dead in 1966, giving the band creative freedom and nearly unlimited studio time for a debut album. The band's self-titled debut album was released in 1967, but critics agreed that with the exception of two tracks where the Dead stretched their improvisational legs—"Viola Lee Blues" and "Morning Dew"—their debut album fell short of the live experience.

Two personnel changes occurred in late 1967. Robert Hunter, one of Garcia's oldest pals from his Palo Alto days, became the band's lyricist after penning the psychedelic lyrics for "Dark Star," which by 1968 emerged as a powerful canvas for the most exploratory improvisation the band had yet attempted. Meanwhile, Kreutzmann met a drummer named Mickey Hart (born Michael Steven Hartman, September 11, 1943; drums) and invited him to sit in with the band on September 30, 1967. Hart likened the experience to being "whipped into a jet stream" and was invited to permanently join the band (McNally 2002, 224).

Warner Bros. released *Anthem of the Sun* in 1968, featuring the suite "That's It for the Other One." This composition sandwiched Weir's "The Other One" between Garcia's "Cryptical Envelopment," and borrowed techniques from the classical avant-garde, including a section of electronic composition created by Lesh's composer friend Tom Constanten. The band invited Constanten to join them on keyboards, as Pigpen was ill-equipped to handle the newer, experimental music and more complex compositional techniques. In 1969, the band released *Aoxomoxoa*, the last of their albums with a strongly psychedelic style. The album was the band's first experience with 16-track recording equipment, and thus took on an experimental quality that Garcia later felt was too heavy-handed (Jackson 1999).

After three studio albums with little to moderate success, the band realized that a live album would be the only effective way to capture the energy and essence of a Grateful Dead concert on record. For their spring 1969 tour, the band utilized a portable 16-track recording console, an unheard-of practice at the time. The result was the late 1969 release of *Live/Dead*. The centerpiece was the opening track, "Dark Star," which musicologist Graeme Boone calls "one of the most memorable performances in rock music"

(Boone 1997, 172). Over 23 minutes long, this version of "Dark Star" showcased the band's comfort on the edge of order and chaos, mellow grooves and intense freak-outs.

The remainder of the album focused on the band's rock and blues basis. "St. Stephen" was a rambunctious blues rocker linked to "The Eleven" (with 11 beats per measure), followed by Pigpen's preacher-like exhortations in the fast blues rave-up of "Turn On Your Lovelight." The slow blues ballad "Death Don't Have No Mercy" highlighted Garcia's melancholy yet gorgeous guitar soloing. Concerts often ended with all three guitarists assaulting the audience with amplifier feedback and distortion, captured as the track "Feedback," while the a cappella spiritual "And We Bid You Goodnight" provided a bit of respite following the noisy barrage. Compiled from three separate nights, *Live/Dead* managed to encapsulate the Grateful Dead concert experience of the late 1960s.

The Dead played a forgettable set plagued by technical problems at Woodstock in August 1969. In December, the band was scheduled to participate in the Altamont Festival in Northern California, but cancelled their appearance following an ugly encounter between members of the motorcycle gang Hell's Angels and Jefferson Airplane.

In late 1969, Garcia and Hunter composed a variety of new songs that leaned heavily on folk, bluegrass, and country traditions in both musical and lyrical style. This return to their roots was a reaction to the complex psychedelia of the previous years while also indicative of a wider-ranging country-rock trend mirrored by Creedence Clearwater Revival, the Band, and albums from the Rolling Stones and Bob Dylan. Lesh described the change as a "commitment to a new simplicity and directness of expression" (Lesh 2005, 171) while Garcia commented that "we weren't feeling so much like an experimental music group, but were feeling more like a good old band" (Jackson 1999, 181). The initial fruit of this endeavor was *Workingman's Dead*, released in early 1970.

The cover of *Workingman's Dead*, a sepia-toned old-time photo of the band, was a stark contrast to the previous colorful, psychedelic album covers. The music matched the nostalgic, old-timey feel of the album cover, as Hunter revisited well-traveled Americana images such as trains, coal mines, and death. Although his lyrics were original, they borrowed heavily from the old-time folk traditions. As Carol Brightman has noted, "[Hunter] was dipping into old ballads mainly for atmosphere" (Brightman 1998, 64).

Later in 1970 the band released *American Beauty,* a counterpart to *Workingman's Dead.* The album saw considerable radio play in the summer and fall of 1970 thanks to singles such as "Truckin'," an autobiographical song about life on the road. It featured perhaps Hunter's most famous lyric, about taking a long strange trip, a phrase that has penetrated many facets of popular culture of the last 40 years.

Acoustic instruments figured prominently on both *Workingman's Dead* (the folky "Dire Wolf") and *American Beauty* ("Friend of the Devil" and "Ripple"). Sweet vocal harmonies were modeled on Crosby, Stills, and Nash anchor "Attics of My Life," while "Sugar Magnolia" showed a considerable pop sensibility. The opening track of *American Beauty* was perhaps Phil Lesh's greatest contribution to the Grateful Dead canon, "Box of Rain," with vividly poetic lyrics by Hunter. While *Workingman's Dead* and *American Beauty* were commercially successful, audiences were initially resistant to the new material since it featured less jamming.

Concerts in the spring of 1970, dubbed "An Evening with the Grateful Dead," included an opening acoustic set that featured many of the *Workingman's Dead* and *American Beauty* songs. The concert from May 2, 1970, in Binghamton, New York, exemplified this era and was officially released as *Dick's Picks vol. 8* in 1997 (the *Dick's Picks* series, a collection of 36 two-track recordings begun in 1993, was named after band archivist Dick Latvala, although in actuality he did not have the final say). The show featured cover songs encompassing a wide variety of American musical styles, including folk, jug band, blues, and gospel. A long "Other One" suite anchored the electric set, and a blistering jam on "Viola Lee Blues" closed out the night. As McNally noted, "they did not simply replace psychedelia with country;

they added new dimensions to an established oeuvre" (McNally 2002, 319).

Constanten parted ways with the band in early 1970; Lesh explained that this was the result of the band's move "away from balls-against-the-wall free-form weirdness toward simpler songs and musical storytelling" (Lesh 2005, 169). That summer, the band discovered that their band manager—Mickey Hart's father, Lenny—had been stealing from the group. Mickey Hart became despondent in the wake of the scandal, despite the band's reassurances that they did not blame him for his father's breach of trust. The guilt became too much for Hart, and he left the band after their gig on February 18, 1971.

In the fall of 1971, a singer named Donna Jean Godchaux (born Donna Jean Thatcher, August 22, 1947; vocals) approached the band and announced that her husband, keyboardist Keith Godchaux (born Keith Richard Godchaux, July 19, 1948, died July 23, 1980; keyboards), intended to join the group. Pigpen's health was deteriorating and his ability to play was compromised; over a decade of hard drinking had taken its toll on his liver. Unbeknownst to Godchaux, the band was in need of a new keyboard player. A quick jam session confirmed that Godchaux was the right man for the job, and Donna Jean later joined the band on vocals.

The *Live/Dead*-era sound and personnel was gone, a change documented on two live albums from 1971 and 1972. Their second self-titled record, released in October 1971, was a double LP culled from performances the previous April. With only one drummer and Pigpen's contributions minimal, the band revealed a tight, leaner style leaning heavily on a mix of country, blues, and folk played at fast rock tempos. The improvisational masterpiece of the album, an 18-minute version of "The Other One," showed an influence from *Bitches Brew*–era jazz fusion (Miles Davis opened for the Dead in 1970). Garcia's soloing alternated between relaxed and intense, while the band's thick texture sounded more controlled than their earlier, wilder experiments.

The other live album was compiled from the Dead's extended tour of Europe in the spring of 1972. Released in the fall of that year, *Europe '72* was a triple LP featuring excellent versions of the country and folk-inspired songs that had premiered over the past year. Improvisational segments included an extended take on "Truckin'" and a powerful version of "Morning Dew." Pigpen sang lead vocal on two songs, the Elmore James blues ballad "Hurts Me Too" and the Pigpen/Hunter original "Mr. Charlie." They would be his final appearances on record, as he died from internal bleeding resulting from excessive alcohol abuse in 1973 at age 27.

In 1973, the band ended their relationship with Warner Bros. and began their own Grateful Dead Records, quickly releasing *Wake of the Flood*. Stand out songs included the recently debuted "Eyes of the World," whose jazzy lilt immediately became a canvas for extended improvisational journeys, and Weir's "Weather Report Suite," a multipart composed piece that showed maturity in its musical complexity, with lyrics penned by Weir's new collaborator, his childhood friend John Perry Barlow.

Sound quality and amplification had always been a primary concern of the band, and in 1973, their technicians realized that their expensive and extensive P.A. system would not fit on most stages. After installing phase-cancelling microphones, the band was able to stack speakers behind them in a giant wall, which would allow the band to always have their ideal sound. The Wall of Sound, as it was called, was an enormous and extravagant sound system that towered behind the band for all of 1974. It was the largest, and one of the best-sounding, P.A. systems in the world.

Yet, 1974 saw internal problems in the Grateful Dead world. Both the band and the crew were road weary, cocaine abuse was straining relationships, and the Wall of Sound was a financial liability. The band decided to take a hiatus, playing a five-night run of "retirement shows" in San Francisco in October 1974. On the final night, Mickey Hart played drums next to Kreutzmann for the first time in over three years.

In June 1976, the band began touring again with Hart back on the roster. Eschewing the psychedelic, jazzy, and sometimes esoteric improvisation of their prehiatus years, the band found itself jamming over more comfortable grooves, with fewer moments of far-out weirdness. The Dead's music in the late 1970s generally moved at slower tempos, while the dual-drum juggernaut solidified the rhythmic pocket, making it exceedingly enjoyable if not slightly less challenging.

One night in particular, May 8, 1977, at Cornell University's Barton Hall, assumed a legendary status among Deadheads. Although the show contained some inspired playing, its mythology owes to the fact that it was one of the first soundboard recordings of extremely high quality to circulate widely among fans. The show's fame was more a reflection of the tape's popularity, rather than the music contained within. Yet because of its iconic status within the Deadhead subculture, the recording of May 8, 1977, was inducted into the Library of Congress's National Recording Registry in 2012.

The year 1977 saw the release of a new album, *Terrapin Station,* for a new label, Arista Records. "Terrapin Station," a multipart suite, began like many of Hunter's lyrics, by borrowing images and ideas from traditional American music for something original. The final guitar solo was one of Garcia's finest composed riffs, yet the lush orchestral additions to the track produced a saccharine sound. Many Dead jams were beginning to take on a more groove-oriented, dance quality, reflecting the mainstream disco aesthetic of the era. The old Motown hit "Dancing in the Street" frequently stretched out to over 15 minutes, with funky, wah-wah pedal soloing from Garcia, while many originals took on a disco flavor. This trend culminated with the release of *Shakedown Street* in 1978, whose title track was a dance club romp.

In September of 1978, the Grateful Dead and their entourage traveled to Egypt to play three concerts at the base of the Great Pyramid at Gizeh. By early 1979, drugs and road weariness had gotten to the Godchauxs and they left the band by the end of the winter tour; Keith died the following summer in a car accident. In March, Weir's keyboard player from a solo project, Brent Mydland, joined the band, learning songs that would comprise a new album released in 1980, *Go to Heaven.*

In the late 1970s, a new constant appeared in the second set, when Kreutzmann and Hart were given a drum solo that would eventually incorporate a significant amount of non-Western percussion instruments. Afterward, the melodic instruments played a formless jam using electronic manipulations of sound, harmonic dissonance, and generally free rhythm. The two sections were named "Drums" and "Space," and they became fixtures in the late second set of nearly every show.

The early 1980s were somewhat stagnant times for the Grateful Dead, characterized by frequent touring but no new studio albums between 1980 and 1987. The biggest change in the early 1980s was the emergence of a traveling Deadhead subculture. In 1979, the band allowed camping on the grass outside the Kaiser Auditorium in Oakland, which attracted a few hundred fans. Some Deadheads began living "on tour," following the band and camping in the parking lots after shows. The parking lots took on the character of a small village, with a barter economy centered on goods, crafts, food, drugs, and especially concert tickets.

A new generation of younger fans came onboard, many seeking the same sense of liberation that had fueled fans in the 1960s. In the Reagan 1980s, the largely underground Grateful Dead scene offered a nostalgic continuation of the 1960s counterculture and an alternative to the conservatism and materialism of the times. In 1984, the Dead established their charitable organization, the Rex Foundation, to support environmental issues, the arts, and social services.

Audience taping of live concerts had been unofficially tolerated for most of the band's career. In October 1984, the band created a taper's section behind their soundboard, with seats available through the band's ticketing service. The practice of tape collecting and trading became "one of the most durable binding threads in the fabric of the Deadhead community" (Shenk and Silberman 1994, 280).

In 1986, with his weight ballooning, Garcia slipped into a diabetic coma. He had begun using heroin in the late 1970s, and his addiction accelerated his condition. Renewed by his brush with death, and the healthiest he had been in years, Garcia breathed new life into the band, and by early 1987 they recorded an album for Arista Records of road-tested material, some of which had been played live since 1982. Of these tunes, the anthemic "Touch of Grey," with its chorus "I will get by/I will survive," took on deeper meaning following Garcia's coma.

In the Dark was released in July 1987 and immediately began to garner considerable press. The poppy single "Touch of Grey," with its smooth production, lumbering groove, and even an MTV video, peaked at number nine on the *Billboard* charts. The commercial success that the band never really desired had finally found them; *In the Dark* was certified platinum by September.

Success had its price, and this was mainly in the influx of new, younger fans (pejoratively called "Touch Heads" due to the timing of their arrival), many of whom did not understand the Deadhead ethos of community. Some were unable to handle psychedelic drugs, lacking the respect for the substances that older Deadheads practiced, leading to well-publicized casualties. Profiteering entered the scene as well, including professional drug dealers who had no interest in the music or the community, ticket scalpers and counterfeiters, and pirate merchandise. Ticketless fans would show up and party in the parking lots, creating a strain on both infrastructure and police resources.

Despite this, the Dead were playing some of their best music in years from 1987 to 1990. Mydland contributed solid originals such as "Blow Away" and "Just a Little Light," and "Dark Star" returned to the stage after a five-year absence. A guest appearance by jazz saxophonist Branford Marsalis in March 1990 precipitated some of the best jamming of the era ("Eyes of the World" with Marsalis was released on the live compilation *Without a Net*).

Tragedy struck the keyboard seat again in the summer of 1990 when Mydland died from an overdose. The band hastily found a replacement in keyboardist Vince Welnick. Bruce Hornsby also joined the band, playing piano for most of the following two years, although he never committed to becoming a regular member of the band.

Despite the occasional high point, the music gradually deteriorated throughout the 1990s. Garcia continued to lapse in and out of addiction, while crowd control problems persisted. In 1995, fans at Indiana's Deer Creek Amphitheater tore down the fence and stormed the venue, causing the band to cancel the following night's show. On July 9, 1995, the Grateful Dead played what would be their final show at Chicago's Soldier Field Stadium.

Garcia checked himself into rehab after the tour that summer, but it was too late. On August 9, 1995, he died of a heart attack, eight days after his 53rd birthday. Over 20,000 people showed up in Golden Gate Park for an impromptu memorial celebration, and that winter the band convened to decide that they would retire the name "Grateful Dead."

Although there would be no more live Grateful Dead concerts, the music lived on both in live releases and performances from the rest of the band. The band began releasing multitrack concerts from the vault on CD in 1991, as well as the two-track *Dick's Picks* series, spanning much of the Dead's history. Archival releases began appearing on the Rhino Records imprint in 2006 and have continued under a variety of series titles (e.g., *Road Trips, Dave's Picks*), although Grateful Dead Productions still controls the live output.

Both Weir and Lesh fronted bands, RatDog and Phil & Friends, which played Grateful Dead music after Garcia's death. However, Weir, Lesh, Kreutzmann, and Hart did not share the stage until 2002. Calling themselves the Other Ones, they played a "family reunion" weekend in Wisconsin, but controversially did not include Welnick. In 2003, they changed their name simply to the Dead.

Lesh and Weir wanted to take the Grateful Dead's music into different, unexpected directions. They felt that the original drummers caused them to play with a certain amount of expectation and complacency (Budnick 2011). They assembled a new group of musicians, including guitarist John Kadlecik, who had founded the Grateful Dead tribute act Dark Star Orchestra, and dubbed themselves Furthur. This was the first time that Weir or Lesh had played with a guitarist who imitated Garcia's playing style. Despite a few rocky months of adjustment, Kadlecik assumed the lead guitarist role in the band, and many Deadheads agreed that Furthur, with Joe Russo on drums and Jeff Chimenti on keyboards, was the best post-Garcia band playing Grateful Dead music.

The Dead's approach to jamming was one of the most identifiable markers of their musical style. Influences changed over the course of their career, but the band's improvisational style drew from rock, bluegrass, bebop, modal jazz, funk, and modern classical music. However, the idea of group improvisation was perhaps the Dead's most important musical attribute. The band generally avoided the practice of soloing over an accompanying background, as musicologist Michael Kaler notes: "the overall group feel is created through continuous and independent although united movement in all the voices" (Kaler 2012, 76). Much of what made the Dead's jamming so unique was intangible, and Deadheads have described the band's best improvisational moments as "The X Factor" or "The Zone" (Shenk and Silberman 1994).

Certain idiosyncrasies of individual band members help separate the Dead's sound from any other band, mainly in the rhythm section. Weir frequently avoids the folk-rock style strumming or riffing that helps to establish an even meter, often choosing to emphasize offbeats. His chord fingerings are extremely varied, favoring the middle of the guitar neck. During jams, his playing is atypical and eccentric, offering accents and color rather than a rhythmic or harmonic grounding.

Lesh is an equally unorthodox rock bassist who formed his style upon his knowledge of music theory and a few favorite jazz bassists. Unlike R&B or soul bass players, Lesh does not lay down a repetitive groove, nor does he walk the bass as jazz players do. The fast tempos of rock and roll cause him to play an extremely active bass part with longer patterns and melodies. He frequently assumes more of a lead instrument role during jams, where he plays countermelodies with Garcia. Between Weir, Lesh, and the interlocking rhythms of Kreutzmann and Hart, the best Grateful Dead jams are in constant flux between rhythmic stability and chaos.

Bands as diverse as Los Lobos, Jane's Addiction, and Henry Rollins have all cited the Dead as influences. Additionally, a newer wave of indie rock bands, including Animal Collective, Bonnie "Prince" Billy, and the Decemberists have either covered the Dead or cited the Dead's importance to their sound (Jarnow 2008). Regarding their business model, their in-house ticketing and production, and their concert-based approach to marketing and revenue, the Dead prefigured many of the modern jambands such as Phish, moe., and String Cheese Incident. These bands follow the Dead's practice of allowing distribution of audience recordings, and their fans often overlap with Deadheads. While each band sounds different, all share a commitment to group improvisation modeled, in part, on the Grateful Dead.

Jacob A. Cohen

Selected Discography
Studio and Contemporary Live Recordings:
The Grateful Dead, Warner Bros. WS-1689, 1967.

Anthem of the Sun, Warner Bros. WS-1749, 1968.

Aoxomoxoa, Warner Bros. WS-1790, 1969.

Live/Dead (2 LPs), Warner Bros. 2WS-1830, 1969.

Workingman's Dead, Warner Bros. WS-1869, 1970.

American Beauty, Warner Bros. WS-1893, 1970.

Grateful Dead (2 LPs), Warner Bros. 2WS-1935, 1971.

Europe '72 (3 LPs), Warner Bros. 3WS-2668, 1972.

Wake of the Flood, Grateful Dead Records GD-01, 1973.

Grateful Dead from the Mars Hotel, Grateful Dead Records GD-102, 1974.

Blues for Allah, Grateful Dead Records LA-494, 1975.

Terrapin Station, Arista AL-7001, 1977.

Shakedown Street, Arista AB-4198, 1978.

Reckoning (2 LPs), Arista A2L-8604, 1980.

In the Dark, Arista AL-8452, 1987.

Without a Net (2 CDs), Arista ACD2–8634, 1990.

So Many Roads (1965–1995) (5 CD compilation), Arista GDCD-4066, 1999.

Birth of the Dead (2 CD compilation), Rhino R2–74391, 2003.

Archival Live Release (Vault):
Date of recording is indicated in parenthesis following the album title. There have been nearly 100 live releases since 1991; the following selections are listed because of historical significance and/or personal preference of the author.

One from the Vault (August 13, 1975), Grateful Dead Records GDCD-4013–2, 1991.

Two from the Vault (August 24, 1968), Grateful Dead Records GDCD-4016–2, 1992.

Dick's Picks vol. 1 (December 19, 1973), Grateful Dead Records GDCD-4019, 1993.

Dick's Picks vol. 3 (May 22, 1977), Grateful Dead Record, GDCD-4021, 1995.

Hundred Year Hall (April 26, 1972), Grateful Dead Records GDCD-4020–2, 1995.

Dick's Picks vol. 4 (February 13–14, 1970), Grateful Dead Records GDCD-4023, 1996.

Dozin' at the Knick (March 24–26, 1990), Grateful Dead Records GDCD-4025, 1996.

Dick's Picks vol. 8 (May 2, 1970), Grateful Dead Records GDCD-4028, 1997.

Dick's Picks vol. 13 (May 6, 1981), Grateful Dead Records GDCD-4033, 1999.

Dick's Picks vol. 16 (November 8, 1969), Grateful Dead Records GDCD-4036, 2000.

Ladies and Gentlemen . . . the Grateful Dead (April, 1971), Grateful Dead/Arista 1110026, 2000.

The Closing of Winterland (December 31, 1978), Grateful Dead Records GDCD-4090 2003.

Road Trips: Vol. 1, No. 1 (Fall 1979), Grateful Dead/Rhino GRA2–6001, 2007.

Three from the Vault (February 19, 1971), Grateful Dead/Rhino R2–162812, 2007.

Road Trips: Vol. 2, No. 4 (May 26–27, 1993), Grateful Dead/Rhino GRA2–6008, 2009.

Formerly the Warlocks (October 8–9, 1989), Grateful Dead/Rhino R2–525760, 2010.

Road Trips: Vol. 4, No. 4 (April 6, 1982), Grateful Dead/Rhino GRA2–6021, 2011.

Dave's Picks Volume 2 (July 31, 1974), Grateful Dead/Rhino R2–529204, 2012.

References

Barnes, Barry. *Everything I Know About Business I Learned from the Grateful Dead: The Ten Most Innovative Lessons from a Long, Strange Trip.* New York: Business Plus, 2011.

Boone, Graeme M. "Tonal and Expressive Ambiguity in 'Dark Star.'" In *Understanding Rock: Essays in Musical Analysis,* edited by John Covach and Graeme M. Boone. New York: Oxford University Press, 1997.

Brightman, Carol. *Sweet Chaos: The Grateful Dead's American Adventure.* New York: Clarkson Potter, 1998.

Budnick, Dean. "Dead Behind, Furthur Ahead." *Relix* 38 (2) (March 2011): 54–59.

Graham, Bill, and Robert Greenfield. *Bill Graham Presents: My Life Inside Rock and Out.* New York: Doubleday, 1992.

Jackson, Blair. *Garcia: An American Life.* New York: Penguin Books, 1999.

Jarnow, Jesse. "How Jerry Got Hip Again." *Relix* 35 (5) (August, 2008): 62–69.

Kaler, Michael. "How the Grateful Dead Learned to Jam." In *Reading the Dead: A Critical Survey,* edited by Nicholas G. Meriwether. Lanham, MD: Scarecrow Press, 2012.

Lesh, Phil. *Searching for the Sound: My Life with the Grateful Dead.* New York: Little, Brown and Company, 2005.

McNally, Dennis. *A Long Strange Trip: The Inside History of the Grateful Dead.* New York: Broadway Books, 2002.

Shenk, David, and Steve Silberman. *Skeleton Key: A Dictionary for Deadheads.* New York: Doubleday, 1994.

Wolfe, Tom. *The Electric Kool-Aid Acid Test.* New York: Bantam, 1968.

Green Day (1987–Present)

Inspired by their formative experiences in suburban California, and shaped by early personal challenges, including like the death of a parent, divorce, and adoption, the members of Green Day pioneered what Matt Diehl has called West Coast "neo-punk" and defined as a genre rooted in 1970s first-wave punk and Seattle grunge. In its early albums, the band appeared to reflect (or perhaps even to caricature) male adolescence with various scatological references in their album titles and in their promotional artwork, and assumed this stance to heighten the "bad boy" image that they sought to portray in their performances. As one observer of Green Day's early output observed, the band reconceived punk as "a bratty ordeal free of revolutionary political pretentions, while retaining the rebellion" (Dimrey, 751).

Later, and as the members of the band matured, Green Day became noteworthy for its political messages, most of which were designed in reaction to the policies of the George W. Bush administration in response to the 9/11 attacks. According to one critic, the band's most famous album, *American Idiot*, harkens back to the protest songs of the 1960s, and "the fire in [Billie Joe] Armstrong's vocals alone made it clear that a powerful protest song, the likes of which pop culture hadn't heard since the heyday of Dylan and Lennon, had arrived" (Spitz, 172). Put simply, Green Day's thematic trajectory from suburban alienation to political disillusionment represents a more general coming-of-age narrative about growing up and becoming politically aware in the United States at the turn of the millennium.

The band was formed under the name "Sweet Children" in 1987 by childhood friends Billie Joe Armstrong (born February 17, 1972; guitar, vocals) and Mike Dirnt (born Michael Pritchard, May 4, 1972; bass). Despite their strong friendship, Armstrong and Dirnt had grown up under very different circumstances in the suburbs of San Francisco, and each suffered an early personal loss that later shaped the themes explored in their music and the "punk" stance that each adopted as a performance practice. The youngest son in a family of five children, Billie Joe was particularly close to his father, Andy, who was an amateur jazz drummer with a passion for modern jazz and who encouraged his son to pursue his own interests in music.

In 1977, the family supported Billie Joe as he sought to record his first single, the self-penned "Make My World Beautiful," written when the youngster was

American punk group Green Day, in Phoenix, Arizona, early 1990s. Left to right: drummer Tré Cool, singer and guitarist Billie Joe Armstrong, and bassist Mike Dirnt. Green Day was responsible for bringing the second wave of punk music to the masses. They parlayed that success into multiple Grammy Awards and induction into the Rock and Roll Hall of Fame in the 2015 class. (Photo by Robert Knight Archive/Redferns)

only five years old. Music would become a safe haven for Billie Joe, particularly after his father's premature death in September 1982. Devastated, the 10-year-old receded into music, MTV, and guitar lessons with his teacher, George Cole. Cole became a surrogate father figure for Billie Joe, who eventually purchased Cole's Stratocaster, named "Blue," as a trademark instrument later used throughout his career and a token of his strong ties to this early teacher. Unlike the comparatively stable family life enjoyed by Armstrong, Mike Dirnt was raised in a difficult adoptive family after he was given up by a biological mother who struggled with heroin addiction. Like Armstrong, he used music

as an escape from difficulties at home, but in his case, these difficulties ended in a divorce that broke up his family. Armstrong and Dirnt met at middle school in Rodeo, California, and bonded over a shared love of music. On the advice of Armstrong, Dirnt eventually enlisted Cole as his guitar teacher.

By the early 1980s, the pair began to forge their musical identities when Armstrong's older sister, Anna, introduced them to the "alternative" rock typically played on college radio stations at the time. Bands like Hüsker Dü, the Replacements, Bad Brains, Camper van Beethoven, and R.E.M. became formative influences, and under the moniker of Sweet Children, the pair added several covers to their set list. Another important source of musical inspiration for the pair was the punk fanzine *Maximumrocknroll* (*MRR*), where interviews with, and discussions about, bands like Black Flag, the Dead Kennedys, and the Germs were regularly featured; their punk resistance was contextualized in terms of the election of Ronald Reagan in 1981 and his subsequent presidency.

While the influence of the fanzine's political overtones on Armstrong and Dirnt might have needed to percolate for a few years, a more immediate effect was that it introduced the pair to the clubs associated with the San Francisco punk scene, notably was the Gilman (at 924 Gilman Street), the Mabuhay Gardens (at 443 Broadway), and the Farm (1499 Potrero Street). Hanging out at the Gilman, in particular, was a formative experience for the duo, both of whom spent weekends as audience members at the club. As Marc Spitz suggested in his 2006 biography of the band, "It would be at 924 Gilman where . . . the pop melodic punk of the Ramones and the politicized early hardcore of the Dead Kennedys (and touring acts like Black Flag, the Bad Brains, and Minor Threat) would collide violently to create a new sound and a new ethos, both of which would heavily influence Green Day in their formative years" (Spitz, 30).

One night at the Gilman, after a concert by a local band called Isocracy, Armstrong and Dirnt decided to invite the drummer, Al Sobrante (born John Kiffmeyer, July 11, 1969; drums), to join Sweet Children. Sobrante was well known on the San Francisco punk scene, and his connections proved useful for the unknown duo. Older and more experienced than his new bandmates, Sobrante appointed himself as the band's manager and secured a gig at the Gilman in November 1988 for his new act. The three played a warm-up show at the restaurant where Armstrong's mother worked, Rod's Hickory Pit restaurant in El Cerrito, California.

At their Gilman gig, the trio distinguished themselves both because they were younger than many of the musicians with whom they shared the stage and because they were more talented than most. Because of the success of this gig, the band was invited to play at various house parties in the East Bay. At one of these parties, the band came to the attention of Lawrence Livermore, a punk impresario who promoted the East Bay punk scene through his own fanzine, *Lookout*, and his recording label, Lookout! Records. Initially designed to promote Livermore's own punk band, the Lookouts, the label soon became central to the careers of Armstrong and Dirnt; but in the short term, the Lookouts also provided a key link between the duo and the drummer who would soon replace Sobrante, a prodigy from Willits, California, named Frank Edwin Wright III (born December 9, 1972; drums). When he invited Wright to join the Lookouts, Livermore dubbed him Tré Cool, which is the stage name that he has since carried throughout his career.

Livermore arranged for Armstrong, Dirnt, and Sobrante (now playing under the name "Green Day") to open at the Gilman for Lookout!'s most established act, Operation Ivy; they had been one of the few East Bay bands to tour the East Coast, where they played in venues in New Jersey, Pennsylvania, and Connecticut. By the time they shared the stage with Green Day on May 28, 1989, Operation Ivy had already released their only studio album, *Energy*, on Lookout! in March 1989, and the concert was designed to promote the release of the album. Despite their seeming success, however, *Energy* would be Operation Ivy's first and only record.

Green Day, by contrast, appeared poised to take their place, and Livermore signed the band to his record label, but, as he has been quoted as saying, he worried that "they were way more pop than the other Gilman bands—too pop, I thought, to have much of a chance at doing well on that scene. But I thought the songs and the performances were so good that they deserved to be captured on vinyl, even if I did end up losing a little money on it" (Spitz, 63). During the 1989 Christmas holiday, when the studio was empty and recording time was cheaper, Armstrong, Dirnt, and Sobrante recorded their debut for Lookout! at Berkeley's Art of Ears studio. *39/Smooth* was released on April 13, 1990, and featured 10 tracks that ranged from raw punk songs as "At the Library" and "The Judge's Daughter" to more introspective ballads as "I Was There." The album sold well in its local market, and the band went on tour in June to promote the album at various indie clubs across the United States.

While on tour, Armstrong met Adrienne Nesser, a 22-year-old student at the University of Minnesota who attended their concert in Minneapolis. Later to become his wife, Nesser became the inspiration for the pop lament "2,000 Light Years Away," which chronicles an emotional bond between a male protagonist and a girl whom he has just met but that he knows he cannot live without. Nesser has been Armstrong's muse ever since, and she has since inspired such songs as "80" (a reference to his nickname for her, "Aidy").

After the promotional tour concluded, Sobrante decided to return to school and enrolled at Humboldt State College in the fall of 1990. This left the two original members of the band without a drummer. As fate would have it, Tré Cool had the opposite problem when his band, the Lookouts, disbanded and left him as a drummer without a band. With Cool in tow, Green Day's lineup was finalized for good, and although Sobrante would play on four tracks on Green Day's second studio album, *Kerplunk* (released on January 17, 1992), he left the band for good when this project was completed.

Kerplunk found itself on the right side of history, since its release corresponded with the rising popularity of the Seattle grunge scene in the Bay Area, marked in particular by the success and popularity of Nirvana's second album, *Nevermind* (released on September 24, 1991). As Spitz has argued, Nirvana's music made "the melodic Beatles-conscious punk rock that Green Day had been defiantly producing for years extremely marketable. Suddenly, the commercial prospects for a young, loud, and snotty trio from the burbs of a major U.S. metropolis seemed limitless" (Spitz, 75). *Kerplunk* was an instant hit on the indie circuit, and the album sold 10,000 copies on the first day of its release. On the heels of this newfound success, Green Day decided to enlist the help of a professional management team and signed with Elliot Cahn and Jeff Saltzman, a Los Angeles firm that went

under the name Cahn-Man and also managed acts like the Offspring, Rancid, and the Seattle grunge band Mudhoney. Under the guidance of their new management team, Green Day was booked into prestigious venues like the Whisky a Go Go in Los Angeles and Slim's in San Francisco and was sent to Europe to promote the album.

Kerplunk was the last Green Day album to be recorded on an independent label, and on August 24, 1993, the band left Lookout! for the Warner Bros. subsidiary, Reprise. Their in-house producer, Rob Cavallo (who has since risen to the chairmanship of Warner Bros.) was a rookie at the Warner offices when he signed Green Day to the label in 1993. Like many punk bands who came before them (notably, the Clash), Green Day faced enormous hostility from fans who accused them of "selling out" to a major label, and the members of Green Day quickly found themselves ostracized by the Gilman, which excluded bands with major-label contracts from their roster. Despite their excommunication from their former venues, or perhaps in response to it, the members of Green Day turned inward and focused on songwriting for their next studio album, *Dookie,* which was the first to be released on the Reprise label and which appeared on February 1, 1994. Like *Kerplunk*, the title of the band's third release was an overt scatological reference that has sometimes contributed to the "frat boy" image attributed to the band, but the nihilism of the album's cover, which features a cartoon bomb released over a hypothetical East Bay scene populated by various cultural icons, began to point toward the political tone assumed by the band in later albums. Chris Smith has noted about the album that "from the potty-humor title to the snotty juvenilia of the material, *Dookie* brought punk and rock and roll's lighter aesthetics to a mainstream audience, while still managing to convey their seemingly dichotomous brand of teenage boredom and garage-rock energy" (Smith 228). *Time* magazine similarly proclaimed that "this is music for people with raging hormones and short attention spans . . . for the sort of kid who, as his burrito rotates in the microwave, impatiently frets 'three minutes is an eternity'" (*Time,* June 1994).

The album produced five hit singles for the band: "Long View," "When I Come Around," "Basket Case," "Welcome to Paradise," and the radio-only single "She." It charted at number two on the American *Billboard* charts and received a Grammy Award in 1995 for Best Alternative Music Album. After the mixing of *Dookie* was completed in 1993, Green Day toured with their Los Angeles punk heroes Bad Religion, and their connection with this older band exposed Green Day to an increasingly wider audience. Soon, Green Day was selling out arenas all over the United States and appearing on television as guests of *The Late Show with David Letterman, Saturday Night Live, Late Night with Conan O'Brien,* and on MTV.

As his career was rising, Billie Joe Armstrong married Adrienne Nesser on July 2, 1994, and discovered the day after the wedding that she was pregnant. The other two members of the band also married their girlfriends in 1994 and, like Armstrong, began to feel that they wanted to slow down the pace of their careers so that they could spend time with their new wives. Despite their personal circumstances, however, Green Day played Lollapalooza in August 1994, skipping one of its tour dates to play at Woodstock, where they started an infamous mud fight with the audience that caused the first of many concert riots to come. Their antics at Woodstock brought international attention to the band, which became a household name in the wake of the mud-slinging event. By December 1994, the band's next promotional event, a concert in Boston, sold 100,000 tickets and ultimately caused another riot.

Perhaps one of the most anticipated releases of 1995, the follow-up to *Dookie* was the studio album *Insomniac,* with cover artwork by the collage artist Winston Smith. Released on October 10, 1995, *Insomniac* has been described as an album that retained Green Day's punk blueprint, but that was a shade darker in tone. As a sample of what was to come, the band released the single "Geek Stink Breath" on September 25, 1995 (although it had previously debuted on December 3, 1994, during the band's appearance on *Saturday Night Live*). Alluding to methamphetamine through the slang "Geek," the song described the effects of the drug on the human body in rather graphic terms. Although the album failed to sell as well as *Dookie,* Green Day launched a world tour in support of its release; however, the European leg of the *Insomniac* tour was canceled before its completion, with the band citing exhaustion and a desire to be at home with their new families. By this time, the band had also fired its management, Cahn-Man, and was managing itself.

After a brief hiatus to rethink the direction of the band, Green Day reconvened in 1997 and began to work on their fifth studio album, *Nimrod.* This album took four months to record and was released on October 14, 1997. Perhaps responding to the criticism that *Insomniac* was too similar in style to *Dookie,* Green Day's music began to hint toward a more diverse musical palette, and *Nimrod* became noteworthy for its musical allusions to ska, folk, and surf. The lyrical themes also showed that the band was maturing, since the songs began to reflect such topics as fatherhood, aging, and failed relationships. *Nimrod* returned the band to the status it had achieved with *Dookie,* and the album charted at number 10 on the *Billboard* charts, where it remained for 70 weeks. The ballad "Good Riddance (Time of Your Life)" also put the band back on the *Billboard* singles charts. (Armstrong had actually written the song several years earlier, after he had been dumped by an early girlfriend, but it had been rejected for the band's earlier albums because it was deemed too sentimental.) The *Nimrod* promotional tour, launched in the fall of 1997, was marked by riots similar to those that had ensued three years earlier. Notably, an in-store signing at Tower Records in Manhattan provoked a riot among Green Day fans when Armstrong overturned a set of CD racks in the store and spray painted its front windows. Despite these negative behaviors, the *Nimrod* tour also spawned another ritual that has endured in the band's performances—one that invokes punk's DIY ethos—as members of the audience were invited to join the band onstage to play the song "Knowledge" (originally by Operation Ivy), chosen principally because it is less demanding than other Green Day songs. This has proven to be a masterful publicity stunt, since the guitarist of the ad hoc band is usually allowed to keep the instrument as a souvenir.

The folk element explored in *Nimrod* became central to the band's next album, *Warning*, released on October 3, 2000, and Marc Spitz has suggested that the turn away from punk and toward acoustic elements in this album might constitute a form of homage to Bob Dylan (specifically, Dylan's 1965 masterwork *Bringing It All Back Home*), whom Armstrong cited as a musical influence. Certainly, Dylan provided a template for the band's expression of their newly awakened political views. Written in the midst of the 2000 election of George W. Bush, the album was the band's most political to date. The song "Minority," for example, was written as an expression of the band's concerns about the election.

Warning debuted on the U.S. *Billboard* Top 200 Chart at number four, where it remained for 25 weeks. Despite the acoustic focus of the album, Green Day decided to promote *Warning* at the annual Vans Warped Tour in 2000—a surprising step, since the tour is commonly known for its promotion of extreme sports and its preference for guitar-based, three-chord punk rock. Late in 2001, Green Day shocked their fans even further when they announced that they would co-headline the "Pop Disaster" tour the following year with the pop-punk band Blink-182. The choice was strategic on both sides. Blink-182 would gain credibility by playing with a band that had established itself as neo-punk, while Green Day would gain exposure to an audience for whom the band might have seemed irrelevant. Despite criticisms about the union of these seemingly disparate bands, the punk scene had begun to coalesce around a set of anti-Bush political ideals. In particular, punks sought to express their opposition to various geopolitical decisions made by the president in the wake of the September 11th attacks. Many bands that had been apolitical, among which one might include Blink-182, were motivated by what they believed to be an unconscionable set of decisions made by the Bush administration that eventually led to the invasion of Iraq.

In this political environment, the band went to work on their next studio album, which promised to be a return to hard-edge punk. This project, tentatively titled *Cigarettes and Valentines,* was abandoned in the summer of 2003, after the master tapes of the album were purportedly stolen. Instead of attempting to revive the project, the members of Green Day decided to turn their attention toward a project they had discussed as early as 1997: a punk opera. The first track to be written, "Homecoming," was a five-song suite in which each member of the band reflected on his particular mood or feeling at the moment the song was written. Dirnt's contribution, "Nobody Likes You," described a songwriter who found himself alone in the studio, while Cool's contribution, "Rock and Roll Girlfriend," described his second divorce. "Homecoming" became the 12th track on Green Day's seventh studio album, *American Idiot,* whose opening title track was intended as a sharp critique of the Bush administration. In composing the critique, the band took an enormous publicity risk. As Spitz explains, "In an age when anything vaguely suggesting a lack of patriotism had been enough to get an artist black-listed, throwing up a spot on this common emotion, as sharp as it was, risked being wildly misconstrued" (Spitz, 162).

The album, and later the opera, depicted the plight of an antihero, "Jesus of Suburbia," described in the second track (another suite of five songs) as he awakened to a town that he despised, a family that did not understand him, and a need to rebel. Running away from home, he met the punk rock rebel "Saint Jimmy" and fell for a girl, "Whatshername." The theme that bound the narrative together was the struggle between the emotional states of rage (embodied in Jimmy) and love (embodied in the girl), the former of which he needed to overcome so that he could embrace the latter. Saint Jimmy committed suicide toward the end of the album, and in the final track, the antihero lost track of Whatshername. The end result was a sense that the protagonist was alienated even from himself as he continued to search for the meaning of life. Released on August 31, 2004, the single "American Idiot" peaked at number 61 on the *Billboard* Hot 100, entered the Canadian charts at number one, and was Green Day's first breakthrough into the top five singles charts in the United Kingdom.

American Idiot was released in the midst of the 2004 presidential campaign, and the band made it clear that they were aggressively anti-Bush. They had the opportunity to show their support for John Kerry when they were booked to appear on the same episode of *The Late Show with David Letterman* on September 22, 2004, and the band had a photo-op with the candidate. The next week, the album was released and entered the U.S. *Billboard* 200 charts at number one. Resonating with young British voters who were disenchanted with Prime Minister Tony Blair and concerned about his close relationship with President Bush, *American Idiot* also sold well in the United Kingdom, where it soared to the top of the U.K. Albums Chart. The political message in *American Idiot* also added to Green Day's "punk" credibility among British listeners, who saw connections with the political critiques leveled by the Sex Pistols and the Clash against the political systems of their day. The album received seven Grammy Award nominations and won best album awards at the American Music Awards, the Brit Awards, the Grammy Awards, the Japan Gold Disc Awards, and Canada's Juno Awards. The rock opera format was retained for the band's next studio album, *21st Century Breakdown,* released to critical acclaim on May 15, 2009. The songs on the album, and the narrative of the proposed opera, center on themes of alienation experienced by individuals who find themselves controlled by institutions in which they play only a passive role (like government, religion, and the media). Set in Detroit, Michigan, the story unfolds as a triptych, with acts provocatively named "Heroes and Cons," "Charlatans and Saints," and "Horseshoes and Hand Grenades."

Of the two rock operas written by Green Day, only *American Idiot* has found its way onto the stage. In 2009, the plot was filled out by Billie Joe Armstrong and Broadway director Michael Mayer, and the opera (perhaps better described as a stage musical) premiered at the Berkeley Repertory Theatre in Berkeley, California. In March 2010, the show was moved to the St. James Theater on Broadway, where

it ran for 422 performances and closed on April 24, 2011. When his schedule allowed, Armstrong appeared in the Broadway production in the role of "St. Jimmy," although the other band members never participated in the show.

The band next began work on a trilogy, titled *¡Uno!, ¡Dos!, ¡Tré!,* of which the first was released on September 24, 2012, and the second was released on November 12, 2012. The third album, *¡Tré!,* was released December 11, 2012. A grayscale photograph of one of the band members appears on the cover of each album, set against a Day-Glo background, with eyes crossed out in heavy pink. The point of the trilogy is to highlight different stages in the creation of a party with different musical "moods." The first album, *¡Uno!,* is meant to set the preparatory stage of a party, with pop songs that invite the listener to dance. The second album, *¡Dos!,* attempts to capture the party in progress with songs that are more derivative of garage rock. By the third album, *¡Tré!,* the band attempts to convey the sense of a party that is over, with songs that reflect back on various compositional styles that mark earlier Green Day albums. The album is a kind of summation of the band's career, with songs that reflect the "punk" attitude struck by the band on their earliest albums, songs that take a more experimental approach reminiscent of the band's middle period, and anthemic songs that are more akin to the band's later "operatic" works. *¡Uno!* debuted at number two on the U.S. *Billboard* 200 chart and sold 139,000 copies during the first week of its release. At the time of this writing, it was still too early to determine the commercial success of *¡Dos!* and *¡Tré!.*

In a career marked at first by frat-boy humor, and later by political activism, Green Day helped to revive an interest in punk through the 1990s by infusing the genre with a pop sensibility. Perhaps its greatest influence can be felt in the music of bands that adopted the pop-punk format pioneered by Green Day, which include Blink-182, Avril Lavigne, My Chemical Romance, Simple Plan, and Weezer. Along with this obvious musical legacy, the band has also been cited by some as an influence on the emo-punk scene that emerged in the mid-1980s in Washington, D.C., and that has been associated with bands like Fall Out Boy, Fugazi, Panic! at the Disco, and Sunny Day Real Estate. Some emo fans might disagree, given the political or frat-boy themes that proliferate in the music of Green Day. Despite their reservations, however, this author would argue that, like emo, whose lyrics are confessional, expressive, and designed to focus on emotions (hence, emo), Green Day is unafraid to stray into thematic territory that is uncommon in punk, particularly in songs about romantic love and loss like "Good Riddance (Time of Your Life)" or "2000 Light Years Away."

Karen Fournier

Selected Discography

1000 Hours (EP), Lookout! Records 017, 1989.

Slappy (EP), Lookout! Records 035, 1990.

39/Smooth, Lookout! Records LK22, 1990.

Kerplunk, Lookout! Records LK46, 1992.

Dookie, Reprise 9362–45529, 1994.

Insomniac, Reprise 9362–46046–2, 1995.

Nimrod, Reprise 9362–46794, 1997.

Warning, Reprise 9362–47613–2, 2000.

International Superhits (compilation), Reprise 9362–48145, 2001.

Shenanigans (B-side compilation), Reprise 9362–48208, 2002.

American Idiot, Reprise 9362–48877, 2004.

Bullet in a Bible, Reprise 9362–48837, 2005.

21st Century Breakdown, Reprise 9362–49802, 2009.

Awesome as Fuck, Reprise 9362–49610–9, 2011.

¡Uno!, Reprise 9362–49487–1, 2012.

¡Dos!, Reprise 533420–2, 2012.

¡Tré!, Reprise 531978–2, 2012.

References

Azzerad, Michael. *Our Band Could Be Your Life: Scenes from the American Indie Underground 1981–1991.* New York: Back Bay Books, 2002.

Boulware Jack, and Silke Tudor. *Gimme Something Better: The Profound, Progressive, and Occasionally Pointless History of Bay Area Punk from Dead Kennedys to Green Day.* New York: Penguin Press, 2009.

Diehl, Matt. *How Neo-Punk Stage-Dived into the Mainstream.* New York: St. Martin's, 2007a.

Diehl, Matt. *My So-Called Punk: Green Day, Fall Out Boy, The Distillers, Bad Religion—How Neo-Punk Stage-Dived into the Mainstream.* New York: St. Martin's Press, 2007b.

Dimrey, Robert, ed. *1001 Albums You Must Hear Before You Die.* New York: Universe, 2005.

di Perna, Alan. *Green Day: The Unauthorized Illustrated History.* Minneapolis: Voyageur Press, 2012.

Doeden, Matt. *Green Day: Keeping Their Edge.* Minneapolis: Lerner Publications, 2007.

Edge, Brian, ed. *924 Gilman: The Story So Far.* San Francisco: Maximum Rock 'n' Roll Press, 2004.

Egerdahl, Kjersti. *Green Day: A Musical Biography (The Story of the Band).* Santa Barbara, CA: ABC-CLIO, 2009.

Garr, Gillian. *Green Day.* London: Omnibus Press, 2007.

Moore, Ryan. *Sells Like Teen Spirit: Music, Youth Culture, and Social Crisis.* New York: New York University Press, 2010.

Myers, Ben. *Green Day: American Idiots and the New Punk Explosion.* New York: IMP Publishing, 2006.

Oakes, Kaya. *Slanted and Enchanted: The Evolution of Indie Culture.* New York: Henry Holt and Company, 2009.

Small, Doug. *Omnibus Press Presents the Story of: Green Day.* New York: Omnibus Press, 2005.

Smith, Chris. *101 Albums That Changed Popular Music.* London: Oxford University Press, 2009.

Spitz, Marc. *Nobody Likes You: Inside the Turbulent Life, Times, and Music of Green Day.* New York: Hyperion, 2006.

Guns N' Roses (1985–Present)

Guns N' Roses can be credited with bringing heavy metal stylings into the mainstream of American popular music during the 1980s. Having launched their career with *Appetite for Destruction,* the best-selling debut studio album in U.S. history, Guns N' Roses opened a Pandora's box of metal onto the airwaves. Noted for living as hard as they play, Guns N' Roses

Guns N' Roses, pictured here in 1987, were largely responsible for bringing the 1980s version of American heavy metal to the masses. The band's influence is enormous and attested to by countless award nominations and their 2011 induction into the Rock and Roll Hall of Fame. (Photo by Paul Natkin/WireImage)

continues to take the music industry on a wild ride. *Appetite for Destruction* would not be the only Guns N' Roses album to set records. The band's sixth and most recent studio album, *Chinese Democracy*, cost a record-setting $13 million to create over its decade of development (Cohen 2009). Influenced by groups such as Queen, the Rolling Stones, AC/DC, and Aerosmith, the signature sound of Guns N' Roses will always include elements of hard rock, heavy metal, blues, and glam rock. To this day their songs "Welcome to the Jungle" and "Sweet Child o' Mine" remain iconic examples of their output. These two songs in particular seem to permeate American mainstream culture, with frequent appearances in a variety of movie soundtracks and other media.

W. Axl Rose (born William Bruce Rose Jr., February 6, 1962; vocals) now stands as the only member to be with Guns N' Roses from its fledgling foundation in 1985. Rose was raised in Lafayette, Indiana, by his mother Sharon and stepfather L. Stephen Bailey. At the time, Rose was raised under the name Bill Bailey but later adopted the last name of his natural father, William Rose (Stenning 2005). Having been given the nickname "Axl" while singing with different bands in the Lafayette area, he legally changed his name to W. Axl Rose in 1986. Rose and his childhood friend, guitarist Izzy Stradlin (born Jeffery Dean Isbell, April 8, 1962; guitarist), moved to Los Angeles in 1982 with dreams of starting a band together and making it in the music scene. Rose and Stradlin had formed the band Hollywood Rose in 1983 with guitarist Chris Weber, but after various personnel changes, including the fortuitous time period when Slash and Steven Adler joined the group, Hollywood Rose collapsed in 1984.

Hollywood Rose got back together in 1985, and eventually Tracii Guns of the band L.A. Guns replaced Chris Weber in the group. Guns brought along bassist Ole Beich and drummer Rob Gardner from L.A. Guns, and the band Guns N' Roses (a merger of Tracii Guns's and Axl Rose's names) was officially formed in March of 1985. This lineup would not come together as a cohesive unit until the addition of members of the band Road Crew later that year.

Slash (born Saul Hudson, July 26, 1965; guitar) was born in England and moved to Los Angeles with his family so his parents could further their careers in the entertainment industry. Slash's mother, Ola Hudson, was a successful costume designer, and his father Tony was a graphic designer who got work creating album sleeves. In middle school, Slash met Steven Adler (born Michael Coletti, January 22, 1965; drums), who introduced Slash to the electric guitar (Slash 2007). It was not long, according to Adler, before Slash's ability and obsession with the guitar quickly overtook his own. Adler decided to take up drums to keep playing with his friend. Bassist Michael Andrew "Duff" McKagan (born February 5, 1964; bass) came from a punk background instead of the hard rock background Slash and Adler shared, but the three came together to form the band Road Crew in 1984. Slash, McKagan, and Adler eventually replaced Guns, Beich, and Gardner in the Guns N' Roses lineup.

This final shuffling of personnel created the famous lineup of Guns N' Roses, which would see the band into its rapid rise to the peak of the music scene. Turbulent lineups became the norm with Guns N' Roses as its career continued. Just a few days after settling in as a band (Axl Rose—vocals and keyboard, Slash—lead guitar, Izzy Stradlin—rhythm guitar, Duff McKagan—bass, and Steve Adler—drums), Guns N' Roses did their first tour, the so-called Hell Tour of 1985. This was a brief tour of a few cities along the West Coast including Seattle and Sacramento, but it was a critical experience for the band.

Called the Hell Tour because of the myriad obstacles they encountered, the time Guns N' Roses spent together further developed their hard rock sensibilities and decadent lifestyles.

Guns N' Roses started playing more and more venues in the Los Angeles scene, scoring headline acts at places such as Whisky a Go Go, the Roxy, the Water Club, the Troubadour, and Scream. The band quickly caught the eye of the A&R department at Geffen Records, who signed Guns N' Roses to their list of bands in 1986, a mere eight months after the five members came together.

Geffen Records wanted Guns N' Roses to release *Appetite for Destruction*, an album based on songs that were still being worked out, in 1986, but in what can only be described as prophetic for Guns N' Roses, the album was not ready. Instead, Guns N' Roses recorded a four-song EP titled *Live ?!*@ Like a Suicide,* which they released on the band's own label, UZI Suicide Records, distributed by Geffen. The four tracks on *Live ?!*@ Like a Suicide* included the two original tracks "Reckless Life" and "Move to the City" as well as two covers songs, "Nice Boys (Don't Play Rock 'n' Roll)" by Rose Tattoo and Aerosmith's "Mama Kin." While the EP was described as "live," it was really nothing more than a studio album with prerecorded crowd sounds added to the tracks to give the illusion of a live album. Only 10,000 copies of *Live ?!*@ Like a Suicide* were released on December 16, 1986.

One of the contributing factors in the delay of *Appetite for Destruction*'s release was the temporary absence of Slash and Stradlin so they could deal with their heroin addictions. Guns N' Roses developed a reputation for being a hard-living and aggressively hedonistic group of men, and they channeled that energy into their music. The British magazine *Kerrang!* ran a feature on Guns N' Roses in 1987, calling them "The Most Dangerous Band in the World." Guns N' Roses would do little in their career to make their fans question this title.

When *Appetite for Destruction* was released on July 21, 1987, it proved to be worth the wait. While *Appetite for Destruction* did not explode onto the music scene immediately, it came to dominate the musical conversation of the time. Eventually hitting number one on the *Billboard* 200, the explicit lyrics and aggressive sound were a stark contrast to the previous year's number-one album, Bon Jovi's *Slippery When Wet*, a clean-cut and straight-laced rock album. *Appetite for Destruction* sold 28 million copies worldwide in 1987, 18 million of those in the United States, setting (and still holding) the record for the best-selling debut album in America. These strong sales of *Appetite for Destruction* were aided by the singles "Welcome to the Jungle," "Sweet Child o' Mine," and "Paradise City."

Guns N' Roses did much to cultivate their reputation as "The Most Dangerous Band in the World." The lyrics of several of their songs on *Appetite for Destruction* were a source of concern for many interest groups at the time. Several songs on the album extoll the virtues of drugs and/or alcohol, including "Night rain," named for a fortified wine. While the liquor's true name is Night Train Express, Guns N' Roses' lyrics clearly show that elision of these two words was mere camouflage and not a reference to evening precipitation, especially in the song's chorus.

"Mr. Brownstone" did for heroin what "Nightrain" did for alcohol. Heroin is anthropomorphized as a dancing man, and the chorus captures the common motivations of a junkie. Seeing as most of the band had either an active or recent heroin habit, the references to the drug are thinly veiled, if one could say they are disguised at all.

"My Michelle" was also a target for activist groups against explicit lyrics for its references to prostitution. The song was supposedly written about a prostitute known by Rose and other members of Guns N' Roses, but it could also be another example of the kind of misogyny audiences came to expect from rock/metal/ glam bands.

The explicit lyrics and topics found on *Appetite for Destruction* were not the only obstacles in getting the music to its eventual record-breaking place in music history. The original proposed album artwork, Robert Williams's print of the same name, caused controversy. The image was rather graphic: a robot in a brown trench coat stands before a young blonde woman who lies against a fence, partially nude and in obvious distress with her panties at her knees while a giant red creature with knives for teeth leaps over the fence. When Geffen refused to release the album with that artwork, the band replaced the cover with a plain black background and the skulls of the five band members in a cross pattern. The Robert Williams image was included in the interior of the album's liner notes.

MTV was reluctant to program the videos for *Appetite for Destruction*. "Welcome to the Jungle" aired only once at 5 A.M. on a Sunday morning. Calls came in requesting the video, and eventually MTV acquiesced. "Welcome to the Jungle" would reach number seven on the *Billboard* Hot 100, and "Sweet Child o' Mine," a ballad Axl Rose wrote about his then girlfriend Erin Everly, would reach number one on the *Billboard* Hot 100; in a reversal of fortune, would be programmed twice an hour on MTV. "Welcome to the Jungle" appeared in films such as *Lean on Me* and was featured in the 1988 Clint Eastwood film *The Dead Pool*. In *The Dead Pool*, Dirty Harry (Eastwood) was meeting with rock star Johnny Squares (played by Jim Carrey) on the set of a video shoot. "Welcome to the Jungle" was used as the song for the video. Guns N' Roses had uncredited cameos as Johnny Squares's bandmates attending his funeral in the film.

The "Appetite for Destruction Tour" was a 16-month tour from August 1987 through December 1988. Guns N' Roses opened for bands such as the Cult, Mötley Crüe, Alice Cooper, Iron Maiden, and Aerosmith. Since the band was actively touring while *Appetite for Destruction* was breaking records, several of the headlining acts were taken aback when journalists were more interested in doing stories on Guns N' Roses than on them.

A follow-up album was eagerly awaited by fans but long in development. On November 29, 1988, Geffen Records released *G N' R Lies* as a stopgap solution. Side A of *G N' R Lies* was a rerelease of the band's *Live ?!*@ Like a Suicide* EP. Side B contained four acoustic tracks: "Patience," the album's only released single, a slow and bluesy version of the *Appetite for Destruction* track "You're Crazy," and the songs "Used to Love Her" and "One in a Million."

Explicit lyrics again brought controversy to Guns N' Roses due to the use of racist and homophobic slurs in "One in a Million." These lyrics caused Guns N' Roses, removal as the headliners for an AIDS benefit at Radio City Music Hall in March of 1989.

Fans of Guns N' Roses were critical of *G N'R Lies* because it contained very little new material. Nevertheless it hit number one on the *Billboard* 200 in 1989. Guns N' Roses delivered more original material than anyone expected with their double-album release *Use Your Illusion I* and *Use Your Illusion II,* which hit stores on September 17, 1991. These two albums released separately but concurrently; they also contained significant changes to the band's lineup. After reportedly needing 30 takes to complete the drum part of "Civil War" due to heroin addiction, original drummer Steve Adler was replaced by the Cult's drummer Matt Sorum (born November 19, 1960). Dizzy Reed (born Darren Arthur Reed, June 18, 1963) also joined the Guns N' Roses lineup as keyboardist.

Again, *Use Your Illusion I* and *Use Your Illusion II* was the product of several years of gestation. The first track on *Use Your Illusion II,* "Civil War," was featured on Guns N' Roses' performance at Farm Aid IV in April of 1990. On June 27, 1990, their cover of Bob Dylan's "Knockin' on Heaven's Door" appeared on the *Days of Thunder* soundtrack. "You Could Be Mine" was featured in the film *Terminator 2: Judgment Day* (theatrical debut July 3, 1991), but the song was not included on the *T2* soundtrack. Sales of *Use Your Illusion II* outpaced *Use Your Illusion I,* due in part to the popularity of *T2.* The video for "You Could Be Mine" also featured Arnold Schwarzenegger reprising his movie role and considering the termination of "The Most Dangerous Band in the World" (his final conclusion was that the band was a "waste of ammo"). *Use Your Illusion II* reached number one on the *Billboard* 200 while *Use Your Illusion I* took the number-two spot.

Videos were important to Guns N' Roses' continued success, and *Use Your Illusion I* and *Use Your Illusion II* both spawned several important videos. "Estranged," "Don't Cry," and "November Rain" all received widely played video treatments. "November Rain," the power ballad that hit number three on the charts, won the Best Cinematography award at the 1992 MTV Video Music Awards (Andy Morahan, director; Daniel Pearl, director of photography/camera).

Seen as the band's magnum opus, this double-album set saw the most singles released. "You Could Be Mine," "Don't Cry," a cover of Paul McCartney's "Live and Let Die," "November Rain," "Knockin' on Heaven's Door," "Yesterdays," and "Civil War" all placed within the top 10 of *Billboard*'s Hot Mainstream Rock chart ("Knockin' on Heaven's Door" and "Don't Cry" reached number one).

Again, explicit lyrics and content were prevalent on *Use Your Illusion I* and *Use Your Illusion II.* Neither Walmart nor Kmart stocked the albums due to their explicit lyric content. A compilation album simply titled *Use Your Illusion* and containing six tracks each from both *Use Your Illusion I* and *Use Your Illusion II* was released on August 25, 1998, in order to appease these markets.

The era of *Use Your Illusion I* and *Use Your Illusion II* did little to deter the image of Guns N' Roses as "The Most Dangerous Band in the World." Performing in St. Louis on July 2, 1991, as a part of the epic 28-month-long "Use Your Illusion Tour," Rose spotted a fan in the crowd with a video camera. When security did not respond quickly enough to Rose's request that the camera be confiscated, Rose leaped into the crowd and tackled the camera operator. After a physical confrontation with the fan, Rose left the stage and refused to continue the performance. The crowd rioted and dozens of people were injured. A similar incident began to play out while the band was on tour in Germany, leading Izzy Stradlin to abruptly quit the band. While touring in Montreal with Metallica, Guns N' Roses took the stage late and left early, citing a bad sound system and Rose complaining of throat issues. Coincidentally, this was the show at which James Hetfield, the lead singer and rhythm guitarist for Metallica, was badly burned when he accidentally stepped into the path of a large stage pyrotechnic as it was igniting. The Guns N' Roses set could have satiated the crowd in the wake of the accident, but instead, Axl cut their set short. The crowd rioted, and Guns N'

Roses received a lifetime ban from the Montreal Olympic Stadium because of the event.

Izzy's sudden departure led to several "Easter eggs" in the video for "Don't Cry," which was filmed after Izzy left the group. Slash can be seen wearing a "Where's Izzy" T-shirt in the video, and Rose sports a St. Louis Cardinals baseball cap, an oblique reference to one of the incidents that prompted Izzy's leaving Guns N' Roses. Gilbert "Gilby" Clarke (born August 17, 1962; guitar) stepped in to fill the void of rhythm guitar in November of 1991 and remained in that capacity through their next album, *The Spaghetti Incident?*

Guns N' Roses never shied away from covering songs by other artists, so it was not out of character for the band's fifth full-length studio album to be devoted entirely to cover songs. *The Spaghetti Incident?* (released on November 23, 1993) contained covers of the Skyliners, the Stooges, T. Rex, Soundgarden, the Misfits, and Nazareth, to name a few. One of the covers on *The Spaghetti Incident?,* the U.K. Subs' song "Down on the Farm," was used in their Farm Aid IV performance, which was further evidence that the band refined their material over an extended period of time.

The Spaghetti Incident? reached number four on the *Billboard* Top 200, and sales were generally disappointing. Singles released included "Ain't It Fun" by Peter Laughner and Cheetah Chrome (Gene O'Connor), "Hair of the Dog" by Nazareth, and "Since I Don't Have You" by the Skyliners.

Another round of controversy struck with the inclusion of "Look at Your Game, Girl," by Charles Manson, as a hidden track tacked on to the end of Fear's "I Don't Care about You." Most of the lineup of Guns N' Roses disagreed with including the track and refused to play on the recording. Rose, Reed, and session musician Carlos Booy recorded the song, and the band received strong criticism for including it.

The Spaghetti Incident? was a game-changing album for Guns N' Roses. After *The Spaghetti Incident?,* Guns N' Roses gradually changed personnel almost completely, leaving Rose as the only consistent member from their 1985 beginnings through the 2008

release of *Chinese Democracy.* First, Gilby Clarke was replaced by Paul Tobias (aka Paul Huge, born August 1963), a childhood friend of Rose's. Paul Tobias was brought on to play rhythm guitar on Guns N' Roses' cover of the Rolling Stone's "Sympathy for the Devil," which they recorded for the *Interview with the Vampire* soundtrack, released on December 13, 1994.

Tensions between Slash and Rose grew steadily over a wide variety of issues, and Slash left Guns N' Roses in October of 1996. Robin Finck (born November 7, 1971; guitar) of Nine Inch Nails was brought on to cover lead guitar. In April of 1997, Matt Sorum was fired, and Duff McKagan resigned later that same year. Bassist Tommy Stinson (born October 6, 1966; bass), previously of the Replacements, was brought on board. After going through a series of several drummers in a rather short amount of time, Josh Freese (born December 25, 1972; drums) became drummer long enough to record the single "Oh My God" for the *End of Days* soundtrack, released on November 2, 1999. In 2002, Slash, McKagan, and Sorum came together to form the core of Velvet Revolver with Dave Kushner on rhythm guitar and former Stone Temple Pilots front man Scott Weiland.

"Oh My God" was also the first recording that included keyboardist Chris Pitman (born November 16, 1961; keyboard), who joined Dizzy Reed on keyboards in 1998. "Oh My God" was to be the emergence of a new and improved Guns N' Roses, but reaction to the song failed to stir much positive publicity. Rose did tell Kurt Loder in a 1999 interview for MTV that he had rerecorded *Appetite for Destruction* with this new lineup and that he replaced two of *Appetite*'s original songs with "You Could Be Mine" and "Patience" since the new lineup was playing those songs on tour. This new recording of *Appetite for Destruction* has not surfaced, and some speculated it was recorded in anticipation of the album's 25th anniversary.

After "Oh My God," Robin Finck briefly returned to Nine Inch Nails and was replaced on lead guitar by Buckethead (born Brian Carroll, May 13, 1969; guitar). Finck later rejoined Guns N' Roses and played alongside Buckethead through most of *Chinese Democracy*. Former Primus drummer Bryan Mantia (born February 4, 1963; drums) replaced Josh Freese in October of 2000 until he was replaced by Frank Ferrer in 2006.

The 14-year gestational period of *Chinese Democracy* continued to take its toll on Guns N' Roses personnel. Eventually the band emerged with Axl Rose on vocals, Dizzy Reed and Chris Pitman on keyboards and backing vocals, Frank Ferrer on drums, Ron "Bumblefoot" Thal (born September 25, 1969; guitar) replacing Buckethead on lead guitar, and Richard Fortus (born November 17, 1966; guitar) replacing Paul Tobias on rhythm guitar. DJ Ashba (born Daren Jay Ashba, November 10, 1972; guitar) joined the band in 2009, after *Chinese Democracy* was released.

This was a tumultuous time for Guns N' Roses. Band members seemed to be in a revolving door. Constant delays and holdups from Rose, the studio, or both were preventing the completion of *Chinese Democracy*. Geffen did whatever it could to keep Guns N' Roses in the public eye. The band was contracted to release a live album, and on November 23, 1999, the two-disc set *Live Era '87–'93* was released. On March 23, 2004, a *Greatest Hits* compilation was released (with no input from the original lineup as to its contents), which included "Sympathy for the Devil," the only track from a non–Guns N' Roses album.

The new Guns N' Roses lineup started the "Chinese Democracy Tour" in 2001, but the band cancelled more performances than they gave until 2006. After about 100 shows in 2006 and 2007, the band stopped touring altogether to complete and finalize the *Chinese Democracy* album.

On November 23, 2008, the wait was over. *Chinese Democracy* was released from its 10 years of development, 14 years after Guns N' Roses, last studio album. Universal Music Group (who acquired Interscope Geffen A&M in 1999) reportedly spent $13 million on the development of *Chinese Democracy*. Changing lineups, changing studios, the writing of as many as 70 original songs, and a rotating array of producers all contributed to the various delays stalling the project. Many believed the disc would never be released. Chuck Klosterman's review in avclub.com confronted the very mythical nature of the album:

> Reviewing *Chinese Democracy* is not like reviewing music. It's more like reviewing a unicorn. Should I primarily be blown away that it exists at all? Am I supposed to compare it to conventional horses? To a rhinoceros? Does its pre-existing mythology impact its actual value, or must it be examined inside a cultural vacuum, as if this creature is no more (or less) special than the remainder of the animal kingdom? I've been thinking about this record for 15 years; during that span, I've thought about this record more than I've thought about China, and maybe as much as I've thought about the principles of democracy. (Klosterman 2008)

While the album earned a fair amount of critical success, *Chinese Democracy* was considered a financial failure. Interscope, who handled the release of the album, entered into an exclusive deal with Best Buy as the sole retailer of the physical release. Other bands had entered similar deals, the most successful of which was between AC/DC and Walmart for the release of that band's *Black Ice*, which came out on October 21, 2008, just six weeks before *Chinese Democracy*. Where *Black Ice* sold 784,000 copies in its first week, *Chinese Democracy* sold a mere 261,000. That number was enough for *Chinese Democracy* to grab the number-three spot on the *Billboard* 200, but *Chinese Democracy* only managed to sell around five million copies worldwide. Two singles were released in 2008, "Chinese Democracy" and "Better," reaching the number-five and number-three spots, respectively, on *Billboard*'s Hot Mainstream Rock 100.

In 2011, the original *Appetite for Destruction* lineup of Guns N' Roses was inducted into the Rock and Roll Hall of Fame, the first year the band was eligible to receive such an honor. Also inducted into the Hall of Fame at this time were the Beastie Boys, the Faces, and the Red Hot Chili Peppers. At the ceremony in April of 2012, band members Slash, McKagan, and Adler were joined by Gilby Clarke and Matt

Sorum. Myles Kennedy served as vocalist for performances of "Sweet Child o' Mine," "Paradise City," and "Mr. Brownstone." Axl Rose chose not to attend the ceremony because he worried that the old lineup would distract from the work he was doing with the band's current incarnation.

Guns N' Roses is still active and touring (the "Up Close and Personal Tour" began in February of 2012) and recently announced they will be performing a residency at the Joint at Hard Rock Hotel and Casino in Las Vegas. The "Appetite for Democracy" poster consists of a modified version of the originally rejected Robert Williams print, including the iconic "Welcome to Las Vegas" appearing behind the wall (which is now painted to look like the Chinese flag). An additional "Welcome to Sin City" sign is leaning in from the bottom right corner, but the word "Sin" has obviously been painted over with "Paradise," making reference to the Guns N' Roses hit "Paradise City." Rumors exist that Guns N' Roses could release another studio album, including the rerecorded version of *Appetite for Destruction* or a product of the *Chinese Democracy* sessions. In the meantime, the band shows no sign of becoming less dangerous in the near future.

Jay C. Batzner

Selected Discography

Live ?!@ Like a Suicide* (EP), UZI Suicide USR-001, 1986.

Appetite for Destruction, Geffen 24148, 1987.

G N'R Lies, Geffen 24198, 1988.

Use Your Illusion I, Geffen 24415, 1991.

Use Your Illusion II, Geffen 24420, 1991.

The Spaghetti Incident?, Geffen 24617, 1993.

Live Era '87–'93, Geffen 490514, 1999.

Greatest Hits, Geffen 9862108, 2004.

Chinese Democracy, Geffen 0602517906075, 2008.

References

Cohen, Jonathan. "Axl Rose: The *Billboard* Q&A," *Billboard,* February, 2009.

Christman, Ed. "*Democracy* in America," *Billboard,* December 2008.

DeTogne, Gregory. "Gun N' Roses: Lose the Illusion," *MIX* January 2007.

Klosterman, Chuck. "Chuck Klosterman reviews *Chinese Democracy,*" avclub.com, 18 November, 2008.

Slash and Anthony Bozza. *Slash.* New York: HarperCollins, 2007.

Stenning, Paul. *Guns N' Roses: The Band That Time Forgot.* New Malden, UK: Chrome Dreams, 2005.

Sugerman, Danny. *Appetite for Destruction: The Days of Guns N' Roses.* New York: St. Martin's Press, 1991.

Tannenbaum, Rob. "The Hard Truth About Guns N' Roses," *Rolling Stone,* November 17, 1988.

Wall, Mick. *Guns N' Roses: The Most Dangerous Band in the World.* New York: Hyperion, 1991.

Wall, Mick. *W.A.R: The Unauthorized Biography of William Axl Rose.* New York: St. Martin's Press, 2008.

Heart (1974–Present)

Heart is a powerhouse female-led band that earned a place in the rock and roll scene in the early 1970s, and with sisters Ann and Nancy Wilson at its core, Heart continues to demonstrate remarkable staying power. Even through personnel shifts over the decades, the band has retained a distinctive sound and remains one of the most successful rock bands of all time. Moreover, their economic status rivals some of the best-known bands in history, in any category. Heart, in all of its manifestations and across four decades, is also highly decorated; they have received four Grammy nods and enjoyed revenues from over 30 million records sold globally, 22 million sold in the United States, from which came 20 top 40 singles. After celebrating a nomination for the 2012 Rock and Roll Hall of Fame, Heart missed induction, but they earned a spot in the class of 2013 alongside Rush, Public Enemy, and Quincy Jones. As songwriters, Ann and Nancy Wilson have also garnered ample attention, winning the ASCAP Founders Award in 2009. As of 2015, Heart has released 15 studio albums, complemented by six live albums, including *The Road Home* (1995) and *Dreamboat Annie Live* (2007), plus nine compilations.

The band started off strong, netting platinum- and gold-status records in the United States and Canada between 1976 and 1980, but *Heart* (1985) was the band's first million-dollar record and the breakthrough album for their widespread commercial appeal. As leaders of a group that shared the stage with 27 different musicians over 40 years, the Wilson sisters have taken multiple paths toward

capitalizing on their initial success, building lucrative relationships with major labels like Sony, Capitol, and Epic (Gaar 2002). Contract negotiations, personal controversies, personnel clashes, and fighting against alternative trends to remain true to rock and folk roots have challenged Heart; to counter downtimes, comebacks have been staged by the band's promoters at various stages, always carefully managed via events designed to cash in on renewed interest in and loyalty to Heart's unique brand of hard rock.

Ann Dustin Wilson (born June 19, 1950; vocals, guitar) and Nancy Lamoureaux Wilson (born March 16, 1954; guitar, vocals) hail from a military family that in 1960 settled in Bellevue, Washington, near a thriving Seattle music scene. Their mother, Lou, played piano, and their Marine Corps father John sang in barbershop quartets and directed a military band. The elder Wilsons dutifully exposed their daughters to opera, bossa nova, and to singers like Ray Charles, and Nancy claims that she learned early on about music theory, always using that foundation to refine her songwriting and guitar playing. With some piano lessons as a foundation, both girls tackled guitar on their own as teenagers, learning every Beatles song. Nancy said, "I, in particular, just flipped for the Beatles . . . We just had to get guitars" (Gaar 2002). Nancy also claims to have mimicked the finger-style of Paul Simon and to have found inspiration in Joni Mitchell's altered tunings (Bergman 1994). The sisters sang together in bands with friends, and close harmonies became one mark of their performances. Longtime friend and collaborator Sue Ennis calls their combined voices "pitch-perfect blood harmony" (Cross 2012).

Heart, pictured here ca. 1977. Clockwise from left: Roger Fisher, Howard Leese, Steve Fossen, Michael Derosier, Nancy Wilson, and Ann Wilson. As the leaders of the group, the Wilson sisters proved that a serious rock band could be fronted by females. The band has enjoyed more than 40 years of popularity and has sold in excess of 30 million records. (Photo by Michael Ochs Archives/Getty Images)

Ann claims high school choir was significant to her musical formation; it was the place where she first learned to breathe (Cross 2012). Her sharp, focused tone was a signature contribution to any band she joined, while younger sister Nancy "went whizzing by me" on guitar. Nancy confirmed, "Ann was the girl who sang. I was the girl with the guitar" (Gaar 2002). With their respective roles, the Wilson sisters came of age alongside the Bob Dylan folk explosion and the British Invasion. In this eclectic climate, the duo created a distinctive fusion that still marks their music decades later. It remains difficult to confine Heart to a single genre or style category. The influence of Led Zeppelin is clear in their ability to transition from dry, acoustic leanings to "totally rocking out," made possible by utilizing each band member's strengths (Bergman 1994); however, Ann suggests that "people sell themselves short when they look at one of our albums and . . . decide what pigeonhole we should be put into. Instead of putting us in categories, they should just listen to the music." Nancy explains, "We are the combo platter of rock and roll" (Wright 2012). Over time, Heart learned to market themselves on that fluidity, and while they were aware that a female-fronted band could not afford to show too much of a "soft side," the Wilsons asserted that gender bias never tainted what they offered as their signature sound.

Both women have contributed to Heart's song writing legacy. Nancy admits to avoiding hard-and-fast rules: "I don't think there's any real methodology to songwriting. It's sort of like catching butterflies [for] inspiration" (Sharken 1999). The process evolved over time, always aligning with the sisters' relationship at that time, so that a "context with the past" colored and defined both practice and content, as the women moved toward creating something independent of their idols (Wright 2012). Ann elaborated, "The vocal melodies are where Nancy and I work together the most. I come up with very natural melodies, but sometimes they will be too commonplace" (Wright 2012). Nancy's approach to harmony has always been unconventional: she avoids thirds to instead feature stacked fourths and tritones (Bergman 1999). Furthermore, the band's practice has always been to learn each song in multiple keys to accommodate Ann's vocal range. Howard Leese said, "90 percent of rock stuff is in easy keys—E and A and B. But our stuff is in A-flat minor, B-flat minor . . . because that's the perfect key for Ann" (Gaar 2003).

The Wilson sisters came into their own long before linking up with other musicians and cementing their first record deal. Ann earned performance experience as the lead in a string of bands, including A Boy and His Dog. In 1968, she took on valuable studio experience with the band Daybreak (Cross 2012), with whom she also played clubs and military bases (with Nancy often singing backup). Ann's many talents impressed those in the business; her first official gig came when she answered an ad to join Roger Fisher's cover band. Fisher (born February 13, 1950; guitar) was the nucleus of a group that had various names over the years (including the Army and White Heart) but kept brother Mike and bassist Steve Fossen at its core. Ann joined as lead singer when the Fishers formed Hocus Pocus, but she shared duties across the group to give the band a wider range (Cross 2012). Active from 1967 to 1982, the band performed in small venues in the Washington area, where Ann recognized her niche; that celebrated vocal sound, which has been described as robust, muscular, and agile, was the ticket. Wanting to thicken the vocal harmonies, Hocus Pocus invited Howard M. Leese (born June 13, 1951; guitar, keyboards) to join; Leese remained with Heart for 24 years, rivaled only by drummer Ben Smith, who has so far racked up 20 years with Heart.

The narrative soon shifted to Ann's relationship with Mike Fisher, who had moved to Vancouver, Canada, to avoid the draft. Their romance began during his visit back to the United States; after a whirlwind courtship (which inspired the song "Magic Man"), Ann followed Mike to Canada, which meant quitting Hocus Pocus. The rest of the group eventually followed to try their luck on the Vancouver scene. Ann's voice, compared by critics to the rasp of Axl Rose and to the power of Jon Bon Jovi, proved vital to getting attention from Mushroom Records (Nagy 2010). An independent studio, Mushroom was unable to sign the whole band, so Ann rejected the offer. Still honing balance and blend, Ann asked Nancy to come from Oregon to join them. Her 19-year-old sister was, however, studying and "living life without Ann," cultivating her own interests (Cross 2012). Nancy expressed her individual musical style mostly in coffeehouses, slanted toward the acoustic, folksy trends popular in Oregon at the time ("Heart Band History" 2008). In mid-1974, Nancy finally dropped out of Portland State University to take part in the fledgling band and subsequently to become Roger Fisher's girlfriend (Cross 2012). For four years, the Fisher brothers and the Wilson sisters were the core of the new band, now labeled Heart. They performed covers in clubs and appointed Mike Fisher as manager in this new locale. His five-year plan included the solidification of a following first, only after which would they branch out to introduce original material to what would hopefully be a receptive, loyal audience.

Finally, a deal was struck with Mushroom to include the entire band, and Heart's first album was on the horizon. They were determined to break into the U.S. market, without moving to the States, since Fisher's draft-dodger status precluded that. The plan required collaboration with Mike Flicker, producer and chief engineer at Mushroom. He fine-tuned the group's makeup so that by 1975, Leese was full-time, and after using various session drummers for early cuts, Mike Derosier was appointed percussionist. The first record, *Dreamboat Annie*, was released in 1976 but did not sell well initially. Although an "enticing mix of ballads and hard rock," the music did not lure followers, and soon the band was disillusioned (Gaar 2002).

A break came with an invitation to open for Rod Stewart in Montreal. Heart was well supported in radio there, and station managers readied the community to welcome Heart live by giving *Dreamboat Annie* singles ample air time. Popular success in Montreal led to better record sales, and soon Heart brought the album to the United States, introducing their music, city by city, to radio stations and record stores (Gaar 2002). With Ann as watchdog on the business end and Nancy keeping a lookout for unreasonable demands and compromises on the creative side, the duo hit their stride (Bergman 1994). Flicker remained behind the scenes as "Magic Man," the second release from *Dreamboat Annie*, became Heart's first top 10 hit, propelling the album to a number-seven spot on the *Billboard* charts. *Dreamboat* found its footing in hard-rocking cities like Detroit and Buffalo, and once Mike Fisher resolved his legal issues, the band was finally free to tour in the United States. The record was picked up and rereleased by Capitol, eventually selling two million copies and remaining on the charts for two years.

Sharp lyrics, inventive harmonies, and the leads' unique vocal styles helped Heart carve a specific niche within the rock and roll milieu. The hard-hitting autobiographical messages engaged listeners, especially females, on a fresh level. The initial release from *Dreamboat* was "Crazy on You," a song that exemplified Heart's signature sound; it remains one of their most recognizable songs and a staple on stage. One of the best examples of the band's mixture of acoustic and hard rock, "Crazy on You" satisfied the fan base on all fronts. The single soared to number 35, leading Nancy to conclude that Heart was appealing in its "new kind of configuration," describing the band as not just a group featuring a "woman singer, but . . . a rock band that had women in it, too" (Gaar 2003). The folksy "Dreamboat Annie" was the next offering; the single revealed Heart's versatility. This gentler aesthetic would remain an integral part of what the band delivered to fans, driven by Nancy, who has clung to that softer side throughout the band's 40-year tenure.

Heart remained loyal to Mushroom through cash-flow problems and courtship of U.S. labels, but eventually their relationship with the studio fractured as negotiations broke down over how to compensate members once *Dreamboat* went platinum (Gaar 2002). When Flicker left the outfit, Heart had the necessary legal point for a contract break: without him, the label could not provide the producer cited in the contract, which voided the agreement. Soon Heart signed with Portrait (later absorbed by Epic) while still in debt to Mushroom for one more record. Heart's former label chose to release a second album, *Magazine*, without the members' oversight of what was yet-unfinished material; eventually that record (featuring five studio recordings and some live tracks) was recalled by a federal injunction, but not before it had sold 50,000 copies. To satisfy the deal with Mushroom once and for all, and to have the legal right to sign with another label, Heart took the same raw material Mushroom packaged up for their release and headed to a Seattle studio to remix, reorder, and rerelease. Thirty days and one million copies later, Heart was free from the Canadian outfit for good.

Administrative changes were looming: manager Mike Fisher was replaced by Ken Kinnear, and a new performer lineup was set, with the Wilsons complemented by DeRosier, Roger Fisher, Fossen, and Leese. This combo assembled *Little Queen* in 1977, an album that went platinum largely thanks to the hit "Barracuda." By now, the band had come into their own as a cohesive unit, in agreement on message, performance, and style, each member enjoying the creative space to exercise a distinct personality. Heart hit the road to play 100 concerts, financially stable enough to lease a jet and enjoy some hard-earned luxuries (Cross 2012).

For the next album, Sue Ennis joined the song writing team. Recruited by the Wilsons during a post-show visit in San Francisco, Ennis's touch is clear throughout *Dog and Butterfly*, as she cowrote all of the releases, including the romantic "Lighter Touch," and helped finish "Mistral Wind," which became the cornerstone of live performance (Gaar 2003). *Dog and Butterfly* hit stores in October 1978, selling one million copies its first month. The title track hit only number 34, but "Straight On" managed number 15; the album stayed on the album charts for most of the year, reaching number 17, to become Heart's fourth consecutive multi-platinum album. In 1980, Ann and Nancy Wilson were enjoying a strong hold on personnel and business decisions, and the band had struck a sophisticated artistic stride. Future member Mark Andes recalled the era as "the best the band ever sounded" (Gaar 2003). *Bebe le Strange*, released in February 1980, was the first musical result of this new era, where a natural shifting of relationships still threatened Heart's momentum. During the making of the record, the Fisher/Wilson alliances were ending, and personal and musical ties seemed to simultaneously fizzle. As Ann and Mike's long-term romance disintegrated, Nancy admitted to having romantic feelings for drummer DeRosier. Inevitably, the core power structure of the group had to be modified, but each side held tightly to business and artistic control ("The Making of *Bebe le Strange*" 2010). Soon enough, the Fisher brothers almost simultaneously left the band as a new lineup coalesced to help Heart weather the early 1980s obsession with the power ballad.

Heart was down from six members to five. Leese remained on lead guitar, and although Nancy was leery that the world was not ready for a female lead guitarist, she took more of a heavy rock role ("The Making of *Bebe le Strange*" 2010). With this lineup, *Bebe le Strange* peaked at number five, becoming the band's

third top 10 album, but stalling at gold status. It did yield the top 40 hit "Even It Up" (number 33), and promotion via a 77-city arena-rock tour meant that by late 1980, Heart could boast their highest-charting single yet, "Tell It Like It Is," a number-eight hit. Although not chart-toppers, "Down on Me" and "Break" were deeply personal songs that earned the sisters "some of the best reviews of our career" (Cross 2012).

Two years separated *Bebe le Strange* and the next studio effort, but a two-disc compilation, *Greatest Hits/Live*, was released in 1981. The album reached number 12 on the U.S. charts, and Heart soon transitioned again by moving from Epic Records to a new brand of management at Sony/BMG. The band planned to work with a new producer, Jimmy Iovine, who suggested that none of the pieces Heart had slated for the next album, *Private Audition*, had chart potential; eventually, the Wilson sisters produced the record on their own. The title track foreshadowed the later trend of power ballads, proving that Heart was again on the cutting edge of pop culture, but *Private Audition* failed to grab attention. It stalled at number 25 and yielded only one top 40 single, "This Man Is Mine." Ann said, "That album tanked," and she lamented that the band's "let's experiment phase" (and notion that they did not have to "listen to what anyone's telling them") proved a dangerous formula ("Ann Wilson on *Inside Track*" 2010).

In 1983, Ann admitted that the band had realized, "hey, we're fallible" ("Ann and Nancy Interview" 1983). Poor sales resulted in a nonrenewal with Sony/BMG, and being without a label for the first time since the Vancouver days solidified that the band needed redirection. Just as a new era in rock swept the country, Heart went back to the drawing board to reinvent and redirect for the mid-1980s reality. DeRosier was replaced with Denny Carmassi, while Fossen's spot was given to Mark Andes, which left only Leese and the Wilsons from the original lineup. A new day—and a new lineup—meant a fresh frontier for Heart: Ann and Nancy relinquished some control to rely on marketing experts and on their new female manager, Trudy Green (whom the sisters thought might be the right prescription for a female-led rock band); soon every detail of the music industry became a focus, from management to makeup to music. The group adapted to additional collaboration on the songwriting front, for which Ann's work with Mike Reno of Loverboy on the pop hit "Almost Paradise" was the catalyst. A breakthrough commercial success came in 1985 with Heart's Capitol release, *Heart*. The album represents the Wilson sisters' tangible move into a new era of rock and roll, where the women submitted to changes in creative procedure, production control, and even appearances for this new era of the MTV video, which trumped music and songcraft to clearly favor the visual. It became their first number-one album, selling five million copies thanks to four top 10 singles.

For *Heart*, the Wilsons relied for the first time on other writers' material (Cross 2012), and for Ann and Nancy, accustomed to being in artistic control, it was a time of transition, but also one of steadfastness to their history. Ann declared that the sisters only really allowed for modest changes, saying, "Heart is an ever-evolving band . . . that stays true to itself, and . . . the way we write the songs and the way I sing them. We don't want to do anything that is meaningless" (Wright 2012). The new look and new business approach paid off with "Nothin' At All," "What About Love?" and "Never" landing in the top 10 ("If Looks Could Kill" charted as well). With Nancy fronting on vocals, "These Dreams" became Heart's first number-one single. Ann said, "It was Nancy's song from the start," and her understated vocals hit a sentimental tone that matched the ethereal lyrics (Cross 2012). Ann admits that the mid-1980s were a "really exciting time" but also "a time of great theater, where . . . everyone had huge hair and . . . high heels . . . After a while it became very hard to maintain the pose" ("Ann Wilson on *Inside Track*" 2010).

In 1987, Heart moved more definitively away from the folk and acoustic aesthetic toward a glossier, arena-rock vibe with *Bad Animals*. It peaked at number seven on the U.K. Album Chart, and in the United States garnered the number-two spot, relying on singles like "Who Will You Run To" and "Alone." Nancy claimed the band was its most cohesive unit at the time, "never . . . more unified as a band," but still accepting outside creative contributions (Cross 2012). "Alone," for example, was a collaboration with Tom Kelly and Billy Steinberg, and even before the tour began, "Alone" had hit number one.

Heart's third effort for Capitol, *Brigade*, was also the band's third consecutive multi-platinum album. As the band moved into a new decade, they seemed eager to return to hard rock and live performance. Even with more personnel changes, a record of success remained unbroken, and a relentless tour was planned for 1990 to reintroduce their latest incarnation. The single "All I Wanna Do Is Make Love to You" (written by Mutt Lange) hit number two, and "I Didn't Want to Need You" and "Stranded" became top 25 hits. Soon enough the Wilsons would require some downtime to focus on making music with friends and to renew the artistic and performing dialogue between sisters.

For their 1993 effort, *Desire Walks On*, Andes was replaced with Fernando Saunders; Leese remained, but Denny Fongheiser was added as drummer. This album was the first recorded in their own studio, and the band luxuriated in the time to dally through songs like "Under the Sky," "Rage," and "Two Black Lambs" (Cross 2012). Alongside what would be their final tour for some time, Heart recorded a 1994 live show from the Backstage in Seattle; the show demonstrated that the band had adequately reacquainted with their earlier sound by featuring leaner, acoustic versions of "Alone" and "Barracuda." Released in 1995 as *The Road Home*, the live compilation was the last album Heart produced under their contract before being dropped by Capitol—a label for whom the band had sold 20 million albums.

While actively performing in venues off the beaten path, Heart stayed out of the studio for over a decade. Nancy had requested the break to focus on family and film scores (she had recently married director Cameron Crowe); in this interim, Ann fronted the Ann Wilson Band and Heart Featuring Ann Wilson, with Leese and various others contributing on guitar, bass, and drums. By 2002, Nancy had warmed to another tour, and an eight-week summer trajectory was scheduled. By early 2003, the newly organized and still touring version of Heart was trying out singles, from hard-rocking songs to ballads, set for release on the long-awaited album *Jupiter's Darling,* to be their first studio effort in 10 years. Newly signed with independent label Sovereign Artists, and satisfied that they were in artistic control with Nancy as producer, Heart settled into the studio to work on singles "The Perfect Goodbye" and "Oldest Story in the World." They were paying close attention to the fan base, which by now had evolved significantly, as had the music market. "Genre-bending" songs were the avenue for sales, in a time when it was common for a country act to open for a rock band. All along, the Wilsons kept their eye on autonomy. *Jupiter's Darling* was financed by the band and the Wilsons retained ownership of all its masters. Despite dismal sales and barely breaking the top 100, this was a new era for the band and an opportunity to apply all that they had learned over the decades.

Another hiatus followed *Jupiter's Darling,* this time a six-year lapse, but Heart resurfaced in 2010 with *Red Velvet Car* and a full-on North American tour to gain "radio traction" (Mitchell 2010). *Red Velvet Car* became a top 10 album (their first in 20 years), reflective of the band's "strong fan base four decades after our start" (Cross 2012). Featuring a newly sober Ann on singles like "Sunflower," Heart again sold out concerts, aided by stellar *Billboard* results, and had one of the band's "best-reviewed albums in years" (Cross 2012). The album offered distinctive, original melodies and a balance of hard rock and folk that defined their earlier efforts. *Red Velvet Car* peaked at number 10 on the *Billboard* 200 and number three on *Billboard*'s Rock Album chart. "Hey You" was a love song that Ann "had in my back pocket for a while" (Mitchell 2010) while "WTF" is an "angry wail" (Nagy 2010).

After a 2012 release of the retrospective box-set *Strange Euphoria,* Heart's 14th studio album came through Sony/Legacy in October 2012, after a year on the road in the United States and Canada. *Fanatic* now ranks as Heart's 12th top 25 album. A 61-year-old Ann related that "*Fanatic* was the perfect thing for us to

lay out a lot of ourselves, at our age and with our experiences" (Wright 2012). Even though Heart's lead singer was now a grandmother, the same themes still resonated in the lyrics: "Mashallah" was "sexy and erotic," and "Dear Old America" celebrated themes of American soldiers active from World War II to Korea to Afghanistan (Wright 2012). The title song was classic Heart, with a wailing guitar introduction and Ann's vocals prominent on top. The Wilsons toured actively during the summer of 2013, meeting dates at large venues like the Farm Bureau Live stage in Virginia Beach, the Jiffy Lube Amphitheater near Washington, D.C., and a stint at the Comcast Center in Mansfield, Massachusetts.

Neither Ann nor Nancy Wilson ever projected themselves from the hard-core feminist platform, nor did either take any active role in the "women's movement" in order to succeed in the business. They also never relied on pioneering women executives similar to Frances Preston or Estelle Axton to head up their business operations; instead, both claim that their music and lyrics always spoke most clearly to their causes and beliefs (Dickerson 1998). Ann and Nancy simply positioned themselves as two members of an integrated five-member band, always wanting to be perceived as legitimate performers first, women second (Gaar 2002). While they deemed it not advantageous to align with gender politics in rock and roll, Ann and Nancy likely sensed their potential for influence and enjoyed the notion that their presence might make possible a similar role for other female artists by equalizing gender roles on stage and in studio. They did, after all, rank at number 40 in VH1's "100 Greatest Women in Rock and Roll," and their work can certainly be considered pioneering. Ann admits to enjoying letters from young women who pursued music with Heart as their model (Sharken 1999). "We've even seen people showing up with kids 10 years and younger" (Mitchell 2010).

A willingness to re-create and to reincarnate is the spirit that has kept Heart relevant for 40 years. In the 21st century, the reality-show television phenomenon brought renewed focus to Heart and their hit songs. Video game *Guitar Hero* and hit TV shows like

Glee and *American Idol* have introduced fresh renditions of Heart songs to the modern stage ("Alone" in particular has been a favorite of *American Idol* contestants), making clear that the band's longevity and legacy are still being celebrated (Mitchell 2010). Perhaps Heart did not pave the way for female rock musicians, but they certainly further smoothed the path after the efforts of Janis Joplin, Grace Slick, Joan Jett, and Stevie Nicks. The Wilsons knew that they had found a place among younger female artists by mostly avoiding expected sexual personas to instead navigate the "in-between," where they struck a more comfortable balance for their particular listenership. As evidence, Grammy-winning singer Kelly Clarkson calls Ann Wilson her "favorite singer of all time" (Cross 2012). A reliance on renewal and on thoughtful songwriting, plus emphasis on vocal health and personal growth, as well as attention to fans, has allowed the women to maintain their rightful place in the recording industry and on live performance calendars of major cities.

Sarah Tyrrell

Selected Discography

Dreamboat Annie, Capitol 46491, 1975.

Dog and Butterfly, Portrait, 35555, 1978.

Bebe le Strange, Epic, 36371, 1980.

Greatest Hits Live, Sony/BMG, 36888, 1980.

Private Audition, Sony/BMG, 38049, 1982.

Passionworks, Sony/BMG, 38800, 1983.

Jupiter's Darling, Sovereign, 1953–2, 1984.

Heart, Capitol, 46157, 1985.

The Road Home, Capitol, 530489, 1995.

These Dreams: Greatest Hits, Capitol, 3765, 1997.

Red Velvet Car, Sony Legacy, 88697 73800 2, 2010.

Fanatic, Sony Legacy, 887254481416, 2012.

References

"Ann and Nancy Interview—1980, part 1." YouTube video, 5:06. October 13, 2010.

"Ann and Nancy Interview—1983, part 1." YouTube video, 3:15. October 13, 2010.

"Ann Wilson (Heart) on *Inside Track,* part 3." YouTube video, 6:53. May 19, 2010.

"Backstage with Nancy Wilson and Her Guitar Tech Jeff Ausley." YouTube video, 3:34. February 10, 2009.

Bergman, Julie. "Nancy Wilson: Guitar Queen of Heart." *Acoustic Guitar* 81 (September 1999): 48–61.

Brophy, Aaron. "Heart's Canadian Confusion: Love, War, and Draft Evasion all Figured into the Band's Early Days." *Huffington Post Canada,* March 19, 2013.

Brown, Jake. *Heart: In the Studio.* Toronto: ECW Press, 2008.

Dickerson, James. *Women on Top: The Quiet Revolution That's Rocking the American Music Industry.* New York: *Billboard* Books, 1998.

Garr, Gillian. "The 3-Decade Journey of Heart." *Goldmine* 29:29 (November 2003): 14–18.

Gaar, Gillian G. *She's a Rebel: The History of Women in Rock and Roll,* 2nd ed. New York: Seal Press, 2002.

"Heart Band History." YouTube video, 9:51. November 20, 2008.

"Heart's Ann and Nancy Wilson in Studio Q." YouTube video, 31:48. April 10, 2013.

Hopper, Jessica. "Juicy Tales from Heart's Ann and Nancy Wilson." *Rolling Stone* September 11, 2012.

"The Making of *Bebe le Strange,* part 2." YouTube video, 10:05. July 1, 2010.

Mitchell, Gail. "Gotta Have Heart." *Billboard* 122:35 (September 4, 2010): 31.

Nagy, Evie. "Heart Red Velvet Car." *Billboard* 122:37 (September 18, 2010): 56.

Newman, Melinda. "The Beat: Wilson Sisters Record New Heart Album for the Fans." *Billboard* 116:27 (July 3, 2004): 13.

Sharken, Lisa. "Nancy Wilson: Heart's Ax-Slinging Sister Goes Solo." *Guitar Player* 33:7 (July 1999): 29.

Waddell, Ray. "Venue Views: Heart's Afire." *Billboard* 115:22 (May 31, 2003): 36.

Wilson, Ann and Nancy, Charles R. Cross. *Kicking and Dreaming: A Story of Heart, Soul, and Rock and Roll.* New York: It Books, 2012.

Wright, Jeb. "Heart and Soul." *Goldmine* 38:13 (November 2012): 46–51.

INXS (1977–2012)

The core of INXS was the three Farriss brothers: Tim (born August 16, 1957; guitar), Andrew (born March 27, 1959; keyboards), and Jon (born August 10, 1961; drums). While their father Dennis and mother Jill were not professional musicians, making music as a family was a normal casual activity at home and each brother was encouraged into their own musical activities. In 1971, the family moved from Perth, where each brother had been born, to a suburb of Sydney and it was here that the brothers formed bands and friendships, which led directly to the creation of INXS.

Tim Farriss befriended fellow guitarist Kirk Pengilly (born July 4, 1958; guitar/saxophone) and the two formed a band with an American pedal steel player named David Stewart. The group, named Guinness, began to develop a certain amount of local success and picked up gigs in the Sydney suburbs. Tim and Pengilly were equally active in Christian ministry work and preached scriptures under the guidance of John Kidson. When Kidson discovered Tim and Pengilly's rock lifestyle of drugs and sex, he made them choose between their preaching activities and their rock and roll activities. The decision was not a difficult one for the boys to make.

When David Stewart left for the United States, Guinness was in need of another band member. Garry Beers (born June 22, 1957; bass) who also went to school with Tim and Pengilly joined Guinness as their bass player. Beers was a former guitarist who started on bass after losing a bet with his pre-Guinness band mates. Through Tim, Beers met the other Farriss brothers and made a musical connection with Andrew as well.

Andrew Farriss made an equally important connection when he met Michael Hutchence (born January 22, 1960, died November 22, 1997; vocals) at Davidson High School in Sydney. Hutchence had recently moved to Sydney from Hong Kong and ran in similar social circles as Andrew throughout their high school days. Hutchence moved to Los Angeles with his mother in 1975 after his parents' divorced. There he attended Beverly Hills High for one year and then moved back to Sydney. Hutchence and Andrew rekindled their friendship upon Hutchence's return to Sydney and the two began to write songs together and formed a band. Dr. Dolphin featured Andrew Farriss on keyboard and guitar, Hutchence on vocals, and Beers on bass with Kent Kearney on guitar and Neil Sandon on drums.

The core lineup of INXS came together for the first time in a joint jam session between Dr. Dolphin and Guinness. Tim Farriss and Pengilly had a storefront in Avalon Beach, which they had converted into band practice space and a recording studio. The two bands got together and jammed on Eric Clapton's cover of Bob Marley's "I Shot the Sheriff." The two groups decided to merge and shortly thereafter Kearney and Sandon departed the scene. Sandon's departure left the band without a drummer and Jon Farris stepped quickly into that role. The sextet, which finally emerged in 1977, of Andrew Farriss on keyboards and guitar, Jon Farriss on drums, Tim Farriss on lead guitar, Kirk Pengilly on rhythm guitar and saxophone, Garry Beers on bass, and Michael Hutchence on lead vocals quickly dubbed themselves The Farriss Brothers. This lineup remained fixed for 20 years,

The members of INXS, ca. 1993. From left to right: Kirk Pengilly, Garry Beers, Tim Farriss, Andrew Farriss, Jon Farriss, and Michael Hutchence. INXS was one of the most famous bands to emerge from Australia, is the third-highest-selling band in the history of that country, and was inducted into the ARIA Hall of Fame in 2001. (Photo by Dan Borris/Corbis)

changing only after the passing of Michael Hutchence in 1997. Throughout this period, Andrew and Hutchence tackled the bulk of the songwriting duties.

The Farriss Brothers started their career playing various surf, beach, and house parties in the Avalon and Northern Beach areas around Sydney, as well as other smaller beach towns. In 1978, the Farriss family moved back across the continent to Perth, and since Jon was still in high school he had no choice but to move with his parents. The rest of the band decided to move to Perth as well in order to follow their drummer and keep the band together. Tim, Pengilly, and Hutchence moved into a small house, which they converted into rehearsal space for their music. They lined the walls of the living room with mattresses as inexpensive soundproofing and held almost constant daylong band practices.

The Perth club scene was a difficult proving ground for the Farriss Brothers. All of the venue booking was controlled by a single person and only cover bands got booked. The band was more interested in working their New Wave/pop style than playing covers. After almost a year of struggling to be accepted by this very closed music scene, the band moved back to Sydney in 1979.

The Sydney music scene was much more suited to the Farriss Brothers' sound. Sydney was steeped more in post-punk and hard rock, and one of the most successful Sydney bands at the time was Midnight Oil. Tim Farriss had a chance meeting with Gary Morris, Midnight Oil's manager, and Morris started to book gigs for the Farriss Brothers and included the Farriss Brothers in a small regional tour with Midnight Oil. More importantly, though, Gary Morris changed the band's name:

"I saw a commercial for a brand of jam called IXL. Their ad featured a guy who said, 'I excel in all I do.' I'd recently seen the English band XTC when they toured Australia, and I loved their name: XTC—Ecstasy. In that moment, I put all those thoughts together. The name needed to be letters, but make a word. I put the IXL jam commercial together with XTC and the concept of a band that was inaccessible and I had it: INXS" (INXS/Bozza, 2005).

Morris had other ideas for INXS, too, including Devo-style outfits and promoting Christian messages and morality. While INXS did appreciate the new name, they were not interested in the rest of Morris's vision. Morris dropped INXS and they signed on with Chris Murphy for their booking agent. Murphy was more business savvy than Morris and was able to book INXS into larger and more prestigious venues in the Sydney area. Murphy only acted as their booking agent until Michael Browning, former manager of AC/DC, heard INXS and saw the potential for international success. Browning funded the recording of INXS's first release: the singles "Simple Simon" and "We Are the Vegetables." "Simple Simon," an up-tempo New Wave pop song, featured rapid-fire lyrics and prominent use of the synthesizer. "We Are the Vegetables" was a rugged post-punk song with heavy distortion on the guitars and vocals. Released on Deluxe Records in 1980, the singles did not generate much buzz, but "Simple Simon" managed to break into the charts in France.

INXS released their first studio album, *INXS,* on Deluxe Records on October 13, 1980. Still well rooted in the New Wave aesthetic, the album contains mostly up-tempo songs with prominent synthesizer use. In addition to the New Wave influence, songs like "Doctor" and "Roller Skating" show off a ska influence with punchy guitar accents and saxophone solos.

INXS contained the band's first single to break into the Australian Recording Industry Association (ARIA) charts. On "Just Keep Walking," Browning made a point of encouraging INXS to focus more on funk and groove elements instead of a New Wave sound. "Just Keep Walking" reached 38 on the top 40, and *INXS* landed in the top 30 in Australia (number 27). INXS was also nominated for a Countdown award (a predecessor to the ARIA Awards) in the New Talent category in 1980 (Johnny O'Keefe won). This newfound success promoted the band from booking clubs to beginning tours.

INXS toured extensively, performing approximately 300 live shows in 1981, and the band began to develop a reputation as a strong live act. Before hitting the studios again for another full album, INXS released a cover of the Loved Ones' "The Loved One," which reached number 18 on the ARIA charts. This slower-tempo R&B groove sounded more reserved than the band's previous energetic recordings, and the single's success encouraged INXS to use more blues, funk, and groove in their music.

Funk and groove elements were more pronounced in INXS's second album, *Underneath the Colours.* Produced by Richard Clapton, this album was released on October 19, 1981, and reached number 15 on the ARIA charts, largely due to their successful single "Stay Young," which reached number 21 on the ARIA charts. *Underneath the Colours* remains a fairly eclectic album, as INXS struggled to merge their various influences. "Barbarian" and "Fairweather Ahead" show the band's synth-pop side while

"Underneath the Colours" draws from upbeat ska. "Stay Young" stands out on the album for its uncanny blend of INXS's earlier New Wave/synth-pop sounds mixed with ska and laid-back funk.

Murphy and INXS became frustrated with Deluxe Records' inability to effectively promote the band's albums on the international scene. In order to shop for a new label, INXS recorded the single "The One Thing" using their own funds and managed to land a recording contract with WEA Australia. Mark Opitz, who produced "The One Thing," was kept on as producer for INXS's third studio album, *Shabooh Shoobah.* Opitz's touch as the producer made a significant impact on INXS's sound, with richer drums, thicker guitars, and more blended synth timbres.

Shabooh Shoobah, released in October 1982, was exactly what INXS needed to break onto the international music scene. Anchored by the success of "The One Thing," *Shabooh Shoobah* spent 94 weeks on the ARIA charts, peaking at number five. INXS finally broke into the U.S. charts, too, with the album reaching number 46 in the *Billboard* Top 200. Their single "The One Thing" reached number 14 on the ARIA charts, number 31 in the Canadian charts, number 30 on the *Billboard* Hot 100, and number two on the *Billboard* Hot Mainstream Rock Tracks.

"The One Thing" wasn't the only successful single from *Shabooh Shoobah.* "Don't Change," a synth-heavy mid-tempo rock song, topped at number 14 on the ARIA charts. "Don't Change" slipped in the United States, peaking at number 80 on the *Billboard* 100. *Shabooh Shoobah* kept INXS in the ARIA charts throughout 1983 as the simmering "To Look at You" reached number 36, while "Black and White," a throwback to INXS's quicker-tempo New Wave style, hit number 24.

INXS also launched their first tour in the United States around the *Shabooh Shoobah* period. Supporting groups such as Adam and the Ants, the Kinks, the Go-Go's, Hall & Oates, Stray Cats, and Men at Work, these tours did much to increase attention to their music. While they were no strangers to making music videos, "The One Thing" was INXS's first video to play on MTV. INXS got even more exposure when three songs from *Shabooh Shoobah* appeared on the soundtrack to the movie *Reckless* in 1984.

While on tour in Canada, INXS recorded a new single with producer Nile Rodgers. Rodgers had previously produced *Let's Dance* with David Bowie, and Michael Hutchence's vocals, as with the song overall, show a strong Bowie influence. "Original Sin," a Bowie-esque song about interracial romance, frequently swaps races and genders of the couple throughout the chorus.

When the time came for INXS to complete their next studio album, they did so at the Manor Studios in Oxford. This time, their producer was Nick Launay, who had previously produced two of Midnight Oil's albums. *The Swing* was released in the spring of 1984 and was an even bigger international success than *Shabooh Shoobah*. *The Swing* reached number one on the ARIA charts, number 14 in France, and number 52 in the United States. *The Swing* was also INXS's first U.S. platinum-certified record and became one of the top five domestic releases in Australian history.

Singles off of *The Swing* received significant airplay in their native Australia as well as in the United States, Canada, New Zealand, and the Netherlands. "Original Sin" became INXS's first number-one hit on the ARIA charts, and it reached number two in France. While "Original Sin" only reached number 58 in the *Billboard* Hot 100, it did reach number one on *Billboard*'s Hot Dance Club Songs. "I Send a Message" and "Burn for You" also fared well in Australia; each song reached number three on the ARIA charts. "Dancing on the Jetty" was less successful and peaked at number 39.

INXS won every Countdown award for which they received nominations that year, including Best Album, Most Popular Australian Group, Most Popular Male (Hutchence), Best Songwriter (for Andrew Farriss and Hutchence), Best Group Performance in a Video and Best Promotional Video for "Burn for You," and Most Outstanding Achievement.

After extensive touring throughout the world, INXS went back to the studio for their fifth album.

Listen Like Thieves was recorded at Rhinoceros Studios in Sydney with producer Chris Thomas. Thomas had previously produced albums by Elton John, Pete Townshend, the Sex Pistols, and Roxy Music. After the bulk of the album had been recorded, Thomas did not feel there was a solid "hit" on *Listen Like Thieves*. Andrew Farriss shared a funk guitar groove he had been working on, and with Thomas's assistance, INXS wrote and recorded "What You Need" over the course of a weekend.

Listen Like Thieves came out on October 14, 1985, and brought INXS even more international success than their previous albums. While the album only hit number three on the ARIA charts, it did even better in the United States than any previous INXS record (number 11 on the *Billboard* Top 200) and became a double-platinum seller.

"What You Need" also became INXS's biggest U.S. single to date, reaching number five on the *Billboard* Hot 100. The video for "What You Need," made of many layers of rotoscope animation, also became a mainstay on MTV throughout 1985 and garnered the band their first MTV Music Award for Best Group Video in 1986. While the Video Music Award (VMA) for that category went to "We Are the World," INXS performed "What You Need" at the awards show (other performers that year included Eurythmics, Tears for Fears, Pat Benatar, and Sting). As another sign of INXS reaching broader American audiences, a snippet of "What You Need" was included in Weird Al Yankovic's "Polka Party!" medley on his fourth album, *Polka Party!*

Internationally, "What You Need" did not perform as well as "Original Sin." The song reached number two on the ARIA charts, number 21 in Canada, and number 14 in New Zealand. While the album did not receive much critical or commercial acclaim in the United Kingdom, *Listen Like Thieves* and "What You Need" were INXS's first entries into the U.K. charts (numbers 48 and 51, respectively).

Again INXS won every category in which they received nominations during the 1985 Countdown Awards. "What You Need" took Best Video, and INXS won both Most Popular Australian Group and Most Outstanding Achievement.

The other releases from *Listen Like Thieves* supported Thomas's instinct that the album lacked another hit. INXS always charted comparatively well in their native Australia, but no other release from *Listen Like Thieves* charted higher than number 40 on international charts. The bright, guitar-driven ballad "Kiss the Dirt" reached number 15 on the ARIA charts while "This Time" only reached number 19. "Listen Like Thieves," another groove- and funk-inspired song, topped at number 28 on the ARIA charts in 1986.

The year 1987 brought many successes to INXS. They collaborated with Jimmy Barnes on two songs for the soundtrack of the popular vampire film *The Lost Boys*. "Good Times," a cover from the Easybeats, brought out a traditional R&B rock sound from the band and reached number two in Australia and number one in New Zealand. The group also collaborated with Barnes on the song "Laying Down the Law," which helped launch Barnes's solo career.

INXS was also busy in the studio again in 1987 creating *Kick* with producer Chris Thomas. When the album was finished, Atlantic was dissatisfied with what they heard. WEA claimed the album contained no singles suitable for release and offered INXS $1 million to scrap the project and try again. INXS released *Kick* on October 19, 1987, against Atlantic's wishes and the gamble paid off. *Kick* became INXS's most popular and commercially successful album. *Kick* reached number one in Australia, number three in the United States, and number nine in the United Kingdom; sales of *Kick* went six times platinum in the United States, three times platinum in the United Kingdom, and reached platinum/diamond status in Canada, France, and Switzerland.

INXS had learned their lesson from *Listen Like Thieves* about successful singles driving record sales. *Kick* spawned five singles throughout 1988 and 1989, more than their previous albums. The first release, "Need You Tonight," dominated international charts. The song reached number one in the United States and Canada, number two in the United Kingdom, and

number three in Australia. The slow, sultry groove, and breathy, sensual vocals from Hutchence were almost unrecognizable from INXS New Wave/ska beginnings seven years earlier.

The video for "Need You Tonight/Mediate" ("Mediate" was never released as a separate single) dominated the MTV Video Music Awards in 1988. INXS won Video of the Year, Best Group Video, Viewer's Choice, Best Editing, and Breakthrough Video. The Richard Lowenstern–directed video was also nominated for Best Concept Video (losing to Pink Floyd's "Learning to Fly") as well as Best Art Direction and Best Special Effects (losing both to "Hourglass," by Squeeze). INXS received a second nomination in Best Editing for their "Devil Inside" video directed by Joel Schumacher.

Success in the music video arena was hardly a surprise given INXS's history with video production. INXS actively made videos throughout their career, beginning with "Simple Simon" and "Just Keep Walking" in 1980, as well as for their first cover of "The Loved One" in 1981 (a new cover of that song appeared on *Kick*). INXS created videos for all of their major releases on *Shabooh Shoobah* and *The Swing,* and they began to make videos for nearly every song on future albums.

While "Need You Tonight" remained the biggest hit of INXS's career, several other singles achieved success on the charts. "Devil Inside," another midtempo yet driving groove, made it as far as number two on the *Billboard* Top 100 in the United States and charted well in Canada (number three), New Zealand (number two), and Australia (number six). The uptempo synth-driven "New Sensation" reached number three in the United States, number one in Canada, and number eight in Australia. The ballad "Never Tear Us Apart" reached number seven in the United States and number nine in Canada, but only made it as far as number 14 in Australia.

Surprisingly, *Kick* was the first album for INXS from which every single charted more poorly in their native Australia than in other countries. "Kick" and "Mystify" were the last two releases from *Kick* in 1988–1989, but neither charted well.

INXS did win the ARIA Award (which replaced the Countdown Awards) for Best Group in 1987. *Kick* was nominated for a Grammy Award in the Rock Vocal category in 1988 but lost to U2's *The Joshua Tree*. In 1989 the band took home Grammys for Outstanding Achievement, Best Group, and Best Video for "Never Tear Us Apart," again winning every category in which they were nominated.

In 1989, INXS took a break from recording and from each other. Throughout their career the various band members pursued side projects, and this year saw much activity on non-INXS collaborations. Hutchence worked on the electronic music band Max Q with Ian "Ollie" Olsen and also starred in the Richard Lowenstein feature film *Dogs in Space*. Garry Beers played bass with Absent Friends during this year while Pengilly and Tim Farriss produced a Crash Politics album.

In 1990, INXS gathered together again and joined producer Chris Thomas to record their seventh studio album. *X* was released on September 25, 1990, and while the album and its singles did not exceed the success of *Kick, X* did very well in all markets. The album reached number one in Australia, number five in the United States, and number two in the United Kingdom (a market that had not previously been impressed with the band). Through 1990, INXS released two singles from *X,* including the harmonica-rich funk track "Suicide Blonde" and the mellow synth-driven ballad "Disappear." "Suicide Blonde" performed quite well and reached number one in New Zealand, number two in Australia, and number nine in the *Billboard* Top 100. The song was further nominated for a Rock Vocal Group Grammy in 1991 but lost to "Janie's Got a Gun" by Aerosmith. "Disappear" performed about as well in the U.S. charts, reaching number eight, but slipped in comparison by only reaching number 23 on the ARIA charts.

Three more songs from *X* were released as singles the following year. "Bitter Tears," "By My Side," and "The Stairs" saw largely diminishing chart placements throughout 1991. "By My Side," an acoustic guitar ballad, performed best on the ARIA charts, reaching number 23. In 1991, INXS also released their first and most popular live album, *Live Baby Live,* on November 11, 1991. *Live Baby Live* performed modestly well in the ARIA charts (number three) but the one single, "Shining Star," only reached number 21 in Australia.

The next studio album, *Welcome to Wherever You Are,* was released on August 4, 1992, and paired INXS once again with producer Mark Opitz. *Welcome to Wherever You Are* featured a much-expanded sound world, including arrangements that used a full symphony orchestra. The songwriting influences expanded as well, with the opening track "Questions" featuring tabla, sitar, and other Indian instruments. Critical response from the album was mixed, but *Welcome to Wherever You Are* managed to reach number two in Australia, though it only reached number 16 in the United States. INXS's clout in the United Kingdom had been on the rise since *Kick,* a detail some attribute to Hutchence's romance with Kylie Minogue, another Australian pop star who had considerable success in the United Kingdom. *Welcome to Wherever You Are* was most successful in the United Kingdom and hit number one in the charts.

Singles from *Welcome to Wherever You Are* slid further below the levels of previous INXS albums. "Heaven Sent" performed best overall, reaching number 13 on the ARIA charts, and while the album was number one in the United Kingdom, none of its singles charted higher than number 20. INXS did receive a Best Short Form Music Video Grammy nomination for "Beautiful Girl" in 1994 but lost the award to Peter Gabriel's "Steam."

Their next album, *Full Moon, Dirty Hearts* was released on November 2, 1993, and again INXS worked with Opitz as their producer. This album also had mixed critical response and did not perform very well in charts outside of Australia (number four) and the United Kingdom (number three). "The Gift," "Time," and "Please (You Got That . . .)" were all released as singles in 1993, but none would chart higher than "The Gift," which reached number 16 in the ARIA charts and number 11 in the United Kingdom. With the disappointing performance of their ninth studio album, INXS decided to take a break from the studio and released their first greatest hits album in 1994.

INXS came together again in 1997 to record and release *Elegantly Wasted,* which was seen by many as a comeback attempt for the band. Again, facing mixed critical attention, the album did not perform as well as anticipated and reached only number 14 in Australia and Canada, number 16 in the United Kingdom, and number 41 in the *Billboard* Top 200. The title single "Elegantly Wasted" tried to recapture the magic of "Need You Tonight" with a sensual and restrained funk groove, but it fell flat. The song gave INXS a number-one hit again on Canadian charts but underperformed everywhere else. The singles "Everything," "Don't Lose Your Head," and "Searching" all saw diminishing chart positions throughout 1997.

INXS embarked on a 20th-anniversary tour in April of 1997 to celebrate the release of *Elegantly Wasted.* On November 22, 1997, near the end of their tour, Michael Hutchence was found dead in his hotel room in Sydney. The final report, after an investigation, stated that Hutchence was caught in a mixture of depression, drugs, and alcohol, and committed suicide by hanging himself.

Without Hutchence's presence, INXS retreated from performances and recordings. INXS performed in one-night-only appearances using guest lead singers, including Terence Trent D'Arby, Russell Hitchcock, and Jon Stevens. Album releases essentially ceased except for a few collections of greatest hits and remixes by other artists. A remix of "Need You Tonight" called "One of My Kind" found its way to number 10 on the ARIA charts in 2003, but otherwise INXS was rarely seen or heard until 2004 when the band announced their quest for a new lead singer.

On July 11, 2005, the reality competition television show *Rock Star: INXS* aired on CBS. Created by INXS and reality show producer by Mark Burnett, 15 contestants competed to be the new lead singer for INXS over the course of 11 weeks. Each singer performed covers of well-known rock songs and viewers voted on their favorite performer for the week. The three singers each week with the least votes were removed from the competition. The band used on the show was the house band of KISS's Paul Stanley. Only the two finalists, Marty Casey and J. D. Fortune, performed with INXS during the final round. The show struggled in the ratings, and eventually CBS moved the program to air on VH1 in August 2005. Canadian singer J. D. Fortune (born September 1, 1973) won the contest, and by November 29, 2005, INXS released their new album, *Switch,* with Fortune on vocals.

Switch charted rather well considering it had been almost a decade since INXS released an original studio record. *Switch* hit number 18 in the ARIA charts and number 17 in the United States. The album performed better in Canada, potentially due to the nationality of Fortune, and went as far as number two on Canadian charts (also achieving platinum sales in that country). Singles from *Switch* flashed in the pan. "Pretty Vegas," the first single, went number one in Fortune's native Canada and reached number nine in Australia. Other releases including "Afterglow," "Devil's Party," and "Perfect Strangers" achieved little to no chart status throughout 2006.

By the end of 2006, it looked as though INXS was at an end. A tour of Australia and New Zealand kept the band active through 2007, although approximately 10 months of the scheduled tour was cancelled. On November 16, 2010, INXS released *Original Sin* as a tribute album to Michael Hutchence. *Original Sin* featured various guest singers performing INXS hits with the band, and in general the project was not very well received. INXS and Fortune had an on-again, off-again relationship until Fortune left the band in September of 2011 and was replaced by Irish singer Ciaran Gribbin. In a concert in Perth with Matchbox Twenty on November 11, 2012, INXS announced that their evening's performance would close the band's musical career after 35 years.

INXS's career stands as one of the most successful rock bands to emerge from Australia. Inducted into the ARIA Hall of Fame on October 30, 2001, INXS was the third-best-selling Australian band in history (behind AC/DC and the Bee Gees). INXS's career also highlighted the significant role that producers play in a band's sound. Only through the careful suggestions of visionary producers such as Mark Opitz and Chris Thomas did the Farriss Brothers' original New Wave pop sound gradually give way to the signature funk/rock blend that made INXS an international legend in the late 1980s and early 1990s.

Kick remains INXS's most enduring success and earned the number 11 spot in the 2010 book *100 Best Australian Albums* (*The Swing* was also on the list at number 56). Beck famously covered the entire *Kick* album with Liars, St. Vincent, and Os Mutantes' Sergio Dias in a 12-hour recording session as part of his "Record Club" project, and "Need You Tonight" remains a mainstay of 1980s radio playlists.

Jay C. Batzner

Selected Discography

INXS, Deluxe/RCA VPL1 6529, 1980.

Underneath the Colours, Deluxe/RCA VPL1 6601, 1981.

Shabooh Shoobah, WEA 600133, 1982.

The Swing, WEA 250389–1, 1984.

Listen Like Thieves, WEA 252363–1, 1985.

Kick, WEA 255080–1, 1987.

X, Atlantic 7–82140–1, 1990.

Live Baby Live, Mercury 510 580–1, 1991.

Welcome to Wherever You Are, Mercury 512 507–1, 1992.

Full Moon, Dirty Hearts, Atlantic 7–82541–2, 1993.

INXS: The Greatest Hits, Atlantic 7–82622–2, 1994.

Elegantly Wasted, Mercury 314 534 531 2, 1997.

Switch, Epic 74776, 2005.

Original Sin, Petrol Electric PE 009X, 2010.

References

Arnold, Gina. "INXS: The Hardest Kick," *Musician* vol. 113, March 1988: 60–66.

Farinella, David John. "INXS: Big-Time Band Returns to Medium-Sized Venues," *MIX,* March 2006: 86–88.

Hutchence, Tina, and Oatrucua Glassop. *Just a Man: The Real Michael Hutchence.* London: Sidgwick & Jackson, 2000.

INXS and Anthony Bozza. *INXS Story to Story: The Official Autobiography.* New York: Atria Books, 2005.

O'Donell, John. *100 Best Australian Albums.* Sydney: Hardie Grant Books, 2010.

Tannenbaum, Rob. "The Sweet Success of INXS," *Rolling Stone,* January 14, 1988: 48–50.

Walsh, Chris. "A New Reality for INXS," *Billboard,* July 27, 2005.

Young, Charles. "INXS: God Rewards the Righteous," *Musician* vol. 144, October 1990: 60–64.

Iron Maiden (1975–Present)

Two working-class young men in London, bassist Steve Harris (born Stephen Percy Harris, March 25, 1956; bass, backing vocals) and guitarist Dave Murray (born David Michael Murray, December 23, 1956; guitar) founded Iron Maiden in the late 1970s. The late 1970s was a period where punk music was the most powerful force in English popular music. What Harris and Murray were critical of was that the music lacked the technical sophistication of more progressive rock groups from the early 1970s, particularly bands such as Jethro Tull. Eventually, Iron Maiden made their name in the early London underground metal scene and quickly came to be considered one of the true New Wave of British Heavy Metal (NWOBHM) artists. Some, such as Harris Berger, considered Iron Maiden to be best described as "power metal," in the vein of fellow British group Judas Priest (Berger 1999, 57). During the 1980s, the band achieved great popularity, finding international fame by the middle of the decade. Toward the end of the 1980s, the group began to experiment with even more elaborate musical approaches. For most of the decade that followed, Iron Maiden lost much of their core fan support, coupled with member changes from their most popular lineup. However, these members returned for the first decade of the 21st century, and the group has reestablished a strong fan base, particularly outside of the United States.

Harris had grown up with a love of playing English football (soccer in the United States), especially as a fan of West Hammersmith (Wall 1998, 17). He started to play bass as a teenager, and after working

Iron Maiden, pictured here in 1982, is credited with bringing heavy metal back to the forefront in the United Kingdom and the United States. The group's "power metal" sound has sustained its popularity for decades, with serious musical virtuosity coupled with aggressive music and provocative lyrics steeped in the mystique of the band's ever-evolving mascot, Eddie. (Photo by Michael Putland/Getty Images)

through a few smaller local bands, Harris began Iron Maiden with Murray and eventually added vocalist Paul Di'Anno (born Paul Andrews, May 17, 1958; singer), guitarist Dennis Stratton (born October 9, 1950; guitar), and drummer Clive Burr (born March 8, 1957; drums). After making a demo recording, the group gave the recording to the DJ at a local metal club known as the Soundhouse. The recordings were later released as the Soundhouse Tapes. The DJ, Neal Kay, added the tape (containing the songs "Iron Maiden," "Invasion," and "Prowler") to the rotation at the club, and it topped the request list for a period of months. Soon, the group was performing live at the Soundhouse (Wall 1998, 73). Manager Rod Smallwood was introduced to the tape and started to find performances for the band in higher-profile venues in London and throughout the rest of the country. Maiden then recorded an independent single, "Running Free," which brought them more attention.

The group was asked to record two new songs, "Sanctuary," and "Wrathchild," which were included in a compilation album, *Metal for Muthas* (1980), highlighting what was considered the emerging NWOBHM movement. EMI Records eventually signed the band to a record contract based on the overall impact of these early releases.

Signature elements of Iron Maiden's style were featured in their first album, *Iron Maiden* (1980). A melodic sheen of guitar harmonies often counteracts the pulsating push of Harris's bass. Harris was quickly becoming one of the most respected bassists in the metal community, particularly with the song "Phantom of the Opera," which featured swift bass playing doubled by both Stratton and Murray. Also present, at least for the group's first two albums, were the vocals of Paul Di'Anno. Known for his gruff vocal style, Di'Anno was a powerful figure on and off the stage. The group's early fans were particularly keen on "Running Free," "Transylvania," and the album's title track. Helping to bring popularity to the group was an appearance as the opening act for Judas Priest on their *British Steel* tour, one of Priest's strongest. They also opened for UFO and KISS (www.ironmaidencommentary.com). A new recording of "Sanctuary" was released as a single in the United States and gained popularity among stateside fans of underground metal, though the song was not initially included on the U.K. version of the album. The new version of "Sanctuary" was much stronger than their *Metal for Muthas* version.

"Wrathchild," the other song from the *Metal for Muthas* album, was rerecorded and included on the group's second album, *Killers* (1981). "Wrathchild" has endured as one of the fans' longest-lasting favorites, and it is often still performed in their regular sets more than 30 years after its release. Other popular songs from the album included "Murders in the Rue Morgue" and the title track, both of which helped the band become a formidable force in the U.K. metal scene. *Killers* included the addition of a new guitarist, Adrian Smith (born Adrian Frederick Smith, February 27, 1957; guitar, backing vocals), who replaced Stratton. Smith's more determined style was a perfect complement to the soaring melodicism of Murray. The tour to support the album's release allowed the group to move to larger venues, opening for significant acts such as Judas Priest and UFO, while co-headlining with Accept.

Another key difference between *Iron Maiden* and *Killers* was that the production was much stronger, via new producer Martin Birch. Birch had previously worked with a string of popular 1970s hard rock/heavy metal artists. Birch recorded metal classics by Deep Purple (*Deep Purple in Rock,* 1970; *Machine Head,* 1972). Rainbow released metal favorites *Ritchie Blackmore's Rainbow* (1975), *Rising* (1976), and *Long Live Rock 'n' Roll* (1978) under Birch's stewardship. Birch produced two albums for Black Sabbath that included Rainbow vocalist Ronnie James Dio: *Heaven and Hell* (1980) and *Mob Rules* (1983), both considered metal classics. Birch was an

important part of the Maiden sound, and he continued to produce the group through 1992. Thanks to Birch and Iron Maiden's partnership, Iron Maiden helped establish the sound of metal for the early 1980s.

Though Iron Maiden was clearly a fan favorite in both the United Kingdom and Japan (as is evident from their four-song live album recorded in Japan, *Maiden Japan* [1981]), the group was not as popular in the United States. Di'Anno's vocals lacked strong range, and considering the musicianship established by Harris and the guitarists, the band began to consider a new singer who would be able to better complement the group. As Di'Anno had personal and substance-abuse issues at this time, it was easy for the group to recruit the lead vocalist from one of their opening acts, Samson (Wall 1998, 232).

The singer, Bruce Dickinson (born Paul Bruce Dickinson, August 7, 1958; lead vocals), joined the band in time for their third album, *Number of the Beast*. This album featured the writing style found in the group's first two albums, with a much better singer. Harris himself wrote many of the songs, with a new level of complexity in both the lyrical and musical senses. One of these songs, "Run to the Hills," became the group's first mainstream hit. The driving force of the song was through its bass line, reinforcing imagery of American Indians escaping from whites during the expansion of the settlements in the early 19th century. The galloping bass line was similar to the running of horses, and similar visual imagery in the music video helped solidify the feeling. Robert Walser noted that this device was important in defining Iron Maiden's style, as it was used often (Walser 1993, 156). The lyrics were sung with clarity and power not seen in earlier Iron Maiden songs.

The album's title track also gained attention, though it was through controversy, not mainstream success. Religious groups were disturbed by the imagery of the album (the group's Eddie mascot controlling a puppet of the Devil, who is in turn controlling a puppet of the Eddie mascot) and by the song's lyrics. To help make the lyrics have more impact, veteran actor Vincent Price recited a verse from the New Testament's Book of Revelations, which seemed to go unnoticed by the religious right. Deena Weinstein remarked that the title track was a "particularly rich source of imagery for heavy metal lyrics" (Weinstein 2000, 39). Weinstein is on solid ground: because of this imagery, the group came to be considered somewhat dangerous, and their teenage fan base embraced them more than ever.

Other important songs were inspired by war and battles ("Invaders"), a continuing story of a prostitute ("22 Acacia Avenue"), or a popular British television show ("The Prisoner"). Each of these songs had an identifiable storyline that was easy for the audience to follow, and reinforcing the text was the clear, powerful singing of Dickinson, which had not been heard prior to this. Another lyrical highlight was the album's closing song, "Hallowed Be Thy Name," describing the thoughts of a condemned man about to be executed by hanging. This final song had very philosophical and developed lyrical content.

The group's fourth album, *Piece of Mind* (1983), featured the addition of new drummer Nicko McBrain (born Michael Henry McBrain, June 5, 1952; drums). McBrain was a polished drummer, less raw than his predecessor Burr, and the overall change in the group's sound opened the door to widespread mainstream popularity (Wall 1998, 252). Lyrical content was becoming even more refined than before. Two songs that featured strong lyrics helped bring the group attention: "Flight of Icarus" and "Revelations." "Flight of Icarus" was inspired by the classical Greek myth of Icarus and his waxen wings. This became one of the few songs released by the band based on stories first exposed in literature and movies. "Revelations" was motivated by the writings of mystic Aleister Crowley (Touchard 1983, 8).

The popular fan favorite "The Trooper," which highlighted a hero's battle in war, was based on Alfred Lord Tennyson's poem "The Charge of the Light Brigade." "Where Eagles Dare" was instigated by the Alistair MacLean novel of the same name; it was made into a film by Brian Hutton starring Clint Eastwood and Richard Burton in 1968. "Quest for Fire" was inspired by the movie of the same name released a few years before Iron Maiden's recording. Of these songs, "The Trooper" was among the band's most popular.

What was peculiar about this song was that it did not include a chorus in the formal makeup. But there were melodic "hooks" that were either sung by Dickinson or played in harmony by Murray and Smith that served as the main idea for the song's popularity. The fan base was becoming more passionate worldwide, and the group began to enjoy a higher degree of success than they had seen ever before. Popular music videos on MTV, including "Flight of Icarus" and "The Trooper," were helping to make the most impact. Iron Maiden was now becoming considered the top metal group of their time.

Iron Maiden's next album, *Powerslave* (1984), brought the group to their height of popularity. The most popular song on the album, "Two Minutes to Midnight," gave a narrative of espionage. Reinforcing the lyrics was a successful video depicting an illegal arms sale by members of the communist resistance in the Soviet bloc. In 1984, the Cold War was in full force and was on the minds of many Westerners. Surprisingly, Iron Maiden was one of the first groups from the West to be allowed to perform in the communist countries of Europe, including Poland, Yugoslavia, and Hungary. The tour was chronicled in a documentary titled *Behind the Iron Curtain,* which received ample time on MTV. The ability of a Western group to tour in this capacity was quite surprising considering the political climate of the period, but the fact that a metal group was allowed to do so highlights the important role that metal had taken in the musical landscape of the time.

The album consisted of other highlights as well, which became fan favorites. Another single, "Aces High," detailed a dogfight between British and German aircraft in World War II. Acts of heroism in a war setting were not new to Iron Maiden's fans, yet this has always been an element of appeal throughout the group's history. Fans supported "Rime of the Ancient Mariner" a 13-minute epic based on a classic English poem by Samuel Taylor Coleridge. This song became the model for long, epic songs that would be featured on the albums that followed. "Flash of the Blade," written by vocalist Dickinson, tells of a sword fight; Dickinson had been involved with fencing in the years surrounding *Powerslave*'s release. The album's title track, featuring a tonality most similar to music of the Middle East, which reinforced the Egyptian motif on the cover, would also become a fan favorite on the tour. The cover inspired the set for their live performances, which was one of the most elaborate tours in their career.

The 13-month tour was quite extensive and was documented on the successful live album *Live after Death* (1985). The accompanying video of the concert was described as the group "at their ferocious best, performing with the most elaborate state and lighting production yet" (Weinstein 2000, 172). Iron Maiden had become the most popular group in the genre at this point, though vocalist Dickinson was leaning toward finding a way of expanding the group's sound. Dickinson's ideas toward acoustic music were ultimately shelved, but the idea of change was occurring regardless (Konow 2002, 224).

It was not until 1986 that Iron Maiden released a new studio album, *Somewhere in Time*. The 1980s were a period in which synthesizer technology was beginning to expand, including the use of the MIDI protocol language and the implementation of FM synthesis. One other development occurred that was less widespread: the development of the guitar synthesizer. Iron Maiden began using guitar synthesizers for *Somewhere in Time,* an album that featured many songs that revolved around issues of time and space. The synthesizers, as well as the implementation of solid-state amplifiers away from the traditional, tube-based Marshall amplifier, gave the album a type of slick sound that was different from previous ones (Wall 1998, 282). Like most of Iron Maiden's albums, the majority of the songwriting included Steve Harris, but how *Somewhere in Time* differed was that Dickinson was not included on any of the songs that were kept for the album. The album's first single, "Wasted Years," written by guitarist Adrian Smith, featured lyrics that discussed the golden years and personal struggle. The album's second single, also by Smith, "Stranger in a Strange Land," focused on an Arctic explorer discovered frozen many years after going missing on an expedition. Both songs were far from the stories of war

and espionage that dominated earlier albums. Most Iron Maiden fans were beginning to view the group differently; though the group's writing maturity and sophistication were growing, the band was beginning to lose the raw power that had been exhibited in their earlier albums.

A final album in the 1980s, *Seventh Son of a Seventh Son* (1989), continued an approach that seemed to alienate younger metal fans interested in the sheer power that the genre provided in Maiden's earlier material and in the group's emerging popularity in the late 1980s. The music of this album had become more progressive, and approximately half of the songs were unified into a type of concept-album approach. This concept was inspired by Orson Scott Card's *Seventh Son* fantasy novel, which Harris had read right before the writing for the album began. Robert Walser acknowledged the album as a song cycle, in the vein of 19th-century composers Schubert and Schumann (Walser 1993, 153). The album featured three singles: "Can I Play with Madness," "The Evil That Men Do," and "The Clairvoyant." The first, which included Dickinson as a songwriter after he did not contribute in that capacity on the previous album, was the story of a man dealing with nightmares with the help of a prophet. Shakespeare's *Julius Caesar* inspired "The Evil That Men Do." "The Clairvoyant" questioned how a psychic cannot view her own death. Like the previous album, there was a reduction in the number of songs of heroic tales of war. "Can I Play with Madness" was described as a "bouncy, cheerful song because of the music, which was played in a major key with a lively beat and included vocal harmonies," which could be seen as the reason for its popularity; however, critics such as Jeffery Jensen Arnett were eager to remark that the song was focused on negative thoughts of fear and anxiety (Arnett 1996, 45). This type of struggle was what metal fans preferred, reinforcing the group's allure. However, even though "Can I Play with Madness" became a successful single, the album as a whole neglected to gain as much attention as its predecessors. It was also the last album to include Adrian Smith until he rejoined the band in 2000.

Bruce Dickinson was approached about writing a song to contribute to a soundtrack recording for the *Nightmare on Elm Street* series—in this case, the fifth movie released in 1990. The resulting song, "Bring Your Daughter . . . to the Slaughter," was a collaboration between Dickinson and English guitarist Janick Gers. Eventually, Dickinson decided to form a band to record a solo album, *Tattooed Millionaire*, with Gers. As with any group, a member recording a solo album runs the risk of alienating the rest of the group. However, Iron Maiden liked the song so much that they rerecorded the single again for their next album, regardless of the controversy the lyrics attracted when the newer version was released.

Iron Maiden began to reevaluate their experimental uses of keyboard technology in preparation for their 1990 album *No Prayer for the Dying*. In years past, the group had recorded in some of the world's top recording studios, such as Compass Point in the Bahamas; in order to recapture a raw approach seen in their earliest albums, the group decided to use the Rolling Stones Mobile Studio. This Mobile, used by many artists for years, would house the recording equipment while virtually any house or other facility could be adapted to serve as the recording area for the group—which in this case was a barn at Harris's farm. Ultimately, this change of mentality affected guitarist Adrian Smith, who left just before the recording sessions, to be replaced by Gers, the lead guitarist from Bruce Dickinson's solo band (Wall 1998, 291). Dickinson was beginning to change the way he sang as well, to a less refined style. The album's overall sound was disappointing for all of the members.

Harris then decided that for the group's next album, *Fear of the Dark* (1992), he would convert his barn into an actual studio. This was also the last album that included Martin Birch on any production decisions, with Harris beginning to take over those duties (Birch had decided to retire after recording the album). Though an improvement sonically from its predecessor, the album lacked effective singles, with only "Be Quick or Be Dead" and "Fear of the Dark" gaining much attention. Dickinson had now begun to venture back into solo recording, and he left the group

after this album. Dickinson then released two albums, *Balls to Picasso* (1994) and *Skunkworks* (1996), with new collaborator Roy Z., with little attention.

Meanwhile, Maiden hired Blaze Bayley (born Bayley Alexander Cole, May 29, 1963; vocals), the singer for the moderately successful Wolfsbane, as Dickinson's replacement. Wolfsbane was moderately known as an English rock group, but most metal fans were very surprised that he was considered for the position. Two albums released with Bayley, *The X Factor* (1995) and *Virtual XI* (1998), were considered musically and commercially unpopular. Produced by Nigel Green, neither album featured a strong single, and reviews of both were quite poor. The latter release was to coincide with the release of an ambitious video game, *Ed Hunter*, which failed to gain much footing in that industry. Further complicating the fans' lack of musical enthusiasm for Bayley were Bayley's frequent health problems, often preventing him from singing on tour.

Much to their fans' satisfaction, Dickinson and Smith both returned to Iron Maiden in 1999. Dickinson's direct replacement of Bayley was simple, but when Smith returned to the group, Iron Maiden still had two guitarists. As such, a three-guitar lineup was introduced. This scenario worked well for the group, as it added versatility to its live performances. Previously, when two guitarists were in the band, they often harmonized melodic lines on their albums with rhythm guitar tracks behind them, which was not possible to do live with just two guitarists. But with the addition of a third, who was also a key songwriting element in the group, the band's sound was powerful yet mature. The group's first album as a six-piece, *Brave New World* (2000), inspired by Aldous Huxley's 1931 eponymous novel that focused on London in the 26th century AD. Two singles were released from the album, "The Wicker Man" and "Out of the Silent Planet"; however, neither helped make the album popular in the United States. Not surprisingly, the album was met with popularity in the band's native United Kingdom. The group's fan base in Brazil was even stronger, highlighted by a final concert in Rio with over 250,000 fans. The concert was released as the album *Rock in Rio* (2001), alongside a DVD version. The album was also the first in a series produced by Kevin Shirley, with whom the band would maintain a relationship for a number of years.

Iron Maiden returned for their 2003 album *Dance of Death*. The lyrical content on this album furthered their maturity, with many of the songs based on historical content. "Paschendale" remarked on the battle from World War I; Dickinson penned a song discussing the fall of a French stronghold, "Montségur," from the pre-Inquisition period during the Albigensian Crusades that stopped the Cathar movement in the 13th century. Others include "Face in the Sand," a comment on the Iraqi War and the eventual failure of whatever new government was set up in its place. Even drummer Nicko McBrain contributed material for the first time, commenting on human cloning in the context of the Christian perspective, with "New Frontier." Most significant was the inclusion of Iron Maiden's only song with complete acoustic instrumentation, "Journeyman," chronicling the life of a musician.

Extensive touring by the group delayed their ability to release another album for three more years. *A Matter of Life and Death* (2006) rose into the top 10 of the *Billboard 200* album charts for the first time, proving that even after an extended absence the group was still respected by its fan base. What makes this point more remarkable is that neither of the singles, "Different World" and "The Reincarnation of Benjamin Breeg," were successful in the United States. Internationally, however, the group maintained strong support in their usual strongholds in the United Kingdom, Europe, and Brazil. The recording process went faster than on earlier albums, and the overall sound was less polished than other Iron Maiden releases since the earliest part of their career.

The group embarked on a tour, called Somewhere Back in Time, in 2008 to promote the rerelease of their classic 1985 concert, Live after Death, that was distributed on DVD for the first time. The tour's stage props/set included the design from their most popular period, the tour in support of 1984's *Powerslave*. The group then released a compilation album, *Somewhere Back in Time: Best of 1980–1989*. Songs written before Dickinson joined the band were showcased in their live format featuring the newer vocalist. In the course of the tour, the group teamed up with heavy metal documentary filmmaker Sam Dunn (known for his movie *Metal: A Headbanger's Journey*) to record portions of the tour. The group traveled the globe on their own jumbo jet, "Ed Force One" (named after their infamous mascot, Eddie), piloted by none other than the group's lead vocalist, Dickinson. Dickinson had become a licensed commercial pilot in the years prior, and the documentary gave fans an insider's look into how the band functioned. The resulting film, *Flight 666* (2009) was very successful for the group. The group also released a second compilation album, *From Fear to Eternity: The Best of 1990–2010,* in 2011; similar to *Somewhere Back in Time,* live versions of songs originally recorded by a different vocalist (in this case, Bayley) were used for compilation purposes.

Another significant gap between studio albums occurred between 2006 and 2010, until the release of *The Final Frontier*. This album was recorded at Compass Point Studios in the Bahamas, the studio that was used in the 1980s for their classic albums. This album marked two milestones for the band: first, at over 76 minutes, the album was the group's longest up to this point of their career. Second, the single "El Dorado" earned the group their first Grammy Award for Best Metal Performance. Critical acclaim was high for this album, as the overall compositional approach was thicker than many of their previous albums, intricate without relying too much on a progressive metal approach. Some of the songs were quite long, between eight-and-a-half and nearly eleven minutes. Even "El Dorado" was over six minutes. But what made "El Dorado" so popular among their fans, regardless of the length and subsequent snubbing by radio stations, was that the song was provided as a free download. This plan worked well, as the group's release technique catapulted the song to a peak of number four on the *Billboard 200* chart made it the top seller in many countries around the world.

There have been consistencies throughout Iron Maiden's career that have earned it recognition among heavy metal fans throughout their history. Among the most significant elements are their solo guitar melodies. Harmonized versions of the melodies help soften the attack of melodic lines and add interest simply because there are two notes occurring. The importance of a "hook," or memorable idea, in music has been prevalent in all genres that fans can relate to. The harmonized melodic lines in such songs as "Phantom of the Opera" (*Iron Maiden,* 1980), "Number of the Beast" (*The Number of the Beast,* 1982), and "The Trooper" (*Piece of Mind,* 1983) played a significant role in solidifying their style early in their career. As the group became a three-guitar band, with Dave Murray, Adrian Smith, and Janick Gers, its sophistication became more pronounced.

Adding to this was a driving rhythm section. Steve Harris became recognized as one of the best bass players in all of rock in the 1980s. Harris's style of arpeggiating chords, with just the root and fifth of the chord played, pushed the underlying lowest parts of the group's harmonies forward. Since the group's fourth album, Nicko McBrain's powerful and precise drum performances have given the group an overall sheen that enabled them to obtain a greater presence in the mainstream. Both the guitars and rhythm sections provide a solid foundation for vocalist Bruce Dickinson. Early in his career, Dickinson relied on the "air raid siren" part of his tessitura, but in later years he has been more comfortable in the lower part of his range, giving the music even greater contrast. With these strictly musical elements, the group's ability to write arrangements of music has been nearly mesmerizing to their dedicated fans.

What has given the fans even more to love is well-thought-out lyrical content. The band members are simply well read, with many songs about historical events, especially in the tales of heroism in battle. Stories of heroes were often well respected by male fans, which made up the large majority of the group's base. They were also motivated by pieces of literature, the occult (a very popular topic in heavy metal of the early 1970s), and mythology in their lyrics, and always delivered the text in a way that captured the audience's attention.

The reception of popular music is not simply restricted to musical interpretation. The live performance must have power, as would be expected in any other genre, but with heavy metal there is this fundamental need for a supporting show that showcases the music. Iron Maiden's touring stage props have been seen by their fans as some of the most stimulating among groups in the genre, and as the group became more popular, the more elaborate the props and lighting became. Adding to the overall image was the continuous impact of their "undead" mascot Eddie. Eddie graced each cover and each stage that the group has been involved with since the very beginning. The evolution of the gothic Eddie has become a storyline in itself since the group's first album was released; he has become an endearing figure to those fans, one that the group is genuinely supportive of (Weinstein 200, 219). Though their music can be quite serious, they have never taken the persona of ultra-serious divas at all. For Iron Maiden fans, the group is part of a community that represents thought and power simultaneously, embraces high degrees of musicianship consistently, has not succumbed to any type of compromise to make them more popular among fringe fans of aggressive rock music, and has ultimately earned respect among a core contingent because of the approach.

Iron Maiden has had an enormous influence on other bands and individual musicians. They have been described as having influenced generations of newer metal acts, from legends like Metallica to current stars like Avenged Sevenfold (Bienstock 2011). A series of individual players cite Iron Maiden's influence. The list is long and diverse, ranging widely from Kerry King of Slayer to Scott Ian of Anthrax to Lady Gaga. Several musicians are on record as saying that without Iron Maiden's influence their bands would not exist, such as Matt Heafy from the band Trivium and M. Shadow from Avenged Sevenfold.

Thomas Harrison

Selected Discography

Iron Maiden, EMI 7–52018–2–6, 1980.

Killers, EMI 7–52019–2–5, 1981.

The Number of the Beast, EMI 7–24387–0–4, 1982.

Piece of Mind, EMI 7–46383–2–2, 1983.

Powerslave, EMI 7–46045–2–9, 1984.

Somewhere in Time, EMI 7–46341–2–0, 1986.

Seventh Son of a Seventh Son, EMI 7–90258–2–4, 1988.

No Prayer for the Dying, EMI 7–95142–2–9, 1990.

Fear of the Dark, EMI 7–99161–2–2, 1992.

The X Factor, EMU 7–24383–2–4, 1995.

Virtual XI, EMI 7–24349–2–9, 1998.

Brave New World, EMI 7–24352–2–0, 2000.

Dance of Death, EMI 7–24359–2–0, 2003.

A Matter of Life and Death, EMI 3–72331–2–2, 2006.

The Final Frontier, EMI 50999–6477712–2, 2010.

References

Arnett, Jeffrey Jensen. *Metalheads.* Oxford: Westview Press, 1996.

Berger, Harris. *Metal, Rock, and Jazz.* Hanover, NH: University Press of New England, 1999.

Bienstock, Richard "Maiden Voyage." *Guitar World* (July 3, 2011), 14–15.

Konow, David. *Bang Your Head.* New York: Three Rivers Press, 2002.

Touchard, Philippe. "Bruce Dickinson Interview." *Enfer Magazine* (December 1983), 8.

Wall, Mick. *Run to the Hills.* London: Sanctuary Publishing, 1998.

Walser, Robert. *Running with the Devil.* Hanover, NH: Wesleyan University Press, 1993.

Weinstein, Deena. *Heavy Metal: The Music and Its Culture.* New York: Da Capo Press, 2000.

The Jackson 5 (1969–1990, 2001, 2012–Present)

Motown owner Berry Gordy described the Jackson 5 as "the last big stars to come rolling off my assembly line" (Gordy 1994, 288). The Jackson 5 began their groundbreaking career as Motown recording artists in 1969, and the impact of their career was acknowledged in their 1997 induction into the Rock and Roll Hall of Fame. The group recorded for Motown Records from 1969 to 1975 and for CBS-Epic from 1976 to 1989. During their Motown years, the group included Sigmund Esco (Jackie) Jackson (born May 4, 1951; vocals), Toriano Adaryll (Tito) Jackson (born October 15, 1953; vocals, guitar), Marlon David Jackson (born March 12, 1957; vocals), Jermaine La Jaune Jackson (born December 11, 1954; bass, vocals), and Michael Joseph Jackson (born August 29, 1958, died June 25, 2009; lead vocals). When the Jackson 5 ended their contract with Motown and moved to CBS-Epic, Jermaine remained a Motown artist, and brother Randall (Randy) Jackson (born October 29, 1961; keyboard, vocals) joined the other four as keyboardist and vocalist. The Jacksons last performed together with brother Michael in September 2001 as a part of the *Michael Jackson 30th Anniversary Special: The Solo Years* in Madison Square Garden. The brothers most recently performed a tour throughout the United States in 2012, three years after Michael Jackson's death.

The success of the Jacksons was directly influenced by the care and management of their parents, Joseph and Katherine. Joseph Walter Jackson (born July 29, 1929) was born in Fountain Hill, Arkansas, to Samuel and Chrystal Jackson, who divorced when Joseph was a teenager. He first lived with his father in Oakland, California, but after his father's third marriage, Joseph returned to his mother, who then lived in East Chicago. Katherine Esther Scruse (May 4, 1930) was born in Alabama to Prince Albert Screws and Martha Upshaw and at 18 months was stricken with polio. The family moved to East Chicago in 1934, and before living there for a year, Katherine's parents divorced. Katherine and Joseph met at a neighborhood party, and they were married on November 5, 1949, in Crown Point, Indiana. Joseph was 20, and Katherine 19. The couple purchased a two-bedroom home on 2300 Jackson Street in Gary, Indiana.

In these humble beginnings, the musical family that would make history had its beginnings. The Jackson children were always surrounded by music as father Joseph Jackson was guitarist with the Falcons (a musical group with his brother and two other men) and mother Katherine played piano and clarinet and sang to their children. Joseph worked as a crane operator and performed with the Falcons in the evenings. When the Falcons disbanded, Joseph's guitar was locked in the closet. This locked instrument was of great intrigue to the older Jackson children, and whenever they had an opportunity, the boys played it. Tito had studied Joseph's playing keenly, and one day, while playing Joseph's precious guitar, he broke a string. After Joseph reprimanded his son, Tito showed his father what he could do with the instrument, and this was the beginning of the family's musical act. Tito, Jermaine, and Jackie then performed throughout Gary.

In 1963, five-year-old Michael participated in Garnett Elementary School's talent show and sang "Climb Ev'ry Mountain" from *The Sound of Music*.

American pop vocal group the Jackson 5 performs on a studio stage set for the TV variety series *The Sonny & Cher Comedy Hour* on September 15, 1972. The group, with lead singer Michael, kept Berry Gordy's Motown label on the charts at the end of the 1960s. The Jackson 5's success launched Michael's solo career and led to the group's induction into the Rock and Roll Hall of Fame in 1997. (Photo by CBS Photo Archive/Getty Images)

After this performance, the Jacksons had discovered their lead singer. Marlon later joined the brothers playing bongos. Since Joseph rehearsed the children for three hours every day, it also kept the Jackson kids out of the street life in urban Gary.

The Jackson 5 began their performing career at a Gary nightclub called Mr. Lucky on January 1, 1964, and eventually performed in clubs throughout Gary and the Chicago area. In 1966, two young musicians from the neighborhood joined the Jacksons: Johnny Jackson (no relation) became their permanent drummer, and Ronny Rancifer their keyboardist. Joseph continued to rehearse the Jackson brothers during weekdays, and then take them on increasingly longer tours during the weekends. By the time the Jacksons played the Apollo Theater in Harlem in 1967 they had already played in St. Louis, Kansas City, Boston, Milwaukee, and Philadelphia as opening acts for already established artists such as the Temptations, the O'Jays, the Emotions, and Bobby Taylor and the Vancouvers. Their performance at the Apollo was for the prestigious Superdog Contest, which they won.

After winning another talent show, the Jacksons signed their first short-term record deal with a small label called Steeltown Records in the spring of 1968. In May of the same year, they returned to the Apollo in New York, and returned to perform in Chicago during the summer. In July, one of their performances was as an opening act for Bobby Taylor and the Vancouvers at Chicago's High Chaparral Club, and it was Bobby Taylor who immediately got in contact with Motown executive Ralph Seltzer to recommend the group for an audition. The Jacksons, with Johnny and Ronny, auditioned in front of Motown executives on July 23, 1968. The audition was videotaped and sent to Motown owner Berry Gordy Jr., who was in Los Angeles. In retrospect, Gordy was pleased that the events occurred in such fashion, as now the tape is world famous. Their audition included their extremely individual renditions of the Temptations' "Ain't Too Proud to Beg," "I Wish It Would Rain," "Tobacco Road," and James Brown's "I Got the Feelin'." The Jackson 5 signed their Motown contract three days later. Their contract was for seven years, and while Joseph was hesitant about this, Gordy believed that an artist needed at least five years to see a return in the company's investment. The length of contract clause was soon changed to a one-year contract; however, the Jacksons recorded for Motown until 1975. Evidently, this was the only part of the contract that Joseph negotiated and effectively read, and it would show when the group left the company years later.

While the Jacksons began recording songs for Motown in 1968, the brothers were still under contract with Steeltown Records, and after a settlement, the Motown contract was fully executed by March of 1969. In August 1969, the Jacksons—including Johnny and Ronny—left their home in Gary, Indiana, and moved to Los Angeles. Katherine remained in LA with the children for three more months. It was here where the Jacksons were to be groomed and rehearsed to become Motown stars, and it was decided that for commercial purposes Diana Ross would become the one who discovered the Jackson 5. Berry Gordy arranged for young Michael to live with Diana Ross so that he could learn from one of Motown's biggest stars. It was also in Motown's West Coast Division where Berry Gordy's team of songwriter–producers began work on original music for the Jackson 5. Motown's creative director of talent, Deke Richards, worked with Freddie Perren and Fonce Mizell on songs for the group. The three of them, along with Berry Gordy, were then known as the Corporation. The final mix of the Jackson 5's first record, "I Want You Back," written by the Corporation, was finished on October 2, 1969, and was released five days later. As soon as this happened, Motown executives, led by Suzanne dePasse, were to give the young performers a makeover, as their first television appearance was just around the corner.

On October 18, the Jackson 5 made their first national television appearance on *The Hollywood Palace,* which was hosted by Diana Ross. On December 14, the Jackson 5 appeared on *The Ed Sullivan Show* in New York, marking another important nationally televised milestone. While "I Want You Back" was released in October 1969, it did not become number one until January 31, 1970, when it replaced "Raindrops Keep Falling on My Head." It sold over two million copies in the United States.

Gordy knew that one number-one hit was not enough, and that he could get these kids to have at least four; that was exactly what he did. Before "I Want You Back" hit number one, Gordy had already started turning the wheels on the next single. Another song, "ABC" (also written by the Corporation), was released on February 24, 1970, and it became number one by April, replacing the Beatles' "Let It Be." "The Love You Saved," their next single, was number one in June of that year. These singles had formulaic structures that made for a recognizable Jackson 5 sound. Their next single was going to be different, a ballad. "I'll Be There" replaced Neil Diamond's "Cracklin' Rosé" in the number-one position, and it became Motown's biggest-selling record at over three million copies. The Jackson 5 made history by becoming the first group to have their first four singles become number-one hits.

Their first concert appearance as Motown artists was on May 2, 1970, at the Philadelphia Convention

Center. While sales had been terrific, it had not prepared the brothers for the success with real fans. The scene at the Philadelphia airport was reminiscent of the Beatles' arrival in New York a few years back, with thousands of fans. The Jackson 5's first hit of 1971 was "Mama's Pearl," which only made it to number two in the charts. It was early in the year when the Jacksons returned to Gary, Indiana, to perform two concerts on behalf of the mayor's reelection campaign. The family returned to their home city as heroes, and both concerts were complete sellouts. On the day of their first comeback performance, the mayor named January 31 Jackson 5 Day, and he also named the street where they lived (Jackson Street), Jackson 5 Street for one week. By this time, the Jackson 5's popularity was skyrocketing with such force that a Saturday morning cartoon, with their voices, was launched. The group also released a Christmas album despite being raised by a mother who was a Jehovah's Witness.

In May 1971, the Jacksons sold their home in Gary and purchased a large estate in Encino, California. Everyone in the Jackson family and the Jackson 5 lived there, including drummer Johnny Jackson and keyboardist Ronny Rancifer. This move corresponded with Gordy's relocation of the Motown label to Los Angeles in 1972.

The Jackson 5 continued to provide audiences with top-selling singles in 1971, such as "Never Can Say Goodbye" and "Maybe Tomorrow," as well as maintaining a busy touring schedule. In July, they taped their first television special, *Goin' Back to Indiana,* which aired in September. In October of that year, Michael Jackson would release his first single as a solo artist, "Got to Be There." The following year, Michael released two more solo singles, "Rockin' Robin" and "Ben," both to great acclaim. The year 1972 also marked the start of Jermaine's solo career, although his first hit as a soloist did not come until 1973, "Daddy's Home." Future releases for Jermaine in Motown did not meet audiences' expectations until about 1980. Jackie's solo career began in 1973, but it did not produce any hits.

In November of 1972, the Jackson 5 embarked on a European tour, which included a command performance for Queen Elizabeth. However, concerns about lagging record sales began to surface within Motown and the family. This may have been because the Jackson brothers were growing up and their target audience was not receiving the changes too well. In June of 1972, Tito was married to Dolores Martes (known as Dee Dee), and in December of the following year, Jermaine married Hazel Gordy, Berry Gordy's daughter. The youthful image of the Jackson 5 was now different. Their 1973 album *Skywriter* was a commercial disappointment for the family, only selling 700,000 copies. However, with the advent of disco, they scored big with "Dancing Machine," which sold over two million copies.

In 1974, Joseph Jackson booked the family to perform at the new MGM Grand in Las Vegas, much to Berry Gordy's distress, as he did not think the boys were ready for such a show. The show included the rest of the Jackson family, Randy, Maureen (Rebbie) Jackson (born May 29, 1950), LaToya Jackson (born May 29, 1956), and little Janet Jackson (born May 16, 1966). Their show ran through April, and they returned for another run from November through early December. While the shows in Las Vegas did not interrupt the Jackson 5's touring schedule, they released fewer records that year. While in Las Vegas, Jackie Jackson married Enid Spann, leaving Marlon and Michael as the only single members of the group. It was in Las Vegas that Michael Jackson first met his first wife, Lisa Marie Presley.

On June 14, 1975, the Jackson 5 released *Moving Violation,* which became their final album with Motown, as two weeks later Joseph announced that the family would move to CBS's record label Epic as soon as their Motown contract expired. Like other Motown artists, the Jacksons felt that they did not have enough creative input in their albums. The brothers wanted to write and produce their own songs and their contract would not allow them to do so. Even though Jermaine and Tito actually played during their live performances, only Motown musicians recorded the instrumental tracks for the albums. Joseph announced the change of record labels at a press conference held on June 30, 1975, at Rockefeller Center.

Their contract with Motown was not set to expire for another nine months. After the announcement, Berry Gordy filed a $5 million lawsuit against the Jackson 5, Joseph, and CBS for signing with a record company before the expiration of their contracts. Joseph countersued, claiming that Gordy's company owed them royalty fees. This, however, only showed that Joseph had not bothered to read the boys' original contract with the company; as it turned out, they actually owed Motown. According to their contract, the Jacksons were responsible for all the costs involved with the songs they recorded, whether they were released or not, and since they recorded 469 songs (only releasing 174) during their time at Motown, they owed the company over half a million dollars in costs for the other 295. The company also kept the name Jackson 5, and since he was married to the boss's daughter, Jermaine remained with Motown. In the end, Gordy and Motown received close to $2 million from the Jacksons, and the group had to surrender their royalties on recordings they had already made. This meant that while the Jacksons were recording for Epic, Motown could release the rest of the songs that the group recorded with them, and Motown did continue to release albums with the Jackson 5.

The Jacksons' deal at CBS was much more profitable than their previous one at Motown, and it also allowed them far more creative input on their product. Before recording their next album, the Jacksons began hosting a variety show on CBS based on their Las Vegas production. With Randy replacing Jermaine and with Motown keeping the Jackson 5 name, their first CBS album, simply titled *The Jacksons,* was released in November of 1976. Produced by Kenny Gamble and Leon Huff, the record included two songs by the Jacksons. Their first single, "Enjoy Yourself," became their most successful one since "Dancing Machine." Their second album at CBS, *Goin' Places,* however, was enough of a disappointment that the label was considering dropping the group from their roster. Michael and Joseph negotiated with the company to allow the brothers even more involvement with their next product. The result was *Destiny* (released in December 1978), in which

the Jacksons wrote all of the songs except for one, "Blame It on the Boogie," their first single. It did not fare well with the public; however, "Shake Your Body (Down to the Ground)," written by Michael Jackson, sold two million copies worldwide. Other hits from this album include "Lovely One" and "Heartbreak Hotel," both written by the Jacksons.

In 1979, Michael launched his solo career on CBS-Epic with *Off the Wall.* Michael, however, expressed to Joseph (who had been the group's manager from the beginning) his dissatisfaction with certain moves with their careers. These included Jermaine's situation with the family, the way in which they left Motown, and their current products with Epic. Since Michael had just turned 21, he fired Joseph from his managing position and hired John Branca as his attorney. Branca renegotiated Michael's contract with CBS such that he was no longer legally bound to record with the brothers again.

Katherine, however, continued to influence Michael's decisions when they related to recording or performing with the family, but only to a certain point. In 1980, the Jacksons' *Triumph* was released in October, and by December, it had sold a million copies. During this time, however, Randy was involved in a car accident in Los Angeles and suffered severe injuries. The doctors first thought that he would lose both legs, then that he may never walk again. Finally, after intense physical therapy, Randy was able to join his brothers for the album's tour. The 39-city tour received rave reviews, and a recording from these performances, *Jacksons Live,* was released in the United States and Britain in November 1981.

Outside of managing his children, Joseph Jackson's business ventures had not always proven the most solid. In 1981, his financial troubles were enough for him to consider selling the Encino home. However, the family's attachment to the home was such that it proved to be wise to sell it to the son who had the fewest monetary concerns: Michael. As soon as he took ownership of the home, Michael demolished the property and built the home that he wanted for the family. He continued to live at the Encino estate until the late 1980s.

In December 1982, Michael released *Thriller,* which made history by becoming the biggest-selling album of all time and garnering seven Grammy Awards. Riding on this success, Michael appeared on television for the first time in years with his brothers at the taping of *Motown 25: Yesterday, Today, and Forever* in March 1983. This performance was also the first time since the group left Motown that Jermaine performed with his brothers. The success of this program motivated the Jacksons to tour together again. Jermaine, with his wife's help, officially left Motown for Arista and was thus able to tour with his brothers. In fact, the release of his first record on Arista Records was to coincide with the Jacksons' new release in 1984, *Victory.* Jermaine's first release on Arista was titled *Jermaine,* and it became the R&B number-one hit. It included hits such as "Dynamite," and "Do What You Do," leading the album to gold record sales. His later releases did not enter the top 100 charts.

For the *Victory* album, Michael wrote and sang in two tracks, and cowrote a third song. While the album was released in the summer of 1984, the first press conference regarding the upcoming tour was held on November 30, 1983. The 40-city tour featured all six brothers, and Joseph and Katherine were involved in the production team (which meant that almost everyone in the family was gaining financially from it). Don King was the tour's promoter, and he was also responsible for the $5 million endorsement by Pepsi. As part of the endorsement deal, the Jacksons were to shoot two commercials for Pepsi. In early 1984, the commercials were shot, and Michael suffered severe burns in the process.

Controversy began to loom over the tour. In June 1984, just a month before the tour was set to start in Kansas City, the plan for ticket distribution for the tour was announced. Tickets would sell at $30 apiece but were only sold in sets of four. While one could order tickets, these were not guaranteed, as a computer would randomly select the coupons with the names of the winners. The coupons had to be cut out of ads in the local newspapers. If selected, the winners were notified two days before the performance (provided tickets were not delayed in the mail), and only then

would they know which performance they were to attend. The controversy over this deal was enormous, and Michael's popularity was suffering as a result. He was the one who put the wheels in motion to change the entire ticket sale plan. This was finally done on July 5, 1984, one day before their first concert. In spite of all of this, the tour was an enormous success, becoming the largest-grossing tour of its time. In it, the brothers performed Motown hits; both Jermaine and Michael performed hits from their recent solo albums, but not a single number from the newly released *Victory* album. The tour ended in Los Angeles on December 9, 1984, while Joseph and Don King were making plans to take the tour to Europe. For Michael, however, this show was his last with his brothers. He donated his proceeds to charity. In March 1985, Marlon, Jackie, Tito, and LaToya joined Michael for the all-star cast recording of "We Are the World," written by Michael and Lionel Richie. The proceeds of the record went to the nonprofit foundation USA for Africa. It sold four million copies and earned $8 million for the foundation.

As Michael's career rose to unprecedented heights through the 1980s, it was clear that the family ties were severely damaged after the *Victory* tour. In August 1987, Jackie's marriage to Enid ended and was followed two months later by Jermaine and Hazel's divorce. That same year, Michael released *Bad* and began a world tour to promote this new album in September 1987: his first solo tour. The final concert of the *Bad* tour was held in Los Angeles, and Diana Ross, Elizabeth Taylor, Katherine and Janet Jackson, Berry Gordy, Suzanne dePasse, and many others were in attendance. When Michael performed his Motown medley, he dedicated it to Gordy, and throughout the performance, Michael was flanked by four dancers, reminiscent of the Jackson 5; Katherine noticed. In 1988, Michael released his autobiography, *Moonwalk,* in which he described Joseph as abusive. He also purchased his estate in the Santa Ynez Valley, which he called Neverland. The property is roughly 100 miles from his family home. Michael never told his family he was moving out. In May of 1989, the Jacksons, now a quartet, released their first single without Michael,

"Nothin'." This was followed by their first release in five years, *2300 Jackson Street* (after their address in Gary), in June with its respective tour (European). This was the last album the Jacksons recorded with Epic, and their contract was not renewed.

The 1990s was a busy decade for the Jacksons. In October 1990, Katherine published her book *My Family, The Jacksons*. The following year, Jermaine released *You Said* on the La Face label, which included a track called "Word to the Badd," a clear attack on his brother that only created headlines. That same year, Michael released his *Dangerous* album. In November 1992, *The Jacksons—An American Dream,* a 5-hour miniseries on the family, was first screened. Becoming the most-watched miniseries in television in the early 1990s, it depicted Joseph as abusive and demanding and began to taint the family image. The trend continued in 1993, when Michael was charged with child molestation while on his *Dangerous* world tour. The charges were eventually dropped after a settlement. The family, however, was kept on the sidelines during this issue; several members released statements of support for Michael, although LaToya publicly condemned his actions from Israel. Almost immediately following, the family wanted to show their unity by producing *The Jackson Family Honors,* a television special from the MGM Grand Hotel in Las Vegas where they honored Berry Gordy and Elizabeth Taylor. All were present except for LaToya. Airing on February 1994, the show was plagued by allegations of financial irregularities and slow ticket sales. The profits of the show went to the family's nonprofit charity, Family Caring for Families. That same year, Tito's ex-wife, Dolores (Dee Dee), drowned in a swimming pool, and Michael married Lisa Marie Presley, Elvis Presley's daughter, on May 26, 1994, to the great surprise of everyone, including the family. The marriage lasted 18 months. In 1995, Michael released *HIStory—Past, Present, and Future, Book 1,* which included 15 remastered hits and 15 new songs. In August 1997, the Jackson 5 were inducted into the Rock and Roll Hall of Fame. Presented by Diana Ross, their induction included the members of the Motown-based group, which meant Randy Jackson was not included.

The new millennium began with another reunion for the Jackson brothers. The *Michael Jackson 30th Anniversary Special: The Solo Years* was held at Madison Square Garden in New York City on September 7 and 10, 2001. As Michael celebrated his solo career, the brothers were simply joining him for a few Motown numbers, and other celebrities were part of the show. This was the last time all of them performed together on stage. That same year Michael was inducted into the Rock and Roll Hall of Fame as a solo artist. The following years were trying times for Michael Jackson and his family. On January 16, 2004, he was arraigned for another set of child-molestation charges. This time, the family provided a united front in support of Michael, who now was the father of three—two from a former marriage to Debbie Rowe, his dermatologist assistant and one from an unknown surrogate. On June 13, 2005, Michael was declared innocent on all charges. While in the 1993 case the family was kept at a distance, they were a strong presence throughout this one.

On June 25, 2009, Michael Jackson was taken to the UCLA Medical Center after suffering from cardiac arrest, and he was declared dead that same day. In his will, Michael named Katherine as the legal guardian of his three children, and if she were not able, the task would go to Diana Ross. A public memorial service was held at the Staples Center in Los Angeles where some of the brothers performed. He was finally laid to rest on September 3, 2009. The previous month, however, filming began for a reality television series for the A&E Channel, *The Jacksons: A Family Dynasty*. The television series aired in January 2010 and depicted the surviving brothers going across the country doing interviews and talk shows. On June 2, 2010, Joseph Jackson announced the plans for a Jacksons Museum and Performing Arts Center to be built in Gary, Indiana. During the summer of 2012, the brothers went on a 16-city concert tour, called the *Unity* tour, where they performed their own solo hits, their Motown hits, and even Michael Jackson's songs. During the summer of 2012, the Jacksons were involved in a scandal involving the guardianship of Michael's three children.

Jonathan Borja

Selected Discography

Diana Ross Presents the Jackson Five. Motown 700, 1970.

ABC. Motown 709, 1970.

Jackson Five Christmas Album, Motown 713, 1970.

Third Album. Motown 718, 1970.

Maybe Tomorrow. Motown 735, 1971.

Goin' Back to Indiana. Motown 742, 1971.

Lookin' Through the Windows. Motown 750, 1972.

Get It Together. Motown 783, 1973.

Dancing Machine. Motown 780, 1974.

Moving Violation. Motown 829, 1975.

The Jacksons. Epic 34229, 1976.

Goin' Places. Epic 34835, 1977.

Destiny. Epic 35552, 1978.

Triumph. Epic 36424, 1980.

The Jacksons Live. Epic 37545, 1981.

Victory. Epic 38946, 1984.

2300 Jackson Street. Epic 40911, 1989.

References

Fong-Torres, Be. *Not Fade Away: A Backstage Pass to 20 Years of Rock and Roll.* San Francisco: Miller Freeman Books, 1999.

Fox, Ted. *Showtime at the Apollo.* London: Quartet Books, 1985.

Gordy, Berry. *To Be Loved: The Music, the Magic, the Memories of Motown, an Autobiography.* New York: Time Warner Books, 1994.

Helander, Brock. *The Rock Who's Who.* New York: Prentice Hall International, 1996.

Jackson, Jermaine. *You Are Not Alone Michael: Through A Brother's Eyes.* New York: Touchstone, 2011.

Jackson, Michael. *Moonwalk.* New York: Doubleday, 1988.

Posner, Gerald. *Motown: Music, Money, Sex, and Power.* New York, Random House, 2002.

Romanowski, Patricia, and Holly George-Warren, eds. *New Rolling Stone Encyclopedia of Rock & Roll.* New York: Fireside, 1995.

Stambler, Irwin. *Encyclopedia of Pop, Rock & Soul.* New York: St. Martin's Press, 1989.

Taraborrelli, J. Randy. *Michael Jackson: The Magic, the Madness, the Whole Story, 1958–2009.* New York: Grand Central Publishing, 2009.

Jane's Addiction (1985–Present)

Jane's Addiction is classified as alternative rock, but their musical style is too difficult to define under a simple heading. Taking the clenched-fist attitude of punk and adding elements of rock, Latin jazz, and funk, the band has managed to produce music that is extremely complex and tightly knit. Refining their skills in the underground bars of Los Angeles, the band learned from their experiences, what they were mentally and physically exposed to, and combined their gatherings into an image that is more iconoclastic than the band. For many who followed in their footsteps, the band gave courage to explore new means of artistic expression, and for those who never quite understood Jane's Addiction's approach, the vagueness itself has added to their mystique.

Although considered a band of the early 1990s, the origins of Jane's Addiction date back to the mid-1980s when Perry Farrell (born Perry Bernstein, March 29, 1959; vocals) helped to found the punk band PSI-Com with friends Aaron Sherer, Vince Duran, and Kelly Wheeler. The year was 1981, and Farrell, who had previously lived in Florida for three years, had been searching Los Angeles for six years trying to find something he could get creatively involved in (Handleman 1987). That something turned out to be PSI-Com, a band that would not only make his name known among talented circles but would ultimately introduce him to the members that would become Jane's Addiction.

PSI-Com lasted five years, but in that short span of time, they released a self-produced cassette of demonstration songs and an EP. There was no debate as to when the demo recording was made: in 1984, PSI-Com released *Worktape 1.* However, there was debate as to when the EP was released: it was believed the self-titled EP was recorded in 1985. For many years it was only available as a CD bootleg of the original vinyl recording until being officially released in 1993 by Triple X Records, well after Jane's Addiction had become popular (Handleman 1987).

In the early 1980s, Perry Farrell was introduced to Eric Avery (born Eric Adam Avery, April 25, 1965; bass) who over a phone conversation learned the two enjoyed similar tastes in music, namely the sound of Joy Division and the Velvet Underground. Farrell, who after the breakup of PSI-Com had been taking a break for two years to work on his rock opera named *Buddy Clear-Eyes*, arrived at the conclusion that to succeed in music he would need to create a new band "that confronted issues like censorship and sexuality" (Handleman 1987). By meeting Avery, Farrell had opened the door to another chance encounter when Eric's sister began dating Dave Navarro (born David Michael Navarro, June 7, 1967; guitar) and later Stephen Perkins (born Stephen Andrew Perkins, September 13, 1967; drums), whom Navarro had been playing with in a speed metal band and performing with at famous Los Angeles hotspots: the Roxy and the Troubadour (Perna 1997).

It seemed an unlikely pairing, speed metal and 1970s punk, but in the spring of 1986, the four friends created Jane's Addiction, with Perry Farrell on vocals, Dave Navarro on guitar, Eric Avery on bass guitar, and Stephen Perkins on drums. In a humorous tale, the younger Navarro and Perkins recount how they could not enter a bar due to their age and were forced to wait outside until it was time to perform; but despite the obvious, the band's career moved quickly. By 1987, the band was being managed by Triple X, a management and record label started by Charley Brown, Dean Naleway, and Peter Heur, who had all previously worked in record distribution. Under the guidance of Triple X, Jane's Addiction released a live performance of a show at the Roxy that became their debut album (Perna 1997).

With the release of their live performance album in 1987, Jane's Addiction was voted the Best Underground Band and the Best Hard Rock/Metal Band by *L.A. Weekly* and in the process garnered the attention of record labels. In the time before social media, bands relied more heavily on large, corporate labels to distribute their albums. Although the band was signed with Triple X Records, the management team at Triple

Portrait of Jane's Addiction in 1988. Pictured are (from left to right): Perry Farrell, Dave Navarro, Stephen Perkins, and Eric Avery. Jane's Addiction was at the forefront of the mid-1990s alternative rock revolution in the United States. The band's influential sound gave rise to a host of imitators throughout the 1990s. (Photo by Paul Natkin/Getty Images)

X realized the band needed a stronger push than their small label could provide. Initially offered a deal by Los Angeles–based, independent label Slash Records, the band was advised to continue searching for a tenured label that had connections and an established track record. The goal was to find a company that would not only take the group to the next level but would also be willing to take a huge financial risk, as their music was not considered radio-friendly or traditional by commercial standards (Handleman 1987).

Several major labels courted the band, Capitol and Geffen being two of the most notable ones to do so, but eventually the band decided on Warner Bros. had a history of working with artists who were on the edge, and the company maintained the unusual strategy of not chasing the music—an approach that was both welcome and unnerving (Handleman 1987).

Cautious about signing with Warner Bros., but also finding themselves attracted to the nonchalant atmosphere and the label's reputation of working with "difficult" acts, Jane's Addiction agreed to accept a deal for a figure believed to have been as high as $300,000. Robert Peterson, who had been working at Warner Bros. for 12 years, signed the band in 1987 (Handleman 1987).

Having a strong label for support, Jane's Addiction began work on their first studio album, *Nothing's Shocking*. Released on August 23, 1988, the album won praise from critics, but scorn from distributors who found the album cover, featuring two Siamese twins fully nude with their hair ablaze, objectionable, resulting in the album being banned by a total of seven distributors. Perry Farrell, when challenged about the direction the band had taken with their choice of album art, reminded all who would listen that their plans should have come as no surprise (Handleman 1987).

Given the bohemian philosophy of Jane's Addiction, Farrell's assessment could have been dismissed as a snappy comment, but to do so would underappreciate the historical context in which rock bands in the late 1980s operated, especially a band that had risen by performing in some of Los Angeles's seediest bars and clubs.

Nothing's Shocking was released at a time when artists were increasing their challenge of the status quo by pushing the envelope when it came to controversial album covers, and record labels were trying to figure out how to get past the censors. A year before *Nothing's Shocking* was released, Guns N' Roses had released *Appetite for Destruction*, with the original album cover depicting a hand-drawn image of a female who had been sexually assaulted by a robot. At the center of the argument was the profane nature of the album itself. *Nothing's Shocking*'s album cover not only contained nudity, as did the video for "Mountain Song," but the lyrics contained profanity, causing the record company to release the album with a parental advisory logo.

Despite the album's lackluster acceptance by mainstream distributors, *Nothing's Shocking* did surprisingly well. The album peaked at 103 on the *Billboard* 200

and was awarded a platinum certificate for sales in excess of one million units sold. The album produced one notable single, "Jane Says," which rose to number six on *Billboard*'s Modern Rock Tracks chart (Ruhlmann 2014). Based on an actual person, "Jane Says" was the story of a young drug addict named Jane Bainter who shared an apartment with Perry Farrell in 1985. It was from her name that the band also derived its name (Raul 2009). In the song, Jane struggled to balance her life between her friends and boyfriend. Produced by David Jerden, who had previously worked with Brian Eno, Talking Heads, and the Rolling Stones, the song featured steel drums against a backdrop of peaceful strumming and harmonic, vocal humming.

The follow-up album to *Nothing's Shocking* was *Ritual de lo Habitual*. Released on August 21, 1990, the album reached number 19 on the *Billboard* 200 and produced two number-one singles: "Stop" and "Been Caught Stealing," both of which appeared on *Billboard*'s Modern Rock Tracks chart, and videos for the songs were played in heavy rotation in MTV. As with *Nothing's Shocking,* the band caused controversy with a painted album cover depicting a ménage à trois. Promotion of the album caused some store owners to get arrested on the charge of obscenity. To accommodate the censors, the band released a generic album cover that only featured the band's name, the title of the album, and "Amendment 1" of the U.S. Constitution (Ruhlmann 2014).

To record *Ritual de lo Habitual,* the band once again brought in producer David Jerden, who had worked with the band on *Nothing's Shocking*. By all standards, Jerden produced a quality album: clean, clear, and tighter than the first. It was Jerden who encouraged the band to experiment, to record live, and to add additional tracks and effects in postproduction. Because of his influence, "Jane Says" had the island sound of steel drums and an acoustic, swing rhythm. Jerden had laid the foundation for the album's success, and many noted the achievements of the album.

Despite revisiting old complaints as to their choice of cover art, Jane's Addiction was able to achieve double platinum sales figures with *Ritual de lo Habitual,* and critics remained enthused with the band's second studio album. The first album had been seen as a revolutionary force to be reckoned with, its edgy message being accessible to a growing number of young, disgruntled listeners seeking guidance in lyrics but not able to receive any thoughtful attention from the commercial albums being promoted by major record companies of the period. Jane's Addiction's second album was thought to be more tailored to a radio audience (*Guitar World* 1990). *Ritual de lo Habitual* possessed more commercial appeal because the songs had a pop design to them, but the album was also missing the crucial elements that made the first stand out, namely the angst and bitter lessons learned from life discovered in not-so-favorable circumstances. Though considered inspirational, what had separated the band from their contemporaries, who were failing to interpret the same tensions, had diminished, and rumors that started during the ramp-up period following the release of *Nothing's Shocking* only seemed to intensify.

It was no secret that the band enjoyed an alternative lifestyle. Drugs had long been established as part of the Los Angeles music scene. Because of their onstage antics and Perry Farrell's casual, off-the-cuff comments about sex and drugs, rumors had started to circulate that Farrell was at one time a male prostitute and consequently had contracted AIDS (Perna 1996). Yet, it was after the release of *Ritual de lo Habitual* that rumors began to surface that the use of drugs within the band had reached a point where it was hampering the music. The speculation resulted from the rumor *Ritual de lo Habitual* had been delayed by one month because of drug issues within the band; a rumor that was not easily dismissed given that the band had fired their manager Gary Kurfirst, resulting in a lawsuit where Kurfirst alleged the band's decision to terminate his employment was clouded by drug use. True or not, the allegation prompted the management team hired to replace Kurfirst, Lippman Kahane Entertainment, to ask Farrell to submit to a urine test. The question and the reason for the sample were met with a swift reply, and new management was immediately sought (Handleman 1991).

An astute observer watching the personalities in the band could predict that Jane's Addiction was on the verge of a time-out or complete breakup. In 1991, Perry Farrell admitted the band was going to break up, but he also claimed that Warner Bros. was not aware of the band's decision. Adding mystery to the question, the band's comanager Tom Atencio found Perry's comments more of a joke than a truthful comment. Yet, the band was leaning toward a collapse, and it was only a matter of time before something would give. That something came in late 1991 when bassist Eric Avery confided in guitarist Dave Navarro that he was going to leave Jane's Addiction to try and renew his love for making music. Shortly after Avery's decision, Navarro too decided to leave. The band was on the first Lollapalooza Festival tour created by Perry Farrell when the two band members made the decision. Lollapalooza, which had been planned before any split was finalized, was created as a way to usher out Jane's Addiction in a slow, nondramatic way while also exposing fans to culture and new ideas. Conflict within the band, however, reached a peak and was made public when a physical altercation ensued on stage between Farrell and Navarro; this caused the remainder of the tour to be fraught with tension as the members tried to isolate each other, leading the band to officially break up in September of 1991 once their tour had completed (Perna 1997).

Touring was a major part of the band's success, and the road can be a lonely place with a lot of temptation. To promote their first, second, and third albums, the band toured heavily between 1987 and 1992.

The first tour in 1987 was confined to the United States and had the band spending most of its time balancing shows on the West Coast and East Coast as they promoted their live album, *Jane's Addiction*. It was also during this period that the band was seeking a larger, more lucrative record label, and justifiably remaining close to Los Angeles, New York, and Florida as a logical strategy. On this tour, the band played a total of 66 concerts (janesaddiction.org).

To promote their first studio album, *Nothing's Shocking,* the scope of the tour expanded, with the band visiting more points in between, spending most of their time touring the hinterland of the United States along with coastal cities and performing in

England, Canada, and Germany. Shorter, but more advantageous, the group played a total of 61 concert dates on their 1988 tour (janesaddiction.org).

Continuing to promote *Nothing's Shocking,* the band scheduled 59 concert dates for 1989 and continued to spend a majority of their time touring the United States, while choosing to perform in Canada, England, Scotland, and Mexico (janesaddiction.org).

It was not until the 1990 tour, and the release of *Ritual de lo Habitual,* that Jane's Addiction toured Europe heavily. The start of the tour had the band beginning on July 7 in Mt. Baldy, California, before taking a break for one month, and on August 8 playing a show in London, England. The band spent the first part of 1990 touring France, Belgium, England, Germany, Italy, Amsterdam, and Scotland before returning to America to finish the tour, performing mainly in the United States but also visiting Canada. As with the three previous tours, the band played a similar number of shows, in 1990, a total of 57 (janesaddiction.org).

Between 1987 and 1990, the band had remained relatively consistent in the number of shows they booked for a specific tour, but with rumors of the band breaking up being confirmed by Farrell, the creation of 1991's Lollapalooza increased their last tour exponentially. The increase in dates was later cited by Dave Navarro as one of the leading factors that caused him to leave the band.

To make Lollapalooza an event to be remembered, a diverse lineup of major acts was invited to join Jane's Addiction on their tour. Some of those invited to perform included Nine Inch Nails, rapper Ice-T, and Siouxsie and the Banshees. The design was to have the visiting artists perform throughout the day, with Jane's Addiction wrapping up the evening with a mesmerizing concert. If all went as planned, the audience would be primed and ready for an experience, not just a show. However, this also meant that the members of Jane's Addiction were exposed to the temptations of the festival. While artists and groups performed throughout the day, the members of one of the most notorious bands on the planet were subjected

to interviews and hours of waiting before finally taking to the stage. By the start of the evening, the band was both exhausted and expected to perform.

Scheduled to coincide with Jane's Addiction's ongoing tour to promote *Ritual de lo Habitual,* Lollapalooza began on July 18 and ended on August 28, 1991. Although the concert dates for this segment of the tour totaled less than two months, the band had already been on the road since January 27, performing shows in the continental United States, Hawaii, Europe, and Australia before returning to perform at Lollapalooza. Once their obligations were complete for July and August, the band continued their tour by going to Australia, before moving onto New Zealand, and finally ending in Hawaii on September 26. In total, Jane's Addiction performed 106 shows in 1991 (janesaddiction.org).

Following the 1991 tour, the band members went in their own directions, dedicating their time to side projects and finding out the best methods of going forward. For Perry Farrell this meant continuing to promote Lollapalooza and performing with his new group Porno for Pyros. For guitarist Dave Navarro the journey out of Jane's Addiction led him to the stage of another very famous Los Angeles band, Red Hot Chili Peppers (RHCP), where he replaced guitarist Jesse Tobias. Drummer Stephen Perkins continued on with Porno for Pyros while also doing session work with Rage Against the Machine for their political mantra, "Know Your Enemy," and RHCP's "One Big Mob." Bassist Eric Avery took a low-profile approach, devoting most of his time to working on his own side project, Polar Bear, and dedicating what was left to working with or helping other musicians such as Alanis Morissette and the Smashing Pumpkins.

In 1997, it was announced that Jane's Addiction would be releasing a new album titled *Kettle Whistle,* a name derived from a song the band had performed in its early days but had never recorded in the studio until the release of the 1997 album. Fans were hopeful that the original lineup would reunite, but only Perry Farrell, Dave Navarro, and Stephen Perkins came together for the project. Eric Avery, the band's original bassist, was invited to join but chose to remain out of the limelight, and Flea from RHCP was signed on as the bassist (Perna 1997).

Released on November 4, 1997, *Kettle Whistle* got its name from the featured song by the same title recorded for the album. The song had been performed years earlier by Jane's Addiction, and the only known circulation until the studio release was a bootleg. This made the album perfect for ridicule because *Kettle Whistle* was a combination of songs from the past and songs rarely performed. It was by all accounts a compilation album. Perry Farrell referred to the tour that followed the release of *Kettle Whistle* as the "Relapsed" tour. A notable track on the album was a live recording of "Jane Says" recorded July 24, 1991, at Irvine Meadows Amphitheater in Irvine, California. The release of the live version of "Jane Says" also led to the creation of a video for the song featuring footage from the Hammerstein Ballroom in New York, recorded on October 31, 1997 (janesaddiction.org).

Although the band toured the album, the tour was brief and the shows were few. In 1997, the band only scheduled 21 concert dates, and still *Kettle Whistle* sold enough units to receive a gold certification (janesaddiction.org). Fans were pleased, but the critics were jaded and gave the album low marks. *Rolling Stone* considered the album a rehashing of nostalgia and marketed through hype (Chonin 1997). *Entertainment Weekly* thought the reunion tour was a waste of time as it seemed nothing more than an altered version of Perry Farrell's side project, Porno for Pyros (Mirkin 1997).

Placing the Relapsed tour behind them, the band members continued to move forward. Farrell and Perkins continued performing with Porno for Pyros and Navarro remained with RHCP. It was also in 1997 that Lollapalooza came to an end.

From its inception, Perry Farrell had insisted that Lollapalooza be a traveling show, a venue for the fans to experience a carnival-like atmosphere, but as the show grew in popularity and became more lucrative for investors, it became increasingly difficult to find locations willing to host the one-day event. Small communities that had allowed the tour to visit on repeated occasions became increasingly concerned about the amount of traffic and local disruption the staging caused; this forced the promoters to search for other venues, sometimes losing money in the process as the formula for financial success had to be modified to meet burgeoning circumstances. Aside from logistics and the maintenance of diplomacy, choosing the correct bands to perform on the tour became an ever more difficult task, especially as the era of music that created Lollapalooza moved closer to the mid-1990s and the commercialization of alternative rock. In some cases, bands went into defensive mode, protecting their domain as headliners and setting aside the friendship and camaraderie that had made the tour a pleasurable experience. At other times, members of the audience lashed out at the artists chosen to play. By the end of 1996, promoters anxious to turn the situation around adopted a new strategy by inviting artists who were creating electronic music. In theory, it should have worked. Electronic music was gaining momentum among young partygoers, but unlike the other tours, the acts were scheduled to play on different dates. For the fans, this meant shows were not consistent in their roster of acts, and many were turned off.

At the close of 1997, a new Lollapalooza was being planned, but a misunderstanding led promoters to believe that Jane's Addiction would reunite and headline the concert. After reaching out for possible contenders and receiving a steady stream of rejections from bands who no longer found the tour appealing, Lollapalooza was officially put on hold (janesaddiction.org).

Meanwhile, Perry Farrell's side project, Porno for Pyros, disbanded in 1998 when it was discovered that guitarist Peter DiStefano had cancer. This set Farrell on a path of self-promotion whereby he put his energy into a solo career, writing music and releasing several tracks online at a time when few artists were taking advantage of digital download distribution.

The year 1998 was also a turning point for guitarist Dave Navarro, who had joined RHCP in 1993. Navarro who had struggled with drug addiction, had relapsed while on tour. When members of RHCP learned of his drug use, they fired him. Like Farrell,

Navarro took time to gather his thoughts and worked on a solo career.

With the new millennium approaching, a renewed interest in trying to revive Lollapalooza began to consume Perry Farrell, but when an attempt in 1999 once again failed to produce a headliner, it seemed the project was better left alone. To help, it was theorized that Jane's Addiction could reunite and perform as the headlining act to fans who had been waiting and wondering if the band would ever return to the stage.

In 2001, the band came back together to perform a series of concerts that carried them into a 2002 tour. Flea, who was working with RHCP, was in no position to set out on the open road. Once again, the band reached out to their old friend and original band member Eric Avery, but he declined the offer and the band turned to Martyn LeNoble, who had been the bassist for Porno for Pyros. While on tour, the gears started to turn, and, pleased by how successful the tour had been, the band prepared not only for a tour in 2002, but also the release of their third studio album since *Ritual de lo Habitual* in 1990.

To record the new material, the band replaced Martyn LeNoble with bassist Chris Chaney, who had worked with Alanis Morissette on her 1995 tour to promote her album *Jagged Little Pill*. They also hired producer Bob Ezrin, who had produced the Kiss album *Destroyer* and had worked with Pink Floyd. Having a reputation for getting the very best out of the artists he worked with, Ezrin was able to get the members to seriously focus on their effort, and the result paid off.

Entering the studio in early 2002, the band returned to the road later that same year to perform 20 concerts (janesaddiction.org). The album that came out of the spring sessions was nothing like anything Jane's Addiction had made before, and the attention was immediate. Within the first week, sales of *Strays*, released on July 22, 2003, by Capitol Records, who had recently signed the band, exceeded 100,000 units, securing for the album a gold certification; critics, who had grown accustomed with interpreting the band's post-1990 achievements with skepticism, were amazed by what they heard. *Entertainment*

Weekly called the album "the stuff of which comeback dreams are made" (Weingarten 2003), and *Rolling Stone* magazine gave the band four stars, noting that "Jane's Addiction have finally come up with music that can stand alongside their previous albums" (Pareles 2003).

To promote *Strays,* the band toured heavily in 2003, booking a total of 104 venues. Between July 5 and August 24, the band performed on the main stage at the revived Lollapalooza. Unlike previous tours, Jane's Addiction started outside the United States, in Auckland, New Zealand, a month before returning to Riverside, California, in February. After performing at Lollapalooza, the band continued touring, but several shows were canceled and the band broke up with no clear reason why.

Lollapalooza also suffered a major setback. A 2004 tour was planned, but fans, not in agreement with the lineup, failed to purchase tickets, and the festival was canceled; this resulted in Perry Farrell reaching out to Capital Sports & Entertainment, and together the partnership purchased the rights to Lollapalooza, changing it from a one-day, traveling festival, to a static, three-day festival. The city of Chicago, which had showed the greatest interest in 2003, was selected to become the home of Lollapalooza and contractually became the host of the festival through 2021 (janesaddiction.org).

After the 2003 tour, Jane's Addiction went silent, making only sporadic appearances. However, in 2008, bassist Eric Avery returned to perform with the band's original lineup at the NME Awards held on April 23, 2008. Though Avery did not record on the band's fourth studio album, *The Great Escape Artist,* released on October 18, 2011, he did tour with the band in 2009 before announcing he was leaving the group. Duff McKagan signed on to play bass, but he left and was replaced by Dave Sitek, who recorded the bass tracks for the album but left the tour to bassist Chris Chaney.

Whereas Jane's Addiction had won praise and compliments with their 2003 release, *The Great Escape Artist* reversed the positive trend. It received on average three-star reviews and never achieved gold certification. Nevertheless, the remaining members of the band, Farrell, Navarro, and Perkins, extensively toured together in the years following its release (Dolan 2011). In fact, Farrell, Navarro, and Perkins continue to play together intermittently as Jane's Addiction to the present time.

Because Jane's Addiction was one of the earliest alternative music bands, although with a hard edge, they were incredibly influential. Stylistically, Jane's Addiction prefigured the nu-metal style of the early 1990s. The list of bands that have claimed immediate influence from Jane's Addiction include Tool, Korn, the Smashing Pumpkins, Limp Bizkit, Candlebox, P.O.D., Stabbing Westward, Incubus, System of a Down, and Oceansize. Additionally, although no longer directly affiliated with Farrell or the band, Lollapalooza remains a destination concert staged over three days every summer in Chicago.

Throughout the 1990s Jane's Addiction's music was compared repeatedly to that of Led Zeppelin, but for millions of young people who tapped into their message, their sound, and their street-level philosophy, the band was unique and not defined. Jane's Addiction can trace its roots back to a different time when attitudes about drugs and sex were reserved with a taboo connotation. If one finds it difficult to get the image out of one's head when first viewing the album cover to *Nothing's Shocking,* then imagine what it was like for a Reagan-era teen who saw the world through a sanitized lens. It appears, in hindsight, that the very thing the band railed against was the same thing they so desperately needed to maintain their cult-like following—a somewhat innocent, naive view of world.

Brooks Kohler

Selected Discography
Nothing's Shocking (CD), Warner Bros. Records 25727, 1988.

Ritual de lo Habitual (CD), Warner Bros. Records 25993, 1990.

Psi Com (CD), (Triple-X) CDPRO 135, 1993.

Kettle Whistle (CD), Capitol Records 90186, 2003.

The Great Escape Artist (CD), Capitol Records 50999–9–65112–20, 2011.

References
Chonin, Nevin. "*Kettle Whistle* Review," Rollingstone.com, December 11, 1997.

Dolan, Jon, "*The Great Escape Artist* Review," Rollingstone.com, October 18, 2011.

Ellerman, Nina. "Jonestown Revisited," *BAM,* December 2, 1988.

Handelman, David. "Local Heroes," *Rolling Stone,* October 22, 1987.

Handleman, David. "Nothing's Shocking: Meet L.A.'s Wildest New Band Jane's Addiction," *Rolling Stone,* February 7, 1991.

Jane's Addition Official Website, 2015. "Discography." Accessed May 2014. www.janesadditiction.org.

Mirkin, Steven. "Kettle Whistle (1997)," EW.com, November 10, 1997.

Pareles, Jon. "Strays: The *Rolling Stone* Review," Rollingstone.com, August 7, 2003.

Perna, Alan di. "Birth of a Nation," *Guitar World,* March 1996.

Perna, Alan di. "A Jane's Addiction Timeline," *Guitar World,* November 1997.

Perna, Alan di. "Shock Exchange," *Guitar World,* November 1997.

Raul. "Jane Bainter Is the Namesake of Jane's Addiction Band Name & 'Jane Says' Song," Feelnumb.com, March 5, 2009.

Ruhlmann, William. "Jane's Addiction." *All Music Guide.* Rovi Corporation, 2014.

Weingarten, Marc. "Strays Review," EW.com, July 25, 2003.

Jethro Tull (1968–Present)

As recounted on the official Jethro Tull website, the band formed in 1968 "from the ashes of various failed regional bands gathered together in hunger, destitution, and modest optimism in Luton, north of London" (jethrotull.com/press). The original lineup consisted of Ian Anderson (born August 10, 1947; vocals, harmonica, guitar, flute), Glen Cornick (born April 24, 1947; bass), Mick Abrams (born April 7, 1943; vocals, guitar), and Clive Bunker (born December 12, 1946; drums). The band began playing two gigs per

Jethro Tull poses in Amsterdam, the Netherlands, in 1972. From left to right: John Evan, Ian Anderson, Barriemore Barlow (Barrie Barlow), Martin Barre, and Jeffrey Hammond. Marked by the sound of Anderson's flute playing, Jethro Tull's mixture of blues, rock, and prog styles made them unique along with their incorporation of the English folk tradition. (Photo by Gijsbert Hanekroot/Redfern)

week in the clubs in London, often playing under different names in order to get a second booking. Dave Robson, a historically minded staff member from the Ellis-Wright Agency (later known as Chrysalis) was the one who suggested the name "Jethro Tull." The original Jethro Tull was an English agriculturalist who lived from 1674 to 1741 and was credited with perfecting the horse-drawn seed drill. According to Anderson, the name stuck with the band because it was the name that they were using when the popular London venue the Marquee Club offered the group a Thursday night residency.

By February of 1968 the band already had a single released for MGM. "Aeroplane" was cowritten by Anderson and Cornick and released with the B-side

"Sunshine Day" by Anderson, and the band name was printed as "Jethro Toe." The typo was, according to Cornick, intentional on the part of producer Derek Lawrence, who thought the name "Jethro Toe" was an improvement on the unhip name Jethro Tull. Lawrence, for his part, claimed it was a misunderstanding in a phone conversation. The single did not fare well, but it did not seem to impede the band one bit.

Jethro Tull began during the late 1960s British blues explosion that fostered the careers of Eric Clapton, the Rolling Stones, and Fleetwood Mac, among others. Anderson was musically influenced by the guitar work of Clapton but soon realized that he would not be able to play guitar on the same level as his idol. So instead of being a second-rate guitarist, Anderson attempted to set himself apart by picking up a very nontraditional blues or rock instrument, the flute.

Anderson's flute playing was influenced in part by the great jazz musician Rashaan Roland Kirk, who played flute on the 1965 album *I Talk with the Spirits*. In this recording Kirk sang and hummed through the instrument while playing to create interesting polyphonic effects. The other great influence on Anderson's playing was, appropriately, Eric Clapton, whom Anderson used as a model for the creation of his melodic and improvisatory content. The flute seemingly came fairly naturally to Anderson, and he began performing on the instrument within weeks of beginning to play.

In June of 1968, Jethro Tull opened for Pink Floyd at the first free rock festival in London's Hyde Park. In August the band was invited to play at the Sunbury Jazz and Blues Festival at London's Kempton Park. This put Jethro Tull onstage in front of about 80,000 people, and before summer's end they had signed a record deal with Island Records.

By October the band had already recorded their debut album, *This Way*. The album was released by Island Records and proved quite successful, peaking at number 10 in the U.K. charts and 62 in the United States. The album placed Jethro Tull soundly in the blues idiom with the help of Abrahams's guitar, vocals, and songwriting. The track "Someday the Sun Won't Shine for You" was about as close to country blues as any British blues band could get, with its sparse arrangement featuring only vocals, guitar, and harmonica. The more blues/rock "It's Breaking Me Up" was equally successful and really showcased the band's soulful side while Abrahams's arrangement of the traditional tune "Cat's Squirrel" proved a fruitful base to showcase his virtuosic abilities as a blues lead man. In an entirely different direction was the Rashaan Roland Kirk instrumental cover "Serenade to a Cuckoo," proving that the band had the skill to play jazz as well as blues and featuring Anderson playing the lead and improvising on the flute, which he had only been playing for a few months prior to the recording. Anderson's talent on the flute was truly remarkable for such an inexperienced player.

This Was served as a document of the foundations of Jethro Tull. Anderson and Cornick both commented that the decision to be a blues band at the time of the band's formation was more of a commercial decision than anything. The album was produced for the blues scene, but perhaps it was Abrahams, the only true blues fanatic in the group, who helped sell the album.

Shortly after *This Was,* Abrahams left the group due to a disparity in the amount the band members wanted to play. Abrahams wanted to limit the number of performances per week and stay within the country, while the other members wanted to make a career of playing music. The two approaches could not coexist. With Abrahams out, Anderson was left to provide all of the material and front the band, a situation that pushed Anderson to isolate himself from the band and drove him to write new material in an obsessive manner.

After Abrahams, Jethro Tull briefly scalped the rock guitar icon Tony Iommi from the band Earth (later Black Sabbath), but he did not stay for long before realizing that the group dynamics of the band were not going to suit his idea of a band. Iommi did stay on for the band's appearance on *The Rolling Stones' Rock 'n' Roll Circus* with the Rolling Stones, the Who, Eric Clapton, Taj Mahal, and John Lennon and Yoko Ono—another incredible break for such a young band.

The band held auditions for a new guitarist and ended up hiring Martin Barre (born November 17, 1946; guitar) for the position. Barre, who had played in the band Gethsemane and opened for Jethro Tull on one occasion, was asked to audition for the spot but failed the initial audition. However, he enjoyed the band so much that he called Anderson and was invited back for a private jam session; he was then offered an audition at a live gig at the Penzance Wintergardens on December 30. Barre was subsequently offered the spot with the band and he has maintained the position of Jethro Tull guitarist ever since.

In January of 1969, Jethro Tull played their first U.S. dates supporting Blood, Sweat, and Tears at the Fillmore East in New York. The band then did some recording in the States, played a series of dates in the United Kingdom, and came back to the States for a two-month run playing large festivals. They were even invited to play Woodstock but backed out after being told by the band Ten Years After that it was rainy and "one of the worst fucking gigs you've ever seen!" (Nollen 2002). The band did make an appearance at the Newport Jazz and Blues Festival performing alongside Anderson's inspiration, Rashaan Roland Kirk.

This Was had its U.S. release in April of 1969 and found a small but loyal fan base, but the band was already changing and recording new material with Barre. *Stand Up* was released in August and became the band's only number-one album. The entirety of the album was written by Anderson with the exception of his jazzy arrangement of J. S. Bach's *Bouree in Em,* the fifth movement from BWV 996.

In only their sophomore release the band had shown a significant movement away from the blues into more "progressive" territory, placing them in the same category as Pink Floyd, King Crimson, Genesis, and Yes.

The album *Benefit* hit the stores in April 1970 and showed the group settling into their future path with Anderson at the helm. On the back cover, appearing above the credits, was "Songs by Ian Anderson." The band had also become more comfortable in the studio and incorporated some more advanced recording tricks, like the backward flute part in "With You There to Help Me."

The year 1970 was one of many changes for the group. First came the addition of keyboardist John Evan (born March 28, 1948; keyboard) who was initially invited as a guest to record on *Benefit* but stayed on as a fulltime member. Then in December, Mick Cornick was asked by management to leave the group and was subsequently replaced by Anderson and Evans's childhood friend Jeffrey Hammond (born July 30, 1945; bass). Hammond was often credited in liner notes as Jeffrey Hammond-Hammond, in homage to the fact that both his mothers' and fathers' surnames were Hammond—there was no relation between the two families.

With this new lineup the band produced their most famous album, *Aqualung,* in 1971. The album broke into the U.S. top 10, peaking at number seven, and topped out at number four in the United Kingdom. Several of the songs; including "Cross-Eyed Mary," "Locomotive Breath," and of course the title-track "Aqualung"; received substantial airplay. Though it did not peak at number one on either side of the pond, the album did sell over a million copies and was rewarded a Gold record in July of 1971 by the RIAA. It has since gone on to be a three times platinum album.

The album *Aqualung* was often referred to as a concept album focused on organized religion, a distinction that Anderson denies. It has served Jethro Tull amazingly well and is still the best-selling album in the band's extensive catalogue. This was also the album that helped Anderson explore and create his style of guitar accompaniment as something separate from the American blues tradition by leaning more heavily on the English folk tradition. The music of some of his contemporaries, such as John Renbourne, Bert Jansch, and Richard Thompson, helped Anderson realize that he could contribute something to his music through his limited guitar abilities.

Following *Aqualung* and due to the band's persistent touring schedule Clive Bunker, the band's drummer, decided to leave the group. His replacement was Barrie Barlow (born September 10, 1949; drums) an old friend from the pre-Jethro Tull days.

In a response to the persistent comments about *Aqualung* being a concept album Jethro Tull released a true concept album, *Thick as a Brick* in April 1972. The entire album was one cohesive track with lyrics supposedly written by an eight-year-old boy by the name of Gerald Bostock. Anderson later stated that the whole thing was intentionally overdone to make it obvious that the album was not written by a child; however, many fans still believed there was truly a Gerald Bostock out there.

The album was written and recorded in sequence often switching between sparse acoustic and full band sections with elements of jazz, folk, theatrical, rock, and even medieval music. Each member was able to contribute to the writing process and got featured in the various improvisational sections in the piece. *Thick as a Brick* was another commercial success peaking at number five in the United Kingdom and number one in the United States on the *Billboard* Top 200.

Later in 1972 the first compilation album, *Living in the Past* was released. Some of the tracks were previously issued while others were previously recorded but had not been released. It included remixed versions of singles, B-sides and outtakes, a live recording from a 1970 Carnegie Hall concert, and a complete version of the *Life is a Long Song* EP. The title track, "Living in the Past," became the band's first single to break into the top 20 peaking at number 11.

To this point the band had been remarkably prolific and had maintained solid footing with both its fan base and the critics. That stretch ran out with the 1973 release of *A Passion Play*. Since *Thick as a Brick* was such a hit the band came to the conclusion that they should record another concept album, but this time the album focused on more serious religious imagery. The album was badly criticized but the public supported it all the way to number one in the United States and number 13 in England. The band also toured the United States in support and again received bad reviews; however, the tour was completely sold out, again illustrating the disparity between the rock press and public opinion.

The band followed *A Passion Play* with a return to convention on 1974s *War Child*. The album presold enough copies to be certified as Gold upon its release. The album was originally conceptualized as a film soundtrack to accompany a film of the same name. Sir Frederick Ashton choreographed the film, Monty Python's John Cleese was hired as the "humor advisor," and Byron Forbes came on as director. Unfortunately, the film never transpired due to issues with the financing and the band had to make the decision to move ahead with the album.

Minstrel in the Gallery was released in September of 1975 and resembled *Aqualung* more than the previous releases in the variation of electric and acoustic material. The album sold well giving Jethro Tull another top 10 showing with the album peaking at number seven in the United States and reaching 20 in the United Kingdom. The material on *Minstrel in the Gallery* was written and recorded in a new mobile studio, which the band parked in front of a radio station in Monte Carlo, France. The album was also recorded in the midst of Anderson's divorce from his wife Jennie Franks and a period of tension in the band. These factors come across on an album full of personal lyrics, sometimes verging on angry or cynical.

David Palmer, the band's longtime orchestral arranger, joined the group to support the tour for *Minstrel in the Gallery* and following the tour Hammond quit. Bassist, John Glascock (born May 2, 1951, Islington, United Kingdom, died November 17, 1979; bass) from a flamenco-rock band named Carmen that had toured as an opener for Jethro Tull replaced Hammond.

The year 1976s *Too Old to Rock 'n' Roll: Too Young to Die* was another Jethro Tull project with a grand origin. The concept came from a single song titled "Too Old to Rock and Roll" and turned into a theatrical piece about an ageing rock star named Ray Lomas. The focus was to be about the cyclical nature of style and to illustrate that a once-popular artist could remain true to their vision if they are patient enough to see it come back into vogue. Inevitably the press pounced on the idea that the album was autobiographical even though Anderson was only 28 at the time. Just like *Passion Play,* the grand production was again scrapped and just the album was released.

The end of the 1970s brought a change of flavor for Jethro Tull. Anderson bought a farm in the English countryside, a move that was mirrored musically by an album with more British folk influence. *Songs from the Wood* was the group's most artistically unified album in quite some time and the first to receive positive reviews from the press since 1972s *Living in the Past*. The album drew heavily on history and culture of the British Isles.

Two albums were released in 1978, *Heavy Horses* and a double live record titled *Bursting Out,* which was recorded during the *Heavy Horses* tour. *Heavy Horses* was a sort of extension of the new pastoral Jethro Tull but where *Songs from the Wood* drew heavily on Elizabethan influence, *Heavy Horses* drew more influence from 18th-century Scottish music. The subject matter largely related to animals like the once-prolific draught horses found through Britain, cats, mice, moths, and Anderson's imaginary Weathercock.

The year 1979s *Stormwatch* found Tull making a bit of a return to rock but still drawing on some of the influence of the prior two albums. While the band was working on the project, bassist John Glascock who had joined just four years prior was having heart problems, which kept him from participating in the bulk of the recording sessions for *Stormwatch*. Glascock performed on three tracks, "Orion," "Flying Dutchman," and "Elegy," and Anderson chose to track the remaining bass parts himself. Anderson said of his bass playing "if I'd been auditioned for the part I wouldn't have got it." Unfortunately the heart problems led to heart surgery and a year later, on November 17, Glascock died when his heart suddenly rejected the replacement valve.

The year 1979 also proved to be the end of an era for Jethro Tull. Glascock passed just weeks before the *Stormwatch* tour and the former Fairport Convention bassist, Dave Pegg, was hired to fill in. Barrie Barlow decided to leave the band after the death of Glascock, his close friend, but Barlow did play the supporting dates for the *Stormwatch* tour. Shortly after the tour Palmer and Evans (and Barlow) were told by Anderson via carbon copy letter he was going to do a solo project and he may use Jethro Tull's name or not but either way they were not to be involved.

Anderson needed to fill his new band and hired Eddie Jobson (born Edwin Jobson, April 28, 1955) to play piano, keyboards, and electric violin. He also hired the first American to join the band, Minnesota (born Mark Craney, August 26, 1952, died November 26, 2005) on drums. Rounding out the players were Fairport Convention bassist, Dave Pegg, and Jethro Tull's Martin Barre on guitar.

The new album was titled *A* and though it set out to be an Ian Anderson solo piece, and the material was significantly different from what Jethro Tull had previously released; however, Chrysalis was of the opinion that the album would sell better under the name of Jethro Tull. All of the players remark how enjoyable of an experience recording *A* was and the entire album was tracked in a matter of 10 days.

A was released in August of 1980 in the United Kingdom and September in the United States and the band began touring in support of the release. They began in the United States, touring from October to November and then moved to the United Kingdom for two dates at the Royal Albert Hall on November 20–21. Beginning February of 1981 they did a more extensive European tour at the end of which Craney and Jobson left the band.

After taking the majority of 1981 to tend to his farm, Anderson again needed new membership to flesh out Jethro Tull. Former Cat Stevens drummer Gerry Conway (born September 11, 1947) and a 25-year-old keyboardist Peter-John Vettesse (born August 15, 1956) were brought on to fill out the group. Vettesse played a large role in the new lineup and his innovative work on the synthesizer added a new element to the band.

The album *The Broadsword and the Beast* differed from *A* in that the recording process took almost an entire year. This was largely due to the hiring of Paul Samwell-Smith as a producer, something that the band had never done. Unfortunately the arrangement did not work, costing the band months in the studio. Following Smith's departure, Anderson took on his usual role as producer.

In 1983, Anderson set out to record another solo project and this time the album was released under the name Ian Anderson. *Walk into Light* was dominated by the sound of synthesizers, a significant change from the Jethro Tull sound. The album performed poorly leading Anderson to reunite Jethro Tull for the 1984 release of *Under Wraps*, an album that pushed the band into more electronic territory. The overuse of new technology led Terry Ellis to tell the band upon hearing the completed album for the first time; "If you think I'm going to release this fucking pile of crap on my label, you can think again!" (Nollen, 177). Chrysalis was persuaded otherwise after Ellis left the company.

After answering an ad in the *Village Voice,* Doane Perry landed the gig as the drummer for the *Under Wraps* tour. Unfortunately, Anderson developed a throat infection that forced the cancellation of the support tour, which may have been a factor in the poor sales. The album debuted at number 76 in the United States and had the poorest sales of any Jethro Tull album to date.

Due to Anderson's reoccurring throat problems, there was not another album released until 1987s *Crest of a Knave.* In the intervening years the group participated in a project to have works of Jethro Tull performed by the London Symphony Orchestra. Chrysalis made up for the lack of new material by releasing a compilation album in October 1985 titled *Original Masters.* In 1986, a recording of the symphonic project titled *A Classic Case: The London Symphony Orchestra Plays the Music of Jethro Tull* was released.

Crest of a Knave was released in September of 1987 and proved to be a major comeback for Jethro Tull. The group was still intertwining the sounds of folk and hard rock but this time it had a harder edge than past recordings. The album sold well and the band set out on a 20th-anniversary tour of the United States, which coincided with the release of a Chrysalis issued boxed set, *20 Years of Jethro Tull.* The big surprise came in February of 1989 when *Crest of Knave* beat out Metallica's seminal album . . . *And Justice for All* and won the Grammy Award for Best Hard Rock/Metal Performance. This win became a topic of debate for the rock press who ultimately attacked the National Academy of Recording Arts and Science for being out of touch with popular culture.

Rock Island was released in 1989 and was similar in style to *Crest of a Knave,* though it did not perform quite as well commercially. The 1991 album *Catfish Rising* toned down the hard rock aspects of their music and somewhat returned to an earlier sound for the band, utilizing some acoustic sounds. The trend back toward the acoustic side of Jethro Tull continued on the 1992 album *A Little Light Music.* Each album following *Crest of a Knave* had lower sales than the previous, leaving *A Little Light Music* to top out at 34 in the United Kingdom and 150 in the United States.

Even with poor album sales the band still played to large audiences through the 1990s. In 1993 Chrysalis released the *Twenty-Fifth Anniversary Boxed Set*, another collection of remixes, live material, and a few new tracks. One of the discs in the box featured new recordings of old material with the current band performing them.

Another lineup change brought Steve Bailey in on bass, replacing Dave Pegg, who chose to focus on Fairport Convention. Bailey's first recording with the group was *Roots to Branches,* the first album in the Jethro Tull catalogue for which Anderson completely relinquished control of the rhythm section arrangements. The album also showed signs of the band reinventing itself musically through the incorporation of world music influence, a trend which the 1999 album *J-Tull Dot Com* continued.

In 1995, Anderson released another solo album. *Ian Anderson Divinities—Twelve Dances with God* was a pop classical recording of instrumental music featuring Anderson on flute with orchestral accompaniment. The album sold reasonably well, appearing at number one on the Classical Crossover chart. Anderson produced two additional solo albums in 2000 and 2003, respectively titled *The Secrete Language of Birds* and *Rupi's Dance.* Both of these albums are song-based collections of primarily acoustic material.

The Jethro Tull Christmas Album was released in 2003 and proved to be the biggest commercial success the band had since 1985's *Crest of a Knave.* The album featured Anderson's arrangements of various Christmas classics.

Between 2002 and 2009 the group released five live albums, *Living with the Past* (2002), *Nothing Is Easy: Live at the Isle of Wight 1970* (2004), *Aqualung Live* (2005), and *Live at Madison Square Garden* (2009).

In 2012, *Thick as a Brick 2: Whatever Happened to Gerald Bostock?* was released as an Anderson solo album. There was also an 18-month tour to promote the new album and the 40th anniversary of the original release of *Thick as a Brick.*

The Jethro Tull lineup since 2011 has consisted of longtime collaborators Ian Anderson and Martin Barre, with Nathan Noyce on bass, Doare Perry on drums, and John O'Hara on keyboards.

Few bands have had the longevity or prolific output of Jethro Tull. Anderson and Barre have been able to work together continuously since 1969. The various other members of the group were each suited to and helped shape the various stylistic periods of the band's development. Though the creative development and the majority of the output are that of Anderson, the rotating cast of band members must have kept the band fresh and original through the years.

Jethro Tull came up in the United Kingdom during a time of intense creativity and musical exploration. American blues were becoming extremely influential and the earliest iteration of Jethro Tull was performing a lot of blues material. Before long the band expanded its repertoire into more progressive territory by incorporating more of the English folk tradition along with elaborate and intricate arrangements showcasing the virtuosity of the players. Other English acts that drove the progressive rock genre include Pink Floyd, Fairport Convention, Genesis, and Yes, among others.

Joshua Rieck

Selected Discography

The London Symphony Orchestra Plays the Music of Jethro Tull, RCA Red Seal, RCD1–7067, 1965.

This Was, Island Records, ILP 985, 1968.

Stand Up, Island Records, ILPS 9103, 1969.

Benefit, Chrysalis, ILPS 9123, 1970.

Aqualung, Chrysalis, ILPS 9145, 1971.

Thick as a Brick, Chrysalis, CHR 1003, 1972.

A Passion Play, Chrysalis, CHR 1040, 1973.

War Child, Chrysalis, CHR 1067, 1974.

Minstrel in the Gallery, Chrysalis, CHR 1082, 1975.

Too Old to Rock 'N' Roll: Too Young to Die!, Chrysalis, CHR 1111, 1976.

Songs from the Wood, Chrysalis, CHR 1132, 1977.

Bursting Out: Jethro Tull Live, Chrysalis, CJT4, 1978.

Heavy Horses, Chrysalis, CHR 1175, 1978.

Stormwatch, Chrysalis, CDL 1238, 1979.

A, Chrysalis, CDL 1301, 1980.

The Broadsword and the Beast, Chrysalis, ZCDL 1380, 1982.

Walk into Light, Chrysalis, CCD 1443, 1983.

Under Wraps, Chrysalis, CDL 1461, 1984.

Crest of a Knave, Chrysalis, CCD 1590, 1987.

Rock Island, Chrysalis, CCD 1708, 1989.

Catfish Rising, Chrysalis, CCD 1886, 1991.

A Little Light Music, Chrysalis, F2–21954, 1992.

Ian Anderson—Divinities: Twelve Dances With God, Angel Records, CDC 552622, 1995.

Roots and Branches, Chrysalis, F2 35418, 1995.

J-Tull Dot Com, Fuel 2000, FLD-1043, 1999.

Living with the Past, Eagle Records, EAGCD231, 2002.

The Jethro Tull Christmas Album, Fuel 2000, 302 061, 2003.

Rupi's Dance, Fuel 2000, 302 061 328 2, 2003.

Jethro Tull's Ian Anderson—TAAB2, Chrysalis, 50999638 72620, 2012.

References

Benson, Raymond. *Jethro Tull.* Harpenden, UK: Oldcastle Books, 2012.

Eder, Bruce. "Jethro Tull." *All Music Guide.* Rovi Corporation, 2012.

Jethro Tull Offiical Website. 2015. "Press." Accessed September 2014. jethrotull.com/press.

Macan, Edwyard, *Rocking the Classics: English Progressive Rock and Counterculture.* New York: Oxford University Press, 1997.

Nollen, Scott Allen. *Jethro Tull: A History of the Band, 1968–2001.* Jefferson, NC: McFarland & Co. Inc., 2002.

The Jimi Hendrix Experience (1966–1970)

The guitar legend that the world knew as Jimi Hendrix was born Johnny Allen Hendrix in Seattle, Washington, on November 27, 1942. Hendrix went on to become one of the most internationally acclaimed guitarist of all time—some still argue that he was the best guitarist of all time. Hendrix's rise to stardom was indeed meteoric, but got off to a ponderous start. During a tumultuous upbringing from which both of his parents were largely absent, Hendrix spent hours playing the guitar. After high school and a short stint in the military, he cut his teeth on the chitlin' circuit as a side man before heading to New York. From connections he made at open jam sessions in New York clubs, Hendrix met Bryan "Chas" Chandler who was the bass player for the original Animals.

Chandler convinced Hendrix that his music would best be received in the burgeoning blues-rock scene in the United Kingdom and in September of 1966 the two departed for London. In London, Chandler set about the business of holding up his promises to Hendrix. He soon introduced the young guitar player to Eric Clapton, who had recently exited John Mayall's Bluesbreakers and formed Cream with Jack Bruce and Ginger Baker. Chandler even got Hendrix on stage with Clapton for a jam on Howlin' Wolf's song "Killing Floor." With this, Hendrix instantly established himself as a force to be reckoned with on the London music scene. Unable to work as a soloist, Hendrix needed to assemble a backing band. Because of his long tenure as a sideman, Hendrix was well able to cover both lead and rhythm guitar parts, so he needed a bass player and a drummer—the rock and roll power trio. Noel Redding (born David Noel Redding, December 25, 1945, died May 11, 2003; bass) learned that Chandler was trying to assemble a group around Hendrix and auditioned on bass, although his first instrument was guitar. The two clicked and Noel joined Hendrix's fledgling outfit. That left the role of drummer yet to fill. Mitch Mitchell (born John Ronald Mitchell, July 9, 1946, died November 12, 2008; drums) played with Hendrix and soon enough rounded out the trio that was given the catchy name the Jimi Hendrix Experience.

The Jimi Hendrix Experience, ca. 1968. Left to right: Noel Redding, Jimi Hendrix, and Mitch Mitchell. Although the group was short-lived (only four years), the Jimi Hendrix Experience has had enormous influence. The group was inducted into the Rock and Roll Hall of Fame in 1992 and will forever be remembered for their version of "The Star-Spangled Banner" delivered on the final day of Woodstock. (Photo by Hulton Archive/Getty Images)

The most expedient route to money was for the Experience to record and release a single that they could sell. Chandler convinced Hendrix to use his cover of "Hey Joe" for the Experience's first single—Hendrix wanted to use "Killing Floor." The B-side to the first single was also a contentious point. Hendrix wanted to use another cover version and Chandler was prodding him to write a song of his own. Chandler prevailed and Hendrix set about the task of writing his first original song, "Stone Free." On December 16, 1966, the Jimi Hendrix Experience released their first single on the U.K. imprint Polydor.

Also in December of 1966, Hendrix and the Experience played a series of club dates at the Ram Jam Club, Guild Hall, the Upper Cut, and Blaises Club. Chris Welch offered the following description of the December 21 show:

Jimi Hendrix, a fantastic American guitarist, blew the minds of the star-packed crowd who went to see him at Blaises Club, London, on Wednesday. Among those in the audience were Pete Townshend, Roger Daltrey, John Entwistle, Chas Chandler, and Jeff Beck. They heard Hendrix's trio blast through some beautiful sounds like "Rock Me Baby," "Third Stone From the Sun," "Like A Rolling Stone," "Hey Joe," and even an unusual version of the Troggs' "Wild Thing." Hendrix has great stage presence and an exceptional guitar technique which involved playing with his teeth on occasions and no hands at all on others! Hendrix looks like he is becoming one of the big club names of 1967. (Potash, 1996, 3)

With this appearance before two-thirds of the Who, as well as other music notables, Hendrix and the Experience were on their way to making a mark on the world.

"Hey Joe" was a song that Hendrix had long been conversant with as it exists in a wide variety of versions. The song was originally written by California folk singer Billy Roberts, who sold it to Dino Valenti, who licensed it under the name Chet Powers. Fast versions of the song exist, but Hendrix was most influenced by folk singer Tim Rose's slow, bluesy version. The earliest known recording of the song comes from a band called the Leaves, which was released in late 1965. The Experience recorded their version in October of 1966 with Chandler handling the production at Pye Studios in London.

The first song that Hendrix wrote, "Stone Free," was an anthem to the freedom of the late 1960s—as well as his own belief in personal freedom. Hendrix sang and played in an uninhibited manner, and the song was much more in the rock style than "Hey Joe." With this song Hendrix asserted his artistic independence and also began discussing his life in the lyrics of his songs. The opening verse began with Hendrix discussing his long-standing traveling ways, referencing being in a different city every week. The verse ended with mention of being singled out because of his clothes and then drove into the chorus, where Hendrix put everything behind him by moving on. The second verse was about the many women who entered and exited Hendrix's life and his desire to keep moving before getting pinned down. With this song, Hendrix asserted his songwriting skills, his independence, and his feeling about living a free life.

In early November of 1966, the Experience had a four-day stand at the German club called the Big Apple, in Munich. From November 8 to 11, the band worked to increase their fan base in Germany.

Additionally, it was during one of these shows that Jim smashed his first guitar on stage. What began as an accident turned into one of Hendrix's signature moves on stage. Hendrix had been pulled into the audience by an overzealous fan and in trying to return to the stage he damaged his guitar. As it was already unplayable, he set about smashing it completely, to the amazement and pleasure of the crowd (Glebbeek and Noble 1996, 26).

Released on March 3, 1967, "Purple Haze" has been considered by many as Hendrix describing a drug-induced haze. The reality of this song was that it was influenced by Hendrix's interest in reading science fiction books. The lyrics were based, at least in part, on the Philip José Farmer book *Night of Light*. Early drafts of the lyrics for "Purple Haze" were as many as 10 pages long. Part of Chandler's role in Hendrix's early songwriting was to work with him to trim such things down into manageable, and marketable, length. In an interview published in the music magazine *New Musical Express*, Hendrix went on record describing his concept for "Purple Haze": "I dream a lot and I put a lot of dreams down as songs. I wrote one . . . called 'Purple Haze,' which was all about a dream I had that I was walking under the sea" (quoted in Shapiro and Glebbeek 1995).

Released as the first B-side of the "Purple Haze" single, "51st Anniversary" was another original song that made a poignant statement about relationships and loss. Hendrix presented the lyrics counting backward through a couple's married life, starting with 50 years, then 30, 20, 10, and 3. The main point that Hendrix was making throughout the song was that he would not be tied down in the manner that others referenced in the song were.

The music of "51st Anniversary" was similar to that of "Purple Haze," but without the heavy dissonance and a little less of a psychedelic quality. Here Hendrix mixed elements of the blues and mid-1960s psychedelia, along with a healthy dose of straightforward story telling. Several standard blues devices were present in the lyrics. Hendrix repeated many lines twice in addition to moving back and forth between singing and speaking in the country blues fashion. Mitch and Noel left the focus on Hendrix's singing and guitar playing, with relatively light beat-keeping on the drums and the bass often doubling the guitar. The song ended by fading out over a repeated note figure that simply faded out.

The final day of March found the Experience booked onto a package tour with a host of unlikely other bands on the lineup. For the entire month of April, the Jimi Hendrix Experience toured England on a concert bill that included Cat Stevens, Engelbert Humperdinck, the Walker Brothers (on their farewell outing), the Californians, and the Quotations. The shows were all booked into large cinemas and the Experience had little time to do more than play a five-song set. As a means of setting the band apart from the other acts on the bill, the idea was hatched to light Hendrix's guitar on fire on stage during the opening show on March 31, 1967, at the Astoria in London.

Back in the studio after the tour, the Experience recorded two more Hendrix originals. The A-side of the release was "The Wind Cries Mary" and the B-side was "Highway Chile." This third single was released on May 5, 1967, and marked the first Experience single that was anticipated by the waiting public. Well adjusted to playing with each other after the April package tour, the Experience recorded "The Wind Cries Mary" in only 20 minutes. This new song was unlike anything Hendrix had played or written in the past. The lyrics were a touching love song to Hendrix's then girlfriend Kathy Etchingham (her middle name is Mary). The song was the first that Hendrix wrote that cast his voice as the main feature, with his guitar serving a support role. The four verses of the song were divided in half by a guitar solo in between verses two and three. Although a solo, it lacked any of the pyrotechnic elements of much of Hendrix's later playing.

"Highway Chile" was the B-side to "The Wind Cries Mary." The basic tracks for the song were laid down at Olympic Studios on April 3, 1967. Stylistically, the song was a rollicking mixture of rock and electric blues. Here Hendrix used a signature guitar hook that opened the song and was repeated in each chorus section. Structurally, Hendrix paired two

verses before moving to the chorus, and the song progressed through this patter twice with a short guitar solo inserted after the second chorus. The content of the lyrics described a wandering guitar player with a guitar slung across his back who was wronged by a girl and will never settle down. Vaguely autobiographical, the lyrics of "Highway Chile" seemed to describe Hendrix's early life without making direct reference to any specific circumstances.

During May of 1967, the Experience toured around England, went back to Germany, and began expanding their traveling. On May 19, the group made its first appearance in Sweden with three shows in various locations. They then played in Helsinki, Finland, before returning to Sweden for two more shows. The concert in Helsinki was a disaster, and the Experience and its road crew were harassed for their appearance. The group never played in Finland again. The month ended with a multi-act show in Lincolnshire called *Barbeque '67*. This concert also featured Cream, Pink Floyd, Zoot Money, and the Move. The Jimi Hendrix Experience was the headliner and performed for a packed house.

The summer of 1967 was extremely eventful for the Experience. In May, the group released its first full-length album, *Are You Experienced?* The record was issued on the Track imprint in the United Kingdom on May 17, only 12 days after the release of "The Wind Cries Mary" single. In June, the Experience made their U.S. debut by appearing in the Monterey International Pop Festival in Monterey, California. *Are You Experienced?* was released in the United States in August on the Reprise label, and the group toured the United States throughout June, July, and August. The original Track label imprint for the U.K. album front was a picture of the band taken by Bruce Fleming. The Reprise-imprint release in the United States was fronted by a circular picture of the group with a pale green background and a list of tracks, with another band picture on the back.

Are You Experienced? was recorded in London over the course of several months, October 1966 to April 1967. Chandler was the producer on the record and Dave Siddle was the engineer at De Lane Lea

Studios. The record was mastered at Olympic Studios by Eddie Kramer and was released on May 17 in the United Kingdom. *Are You Experienced?* was a smash hit and spent 33 weeks on the charts, peaking at number two, behind the Beatles' *Sgt. Pepper's Lonely Hearts Club Band*. The record was then released in the United States on the Reprise imprint on August 8, strangely, with a slightly different song list. Stylistically, the album contained solid rhythm section playing that served as a backdrop to Hendrix's guitar mastery, often soaked in feedback. Lyrical content ran from love, to loss, to science fiction.

A month after *Are You Experienced?* was released in the United Kingdom, the single "Purple Haze" with B-side "The Wind Cries Mary" was released in the United States. Now that the Experience had conquered the United Kingdom, it was time for them to invade the United States. The band's takeover began with an appearance at the Monterey International Pop Festival on June 18. Earlier in the day, the Who had played a blistering set that Hendrix feared would upstage his own band. After the Who, the Grateful Dead played, and then the Jimi Hendrix Experience took the stage. Hendrix pulled out all the stops and used every one of his tricks accumulated over the course of trying to get noticed early in his career. He played with his teeth and behind his back, and he created great waves of feedback sliding the neck of his guitar over his mic stand and on the edge of his amplifier cabinets. Noel and Mitch matched Hendrix's energy, and the Experience put on a set that remains remarkable 40 years later.

After making a huge impression at Monterey, the Jimi Hendrix Experience spent the summer of 1967 touring the United States. From June 20 to June 24, the Experience took up residence at the Fillmore West in San Francisco, California. They followed this with other California shows, playing in Santa Barbara and then moving on to Los Angeles for a night at the storied Whisky a Go Go.

Riding the wave of success from the early singles and successful U.K. and U.S. tours, the Jimi Hendrix Experience returned to London in the fall of 1967 for the purpose of going into the studio to cut their sophomore album. Enshrined in London's Olympic Studios, the trio set about the work of recording new songs. In the studio for this record were Hendrix, Noel, and Mitch, along with Chandler handling production and "song shortening" duties. Eddie Kramer was the engineer of record for all the sessions and George Chkiantz was tape operator. The product of the work done by all over the next several months was *Axis: Bold as Love,* the second official Jimi Hendrix Experience album, which was released in the United Kingdom on Track in December of 1967 and on Reprise in the United States in January of 1968. The record went to number five in the United Kingdom, where it sat on the charts for 16 weeks, and to number three in the United States, where it charted for 43 weeks. The album was released in a gatefold sleeve that allowed the full album art to be viewed when the jacket was unfolded. The image was of the Hindu devotional painting called "Viraat Purushan-Vishnuroopam," which illustrated the various forms of Vishnu with Hendrix, Noel, and Mitch's faces superimposed. The inside of the gatefold sleeve was a large black-and-white image of the group painted by Roger Law. The U.S. issue on the Reprise label included lyrics for each song surrounding the painting. The style of playing on the record was an amplification of the first album. Here Hendrix also continued to lyrically explore his fascination with science fiction, love, and relationships.

Musically, the song "Burning of the Midnight Lamp" contained several additions to the typical Experience power trio. Hendrix added a harpsichord line to broaden the sound of the usual three pieces. Mitch's drums were phased, meaning that the recorded drum sound was split into two signals and altered to allow for the effect that the sound was sweeping back and forth from one speaker to the other. The session engineers Eddie Kramer and George Chkiantz created this effect for the song. About phasing, Hendrix reportedly said, "That's the sound I've been hearing in my dreams" (Glebbeek and Noble 1996, 59). A unique feature of the song was that after the section containing lyrics was complete, the group ripped into an equally long instrumental section with soaring guitar lines and pounding rhythm section accompaniment. The song actually seemed to come to a close before reaching new heights in this second section. The song faded out at over 4 minutes, drawing the second Jimi Hendrix album to a close. In April 1968, Jim Miller reviewed this album for *Rolling Stone* magazine, and amid an uneven and at times unflattering review called Hendrix "the Charlie Mingus of Rock" and said that "*Axis* demonstrates conclusively that he is one of rock's greatest guitar players in his mastery and exploration of every conceivable gimmick" (quoted in Potash 1996, 55).

After *Axis: Bold as Love* sessions were complete, the Experience resumed their aggressive live-show schedule in earnest. In early November, the Experience played at Manchester University, then hopped a plane to Rotterdam to film the TV show *Hoepla* in the afternoon, followed by an evening show as part of the *Hippy Happy Event*. The group then returned to London for a show at Sussex University in Brighton with the band Ten Years After.

Next, the Experience kicked off a 15-day tour of the United Kingdom with Pink Floyd, the Move, Amen Corner, the Nice, the Outer Limit, and Eire Apparent. With the package tour in place, the six bands played a series of venues. The tour was a grind with only five days off in a month. The Experience spent the rest of December in London with Hendrix playing jam sessions at the Speakeasy Club. On December 22, the group played a holiday concert called *Christmas on Earth* in London, with Eric Burdon and the Animals, the Who, Pink Floyd, the Move, Soft Machine, and Tomorrow. At the dawn of 1968, Hendrix was still in London playing in jam sessions at the Speakeasy and Klook's Kleek.

On January 5, the Experience embarked on an outing to Sweden and Denmark warming up for their next American tour. Next, the group began a series of West Coast shows with a concert at the Fillmore West. On February 12, 1968, Hendrix was back in his hometown of Seattle, Washington, to play at the Seattle Center Arena. The February shows then carried the Experience to Colorado, Texas, New York, Pennsylvania, Michigan, Toronto, and Wisconsin before returning to New York. On March 2, the Experience

played Hunter College in New York with the Troggs, whose song "Wild Thing" Hendrix had been covering (quite famously at Monterey) for quite some time.

On April 12, the album *Smash Hits* was released in the United Kingdom. The record was issued by Track Records as a means to fill the gap in between new Experience albums as *Axis: Bold as Love* had been released in December of 1967. *Smash Hits* contained little new material and was not sanctioned by the group. The *Smash Hits* release was technically the Jimi Hendrix Experience's third album, but because it was a greatest hits type of release it was not a true third release. Track was looking to cash in on the international success of the band, but the Experience was still working on the songs that would become their third album of new material, *Electric Ladyland*.

The Experience spent most of the second half of April in the studio. They recorded "Long Hot Summer Night," "Little Miss Strange," "South Saturn Delta," "1983 . . . (A Merman I Should Turn to Be)," "Moon Turns the Tides . . . Gently Gently Away," and "Gypsy Eyes" at the Record Plant through the middle of the month. Throughout these sessions, Hendrix worked at a maddening speed, outpacing the staff at the record plant. He was now exerting significant control over his own sound, song choice, structure, and lyric content. This ever-growing individuality and creative control was often putting him at odds with Chandler, whose job (as producer) had been to control these dynamics. By the end of May 1968, Chandler relinquished his creative control on Hendrix and stopped working as his producer. He continued as a comanager, but stopped being with Hendrix on a day-to-day basis.

Just prior to the official launch of the U.S. tour, the Experience were called to Europe for a pair of important dates. On July 6, they played the second Woburn Music Festival with T-Rex, Geno Washington, and the Family. The concert was a sellout and an enormous success, with approximately 14,000 audience members. The second special European show was on July 18 at a new club called the Sgt. Pepper Club in Palma, Majorca, Spain. The Experience was the first band to play the new venue as it was opened by Chandler and Jeffery.

The tour began in earnest on July 30 with a show at Independence Hall in Baton Rouge, Louisiana. After several other Louisiana dates, the tour moved on to Texas for four shows. The Experience then played Illinois, Iowa, and Maryland. Prior to the August 17 show at Municipal Auditorium in Georgia, the band Vanilla Fudge was added to the package. According to several reports from the time, Vanilla Fudge was not a welcome addition to the tour. Instead, they were brought on by the demands of the Mafia. The Fudge was connected to the mob, and essentially forced their way onto the tour for the Southern and West Coast legs. Although Vanilla Fudge was on the tour through August and early September, they had little to do with the other bands and were kept separate by their handlers.

With the package now including four bands (the Jimi Hendrix Experience, Soft Machine, Eire Apparent, and Vanilla Fudge), the tour continued. The bands next moved to Florida, Virginia, New York, Connecticut, and Massachusetts. These dates included several stadium shows and the New York Rock Festival on August 23 with the Chamber Brothers, Janis Joplin with Big Brother and the Holding Company, and the other packaged bands. By the end of the month, the tour moved west through Utah and Colorado. In early September the bands played six venues in California and shows in Arizona and British Columbia. On September 6, Hendrix was able to again return home with a tour stop in Seattle for a concert at the Seattle Center Coliseum. In the midst of all this, "All Along the Watchtower" with B-side "Burning of the Midnight Lamp" was released on September 2 as a U.S. single.

By early October of 1968, Hendrix and the Experience were showing signs of wear in the wake of an aggressive touring and recording schedule. It was now obvious that Noel was chaffing under the control that Hendrix exerted over the band's sound. In fact, at the end of the summer, Noel had begun to form his own band with a group of players he knew from his pre-Experience days. Noel's new band would go on to play under the name Fat Mattress. With Noel's time now progressively being split between the two groups, the end of the original Experience began to

seem imminent. This situation was exacerbated by Hendrix continually jamming with non-Experience artists—even bringing them into the studio to record with the group. The Experience unwound slowly over the next following six months. During that period, Fat Mattress even served as an opening act for the Experience. Hendrix was aware of the distance desired by Noel. Although it seemed like the beginning of the end, the anticipated separation was considered by the group to be a positive move geared toward reinvigorating the band and allowing them to come back together later at even greater potency.

The creation of Fat Mattress began as an attempt to improve the relationship between Hendrix and Noel. This was attested to by Hendrix's involvement in the Fat Mattress recording sessions. Hendrix even played percussion on the Fat Mattress song "How Can I Live?" Chandler took Fat Mattress on and got them a record deal through Polydor as another sign that this musical diversification was originally intended to benefit the Experience and its members and not to lead to the group's ultimate demise. Even as the bedrock foundation of the Experience was being tested, Eddie Kramer wrapped up the session tapes for the *Electric Ladyland* album and sent them off to mastering. The new album was issued on September 17 in the United States and on October 25 in the United Kingdom—with a different cover design.

The *Electric Ladyland* album was released separately in the United Kingdom and the United States, as were the band's first two records. The U.S. version was released on Reprise with a gatefold album sleeve. Unlike *Axis: Bold as Love,* the new record needed the gatefold sleeve as it was a double album. The U.S. cover was a head shot of Hendrix in mid-performance with red and orange coloring on a black background. The inside of the gatefold listed the name of the band, the name of the album, the track list for each record, the musicians who appeared and their instrument specialization, and the production credits—Hendrix was listed as producer and director.

At the beginning of the year, the group again returned to England and Hendrix settled in with Kathy Etchingham at 23 Brook Street. The group had an existing run of shows booked as well an appearance on the television show *Happening for Lulu*. They played the TV show on January 4. They were not alone on the bill as the Iveys (who would go on to be the group Badfinger) also appeared. The Experience was slated to play "Hey Joe," but Hendrix made an abrupt change—on live television—and sent the band into Cream's "Sunshine of Your Love." This caused some confusion on stage and pushed the producers of the show into a fit. With this, the Experience kicked off 1969 in England.

The Experience began another swing through Europe on January 8 at Lorensberg Cirkus in Göteborg, Sweden, with support from Amen Corner and Burning Red Ivanhoe. Chandler turned up to see the group play and Hendrix asked him to return to the band's management. Chandler declined the offer, but the olive branch had been extended. The tour then played in Stockholm with Jethro Tull, and Copenhagen before moving on to Germany. In Germany the band played a series of dates supported by Erie Apparent. While in Germany, Hendrix met Monika Dannemann, who according to Hendrix "managed to turn my life upside down, and it would never be the same again" (quoted in Glebbeek and Noble 1996, 79). Next the Experience moved into France for a show in Strasbourg, then Vienna and Berlin before a two-night stand at the Royal Albert Hall in London—supported by Fat Mattress, Van der Graaf Generator, and Soft Machine. Beginning with these shows, Fat Mattress was the support group for the Experience for the next month.

In March, Hendrix returned to the United States and more work in the studio. He recorded at Mercury Sound Studios, in New York, tracking "Blue Window" and "Message to Love." At the Record Plant he tracked "The Star-Spangled Banner" and "Hey Gypsy Boy." Also at the Record Plant, with John McLaughlin, Hendrix worked up "Drivin' South" and "Everything's Gonna Be Alright." At the end of the month, Hendrix made a trip to pursue one of his few non-music passions: the Corvette Stingray. On March 29, Hendrix flew to Los Angeles to take delivery of his latest Corvette.

The summer began with the Experience completely worn out from the road, recording, and internal band strife. Hendrix continued to pursue his dream studio with work on Electric Lady Studios continuing as money allowed—strange for an internationally renowned recording artist, but an indication of the problems Hendrix was having with his management. In an effort to recharge, Hendrix booked himself into a room in the Beverly Rodeo Hotel, Beverly Hills, where he spent time working out songs, doing interviews, and occasionally leaving to jam with various local musicians.

The 1969 American tour concluded with the Denver Pop Festival at Mile High Stadium in Denver, Colorado, on June 29. The 30,000 people in attendance witnessed the final concert by the Jimi Hendrix Experience in its original incarnation, as Hendrix had announced the day prior that he was expanding the band. An oddity of this was that Hendrix did not formally remove Noel. Instead he made public that "his bassist will be former Army buddy Billy Cox, but Noel Redding and Mitch Mitchell are not necessarily out of the band" (Black 1999, 194). Although Hendrix did not formally remove Noel, he also did not make all of his intentions clear to his original bassist. The Experience took the stage and during their set the crowd came through the barriers. The police intervened and tear gas was deployed into the crowd. A riot ensued and the band was rushed off stage and whisked away in the back of a truck. After the group got to safety, Noel told Hendrix that he was leaving the band. With the chaos of the Denver Pop Festival, the Jimi Hendrix Experience, as the collective of Hendrix, Noel, and Mitch, came to an end. Noel quickly departed for London while Mitch stayed on to work with Hendrix in whatever capacity that he could.

Amid the tumult of the summer of 1969, Hendrix recognized that he still had a great deal of work to do. His dreams of building his own studio were slowly coming to fruition, but the construction was often slowed by lack of a direct money stream. Further, Hendrix now needed to build a new band. He had Mitch waiting in the wings and Miles and Cox were ready to work with him on short notice—regardless of how his management felt about it. In addition, Hendrix had been jamming with a percussionist named Geraldo "Jerry" Velez. In fact, Hendrix was looking to make his new expanded band quite large—with two percussionists. The other was Juma Sultan, who brought more of a traditional African approach in his drumming.

Although the future of the Experience was unknown, Hendrix went into rehearsals in preparation for the Woodstock music festival. The rain delays and deteriorating stage conditions at Woodstock are well documented. Hendrix was slated to close the festival with the Experience. Instead, the group surrounding him was called the Band of Gypsys and included Mitch (drums), Billy Cox (bass, backing vocals), Larry Lee (rhythm guitar), Juma Sultan (percussion), and Jerry Velez (percussion). The group's set culminated in Hendrix's famous rendition of "The Star-Spangled Banner."

By early 1970, Hendrix's group the Band of Gypsys was not the same outfit that played Woodstock; by October it was Hendrix, Miles, and Cox. Throughout the month of November, Hendrix and his new rhythm section tracked the songs that would become the next chapter of his musical journey. Recording of the songs "Izabella," "Ezy Ryder," "Shame, Shame, Shame," and "Room Full of Mirror" took place at the beginning of the month. After further studio time, the Band of Gypsys played a series of live shows and released a six-song album in June of 1970. With this, the Band of Gypsys were no more.

In the wake of the short-lived Band of Gypsys, Hendrix announced in early February that the Experience was re-forming. In the statement announcing the return of the Experience, Hendrix was careful to note that there would still be time for side projects and that he intended to continue to work with other musicians. Also at this time, work on the Electric Lady Studio construction again halted. Hampered by lack of money, the studio was creating a great financial drain, which was made much worse by the fact that Hendrix had basically stopped playing live shows. By early 1970, the work on building the studio could only progress with a loan from Warner Bros.

Records guaranteed against future royalty earnings. Hendrix really needed his own studio as he was basically in residence at the Record Plant and was racking up enormous studio bills.

With the now-impending reformation of the Experience, Hendrix needed to somehow reconcile his situation with Noel. After the pair had parted company on such bad terms, it seemed unlikely that they would be able to mend their fences. Hendrix turned to Mitch for advice and it was agreed that bringing Noel back into the fold would be tricky—regardless of the fact that it seemed that Noel was game to return. Instead, Hendrix again enlisted the help of Billy Cox. While the new collective was still not the original Experience, it was closer than the three musicians that had formed the Band of Gypsys. This point has led to a great deal of debate concerning what to call the band that Hendrix toured with for the rest of his life. The collection of Hendrix, Mitch, and Cox was sometimes billed as "the New Jimi Hendrix Experience," and on other concert announcements only Hendrix's name appeared.

In April, Hendrix began gearing up for a U.S. tour with Mitch and Cox backing him on stage. Several months of dates were scheduled and the tour was set to kick off in Los Angeles on April 25. The tour commenced at the Forum in Inglewood, California. Hendrix's band was the headliner, and the Buddy Miles Express and Ballin' Jack were the openers. The tour included studio time at Electric Lady Studios and a sojourn to Hawaii for an ill-conceived movie project. After Hawaii and the "official" opening of Electric Lady Studios, the tour continued on to Europe for dates such as the Isle of Wight Festival.

While in Europe in mid-September 1970, Hendrix appeared to be burning out from the road. Hendrix spent time with Monika Dannemann at the Samarkand Hotel for a few days as he planned his future. On the morning of September 18, Dannemann woke before Hendrix and went out for cigarettes. When she returned Hendrix had vomited in bed and she was unable to wake him. She called an ambulance. The paramedics on the scene tried to revive Hendrix without success. He was taken to St. Mary Abbots Hospital where doctors cleared his airway and attempted to resuscitate him. It was reported that Hendrix's stomach contents contained quite a bit of red wine and that he had taken sleeping pills before bed. At age 27 Hendrix was pronounced dead by Dr. John Bannister at 12:45 P.M. The official cause of death was inhalation of vomit due to barbiturate intoxication.

When Hendrix died, he had not released a studio album in almost two years. The vault of unreleased material that he, and various other musicians, had recorded during that period represents a substantial catalogue. He had spent countless hours in the studio with a host of musicians and he left behind a treasure trove of unreleased material. Progressively, since his death, these songs have been coming to light. Immediately following his death, a host of albums were released—some sanctioned, most not. Since then, new songs and new versions of previously released material have continued to surface. As a true testament to Hendrix's songwriting and performing skills, the world continues to wait for future releases. To satisfy this insatiable appetite for all things Jimi Hendrix and the Experience, further releases continue to trickle out of the vaults.

The Jimi Hendrix Experience is very often cited as an influence on other subsequent bands. The bands that have gone on record as having fallen under that influence include: Prince, members of Parliament Funkadelic, members of Red Hot Chili Peppers, De La Soul, A Tribe Called Quest, Digital Underground, Run-DMC, the Beastie Boys, and many others. The band's legacy is well documented through multitudes of awards. Hendrix was voted 1967 Pop Musician of the Year by *Melody Maker* magazine. He was named *Billboard* artist of the year in 1968. *Rolling Stone* included all three of the Jimi Hendrix Experience albums released during Jimi's life among the 500 Greatest Albums of All Time.

David V. Moskowitz

Selected Discography

Are You Experienced?, Track 613 001, 1967.

Axis: Bold as Love, Track 613 003, 1967.

Smash Hits, Track 613 004, 1968.

Electric Ladyland, Track 613 008, 1968.

Band of Gypsys, Track 2406 002, 1970.

Woodstock, Cotillion SD 35000, 1970.

Isle of Wight, Polydor 2302 016, 1971.

References

Black, Johnny. *Jimi Hendrix: The Ultimate Experience.* New York: Thunder's Mouth Press, 1999.

Glebbeek, Caesar, and Douglas J. Noble. *Jimi Hendrix: The Man, the Music, the Memorabilia.* New York: Thunder's Mouth Press, 1996.

Jimi Hendrix Official Website. 2015. "Life." Accessed November 2014. www.jimihendrix.com/us/jimi.

McDermott, John with Eddie Kramer. *Hendrix: Setting the Record Straight.* ed. Mark Lewisohn. New York: Grand Central Publishing, 1992.

Perone, James. *Woodstock: An Encyclopedia of the Music and Art Fair.* Westport, CT: Greenwood Press, 2005.

Potash, Chris. *The Jimi Hendrix Companion: Three Decades of Commentary.* New York: Schirmer Books, 1996.

Shapiro, Harry, and Ceasar Glebbeek. *Jimi Hendrix: Electric Gypsy.* New York: St. Martin's Griffin Press, 1995.

Journey (1973–Present)

Journey is one of the most popular rock bands of the past 30 years. They have maintained a spot in current popular culture and continue to tour to this day. The band has attained 19 top 40 singles and 25 gold and platinum albums. Journey's album *Greatest Hits* (1988) has sold over 25 million copies and has been certified platinum 15 times, making it the best-selling compilation in music history. Journey's music has stayed in the public's ear through its appearance on popular television shows including *Glee, Family Guy,* and the finale episode of *The Sopranos,* which featured Journey's 1981 song "Don't Stop Believin'."

The original band was formed in 1973. The only founding and constant member of Journey has been Neal Schon, the lead guitarist. At the age of 15, Neal Schon (born Neal George Joseph Schon, February 27, 1954; lead guitars/backing vocals) quit high school and left his home in Oklahoma to be a

American rock band Journey in 1981. From left to right: Ross Valory, Steve Perry, Neal Schon, Jonathan Cain, and Steve Smith. Journey is indisputably one of the most popular rock bands of the mid-1970s. The band has 25 gold or platinum albums and has sold over 25 million records with its special breed of arena-friendly rock. (Photo by Chris Walter/ WireImage)

professional guitarist. Schon credits his early start to playing the Keystone Korner Club in San Francisco every Tuesday night. On Tuesdays, the club had a jam night for guitar players from all across the Bay Area. It was here that he was introduced to Elvin Bishop and Michael Bloomfield, both famous American Blues guitarists. By the age of 17 he was touring and recording with the band Santana.

In early 1973, the manager for Santana, Walter "Herbie" Herbert (born Walter James Herbert II, February 5, 1948; manager) approached Schon about forming a new band in the San Francisco Bay area. Schon agreed to the idea and joined with Ross Valory (born Ross Lamont Valory, February 2, 1949; bass, backing vocals) and George Tickner (born George Tyndall Tickner, September 8, 1946; rhythm guitar). Both men were members of a local band

called Frumious Bandersnatch. They added Prairie Prince (born Charles Lempriere Prince, May 7, 1950; drums) as the final piece of the new band. The first incarnation of the band was an all-instrumental group called the Golden Gate Rhythm Section (GGRS), which had a strong following in the Bay area. The initial goal of GGRS was to be the first call studio team in San Francisco to back up any performers and to be one of the best jam bands. There are two different stories about how the band went from GGRS to Journey. One is a contest by a local FM station, KSAN, which is credited with coming up with the name. The real story is that a roadie by the name of John Villanueva came up with "Journey."

By the summer of 1973, Santana keyboardist Gregg Rolie (born Gregg Alan Rolie, June 17, 1948) joined the band. On New Year's Eve of 1973, Journey made their live debut at San Francisco's Winterland Ballroom in front of 10,000 people. The next day they went on to play for an audience of 100,000 people at the Sunshine Festival in Hawaii. At this time the band was developing a mostly instrumental, progressive rock and jazz-rock sound that included improvised solos from each of the members. Two months later, drummer Prince left the group to pursue a career with the Tubes and was replaced by Aynsley Dunbar (born Aynsley Thomas Dunbar, January 10, 1946; drums). Dunbar had previously performed with Jeff Beck, Frank Zappa, and John Lennon. On February 5, 1974, the new members made their debut at the Great American Music Hall. Later that year, Tickner also left the group to earn a medical degree at Stanford Medical School. Tickner's exit left all guitar duties to Schon, orienting the sound of the band around the solo guitar.

The group signed with Columbia Records in November of 1974. Journey's first three albums, *Journey* (1975), *Look into the Future* (1976), and *Next* (1977), were representative of their jazz-rock sound that was almost exclusively instrumental. In addition to recording three albums in three years, the band also maintained a demanding touring schedule and was on the road nine months of the year. Despite touring extensively and selling records, the profits were not sufficient for the label, and Journey was asked to hire a full-time vocalist.

Robert Fleischman (born March 11, unknown year) was the first vocalist to join Journey and toured with the band in the summer of 1977. Fleischman also contributed as a lyricist by cowriting "Wheel in the Sky," and "Winds of March" with Neal Schon. In November of 1977, Fleischman was fired by Herbert and was replaced by a young singer named Steve Perry (born Stephen Ray Perry, January 22, 1949; lead vocals), who was brought in on the recommendation of a Columbia Records executive. Perry was the former frontman for the band Alien Project and had left the group, almost giving up music entirely, due to the sudden death of the bassist, Richard Michaels.

The switch to the pop-rock sound associated with Journey's music today happened in 1978 with the addition of Perry's vocals to the music on their fourth album, *Infinity*. Roy Thomas Baker, who was brought in to give the band a new sound, produced the album. Baker had previously worked with Queen and was considered to be the secret weapon for the album. *Infinity* immediately went platinum and stayed on the *Billboard* charts for over two years, reaching number 21 on the *Billboard* 200 album chart. The two breakout singles for this album were "Wheel in the Sky" and "Lights." The album has sold over three million copies to date. Schon and Perry collaborated on five of the tracks and wrote "Lights" together in 40 minutes. Journey drummer, Aynsley Dunbar, was not happy with the direction the band was heading and left to join Jefferson Starship. Journey immediately hired former drum roadie Steve Smith (born Steve Elliott Smith, August 21, 1954; drums).

Journey's next album, *Evolution,* was released in 1979, leading to the band's first top 30 single, "Lovin, Touchin', Squeezin'." *Evolution* reached number 16 in July of 1979, and became the band's second million-selling album. This was the beginning of a successful output of hit albums for Journey. This same year, Journey recorded a song for Budweiser that was featured in several of their commercials. Their popularity skyrocketed. Less than a year later, in 1980, Journey's album *Departure* was released. This became their first top 10 album and included the single "Any Way You Want It." The single reached a height of number eight on *Billboard*.

The next year, Journey released its fourth consecutive platinum recording, *Captured,* which was recorded live during the 1980 *Departure* world tour. After the release of *Captured,* founding member Gregg Rolie left Journey to start a family and was replaced by Jonathan Cain (born February 26, 1950; keyboards). Cain was originally a member of the band the Babys, but on the recommendation of Rolie, he left his band and joined Journey. Cain was an important addition to the band. He believed his job was "to define Journey, to give it a conscience and a heart, and write songs for the people who adored the band." Cain considered himself to be a songwriter first and a keyboard player second. Once again Journey developed a new sound, which included Cain's use of a synthesizer and his talent as a songwriter. Schon, Perry, and Cain worked together to create the defining Journey sound. As a result of their teamwork, the pinnacle of Journey's success came with the release of *Escape (E5C4P3)* in 1981.

Escape produced three top 10 hits and was the group's first chart-topping number-one album. It spent over a year on the top 40 chart and has been certified platinum eight times. The three top 10 singles from this album are some of Journey's best-known songs: "Don't Stop Believin'" reached number eight, "Who's Crying Now" reached number nine, and "Open Arms" reached the number-two spot in January of 1982. "Open Arms" was the first songwriting collaboration between Perry and Cain and became the band's signature song during the 1980s. In 1983, Journey released a follow-up album to *Escape* titled *Frontiers*. Following on the success of *Escape*, *Frontiers* reached and stayed at number two on the *Billboard* album chart for nine weeks. "Separate Ways" was the one hit single from *Frontiers*, and it reached number eight on the *Billboard* singles chart in February of 1983.

The success of *Frontiers* and *Escape* cemented Journey's place in pop-rock music history. The last four shows on the *Escape* tour changed the standards for video and audio production in concerts. The band implemented computerized lighting and added giant video monitors to the sides of the stage for the fans in the back of the stadiums—for the first time all audience members could see the band perform up close. Journey could be seen on MTV, heard in commercials, and was featured in video games. In 1983, the video game company Bally Midway released an arcade game called *Escape*. Fans and nonfans alike helped the band members retrieve their instruments from different planets in order for them to perform a concert at the end.

Much of Journey's success can be credited to the addition of Steve Perry. The group went from a well-known rock band to international superstars. Perry's voice gave the band its defining sound, and his songwriting skills helped create several of their chart-topping singles, including "Lights," "Who's Crying Now," and "Separate Ways (Worlds Apart)." *Rolling Stone* magazine has placed Perry as number 76 in their Top 100 Greatest Singers list. His voice influenced many singers, including Chris Daughtry and Rob Thomas. In a 2011 interview, Neal Schon was asked to summarize Perry's contribution to the band's legacy:

> Steve Perry is an amazing singer, one of the best ever, in the world . . . He knew exactly what he loved, and he could really do it like nobody's business. I love what he brought to the band because of the mixture with my playing; my job was to bring the rough edge to everything. When Jon and Steve wrote, it was all melody, beautiful songwriting. I loved that Perry brought the soul factor in with the rock, it made it sound to me way different than what we used to get categorized as. (Waddell 2011)

Despite huge commercial success, critics were not always impressed with Journey's output. *Rolling Stone* reviewer Deborah Frost reviewed *Escape* in 1981:

> "Who's Crying Now," the hit single off Journey's hit LP, isn't super hip, super deep or even real, real hooky. But it does sound good. What I'm talking about is the way the song's soft, soapy bass redeems its soft, dopey sentiment by diving beneath tiny fillips of acoustic guitar and bubbling up around a dream-sized dollop of fat harmonies. Every shimmery cymbal tick pays tribute to the state of modern engineering. The funny part is that Journey's current success doesn't have much to do with the hard-rock pose they've been trying to fool us with for nearly eight years now. Instead, *Escape* is a triumph of professionalism, a veritable march of the well-versed schmaltz stirrers. Then again, when heroes are hard to find, the first thing you'll see are the showoffs. On second (or is that third?) thought, maybe there really are a lot of "streetlight people" out there. If so, my guess is that they'll soon glow out of it. (Frost 1981)

Even in the 1992 *Rolling Stone Album Guide, Escape* and *Frontiers* received two and a half stars out of a possible five. The "albums in the two-star category either fall below an artist's established standard or are, in and of themselves, failures." Mark Coleman, a *Rolling Stone* record reviewer since 1980, claims Journey's albums to be:

> chrome synthesizer plating, super-charged vocal capacity, dependable rhythmic drive, white-wall guitar flash: Journey's slick, comfortable sound is custom-built for the expressway. There's a unifying blandness to Journey's work: the individual albums are largely interchangeable. Despite the group's popularity and undeniable influence, the memory of Journey quickly faded. (Coleman 1992)

There were many disputes among band members during the years 1984 to 1989. The numerous creative differences resulted in solo experiments, members departing, and the eventual breakup of the band. By 1986 there were only three members of Journey: Perry, Schon, and Cain. Many conflicts arose around the time of the release of *Frontiers*. Due to being on the road constantly, personal relationships started to suffer. Perry commented on the strain of success in a 2006 interview: "What happens is relationships suffer because they need attention, they need support, too. But at some point your music is your girlfriend and the performing is your girlfriend and she really needs all of your time and you cannot give her anything short of that" (Sharp 2006). Cain had coproduced and cowritten an album with his wife and wanted to explore new possibilities. By this point, Schon had recorded two albums, *Untold Passion* (1981) and *Here to Stay* (1982), with Czechoslovakian composer and pianist Jan Hammer (born April 17, 1948). Perry was also exploring other options and recorded a single with Kenny Loggins called "Don't Fight It" (1982). When the Frontiers tour wrapped up, Schon recorded a live album, *Through the Fire,* with another band, HSAS (Hagar Schon Aaronson Shrieve). HSAS was short-lived, lasting one year. Drummer Steve Smith

also recorded a separate jazz album, *Vital Information* (1983), with a band of the same name. In 1984, Perry recorded a solo album, *Street Talk,* which resulted in a platinum album and the popular single "Oh Sherrie." The next year, Perry fired drummer Steve Smith and bassist Ross Valory due to creative differences. Smith and Valory went on to create their own group and teamed up with Gregg Rolie, Keving Chalfant, and Josh Ramos to form the Storm.

Despite members going their own ways and recording solo projects, Journey released a new album in 1986, *Raised on Radio*. The sound of the album was unlike any of the band's previous albums. The new sound was partly due to the new studio musicians brought in for the record. Ross Valory had been replaced by Randy Jackson (born June 23, 1956; bass), and Steve Smith was replaced by Mike Baird (born May 18, 1951; drums). The band's sound was now more heavily influenced by R&B rather than the synthesizer, guitar-heavy, rock-influenced sound of its previous records. "Be Good to Yourself" was the one top 10 single, reaching number nine on the charts. In 1987, Schon, Cain, and Perry all won awards at the Bay Area Music Awards, but this would be the last time all three would appear together for several years. In 1988, Journey released their best-selling album *Greatest Hits/Best of Journey,* which has become the best-selling compilation of all time. The record also served as a memorial to the history of the band. Journey officially disbanded in 1989 to allow band members to pursue individual projects.

Once Journey had completely finished, Cain and Schon were free to form Bad English with ex-Babys vocalist John Waite (born July 4, 1952). The new group recorded two albums and recorded the hit single "When I See You Smile." After the second album Schon left with drummer Deen Castronovo (born August 17, 1965; drums) to form the short-lived group Hardline. Journey briefly reunited in 1991 for a memorial concert for San Francisco area promoter Bill Graham. This reunion included previous band members Schon, Cain, and Perry. A second reunion happened in 1993 (minus Perry) at a concert honoring Journey's manager Walter Herbert. Other than the reunion, Perry would remain in seclusion until his 1994 solo album, *For the Love of Strange Medicine.* Schon, Cain, and Perry joined forces once more to create a new Journey album in 1996. The trio wrote all of the songs in just two weeks, and the result was *Trial by Fire,* a million-selling album featuring the top 20 single "When You Love a Woman." The new album debuted at number three, and the single earned the band their first Grammy nomination. After the release, Journey was set to start a 25-date tour and Perry moved to Hawaii to get in shape. Unfortunately, the tour never took place due to Perry's degenerative bone disease, which required hip-replacement surgery. Perry's departure was perceived to be the end of Journey.

In 1998, Schon, Cain, and Valory decided they wanted to keep Journey moving forward. Deen Castronovo was hired to be the new drummer. Along with being the drummer for Bad English, Castronovo had previously worked with artists such as Ozzy Osbourne, Paul Rodgers, and Geezer Butler of Black Sabbath. Steve Augeri (born January 30, 1954) was brought in to be the new vocalist. Augeri was the former front man for the bands Tyketto and Tall Stories. Despite a strong resemblance in appearance and sound, most fans missed Steve Perry. In a 2012 interview Cain claimed, "I was worried about him [Augeri] getting shot. We took a lot of flack. We used to get hate mail. Somebody got my number and would call me: 'You song of a bitch!' They were reading us the riot act because how dare us be Journey without Steve Perry?" (Appleford 2012). The same year, the new group recorded "Remember Me" for the movie *Armageddon.* Then in 2001, Journey released their 11th studio album, *Arrival.* The single "All the Way" became a minor hit in the adult contemporary category. In 2003, they released a four-track album titled *Red 13* that featured fan art on the cover.

In 2005, Journey released their 12th album, *Generations.* This unique album features every member of the band performing lead vocals on at least one track. After the release of *Generations,* the group embarked on a 30th-anniversary tour. The tour included 3-hour-plus shows that highlighted the band's entire career. The 30th-anniversary year culminated in the group receiving a star on the Hollywood Walk of Fame.

In July of 2006, Augeri developed a throat infection. Once again, Journey had to find a new singer. Jeff Scott Soto (born November 4, 1965) was a former member of the Talisman. Soto's career in Journey was short-lived. His first appearance as lead vocalist was on July 7, 2006. The band announced on June 12, 2007, that he would no longer be the lead singer; they wanted to move in a new direction. At this same time "Don't Stop Believin'" had reached the number 30 spot on the *iTunes Top Songs* list after being heard on *The Sopranos'* finale on June 10.

Still wanting to further Journey's career, Neal Schon began his search for a new front man. Schon did not want to find a new singer in the usual audition process; he thought it was too expensive and time consuming and also did not trust CD recordings, claiming anyone could sound great using Pro Tools. Using a nightly ritual of searching YouTube, Schon began his search for a new lead singer. Schon describes his process and discovery in a 2008 interview for the magazine *Guitar Player.*

Once I checked out YouTube for a second, I loved it. I loved the idea of watching clips of people performing in truly live setting. I punched in the words "male vocalist rock and soul" and looked at everybody until finally, after about two or three days, I fell upon a clip of Arnel. He was doing a Survivor song. It was a tough tune with lots of vibrato and high held notes, and it was all live. I was like, "wow, this guy's amazing. If it sounds this good through a funky little condenser mike in a club in Manila streaming across the 'Net through my computer speakers, then the guy's got some serious pipes." At first I couldn't believe how good he sounded— I thought perhaps I was delirious from being online for three days—so I left, got some dinner, came back, and watched some more clips, and he still sounded insanely good. (Gold 2008)

Neal Schon decided to call Arnel Pineda (born September 5, 1967). Pineda had been performing with a 1980s cover band called the Zoo in Manila. Pineda's voice was remarkably close to that of Steve Perry's.

When Pineda first received the call from Schon he thought it was a prank and demanded that Schon call from a webcam. Six weeks later Pineda was flown out to San Francisco to audition for Schon and Cain and was immediately hired.

On June 3, 2008, Journey introduced their new lead singer to the world with the release of their 14th studio album, *Revelation*. Along with having a new front man, this album earned the band its biggest first-week sales in over a decade and debuted at number five on the *Billboard* album chart and at number one on *Billboard*'s independent album chart. Schon and Cain cowrote the album and achieved a balance between the familiar and the new. *Revelation* was also the first studio album Journey recorded that was not released on Columbia Records. Instead, Neal Schon released it on his own personal label, Nomota LLC. The album was a two-disc recording featuring new songs and rerecordings of their hits, including "Faithfully," "Who's Crying Now," and "Open Arms," all featuring Pineda as the lead vocalist.

After the release, Journey embarked on a two-year world tour showing off their new vocalist. Pineda's sudden fame proved to be difficult at first. Pineda was nervous before the first show of the tour; he turned to Schon and told him he wanted to back out. Schon replied that it was too late to back out now and pushed him onto the stage. In a 2008 *Rolling Stone* interview, Pineda spoke about missing his girlfriend and son, the grueling pace of the tour, and how he would sometimes break down and cry. Journey also had to deal with the backlash to the new, foreign singer. The band received racist messages and negative reactions to hiring a Filipino and for attempting to have another Perry replacement. Fans called Pineda garbage, copycat, and a monkey. There were also some good moments on the tour. The most notable stop occurred on March 14, 2009, when Journey played for 30,000 people in Pineda's hometown of Manila.

Journey found renewed life with the addition of Pineda's voice. During the world tour, the group started to write new songs together. The chemistry of the group inspired the album *Eclipse* or *ECL1P53*. The album was released on May 24, 2011. This new recording featured the songwriting skills of Pineda, Schon, and Cain. They decided as a group not to rehearse the material before recording in order for the tracks to have a more impromptu sound. Cain describes the record as "a concept record with some spiritual themes to it . . . pretty tough, hard-hitting stuff. The concept of Eclipse is the tantric way of looking at life—the concept of the album was about belief and enlightenment" (Journey Official Website 2011). Eclipse reached number 13 on the *Billboard* 200 album chart.

Director Ramona S. Diaz heard of Pineda's pluck from obscurity and wanted to make a film documentary about the new singer for Journey. The result was the 2012 film *Don't Stop Believin': Everyman's Journey*. This movie depicts the journey of Pineda from his Third World life in Manila to being the lead singer for Journey and the large impact on the American Filipino community. There is also a depiction of the parallels happening in the early 1980s between Journey's success and Pineda's life as a homeless child after the death of his mother. The older members of Journey have nothing but praise for their new singer. Every night they play, each is stunned that Pineda can sing all their songs just as well as Perry did. The band's tours are selling out all over the world, and most of the response to Pineda has been positive. Throughout the 40 years of Journey's presence on the music scene, they have continued to have significant influence on subsequent generations of musicians. The band's high sales records have earned it a permanent place in rock and roll history. Even today Journey can be heard on television and current popular radio stations, and Journey continues to tour for packed arenas around the world. Journey is seemingly unstoppable.

Jennifer Wagner

Selected Discography

Journey, Columbia Records PC 33388, 1975.

Next, Columbia Records PC 34311, 1977.

Infinity, Columbia Records HC 44912, 1978.

Evolution, Columbia Records PCT-35797, 1979.

Departure, Columbia Records FCA 36339, 1980.

Captured, Columbia Records KC 237016, 1981.

Escape, Columbia Records HC 47408, 1981.

Frontiers, CBS AL 38504, 1983.

Greatest Hits, Columbia Records CK 44493, 1988.

Trial by Fire, Columbia Records 82876 858932, 1996.

Arrival, Columbia Records CK 69864, 2001.

Revelation, Nomota LLC 4506–2, 2008.

Eclipse, Nomota LLC N0104, 2011.

References

Coleman, Mark. *The Rolling Stone Album Guide: Completely New Reviews: Every Essential Album, Every Essential Artist.* Edited by Anthony DeCurtis, James Henke, and Holly George-Warren. New York: Random House, 1992.

Diaz, Ramona S. *Don't Stop Believin': Everyman's Journey.* DVD. New York: New Video Group, 2012.

Frost, Deborah. "Journey: Escape." *Rolling Stone Online,* October 29, 1981. Accessed October 16, 2012. http://www.rollingstone.com/music/albumreviews/escape-19811029.

Gold, Jude. "Phoenix Rising." *Guitar Player* 42.11 (2008): 95–100, 102, 105–106, 108, 110, 113–14, 191.

Greene, Andy. "R&R: Sad 'Journey' for New Singer." *Rolling Stone* (Oct 2008): 24.

Haid, Mike. "Deen Castronovo: The Journey of a Decade, the Career of a Lifetime." *Modern Drummer* 32:8 (2008): 76–80, 82–83, 85, 87, 89–90.

Journey Official Website. 2015. "Band Biography." Accessed July 2014. www.journeymusic.com/pages/theband.

Lindblad, Peter. "The Musical Journey of Neal Schon." *Goldmine* 39:2 (2013): 52–55.

Reesman, Bryan. "Journey's Wheels Keep on Turnin': Side Projects, Revisiting Old Songs in Concert Keep Band Members Fresh." *Goldmine* 30.24 (2004): 14–15.

Regen, Jon. "Jonathan Cain: Hartfelt Songwriting Propels Journey into the 21st Century." *Keyboard* 34:12 (2008): 30–32, 34, 36.

Rule, Greg. "411 Backstage Pass Journey–Jonathan Cain." *Keyboard* 25:13 (1999): 28.

Sharp, Ken. "Steve Perry Gets Emotional Over 'Live in Houston 1981—Escape Tour.'" *Goldmine* 32.6 (2006): 30.

Waddell, Ray. "Journey's Reward." *Billboard—The International Newsweekly of Music, Video and Home Entertainment* 123:41 (2011): 32, 34.

Judas Priest (1969–Present)

In the first edition of *The Rolling Stone Record Guide,* editor Dave Marsh described Judas Priest as "[g]runting, flailing Seventies hard rock as vulgar as its name, but less euphonious" (Marsh 1979). He went on to warn listeners that Judas Priest is for "lovers of recycled Led Zeppelin riffs only" (Marsh 1979). Marsh gave each of the three Judas Priest albums released up to that time one star. In 1979, Judas Priest's prospects for true stardom seemed less than promising. There was little indication of their future chart success, or that heavy metal would explode in popularity in the 1980s even as it evolved as a genre.

Two of the three albums to which Marsh gave one star were in fact among the most influential metal records ever released, and in the years after his review Judas Priest would take its place as one of the most important metal bands of all time. Priest constituted a bridge between the blues-based metal of first-generation heavy metal bands like Black Sabbath, Deep Purple, and Led Zeppelin and the speed and thrash metal of the 1980s. It is almost impossible to imagine bands such as Anthrax, Slayer, Megadeath, and Metallica without Judas Priest's *Stained Class* or *Killing Machine.* Priest even paved the way for more commercially successful hair metal bands like Poison and Mötley Crüe. Metal anthems such as "Breakin' the Law," "You've Got Another Thing Comin'," and "Livin' After Midnight" opened the door for second-generation heavy metal music to appear on mainstream radio as well as on the new, more visual, medium of MTV. Judas Priest did far more than simply recycle Led Zeppelin riffs. The band in fact laid the groundwork for much of what heavy metal would become in the 1980s and beyond.

Judas Priest did not achieve success, nor did they arrive at their innovative sound, overnight. Priest in its earliest incarnations was a straightforward hard rock band. What was perhaps the first incarnation of Judas Priest came together in 1969 when Birmingham, England, singer Al Atkins (born Alan John Atkins, October 11, 1947; vocals) formed a hard rock act called Judas Priest, a name ostensibly borrowed from the Bob Dylan song "The Ballad of Frankie Lee

Pictured here in 1986, Judas Priest has had a long and lasting impact on heavy metal music. Together, the band has carved a niche with hard, fast, and loud songs and a unique leather-clad appearance. (Photo by Chris Walter/WireImage)

and Judas Priest." This band broke up in April 1970 after a tour of Scotland. Later that year, Atkins joined with guitarist K. K. Downing (born Kenneth Downing Jr., October 27, 1951; guitar), bassist Ian Hill (born Ian Frank Hill, January 20, 1951; bass), and drummer John Ellis (born September 19, 1951; drums). The latter three were also from Birmingham and had attended school together. They played in a band called Freight and needed a lead singer. Atkins joined them and suggested that the band borrow the name Judas Priest now that the original band with the name had broken up. They agreed, and the new lineup of Judas Priest played its first show at a community center in South Staffordshire in March 1971.

Judas Priest toured the West Midlands, an industrial region that was the cradle of British heavy metal, for the next two years. Atkins then left the band in order to have a regular job that could support his young family. He would later resurface in the 1990s and release several solo heavy metal albums, including recordings of early Judas Priest songs that he helped write. Downing set about looking for a new lead singer. His girlfriend at the time told him that her brother, Rob Halford (born Robert John Arthur Halford, August 25, 1951; vocals), sang in a band called Hiroshima and might be a good fit for Judas Priest. Downing liked Halford's voice and invited him to join. Because Judas Priest had yet to find a steady replacement for Ellis, who left the band shortly after Atkins joined, Halford brought along Hiroshima drummer John Hinch (born John Frederick Hinch, July 19, 1947; drums) as well.

This new lineup continued to tour the United Kingdom, opening for various hard rock bands. They even headlined shows in Germany and the Netherlands. Judas Priest signed a record contract with the United Kingdom's independent label Gull and released their debut album, *Rocka Rolla,* in 1974. By this time, Glenn Tipton (born Glen Raymond Tipton, October 25, 1947; guitar) had also joined the band as a second lead guitarist. Like Thin Lizzy, Priest's twin leads would become a hallmark of their sound. *Rocka Rolla* was, however, a rather pedestrian hard rock album that displayed a heavy Black Sabbath influence, which was not surprising given that former Black Sabbath producer Rodger Bain produced *Rocka Rolla,* as well. The album did give a few hints, however, of Judas Priest's future direction. The progressive hard rock sound of the nine-and-a-half-minute suite "Winter/Deep Freeze/Winter Retreat/Cheater" and the opening track "One for the Road" both highlighted Halford's wailing vocals, and the title track contained a number of guitar riffs that sounded familiar to fans of later Judas Priest records. For the most part, however, *Rocka Rolla* displayed bluesy hard rock rather than the more classically tinged progressive and speed metal of their later releases.

Rocka Rolla was a commercial flop. Hinch left after its release, but Judas Priest continued to play live. Alan "Skip" Moore (born 1947; drums), who had played drums for Priest during the Al Atkins days, returned for the second album *Sad Wings of Destiny* (1976). Like *Rocka Rolla,* it failed to crack the charts. At the same time, it was a tremendously influential album. The opening track, "Victim of Changes," announced Halford as one of the most distinctive and talented vocalists in all of heavy metal. "Tyrant," "The Ripper," and "Deceiver" were perhaps the first songs to display fully the Judas Priest style of driving rhythms coupled with fast twin lead guitar runs. *Sad Wings of Destiny* should take its rightful place next to two other releases from 1976—Rainbow's *Rising* and Scorpions' *Virgin Killer*—as marking a turning point in metal as a whole.

Indeed, *Sad Wings of Destiny* was the jumping-off point not only for Judas Priest's future releases,

but also for the New Wave of British Heavy Metal. Judas Priest, along with Motörhead and the extremely influential but relatively unknown Welsh metal band Budgie, formed the vanguard of the movement. The New Wave of British Heavy Metal was harder, faster, darker, and more influenced by classical music than earlier incarnations of the genre. The movement included bands like Iron Maiden, Saxon, Angel Witch, Diamond Head, Samson, Demon, Girlschool, Tygers of Pan Tang, and early Def Leppard. The New Wave crested in the early 1980s, but later speed, thrash, and death metal acts almost universally looked back to the bands involved with the movement as influences.

Sad Wings of Destiny garnered attention from CBS Records, and with a new contract Judas Priest's fortunes began to change. The band continued to have trouble keeping drummers, and their third release saw them replace Alan Moore with 19-year-old virtuoso Simon Phillips (born February 6, 1957; drums). Phillips moved *Sin After Sin* (1977) even further down the road toward what would become progressive and speed metal in the 1980s. Although Priest experimented with softer sounds on this album ("Last Rose of Summer" sounds more like an AM adult contemporary song than something Judas Priest would do), *Sin After Sin* introduced a generation of metal fans to a new brand of hard rock. "Sinner" was classic Judas Priest, with excellent guitar work from Tipton and Downing. Surprisingly enough, the Joan Baez cover "Diamonds and Rust" was one of the strongest tracks on the album. Judas Priest would in fact cover a number of songs with great success throughout their career. "Starbreaker" similarly foreshadows the band's obsession with otherworldly monsters. "Let Us Prey/Call for the Priest" features classic speed metal riffs. The final track, "Dissident Aggressor," may have been the heaviest of all metal songs to date, with Halford's opening scream announcing to the world that hard rock would never be the same.

After *Sin After Sin,* Judas Priest toured America in support of rock lightweights Foreigner and REO Speedwagon. They then returned to the studio to record their fourth album, *Stained Class* (1978). Judas Priest also employed their fourth drummer, Les Binks (born James Leslie Banks, April 5, 1948; drums). As with each previous release, Priest chose an excellent opening track in "Exciter." In fact, the entire album displays the full range of the band's talents as songwriters and musicians. Even "Beyond the Realms of Death," the one song on the album that might pass for a ballad, incorporates the driving rhythms and guitar riffs that define the Judas Priest sound. Judas Priest has perhaps never released an album as important as *Stained Class*. In many ways it stands as a culmination of what hard rock had been and a promise of what heavy metal would be for the next 20 years. According to Steve Huey of *All Music,* it was "impossible to overestimate the impact *Stained Class* had on virtually all of the heavy metal that followed it, from the [New Wave of British Heavy Metal] through thrash and speed metal onward, and it remains Judas Priest's greatest achievement" (Huey 2013).

Although *Stained Class* remains a heavy metal milestone, at the time of its release it sold poorly, reaching only number 173 on the album chart. Even with such meager sales, it still outperformed Priest's first three albums. Their fifth album, *Killing Machine* (1979), inched up the charts a little further, peaking at 128. Retitled *Hell Bent for Leather* for the American market, the album contained shorter, more commercial songs. "Evening Star" and "Take on the World" sound more radio-friendly than almost anything from their first four albums. *Killing Machine* definitely displayed continuities with their previous releases, however. "Delivering the Goods" and "Hell Bent for Leather" sounded as if they could have appeared on *Stained Class* or *Sin After Sin.* Judas Priest also included another excellent cover with Fleetwood Mac's "The Green Manalishi (With the Two-Pronged Crown)." Perhaps more important than the musical direction of the album, *Killing Machine* was the occasion for Judas Priest's transition to their new "studs-and-leather" image. Just as later metal bands would copy Priest's musical style, they would also adopt their fashion.

Next, Judas Priest released a live album recorded in Japan. In many ways *Unleashed in the East* (1979) displayed the band's energy in ways that their studio albums had failed to do up to that time. *Unleashed* generated some controversy, however, because Priest added studio-recorded overdubs and other postshow enhancements. The controversy did not hurt the album's popularity with fans as sales again topped those of Priest's previous releases. In fact, *Unleashed in the East* eventually went platinum and peaked at number 70. Highlights include excellent versions of "Sinner" as well as "Diamonds and Rust" and "The Green Manalishi (With the Two-Pronged Crown)."

It was perhaps too much to hope that Judas Priest would keep a drummer for more than two studio albums. Les Binks departed before the recording and release of Priest's sixth studio release, *British Steel* (1980), and was replaced by Dave Holland (born David Holland, April 5, 1948; drums). *British Steel* was the most commercial Priest release to date, reaching number 34 in the United States and number three in the United Kingdom. Although the singles from the album failed to chart in the United States, "Living After Midnight" and "Breaking the Law" both made it to number 12 in the United Kingdom. The album went platinum in the United States and announced Judas Priest as a commercial as well as an artistic force. The songs on *British Steel* were on the whole simpler than on previous albums, but the driving rhythms and fast lead guitar parts were still there. As a result, *British Steel* influenced a generation of metal listeners and bands. In 2010, Judas Priest devoted an entire tour to the album's 30th anniversary, playing it in its entirety each night.

Dave Holland not only stayed with Judas Priest on their next album, *Point of Entry* (1981), but also on the four studio albums after that. The six albums on which Holland appeared turned out to be the most successful of the band's career. *Point of Entry* continued the trend toward more radio-friendly music. It was, however, not as well received as *British Steel,* nor did it sell as well. It peaked at number 39 in the United States and failed to reach platinum status, as had the two previous Priest albums. "Heading Out on the Highway," one of the album's highlights, reached number 10 on the Mainstream Rock charts. "Solar Angels," with its return to more rhythmic, blues-based metal, was a breath of fresh air in an otherwise mediocre album. Other songs such as "Don't Go," "Hot Rockin'," "On the Run," and "Turning Circles" come across as mere filler.

Judas Priest bounced back in 1982 with *Screaming for Vengeance,* which reached number 17. The single "You've Got Another Thing Comin'" reached number 67 on the Hot 100 chart. It was Priest's most commercially successful album and an artistic improvement over *Point of Entry.* "You've Got Another Thing Comin'" also entered rotation on the new MTV cable network. Like many of their contemporaries who experimented with the new medium, Judas Priest videos often came across as somewhat silly, if not extremely odd. For "Breakin' the Law," the members of the band robbed a bank of its stash of gold records while using guitars as weapons. The video for "You've Got Another Thing Comin'" consists mainly of live shots of the band interspersed with scenes of a staid British gentleman walking toward the stage where the band is playing. Halford then uses telekinesis to explode the man's head.

Judas Priest continued its torrid pace of album release with *Defenders of the Faith* (1984). It sold very well, reaching number 18. Despite the album's excellent sales, there was no standout single. Nevertheless, "Freewheel Burning," "Jawbreaker," and "Rock Hard, Ride Free," the first three tracks on the album, are standout metal songs. The mediocre track "Eat Me Alive" gained notoriety when the Parents' Music Resource Center, led by Tipper Gore, named it one of their "Filthy Fifteen." Priest later responded with the track "Parental Guidance" on *Turbo.* This brush with censors was in fact a harbinger of more significant entanglements with anti-rock protestors during the early 1990s.

Defenders of the Faith also foreshadowed the end of Priest's run of commercial success as well as their influence over the future of the genre. In some ways, *Defenders of the Faith* constituted an unintentional parody of heavy metal up that point. The cover featured a horned hybrid tank-tiger dubbed "the Metallian," a creature described on the back cover as "rising from the darkness of hell" and known as the "Master of

all metal." Despite what some saw as Priest's descent into spinal tap–like silliness, the follow-up to *Defenders, Turbo* (1986), sold well. It eventually went platinum and reached number 18. Longtime Judas Priest fans and critics for the most part did not like it, however. It featured synthesizers and radio-friendly melodies, with the result that tracks like "Wild Nights, Hot and Crazy Days" sound like hair metal more than the speed metal that Judas Priest inspired.

After *Turbo,* Priest's popularity began to wane as the hair metal and thrash that they inspired took over the airwaves. A live album, *Priest . . . Live!* (1987) reached number 38, but it largely failed to capture the energy of Judas Priest live shows in the same way as *Unleashed in the East.* Priest's next studio album, *Ram It Down* (1988), featured a return to Judas Priest's signature style, but the album lacked the overall creativity and excitement of earlier releases. Nevertheless, Priest fans bought enough copies to push the album over the million mark and up to number 31. Aside from the pure speed metal of the title track, *Ram It Down* unfortunately offered few memorable songs. Their forgettable version of "Johnny B. Goode" constitutes the only ill-advised cover in the entire Judas Priest catalogue.

The mediocrity of *Turbo* and *Ram It Down* made the critical success of *Painkiller* (1990) much more surprising. Dave Holland left after *Ram It Down,* as did longtime producer Tom Allom. The differences were apparent from the very beginning of the album. Former Race X drummer Scott Travis's (born September 6, 1961; drums) intense double bass sounds years ahead of its time, and Halford's voice is fiercer and more menacing than perhaps on any previous Priest album. "Painkiller" and "Metal Meltdown" almost define speed metal. "Between the Hammer & the Anvil" reminds listeners of the *Screaming for Vengeance* era, yet with much harder rhythms and increased virtuosity from Tipton and Downing. Judas Priest left behind any pretense of being a commercially driven band on *Painkiller,* and the decision resulted in some of the most enjoyable music of their career. Fans rewarded Priest's efforts by again sending the album over the platinum mark and up to number 26.

At the same time that the band was preparing for the release of *Painkiller,* they were also dealing with a lawsuit brought by the parents of Randy Belknap and James Vance. The two Judas Priest fans from Sparks, Nevada, made a suicide pact in 1985. Belknap shot himself in the head and died instantly. Vance also attempted to shoot himself but survived. He later died of a drug overdose. Their parents believed that subliminal messages in Priest's cover of Spooky Tooth's "Better by You, Better Than Me," which appeared on *Stained Class,* drove the men to attempt suicide. Specifically, the plaintiffs claimed that the song contained the message "do it." Both Belknap and Vance apparently had experienced abuse from parents and had experimented with hard drugs from an early age. In an effort to prove the absurdity of the charges, Halford took the stand and played "Invader" backward. The courtroom "heard" such preposterous statements as "it's so fishy, personally I'll owe it" and "hey look Ma, my chair's broken." Convinced that anti-rock protestors hear what they want to hear when playing records backward, and that Belknap and Vance committed suicide for a host of reasons having nothing to do with Judas Priest, the judge decided that there were no subliminal messages and so exonerated Judas Priest from any wrongdoing.

The stress of the trial coupled with sheer fatigue led Judas Priest to take a break after *Painkiller.* Halford left Priest entirely due to some as-yet undisclosed conflicts with his bandmates. He formed a new group, Fight, and continued down the path laid out on *Painkiller.* Scott Travis also joined him, with the result that Fight's debut album, *War of Words* (1993), was a hit among speed metal fans. It even met with moderate chart success, peaking at number 83. Fight released the EP *Mutations* in 1995, and a second full-length album, *A Small Deadly Space,* in 1995. It reached only number 120, however, and Halford disbanded Fight in order to explore different musical territory. He then formed a band called Two with guitarist John Lowery. Produced by Trent Reznor, Two's lone album *Voyeurs* (1997) sounds a great deal like Nine Inch Nails. Computers in fact played most of the instruments on the album. *Voyeurs* reached only 176,

but the single "I Am a Pig" made it to number 22 on the mainstream rock chart.

Shortly after the release of *Voyeurs,* Halford revealed to reporters that he is in fact gay. Many fans had long speculated about Halford's sexuality. Although the "studs-and-leather" image would become a hallmark of later metal acts, Halford adopted it as a way of expressing his sexuality without actually coming out as a gay man. Longtime fans who listened closely might have discovered that some Priest songs reference homosexual behavior. For example, "Raw Deal" on *Sin After Sin* was explicitly about visiting a gay biker bar on New York's famous homosexual haven Fire Island. "Island of Domination" on *Sad Wings of Destiny* contains similar imagery. While fans and associates might have figured out that Halford was gay long before 1998, his revelation was groundbreaking in a genre that has often glorified virility and overtly objectified women.

After the release of *Voyeurs,* Halford disbanded Two and left behind his techno experiments. He resurfaced in 2000 with a band known simply as Halford. Halford released *Resurrection* that same year to critical acclaim. It also sold well, making it to number five on the Heatseekers Chart and number 16 on the Internet albums chart. The album's cover features a leather-clad Halford on a motorcycle, signaling his return to Priest-era metal. "Resurrection" and "Made in Hell," the album's first two tracks, are highlights. Iron Maiden's Bruce Dickenson joins Halford on "The One You Love to Hate." Halford again impressed on the band's next two releases, a live album titled *Live Insurrection* (2001) and another studio album titled *Crucible* (2002).

While Halford continued to work and tour with his various bands, Judas Priest went on hiatus. In 1993, to commemorate the Halford years, the band released a double-disc retrospective entitled *Metal Works, '73–'93.* Although the band sorely needed a greatest hits release, and this one contained a number of excellent songs, copyright issues prevented the inclusion of any tracks from the first two albums. Furthermore, the album was a chronological jumble, and so gives little sense of Judas Priest's development over time.

It nevertheless stands as the most complete introduction for those new to Priest's body of work.

In 1997, the same year that Two released *Voyeurs,* Judas Priest returned to the charts with *Jugulator.* For the first time, a singer other than Halford appeared on a Priest record. The new singer was Tim "Ripper" Owens (born September 13, 1967; vocals), leader of the Judas Priest cover band British Steel and a Rob Halford sound-alike. Scott Travis's girlfriend heard Owens sing at a bar one night and arranged for him to audition with the band. After singing "Victim of Changes," Judas Priest hired him. *Jugulator* reached number 82, but the songs sounded largely like a rehash of *Painkiller.* The next year, Judas Priest released their third live album, *'98 Live Meltdown.* Priest's second studio album with Owens, *Demolition* (2001), was perhaps the closest Judas Priest ever came to death metal. A full 15 years after the Parents Music Resource Center (PMRC) controversy over "Eat Me Alive," it was also the first Judas Priest album to bear the "Parental Advisory" label.

Deciding that the "Ripper" Owens story was too good to pass up, Warner Bros. attempted to make a movie about the new Judas Priest singer. Priest was initially involved, but decided to pull out of the project. This was not the first time the band flirted with Hollywood, as the song "Reckless" from *Turbo* was originally slated to appear in *Top Gun* before Priest decided that the movie would likely flop. They showed much better judgment with their decision to dissociate themselves from the "Ripper" Owens movie. Originally called *Metal God,* it became a vehicle for Mark Wahlberg and Jennifer Aniston titled simply *Rock Star,* and references to Owens and Judas Priest were removed. It performed poorly in theaters and critics generally panned it.

After another live album, *Live in London* (2003), Owens and Judas Priest parted ways so that Halford could return as lead singer. Halford had worked with the band as they compiled the liner notes and songs for the *Metalogy* box set released in 2004. In 2005, the reunited Priest released *Angel of Retribution.* The album offered nothing new in terms of sound. As with

many Judas Priest albums, the opening track ("Judas Rising") was the best. Continuing their fascination with the monstrous ("Metal Gods," "Starbreaker," "Jugulator," the Metallian), *Angel of Retribution* closed with a 13-minute song about the Loch Ness monster. Although not their best offering, it was far from their worst. Moreover, fans eager to hear Halford with Priest again bought enough copies to push *Angel of Retribution* to number 13.

The bloated *Nostradamus* (2008) does not contain as many good metal tracks as its predecessor, although it was the most adventurous Priest to date. This double-album story about the supposed French prophet of the same name clocks in at almost two hours and contains a number of extended songs and suites that feature symphonies, organs, and even full choirs. Although metal as a genre had often featured such musical devices, their prominence on a Judas Priest album was a new phenomenon. Fans were intrigued, and the album made it to number 11.

Priest followed up their success with another tour and their fifth live album, *A Touch of Evil—Live* (2009). The album featured only three songs from their two post-Ripper studio albums. The band also dispensed with most of their major hits in favor of older album tracks popular with fans. The result was their best live album since *Unleashed in the East.*

In the meantime Halford continued to release albums on its own label—Metal God Entertainment. In 2008, Halford produced *Live at Rock in Rio III.* It was followed in 2009 by, of all things, the Christmas album *Halford III: Winter Songs.* Listeners were surprised to hear Rob Halford sing metal versions of Christmas hymns such as "What Child Is This?" and "O Come O Come Emmanuel." The band followed up that interesting detour with the more traditionally metal *Halford IV* in 2010. A live album, *Live at Saitama Super Arena* (2011), featured Halford versions of "Diamonds and Rust" and "The Green Manalishi (With the Two-Pronged Crown)." None of Halford's albums sold particularly well, the most successful being *Halford III,* which peaked at number 36 on the Holiday Album Chart. Metal fans were nevertheless pleased with each release. As Rob Halford shows no signs of either disbanding Halford or leaving Judas Priest, metal fans can look forward to more albums from both bands.

Judas Priest hit the road again in 2011, this time for what they claimed was their final tour. Taking its name from a song on *Sad Wings of Destiny*, the epic Epitaph World Tour lasted until the end of 2012. In the middle of the tour, K. K. Downing, who along with Ian Hill had been in the band longer than anyone, announced his retirement. Richie Faulkner, who also worked on 90-year-old actor Christopher Lee's heavy metal album *Charlemagne: The Omens of Death,* took over guitar duties. *Redeemer of Souls*, the band's 17th studio album, was released in July of 2014. On the heels of the release, the band again took to the road in support. In 2014 and 2015, the band toured extensively delivering heavy metal the way the audience has come to expect—hard, fast, loud, and excellent.

The impact that Judas Priest exerted on music from the late 1970s to the present is substantial. They were named the 78th Greatest Artists of All Time by VH1 and the second Greatest Metal Band by MTV (surpassed only by Black Sabbath). The list of bands that cite them as an influence in music, style, fashion, or all of the above include Iron Maiden, Metallica, Slayer, Def Leppard, Dream Theater, Megadeth, Pantera, Ratt, Anthrax, Dokken, Guns N' Roses, and W.A.S.P., just to mention a few.

Nathan Saunders

Selected Discography

Rocka Rolla, Gull IMP 7001, 1974.

Sad Wings of Destiny, Gull GRT 5098, 1976.

Sin After Sin, Columbia PC 34787, 1977.

Stained Class, Columbia JC 35296, 1978.

Killing Machine (Hell Bent for Leather), Columbia JC 35706, 1978.

Unleashed in the East, Columbia PC 36179, 1979.

British Steel, Columbia JC 36443, 1980.

Point of Entry, Columbia FC 37052, 1981.

Screaming for Vengeance, Columbia FC 38160, 1982.

Defenders of the Faith, Columbia FC 39219, 1984.

Turbo, Columbia OC 40198, 1986.

Priest . . . Live!, Columbia C2 40794, 1987.

Ram It Down, Columbia CK 44244, 1988.

Painkiller, Columbia CK 46891, 1990.

Metal Works, '73– '93, Columbia C2K 53932, 1993.

Jugulator, CMC International, 06076 86224–4, 1997.

'98 Live Meltdown, International 06076 86261–2, 1998.

Demolition, Atlantic 83480–2, 2001.

Live in London, SPV 092 74262 DCD E, 2003.

Metalogy, Columbia, 88697361602, 2004.

Angel of Retribution, Epic EK 92933, 2005.

Nostradamus, Epic 88697307082, 2008.

A Touch of Evil—Live, Columbia 88697552672, 2009.

References

Bashe, Philip. *Heavy Metal Thunder: The Music, Its History, Its Heroes.* New York: Doubleday, 1985.

Bayer, Gerd. *Heavy Metal Music in Britain.* Burlington, VT: Ashgate, 2009.

Bowe, Brian J. *Judas Priest: Metal Gods.* Berkeley Heights, NJ: Enslow, 2009.

Bukszpan, Daniel. *The Encyclopedia of Heavy Metal.* New York: Barnes & Noble, 2003.

Considine, J.D. "Purity and Power—Total, Unswerving Devotion to Heavy Metal Form: Judas Priest and the Scorpions." *Musician,* September 1984, 46–50.

Daniels, Neil. *The Story of Judas Priest: Defenders of the Faith,* 2nd ed. New York: Omnibus, 2010.

Erlewine, Stephen Thomas. "Judas Priest." *All Music Guide.* Rovi Corporation, 2013.

Huey, Steve. "Sad Wings of Destiny." *All Music Guide.* Rovi Corporation, 2013.

Huey, Steve. "Stained Class." *All Music Guide.* Rovi Corporation, 2013.

Marsh, Dave, and John Swenson, eds. *The Rolling Stone Record Guide.* New York: Random House/Rolling Stone, 1979.

Popoff, Martin. *The Top 500 Metal Albums of All Time.* Toronto: ECW Press, 2004.

Walser, Robert. *Running with the Devil: Power, Gender, and Madness in Heavy Metal Music.* Middletown, CT: Wesleyan University Press, 1993.

Weinstein, Deena. *Heavy Metal: The Music and Its Culture.* New York: Da Capo Press, 2000.